Psychology A2

The Complete Companion
for WJEC

Cara Flanagan • Julia Russell

Consultant Editors: John Griffin • Andrew Favager

OXFORD

UNIVERSITY PRESS

OXFORD
UNIVERSITY PRESS

Great Clarendon Street, Oxford OX2 6DP

Oxford University Press is a department of the University of Oxford.
It furthers the University's objective of excellence in research, scholarship, and education by publishing worldwide in

Oxford   New York

Auckland Cape Town Dar es Salaam Hong Kong Karachi Kuala Lumpur
Madrid Melbourne Mexico City Nairobi New Delhi Shanghai Taipei
Toronto

With offices in

Argentina Austria Brazil Chile Czech Republic France Greece
Guatemala Hungary Italy Japan Poland Portugal Singapore South Korea
Switzerland Thailand Turkey Ukraine Vietnam

Oxford is a registered trade mark of Oxford University Press in the UK and in certain other countries

© Cara Flanagan, Mike Cardwell and Julia Russell 2011

The moral rights of the authors have been asserted

Database right Oxford University Press (maker)

First published 2011

British Library Cataloguing in Publication Data

Data available

ISBN 978 1 85008 571 3

10 9 8 7 6 5 4 3 2

Printed by Printplus, China

Paper used in the production of this book is a natural, recyclable product made from wood grown in sustainable forests. The manufacturing process conforms to the environmental regulations of the country of origin.

Acknowledgements

Project development: Rick Jackman (Jackman Publishing Solutions Ltd)
Editorial & project management: GreenGate Publishing Services, Tonbridge
Design & layout: Nigel Harriss
Cover design: Patricia Briggs & Chris Cardwell
Cover photography: Chris Cardwell

Picture credits
Allen D. Bragdon Publishers, Inc. © 2011: p.181; Alamy: © Mary Evans Picture Library p.180(b), 196(tl); © North Wind Picture Archives p.79; © Photos 12 p.212; © Aflo Foto Agency p.189; © Dennis Hallinan p.149(t); © Editorial Image, LLC p.231; © imagebroker p.111(r); © INTERFOTO p.68; © Larry Lilac p.142; © RIA Novosti p.118(b); © The Photolibrary Wales p.74(b); © TravelStockCollection – Homer Sykes p.111(l); British Psychological Society, 'Code of Ethics and Conduct' © 2009: p.57; Cartoonstock.com: pp.55, 65, 77, 123, 140, 191, 214; Corbis: © John Drysdale p.20; © Farrell Grehan p.118(t); © H. Armstrong Roberts p.139; © Sean Adair/Reuters p.90; © Christian Liewig/TempSport: p.60(t); © Yann Arthus-Bertrand: p.58; Dr William Swann: p.25(b); Daniel Weinberd: p.232; EMPICS Sport: p.85; Fotolia: © Africa Studio p.166; © Alexander Yakovlev p.163; © alunico pp.137, 144; © AHMAD FAIZAL YAHYA p.86; © Amy Walters p.83; © Andre p.13; © Andres Rodriguez pp.15(m), 195; © Anyka p.195; © Ashley p.132; © Beboy p.136; © biker3 p.213(t); © Blaz Kure p.165; © BlessEdd p.74(t); © CandyBoxPhoto p.180(tr); © Cheryl Casey p.230; © chinatiger p.110; © chrisharvey p.8(t), 124, 128; © crabshack photos p.163; © crystal kirk p.37; © Csák István p.165; © Danomyte p.222; © Dave p.220; © diego cervo pp.31, 164, 165, 171; © Douglas Ng p.157; © dundanim p.215, 225; © EastWest Imagin p.221; © ExQuisine pp.54(l), 62, 165; © francovolpato p.131; © Franz Pfluegl p.165; © fred goldstein pp.163, 237; © Galyna Andrushko p.211; © Gary p.30(t); © GLUE STOCK p.133; © godfer p.99(l); © gormonrosta p.233; © Harald Lange p.42; © Harvey Hudson p.217; © ioannis kounadeas pp.135, 144; © iQoncept 212(b); © Jaimie Duplass p.107, 112(b); © Jason Stitt p.53(b); © jeanphilippe delisle p.195; © JJAVA pp.17, 197; © Joe Gough pp.61, 63; © JoeBreuer p.84; © Jovana Dadic p.163; © Julien BASTIDE p.218; © Kira Nova p.206; © Konstantin p.15(t); © KonstantinosKokkinis pp.29, 46, 48; © ktsdesign p.183; © Leonid Nyshko pp.88, 96; © Lisa F. Young pp.165, 174; © Lucky Dragon USA pp.216, 225; © luSh pp.202, 208; © Mau Horng p.100; © modellocate p.9(t); © Monika Adamczyk p.163; © Monkey Business pp.165,180(tl); © Mr.Mizar p.152; © Oleg Kozlov p.10(t); © Olga Ekaterincheva p.66; © patrimonio designs p.25(t);

Dedications

Acknowledgements
The authors would like to thank the special team of people behind the production of this book. First is the unique Rick Jackman, our publisher and friend, who makes things possible and has become ever more proficient at pouring oil on troubled waters! Our thanks also to Dave Mackin and Carrie Makin at GreenGate for their willingness to accommodate our every whim (as long as it didn't cost too much), and to Nigel Harriss, who has had the difficult task of making everything fit on the page and look beautiful. We would also like to express our appreciation to Simon Tanner-Tremaine and Sarah Flynn at OUP for their support and enthusiasm for the book in its new home. Finally, we thank Alison George, the exam officer at WJEC, for her unfailing help and guidance throughout this project.

Cara Flanagan and Julia Russell

John Griffin and Andy Favager

© Peter Polak p.9(b); © Photosani p.195;© picsfive p.33; © Piotr Marcinsk p.109; © pressmaster pp.15(b), 179; © Queen p.26; © Randy McKown p.138; © Ricardo Verde Costa p.51; © S. Mohr Photography p.200; © Samo Trebizan p.223; © Séb_compiegne p.10(b); © Sergi Terendyak p.8(bl); © sonya etchison p.99(ml); © Stephen Coburn p.18; © Stephen VanHorn p.15(l); © terra pp.60(b), 62(l); © tracyhornbrook p.127; © treenabeena pp.71, 115; © Uschi Hering p.112(t); © V. Yakobchuk p.12; © Vally p.182; © Vladimir Grinkov p.78; © windu p.186; © Yuri Arcurs pp.40(x5), 99(r),184; Getty images: © Tom Stoddart/Contributor p.125; © Lisa Maree Williams/Stringer p.121; © Time & Life Pictures p.155; © Getty Images p.228(b); iStock: © Andrejs Pidjass p.102; © Baris Simsek p.227; © Dirk Freder p.84(l); © Jordan Simeonov p.158; © Steve Cole p.143; Jorvik centre, York: pp.93, 97; Mary Evans Picture Library: p.151; Philip Zimbardo: p.22; PNAS National Academy of Sciences, USA: p.149(b); R. Sampson and B. Spencer 1999 'A conversation with I. Richard Savage', Statistical Science, 14: p.41; Reprinted by permission of the publisher from "Fetus Into Man: Physical Growth from conception to maturity" by J.M. Tanner, P. 121, Cambridge, MASS. Harvard University Press, copyright 1978, 1989, p. 72(t); R. DeVries: p.117; Rex Features: p.199; Sipa Press p.56; Everett Collection p.228(t); Geoff Robinson p.228(m); Jim Smeal/BEI p.228(tr); MGM/Everett p.229(tl); Nils Jorgensen p.228(br); Richard Young p.229(bl); Steve Back p.38; Science & Society: p.53(t); Science Photo Library: Photo researchers p.58(l); Shutterstock: © ArrowStudio, LLC p.99(t); © FreshPaint p.19; © Ingrid W. p.168; Texas A & M College of Veterinary Medicine & Biomedical Sciences: p.72(b); The Big Issue: p. 52; Thompson, 'Margaret Thatcher: a new illusion' Perception, 1980, 9, pp 483–4. Pion Limited, London: p.205; Topham Picturepoint © 2003 TopFoto.co.uk: p.105; UCL Department of Psychology: p.35; www.beautycheck.de/english: p.101; www.britishbirds.co.uk: p.116; www.savagechickens.com: p.159; www.speedtracktales.co.uk: p.212(l).

Every effort has been made to contact copyright holders of material reproduced in this book. If notified, the publishers will be pleased to rectify any errors or omissions at the earliest opportunity.

Contents

p4   How to use this book
p6   The A2 examination
p8   Writing effective essays for A2
p10   Effective revision

p11   **Introduction: approaches in psychology**   Introduction

Unit 3   Research methods and issues in research

p15   **Research methods**   Chapter 1A
p51   **Issues in research**   Chapter 1B

Unit 4   Controversies, topics and applications

Section A Controversies

p65   **Controversies**   Chapter 2

Section B Topics

p83   **Memory**   Chapter 3
p99   **Relationships**   Chapter 4
p115   **Intelligence**   Chapter 5
p131   **Adolescence and adulthood**   Chapter 6
p147   **Levels of consciousness**   Chapter 7

Section C Applications

p163   **Health psychology**   Chapter 8
p179   **Educational psychology**   Chapter 9
p195   **Forensic psychology**   Chapter 10
p211   **Sport psychology**   Chapter 11
p227   **Abnormal psychology**   Chapter 12

p243   References
p267   Index and glossary

HOW TO USE THIS BOOK

The contents of this book are mapped exactly onto the WJEC A2 specification. In total the book is divided into 13 chapters, which match areas in the specification. These chapters are separated into the following units and sections.

PY3 (Unit 3) Research methods and Issues in research
There are two chapters on the topics in PY3: Chapters 1A and 1B. You must study both of these chapters.

PY4 (Unit 4) Controversies, Topics and Applications
Section A Controversies (questions 1 and 2 in the exam), covered in Chapter 2.
Section B Topics (questions 3–7 in the exam), covered in Chapters 3–7.
Section C Applications (questions 8–12 in the exam), covered in Chapters 8–12.
You must study Chapter 2. You must also study **three** other chapters – at least **one** chapter from section B and at least **one** from section C.

Each chapter begins with a list of the topics covered in that chapter. _____

The full details of the **specification** to be covered by this chapter are presented on the opening page of each chapter. _____

The first spread in each chapter presents an introduction to the topic and some suggestions for activities.

The main content of each chapter consists of five double-page spreads (except the research methods chapter which is longer). The features on these spreads are illustrated on the sample spreads on the right. The main text, together with all the other features, will help turn your psychological knowledge into effective exam performance.

The **introduction** at the top left of each spread explains what the topic is about and often identifies some key issues or links to previous topics. _____

The **main text** for the spread is in the middle of the page.
On the left hand side of each spread we have presented **description (AO1)** of the topic area. _____
On the right hand side there is **evaluation (AO2)**. _____
In your exam answers you will need to present a mixture of these skills, so we thought it was helpful to separate them clearly in this way.

Sometimes we've added a **comment** to enhance understanding.

We have also included the occasional **website** but as sites come and go, don't be disappointed if such links turn out to be non-existent.

We have tried to include recent research, but a book can become out of date very quickly. To help keep you up to date you can look at our website. We are constantly adding information about new research that we think might interest students. See www.oxfordschoolblogs. co.uk/psychcompanion/blog

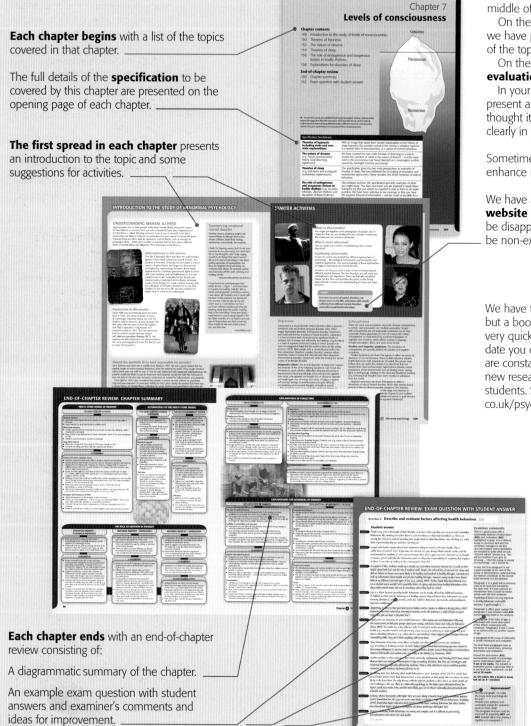

Each chapter ends with an end-of-chapter review consisting of:

A diagrammatic summary of the chapter. _____

An example exam question with student answers and examiner's comments and ideas for improvement. _____

Synoptic signposts appear at the top of each spread, offering suggestions about synoptic material that might be included in an essay. This is something we have usually left for you to develop.

Synopticity is explained on page 13.

Around the edge of each spread we have highlighted some points of special importance. These are often intended to help you with the requirement to be **synoptic** in examination answers. For example:

In the green boxes you will find detailed information on key **research studies** to help you gain a real understanding of some areas of research. Such studies can generally be used for description or commentary – it depends on how you choose to present them.

Information in orange boxes is about **research methodology**. For example, we might discuss the validity of the research described on the spread or look at the problems of using case studies.

Red boxes contain information on **controversies – issues** and **debates**. This includes topics such as gender and cultural bias, determinism, ethics and so on.

There are also yellow boxes which relate to **approaches**.

The blue boxes contain extra material that can be used as evaluation, such as **real-world applications**.

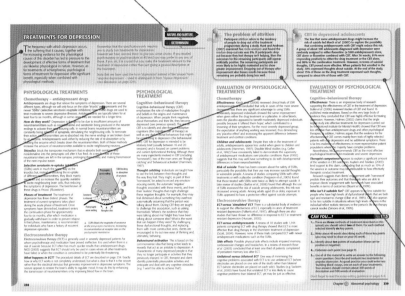

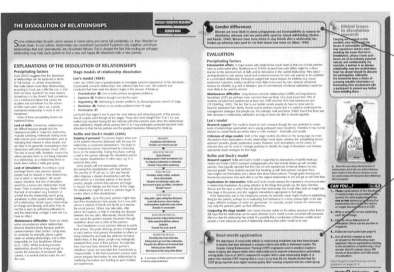

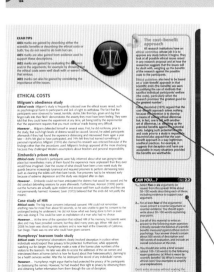

We have provided **exam tips** all over the place but occasionally we have thought of a special one.

We have tried to find a balance between making material interesting and informative, but at the same time useful for your exam.

In order to help you focus on what will be required for the exam, we have included *'CAN YOU...?'* boxes. These suggest how you might select material from the spread in order to construct an answer to the exam question for the topic, and to ensure that you at least have that minimal level of understanding that will enable you to perform well in the exam.

THE A2 EXAMINATION

The A2 examination consists of two papers – Unit 3 (PY3) and Unit 4 (PY4).
You can take either of these in January or June.

Unit 3 Research methods and Issues in research
1½ hours.
This paper is worth 40% of your A2 exam (20% of your whole A level).

The exam is divided into three sections.
You must answer **ALL** questions in Sections A and B, and **TWO** questions in Section C.

Section A Research methods
All questions are compulsory.

This section begins with some material about a research study. The questions that follow are short-answer ones that develop from the research material. See pages 27, 33 and 52 for examples of this type of question.

Candidates are advised to spend at least five minutes reading and understanding the research material before starting to answer the questions. The time spent on each question is determined by the number of marks allocated.

Section B Research methods
All questions are compulsory.

This section also starts with research material and has a series of short-answer questions, as in Section A.

Section C Issues in research
There are **THREE** questions related to Issues in research (covered in Chapter 1B) and you must answer **TWO**.

Each question is worth 15 marks. See page 52 for a detailed explanation of the questions.

Timing – you have about 30 minutes for each section of this paper.

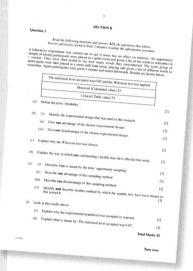

Unit 4 Controversies, Topics and Applications
2½ hours.
This paper is worth 60% of your A2 exam (30% of your whole A level).

The exam is divided into three sections.
You must answer **ONE** question from each of the three sections and **ONE** additional question from either Section B or Section C. A total of **FOUR** questions must be answered.

Section A Controversies
You must answer **ONE** question in this section from a choice of **TWO**. The questions relate to Controversies and are covered in Chapter 2. See page 66 for a detailed explanation of these questions.

Section B Topics
In total there are **FIVE** topics, which are covered in Chapters 3–7 of this book. The contents of Chapter 3 are assessed in question 3 of the exam, Chapter 4 is assessed in question 4 and so on.

Section C Applications
In total there are **FIVE** applications, which are covered in Chapters 8–12 of this book. The contents of Chapter 8 are assessed in question 8 of the exam, Chapter 9 is assessed in question 9 and so on.

Timing – you have about 35–40 minutes for each question to be answered on this paper. Each question is worth 25 marks.

HOW YOUR ANSWERS ARE MARKED

There are four types of question on the A2 exam.

Type 1 Research methods
These questions appear in Sections A and B on Unit 3 (PY3). You are given some research material to read and a number of short questions. You can see examples on pages 27, 33 and 52. The answers are assessed in terms of **AO1** and **AO2**.

Type 2 Research issues
These questions appear in Section C of Unit 3 (PY3). They test **AO3** and are worth 15 marks each.
See page 52 for an explanation of how these questions are marked.

Type 3 Controversies
These questions appear in Section A of Unit 4 (PY4). They are always parted with part (a) worth 3 marks **AO1** and part (b) worth 7 marks **AO1** and 15 marks **AO2**.
See page 52 for an explanation of how these questions are marked.

Type 4 Topics and Applications
These questions appear in Sections B and C of Unit 4 (PY4). They are worth 25 marks, consisting of 10 marks **AO1** and 15 marks **AO2**.
The mark scheme for these questions is shown below.

Assessment objectives AO1, AO2 and AO3

Assessment objective 1 (AO1)
Knowledge and understanding of psychological theories, terminology, concepts, studies and methods.
Assessment objective 2 (AO2)
Analysis and evaluation of psychological theories, terminology, concepts, studies and methods.
Assessment objective 3 (AO3)
How science works in psychology. Designing, conducting and reporting psychological investigation(s), and taking into account the issues of reliability, validity and ethics.

Mark scheme for PY4 (questions 3–12)

AO1 marks	Knowledge	Detail and breadth	Use of language (including grammar, punctuation and spelling)
8–10	Accurate and well-detailed	Depth *and* breadth, though not necessarily in equal measure	Coherent and accurate
6–7	Reasonably accurate, less detailed	Depth *or* breadth	Accurate, structured and clear
4–5	Appropriate	Basic in detail	Some inaccuracies
1–2	Superficial and muddled		Errors
0	No relevant knowledge or understanding		

AO2 Marks	Evaluation	Depth and breadth
12–15	Relevant, clearly structured and thorough	Depth *and* breadth, though not necessarily in equal measure
8–11	Relevant, structured and shows some coherence	Depth *or* breadth
4–7	Some relevance	Basic and limited
1–3	Very limited but relevant	
0	None relevant	

Using banded mark schemes

The mark schemes on the left are called 'banded mark schemes'.

In order to use these to mark a student essay, an examiner first reads the student answer and then decides which mark band best describes the response.

To determine the actual mark within the band, the examiner decides whether they were tempted by the band above (and therefore awards the top mark in the band), or tempted by the band below, or neither. We call this the *magnet effect*.

At the end of each chapter we have presented a student essay with examiner's comments. It is worth reading all of these to help you understand how essays are marked.

WRITING EFFECTIVE ESSAYS FOR A2

There are three different types of extended writing (essay) question in the A2 psychology exam:

- The 15-minute short form in the *Issues in research* of PY3.
- The 30-minute two-part questions in the *Controversies* section of PY4.
- The 30-minute questions in the *Topics* and the *Applications* sections of PY4.

Each type of essay requires a different mix of skills and knowledge. The specific skills for *Issues in research* and *Controversies* are discussed at the beginning of the relevant chapters. On this spread we will look at the general factors that are important in all essay questions.

Clear, logical structure

This means that there is a narrative structure, a story, a tale about the topic. You should logically unfold your material in response to the question. Structure is a way to demonstrate that you have a good grasp of the topic. Structure can involve dividing your essay into small paragraphs, dealing with one subtopic in each. This helps the reader understand the points you are making. Imagine if all the text on this page was presented as just two or three paragraphs – it would make it much more difficult to read.

Structuring your essays makes a high-level demand on literacy skills, and needs practice – so allow time to practise structuring your answers in your revision.

Provide depth and breadth

Consider the following essay question: *Discuss ethical issues in the use of human participants in research in psychology*. There are two possible ways to answer this:

1. You might describe and evaluate ten different ethical issues. In a timed exam answer you would be able to give only the briefest description of each of these issues. Your answer would have lots of *breadth* but little *depth*/detail.
2. You might describe and evaluate three different ethical issues. In an exam you would have time to provide lots of information about each issue. Your answer would have lots of *depth*/detail but little *breadth*.

For top marks in an essay you need to provide evidence of depth *and* breadth, though they don't have to be balanced. If your essay has very little of either breadth or depth your mark will be restricted to one of the lower bands.

Answer the question

Many candidates in psychology exams leave the exam room feeling they've written loads and done well, and are shocked and confused when they get a poor mark. Often it is the candidates who write the shorter answers who get higher marks. Why? Poor essays typically consist of 'everything I know about this topic' and fail to specifically focus on the question that was set. For example, in an essay about the aetiology (origins and development) of depression, a candidate might also describe several therapies for depression. The examiner is under strict instructions to only credit material relevant to the question, not to give general marks for your wider knowledge – unless of course this has been made relevant.

Cloned answers

Everyone wants to get great marks for their exam answers and one strategy is to memorise Grade A answers. However, for this strategy to work, you'll need to memorise something like 25 essays for all the question possibilities.

Examiners hate cloned answers and because they often do not illustrate your knowledge and understanding, nor skills of analysis and evaluation. The reason why we have shown you Grade A answers is so that you can understand the underlying strategy that is needed to attract top marks. On this spread we have provided more clues about successful strategies. Since when have you ever wanted to be like everyone else? Don't be a clone, learn to produce your own masterpieces.

> For AO2, it's not just what you say but how you say it.

> There are no right answers in psychology – you can take any view you wish… but you must be able to support it with research.

Provide detailed answers

On the left are two pictures of flowers. The one on the far left has much less detail; it lacks specific information. In an essay, 'detail' doesn't necessarily mean writing more, it means including more specific information. For example, compare the following:

- One study found that children learned by watching others, getting rewarded and imitating behaviour.
- Bandura *et al.* (1961) found that children learned by observation, vicarious reinforcement and modelling this behaviour.

Both answers contain the same number of words but the second one includes the researcher's name and the date of the study plus psychological terms – all making it more detailed.

Evaluation (AO2)

On the previous spread we outlined the three assessment objectives **AO1**, **AO2** and **AO3**. Evaluation (**AO2**) is the one that causes the most difficulty for exam candidates, for two reasons:

1. It is the more challenging of the assessment objectives.
2. There are more **AO2** marks than **AO1** or **AO3** marks, so if you don't get it right, it has a major effect on your overall mark.

So what is 'evaluation'? It literally means establishing the value of something. So in your essay, when you describe (**AO1**) a theory or research study or concept, it is then important to comment on its value. There are many ways to do this, for example:

- *Research support* – present a study or another theory that supports the **AO1** material.
- *Challenge* – identify flaws with your **AO1** material. This could be a logical flaw or a piece of research evidence that is not in agreement. It could also be a criticism of the research methodology.
- *Alternative research* – contrast one theory or study with another – but don't describe the other research (that would be **AO1**), you should compare and contrast, identify the strengths and/or weaknesses.
- *Application* – how can this knowledge be applied? Real-life applications are a strength of any research.
- *Implication* – what conclusions can we draw? The **AO2** assessment objective is termed 'analysis and evaluation', so analysis is also credited.

There is no simple formula for 'doing' AO2 – there are no clones – because what is appropriate in one essay is not appropriate in another essay. You need to grasp the essence of AO2 in order to be able to provide it. That's why AO2 matters – it is a challenging skill, and requires thoughtfulness.

Making your AO2 points effective

The trick to **AO2** is not just providing research support or challenge, identifying the strengths and/or weaknesses of alternative research, or looking at real-life applications or implications – you have to make this material *effective*.

Verbal indications Start any **AO2** sentence with a key word/phrase to indicate this is **AO2**.

- Use *compare phrases* such as 'In support of this theory…' or 'Supporting evidence comes from…'.
- Use *contrast phases* such as 'In complete opposition to this comes the evidence from…', 'This was clearly disproved by…', 'However' or 'On the other hand'.
- Use *critical phases* such as 'One advantage of this is…', 'One disadvantage…' or 'One problem has been…'.
- *Other phrases* such as 'A useful application is…' or 'One consequence of this research is…'.

Don't be afraid of highlighting verbal indication words by using CAPITALS or underlining. You will NOT be penalised.

Structural indicators Use paragraph breaks to flag up different activities. Description and evaluation can be separated by starting a new paragraph.

Elaboration Throughout this book we have included 'Can You' exercises, and each time we have said to 'elaborate' each point of evaluation. There is very limited credit for presenting criticisms such as 'One limitation of this study was that it lacked ecological validity' or 'One strength of this theory is that it can be applied to the real world'. These criticisms lack elaboration. To attract high AO2 marks you need to write more (i.e. elaborate). So what else can you write? Our answer to elaboration is the three-point rule:

1. Identify your point (e.g. a strength or limitation).
2. Justify it (present evidence to explain why it is a strength or limitation in this particular instance).
3. Explain it (How does this affect the topic being evaluated? Is this good or bad for it and why?).

For example, if your criticism of a study is 'lack of ecological validity' then you have identified it. You need to justify your claim in this context (e.g. studies of this phenomenon in other settings haven't produced the same results). Finally, you need to indicate why ecological validity is a problem in this study (e.g. this means that we can't generalise from the original study to other settings, which limits its explanatory usefulness).

▲ *'Mmmm, fruity aromas and a peachy finish, with a touch of toasty oak.' Is that description or evaluation? The bottom line is that it isn't always easy to know – that's why you have to make your evaluation very clear, otherwise it ends up being credited as description (AO1).*

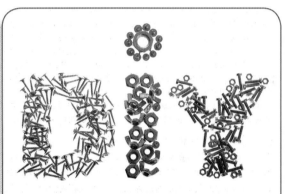

Invent your own AO2

In this book we have given you lots of evaluation material but we have really only just scratched the surface – there just isn't room. We have provided the bare minimum to pass the exam, but for a top A level student it should be just the starting point. Many students think of the textbook as the end, but in fact it's only the beginning. Use the internet or specialist textbooks to read further and find your own research studies to support or challenge what we have written. Remember, new evidence is published every day.

Make it synoptic (see page 13) You can also 'create' your own AO2 points using the issues and debates. However, if you choose to make a synoptic comment then you must make sure that this is contextualised, i.e. make it relevant to the theory or study you are commenting on.

The AO2 description trap It is very easy to find yourself describing something when you're meant to be evaluating it. Just take special care and follow the advice on this page to avoid the *AO2 description trap*. There are situations where candidates feel drawn into *describing* AO2 material rather than using it as part of a *sustained* evaluation. For example, if you want to use psychological therapies to evaluate explanations of depression, make sure you do use them as sustained effective evaluation rather than ending up just describing them.

EFFECTIVE REVISION

Get yourself motivated

People tend to do better when they are highly motivated. We have taught many mature students who all wished they had worked harder at school the first time around. You don't owe success to your teachers or your parents (although they would be delighted); you owe it to the person you will be ten years from now. Think what you would like to be doing in ten years' time, and what you need to get there, and let that thought prompt you into action now. It is always better to succeed at something you might not need later than to fail at something you will need.

Work *with your memory*

In an exam it is harder to access information learned by rote. When someone feels anxious it is easier for them to recall knowledge they *understand* well. Just reading or writing out notes may do little to help you create enduring memories or to understand the content. However, if you do something with your knowledge it will increase your understanding and make it more likely that material is accessible when you need it. Psychologists call this 'deep processing' as opposed to the 'shallow processing' that takes place when you read something without really thinking about it. Constructing 'spidergrams' or mind-maps of the material, or even explaining it to someone else, involves deep processing and makes material more memorable.

Become multisensory

Why stick to using just one of your senses when revising? Visual learners learn best by seeing what they are learning, so make the most of text, diagrams, graphs, etc. By contrast, auditory learners learn best by listening (and talking), taking in material using their sense of hearing. You might associate more with one of these styles than the other, but actually we can make use of *both* these types of learning styles. As well as *reading* your notes and *looking* at pictures and diagrams, try *listening* to your notes and *talking* about topics with other people – and even *performing* some of the material such as role-playing a study.

Short bursts are best

One of the problems with revision is that you can do too much of it (at one go that is…!). As you probably know all too well, your attention is prone to wander after a relatively short period of time. Research findings vary as to the optimum time to spend revising, but 30–45 minutes at a time appears to be the norm. What should you do when your attention begins to wander? As a rule, the greater the physiological change (i.e. go for a walk rather than surfing the internet), the more refreshed you will be when returning for your next 30–45-minute stint. There is another benefit to having frequent planned breaks – it increases the probability of subsequent recall.

Revisit regularly

Have you ever noticed that if you don't use an icon on your computer for a long time, the cunning little blighter hides it? Your computer seems to take the decision that as you are not using it regularly, it can't be that important, so neatly files it away somewhere. Your brain works in a similar way; knowledge that is not used regularly becomes less immediately accessible. The trick, therefore, is to review what you have learned at regular intervals. Each time you review material, it will take less time and will surely pay dividends later on!

Work with a friend

Although friends *can* be a distraction while you are trying to study, they can also be a very useful revision aid. Working together (what psychologists call 'collaborative learning') can aid understanding and make revision more interesting and more fun. Explaining something to someone else is a useful form of deep processing (see above), and by checking and discussing each other's answers to sample questions, you can practise your 'examiner skills' and therefore your understanding of what to put into an exam answer to earn the most marks.

AS IS DEAD, LONG LIVE A2!

Welcome to the second part of your A level course in psychology! By now you have (hopefully) passed the AS part of the course and are ready for some more in-depth study of specialist topics. You may have packed away your well-used AS textbook and carefully organised AS notes – but not so fast – your AS course was not just an end in itself but is also intended as a foundation for the A2 topics. So let's remind you about what you know!

Approaches in psychology

One part of your AS course focused on the four main approaches in psychology: the **biological**, **behaviourist**, **psychodynamic** and **cognitive** approaches. You learned that each of these approaches has a set of assumptions – the signature tune of the approach. In order to help you understand this 'tune', you looked at some examples of each approach – one theory and one therapy. You also studied strengths and weaknesses of each approach and finally looked at the methodology used by each approach (including examples and strengths and weaknesses).

All of this knowledge about approaches from your AS course is going to come in useful during the second part of your A level course.

This is a very brief outline of the four main approaches:

- The **biological approach** believes that behaviour can be explained in terms of physical factors, such as activity in the brain (activity of **neurons** and **neurotransmitters**) as well as in the body (e.g. **hormones**). The biological approach also includes the influence of **genetic** factors.

- The **behavioural approach** believes that the way a person is and behaves is due to life experiences. A person might learn new stimulus–response associations (**classical conditioning**) or may learn new behaviours from being rewarded or punished (**operant conditioning**) and this determines how they behave in future. They might also imitate what they see someone doing (**social learning theory**).

- The **psychodynamic approach** believes that our behaviour is influenced by early childhood experiences (**psychosexual stages**) and by emotions that are buried in the **unconscious**. It is also influenced by **ego defence mechanisms** such as **repression** and **projection**. Behaviour and emotions can be explained in terms of the interaction between the **id**, **ego** and **superego**.

- The **cognitive approach** believes that behaviour is best explained in terms of how mental activity shapes our behaviour. The cognitive approach often uses a computer analogy to understanding the way the mind works (input, process, output) and prefers controlled, experimental research.

However, these four approaches are by no means the only approaches in psychology. On the next spread we introduce some 'new' approaches.

Do It Yourself

If you can resist reading this page, first try an exercise in recall, working in pairs or small groups:

List the four approaches you studied at AS and for each of them write down:
- Some assumptions of the approach.
- The theory you studied that represented the approach, and at least **five** key points about this theory.
- The therapy you studied that represented the approach, and at least **five** key points about this therapy.
- **Two** strengths and **two** weaknesses of the approach.
- **Two** methodologies used to conducted research into the approach, and strengths/weaknesses of the methodology.

List the ten core studies. For each study write at least **one** sentence for each of the following: aims, procedures, results and conclusions. Add anything else you can remember.

Core studies

Another key element of your AS course was the ten core studies. You will find that we refer to many of these in this book.

Research methods

The third key element of the AS course was research methods and you will revisit and extend your knowledge of these concepts in the first two chapters of this book. In addition, concepts such as **validity** and **sampling** crop up here, there and everywhere – research methods provide a means of assessing the value of any research.

Issues and debates

In addition to the approaches, you also probably learned about some of the key issues and debates in psychology during your AS year, such as **nature versus nurture**, **free will** or **determinism**, **reductionism** or **holism**, and **idiographic** or **nomothetic**. In our AS book we used these issues and debates as a means of evaluating each of the approaches – for example, a strength of the biological approach is that it is determinist but a weakness is that it is reductionist.

At A2 level you will continue using these concepts as a means of evaluating theories, so you need to revisit these concepts.

There is also a specific part of the A2 course that focuses on issues and debates. It is called *Controversies* (see Chapter 2) and in this chapter you will study some old and some new issues and debates, such as determinism and free will (a classic debate in psychology), and gender bias and cultural bias (two important issues in psychology).

INTRODUCTION: APPROACHES IN PSYCHOLOGY

MORE APPROACHES

Approaches in psychology were once called 'schools of thought'. Adherents of a particular approach hold assumptions (ways of thinking) about the causes of behaviour and use a common set of concepts when giving an explanation. 'Approaches' have also been called 'perspectives' because they provide us with a way to view the world.

The evolutionary approach

The biological approach includes **genetic** explanations, for example the suggestion that your intelligence is related to the genes you inherit from your parents, or inheriting genes for **schizophrenia** increases the likelihood that you might develop the disorder.

Genetic explanations can also be related to the evolutionary approach. The key concept of the **evolutionary** approach is **natural selection**. If a genetically determined behaviour promotes survival and reproduction, the genes for that behaviour will be selected because they ensure their own continuation. This works in a similar way to *artificial selection* – for example, a dairy farmer deliberately selects the cows that are the best milk producers as breed stock for future generations. The farmer is selecting the best genes (assuming that high milk production is genetically determined) – but in nature no one selects the best genes, they are *naturally* selected because they produce the best, most **adaptive** behaviours. We say that **selective pressures** shape future generations. Evolutionary psychologists suggest that such selection took place largely in the **EEA** (*environment of evolutionary adaptation*).

Strengths One strength of the evolutionary approach is that it is able to explain behaviours that appear dysfunctional, but were not dysfunctional when first 'selected' (such as aggression) or which make little sense in a modern context (for example, the stress response might be good when being attacked by a lion but is less adaptive when facing a bank overdraft).

Another strength is that evolutionary theory considers the function (meaning) of a behaviour, and in this way is not **reductionist**. In particular, such explanations are concerned with the ultimate function of a behaviour rather than being restricted to its *proximate* function (the here-and-now function of the behaviour).

Weaknesses One of the weaknesses of this approach is that evolutionary explanations often ignore cultural influences on our behaviour, or need to be used in conjunction with such explanations. For example, evolutionary influences lead men to select physically attractive women but the exact details of what constitutes physical attractiveness is partly determined by culture (as you know from your AS core study by Buss, 1989, on mate preferences).

Another weakness is that evolutionary explanations are often seen as **determinist** because they suggest that our behaviour is affected by factors other than free will – however evolutionary psychologists argue that genetically based behaviours are better understood as predispositions rather than certainties and thus are not determinist.

A further issue relates to the nature of research on evolutionary theory. The arguments presented by evolutionary psychologists are often speculative. For example, assumptions are made about the EEA and descriptions provided which fit these assumptions but which cannot be falsified.

Finally, there is the question about why humans have not evolved after the EEA. According to this concept humans last evolved two million years ago. However, there have been selective pressures since then (for example, surviving urban life) which should have changed human behaviour but don't appear to have had an effect.

▲ *A building looks different depending on your perspective. The same is true of psychological perspectives or approaches (of course psychologists aren't looking at buildings!). Different psychologists are looking at behaviour from a particular perspective and the result is quite a different picture of human behaviour.*

The humanistic approach

The **humanistic approach** is a reflection of modern-day society in the same way that both psychoanalysis and behaviourism were in their time. Humanistic psychologists reject **behaviourist** and **psychodynamic** perspectives as being reductionist and determinist. They portray individuals as being in control rather than being controlled by external forces. They also feel that other approaches lack a key element when explaining behaviour – the sense of being the one who is having the experience. What matters is each person's subjective view rather than some objective reality. Reality is defined by the individual's perspective.

The emphasis of the humanistic approach is on the unique qualities of each individual and their capacity to be self-determining and responsible. Human nature is seen as positive and inherently good. Each person strives for growth, self-acceptance and **self-actualisation**.

Strengths The humanistic approach focuses on free will rather than taking a determinist view. Carl Rogers, the 'father' of the counselling movement, proposed that taking responsibility for oneself is the route to healthy self-development. As long as individuals remain controlled by other people or other things, they cannot take responsibility for their behaviour and therefore cannot begin to change it. The link to counselling and other forms of client-centred therapies is evidence of the widespread application of this approach.

The humanistic approach is also an **idiographic** approach because it regards each person as unique. This makes the approach quite different to other approaches.

Weaknesses The humanistic approach has been criticised for being vague, unscientific and untestable. This is because humanistic psychologists believe that psychological theories should be humanly rather than statistically significant, claiming that objective data can tell us little about subjective experience. Qualitative methods are used which include discourse analysis (analysing human communications such as books or films) and naturalistic observations.

Some humanistic concepts are culturally relative, for example the emphasis on self-determination is a Western ideal and not as applicable to those societies where the group is more important than the individual (called **collectivist** societies).

Other approaches

Your ten AS core studies were drawn from five topic areas: social psychology, physiological psychology, cognitive psychology, developmental psychology and individual differences. The core studies were selected to give you a 'taste' of each of these topic areas, which in a sense are also approaches.

The social approach was represented at AS by the studies by Asch (1955) and Milgram (1963). It focuses on the influence of other people on our behaviour, which includes interpersonal influences and cultural influences. There are many examples of this throughout the A2 course, but Chapter 5 in particular looks at relationships and how these benefit our well-being. In Chapter 9 we examine how teachers affect our ability to learn and in Chapter 11 we see how coaches may enhance sport motivation.

The physiological approach was represented at AS by the studies by Rahe, Mahan and Arthur (1970) and Bennett-Levy and Marteau (1984). The physiological approach is specifically concerned with the physical elements of the body (e.g. neurons, hormones, etc.), whereas the biological approach includes physiology as well as genetics and evolutionary theory. Many explanations in this book are physiological, such as explanations for dreams in Chapter 7 and for mental illness in Chapter 12. Such physiological explanations are generally seen as reductionist and can be contrasted with less reductionist psychological approaches.

The cognitive approach was represented at AS by the studies by Loftus and Palmer (1974) and Gardner and Gardner (1969). You will come across it when looking at cognitive–behavioural therapies, for example in Chapter 12.

The developmental approach was represented at AS by the studies by Langer and Rodin (1976) and Gibson and Walk (1960). This approach is concerned with looking at how people change as they grow from infancy to adulthood and into old age. There are examples of the developmental approach in this book – we have cognitive development and the development of intelligence in Chapter 5, and theories of adolescence and adulthood in Chapter 6.

Individual differences was represented at AS by the studies by Buss (1989) and Rosenhan (1973). It focuses on how people differ in their behaviour and personal qualities, and also is concerned with measuring these differences as in Chapter 5, which includes intelligence testing. Chapter 12 looks at individual differences in mental health.

Approaches and paradigms

Thomas Kuhn (1962) used the term paradigm to refer to 'approaches'. He suggested that a scientific subject such as biology has one shared set of assumptions that defines the subject, i.e. one approach or paradigm. By contrast, according to Kuhn, psychology has yet to settle on one approach to explaini.ng phenomena and therefore is best described as pre-science. This topic is discussed further in Chapter 2.

Synopticity

Synoptic assessment is a feature of all A2 courses. It refers to being able to understand the connections between different elements of the topic you are studying.

As this is an Advanced level qualification it seems reasonable that, at the end of the course, you should have a sense of what psychology is all about – a broad view. Over the course of your A level studies, you will learn about many different areas of psychology, such as therapeutic techniques used to treat mental illness and explanations for learning. You might also learn about memory or relationships or intelligence and so on. But what do all these bits of psychology have in common?

These bits of psychology have lots of things in common. All psychologists use similar research methods, all psychologists are concerned with ethical issues in their research, and they are also concerned with possible problems occurring in their explanations (issues such as gender bias). Psychologists debate topics such as how (or whether) behaviour is determined and whether nature or nurture offers a better account of behaviour in different areas of psychology. Psychologists also apply similar approaches to explain behaviour – for example, mental illness can be explained using the biological and cognitive approaches, dreams can be explained with the psychodynamic and physiological approaches. Research methods, issues, debates and approaches are all synoptic topics – the threads that run across the whole specification.

'Synopticity' also refers to any links between topics, for example making a link between Langer and Rodin's study at AS and other research on the locus of control in your A2 topics (for example see pages 165 and 174).

Synopticity and the exam Synopticity is embedded in PY3. Candidates will be expected to draw upon their prior study of theory and research at AS level to inform the application of Research methods (covered in Chapter 1A) and Issues in research (covered in Chapter 1B).

Synopticity is also embedded in PY4. The compulsory topic of Controversies (in Chapter 2) requires the critical application of knowledge about issues and debates to other topics you have studied through your A level course. In addition, your other topics of study (in Chapters 3–12) can be evaluated using your synoptic toolkit.

▲ *Synoptic toolkit at the ready!*

A toolkit is a set of tools that enable a person to carry out his or her trade. Psychologists also have a toolkit, but in this case it doesn't contain physical tools. Instead it consists of abstract concepts – such as 'determinism', 'behaviourism', 'ethical issues' and so on. Every specialist group (like biologists or mathematicians) has such a toolkit. When you study a subject you learn about its particular defining (or 'synoptic') concepts – the toolkit is one of the features that defines a subject.

In the case of psychology, such 'tools' are used to explain behaviour and also to evaluate theories and studies. You have already learned quite a bit about this toolkit when studying AS level psychology.

Research methods

Chapter contents

16   Introduction to the study of research methods

18   Validity and reliability

20   Research methods

22   Other research methods

24   Research design

26   More on research design

28   Ethical issues and ways of overcoming these issues

30   Inferential statistics

32   More on inferential statistics

Statistical tests:

34   Spearman's Rank Order Correlation Coefficient

36   Chi-squared (χ^2) Test

38   Sign Test

40   Wilcoxon T Test

42   Mann–Whitney U Test

44   Descriptive and inferential statistics

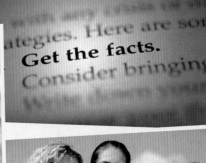

Get the facts.
Consider bringing

End-of-chapter review

46   Chapter summary

48   Exam question with student answer

Specification breakdown

General comments

The specification content on the right shows all the concepts with which you need to be familiar. Most of these concepts and terms were covered as part of your AS level course, so this chapter will serve as a reminder of them.

However, there are also some new topics, most particularly statistical tests and significance.

This chapter contains guidance on all the concepts in the specification (old and new) and provides lots of opportunities for you to check your understanding in the 'Can You' questions.

In some places we have gone beyond the specification because we felt it was a shame to miss out certain key concepts (such as Type 1 and 2 errors). Questions in the exam will only be asked on the topics listed on the right.

Before you begin this chapter it may be useful to look at a typical exam question on research methods (see pages 2, 3, 4). This will help you focus on how you ultimately need to use the knowledge contained in this chapter.

Please note that, in this chapter, we have not followed the order of the specification because it made better sense to cover the concepts/terms in a different order.

The A2 specification

Aims and hypotheses (directional, non-directional and null hypotheses)

Design issues relating to specific research methods, and their relative strengths and weaknesses

Operationalisation of independent variables, dependent variables and co-variables

Ways of overcoming confounding variables

Ethical issues and ways of overcoming these issues

Procedures, including sampling and choice of apparatus

Appropriate selection of descriptive and inferential statistics for analysis of data

Levels of significance

Levels of measurement which include: nominal level, ordinal level, interval and ratio level

Statistical tests including Chi-squared Test, Sign Test, Mann–Whitney U Test, Wilcoxon Matched Pairs Signed Ranks Test and Spearman's Rank Order Correlation Coefficient

Issues relating to findings and conclusions, including reliability and validity

WHY DOES IT MATTER?

We can think of three main reasons why it is important to study research methods.

1. Psychological research is entertaining, exciting and informative.
2. Research studies underpin everything you learn about in psychology, so it is necessary to understand the strengths and limitations of these studies in order to assess what they do actually tell us.
3. We are surrounded by research in our daily lives, such as adverts on TV telling us that 'Brand X face cream has been scientifically proven to be effective'. Are you willing to be taken in by such blatant hogwash? If not, then you need to understand the principles of scientific research in order to challenge it.

2. Research studies are psychology

Everything psychologists know is based on research evidence. It wouldn't be a scientific subject if psychologists didn't seek objective evidence to support their theories and explanations.

For example, in your AS year you studied Hans Selye's (1936) general adaptation syndrome – his view of how the body deals with being stressed. It was important that this study was supported by research studies. In the AS course you also learned about particular core studies, such as Rahe, Mahan and Arthur's (1970) study of stress and illness. This study was important in supporting the explanation that stress may cause physical illness. In other words, your psychology course is rich in research evidence to support what psychologists believe.

In psychology anyone is entitled to their own opinion – but it must be supported by research and this research must be valid and reliable.

EVERYONE IS ENTITLED TO MY OPINION

1. Psychological research is entertaining, exciting and informative

There are so many studies that have impressed or amused us, such as some of those you studied at AS level – Milgram's (1963) study of obedience and Rosenhan's (1973) study of unreliable diagnosis. Both of these regularly feature in lists of the best psychology experiments ever. But here's another one, on inattentional blindness. In fact, before you read on you should probably watch the following video on YouTube, entitled a 'selective attention test': www.youtube.com/watch?v=vJG698U2Mvo

Amused? Impressed? Inattentional blindness refers to being unable to see things that are in plain sight. You could also look at Richard Wiseman's replication of this at www.youtube.com/watch?v=0AwwlJtnwA8

What does it tell us about human behaviour? It could explain some of the problems faced in obtaining accurate eyewitness testimony – and how would we know this without psychological research?

A related field of study is change blindness, which will also amuse you. Change blindness refers to the fact that we are not very good at noticing when things change. Again have a look at YouTube (for example www.youtube.com/watch?v=mAnKvo-fPs0 or www.youtube.com/watch?v=FWSxSQsspiQ) and enjoy.

3. Research is all around us

The science journalist Ben Goldacre (2009) has written a book called *Bad Science* and also writes a column in the *Guardian* and a blog (www.badscience.net) with the same name. His book and blog focus on examples of (not surprisingly) bad science – cases where individuals try to sell products that are apparently supported by 'scientific research'. Such cases range from the relatively trivial to the downright dangerous.

An example of the relatively trivial is the purported benefits of various detox programmes which may be sold to you as effective remedies for all sorts of ailments. If such programmes do remove toxins, we should be able to find evidence of the removed toxins – but no one has. In fact no one has produced evidence of these toxins in your body in the first place. It sounds good, but what you are really being sold is sugar water, i.e. something that has no physiological benefit. It may lead you to feel better because you *believe* it to be true – and it certainly makes the manufacturers feel better because they get your money.

A more serious example concerns the myth of the MMR (measles, mumps and rubella) vaccine. Dr Andrew Wakefield published research in 1998 demonstrating that children who had received this vaccine were likely to develop autism as a result. This finding was picked up by the media and led to a whole generation of children not being vaccinated because parents were afraid their children would develop autism. It was quite an understandable reaction – who would vaccinate their child if there was a small possibility of their child developing autism? Headlines such as 'MMR causes autism' are bound to lead people to jump to conclusions.

However, Wakefield's research has now been shown to be extremely poor science. It was based on a sample of 12 children and any subsequent support has been correlational (i.e. it shows that some children who develop autism did have the MMR vaccine but does not show that the vaccine caused it). In addition, Wakefield was found to have been employed by a company wishing to produce an alternative vaccine, which suggests that he had a financial incentive for discrediting the existing vaccine.

Measles is a dangerous and even fatal childhood illness so there were serious repercussions of this hiatus in the use of this potentially life-saving vaccine. In 2010 the *General Medical Council* struck Wakefield off the medical register, finding him 'dishonest', 'unethical' and 'irresponsible', but some people are still cautious about using the MMR vaccine.

Knowledge

knowl•edge *n.*

1. The information and facts gained through education, time and experience.

YOU ALREADY HAVE THE KNOWLEDGE!

You already know a lot about research methods because it was a big part of your AS course. So what do you remember?

1. Work with a partner and write down all the research methods terms and concepts you can remember from last year.

2. Compare your list with what other students in your class remembered and add any terms/concepts that you forgot.

3. Working with your partner again, write an explanation for each of the terms/concepts. Look up any you can't remember.

4. Get together with another pair of students and compare your explanations. Decide which ones are best.

TIME TO PLAY SOME GAMES

Devise a game based on research methods. You could create a board game (e.g. when you land on a square that says 'Research methods' you have to answer a question and correct answers win prizes) or produce a set of *top trumps* cards (see right).

You can play each other's game – and use them for revision.

The game is played by dealing all the cards between players. Player 1 looks at their first card and selects a category and then chooses another player. If player 1's card beats the other player on the selected category then the player wins their opponent's card. The game continues until one player has all the cards.

You can create your own set of top trump cards for different research methods concepts and have categories such as frequency of usage, conceptual difficulty, etc. You then decide a rating for the concept in each of these categories. For example, in the card on the right, the concept is 'correlation' which has been rated a 7 out of 10 for frequency of use.

You could also make a pack for different research studies.

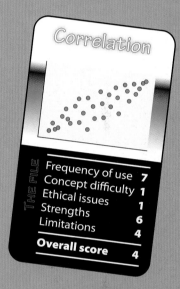

Correlation

THE FILE	
Frequency of use	7
Concept difficulty	1
Ethical issues	1
Strengths	6
Limitations	4
Overall score	**4**

▲ *Top trumps is played with a pack of cards. Each card represents an item – a person, film, country or anything you like. Each item is rated on a list of categories.*

Try this

Conduct your own research project

The fascinating topics of inattentional blindness and change blindness are described at the top of the facing page.

Why not conduct your own research to further understand these phenomena?

For example, you might investigate one of the following hypotheses:

● In the inattentional blindness study, people are more likely to notice the gorilla if they have been told beforehand to take extra special care in observing everything. How could you test this?

● In the change blindness study, people are more likely to notice a change if the confederates are the same age group as the participant rather then being in a different age group. How could you investigate this?

Validity and reliability are the two key concepts in understanding and evaluating research. The findings of a study are meaningless if the study or any measurement used in the study lacks validity and/or reliability.

Validity is concerned with legitimacy. It is the extent to which a measurement is well founded and to which the measurement corresponds accurately to the real world. Students often get confused and think that a valid study is one where the researcher found support for his (or her) hypothesis. This is not the case. A valid result is a correct result in terms of what is really true as opposed to what the researcher thought would be true.

Reliability is about consistency. It refers to how much we can depend on any particular measurement, for example the measurement of a table, or the measurement of a psychological characteristic such as intelligence, or the findings of a research study. In particular we want to know whether, if we repeat the measurement/test/study, we can be sure that we would get the same result. If not, our measurement/findings are unreliable.

Validity is related to reliability because, if a measurement is not reliable (consistent) then a study cannot be valid, i.e. it cannot be 'true' or legitimate. For example, a researcher might measure intelligence using an **IQ test**. If one person is tested on several occasions using the same test and the results change each time, then the IQ test lacks reliability – and any study using the test lacks validity because the scores are meaningless.

However, a measurement may be reliable but still lack validity. For example, a person may take an IQ test and then take the same test several months later. Their score may be consistent, so it is a reliable test. However, the items on the test may simply assess what a person learned at school rather than 'intelligence', in which case the test is lacking validity (i.e. lacks meaningfulness), and any study using the test would lack validity.

Extraneous variables

There is a subtle but important difference between extraneous variables (EVs) and confounding variables. An EV is a variable other than the IV that may affect the DV and should be controlled to prevent this happening. A confounding variable is a variable other than the IV that *has* affected the DV and has thus *confounded* the findings of the study. In other words, the researcher should identify EVs and control them but it is too late to control the confounding variables. All you can do is identify them and suggest how this might affect the validity of any study.

In your AS course you studied extraneous variables and considered how they might threaten validity. The list of possible extraneous variables included:

- **Situational variables** – any environmental variables (such as noise or time of day) that might affect participants' behaviour. The researcher can deal with these by using **standardised procedures**.
- **Participant variables** – characteristics of the participants that might lead one group to perform better than another group. The researcher can deal with these by using **matched pairs** or **repeated measures design**.
- **Investigator effects** – cues from an investigator that alter participants' behaviour (such as **leading questions**). The researcher can deal with these by using the **double blind technique**.
- **Demand characteristics** – cues arising in the research situation that affect participants' behaviour. The researcher can deal with these by improving the design of the experiment.

VALIDITY AND DEALING WITH THE PROBLEMS THAT MAY ARISE

All research strives to be high in validity. Any flaws must be minimised in order to draw valid conclusions from a study. There are two kinds of validity:

- **Internal validity** concerns what goes on inside a study – whether the researcher tested what he or she intended to test.
- **External validity** concerns things outside a study – the extent to which the results of the study can be generalised to other situations and people. The term **ecological validity** is often used as another term for external validity.

Experimental research

Internal validity may be affected by **extraneous variables** (EVs) that may act as an alternative **independent variable** (IV). These are discussed in the box on the left. Conclusions about the effect of the IV on the dependent variable (DV) are erroneous if changes in the DV are due to EVs/**confounding variables**.

Internal validity of an experiment may also be affected by the use of measurements that lack validity. For example, a study on gender differences in conformity may use a **questionnaire** to assess conformity. If the questionnaire lacks validity, this means the experiment in general lacks validity. It could also be that the study assessed conformity by *observing* the behaviour of participants. If the observations lacked validity, this would affect the internal validity of the whole study. See right for a discussion of validity in relation to observational techniques and questionnaires.

External validity Many people think all **lab experiments** are low in external validity whereas **field experiments** and **natural experiments**, conducted in more natural surroundings, are seen as high in external validity. This is not necessarily true. In some cases the contrived, artificial nature of the lab setting is immaterial to the behaviour being observed (such as a memory task) and therefore it can be generalised to everyday situations (high external validity). In some cases, field and natural experiments can be very contrived and artificial.

It is often more important to consider issues such as whether the participants were *aware* of being studied (which reduces the realism of their behaviour) and whether the *task* itself (rather than the setting) was artificial and thus low in **mundane realism**, which reduces the generalisability of the results.

RELIABILITY AND DEALING WITH PROBLEMS THAT MAY ARISE

Experimental research

In the context of an experiment, reliability refers to the ability to repeat a study and obtain the same result, i.e. **replication**. It is essential in a replication that all conditions are the same otherwise any change in the result may be due to changed conditions rather than a failure to demonstrate the same effect.

Observational techniques

Observations should be consistent which means that ideally two observers should produce the same record. The extent to which two (or more) observers agree is called inter-rater or **inter-observer reliability**, calculated by dividing total agreements by the total number of observations. A result of +0.80 or more suggests good inter-observer reliability.

The reliability of observations can be improved through training observers in the use of a coding system/behaviour checklist so they understand the operational definitions.

Questionnaires and interviews

Internal reliability is a measure of the extent to which something is consistent within itself. For example, all the questions on an IQ test (which is a kind of questionnaire) should be measuring the same thing. This can be assessed using the **split-half method** to compare a person's performance on two halves of a questionnaire or test. If the test is assessing the same thing in all its questions then there should be a close correlation in the scores derived from both halves of the test, a measure of internal reliability.

External reliability is a measure of consistency over several different occasions. For example, if the same interview by the same interviewer with the same interviewee was conducted one day and then again a week later, the outcome should be the same – otherwise the interview is not reliable. This can be assessed using the **test–retest method** where a person is given a questionnaire/interview/test on one occasion and then this is repeated again after a reasonable interval (e.g. a week or a month). If the measure is reliable the outcome should be the same every time.

Reliability also concerns whether two interviewers produce the same outcome. This is called **inter-interviewer reliability**. This can be assessed by comparing the results from both interviewers.

▲ *Reliable and valid – consistent and accurate.*

Observational techniques

Internal validity Observations will not be valid (nor reliable) if the **coding system/behaviour checklist** is flawed. For example, some observations may belong in more than one category, or some behaviours may not be codeable, which reduces the internal validity of the data collected. (See page 26 for information on coding systems and behaviour checklists.)

The internal validity of observations is also affected by **observer bias** – what someone observes is influenced by their expectations. This reduces the objectivity of observations.

External validity Observational studies are likely to have high ecological validity because they involve more natural behaviours – though, as we have seen, naturalistic research is not necessarily higher in ecological validity.

Questionnaires and interviews

Internal validity There are several ways to assess the internal validity of **questionnaires**, **interviews** and also **psychological tests**:

- **Content validity** Is the test/questionnaire/interview measuring what you intended to test? For example, are the questions obviously related to the topic?
- **Concurrent validity** This can be established by comparing performance on a new test with a previously established test on the same topic.
- **Construct validity** Does the test measure the target construct? For example, an intelligence test based on Gardner's (1983) theory of multiple intelligences should assess many different kinds of intelligence.

External validity of self-report techniques is likely to be affected by the **sampling** strategies used which may create a biased sample.

CAN YOU...?   No. 1A.1

1... Explain what is meant by validity and reliability, internal and external validity, and internal and external reliability.

2... In each of the following studies describe **two** features of the study that might be a threat to the validity of the study and how the validity could be improved.
   (a) A psychologist conducts interviews with students about their attitudes towards exams.
   (b) A psychologist conducts a study to see if students do more homework in the winter or spring term. To do this he asks students to keep a diary of how much time they spend on homework each week.

3... In each of the following studies suggest how reliability could be assessed and how the reliability could be improved.
   (a) A psychologist intends to use a repeated measures design to test participants' memories in the morning and afternoon. He uses two tests of memory.
   (b) A psychologist interviews teenage girls about their dieting.

4... A group of psychology students plan to conduct on observational study on the effects of different dress styles – to see if men look more at girls dressed casually or smartly.
   (a) Identify **one** way in which you could ensure reliability among the different observers and explain how to do this.
   (b) Explain **one** feature of the study that might threaten the validity of the data being collected.

5... A research team receives funding to assess the effectiveness of a new drug. It intends to give one group of participants a placebo (a substance which has no physiological effect) and the other group will receive the actual drug. Effectiveness will be assessed by comparing the severity of the patients' symptoms before and after the study to see if there has been any improvement. Discuss potential issues of validity and reliability that might arise in this study and suggest how they might be dealt with.

The title of this spread may be confusing because the whole chapter is called 'Research methods' – so why is there just one spread with that title? The term 'research methods' is used to refer generally to everything to do with research but also to refer specifically to the overarching technique used when conducting an investigation – such as an experiment or an observational study.

On this spread we will review the research methods and techniques that you studied at AS level. On the next spread we will look at a range of other research methods, many of which will be familiar to you.

On pages 24–27 we will consider the design of all the different kinds of research methods.

On pages 24–27 we will consider the design of all the different kinds of research methods.

EXAM TIP

Exam questions are likely to focus on asking you to explain **one** advantage and **one** disadvantage of any of the research methods listed on this spread. Questions may also ask you to produce a definition e.g. 'Define what is meant by the term "laboratory experiment"'.

Experiments

All **experiments** involve an **IV (independent variable)** and **DV (dependent variable)**. The IV is varied in order to see how this affects the DV, thus demonstrating a causal relationship. As far as possible all other variables are controlled, so any changes in the DV are due to the IV rather than **extraneous variables (EVs)**.

Lab experiment An experiment conducted in a controlled environment which therefore tends to be high in terms of **internal validity** because many EVs can be controlled – though some EVs (such as **experimenter effects** and **demand characteristics**) may reduce internal validity. Control also increases **replicability**, which is desirable, but reduces **external (ecological) validity** because a highly controlled situation may be less like everyday life.

Field experiment An experiment conducted in a more natural environment but the experimenter still has control over the IV. It may be possible to control EVs, though such control is more difficult than in a lab experiment. Experimenter effects are reduced because participants are usually not aware of being in a study. However, demand characteristics may still be problematic, for example the way an IV is **operationalised** may convey the experimental **hypothesis** to participants.

Natural experiment An experiment that makes use of existing IVs, such as a treatment used for people with mental illness. Strictly speaking, an experiment involves the *deliberate* manipulation of an IV by an experimenter, so causal conclusions cannot be drawn from a natural experiment. In addition, participants are not **randomly allocated** to conditions in a natural experiment (which may reduce validity) but it is often the only way to study certain behaviours or experiences, such as the effects of a poor diet on intellectual development.

Questionnaires and Interviews

Psychologists use **questionnaires** and **interviews** to find out what people think and feel. Interviews are essentially real-time, face-to-face (or over the phone) questionnaires, although in an interview there is the option to conduct a fairly **unstructured interview** where the questions are developed by the interviewer as a response to the answers given by the interviewee.

Advantages and disadvantages Questionnaires/structured interviews can be more easily repeated than unstructured interviews, which is an advantage. However, unstructured interviews may provide unexpected insights and more detailed information can be gained, increasing validity.

The main problem for **self-report methods** is honesty because, for example, the **social desirability bias** means that respondents may provide answers to put themselves in a good light.

The advantages or disadvantages of a questionnaire or interview depend on the kind of questions used. If **open questions** are used, rich data may be collected providing detailed and new insights into what people think and feel. However, such questionnaires/interviews produce **qualitative data** which is more difficult to analyse than **quantitative data**. The opposite is true of questionnaires/interviews with **closed questions**. Here, data analysis is straightforward but answers are limited and participants may be forced to give answers that don't fully represent what they think and feel.

Correlational analysis

Some studies are concerned with the relationship between two variables, such as IQ and A-level results (which we would expect to be **positively correlated**) or reaction time and age (which might be **negatively correlated**).

Advantages and disadvantages
A **correlational analysis** does not demonstrate a cause but is useful in identifying where relationships between **co-variables** exist. Such studies can be done with large data sets and can be easily repeated. However, there may be other, unknown (**intervening) variables** that can explain why the co-variables being studied are linked. Such studies may lack internal/external validity, for example the method used to measure IQ may lack validity or the sample of participants selected may lack generalisability.

▼ *Experimental control is a balancing act.*

▶ *In a lab experiment you have lots of control which is good because it means you can control extraneous variables. However, it is bad because it means the tasks involved may not be very much like everyday tasks (lacks mundane realism).*

◀ *In a field experiment behaviour may be more 'natural' but there is less control which means it is difficult to draw clear conclusions because of confounding variables – variables other than the IV which have affected the DV.*

When answering these questions you may wish to refer to your AS notes on research methods.

1... Write down every key word on this spread (they are in red). These should all be familiar to you so try to write your own explanation using examples. Check your explanation against the definitions given at the end of this book in the Glossary/Index.

2... Draw a table with four columns and at least eight rows. In the first column write down all the different research methods on this spread (and you can include some from the next spread if you wish). In the second column write a brief description of the method. Your description should *clearly* distinguish it from the other methods. In the third column write **one** advantage of using this method and in the final column record **one** disadvantage of the method.

3... For each of the research methods named on this spread identify an example from your psychology studies, and for each example explain **one** advantage of using this research method and **one** disadvantage *in the context* of your research example.

4... In the green box below are some brief descriptions of research studies. Try to answer the following questions in relation to each of these studies (or use some other studies you have looked at during your Psychology course – even your AS core studies).

(a) Identify the research method(s) and/or research technique(s) used in this study and explain your choice(s).

(b) Explain **one** advantage of using this research method in the context of this research example.

(c) Explain **one** disadvantage of using this research method in the context of this research example.

(d) Explain **two** factors that might have affected the validity of this study and how they could be dealt with.

(e) Explain **two** factors that might have affected the reliability of this study and how they could be dealt with.

(f) Describe **one** conclusion that could be drawn.

Observational studies

Perhaps one of the most obvious research methods is simply to watch what people do (**observational techniques**). Observational techniques may be used in an experiment, as a means of measuring the DV, or may form the whole of a research project, such as when observing behaviour of animals in the wild.

It is not that simple to observe behaviour because there is so much information to collect. For this reason, psychologists use structured techniques such as **sampling methods** and **behaviour checklists** to record particular instances of behaviour. These methods are discussed on the spread on research design (see pages 25 and 26).

Even **naturalistic observations** (as distinct from **controlled observations**) use structured techniques to study behaviour.

Advantages and disadvantages Observational studies provide a rich picture of what people actually do (rather than what they say they do) and so are potentially more valid. However, observers may be biased – their observations can be affected by their expectations (**observer bias**). Observations may also lack **reliability**.

Content analysis

Content analysis is a form of observation – observing behaviour by looking at the content of things produced by people, for example looking at magazines, advertisements, books and so on. It is a form of indirect rather than direct observation and can be qualitative (when individual examples of the content are recorded) or quantitative (when examples in each category are counted).

Advantages and disadvantages This method has high ecological validity because observations are made of things that people actually do; however there may be problems with observer bias.

Case studies

A **case study** is a detailed study of a single individual, institution or event. It uses information from a range of sources, such as from the person concerned and also from their family and friends. Many techniques may be used, such as interviews, psychological tests, observations and experiments. Case studies are generally **longitudinal**, in other words they follow the individual or group over an extended period of time.

Advantages and disadvantages The complex interaction of many factors can be studied, in contrast to experiments where only a few variables are studied. However, it is difficult to generalise from individual cases as each one has unique characteristics. Another disadvantage is that it is often necessary to use recollection of past events as part of the case study and such evidence may therefore be distorted. The interpretation of data may also lack objectivity.

Research studies

Study A: Kiecolt-Glaser *et al.* (1984) investigated the effects of stress on our immune system – when a person is stressed they produce high levels of a hormone called cortisol and this reduces immune system activity. In this study blood samples were taken from students one month prior to their exams (low stress) and were taken during the exam period itself (high stress). The samples were analysed to see whether the immune system was functioning normally or not. It was found that levels of immune system activity were lower during the exam period.

Study B: In the USA there is a large-scale research project running which regularly assesses a group of 1000 children who spent their early years attending day nursery schools. *The National Institute of Child Health and Human Development* (NICHD) reports its results regularly. In 2003, when the children were aged five years, the study reported that the more time a child had spent in day care, the more they were rated as assertive, aggressive and disobedient.

Study C: Smith and Lloyd (1978) investigated the way mothers treat babies in terms of gender stereotypes. Each mother was introduced to one baby. The baby was dressed like a boy or girl and given an appropriate name. The mothers were told that the study was about analysing play so they were videotaped while playing with the baby. Seven toys were present – some masculine (a squeaky hammer and a stuffed rabbit in trousers), some were feminine (a doll and a squeaky bambi) and some were neutral (a squeaky pig, a ball and a rattle). Smith and Lloyd found that the mothers selected toys differently depending on what gender they thought the baby was.

Study D: Garner *et al.* (1980) investigated changing attitudes to the female body by looking at the centrefold pictures from *Playboy* magazine over a period of 20 years. They found that, in the years from 1959 to 1978, there was a definite change in the preferred shape for women toward a more angular and thinner physique. The women weighed less and also bust and hip measurements became smaller. The study also involved looking at articles about dieting in six popular women's magazines, where they found an increase in articles about dieting. They also looked at the vital statistics for winners of the Miss America beauty pageant.

The AS Psychology research methods course only names some of the methods and techniques that are used by psychologists. On this spread we will very briefly mention some other methods and techniques that you are likely to encounter when you read about research in psychology. It is useful to know something about them, and their advantages and disadvantages, for making general evaluations of research in psychology as well as for answering questions specifically on research methods.

The research methods discussed on this spread are not identified in the specification, which means that exam questions won't be set on them. This means you can skip this spread entirely if you wish! However, knowledge of advantages and disadvantages of meta-analysis and cross-cultural studies, to name just two, may come in useful when evaluating psychological research in your essays.

▲ An example of role play. Zimbardo et al. (1973) ran the infamous Stanford Prison Experiment to study whether dispositional factors or situational factors would explain the behaviour of prisoners and guards. Student volunteers were randomly assigned to the role of prisoner or guard and required to play these roles.

The multi-method approach

In reality very few studies simply use one method. Many studies reported in this book and your AS book use the *multi-method approach* – a combination of all sorts of different techniques and methods to investigate a target behaviour. Some examples are given on this spread.

Milgram (1963) conducted a controlled observation in a lab, but he also extensively interviewed his participants after the study to find out their views on why they did or didn't obey. For instance, Jan Rensaleer, an industrial engineer, stopped at 225 volts, saying 'I know what shocks do to you. I'm an electrical engineer'. When asked who was responsible for the shocks he said 'I would put it on myself entirely'. Karen Dontz, a nurse who administered the full 450 volts said, 'in hospital I know what rights I have, here I didn't know'. In hospital she would have felt in a position to question authority because of the knowledge she had, but she didn't feel able to do it here (Milgram, 1974). Such interviews supplied important insights into obedience.

Rosenhan (1973) conducted an observational study of the behaviour of psychiatrists and other staff in the psychiatric hospital. However, the study also involved a mini-experiment to see how long hospital staff would spend talking to a person if they were either a patient or a 'normal' young woman.

Meta-analysis

A **meta-analysis** is a technique used in a number of the research studies we have looked at in this book. Researchers combine the results from several studies that have addressed similar **aims/hypotheses** and use the combined results to reach a general conclusion about a particular hypothesis. Because the **independent variables (IVs)** in these studies tend to be measured in different ways, the researcher(s) use **effect size** as the **dependent variable (DV)** in order to assess overall trends. Effect size is a measure of the strength of the relationship between two variables. We use effect sizes in our everyday lives, for example a weight-loss programme may boast that it leads to an average weight loss of 30 pounds. This is the size of the effect.

One example of a meta-analysis is the study by Butler *et al.* (2006) who reviewed 16 meta-analyses of studies of **cognitive–behavioural therapy** (CBT) (see page 239). This was a meta-analysis of meta-analyses. The researchers found large effect sizes when CBT was used for **unipolar depression** and various **anxiety disorders**. Effect sizes were more moderate when CBT was used with marital distress, anger and chronic pain. They also found that CBT was somewhat superior to **antidepressants** in the treatment of adult depression.

Advantage Analysing the results from a group of studies rather than from just one study can allow more **reliable** conclusions to be drawn. Studies often produce rather contradictory results (e.g. some studies may find no effect, some studies find a small effect while others find a larger effect). A meta-analysis allows us to reach an overall conclusion.

Disadvantage The research designs in the different studies sampled may vary considerably which means that the studies are not truly comparable and thus the conclusions are not always **valid**.

Role play

In some investigations participants are required to take on a certain role and then their behaviour can be observed as if it were real life. For example, they might be asked to imagine that they are lying, or to pretend that they are a prison guard as in Zimbardo's study. **Role play** is a form of a **controlled observation** in which participants are asked to imagine how they would behave in certain situations, and act out the part.

Advantages This enables researchers to study behaviour that might otherwise be impractical or unethical to observe. For example, in Zimbardo's study he arranged for participants to play the role of prisoners and guards because you could not randomly allocate such roles in real life.

The researcher may also gain valuable insights into the behaviour being studied by asking participants afterwards to discuss their experiences and behaviour.

Disadvantages The question is whether people really do act as they would in real life. In Zimbardo's study the participants acting as guards may have been following what they *thought* was guard-like behaviour, as seen in films. If they were real guards they may have acted more in accordance with personal principles rather than according to social norms.

There are also **ethical issues** about placing people in uncomfortable situations, such as the prison experiment where those participants assigned the role of prisoners became extremely distressed even though they knew it was only role play.

▲ You can study the effects of ageing on behaviours such as intelligence by testing and interviewing the same person repeatedly as they get older. This is called a longitudinal study – it is also a kind of natural experiment because the IV is age and the DV is whatever behaviour we wish to study (such as intelligence). You would begin such a study when the individuals are young and revisit the same participants at regular intervals over time.

The alternative is to use a cross-sectional design and test/interview separate groups of people representing the different ages we are interested in.

Longitudinal and cross-sectional studies

When a study is conducted over a long period of time it is said to be a **longitudinal study** (it's long!). The need for such studies is to be able to observe long-term effects and to make comparisons between, for example, the same individual at different ages or the same institution at different historical periods.

An alternative way to do this is to conduct a **cross-sectional study**. In this instance one group of participants of a young age are compared with another older group of participants at the same point in time with a view to investigating the influence of age on the behaviour in question. This method is sometimes called a **snapshot study** because a snapshot is taken at a particular moment in time.

Advantage Both methods enable the effects of age or time to be studied. Longitudinal studies control for **participant variables** whereas cross-sectional studies are relatively quick.

Disadvantages Attrition is problem in a longitudinal study. Some of the participants inevitably drop out over the course of a study. The difficulty is that the ones who drop out are more likely to have particular characteristics (e.g. be the ones who are less motivated or more unhappy or who have done less well), which leaves a biased sample or a sample that is too small.

A problem with cross-sectional studies is that the two groups of participants may be quite different. The **participant variables** in a cross-sectional design are not controlled because the participants in each group are different (just like an **independent groups design**). This means that, in a cross-sectional design, differences between groups may be due to participant variables rather than the independent variable.

In a longitudinal study participants are likely to become aware of the research aims and their behaviour may be affected (just like in a **repeated measures design**). Another problem is that such studies take a long time to complete, and therefore are difficult to finance and also to staff.

Cohort effects cause difficulties for both longitudinal and cross-sectional studies. A group (or cohort) of people who are all the same age share certain experiences, such as the fact that children born just after the war had poor diets in infancy due to rationing. In a longitudinal study we may not be able to generalise the findings from a study that looks at only one cohort because of the unique characteristics of that cohort.

In a cross-sectional study cohort effects may produce spurious results, for example one study might compare the IQs of 20-somethings with 80-somethings and find that the IQs of the latter group were much lower, concluding that ageing led to a decreased IQ. The reason, however, might well be because the 80-somethings had lower IQs when they were 20-somethings (due to e.g. poorer diet). This is a cohort effect.

So, cohort effects are problems in longitudinal studies because the group studied is not typical and problems in cross-sectional studies because one group is not comparable with another.

Cross-cultural studies

In **cross-cultural studies** psychologists compare behaviours in different cultures. This is a way of seeing whether cultural practices affect behaviour. It is a kind of **natural experiment** where the IV is, for example, child-rearing techniques in different cultures and the DV is a behaviour, such as aggression. This enables researchers to see if variations in levels of aggression are due to different culturally determined child-rearing techniques.

Advantage Such studies enable us to consider whether behaviours are innate – if a behaviour is the same in all cultures, it suggests that it must be part of our **genetic** make-up.

Disadvantages There are many problems with such studies. For example, researchers may use tests or procedures that have been developed in the USA and are not valid in the other culture. This may make the individuals in the other culture appear 'abnormal' or inferior. The term that is used to describe this is an **imposed etic** – when a technique or psychological test is used with (i.e. imposed upon) one culture even though it was designed for use in another culture. A key example of this is the use of intelligence tests that are designed for Western populations but used worldwide. The poorer performance of non-Western people may be due to the fact that the test is based on Western assumptions about intelligence (see page 122).

A second problem is that the group of participants may not be representative of that culture and yet we make generalisations about the whole culture – or even the whole country.

In addition there are problems of **observer bias**, where the observer's expectations alter what they 'see', and problems of **investigator effects**, where participants try to guess what answers the researcher would like and provide those answers.

CAN YOU...? (No. **1A.3**)

In each of the following, identify the research method and, where relevant, the research technique(s) or design.

1... Scores from a questionnaire 'How good is your memory' are related to GCSE results.

2... A male or female confederate stands by the roadside with a broken-down car to see if people are more likely to help males or females.

3... Psychology exam results from two classes are compared to see if teacher A's teaching style was better than that of teacher B.

4... Children view two films, one that shows a child being helpful and another that shows a child not being helpful. They then are given free play time and watched to see if they are more helpful.

5... Students are asked to explain what methods they find most successful for revision.

6... A group of children are assessed every year on various measures such as IQ, self-esteem and personality.

7... Interactions between first-time mothers and their newborn babies are compared with interactions of second-time mothers and their newborn babies.

8... A study on gambling is based around the experiences of one individual.

9... The effect of age on IQ is studied by comparing a group of young people with a group of older people.

Research design refers to the detailed plan used within a research method, i.e. experimental design (discussed on this spread) and questionnaire, interview and observational design (discussed on the next spread). There are general design issues, common to all research methods, such as producing a testable hypothesis and sampling techniques, both of which are covered on this spread.

Aims and hypotheses

Researchers start any research study by identifying what they intend to study (the **aims**) and then make a formal statement of their expectations using a **hypothesis**. This hypothesis might state a *difference*, for example:

- Students tested in the morning get better marks than students tested in the afternoon (a directional hypothesis).
- Students tested in the morning perform differently from students tested in the afternoon (a non-directional hypothesis).

Or may state an *association/correlation*:

- Exam results are positively correlated with intelligence test scores (a directional hypothesis).

A hypothesis may be **directional** or **non-directional** (i.e. the direction of a difference or correlation is or is not stated).

Operationalising a hypothesis
A good hypothesis must be **operationalised** so that the variables are in a form that can be easily tested. For example, if your hypothesis states 'People who own pets are happier than people who don't own pets' you need to operationalise the dependent variable 'happiness'. You might do this by devising a **questionnaire** to assess happiness. The operationalised hypothesis would then be 'People who own pets score higher on a happiness questionnaire than people who don't own pets'.

Operationalising in observational studies
Operationalisation is also important when developing **behavioural categories** because what you are doing is breaking down target behaviours into a set of components. For example, if you are observing whether people are happier when they have a pet or not, you would identify a number of observable behaviours that demonstrate happiness, such as smiling and laughing. You might also have behaviours that don't demonstrate happiness, such as staring vacantly or crying.

EXPERIMENTAL DESIGN

In any **experiment** there are several levels of the **independent variable** (IV). For example, in the AS core study on eyewitness testimony by Loftus and Palmer (1974) participants were given a sentence with one of five verbs (hit, smashed, bumped, etc.), so there were five levels of the IV. Experimenters have a choice – either each participant is tested on all of the IVs (**repeated measures**) or there are separate groups for each IV (**independent groups**). There is also a third possibility – the participants in each independent group can be matched with participants in the other group(s) on key variables such as age and IQ (**matched pairs** design).

Repeated measures
The same participants take part in every condition being tested. For example, if you were testing the effect of temperature on ability to work, each participant would do a task in a warm environment and again, later, in a cold environment.

This means there is good control for **participant variables** and fewer participants needed. But **order effects** may occur (e.g. boredom, practice) or participants may guess the purpose of the experiment and their behaviour would be affected.

Independent groups
Participants take part in only one condition. For example, some participants do the task in the warm environment and some do it in the cold environment and their performance is compared.

This technique avoids problems that occur with repeated measures design but needs more participants. There is no control of participant variables, although this can partly be overcome using **random allocation** of participants to conditions.

Matched pairs
Participants matched on key participant variables. This technique avoids order effects and partially controls participant variables but matching is difficult.

Experimental control
We have discussed the importance of controls in experimental research – to control **extraneous/confounding variables**. However, researchers also use the word 'control' in a different context – as a means of establishing a baseline in an experiment. You may recall seeing the words *experimental group* and *control group*. For example: A researcher might want to investigate the effects that rewards have on performance. To do this children are asked to collect rubbish from a playground and offered a chocolate bar as a reward. They collect ten bags of rubbish.

We cannot conclude anything about the effects of the reward because we don't know if ten bags of rubbish is more or less than 'normal'. We don't know if they would have collected as many bags even if offered no reward. We need to have a control group so that we can make a comparison.

We could do the study with two groups of children (i.e. an independent groups design): an **experimental group** (offered a reward) and a **control group** (offered no reward). This allows us to compare the effects of the reward (IV) on collecting rubbish (**dependent variable, DV**).

Or we can carry out a repeated measures study with just one group of participants but two *conditions*: an **experimental condition** (children offered a reward on one occasion) and a **control condition** (offered no reward on another occasion).

Populations, sampling and hypotheses

The '**population**' is all the people about whom a researcher wishes to make a statement. (The phrase '**target population**' is sometimes used). The hypothesis is a statement about the population not the **sample**. The aim is to select a *representative* sample from the target population – a small group who *represent* the target population in terms of characteristics such as age, IQ, social class, relevant experiences and so on.

The importance of representativeness is in order to be able to *generalise* from the sample to the target population. A sample that is not representative is described as **biased**, i.e. leaning in one direction. A biased sample means that any generalisations lack **external validity**.

SAMPLING TECHNIQUES

The aim of all psychological research is to be able to make valid generalisations about behaviour. In a research project only a small number of participants are studied because you could never study the whole population. Psychologists use **sampling** techniques which maximise generalisability.

Opportunity sample Participants are selected by using those people who are most easily available. This is the easiest method to use but it is inevitably biased because the sample is drawn from a small part of the target population. For example, if you selected your sample from people walking around the centre of a town on a weekday morning then it would be unlikely to include professional people (because they are at work) and is therefore biased.

Self-selected (volunteer) sample Participants are selected by asking for volunteers, for example placing an advertisement in a newspaper or on a college noticeboard asking for participants. This method can access a variety of participants if the advertisement is, for example, in a national newspaper, which would make the sample more representative. However, such samples are inevitably biased because volunteer participants have special characteristics, for example they are highly motivated (= **volunteer bias**).

Random sample Participants are selected using a random number technique. First, all members of the target population are identified (e.g. all the members of one school) and then individuals are selected either by the lottery method (names drawn from a 'hat') or using a random number generator.

This method is potentially unbiased because all members of the target population have an equal chance of selection, although in the end a researcher may still end up with a biased sample because some people refuse to take part.

Systematic sample Participants are selected using a predetermined system, such as selecting every tenth person.

This method is unbiased as participants are selected using an objective system. It is not truly random unless you select a number using a random method and start with this person, and then you select every tenth person.

Stratified and quota samples Subgroups (strata) within a population are identified (e.g. boys and girls or different age groups). Then a predetermined number of participants are taken from each subgroup in proportion to their numbers in the target population, e.g. if there are twice as many boys than girls in the target population then the sample will consist of twice as many boys. In stratified sampling participants in each strata are selected using random techniques, in quota sampling it is done using opportunity sampling.

This method is more representative than other methods because there is proportional representation of subgroups. However, selection within each subgroup may be biased because of opportunity sampling, for example.

Sampling techniques are also used in observational studies – **time sampling** and **event sampling** (see next spread).

A systematic sample is often mistaken for a random sample but it isn't – it is systematic, for example taking every tenth person from a register. However it is random if the first person is selected randomly!

A few other things

Pilot studies

If you have tried any of the studies in this book you probably were aware that there were flaws in your design. Did you realise that there would be flaws beforehand? Or did some of the flaws become apparent after conducting the study?

Scientists deal with this problem by conducting a **pilot study** first. A pilot study is a small-scale trial run of a research design before doing the real thing. It is done in order to find out if certain things don't work. For example, participants may not understand the instructions, or they may guess what an experiment is about, or they may get very bored because there are too many tasks or too many questions. If you try out the design using a few typical participants you can see what needs to be adjusted without having invested a large amount of time and money.

Confederates

Sometimes a researcher has to use another person to play a role in an experiment or other investigation. For example, you might want to find out if people respond differently to orders from someone wearing a suit or dressed in casual clothes. In this experiment the IV would be the clothing worn by someone briefed to behave in a certain way by the experimenter. The experimenter would arrange for this person to give orders either dressed in a suit or dressed casually. This person is called a confederate.

▶ *The woman on the left (a confederate) talks 'blirtatiously' (loudly and effusively) to see what this effect this has on the person who is studying.*

CAN YOU...?　　　No. **1A.4**

1... Draw a table with four columns and three rows. In the first column list the three kinds of experimental design. In the second column write a brief description of the design. In the third column describe **one** advantage and in the final column write **one** disadvantage.

2... Draw another table with four columns and six rows. In the first column list the sampling methods described on this page. Fill in the other three columns as for question 1.

3... Produce your own example of an experimental hypothesis which is not operationalised and then operationalise the IV and DV.

4... On page 21 **four** research studies are described. For each study:

(a) Write a suitable operationalised hypothesis.

(b) Identify whether your hypothesis is directional or non-directional and explain why you chose this kind of hypothesis.

(c) If appropriate, identify the type of experimental design used in the study and explain why the researcher would have chosen this experimental design.

(d) Suggest a suitable sampling method.

(e) Give **one** advantage and **one** disadvantage of the sampling method in the context of the study.

(f) Identify **one** possible confounding variable that could be a problem in this study and explain how it might have been dealt with.

On this spread we look briefly at the main issues involved in the design of observational studies and studies using questionnaires or interviews.

Try this

Observational study at a zoo

Jordan and Burghardt (1986) undertook a study of black bears in a zoo to determine whether the presence of observers altered the animals' behaviour. They did this to establish whether naturalistic observations of animals was in fact 'naturalistic' – if the animals' behaviour was affected by the presence of observers then it wasn't so natural after all.

In this study they selected two bear enclosures in parks in the USA, one at *Dollywood* (less observed by people) and the other at *Tremont*. They found a much higher activity level at Tremont where the bears had more human contact.

You could conduct your own observational study at a zoo based on some of the procedures of this study. The researchers spent one hour each day making recordings over a two-and-a-half-year period. Observations were recorded every 30 seconds (time sampling) using a behaviour checklist/coding system similar to the one below.

Behaviour checklist and coding system for recording postures and locations of captive black bears

Activity level 1: Reclining postures
> Lying on back (P6)
> Lying on front (P7)
> Lying on side (P8)
> Lying/sitting in a tree (P28)

Activity level 2: Sitting or standing
> Standing on all fours (P3)
> Standing on two feet (P29)
> Sitting erect or semi-erect (P4)

Activity level 3: Bipedal standing and slow locomotion
> Standing on two feet while touching an object (P1)
> Walking on all fours (P11)
> Rolling over (P18)

Activity level 4: Vigorous activity
> Running (P19)
> Ascending (e.g. trees) (P24)
> Descending (e.g. trees) (P27)
> Running a short distance and then walking (P32)
> Jumping (all legs off ground) (P35)

Designing observations

Observational techniques may be used in all sorts of studies. For example, in an experimental study you might look at whether people work better in a library or their own room. In order to assess the quality of their studying you might observe participants and record how much of the time they are actually studying as opposed to daydreaming! The study is an **experiment** because there is an **independent variable** (studying in the library or at home). The **dependent variable** (quality of study) is assessed using observational techniques.

Other research studies are solely observational. For example, a researcher might wish to look at students' study habits and therefore observe students studying and record the different behaviours. This might be conducted as a **naturalistic observation** where all variables are free to vary, or could be a **controlled observation** where certain elements of the situation are controlled by the researcher.

Making reliable observations In order to produce **reliable** observations it is necessary to devise objective methods to separate the continuous stream of action we observe into separate behavioural components, i.e. **operationalise** the target behaviour(s). This can be done by creating **behavioural categories**. Such categories should:

● Be clearly *operationalised* and *objective* – the observer should not have to make inferences about the behaviour.
● Cover *all possible component behaviours* and avoid a 'waste basket' category.
● Be *mutually exclusive*, meaning that you should not have to mark two categories at one time.

The behavioural categories can be presented in the form of a **behaviour checklist** (a list of component behaviours) or as a **coding system** (a code is given to individual behaviours for ease of recording).

Sampling In many situations, continuous observation is not possible because there would be too much data to record, therefore systematic methods of sampling behaviour are used. **Event sampling** involves counting the number of times a certain behaviour (event) occurs in a target individual in a fixed period of time. **Time sampling** involves recording behaviours at regular intervals, for example every 30 seconds, identifying which behaviours on your behaviour checklist are occurring.

Structured and unstructured In a **structured observation** the observer uses behavioural categories and sampling procedures to control or structure the observations. (The behaviour of the individuals being observed may be uncontrolled, i.e. naturalistic.) In an **unstructured observation** the observer records all relevant behaviour but has no system. This technique may be chosen because the behaviour to be studied is largely unpredictable.

Overt and covert If a participant is aware of being observed (**overt observation**) they may alter their behaviour so validity is reduced. Observations can be made without a participant's knowledge (**covert observation**), such as using one-way mirrors. This may raise **ethical issues** regarding invasion of **privacy**.

It is easy to make the mistake of thinking that naturalistic observations are unstructured. All variables are free to vary but the researcher is still likely to use a behaviour checklist and a sampling method, i.e. use structured observation techniques.

Becoming an expert

The best way really to understand research methods and techniques is to conduct some research yourself. In days gone by A level psychology students had to produce coursework as part of their exam. There now is no required coursework element but you can still conduct mini-research projects to get a feel for the whole process. Various project ideas have been suggested in the section in this chapter on statistical tests (see pages 34–43).

Designing questionnaires and interviews

Both **questionnaires** and **interviews** involve a series of questions or statements that have to be answered by participants. There are two key issues – the first is about writing good questions and the second is about writing good questionnaires/interviews.

Writing good questions A 'good question' should:

- Be clear and unambiguous so the respondent is not confused and can give an appropriate answer.
- Avoid eliciting answers that display a **social desirability bias**, for example asking whether a person is truthful – people will tend to answer yes because they don't want to be seen in a bad light. Such questions need to be phrased more carefully.
- Be unbiased, for example not a **leading question**.

The person designing the questionnaire may decide to use closed or open questions.

Closed questions have a range of answers from which respondents select one. They produce **quantitative data** that are easier to analyse. However, respondents may be forced to select answers that don't represent their real thoughts or behaviour.

Open questions invite respondents to provide their own answers rather than select one of those provided. They tend to produce **qualitative data** and can provide unexpected answers and rich detail, thus allowing researchers to gain new insights. However, they are more difficult to analyse because there may be such a wide variety of different answers.

Writing good questionnaires and interviews Questions should start off being unthreatening and easy to answer. More challenging questions will be answered more truthfully once trust is established. Filler questions may be used to disguise the true aims of the questionnaire/interview so that respondents are more honest. **Sampling** techniques (see previous spread) are important in obtaining a representative sample.

Using a **pilot study** enables questions to be tested on a small group of people. This means you can refine the questions in response to any difficulties encountered.

The questions below relate to other spreads as well as the current one.

1... A psychologist intends to study the behaviour of car drivers in traffic, looking particularly for aggressiveness. Suggest **three** behavioural categories that could be used.

2... The government plans a new campaign related to speeding. They decide to find out about attitudes towards speeding in order to make the campaign effective.

   (a) Suggest **one** closed question and **one** open question that might help the researchers find out more about people's attitudes towards speeding.

   (b) Write a question that might elicit social desirability bias.

   (c) Write a leading question that might be used on this questionnaire and then rewrite it so it is not leading.

3... Design a study to investigate the relationship between success at school and attitudes towards school. You should include sufficient detail to permit replication, for example a hypothesis, variables being studied, and detail of design and procedures.

4... In each of the following identify the experimental design used and the experimental and control group/condition.

   (a) A study looking at the effects of lack of sleep on memory: one group have stayed up all night and the other group slept normally.

   (b) The same study is conducted but this time all participants are tested beforehand on their memory abilities and intelligence so participants in each group are paired.

   (c) A study looking at the effects of day care on IQ at age ten: some children have had two years in nursery school and the others have not attended nursery school.

   (d) A study looking at the effects of alcohol: each participant is asked to learn and recall a list of words and then given four units of alcohol and asked to repeat the same task.

5... Explain the following terms: demand characteristics, pilot study, confederate, participant variables, situational variables, investigator effects, order effects, counterbalancing, single and double blind.

An exam-style question for you

A dental school was interested to find out what factors might reduce anxiety in dental patients. In one study the focus was on anxiety levels before the patients even got to see the dentist – looking at how the waiting room environment might affect anxiety. For example, some dentists have fish tanks in their waiting rooms, while others play soft music.

An observational study was designed involving a number of different dental practices. Some were classed as 'relaxing' because they played soft music and had calming decor. Others were classed as 'normal' because they were just a typical waiting room with hard chairs and magazines. In each waiting room observations were made of how anxious each patient was. These observations were recorded by the dental receptionist so that the participants were not aware that they were being observed. The observations were used to produce an anxiety score.

(a) (i) What is meant by a directional hypothesis? [2]
     (ii) Write an appropriate directional hypothesis for this study. [2]

(b) (i) Describe what is meant by an independent groups design. [2]
     (ii) Give **one** advantage and **one** disadvantage of this experimental design. [4]

(c) (i) Define the term reliability. [2]
     (ii) Outline **one** problem with the reliability of this study. [2]

(d) The researcher used a opportunity sample for this study. Describe **one** advantage and **one** disadvantage of this sampling method. [4]

(e) Identify **one** possible confounding variable and say how you would deal with it. [3]

(f) Describe how the researcher might design a form for the receptionist to use when recording behaviour. [4]

Total = 25 marks

ETHICAL ISSUES AND WAYS OF OVERCOMING THESE ISSUES

Any professional group, such as psychologists or doctors or solicitors, has a duty to behave in an ethical manner, i.e. to behave with a proper regard for the rights and feelings of others. For psychologists this encompasses the treatment of patients and the responsibilities of researchers towards their participants – human or non-human.

There is an important point to remember where ethical issues are concerned – there are no right or wrong answers because these are *issues*, i.e. topics where there are conflicting points of view. Professional organisations such as the BPS (*British Psychological Society*) and APA (*American Psychological Association*) provide guidance for psychologists about how to behave. Such guidance is always being updated in order to keep up with changing viewpoints and new moral dilemmas (e.g. research on the internet). The BPS published a revised *Code of Ethics and Conduct* in 2009.

There is further discussion of ethical issues in Chapters 1B and 2, see pages 56, 60 and 70–71.

You might also read about ethical issues related to the use of non-human animals, see page 58.

Ethical issue	INFORMED CONSENT	DECEPTION	RIGHT TO WITHDRAW
What is it?	**Informed consent** entails giving participants comprehensive information concerning the nature and purpose of a study and their role in it.	**Deception** occurs when a participant is not told the true aims of a study nor told what participation will entail. This may involve withholding information or may involve lying.	The **right to withdraw** means informing participants that they can decline to continue participation in a study at any time. This ensures that they feel comfortable at all times.
The participant's point of view	This is necessary in order to be able to make an informed decision about whether to participate in a study.	Prevents participants being able to give truly informed consent. Honesty is an important ethical principle.	Participants may feel they shouldn't withdraw because it will spoil the study. In some studies participants are paid or rewarded (e.g. University credits) so they may not feel able to withdraw.
The researcher's point of view	Gaining informed consent may reduce the meaningfulness of the research because such information will reveal the study's aims and affect participants' subsequent behaviour.	Some deception is relatively harmless and/or can be compensated for by adequate debriefing.	The loss of participants may bias the study's findings.
How the issue could be dealt with	Ask participants to indicate formally their agreement in writing. Offer participants the right to withdraw. Seek retrospective consent during debriefing, offering participants the right to withhold their data. Use **presumptive consent** (see facing page).	Seek permission from an **ethical committee** (see facing page) that considers costs versus benefits. Use debriefing (see below), although this doesn't turn back the clock and participants may, for example, still feel embarrassed or ashamed.	The right to withdraw should be emphasised at the start and participants should be reminded of this throughout the study. Participants should be assured that any money or rewards will be forthcoming even if they do withdraw.

Debriefing

Before conducting an activity researchers give participants a **briefing** about what to expect in the task ahead. After engaging in a task, especially a stressful task or experience, participants are given a debriefing. A debriefing is a semi-structured conversation – in other words some aspects of the **debriefing** are predetermined whereas other questions/responses develop during the debriefing. In a research study a debriefing provides the opportunity to tell participants the full details of the study (aims, full procedures, etc.) and also to discuss any concerns they may have about their behaviour in the study or the implications of the study.

Debriefing is particularly important when informed consent has not been available at the start of the study and when participants need to be returned to the state they were in at the beginning of the study (e.g. the same level of self-esteem). Debriefing is not a substitute for designing ethically sound research.

There is some debate about what constitutes an ethical issue. For example, informed consent isn't an issue – the issue is really when there is a *lack* of informed consent. Some people take the view that only deception, protection from harm and confidentiality are issues. However, from the point of view of your studies, all six issues below would gain credit as examples of ethical issues.

The researcher wants to conduct meaningful research.

The participant wants his/her rights protected.

PROTECTION FROM HARM	CONFIDENTIALITY	PRIVACY
Harm includes any negative physical effects, such as physical injury, and any negative psychological effects, such as embarrassment.	**Confidentiality** concerns the communication of personal information from one person to another, and the trust that this information will be protected.	**Privacy** concerns a person's right to control the flow of information about themselves.
Participants have no desire to be harmed!	The *Data Protection Act* makes confidentiality a legal right.	People have an expectation of privacy.
It may not be possible to estimate the risks before conducting a study.	It may not be possible to keep information confidential because details of a study may lead to an individual's identification.	If participants know they are being observed they may change their behaviour.
Avoid any risks greater than those encountered in everyday life. Any study should be stopped as soon as harm is apparent.	Researchers should not record the names of any participants; they should use numbers or false names. Any confidential information should be stored securely, following the requirements of the *Data Protection Act*.	Do not observe anyone without their informed consent unless it is in a situation where a person would expect to be observed by others. Use presumptive consent (see below). If privacy is invaded, confidentiality should be protected.

CAN YOU...? No. 1A.6

For each of the following studies, identify **one** ethical issue that might arise and suggest how the researcher might deal with it.

1... A correlation of pupil IQ scores and GCSE results.

2... A cross-cultural study of child-rearing practices was conducted by observing small groups of mothers with their children.

3... Interviewing teenage girls about their dieting habits.

4... An observational study of the way in which children cross the road going to and from school.

5... A field experiment to see whether people are more likely to obey someone in a uniform or dressed in a casual suit.

6... A school decides to conduct a natural experiment to see if the students doing a new maths programme do better in their GCSE maths exam than a group of students using the traditional learning methods.

7... A group of adopted children are followed from the age of one until they are 18 to see if they do less well in school than non-adopted peers. The children are given annual tests related to intelligence, reading and maths and teachers are interviewed about their social relationships. The children themselves are also interviewed about social and emotional development.

8... Some students design a questionnaire to assess the attitude of students to teachers at their college.

9... An experiment to test the effect of self-esteem on performance. Participants are given a self-esteem questionnaire and then given a false score (told they either have high or low self-esteem).

10... A teacher asks her students to take part in a research project, telling them it is about eating habits whereas it is really about eating disorders.

11... Observing people in a supermarket to see what foods they prefer to buy.

12... A study was conducted to compare rates of aggression in various different countries. Aggressiveness was assessed using published crime rates.

Presumptive consent

Presumptive consent is another method of dealing with lack of informed consent or deception. A group of people who are similar to the participants are told the full details of the study and asked whether they would agree to take part in the study. If this group of people consent it is presumed that the real participants would have agreed if given the opportunity.

Ethical committee

An ethical committee is a group of people within a research institution who discuss research proposals to decide whether they are ethically acceptable. Sometimes the term *institutional review board* (IRB) is used instead. The committee considers the potential costs and benefits of the research, and how the researcher proposes to deal with any ethical issues that arise.

INFERENTIAL STATISTICS

Y ou may have heard the phrase 'statistical tests' – for example a newspaper might report that 'statistical tests show that women are better at reading maps than men'. If we wanted to know if women are better at reading maps than men we could not possibly test all the women and men in the world, so we just test a small group of women and a small group of men. If we find that the sample of women is indeed better with maps than the sample of men, then we *infer* that the same is true for all women and men. However, it isn't quite as simple as that because we can only make such inferences using statistical (or inferential) tests. Such statistical tests are based on probabilities, so we will start the topic of **inferential statistics** by looking at **probability**.

This spread and the next six spreads are concerned with inferential statistics. We have covered this topic in considerable depth so that it will make sense (hopefully). However, you don't need to know most of it for your exam – all you could be asked is to identify an appropriate statistical test and explain your choice. You might also be asked to state a conclusion, based on a statistical test, to write a null hypothesis or to explain why statistical tests are used. You won't need to explain probability nor Type 1 and Type 2 errors, nor would you be asked to calculate the value of Wilcoxon's *T* or any other statistic. Nevertheless, we think it is good to try to grasp some of the underlying principles and to try your hand at calculating some test statistics.

▲ *We all have an intuitive sense of probability. Would you like to buy a £50 raffle ticket to win this car? If the promoter is only selling ten tickets your answer would probably be 'yes' because your chances of winning would be fairly high whereas, if he is selling 1000 tickets, you might think again. Probability is about chance – how probable is it that you would win if 1000 tickets are sold? You have a 1 in 1000 chance of winning or 0.1% probability (one divided by a thousand = 0.001 or 0.1%).*

UNDERSTANDING INFERENTIAL STATISTICS

Probability

Inferential statistics allow psychologists to draw conclusions from their findings. These conclusions are based on the probability that a particular pattern of results could have arisen by chance or not. Consider the example about gender differences in ability to read maps. One study might test 20 women and 20 men to see who had a better understanding of maps. The findings showed a difference favouring the women. The big question is: *Is this difference due to chance?* Or is there a *real* effect (i.e. women are actually better than men). If the findings are not due to chance, then the pattern is described as **significant**, i.e. there is a real effect.

Samples and populations

Consider the following example from the psychologist and statistician Hugh Coolican (2004): *At my local chippy I am convinced that they save money by giving some people rather thin chips (because they then can get more chips from each potato). There are two chip bins under the counter – the owner of the chippy claims the two bins contain the same kind of chips but I suspect they are different. So I (sadly) tried an experiment. I asked for one bag of chips from each of the chip bins, and I went home and measured the width of the chips in each bag.*

Belief 1 is 'The two bins contain chips of an equal average width'.

Belief 2 is 'One bin has thinner chips on average than the other'.

In fact I found a very small difference between the average width of the chips in each bag (as you can see in the bar chart on the left), but nothing to shout about.

We would expect small differences between samples (bags of chips) just because things do vary a little – this is simply random variation or 'chance'. What we are looking for is a sufficiently large difference between the samples to be sure that the bins (the total population) *are* actually different. Otherwise we assume the bins are the same, i.e. the samples are drawn from a single population rather than from two different populations.

- The *bins* are **populations** – in the earlier example about gender differences in map reading, the population is all the men and women in the world.
- The *bags* of chips are **samples** – in our other example, the 20 women and 20 men comprise our samples.
- The belief that the two bins contain chips of the same width or the belief that there is no gender difference in map reading is called the **null hypothesis**. This is a statement of *no effect* – the samples are not different.
- The alternative belief is that one bin has thinner chips or that women are better than men – this is called the **alternative hypothesis**. This is a statement that *something is going on*, there is an effect – the samples are different.

Ultimately we are interested in making a statement about the population(s) from which the samples are drawn.

▶ *The chippy with his two bins of chips. He claims the chips in each bin are identical but Hugh thinks one bin has thinner chips to save money. What can we conclude from the graph below about the bins?*

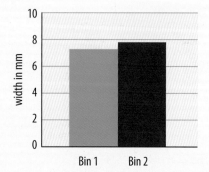

Levels of measurement

One of the factors involved in statistical tests is the **level of measurement** used – some statistical tests are restricted to only certain levels.

Nominal data are in separate categories, such as grouping people in your class according to their height – one group might be tall, another group would be medium and the final group is small. In this case measurement is not very detailed.

Ordinal data are ordered in some way, for example each person in your class lines up in order of size. The 'difference' between each person is not the same.

Interval and ratio data are measured using units of equal interval, such as measuring everyone's height in centimetres. Such units of measurement have equal intervals therefore the level of measurement is more precise. A ratio scale has a true zero.

There is a special problem with **rating scales**, which are often used in psychological research. For example, the AS core study on mate preferences (Buss, 1989) involved participants rating 18 characteristics on a four-point rating scale from 3 (indispensable) to 0 (unimportant). This kind of data is not a true interval scale because the difference between a rating of 0 and 1 is not necessarily the same as the difference between 1 and 2. But this scale is not ordinal either. It is sometimes called a **plastic interval scale**.

NOIR An acronym to help remember the four levels of measurement of data: nominal, ordinal, interval and ratio.

▼ Is something going on (the alternative hypothesis)? You see your friend's boyfriend kissing another girl. He says there is nothing going on between them but you feel pretty certain this is wrong. What has this got to do with the null hypothesis?

The null hypothesis

The null hypothesis is a statement of no difference or no correlation. It is a statement that *nothing is going on* (see photo on right). Inferential statistics require that we accept or reject the null hypothesis.

The null hypothesis isn't as strange as it sounds. For example, your friend might see your boyfriend kissing another girl and says to herself 'How likely is it that he would be kissing her if there is nothing going on?'

- The null hypothesis is 'There is nothing going on, there is no relationship between them'.
- The alternative hypothesis is 'There is something going on, there is a relationship between them'.

It isn't very likely that he would be kissing her if there was nothing going on, therefore you reject the null hypothesis and accept the alternative hypothesis – and tell your friend he is obviously cheating on her.

Chance

In the example above you probably would have an intuitive sense of the *likelihood* that the effect was real, but in research we need to be a bit more precise than that. In order to work out whether a difference is or is not significant we use inferential statistical tests. Such tests are based on some cunning maths that you don't need to know about. They permit you to work out, at a given probability, whether a pattern in the data from a study could have arisen by **chance** or whether the effect occurred because there is a real difference/correlation in the populations from which the samples were drawn.

But what do we mean by 'chance'? We simply decide on a probability that we will 'risk'. You can't be certain that an observed effect was not due to chance but you can state *how* certain you are. In the kissing example above you might say to your friend that you are 95% sure he is cheating. Which means you are fairly confident that you are right but nevertheless have a little bit of doubt.

In general, psychologists use a probability of 95%, which means that there is a 5% possibility that the results did occur by chance. In other words a 5% probability that the results occurred even there was no *real* difference/association between the populations from which the samples were drawn (i.e. the null hypothesis is true). This probability of 5% (or less) is recorded as $p \leq 0.05$ (where p means probability).

In some studies psychologists want to be more certain – such as when they are conducting a replication of a previous study or considering the effects of a new drug on health. Researchers use a more stringent probability, such as $p \leq 0.01$ or even $p \leq 0.001$. This chosen value of 'p' is called the **significance level**, which we will discuss on the next spread.

CAN YOU...? (No. **1A.7**)

1... Explain the reason for using statistical (inferential) tests.

2... Explain the difference between a null hypothesis and alternative hypothesis.

3... A study on memory had the following alternative hypothesis 'People who work in a noisy environment will do less well on a memory test than people who work in a quiet environment'.

  (a) Which of the following would be the null hypothesis: 'There is no difference in memory scores' or 'People do better in a noisy environment'?

  (b) Is the alternative hypothesis above directional or non-directional?

4... Another study investigated the relationship between sleep and exercise, with the following alternative hypothesis: 'The more exercise a person takes in a day, the more sleep they will have at night'.

  (a) Write an appropriate null hypothesis for this study.

  (b) Is the alternative hypothesis directional or non-directional?

5... Explain what is meant by the phrase 'significant at $p \leq 0.05$'. You must mention the null hypothesis in your answer.

6... Suggest why a researcher may choose to use $p \leq 0.01$ in preference to $p \leq 0.05$. (Try to give **two** reasons.)

7... Identify the level of measurement that would be used in the following examples:

  (a) Rating how stressful certain experiences are.

  (b) Counting the days a person has had off school.

  (c) Asking people to indicate their reasons for days off school.

The previous spread ended with the concept of **significance levels**. We will now look at how these are determined when using **statistical tests**, also called **inferential tests** because they allow us to draw inferences from a research sample to the wider population we are interested in.

What is an 'inference'? The word 'infer' means to draw a conclusion on the basis of reasoning or evidence. For example, 'The young girl inferred that her mother was angry from the sharp tone of her voice'.

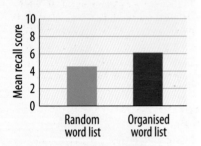

▲ *Bar chart showing the findings from a study on the effects of organisation on memory. We can draw conclusions about the samples from this graph but not about the population. We need a statistical test to be able to draw conclusions about the population.*

USING STATISTICAL TESTS

Drawing conclusions

Inferential statistical tests help us to draw inferences (**conclusions**) about **populations** from the **samples** of data tested. The main aim of any research study is to make some sense of the findings and use these to help explain human behaviour. This is what we mean when we 'draw conclusions'. What does the data show us about human behaviour in general (the population rather than the sample)?

In your AS course you studied **descriptive statistics**. These can be useful when it comes to drawing conclusions because they provide a *summary* of the data. They help us detect general patterns and trends. However, you cannot truly draw conclusions from such statistics because you cannot go beyond the particular sample to draw inferences about people in general (the 'population').

For example, you can conclude from the bar chart on the left that people who studied an organised word list were able to remember more words compared with people who studied a random word list. However, you cannot conclude that people remember organised word lists better (i.e. organisation aids memory) because then you are assuming that people in the population will behave the same as the participants in your study. In order to draw such inferences, we need inferential statistical tests.

Different statistical tests

Different statistical tests are used for different research designs and for data with different **levels of measurement** (see previous spread). For example, if a study involves looking at the **correlation** between two variables then the test used to determine whether or not there is a significant correlation is a correlational test such as Spearman's Correlation Test. There are five statistical tests that you are required to study and these are each examined on the next five spreads – Spearman's Rank Order Correlation Coefficient (Spearman's Correlation Test), the Chi-squared Test, the Sign Test, the Wilcoxon Matched Pairs Signed Ranks Test (Wilcoxon T Test) and the Mann–Whitney U Test.

Observed values

Each statistical test involves taking the data collected in a study and doing some calculations which produce a single number called the **test statistic**. In the case of Spearman's Rank Order Correlation Coefficient that test statistic is called *rho* whereas for the Mann–Whitney Test it is U. The *rho* value calculated for any set of data is called the **observed value** (because it is based on the observations made). This is sometimes also called the **calculated value** because it is the value you calculate.

Type 1 and Type 2 errors

In general psychologists use a 5% level of significance level. One reason for this is because it is a good compromise between being too lenient and too stringent. Consider the top table on the right about a criminal. Which is worse – to let a guilty man go free (a **Type 2 error**) or to convict an innocent man (a **Type 1 error**)?

The same question can be asked about accepting or rejecting the **null hypothesis** (H_0) (see bottom table) – is it worse to reject a null hypothesis which is in fact correct or to accept a null hypothesis which was wrong?

Consider the following example. A research study is conducted with the following hypotheses:

- **Alternative hypothesis (H_1)** *Women have better map-reading abilities than men.*

- **Null hypothesis (H_0)** *There is no difference between men and women in terms of map-reading abilities.*

The study tests 20 men and 20 women and finds a difference between these samples. This leads the researcher to reject H_0 and accept H_1 – but the real truth is that there is no difference in the **target population**. Our samples were biased. Therefore we have committed a Type 1 error. We have concluded that there is something going on when in fact there is nothing going on.

If the significance level is lenient (e.g. 10%) we are more likely to reject H_0 because the difference between men and women can be smaller.

Trial result	Truth	
	Guilty	**Not guilty**
Guilty verdict	True positive	False positive (guilt reported) TYPE 1 ERROR
Not guilty verdict	False negative (guilt not detected) TYPE 2 ERROR	True negative

Test result	Truth	
	H_1 is correct There is something going on	**H_0 is correct There is nothing going on**
Reject H_0	True positive	False positive (likely when p too lenient, i.e. 10%) TYPE 1 ERROR
Accept H_0	False negative (likely when p too stringent, i.e. 1%) TYPE 2 ERROR	True negative

Critical values

To decide if the observed value is **significant** this figure is compared with another number – the **critical value** (found in a **table of critical values**) – which is the value that a test statistic must reach in order for the null hypothesis to be rejected. There are different tables of critical values for each different statistical test (see for example, the bottom of page 35). To find the appropriate critical value in a table you need to know:

1. **Degrees of freedom** (*df*) In most cases you get this value by looking at the number of participants in the study (*N*). In studies using an independent groups design there are two values for *N* (one for each group of participants) which are called N_1 and N_2. In the case of the Chi-squared Test you calculate *df* on the basis of how many 'cells' there are.

2. **One-tailed** or **two-tailed test** If the hypothesis was a **directional hypothesis**, then you use a one-tailed test, if it was non-directional you use a two-tailed test.

3. **Significance level** selected, usually $p \leq 0.05$.

The 1% or 5% level

On the previous spread we noted that the 1% level is likely to be used when you want to be more confident that you should reject the null hypothesis and accept the alternative hypothesis. The 5% level is chosen because it is a good compromise between being too stringent and too lenient (see Type 1 and 2 errors on the facing page). People intuitively feel that 5% is about when you would feel fairly certain that there is an effect – read the betting story on the right!

The importance of R

Some tests are significant when the observed value is equal to or exceeds the critical value, for others it is the reverse (the size of the difference between the two is irrelevant). You need to know which and you will find it is stated underneath each table. One way to remember is to see if there is a letter R in the name of the test. If there is an R then the observed value should be g**R**eate**R** than the critical value (e.g. for Spearman's Correlation and the Chi-squared Tests). If there is no R (e.g. Sign, Mann–Whitney *U* and Wilcoxon *T* Tests) then the observed value should be less than the critical value.

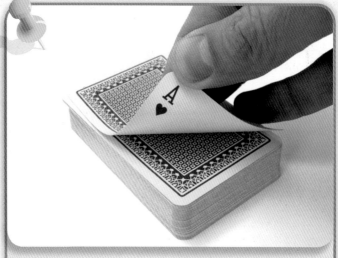

A good bet

I have two packs of cards – one of them is in random order (i.e. there is *nothing going on*, a null hypothesis). The other pack has been arranged so all the red cards are first (i.e. there is *something going on*, an effect, an alternative hypothesis).

I choose one pack and turn over the first card – which turns out to be red. Would you bet that this is the arranged pack? Would you be prepared to reject the null hypothesis after seeing this one card?

I turn over the second card, and it is red. And the third card is red, and the fourth card is red.

Do you now feel fairly confident that this is the arranged pack? Is there *something going on*? Would you bet on it? Probably. This means you are rejecting the null hypothesis that there is no effect at about a 6% level of certainty.

Consider the odds of getting four red cards in a row *if there is nothing going on* 0.5 {×} 0.5 {×} 0.5 {×} 0.5* = 0.0625 or 6%

This shows that intuitively we are prepared to reject the null hypothesis around the 5% level.

Thanks again to Hugh Coolican for this example.

* It isn't quite 0.5 because the cards aren't replaced, which means that the probability of drawing a red card is less than 0.5 after the first red card, but not by much.

An exam-style question

A local hospital decides to have mixed wards rather than separate wards for men and women. Before introducing this new scheme to all wards, the hospital management employ a psychologist to conduct a study into the effects of mixed versus single-sex wards on the health and happiness of patients. Health outcomes are assessed by comparing the blood pressure of patients in the two different wards (low blood pressure suggests healthier patients).

(a) (i) Identify the independent variable and the dependent variable in this study. [2]
    (ii) Suggest **one** way in which you could operationalise the independent variable. [2]
(b) Write a suitable null hypothesis for this study. [2]
(c) (i) Identify the experimental design used in this study. [2]
    (ii) Describe **one** disadvantage of this design in the context of this study. [2]
    (iii) Explain **one** way of dealing with this disadvantage. [2]
(d) Describe the level of measurement used when measuring the health outcomes of patients. [2]
(e) (i) Define the term validity. [2]
    (ii) Outline **one** potential problem with validity in this study. [2]
(f) The researchers will use a statistical test to assess the significance of their results.
    (i) Explain why such tests are used. [3]
    (ii) Identify a suitable level of significance that could be used in this study and explain your choice. [3]

Total = 24 marks

CAN YOU...?   No. 1A.8

1... Explain what is meant by 'significance level'.

2... Give the general name for the value that is worked out using a statistical test.

3... What other name is sometimes used for this value?

4... Give the general name given to the number, found in a significance table, that is used to judge the observed value produced by a statistical test.

5... Identify the **three** pieces of information used to find this value.

6... Explain when a one-tailed test is used instead of a two-tailed test.

7... Explain the difference between a Type 1 error and Type 2 error.

The **first statistical test** we will look at is a test of **correlation** – Spearman's Rank Order Correlation Coefficient. It is used to determine whether the correlation between two **co-variables** is significant or not. For example, the study of stress and illness by Rahe, Mahan and Arthur (1970, one of your AS core studies) found a correlation of +.118 between the number of times a participant was ill and their stress score as measured by the SRRS (social readjustment rating scale). A figure of zero would be no correlation whereas a figure of +1.0 would be a perfect **positive correlation**. A correlation of +.118 may sound like a rather insignificant correlation but in fact it is **significant**.

The **observed value** of +.118 was calculated using an statistical test such as Spearman's Rank Order Correlation Coefficient. This observed value is then compared with the **critical value** found in a table of critical values (such as the table on the facing page) to see whether the observed value is significant. In this study the number of participants was over 2700 and therefore +.118 was significant (as the number of participants increases the value needed for significance decreases). Incidentally if the observed value had been –.118 this would still be significant; it would be a significant **negative correlation**.

HEALTH WARNING – ETHICS

If you do conduct your own research studies, make sure no participants are younger than 16 and that you seek fully **informed consent**. If you are using sensitive information, such as tests of maths ability, then you must protect participants' **confidentiality**.

CAN YOU...? (No. **1A.9**)

1... Identify **two** ethical problems that might arise when conducting a study on finger length and numeracy, and state how these could be dealt with.

2... Suggest problems that might occur when dealing with the ethical problems in the manner you suggested.

3... Identify the co-variables in the study by Brosnan (above right).

4... Identify an intervening variable in this study (the variable that links finger length to numeracy, for example).

5... If you were going to study the relationship between digit ratio and literacy, state a possible alternative and null hypothesis for this study.

6... Draw a scattergraph of the results on the facing page to check the outcome of the statistical test – does your graph show the same relationship as reported for the statistical test?

7... If you conduct a study yourself, produce a report of the study using the normal conventions (as in your AS core studies, use the following sections: context and aims, procedures, findings and conclusions). Use a scattergraph to 'eyeball' your data as well as conducting a statistical test.

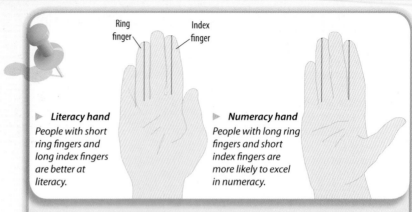

▶ **Literacy hand**
People with short ring fingers and long index fingers are better at literacy.

▶ **Numeracy hand**
People with long ring fingers and short index fingers are more likely to excel in numeracy.

Finger length and exam performance

A number of studies have looked at the relationship between finger length and various abilities such as numeracy or literacy. For example a recent study by Brosnan (2008) examined finger length in 75 British children aged between six and seven (boys and girls), and found that children with a higher digit ratio between their index and ring fingers were more likely to have a talent in maths, while those with a shorter digit ratio were more likely to have a talent in literacy.

This relationship is thought to be due to biological factors, specifically the production of **testosterone** and **oestrogen** in the brain. Male babies are exposed to more testosterone (a male hormone) during prenatal development and this affects their finger length. At the same time testosterone promotes the development of the areas of the brain which are often associated with spatial and mathematical skills, whereas oestrogen (a female hormone) is thought to do the same in the areas of the brain which are often associated with verbal ability.

In order to study the correlation between finger length and numeracy/literacy the researchers took photocopies of both the right and left hands of the children and measured the length of the index and ring fingers. They divided the length of the index finger by the length of the ring finger to calculate each child's 'digit ratio'.

The digit ratios were then correlated with the results from their *National Standard Assessment* Tests (SATs) for numeracy and literacy.

DO IT YOURSELF

You can repeat (**replicate**) this study using GCSE scores instead of SATs results, or you could use online tests of literacy and/or numeracy. In order to determine if your results are significant follow the worked example on the facing page.

MORE DO IT YOURSELF – ideas for studies using a correlational analysis

- **Life events and illness** In your AS studies you looked at the relationship between stressful life events or and illness (the study by Rahe, Mahan and Arthur). You can replicate this study and check whether your correlations are significant.

- **Reaction time and number of hours of sleep** Does lack of sleep have any effects? For example it might be related to poor reaction time. You can measure reaction time using an online test.

- **Reaction time and time spent playing computer games** Perhaps playing computer games is related to reaction time.

- **Working memory and IQ** are predicted to be positively correlated. You can find tests for both at www.bbc.co.uk

When to use Spearman's Rank Order Correlation Coefficient

- The hypothesis predicts a *correlation* between two co-variables.
- The two sets of data are pairs of scores from one person or thing, i.e. they are *related*.
- The data are at least ordinal (i.e. not nominal). See page 31 for an explanation.

◀ *Charles Edward Spearman (1863–1945)*

SPEARMAN'S RANK ORDER CORRELATION COEFFICIENT – A WORKED EXAMPLE

STEP 1. State the alternative and null hypothesis
Alternative hypothesis: The digit ratio between index finger and ring finger is positively correlated to numeracy skills. (This is a **directional hypothesis**, therefore requiring a one-tailed test.)
Null hypothesis: There is no correlation between digit ratio and numeracy skills.

STEP 2. Record the data and rank each co-variable and calculate the difference
Rank A and B separately, from low to high (i.e. the lowest number receives the rank of 1). If there are two or more of the same number (tied ranks), calculate the rank by working out the mean of the ranks that would have been given.

Participant number	Digit ratio	Numeracy score	Rank A	Rank B	Difference between rank A and rank B (d)	d^2
1	1.026	8	10	2.5	7.5	56.25
2	1.000	16	5.5	9	−3.5	12.25
3	1.021	10	9	5	4.0	16.0
4	0.991	9	4	4	0	0
5	0.984	15	3	8	−5.0	25.0
6	0.975	14	1	7	−6.0	36.0
7	1.013	12	7	6	1	1.0
8	1.018	8	8	2.5	5.5	30.25
9	0.982	17	2	10	−8.0	64.0
10	1.000	5	5.5	1	4.5	20.25
N = 10					Σ d^2 (sum of differences squared) = **261.0**	

STEP 3. Find observed value of **rho** (the correlation coefficient)
$$rho = 1 - \frac{6\Sigma d^2}{N(N^2-1)} = 1 - \frac{6 \times 261.0}{10 \times (100-1)} = 1 - 1566/990 = 1 - 1.58 = -0.58$$

STEP 4. Find the critical value of **rho**
$N = 10$, the hypothesis is directional therefore a one-tailed test is used.
Look up the critical value in the table of critical values (on right).
For a one-tailed test where $N = 10$, the critical value of *rho* ($p \leq 0.05$) = 0.564

Note that the observed value is negative – when comparing this figure with the critical value, only the value, not the sign, is important. The sign does, however, tell you whether the correlation is positive or negative. If the prediction was one-tailed and the sign (and therefore the correlation) is not as predicted, then the null hypothesis must be retained.

STEP 5. State the conclusion
As the observed value (0.58) is greater than the critical value (0.564) it might appear that we should we reject the null hypothesis (at $p \leq 0.05$), **however in this case the sign is in the wrong direction – a positive correlation was predicted but a negative correlation was found**. This means that we have to accept the null hypothesis and conclude that there is no correlation between digit ratio and numeracy skills.
If we had predicted a negative correlation then we could have rejected the null hypothesis.

Alternative and null hypothesis

The term 'alternative hypothesis' (H_1) is used because it is the alternative to the null hypothesis (H_0). The null hypothesis is required because statistical tests are looking at whether our samples come from a population where there is no effect or no relationship (in which case the null hypothesis is true, i.e. any relationship is due to chance) or whether our samples come from a population where there is a relationship (in which case we can reject the null hypothesis and accept the alternative).

The null hypothesis is a statement of no relationship (in a correlational analysis) or no difference. So it should always begin 'There is no correlation between…' or 'There is no difference between…'.

▼ *Table of critical values of* rho *at 5% level (*$p \leq 0.05$*)*

N =	One-tailed test	Two-tailed test
4	1.000	
5	0.900	1.000
6	0.829	0.886
7	0.714	0.786
8	0.643	0.738
9	0.600	0.700
10	0.564	0.648
11	0.536	0.618
12	0.503	0.587
13	0.484	0.560
14	0.464	0.538
15	0.443	0.521
16	0.429	0.503
17	0.414	0.485
18	0.401	0.472
19	0.391	0.460
20	0.380	0.447
21	0.370	0.435
22	0.361	0.425
23	0.353	0.415
24	0.344	0.406
25	0.337	0.398
26	0.331	0.390
27	0.324	0.382
28	0.317	0.375
29	0.312	0.368
30	0.306	0.362

Observed value of *rho* must be EQUAL TO or GREATER THAN the critical value in this table for significance to be shown.

Source: J.H. Zhar (1972) Significance testing of the Spearman's Rank Correlation Coefficient. *Journal of the American Statistical Association*, 67, 578–580. With kind permission of the publisher.

The second **statistical test** we will look at deals with **nominal data**, i.e. data that are in categories. We use this test when we have counted how many occurrences there are in each category – called 'frequency data'. For example, we might be interested to find out whether men and women do actually differ in terms of their finger length ratio (as discussed on the previous spread). Research has found that adult women usually have ratios of one, i.e. their index and ring fingers are of equal length. The average for men is lower at 0.98, since they tend to have longer ring fingers than index fingers, suggesting greater exposure to testosterone in the womb. Of course, the Chi-squared Test (see below) does not prove this but can support this gender difference.

'Chi' is one of the letters of the Greek alphabet (pronounced as 'kie' to rhyme with 'pie'). The Greek symbol for chi is χ, which is why this symbol is used as the statistic for the Chi-squared Test.

CHI-SQUARED TEST – A WORKED EXAMPLE FOR A 2 × 2 TABLE

STEP 1. State the alternative and null hypothesis
Alternative hypothesis: There is a difference between men and women in terms of digit ratio (the ratio between the index and ring fingers). (This is a **non-directional hypothesis** that therefore requires a **two-tailed test**.)
Null hypothesis: There is no difference between men and women in terms of digit ratio.

This is a 2 × 2 *contingency table* as there are two rows and two tables. On the facing page there is a 3 × 2 contingency table as there are three rows and two columns. The first number is always rows and the second number is columns (to remember rows then columns, think of RC as in Roman Catholic).

STEP 2. Draw up a contingency table

	Male	Female	Totals
Digit ratio ≥ 1.00	5 (cell **A**)	12 (cell **B**)	17
Digit ratio < 1.00	10 (cell **C**)	9 (cell **D**)	19
Totals	15	21	36

STEP 3. Compare observed and expected* frequencies for each cell
The expected frequencies are calculated by working out how the data would be distributed across all cells in the table if there were no differences, i.e. it was random.

	row × column / total = expected frequency (E)	Subtract expected value from observed value, ignoring signs (O − E)	Square previous value (O − E)²	Divide previous value by expected value (O − E)² / E
Cell **A**	17 × 15 / 36 = 7.08	5 − 7.08 = 2.08	4.3264	0.6110
Cell **B**	17 × 21 / 36 = 9.92	12 − 9.92 = 2.08	4.3264	0.4361
Cell **C**	19 × 15 / 36 = 7.92	10 − 7.92 = 2.08	4.3264	0.5463
Cell **D**	19 × 21 / 36 = 11.08	9 − 11.08 = 2.08	4.3264	1.3905

In some books Yates's correction is recommended but Coolican (1996) says this is no longer modern practice.

STEP 4. Find the observed value of Chi-squared (χ^2)
Add all the values in the final column in the table above.
This gives you the observed value of Chi-squared as 1.984

STEP 5. Find the critical value of Chi-squared (χ^2)
Calculate degrees of freedom (*df*) by multiplying
(rows − 1) × (columns − 1) = 1
Look up the value in the table of the critical values (right).
For a two-tailed test, $df = 1$, the critical value of χ^2 ($p \le 0.5$) = 3.84

STEP 6. State the conclusion
As the observed value (1.984) is less than the critical value (3.84) we must accept the null hypothesis (at $p \le 0.05$) and therefore we conclude that there is no difference between men and women in terms of digit ratio.

▼ *Table of critical values of Chi-squared (χ^2) ($p \le 0.05$)*

df	One-tailed test	Two-tailed test
1	2.71	3.84
2	4.60	5.99
3	6.25	7.82
4	7.78	9.49
5	9.24	11.07

Observed value of χ^2 must be EQUAL TO or GREATER THAN the critical value in this table for significance to be shown.

Source: abridged from R.A. Fisher and F. Yates (1974). *Statistical Tables for Biological, Agricultural and Medical Research* (6th edition). London: Longman.

* Many students get confused about the expected frequencies. These are not what the researcher expects – they are the frequencies that would occur if the data were distributed evenly across the table in proportion to the row and column totals.

The Chi-squared Test can be used to investigate a difference (as in the worked example on this page) or an association (as on the facing page).

There are online programmes that will calculate Chi-squared for you, see for example http://math.hws.edu/javamath/ryan/ChiSquare.html (scroll about half way down the page). You could also use the statistics functions in Excel to calculate the statistic from your data table.

When to use the Chi-squared (χ^2) Test

- The hypothesis predicts a *difference* between two conditions or an *association* between variables.
- The sets of data must be *independent* (no individual should have a score in more than one 'cell').
- The data are in *frequencies* (i.e. **nominal**) See page 31 for an explanation. Frequencies must not be percentages.

Note This test is unreliable when the *expected* (i.e. the ones you calculate) frequencies fall below 5 in any cell, i.e. you need at least 20 participants for a 2×2 contingency table.

Parental style and self-esteem

Psychological research has identified three different parenting styles: *authoritarian* (parents dictate how children should behave), *democratic* (parents discuss standards with their children) and *laissez-faire* (parents encourage children to set their own rules). Buri (1991) found that children who experienced authoritarian parenting were more likely to develop high **self-esteem**.

DO IT YOURSELF

You can access the *Parental Authority Questionnaire* (PAQ) at http://faculty.sjcny.edu/~treboux/documents/parental authority questionnaire.pdf

There are various self-esteem questionnaires on the internet.

MORE DO IT YOURSELF – Ideas for studies using a Chi-squared Test

Gender and conformity Are women more conformist than men? Some studies have found this to be true though Eagly and Carli (1981) suggest this is only true on male-oriented tasks. Try different types of conformity tasks and see whether some have higher or lower levels of female conformity, for example ask questions on a general knowledge test which are related to male or female interests. The answers from previous 'participants' should be shown so you can see if your real participant conforms to the majority answer.

Sleep and age Research suggests that people sleep less as they get older. Compare older and younger participants in terms of average number hours of sleep.

CHI-SQUARED TEST – A WORKED EXAMPLE FOR A 3×2 TABLE

STEP 1. State the alternative and null hypothesis
Alternative hypothesis: Certain parental styles are associated with higher self-esteem in adolescence. (This is a **non-directional hypothesis** and therefore requires a **two-tailed test**.)
Null hypothesis: There is no association between parental style and self-esteem in adolescence.

STEP 2. Draw up a contingency table
In this case it will be 3 by 2 (rows first then columns)

Parental style	Self-esteem High	Self-esteem Low	Totals
Authoritarian	10 (cell **A**)	4 (cell **B**)	14
Democratic	5 (cell **C**)	7 (cell **D**)	12
Laissez-faire	8 (cell **E**)	2 (cell **F**)	10
Totals	23	13	36

STEP 3. Compare observed and expected frequencies

	row × column / total = expected frequency (E)	Subtract expected value from observed value, ignoring signs (O – E)	Square previous value (O – E)²	Divide previous value by expected value (O – E)² / E
Cell **A**	14 × 23 / 36 = 8.94	10 – 8.94 = 1.06	1.1236	0.1257
Cell **B**	14 × 13 / 36 = 5.06	4 – 5.06 = 1.06	1.1236	0.2221
Cell **C**	12 × 23 / 36 = 7.67	5 – 7.67 = 2.67	7.1289	0.9294
Cell **D**	12 × 13 / 36 = 4.33	7 – 4.33 = 2.67	7.1289	1.6464
Cell **E**	10 × 23 / 36 = 6.39	8 – 6.39 = 1.61	2.5921	0.4056
Cell **F**	10 × 13 / 36 = 3.61	2 – 3.61 = 1.61	2.5921	0.7180

STEP 4. Find the observed value of Chi-squared (χ^2)
Add all the values in the final column in the table above.
This gives you the observed value of Chi-squared (χ^2) = 4.0472

STEP 5. Find the critical value of Chi-squared (χ^2)
Calculate degrees of freedom (*df*): by multiplying (rows – 1) × (columns – 1) = 2
Look up the critical value in the table of critical values (on facing page).
For a two-tailed test, $df = 2$, the critical value of χ^2 ($p \leq 0.05$) = 5.99

STEP 6. State the conclusion

CAN YOU...? (No. **1A.10**)

1... State the conclusion for the test above.

2... Draw a contingency table to show the following data – old and young participants are asked whether they sleep more or less than eight hours per night on average. Of the old people 11 said they sleep more and 25 said they sleep less. Of the younger participants 31 said they sleep more than eight hours and 33 said they sleep less.

3... State an appropriate alternative hypothesis (directional) and null hypothesis for this investigation.

4... The observed value of Chi-squared for the data from question 1 is 3.02 (one-tailed test). Is this value significant? Explain your decision and state whether this means you can reject the null hypothesis.

The final three **statistical tests** are 'tests of difference' (on this spread and the next two spreads). What does this mean? A test of difference enables us to consider whether or not two samples of data are different from each other. For example, we might want to know whether people produce more accurate work in a noisy or quiet environment – we would be looking at a difference in participants' performance in the two conditions. The Chi-squared Test (on the previous spread) is both a test of difference and a **test of association**. Tests of association look at whether two variables both increase at the same time (positive association/correlation) or as one increases the other decreases (negative association/correlation).

Tests of difference are generally used for experiments. For example we might conduct an experiment to see if noisy conditions reduce the effectiveness of revision.

Case A – we could have two groups of participants:
- Group 1: participants revise in a silent room and are tested.
- Group 2: a different group of participants revises in a noisy room and is tested.

Case B – we might have two conditions:
- Condition 1: participants revise in a silent room and are tested.
- Condition 2: the same participants revise in a noisy room and are tested.

Case A is an **independent groups design** (we have two separate groups of participants). Case B (we have two conditions but just one group of participants) is a **repeated measures design** as the same participants are tested twice.

The Sign Test (on this spread) and the Wilcoxon *T* Test (on the next spread) are used for repeated measures designs. The Mann–Whitney *U* Test (on pages 42–43) is used for independent groups designs.

In some experiments there are more than two conditions or groups – for example the AS core study by Loftus and Palmer (1974) on leading questions had five different groups according to which verb was in the sentence (smashed, hit, etc.). There are specific statistical tests that are used for designs with more than two conditions/groups – but you don't need to worry about those.

Note There are **three** kinds of experimental design – repeated measures, independent groups and finally, **matched pairs**. In a matched pairs study there are two groups of participants (as in independent groups design) but the groups are not independent, they are matched (e.g. on characteristics such as IQ, age, etc.). Therefore matched pairs experiments use repeated measures tests.

▶ *Can we explain interpersonal attraction in terms of matching? That is, people seek partners who are similar to themselves in terms of attractiveness rather than seeking the most attractive individuals.*

The matching hypothesis

Who do you find attractive? If everyone selected the most attractive people as potential partners we all might be fighting over a small group of beautiful men and women, but the **matching hypothesis** (Walster *et al.*, 1966, see page 103) suggests that people are actually attracted to those individuals who most closely match their perceptions of their own level of attractiveness. Thus, although we may be attracted to physically attractive individuals as potential partners, a compromise is necessary to avoid rejection by our more attractive choices.

A number of studies has tested this hypothesis. For example, Murstein (1972) arranged for photos of dating and engaged couples to be rated in terms of attractiveness. The ratings showed a definite tendency for dating or engaged couples to have similar levels of attractiveness.

In statistical terms a test of difference is looking at whether two sets of scores are drawn from the same population (this is the null hypothesis) or from two different populations (this is the alternative hypothesis). For example, if we are looking at whether noise or no noise is better we either:

- Believe that there is no difference (the null hypothesis) – the scores from the two conditions inevitably will differ slightly but this difference is due to chance factors.
- Believe that there is a difference (the alternative hypothesis) – the fact that the scores from the two conditions differ is because each sample is drawn from a different population.

DO IT YOURSELF
You can replicate this study using photographs of couples from magazines or the internet. Separate the photos so you can put all the males together and all the females together. Place all photos in a random order. Ask 'judges' to rate each individual for attractiveness. If you use a rating scale from 1 to 10 you might decide that similarity counts as having scores that are within 2 points of each other.

MORE DO IT YOURSELF – Ideas for studies using a Sign Test

Evidence for extra sensory perception (ESP) In the early days of ESP testing Zener cards (also called ESP cards) were used (above). Each pack consisted of 25 cards, five of each design. The cards were intended to be emotionally neutral to remove any response bias. A 'sender' (or agent) views each of the cards in the pack in turn and a 'receiver' guesses the symbol on that card. Before a trial begins the cards are placed in a random order. In order to demonstrate ESP a person must get more than five cards right – five is the level that would be expected by chance. If more than five cards are right you score a plus, otherwise you score a minus.

Change blindness If you conduct the 'gorilla' study on page 16 you could use the Sign Test to analyse your findings.

When to use the Sign Test
- The hypothesis predicts a *difference* between two sets of data.
- The two sets of data are pairs of scores from one person (or a matched pair) = *related*.
- The data are nominal (i.e. not ordinal or interval). See page 31 for an explanation.

THE SIGN TEST – A WORKED EXAMPLE

STEP 1. State the alternative and null hypotheses
Alternative hypothesis: Partners who are dating or engaged have a similar level of attractiveness (i.e. match in terms of attractiveness). (This is a **non-directional** hypothesis and therefore requires a **two-tailed test**.)
Null hypothesis: There is no relationship between the level of attractiveness of dating or engaged couples.

STEP 2. Record the data and work out the sign
For each couple record the average rating score given to the male and female partners.
Then score a plus (+) if their average rating scores were the same and a minus (−) if their average rating scores were different. In the example below a rating scale of 1 to 5 was used and scores were expected to be identical to count as similar.

Couple	Average rating for male partner	Average rating for female partner	Similar or different?
1	3	4	−
2	4	3	−
3	5	5	+
4	1	2	−
5	1	1	+
6	3	3	+
7	5	5	+
8	4	4	+
9	3	1	−
10	4	4	+
11	5	2	−
12	4	4	+

STEP 3. Find the observed value of S
S = the number of times the less frequent value occurs.
In this case the less frequent sign is minus, so $S = 5$

STEP 4. Find the critical value of S
N = The total number of scores (less any zero values).
In this case $N = 12$ (no scores omitted). The hypothesis is non-directional therefore a one-tailed test is used.
Look up the critical value in the table of critical values (see above right).
For a one-tailed test, $N = 12$, the critical value of S ($p \leq 0.05$) = 2

STEP 5. State the conclusion
As the observed value (5) is greater than the critical value (2) we must accept the null hypothesis (at $p \leq 0.05$) and conclude that there is no relationship between the level of attractiveness of dating or engaged couples (i.e. they do not match).

▼ *Table of critical values of S (p ≤ 0.05)*

N =	One-tailed test	Two-tailed test
5	0	
6	0	0
7	0	0
8	1	0
9	1	1
10	1	1
11	2	1
12	2	2
13	3	2
14	3	2
15	3	3
16	4	3
17	4	4
18	5	4
19	5	4
20	5	5
25	7	7
30	10	9
35	12	11

Observed value of S must be EQUAL TO or LESS THAN the critical value in this table for significance to be shown.

Source: abridged from R.F. Clegg (1982) *Simple Statistics*. Cambridge: Cambridge University Press.

CAN YOU...? No. 1A.11

1... Identify **one or more** ethical problems that might arise when conducting a study on the matching hypothesis.

2... Suggest how you might deal with the ethical problem(s).

3... If you were going to study ESP using the Zener cards, state possible alternative and null hypotheses for this study.

4... Is your alternative hypothesis directional or non-directional?

5... Describe how you could obtain a volunteer sample for this study.

6... Suggest an alternative sampling method and explain in what way this would be a better method than using a volunteer sample.

7... Either invent some dummy data for the ESP study or collect your own and analyse it using the Sign Test, including a decision on whether to accept or reject the null hypothesis.

8... Explain why the Sign Test would be the appropriate test to use with this data.

9... If you conduct a study yourself, produce a report of the study using the normal conventions (as in your AS core studies: context and aims, procedures, findings and conclusions). Use a bar chart to 'eyeball' your data as well as conducting a statistical test.

Like the Sign Test, the Wilcoxon Matched Pairs Signed Ranks Test is a **test of difference** for **repeated measures** or **matched pairs**. Whereas the Sign Test is only suitable for **nominal data**, the Wilcoxon *T* Test is suitable for **ordinal** or **interval data**. There are more 'powerful' tests that can be used with interval data – such as *t*-tests – but these are beyond the specification so you don't need to worry about them. The concept of 'power' refers to the fact that *t*-tests are better able to detect **significance** – this means that if you use the Wilcoxon *T* Test you might not find that your results are significant but if you used a *t*-test you might detect a significant difference – a bit like using a higher magnification microscope.

Wilcoxon Matched Pairs Signed Ranks Test – what a mouthful! The reason for this name is that Frank Wilcoxon produced another well-known statistical test, called the *Wilcoxon Rank Sums Test*, therefore neither test can simply be called the *Wicoxon Test*. For ease of reference we have called it the Wilcoxon *T* Test because the statistic that is calculated for the Wilcoxon Matched Pairs Signed Ranks Test is called *T*.

Note Matched pairs is also a related design – there are two groups of participants but each participant in one group is matched with a participant in the other group on key variables, so in a sense it is like testing the same person twice.

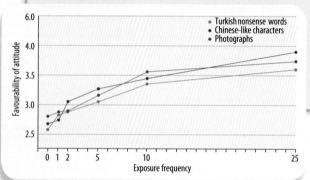

The mere exposure effect

There is a saying that 'familiarity breeds contempt', but psychological research has found that the opposite is generally true – we come to like things because of their familiarity. For example, people generally like a song more after they have heard it a few times, and advertisements often aim to increase our liking for a product through repeated exposure. Things that are familiar are less threatening and thus more likeable.

Robert Zajonc (pronounced 'zie-unts') conducted various experiments to demonstrate the *mere exposure effect*. For example, in one study Zajonc (1968) told participants that he was conducting a study on visual memory and showed them a set of photographs of 12 different men (face only). Each photograph was shown for two seconds. At the end participants were asked to rate how much they liked the 12 different men on a scale from 0 to 6. The key element of the study is that some photos were shown more often than others. For example, one photo appeared 25 times whereas another only appeared once.

Overall the frequencies were 0, 1, 2, 5, 10 and 25. The same experiment was repeated with invented Chinese symbols and also with Turkish words. All the results are shown in the graph on the left.

DO IT YOURSELF

You can replicate this study but don't need to have all six conditions. The final analysis can involve just comparing two of the stimuli – one frequent and one infrequent as shown in the worked example on the facing page.

MORE DO IT YOURSELF – Ideas for studies using a Wilcoxon *T* Test

Mere exposure again The *mere exposure effect* can also be used to explain the fact that people prefer pictures of themselves that are reversed as in a mirror – because that is the way you usually see yourself and so it is more familiar (Mita *et al.*, 1977). You could take a few pictures of each participant with a digital camera and create a mirror image of each. Show them the photographs and record their ratings (on a scale of 1 to 5) for each photograph. Compare the ratings.

Right brain left brain If you perform two tasks that involve the same brain hemisphere you should be slower on both tasks than if performing two tasks that involve the right and left hemispheres separately. For example, tap your right finger while reading a page from a book (both involve the left hemisphere). Then repeat the finger tapping without doing any reading. On each occasion count how many finger taps you manage in 30 seconds and compare these scores.

Smiling makes you happy You might think that you smile because you are feeling happy but psychological research shows it works the other way round too, i.e. you become happy because you are smiling. Laird (1974) told participants to contract certain facial muscles so he could measure facial muscular activity using electrodes. The instructions either resulted in something like a smile or like a frown. Participants who were made to 'smile' while rating cartoons for funniness, rated the cartoons as funnier than those who were made to produce a frown. You could replicate this by asking people to smile for some cartoons and frown for others, and rate each cartoon for humour.

▲ *Whose face is nicest? According to the mere exposure effect you should like the one you see most often.*

THE WILCOXON T TEST – A WORKED EXAMPLE

STEP 1. State the alternative and null hypotheses
Alternative hypothesis: Participants rate the more frequently seen face as more likeable than the less frequently seen face. (This is a **directional hypothesis** and therefore requires a one-tailed test.)
Null hypothesis: There is no difference in the likeability score for faces seen more or less often.

STEP 2. Record the data, calculate the difference between scores and rank
Once you have worked out the difference, rank from low to high, ignoring the signs (i.e. the lowest number receives the rank of 1).
If there are two or more of the same number (tied ranks) calculate the rank by working out the mean of the ranks that would have been given.
If the difference is zero, omit this from the ranking and reduce N accordingly.

Participant	Likeability for more frequently seen face	Likeability for less frequently seen face	Difference	Rank
1	5	2	3	9.5
2	4	3	1	3
3	3	3	omit	
4	6	4	2	6.5
5	2	3	−1	3
6	4	5	−1	3
7	5	2	3	9.5
8	3	4	−1	3
8	6	3	3	9.5
10	4	6	−2	6.5
11	5	2	3	9.5
12	3	4	−1	3

STEP 3. Find the observed value of T
T = the sum of the ranks of the less frequent sign.
In this case the less frequent sign is minus, so $T = 3 + 3 + 3 + 6.5 + 3 = 18.5$

STEP 4. Find the critical value of T
$N = 11$ (one score omitted). The hypothesis is directional therefore a one-tailed test is used.
Look up the critical value in the table of critical values (see right).
For a one-tailed test, $N = 11$, the critical value of T ($p < 0.05$) = 13

STEP 5. State the conclusion
As the observed value (18.5) is greater than the critical value (13) we must accept the null hypothesis (at $p \leq 0.05$) and conclude that there is no difference in the likeability score for faces seen more or less often.

CAN YOU...? (No. 1A.12)

1... Identify the maximum observed value of T that would be required for significance with a two-tailed test with 25 participants.

2... In a psychology experiment, 15 students were given a test in the morning and a similar test in the afternoon to see whether they did better when tested in the morning or afternoon. The researcher expected them to do better in the morning.

   (a) Write an appropriate alternative and null hypotheses for this study.

   (b) Invent data for the study – you need 15 pairs of scores.

   (c) Explain why the Wilcoxon T Test would be the appropriate test to use with this data.

   (d) Follow the steps outlined above to calculate T for your data and then state the conclusion you would draw about the significance of the results.

   (e) One problem with this study is that the students might do better in the afternoon because they had done a similar test in the morning. Therefore the study was conducted again using a matched pairs design. Explain how this might be done (including the variables you would use for matching).

   (f) Explain how **counterbalancing** could be used to deal with the **order effects** if a repeated measures design was used.

When to use the Wilcoxon T Test

- The hypothesis predicts a *difference* between two sets of data.
- The two sets of data are pairs of scores from one person (or a matched pair) = related.
- The data are at least ordinal (i.e. not nominal). See page 31 for an explanation.

▶ *Frank Wilcoxon (1892–1965), an American chemist and statistician.*

▼ *Table of critical values of* T (p ≤ 0.05)

N =	One-tailed test	Two-tailed test
5	T≤0	
6	2	0
7	3	2
8	5	3
9	8	5
10	11	8
11	13	10
12	17	13
13	21	17
14	25	21
15	30	25
16	35	29
17	41	34
18	47	40
19	53	46
20	60	52
21	67	58
22	75	65
23	83	73
24	91	81
25	100	89
26	110	98
27	119	107
28	130	116
29	141	125
30	151	137
31	163	147
32	175	159
33	187	170

Observed value of must be EQUAL TO or LESS THAN the critical value in this table for significance to be shown.

Source: R. Meddis (1975). *Statistical Handbook for Non-statisticians.* London: McGraw Hill.

The final **statistical test** you need to study is one that is appropriate for tests of difference where there are **independent groups**, i.e. where the study involved two groups of participants each given a different level of the **independent variable**. One group might work in a noisy condition whereas the other group works in silence, or one group might be tested in the morning and the other group tested in the afternoon to see if time of day affects performance.

◄ *The Capilano Suspension Bridge was used in the study by Dutton and Aron (see right). The bridge is narrow and long and has many arousal-inducing features: a tendency to tilt, sway and wobble, creating the impression that one is about to fall over the side; very low handrails of wire cable; and a 230-foot drop to rocks and shallow rapids below.*

Falling in love

Psychologists have sought to explain the process of falling in love. One suggestion is that love is basically physiological arousal – arousal of your **sympathetic nervous system** which occurs when you are feeling scared or stressed or find someone physically attractive. Hatfield and Walster (1981) suggested that love is simply a label that we place on physiological arousal when it occurs in the presence of an appropriate object. A man or woman who meets a potential partner after an exciting football game is more likely to fall in love than he or she would be on a routine day. Likewise, a man or woman is more likely to fall in love when having experienced some bitter disappointment. The reason, in both cases, is to do with the two components of love: arousal and label.

This has been supported by various experiments, such as a memorable study by Dutton and Aron (1974). A female research assistant (unaware of the study's aims) interviewed males, explaining that she was doing a project for her psychology class on the effects of attractive scenery on creative expression. The interviews took place on a high suspension bridge (high arousal group, see left) or a narrow bridge over a small stream (low arousal).

When the interview was over, the research assistant gave the men her phone number and asked them to call her if they had any questions about the survey. Over 60% of the men in the high arousal condition did phone her compared with 30% from the low arousal group, suggesting that the men had mislabelled their fear-related arousal as sexual arousal.

DO IT YOURSELF

Another study which investigated the two-factor theory of love was conducted by White *et al.* (1981). In this experiment high and low arousal was created by asking men to run on the spot for two minutes or 15 seconds respectively, and then showing them a short video of a young woman (There is a similar study by Valins described on page 150). The more highly aroused men rated the woman as more attractive.

MORE DO IT YOURSELF – Ideas for studies using a Mann–Whitney *U* Test

Digit ratio and gender (see page 34). You can collect data on the digit ratios of men and women and analyse them using the Mann–Whitney test by comparing the scores for men and women.

Time of day A number of studies have looked at how time of day affects our performance. For example, Gupta (1991) found that performance on IQ tests was best at 7pm as compared with 9am or 2pm, a factor which might be an important consideration when taking examinations.

Eyewitness testimony You could repeat the AS core study by Loftus and Palmer (1974) using just two conditions (e.g. leading question contains the word 'hot' or 'smashed') and compare the speed estimates given by the two groups of participants.

CAN YOU...? (No. **1A.13**)

1... In a study to compare the effects of noise on performance a **matched pairs design** was used. Explain how this would be done, including a description of at least **two** variables that would be used for matching. Explain why you choose these variables for matching.

2... What would be a suitable statistical test to use with this study? Justify your choice.

3... Use descriptive statistics to summarise the results given in the worked example on the facing page, i.e. calculate measures of central tendency and dispersion, and also sketch an appropriate graph (see page 44 if you need a reminder about these concepts).

4... A psychology class decides to replicate the study by White *et al.* on the right. Write appropriate alternative and null hypotheses for this study.

5... Is your alternative hypothesis directional or non-directional?

6... The students check the significance of their results using the Mann–Whitney test and find that $U = 40$ (there were 9 participants in one group and 13 in the other group). State what conclusion they could draw from their results.

7... Repeat questions 2–5 with any of the other studies on this page.

When to use the Mann–Whitney U Test

- The hypothesis predicts a *difference* between two sets of data.
- The two sets of data are from separate groups of participants = *independent groups*.
- The data are at least ordinal (i.e. not nominal). See page 31 for an explanation.

The Mann–Whitney U Test is named after the Austrian-born US mathematician Henry Berthold Mann and the US statistician Donald Ransom Whitney who published the test in 1947. They adapted a test designed by Frank Wilcoxon that was for equal sample sizes (called the Wilcoxon Rank Sums test – not the same as the one on page 40).

THE MANN–WHITNEY U TEST – A WORKED EXAMPLE

STEP 1. State the alternative and null hypotheses
Alternative hypothesis: Male participants interviewed on a high bridge give higher ratings of the attractiveness of a female interviewer than those interviewed on a low bridge. (This is a directional hypothesis and therefore requires a one-tailed test.)
Null hypothesis: There is no difference in the ratings of attractiveness given by those interviewed on a high or low bridge.

STEP 2. Record the data in a table and allocate points (see right)
To allocate points consider each score one at a time.
Compare this score (the target) with all the scores in the other group.
Give 1 point for every score that is higher than the target score and ½ point for every equal score. Add these up to calculate the score for the target score. Repeat for all scores.

STEP 3. Find the observed value of U
U is the lower total number of points. In this case it is 16.5

STEP 4. Find the critical value of U
N_1 = number of participants in group 1
N_2 = number of participants in group 2
Look up the critical value in the table of critical values (below).
For a one-tailed test, $N_1 = 10$ and $N_2 = 14$, and the critical value of U $(p < 0.05) = 41$

Note When you have a directional hypothesis, remember to check whether the difference is in the direction that you predicted. If it is not, you cannot reject the null hypothesis.

STEP 5. State the conclusion
As the observed value (16.5) is less than the critical value (41) and the results are in the predicted direction we can reject the null hypothesis (at $p \leq 0.05$) and therefore conclude that participants interviewed on a high bridge give higher ratings of attractiveness to a female interviewer than those interviewed on a low bridge, i.e. that physiological arousal leads to greater perceptions of attractiveness.

Attractiveness ratings given by high bridge group	Points	Attractiveness ratings given by low bridge group	Points
7	1.5	4	10.0
10	0	6	8.5
8	1.0	2	10.0
6	3.5	5	9.5
5	7.0	3	10.0
8	1.0	5	9.5
9	0.5	6	8.5
7	1.5	4	10.0
10	0	5	9.5
9	0.5	7	7.0
		9	3.0
		3	10.0
		5	9.5
		6	8.5
$N_1 = 10$	16.5	$N_2 = 14$	123.5

The two samples in the table above are unequal, which may happen when using an independent groups design.

Tables of critical values of U (p≤0.05)

CRITICAL VALUES FOR A ONE-TAILED TEST

N_2 \ N_1	2	3	4	5	6	7	8	9	10	11	12	13	14	15
2				0	0	0	1	1	1	1	2	2	2	3
3		0	0	1	2	2	3	3	4	5	5	6	7	7
4		0	1	2	3	4	5	6	7	8	9	10	11	12
5	0	1	2	4	5	6	8	9	11	12	13	15	16	18
6	0	2	3	5	7	8	10	12	14	16	17	19	21	23
7	0	2	4	6	8	11	13	15	17	19	21	24	26	28
8	1	3	5	8	10	13	15	18	20	23	26	28	31	33
9	1	3	6	9	12	15	18	21	24	27	30	33	36	39
10	1	4	7	11	14	17	20	24	27	31	34	37	41	44
11	1	5	8	12	16	19	23	27	31	34	38	42	46	50
12	2	5	9	13	17	21	26	30	34	38	42	47	51	55
13	2	6	10	15	19	24	28	33	37	42	47	51	56	61
14	2	7	11	16	21	26	31	36	41	46	51	56	61	66
15	3	7	12	18	23	28	33	39	44	50	55	61	66	72

CRITICAL VALUES FOR A TWO-TAILED TEST

N_2 \ N_1	2	3	4	5	6	7	8	9	10	11	12	13	14	15
2					0	0	0	0	1	1	1	1
3			0	1	1	2	2	3	3	4	4	5	5
4		0	1	2	3	4	4	5	6	7	8	9	10
5	0	1	2	3	5	6	7	8	9	11	12	13	14
6	1	2	3	5	6	8	10	11	13	14	16	17	19
7	1	3	5	6	8	10	12	14	16	18	20	22	24
8	0	2	4	6	8	10	13	15	17	19	22	24	26	29
9	0	2	4	7	10	12	15	17	20	23	26	28	31	34
10	0	3	5	8	11	14	17	20	23	26	29	33	36	39
11	0	3	6	9	13	16	19	23	26	30	33	37	40	44
12	1	4	7	11	14	18	22	26	29	33	37	41	45	49
13	1	4	8	12	16	20	24	28	33	37	41	45	50	54
14	1	5	9	13	17	22	26	31	36	40	45	50	55	59
15	1	5	10	14	19	24	29	34	39	44	49	54	59	64

For any N_1 and N_2 observed value of U must be EQUAL TO or LESS THAN the critical value in this table for signicance to be shown.
Source: R. Runyon and A. Haber (1976). *Fundamentals of Behavioural Statistics (3rd edition)*. Reading, Mass: McGraw-Hill.

DESCRIPTIVE AND INFERENTIAL STATISTICS

In the examination you may be asked to identify appropriate **descriptive statistics** and/or **statistical tests** that could be used for a particular psychological study. Examples of such questions are shown on the facing page.

On this page we present a reminder of all the different kinds of statistical method you should be familiar with and how you can decide which statistic(s) would be appropriate in any situation. Such decisions are not always black and white, which means that you need to take relative advantages and disadvantages into account.

Descriptive statistics

This is a summary of the descriptive statistics covered at AS, and their advantages and disadvantages.

Measures of central tendency inform us about central (or middle) values for a set of data. They are 'averages' – ways of calculating a typical value for a set of data. An average can be calculated in different ways:

- The **mean** is calculated by adding up all the scores and dividing by the number of scores. It makes use of the values of all the data but can be unrepresentative of the data as a whole if there are extreme values. It is *not* appropriate for **nominal data**.
- The **median** is the middle value in an ordered list. It is unaffected by extreme scores but is not as 'sensitive' as the mean because not all values are reflected in the median. It is *not* appropriate for nominal data.
- The **mode** is the value that is *most* common in a data set. It is the only method appropriate when the data are in categories (such as number of people who like pink), i.e. nominal data, but can be used for all kinds of data. It is not a useful way of describing data when there are several modes.

Measures of dispersion inform us about the spread of data.

- **Range** is calculated by finding the difference between the highest and lowest score in a data set. This is easy to calculate but may be affected by extreme values.
- **Standard deviation** expresses the spread of the data around the mean. This is a more precise measure than the range because all of the values of the data are taken into account. However, some characteristics of the data are not expressed, such as the influence of extreme values.

Graphs A picture is worth a thousand words! Graphs provide a means of 'eyeballing' your data and seeing the results at a glance.

- **Bar chart** The height of the bar represents frequency. Suitable for both words and numbers, i.e. all levels of measurement.
- **Scattergraph** Suitable for **correlational** data, a dot or cross is shown for each pair of values. If the dots form a pattern going from bottom left to top right this indicates a **positive correlation**, whereas top left to bottom right suggests a **negative correlation**. The closer the dots are to a diagonal line, the stronger the correlation. If there is no detectable pattern this suggests a **zero correlation**.

Statistical tests

Statistical tests are the only way to determine whether the results of a study are **significant**, i.e. a real effect has been demonstrated as opposed to a chance pattern that *looks* meaningful.

There are a large number of statistical tests that are used by researchers and statisticians; however you only need be concerned with the five in the specification. When deciding which test is appropriate in any situation you can ask yourself the questions in the diagram below:

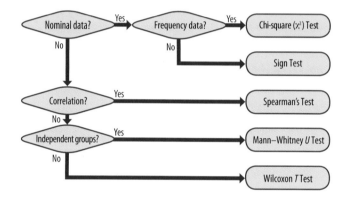

Justifying your choice In an exam question, you may be asked to choose an appropriate statistical test and then *justify* your choice. Below is a variety of possible justifications that could be used. *However, be warned that such justifications need to be adapted to suit the particular circumstances.*

- **Spearman's Rank Order Correlation Coefficient** would be selected because the hypothesis predicted a **correlation**, i.e. predicts that two related variables covary systematically. The data are 'better' than nominal (i.e. **ordinal** or **interval data**). Therefore Spearman's Rank Order Correlation Coefficient is selected (test of correlation, related data, better than ordinal data).
- **Chi-squared Test** would be selected because the data have been put into categories and are classified as nominal data. The results are independent in each cell, and the *expected* frequencies in each cell are at least 5. The appropriate statistical test to use is therefore a Chi-squared Test (test of association, independent groups, nominal data).
- **Sign Test** would be selected because a **test of difference** is required as the **hypothesis** predicts that there will be a positive or negative difference between the two sets of data. The two sets of data are related as all the participants were tested twice. The data are nominal because each participant is placed in a + or − category. Therefore the Sign Test is suitable (test of difference, related groups, nominal data).
- **Wilcoxon T Test** would be selected because a test of difference is required as the hypothesis predicts that there will be a difference between the two conditions. The design is **repeated measures** as all the participants were tested twice. The data were ordinal/interval (select whichever is appropriate and explain why the data are at this level of measurement). Therefore a Wilcoxon T Test was chosen (test of difference, related groups, better than ordinal data).
- **Mann–Whitney U Test** would be selected because a test of difference is required as the hypothesis predicts that there will be a difference between the two groups. The design is **independent groups** as participants were allocated to one of two treatment groups, and the data were ordinal/interval (select whichever is appropriate and explain why the data are at this level of measurement). Therefore the Mann–Whitney test is suitable (test of difference, independent groups, better than ordinal data).

Your own revision flash cards

Now that you have come to the end of this chapter you might think about producing your own set of revision flash cards. The specification table at the beginning of this chapter provides the elements that you must cover. For each topic be sure to include advantages and disadvantages where appropriate.

The secret of good flash cards is that the information is very brief – just a few key words to act as a reminder.

You also might try recording your flash cards as a podcast and listen to your recordings as a way to revise.

CAN YOU...? No. 1A.13

Question 1

*In the following research studies suggest a suitable **alternative** and **null hypothesis** for the study, briefly explain how you might conduct the study, invent a hypothetical set of data that might be produced and finally select an appropriate statistical test, justifying the reason for your choice.*

(a) An experiment where reaction times are compared for each participant before and after drinking coffee.

(b) A study looking at whether old or young people watch more violence on TV.

(c) An investigation to see if reaction time is related to age.

(d) An experiment to compare stress levels in doctors and nurses.

(e) A study where two groups of participants were matched on memory ability. Each group used a different revision technique to learn a topic and then their performances were compared.

(f) A study to see whether people who have a pet are happier than those who don't.

Question 2

For each of the following data sets identify an appropriate measure of central tendency and dispersion and justify your choice.

(a) 8, 11, 12, 12, 14, 15, 16, 16, 17, 19, 22, 27

(b) 15, 17, 21, 25, 28, 29, 32, 34, 25, 35, 38, 41, 45

(c) yes, yes, no, no, no, yes, no, no

Question 3

*A student designed an experiment that used a **repeated measures design** to investigate obedience to male and female teachers. The student decided to do this by observing how pupils behaved with different teachers. She asked various friends to record student behaviours in their classrooms.*

(a) State a possible **directional hypothesis** for this study.

(b) Suggest **two** possible **confounding variables** that might be a problem for this study and describe the possible effects they could have.

(c) Suggest **three** behavioural categories that might be used to record the students' behaviours.

(d) Identify the **sampling** method that is likely to have been used in this study and explain why it would be chosen.

(e) Suggest some appropriate statistical measures that could be used when analysing the data (both descriptive and inferential). Justify your choice.

Question 4

A psychologist designs a set of questions to collect data about smokers' and non-smokers' attitudes to smoking.

(a) Write **one** open and **one closed question** that might be used.

(b) For each question the psychologist would like to summarise the answers that are given. Suggest **two** ways that data could be summarised from the questions you have written.

(c) Suggest **one** advantage and **one** disadvantage of presenting the questions in writing rather than conducting face-to-face interviews.

(d) Why would **standardised instructions** be necessary?

(e) What statistical test might be used in this study? Justify your choice.

(f) How might **demand characteristics** be a problem in this study?

An exam-style question

Researchers conducted a study to test the effect of mental factors on athletic performance using 40 university Sports and Exercise students as participant volunteers.

The students were matched in pairs according to their recorded maximum bench press (a measure of press-up strength), and they were also paired by gender. They were given a standard personality test that measured 'determination' as one co-variable in this study.

A competition was staged with the other participants as audience, where the paired students competed to see who could do the most press-ups before exhaustion. The reason for this part of the study was to push students to produce their best bench press scores.

A correlation test was completed, each student providing their 'determination' score and their maximum press-up score as the variables. 'Determination' was plotted against 'maximum pressup' and Spearman's Rank Order Correlation Coefficient used to calculate the correlation coefficient.

The result was rho = +.22 (which is non-significant).

(a) Give **one** advantage and **one** disadvantage of using a correlational analysis. [4]

(b) The students were matched by bench press and gender. Explain why they were matched by gender. [2]

(c) Describe how the researchers could establish the **validity** of the 'determination' score on the personality test. [2]

(d) Explain why Spearman's Rank Order Correlation Coefficient was chosen to assess the significance of the results. [2]

(e) Describe **one** potential confounding variable, and explain why this might affect the validity of the findings. [3]

(f) Identify **one** potential **ethical issue** in this study and suggest how it could be dealt with. [3]

(g) The researchers used a volunteer sample. Identify an alternative method of sampling and explain how it would be implemented in this study. [3]

(h) The **correlation coefficient** was calculated to be +.22. Explain what '+.22' indicates. [2]

(i) State a suitable null hypothesis for this study. [2]

(j) Explain whether this null hypothesis would be accepted or rejected and why. [2]

Chapter 1A Research methods **45**

VALIDITY AND RELIABILITY

VALIDITY

- Validity is about legitimacy.
- Internal validity is about whether the researcher tested what they intended to test.
- External validity is about whether results generalise to other situations/people – sometimes called ecological validity.

Experimental research
- Variables other than the IV which *could* affect the DV (and therefore lower internal validity) are called extraneous variables. Those which *do* are called confounding variables.
- Possible extraneous variables include:
- Situational variables (environmental variables, e.g. noise), reduced by standardising procedures.
- Participant variables, dealt with by using matched pairs or repeated measures designs.
- Investigator effects (e.g. leading questions) can be solved with the double blind technique.
- Demand characteristics (cues from the research situation that affect participants' behaviour) reduced by improving the design of the experiment.
- If the measures (e.g. questionnaires) used lack validity the experiment will lack internal validity.

- Lab experiments *may* be low in external validity but if the artificial setting is unimportant (e.g. in a memory study) the findings will generalise to everyday situations (high external validity).
- Field experiments may be low in external validity if participants are aware they are being studied or if the task itself is artificial (i.e. low mundane realism); this reduces generalisability.

Observational techniques
- Internal validity (and reliability) of observations depend on the coding system/behaviour checklist, (a) having categories that don't overlap, and (b) including all possible behaviours.
- Internal validity is also threatened by observer bias as observers' expectations reduce objectivity.
- Naturalistic observations tend to have high ecological/external validity.

Questionnaires and interviews
- Internal validity of questionnaires/interviews/psychological tests can be assessed using: content validity (does it look like it is measuring what was intended?), concurrent validity (does it produce the same results as an established test?), or construct validity (does the test assess the intended phenomenon, e.g. intelligence?).
- External validity is threatened if there are sampling biases.

RELIABILITY

- Reliability is about consistency.

Experimental research
- Reliable experiments produce the same result when replicated.

Observational techniques
- High inter-observer reliability (e.g. at least +.80) means different observers produce the same record.
- Reliability in observations is increased by training observers to use checklists, etc.

Questionnaires and interviews
- Internal reliability is whether something is consistent within itself (e.g. do all the items in a test measure the same thing?). The split-half method compares performance on two halves of a test. If all items assess the same thing scores from each half should correlate.
- External reliability is a measure of consistency over different occasions. The test–retest method compares the same people doing a test twice, e.g. a week or a month apart. High positive correlation indicates high external reliability.
- Inter-interviewer reliability concerns whether two interviewers produce the same outcome.

RESEARCH METHODS

RESEARCH METHODS IN THE SPECIFICATION

Experiments
- All experiments have an independent variable (IV) which is varied to investigate changes in a dependent variable (DV) which is measured.
- Advantages: Experiments can therefore demonstrate causal relationships, as long as changes in the DV are due to the IV not extraneous variables (EVs).
- Lab experiments are conducted in controlled environments.
- Advantages and disadvantages: tend to have high internal validity and replicability, though experimenter effects and demand characteristics still threaten internal validity. Controls reduce external validity as the situation may be less like everyday life.
- Field experiments are conducted in more natural environments.
- Advantages and disadvantages: only some variables can be controlled. Experimenter effects are lower (because participants unaware of study) but operationalisation of the IV may cue participants' behaviour (demand characteristics).
- Natural experiments use existing (not deliberately manipulated) IVs.
- Advantages and disadvantages: causal conclusions can't be drawn. Participants aren't randomly allocated to conditions, a threat to validity, but some behaviours or experiences can only be studied in this way (e.g. poor diet).

Questionnaires and interviews
- Self-report techniques investigate what people think and feel.
- Interviews are verbal, questionnaires are written.
- Advantages and disadvantages: questionnaires are structured – fixed questions (therefore easily repeated), interviews can be unstructured – questions developed by interviewer (thus unexpected and detailed information can be gained, increasing validity).
- Social desirability bias may be a problem.
- Open questions produce detailed data which can gain new insights but produce qualitative data which are harder to analyse than quantitative data. Closed questions offer limited answers, thus may not represent participants' views.

Correlational analysis
- Correlational analyses explore the relationship between two variables and may find a positive or negative correlation.
- Advantages and disadvantages: can use large data sets and be easily repeated but can't demonstrate a cause. Validity may be threatened by other, unknown (intervening) variables, using measures that lack validity or if the sample lacks generalisability.

Observational studies
- Observational techniques can be used to measure the DV in an experiment or may be the sole research method.
- Behaviour checklists are used to structure observations and may be used in naturalistic or controlled observations.
- Advantages and disadvantages: observations record what people do (rather than what they say they do) so are more valid, but expectations can cause observer bias and observers may lack reliability.

Content analysis
- Content analysis is an indirect observation – of the content of things produced by people, e.g. adverts or books.
- Categories are identified and examples can be qualitative (individual examples, e.g. quotes) or quantitative (examples counted).
- Advantages and disadvantages: it has high ecological validity as based on things that people actually do, but observer bias can be a problem.

Case studies
- Case studies are detailed investigations of a single individual, institution or event using techniques such as interviews, tests, observations and experiments.
- They are often longitudinal (over an extended time) and allow complex interactions of factors to be studied.
- Advantages and disadvantages: difficult to generalise as each case is unique. The use of recollection and subjectivity of interpretation can lower reliability.

OTHER RESEARCH METHODS

The multi-method approach
- Few studies use only one method, most use a multi-method approach, e.g. combining controlled observation and interviews (e.g. Milgram) or observation and experiment (e.g. Rosenhan).

Meta-analysis
- A meta-analysis combines results from several studies with similar aims and uses effect size to assess the relationship between two variables.
- Advantage: analysing results from many studies makes conclusions more reliable than from just one.
- Disadvantage: differences in research designs may mean the studies aren't comparable so conclusions may be invalid.

Role play
- Researchers ask participants to take on a role. Their behaviour is observed as if it were real life (e.g. Zimbardo's study).
- Advantages: allows researchers to study otherwise impractical/unethical situations and to gain insights by interviewing participants afterwards.
- Disadvantages: people may not act as they would in real life and making people uncomfortable raises ethical issues even when it is only a role play.

Longitudinal and cross-sectional studies
- A longitudinal study is conducted over a long time so can investigate long-term effects and comparisons between the same individual/institution at different ages/historical periods.
- A cross-sectional study compares groups of participants of different ages at the same point in time (so is a snapshot study).
- Advantages: both methods allow the effects of age or time to be studied. Longitudinal studies control for participant variables whereas cross-sectional studies are quicker.
- Disadvantages: participants in longitudinal studies may become aware of the aims and participant drop-out (attrition) is a problem if the drop-outs have similar characteristics biasing the sample (and making it smaller). The two groups in a cross-sectional study may be different (no control over participant variables). A group of people of the same age at the same time (a cohort) share experiences which may cause differences. Cross-sectional studies may confound real age-related differences, whereas in longitudinal studies unique characteristics of the cohort may make the findings ungeneralisable.

Cross-cultural studies
- Cross-cultural studies compare behaviours between cultures to see whether cultural practices affect behaviour.
- Advantage: can investigate whether behaviours are innate (if the same in all cultures).
- Disadvantages: tests developed in one culture may not be valid elsewhere (an imposed etic) making other cultures appear abnormal or inferior, the group studied may not be representative, observer bias may arise and investigator effects occur if participants try to give the answers they think the researcher would like.

RESEARCH DESIGN

AIMS AND HYPOTHESES

- The aim is what the researchers intend to study.
- A hypothesis may be directional, stating which level of the IV will be 'better' or whether a correlation will be positive or negative. Non-directional hypotheses just say there will be a difference/correlation.
- Variables in hypotheses should be operationalised so they can be tested.

EXPERIMENTAL DESIGN

- Each participant may be tested on all levels of the IV (repeated measures design), separate groups may be used for each level of the IV (independent groups design) or each participant may be matched on key variables with a participant in the other group(s) (matched pairs design).
- A repeated measures design controls participant variables and fewer participants are needed but order effects can occur (e.g. boredom, practice) and participants may guess the aim.
- An independent groups design avoids order effects but needs more participants and participant variables can be a problem (but random allocation reduces this).
- A matched pairs design avoids order effects and partially controls participant variables but matching is difficult.
- A control group or condition is used to establish a baseline in an experiment (in comparison with an experimental group/condition).

SAMPLING TECHNIQUES

- Opportunity sample: participants selected by availability. It is easy but biased as the sample comes from a small part of the population.
- Self-selected (volunteer) sample: participants selected by asking, e.g. using an advert. Depending on how/where they are asked, a variety of people may be accessible (more representative) but there may be a volunteer bias (volunteers are motivated).
- Random sample: participants selected by identifying all members of the target population and use a lottery method or random number generator. Potentially unbiased as equal chance of selection for everyone but a bias can arise if people refuse to take part.
- Systematic sample: participants selected using a system such as taking every tenth person. Unbiased but not truly random unless you start with a person determined by a random method.
- Stratified sample: randomly selects a predetermined number of participants from subgroups (strata) in proportion to their numbers in the target population. In quota sampling the participants are chosen by opportunity. These methods provide proportional representation of subgroups but selection within each subgroup may be biased.

DESIGNING OBSERVATIONS

- To produce reliable observations, the continuous stream of action must be separated into target behaviour(s). The categories should: be operationalised and objective, cover all possible component behaviours, avoid a 'waste basket' category and be mutually exclusive.
- A behaviour checklist (list of behaviours to tally) or coding system (code for each behaviour) can be used in structured observations (as opposed to unstructured observations). Naturalistic observations may be structured.
- Event sampling counts occurrence of each behaviour in a fixed period of time and time sampling records behaviours at regular intervals.
- In an overt observation a participant may be aware of the observer; this may alter behaviour reducing validity. In a covert observation a participant is unaware, which raises ethical issues, e.g. privacy.

DESIGNING QUESTIONNAIRES AND INTERVIEWS

- Good questions are clear and unambiguous so should avoid eliciting social desirability and not be leading. Questions may be open or closed.
- Good questionnaires and interviews start with unthreatening and easy questions to establish trust and decrease dishonesty. Filler questions may help hide the aims.
- A pilot study is a small-scale trial which can be used to refine the questions.

ETHICAL ISSUES AND WAYS OF OVERCOMING THEM

- The BPS published a revised Code of Ethics and Conduct in 2009.
- Informed consent: comprehensive information about the nature and purpose of a study and participants' role in it. This may affect participants' behaviour so reduce the meaningfulness of the research. Participants should give consent in writing and be offered the right to withdraw or to withhold their data. Retrospective consent can be sought during debriefing or presumptive consent used.
- Deception: withholding information or lying about the aims of a study or what participation will entail. Prevents participants giving informed consent. Some deception is relatively harmless and/or can be compensated for by adequate debriefing.
- Right to withdraw: participants should be told at the start (and reminded later) they can cease participation (even if they are rewarded). The loss of participants may bias findings.
- Protection from harm: physical (e.g. injury) or psychological (e.g. anxiety) but risks may be unknown before the study. Risks should be no greater than in everyday life and a study should be stopped if harm becomes apparent.
- Confidentiality: a legal right. Personal information should be protected, e.g. by not recording names and storing confidential information securely. Maintaining confidentiality is impossible if details of a study automatically identify individuals.
- Privacy: individuals have a right to control information about themselves but knowing they are being observed may change their behaviour. Observation without informed consent should only be done where people would expect to be observed by others.
- Ethical committees consider the potential costs and benefits of the research and how the researcher intends to resolve ethical issues. Their job is to balance the protection of the participants' rights against conducting meaningful research.
- Debriefing: given after the study to tell participants the full aims, procedures, etc. and to discuss their concerns but shouldn't be a replacement for designing ethically sound research. Especially important if the study was stressful to return the participant to their previous state or if no informed consent.
- Presumptive consent can be gained from a similar group of people to the participants. If they consent it is presumed that the real participants would also agree.

INFERENTIAL AND DESCRIPTIVE STATISTICS

UNDERSTANDING INFERENTIAL STATISTICS

- Probability: conclusions from inferential statistics are based on the probability that a particular pattern of results could have arisen by chance. If the findings aren't due to chance, the pattern is significant.
- Samples and populations: samples are drawn from a target population in order to determine whether there is one single population or two separate ones.
- The null hypothesis (H_0) is a statement of no difference or no correlation in the target population. The alternative hypothesis (H_1) states that there is a real difference/correlation.
- Inferential statistical tests permit you to conclude, at a given probability, whether a pattern in the data from a study could have arisen by chance (accept null hypothesis) or whether the effect occurred because there is a real difference/correlation in the populations from which the samples were drawn (accept alternative hypothesis).
- Psychologists generally use a probability of $p \leq 0.05$, i.e. there is less than or equal to a 5% probability that the results could have occurred if the null hypothesis was true.
- To be more certain (e.g. in a replication) more stringent probabilities (significance levels) e.g. $p \leq 0.01$ or $p \leq 0.001$ can be used.

USING STATISTICAL TESTS

Levels of measurement
- The level of measurement matters to the choice of inferential test.
- Nominal data are data in separate categories.
- Ordinal data are ordered data, the intervals aren't equal.
- Interval and ratio data use units of measurement with equal intervals (so are more precise). Ratio data come from scales with a true zero.
- Rating scales aren't true interval scales but can be called plastic interval scales.

Observed and critical values
- Each statistical test produces a single number (the test statistic) with a name (e.g. rho for Spearman's). The value for any data set is the observed (or calculated) value.
- The observed value is compared with the critical value using a table of critical values for that statistical test.
- To look up a critical value you need to know: the degrees of freedom (df) (generally the number of participants = N); whether the hypothesis was a directional (one-tailed test) or non-directional (two-tailed test); and the significance level (e.g. $p \leq 0.05$).
- If the statistical test finds a significant pattern but the hypothesis was directional, you can only reject the null hypothesis if the difference or correlation is in the predicted direction.
- Type 1 errors occur when rejecting a null hypothesis which is true. This is more likely to happen with a lenient significance level, e.g. 10%. Type 2 errors occur when accepting a null hypothesis which is false.

CHOOSING WHICH STATISTICAL TEST

Spearman's Rank Order Correlation Coefficient
- Spearman is used when: the hypothesis predicts a correlation, the two sets of data are pairs of scores (e.g. from one person, i.e. are related) the data are better than ordinal (i.e. not nominal).

Chi-squared (X^2) Test
- Chi-squared is used when: the hypothesis predicts a difference (between conditions) or an association (between variables), the data sets are independent (no individual has a score in more than one 'cell'), and the data are nominal (frequency data counted in categories).
- The degrees of freedom (df) = (rows − 1) × (columns − 1).
- The test is unreliable if the expected frequencies (the ones based on a random distribution) fall below 5 in any cell (square).

Sign Test
- The sign test is used when: the hypothesis predicts a difference between conditions, the experiment has a repeated measures (or matched pairs) design and the data are nominal.

Wilcoxon T Test
- Wilcoxon is used when: the hypothesis predicts a difference between conditions, the experiment has a repeated measures (or matched pairs) design (i.e. related designs) and the data are better than ordinal (i.e. not nominal).

Mann–Whitney U Test
- Mann–Whitney is used when: the hypothesis predicts a difference between conditions, the experiment has an independent groups design and the data are better than ordinal (i.e. not nominal).

DESCRIPTIVE STATISTICS

Measures of central tendency
- Describe the central values (averages) for a data set.
- The mean is calculated by adding up all the scores and dividing by the number of scores. It uses all the data but can be unrepresentative if there are extreme values. It can't be used on nominal data.
- The median is the middle value in an ordered list. It is unaffected by extreme scores but is less 'sensitive' than the mean as it doesn't use all the scores. It can't be used on nominal data.
- The mode is the most common value in a data set and can be used with any level of measurement. It isn't useful if there are several modes.

Measures of dispersion
- Describe the spread of data.
- The range is the difference between the highest and lowest score in a data set. It is easy to calculate but may be affected by extreme values.
- The standard deviation calculates the spread of the data around the mean. It is more precise than the range as all the scores are used but the influence of extreme values isn't represented.

Graphs
- A bar chart is a graph where the height of the bar represents frequency and is suitable for any level of measurement.
- A scattergraph is used for correlational data, showing each pair of values as a dot. Positive, negative or zero correlation indicated by pattern of dots. The closer the dots lie to a line, the stronger the correlation.

Question

Does the style of leadership in a work situation affect the results of the work? Do authoritarian leaders (who direct everything) get better results than democratic leaders (who involve the workers in decision making)?

A field experiment using an independent measures design was set up using an after-school club in Technology in a local comprehensive school. The club was aimed at producing flying model airplanes. Advertisements were placed around school and a total of 20 students applied to join the club. They were split alphabetically into two groups each consisting of ten students. Group A had ten males and Group B had seven males and three females. The club ran for 20 weeks and ended with a flight-testing afternoon, followed by a satisfaction questionnaire.

The teacher leading group A directed the group in everything (authoritarian style). Students worked largely alone, and meetings were only for the leader to show the group how to do something. The teacher leading group B encouraged discussion of progress, sharing of ideas and helping each other (democratic style).

Results

	Flew successfully	Did not fly
Group A	7	3
Group B	5	5

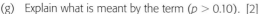

Using the Chi-squared Test gave a non-significant result ($p > 0.10$).

Contextualisation

In the AS research methods exam each of the questions required you to relate your knowledge to the particular study described in the scenario. This is called *contextualisation*. You had to contextualise all of your answers in order to gain high marks in the exam. For example, if you simply described one advantage of using a correlation that would only get part marks; for full marks you had to explain why it is an advantage in the case of the *particular* study.

This is not the case at A2 because the questions are *not* always **AO3**, such as question (a) (ii). This is not an AO3 question and does not require contextualisation. In contrast question (b) (ii) does require a contextualised answer – it would be difficult to see how you could answer the question without contextualising your answer.

The bottom line is, if in doubt – contextualise!

(a) (i) Describe what is meant by an independent measures design. [2]
 (ii) Explain **one** advantage and **one** disadvantage of this design. [4]

(b) (i) Describe what is meant by the term 'confounding variable'. [2]
 (ii) Explain the way in which **one** confounding variable may have affected this study. [2]

(c) (i) What is meant by the term 'reliability'? [2]
 (ii) Explain **one** problem with the reliability of this study. [2]

(d) (i) Explain **one** ethical problem with this study. [2]
 (ii) Explain how this ethical problem might be overcome? [2]

(e) Give **one** advantage and **one** disadvantage of the method of sampling used. [4]

(f) Describe how an alternative method of sampling could be used for this study. [2]

(g) Explain what is meant by the term ($p > 0.10$). [2]

Student answer 1

(a) (i) There are separate conditions of the IV (and usually a control condition), in this case the two differently led groups. Different participants are assigned to each condition.

(a) (ii) Using independent groups design controls for order effects. In this case if students had one type of leadership and then another, the first experience would alter their attitudes and behaviour and would not allow a proper comparison. However, one obvious disadvantage is that you would have to recruit a lot of participants, especially a problem if you had more than the two conditions in this study.

(b) (i) This is an uncontrolled variable present in the study situation that has acted as a separate IV and affected the DV in some way. This makes a study invalid.

(b) (ii) An example here would be that the groups might have different levels of ability in technology due to the way they were sampled.

(c) (i) Reliability refers to consistency, such as whether the same person would get the same score on a test if they took it again.

(c) (ii) One problem with reliability might be in terms of the consistency of teaching styles. For example, the teacher leading group A might have been authoritarian some of the time but sometimes adopted a more democratic style.

(d) (i) Students have been deceived about the nature of the after-school clubs and therefore did not give their consent to take part in a psychology study.

(d) (ii) It would be important to debrief the participants and ensure with follow-up interviews that they did not have any problems with the study.

(e) Volunteer or self-selected samples are usually very easy to organise as you just have to advertise and people apply to take part. This means you would have lots of participants to choose from.
However, the kind of people who volunteer for psychology studies tend to be confident people who are psychologically different from those who don't (e.g. more motivated) so they're not representative of the whole population in personality terms.

(f) Students could be selected for the study systematically by taking every fifth student on a year register, for example.

(g) The probability of obtaining the results in this study if the null hypothesis was true.

Examiner comments

Correct and clear explanation, sufficient for the full 2 marks. There is no requirement for contextualisation.

The advantage is very well explained and has been contextualised, though this is not required in the question. This is nevertheless a good way to gain marks. The full 2 marks.

The disadvantage is also well explained, this time not made specific to this study but still worth the full 2 marks.

The two crucial elements of this answer are 'uncontrolled variable' and 'affected the DV' for the full 2 marks.

A correct answer to this question must be contextualised, as this one is, and therefore gains the full 2 marks. A candidate who simply defined the term 'confounding variable' would not gain marks. There are several possible creditworthy answers, such as other differences between the students that could affect the dependent variable (DV) or differences between the teachers other than leadership style or differences in the task – anything that arguably might affect the DV.

Detailed and concise for the full 2 marks.

This is a good answer, providing a full explanation and the reasoning behind it for the full 2 marks.

The answer goes beyond the simple statement that they were deceived, explaining why this is an ethical issue – therefore the full 2 marks.

Again it is important to go beyond simply identifying the answer and therefore you should include an explanation of what would be done. The full 2 marks.

There is no requirement for a contextualised answer. Neither the advantage and disadvantage are contextualised but both are accurate and detailed for the full 4 marks.

As this question is only worth 2 marks, it is sufficient to identify a method and provide a brief description, as in this answer.

This is a fully correct answer, there is no requirement to explain the actual level (i.e. 10%) in a question worth 2 marks. Many students fail to score full marks because they do not mention the null hypothesis. 2 marks.

Total = 26 out of 26 marks.
This result illustrates that it is not difficult to get maximum marks, but students have to be precise and explain everything fully instead of relying on the examiner to understand what they mean.

Student answer 2 is on the next page.

Student answer 2

Examiner comments

(a) (i) Different groups are used.

This answer is not clear. In what way are different groups used? What is meant by this? Not made clear at all, therefore 0 out of 2 marks.

(a) (ii) You don't get order effects because there are different people in each group so they only do things once. You need a lot of people unlike if they all do all the conditions.

The advantage is identified and explained, so the full 2 marks. The disadvantage is correct but it is a limited answer that needs a fuller explanation, therefore 1 mark and not the full 2.

(b) (i) Something that goes wrong and affects the study, it is an error variable not controlled.

This answer is not clearly explained but demonstrates sufficient understanding for a weak 2 out of 2 marks.

(b) (ii) The kids might not be that interested, got bored. Also they might know the teacher already so they behave like they do normally.

This answer provides two possible confounding variables whereas the question requires only one. Examiners will credit the best one, but in any case neither is fully and clearly explained, therefore 1 mark only.

(c) (i) Consistency.

A very brief though correct answer, therefore just 1 out of 2 marks.

(c) (ii) You would have to repeat this study in different schools and with different teachers and see if you get the same results.

So many students get confused about reliability. If you repeat a test or even a study with different people then you are looking at validity and not reliability. Furthermore the question didn't ask how to deal with reliability, it just asked for a possible problem to be identified. 0 marks.

(d) (i) The kids wouldn't trust the teachers again.

In the scenario presented this might be an issue, so must get credit. However there is insufficient explanation for more than 1 mark.

(d) (ii) Don't let them have those teachers again.

This is not really addressing the issue properly. A much better answer would be to use debriefing or having a discussion with the teachers, which might strengthen the relationship in the future. Therefore 0 marks for this answer.

(e) Volunteers are really motivated so will usually complete the study and not drop out.
  Volunteers are very confident usually so they are not really representative.

The advantage is accurate and sufficiently detailed. The disadvantage lacks some clarity because it does not explain in what way the volunteers are not representative. Therefore the answer would get 2 out of 2 marks + 1 out of 2 marks.

(f) You could take a random sample by drawing names out of a hat.

This answer only gets 1 out of 2 marks because there is insufficient detail about how it would be done.

(g) You've a one in ten chance of being wrong.

This answer would be just about worth 1 mark as it displays some knowledge of what $p > 0.10$ means but really should include 'probability' for 1 mark and then the second mark would be given for explaining that this probability is the certainty with which we accept or reject the null hypothesis.

Total = 13 out of 26 marks.
Many students get this level of mark simply by not writing answers out clearly and in full, explaining everything. You must imagine the examiner listening to you and needing you to spell out precisely what you mean.

Chapter 1B
Issues in research

Chapter contents

52 Introduction to issues in research
54 The use of the scientific method in psychology
56 Ethical issues and human participants
58 Ethical issues and non-human animals
60 Ethical issues in applications of psychology

End-of-chapter review

62 Chapter summary
64 Exam question with student answer

Specification breakdown	
The advantages of the use of the scientific method in psychology	The scientific method is a successful way of acquiring knowledge in the physical world and is the main method employed in modern psychology. The scientific method has many advantages, which can be illustrated with examples from psychology.
The disadvantages of the use of the scientific method in psychology	Not all is sweetness and light, alas! There are also disadvantages with the use of the scientific method. Psychology provides many examples of artificiality in studies and there are also limitations of humans investigating their own brains.
Ethical issues in the use of human participants in research in psychology	Ethical standards and basic human rights can be easily compromised in the process of investigating human behaviour. Apart from the necessary deception so often needed in research, there are many examples where ethical standards may appear less than ideal.
Ways of dealing with ethical issues when using human participants in research in psychology	Both historically and in modern research, ethical issues have arisen and been dealt with, well or badly. There are many examples in psychology that illustrate the ways used.
Ethical issues in the use of non-human animals in research in psychology	For the British in particular, research on non-human animals seems to raise the emotional temperature more than that on humans. The way non-human animals have been used in research raises issues of scientific benefit versus moral considerations – can, and should, we justify animal research when psychology increasingly finds evidence of thought and emotion in non-human animals? This area focuses strictly on psychological research alone.
Ethical issues arising from two applications of psychology in the real world (e.g. advertising, military)	Psychological findings can be used outside the research domain, especially when funded by organisations like retail businesses or governments. The ethical issues arise when ideas are used for financial gain, to oppress people, to deny rights or even to damage them, physically or mentally. Examples can be drawn from any two applications of psychology, not just advertising or military uses. We have covered the media and the military but you could use any of the topics.

INTRODUCTION TO ISSUES IN RESEARCH

What is an issue?

The decision to preface the word 'Issue' with the modifier 'Big' for the magazine sold by and for homeless people, was made because it suggested to us that homelessness was important, vital, not to be ignored. The same is true in psychology – there are some 'issues' that are so important that we really can't ignore them. These may potentially undermine the value of psychological theories and research (e.g. if we can demonstrate that the scientific method is flawed) or they may focus us on important aspects of the subject's integrity (e.g. the use of non-human animals in research). All of these issues are 'big' because we ignore them at our peril.

Link to chapter 1A

Many of the topics in this chapter are linked to Chapter 1A. For example ethical issues in relation to research with human participants were considered on pages 28–29. In this chapter the focus has changed from answering short questions on potential ethical issues in research to answering longer essay questions where you discuss these issues. The material in this chapter builds on the knowledge you gained in your AS studies and also in Chapter 1A. There are also links to the controversies in Chapter 2 where you will again consider science and ethics.

The exam

Possible questions

The PY3 exam is divided into three sections. Sections A and B each contain a parted question on research methods (covered in Chapter 1A). Section C contains **three** essay questions from which you must select **two**.

Altogether you have 1½ hours to answer this paper – about a minute per mark which leaves about 15 minutes for each Section C question.
The three questions will be drawn from the following list:

- *Discuss the advantages of the use of the scientific method in psychology.* [15]
- *Discuss the disadvantages of the use of the scientific method in psychology.* [15]
- *Discuss ethical issues in the use of human participants in research in psychology.* [15]
- *Discuss ways of dealing with ethical issues when using human participants in research in psychology.* [15]
- *Discuss ethical issues in the use of non-human animals in research in psychology.* [15]
- *Discuss ethical issues arising from* **two** *applications of psychology in the real world.* [15]

Note the command word in the above questions is 'discuss'. Other command words may be used.

In this chapter we have covered all six essay possibilities, although some of them have been combined on one spread (thus there are only four spreads in this chapter).

Writing Grade A answers

On pages 8–9 we have discussed how to write Grade A answers for essay questions. The advice offered there is appropriate for essays on PY4; however PY3 essays are different. The essay questions on this paper (Section C) are marked out of 15 marks and there are no separate description and evaluation marks. The assessment objective in this essay is just **A03** – analysing how science works. Your answers are purely assessed on the extent to which you discuss the research issues covered in this chapter.

Such theoretical discussions are difficult and therefore the exam board recommends that you use examples and psychological evidence to develop and support your theoretical discussion. Such examples will help make your essay effective – an important criterion as shown in the mark scheme below. This mark scheme further identifies the key elements required for a Grade A essay.

A summary of the mark scheme for PY3 Section C*

Marks	Appropriateness	Detail	Effectiveness and elaboration	Depth or range of material	Specialist terms
12–15	Appropriate	Well detailed	Effective, and coherent elaboration	Both depth *and* range covered, though not equal	Used throughout
8–11	Reasonable	Less detailed	Effective	Depth *or* range covered	Some evident
4–7	Basic	Relevant			Few evident
1–3	Superficial	Muddled and/or incorrect			Absent or incorrectly used
0	No relevant material presented				

* A full version of this mark scheme is available to all teachers from the exam board, and it's always wise to check if any changes have been made.

STARTER ACTIVITIES

GET TO GRIPS WITH SCIENCE

In this chapter and in Chapters 1A and 2 one of the key issues is looking at psychology as a science. So it's a good idea to get your head round the concept of science. One of the great ways to do this is to look at '**pseudoscience**'. A pseudoscience is a field of study that masquerades as a science but lacks certain important characteristics. A prime example of a pseudoscience is the study of paranormal activity – such as extra sensory perception (ESP), ghosts, aliens, psychic mediums and so on. Of course, some of you may believe in such phenomena and that's fine, but what we scientists want is evidence.

Your task is to put on your sceptical 'hat' (good scientists are sceptics) and select one or more studies of paranormal phenomena (search on the internet) and subject it to the scrutiny of *science*.

- **Can you find a replication?** One of the key features of the scientific approach is that scientists record their procedures exactly so that others can try to reproduce the same study and check that they do produce the same results. Pseudoscientific researchers tend to be secretive and this means we cannot verify their findings.
- **Is the hypothesis irrefutable?** The aim of the scientific process is to test **hypotheses**. It is not possible to prove a hypothesis correct but you can prove it is wrong (i.e. falsify it). Pseudoscientists frequently investigate phenomena that cannot be proven wrong. For example, a study may find no evidence of ESP. This would appear to suggest that ESP doesn't exist. However, some paranormal psychologists then claim the lack of supporting evidence occurs because sceptics are present and the phenomena disappear under such conditions. The end result is a non-falsifiable hypothesis. Many of the hypotheses related to paranormal experience are of this nature.
- **Is there a theory to explain the effects?** The aim of scientific research is to construct explanations for observations made about the world. Many paranormal phenomena have not, as yet, been given explanations that are likely. Without a theory, evidence is meaningless.

▲ *The Cottingley fairies.*

The photograph above was regarded as definite proof of the existence of fairies. One of its notable believers was Sir Arthur Conan Doyle who wrote the Sherlock Holmes stories. There were five photographs taken between 1916 and 1920 by cousins Elsie Wright and Francis Griffiths who lived in Cottingley near Bradford, England. The girls claimed to play with fairies but no one believed them so they produced photographic evidence. Various attempts to prove that the photos were fake failed and it was not until 1983 that the women finally admitted the hoax (www. cottingleyconnect.org.uk).

People continue to accept photographic evidence as proof for anomalous phenomena (such as photos of unidentified flying objects and ghosts), despite the fact that photographs are easily faked. The burden of proof is on the sceptic who is asked 'Explain this photograph' in contrast to scientific research where the burden of proof is on the believer.

> **> WWW**
>
> There is a lot of information about 'bad science' on Ben Goldacre's blog (www.badscience.net), or read his book also called *Bad Science* – it'll change your life (and help you understand science a lot better)!

ETHICAL ISSUES

The other key issue in Chapters 1A, 1B and 2 is ethical issues – those concerning both human and non-human participants and in real-world situations such as advertising.

A bit of debating might be a good idea. Select a meaty ethical issue, and then consider the following:

- Is it unethical? Look at the top ten unethical psychology experiments (see http://listverse.com/2008/09/07/top-10-unethical-psychological-experiments). One team has to defend these studies while the other team argues for their ethical unacceptability.
- Use of non-human animals in research, see www.bbc.co.uk/ethics/animals
- Ethics in advertising or the media or any application; search online.

THE USE OF THE SCIENTIFIC METHOD IN PSYCHOLOGY

The core of your study of psychology is an understanding of 'how science works'. This has been inherent in all of the psychology you have studied. Psychologists, like all scientists, use the **scientific method** to produce valid explanations about the world around them. This method has both advantages and disadvantages.

EXAM TIP

On the previous spread we discussed the importance of using examples and psychological evidence in your essay answers for PY3 Section C – these will help you to develop and support your theoretical arguments (and gain higher marks). The examples and evidence provided on this spread are by no means the only ones – feel free to use your own!

An empirical test

▲ *The picture above left is of a burger from a well-known fast food outlet. Or at least this is what you are led to expect you will get, but what about reality? You may think you know something but unless you test this empirically you cannot know if it is true. Above right is the empirical evidence of what the burgers are really like. 'Empirical' refers to information gained through direct experience. Science uses empirical methods to separate unfounded beliefs from real truths.*

(Thanks to Professor Sergio della Sala for this tasty and memorable example of empiricism.)

The scientific method

The scientific process starts with observations of phenomena in the world. In the **inductive model** this then leads to the development of hypotheses. Hypotheses are tested which may lead to new questions and new hypotheses. Eventually such data may be used to construct a theory.

The **deductive model** places theory construction at the beginning of the process, after making observations.

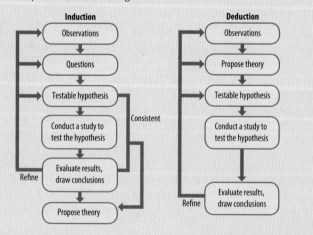

A 'good' theory is one that can be empirically tested. Unless you can test a theory there is no means of knowing if it is right or wrong. So a good theory should produce a variety of testable hypotheses, thus allowing falsification.

ADVANTAGES OF THE USE OF THE SCIENTIFIC METHOD IN PSYCHOLOGY

1. The scientific method is empirical

Empirical data are information gained through direct observation or experiment rather than by reasoned argument or unfounded beliefs. The scientific method aims to collect facts.

Why is this an advantage? People can make claims about the truth of a theory or the benefits of a treatment but the only way we know such things to be true is through empirical evidence.

For example… Testing a drug to see if it reduces anxiety.

2. The scientific method is objective

An important aspect of empirical data is that they are objective, i.e. not affected by the expectations of the researcher. Systematic collection of measurable data is at the heart of the method.

Why is this an advantage? Without objectivity we have no way of being certain that data collected are valid.

For example… In the AS core study by Gardner and Gardner (1969) the observers might have judged that Washoe was using real words because they wanted her to succeed. For that reason the Gardners developed a strict set of criteria to make judgements.

3. The scientific method is falsifiable

The aim of the scientific method is to test hypotheses by falsifying them, i.e. rejecting a **null hypothesis**.

Why is this an advantage? It is not possible to prove a hypothesis correct but you can prove it is wrong, i.e. falsify it.

For example… One of the issues with Freud's (1917) theory of **psychoanalysis** is the lack of proof. His theory produces claims that are untestable because they are unfalsifiable. For instance, his view that all men have repressed homosexual tendencies cannot be disproved. If you do find men who have no homosexual tendencies then it could be argued that the men do have the feelings but these are not apparent as they are repressed.

The **validity** of the theory is important if we want to use it to generate methods of treating people who are mentally ill. If the theory is unfounded then the therapy should not be used. The same arguments could be applied to the use of drugs or ECT in treating the mentally ill.

4. The scientific method is controlled

The ideal form of the scientific method is a **lab experiment** because it enables researchers to demonstrate causal relationships. The **experimental** method is the only way to do this – where we vary one factor (the **independent variable**) and observe its effect on a **dependent variable**. In order for this to be a 'fair test' all other conditions (**extraneous variables**) must be controlled, and the best place for this is the lab.

Why is this an advantage? If we can't demonstrate causal relationships then we can't be sure that, for example, a person's anxiety was reduced by the drug used.

5. The scientific method permits replication

Scientists record their methods and standardise them carefully so the same procedures can be followed in the future, i.e. replicated.

Why is this an advantage? Repeating a study is the most important way to demonstrate the validity of any observation or experiment. If the outcome is the same this affirms the truth of the original results.

For example… One of the issues with Milgram's (1963) study was its **ecological validity**. But the fact that it has been replicated suggests that the study does have ecological validity.

54

"More decisive? How can I be more decisive?
- I live by the uncertainty principle!"

Be careful

It is easy to fall into the trap of believing that the scientific method means lab experiments and you end up criticising lab experiments when you are meant to be considering disadvantages of the scientific method. This is a limited view of the scientific method which in reality embraces all the different research methods.

There is a discussion in Chapter 2 about psychology as a science (see pages 68–69). The interest there is on the wider issue of whether or not psychology can be considered to be a science. On this spread our focus is on the scientific method as a research method.

DISADVANTAGES OF THE USE OF THE SCIENTIFIC METHOD IN PSYCHOLOGY

1. The scientific method may lack internal validity

Psychological research is fraught with problems such as investigator effects and **demand characteristics**, which compromise the **internal validity** of the research.

Why is this a disadvantage? The observed effects may be due to variables other than the research manipulation.

For example ... A questionnaire may have a number of **leading questions**, which means that the findings are not valid.

2. The scientific method may lack external validity

Findings from psychology experiments are not always supported by real-life, everyday observations.

Why is this a disadvantage? This suggests that the findings of psychological research cannot be generalised beyond the particular settings in which they were conducted.

For example ... Mandel's (1998) analysis of obedience research showed that Milgram's (1974) findings bore very little relationship to behaviour in the real world. For instance, Milgram found that being in close proximity to the 'victim' produced lower levels of obedience, yet this constraining factor did not explain obedience in the Nazi death camps.

3. The scientific method can be reductionist

In order to conduct psychological research, behaviour must be *reduced* to a set of individual **operationalised** variables. This is true in experiments and also in observational studies where **behavioural categories** are operationalised.

Why is this a disadvantage? The result of this reductionism is that we may oversimplify something that cannot be simplified and, in doing so, are no longer studying what we meant to study.

For example ... The psychiatrist R.D. Laing (1965), in discussing the causes of **schizophrenia**, suggested that it is inappropriate to view a person experiencing distress as a complex physical–chemical system that has gone wrong. Laing claims that treatment can only succeed if each patient is treated as an individual case (the **idiographic approach**).

4. The scientific method tends to ignore individual differences

Science takes the **nomothetic** approach, looking to make generalisations about people and find similarities.

Why is this a disadvantage? The result is that gender, culture, age and other individual differences are overlooked.

For example ... Most research in psychology has involved American participants who are men and college students. The underlying assumption is that the behaviour of this group of people can be generalised to the whole population, ignoring the possibility that this group of people have unique characteristics, such as higher intelligence than average, interests that are typical of young male adults and so on.

5. The scientific method raises ethical issues

In psychological research there are often **ethical** costs.

Why is this a disadvantage? The issue to consider is whether the benefits of the research outweigh the ethical costs (a topic discussed in Chapter 2, see page 71). Even if the ethical costs are 'excusable' the end result is that the participants may have been harmed in some way.

For example ... Many people feel that the knowledge gained in Milgram's study excuses the **psychological harm** experienced by participants. Nevertheless, individual participants may feel that their rights have been infringed.

Investigator effects

One criticism of the use of the scientific method in psychology is that the findings of a research study may be negatively affected by the way the investigator's behaviour affects participants. This is also a problem in the 'hard' sciences. Heisenberg (1927) argued that it is not even possible to measure a subatomic particle without altering its 'behaviour' in doing the measurement. This so-called uncertainty principle is a kind of investigator effect: the presence of an experimenter changes the behaviour of what is observed, even in physics.

EXAM TIP

You could be set one of the following essays related to the content on this spread:

- *Consider the advantages of the use of the scientific method in psychology.* [15]
- *Consider the disadvantages of the use of the scientific method in psychology.* [15]

Note The *command term* may vary – it could be analyse, assess, consider, discuss, evaluate, examine, explain or identify and explain – whatever it says, you are still required to do the same thing, i.e. present either advantages *only* or disadvantages *only*.

CAN YOU...? No. **1B.1**

1... For each of the **five** advantages and **five** disadvantages select **two** key phrases or concepts (i.e. ten key phrases).

2... For each key phrase/concept write **four or five** sentences explaining the phrase.

3... For each of the **five** advantages and **five** disadvantages try to think of your own examples.

4... Use all of this material to write an answer to the following exam questions: (a) *Discuss the advantages of the use of the scientific method in psychology.* (b) *Discuss the disadvantages of the use of the scientific method in psychology.* Your answers should be about 500 words.

Don't forget to read the essay-writing guidance on pages 8 and 9, as well as the notes for Section C of PY3 on page 52.

In this chapter there are three spreads on **ethical issues** – this spread and the next two spreads. On this spread we look at *human* participants and on both the ethical issues *and* ways of dealing with them. Both of these topics are familiar to you as they were part of your AS studies and have been revisited in Chapter 1A of this book. The aim of this spread is to expand your knowledge and organise new knowledge in a way that will fit the demands of the exam.

The ethical issues described below have also been described on pages 28 and 29, so an explanation is not always provided.

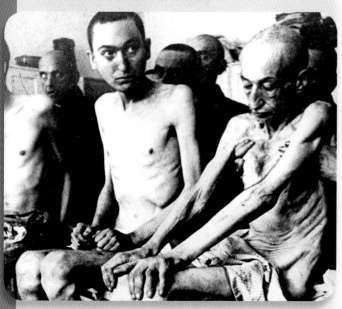

▲ *Concern for the protection of human participants in research has its roots in the Nuremberg Code (1947), a document designed to protect against atrocities such as those uncovered by the Nuremberg Trials following World War II. The Nuremburg Code was the first ethical code of practice. The* American Psychological Association *(APA) produced the first code for psychologists in 1953, a document of 170 pages.*

Socially sensitive research

Ethical guidelines do not cover broader ethical issues that arise in 'socially sensitive' areas. Sieber and Stanley (1988) defined **socially sensitive research** as 'studies in which there are potential social consequences or implications, either directly for the participants in research or the class of individuals represented by the research' (Sieber and Stanley, 1988).

One of the most controversial avenues of research has been consideration of inter-racial differences in IQ (see page 123). Some evidence suggests that, in terms of IQ, black children may be innately inferior. Even though this research may be flawed (e.g. it ignores social conditions) such 'scientific' evidence can be used to support divisive and discriminatory social policies. Other areas of social sensitivity include research on drug abuse or sexual orientation.

The ethical question concerns whether or not such research should be conducted. If research is conducted the findings may be abused. If research is not conducted such groups may miss out on the potential benefits from the research (e.g. increased funding or wider public understanding). However, ignoring these important areas of research is an abdication of the 'social responsibilities' of the psychological researcher (i.e. their duty to society to study important areas of human behaviour).

ETHICAL ISSUES WITH HUMAN PARTICIPANTS

1. Informed consent

Ideally, participants should be given the opportunity to know about all aspects of any research before agreeing to take part, i.e. give their **informed consent**. This is a basic right stemming from the inhumane experiments conducted in concentration camps such as Auschwitz-Birkenau in World War II.

Why is it an issue? Such an issue arises because full information may compromise the integrity of a study (e.g. knowing the full aims may alter a participant's behaviour, rendering the results meaningless). However, informed consent is especially important in cases where there may be issues of harm because participants would not have had the opportunity to decline to participate.

For example... in Milgram's (1963) study participants experienced extreme distress but arguably did not have the opportunity to decline to take part. In studies where harm is not an issue (such as memory studies) then informed consent is less of an issue.

2. Deception

Why is it an issue? Honesty is an important ethical principle and therefore breaches need to concern researchers as studies should only be conducted when circumstances excuse it (see '*BPS Code of Ethics and Conduct*' on the facing page). It is especially an issue because lack of honesty prevents participants from being able to give informed consent.

For example... In Rosenhan's (1973) study the hospital staff were deceived about the nature of the pseudopatients. This may have led them in future to be mistrustful of patients and therefore not offer the best treatment.

3. Right to withdraw

If participants do not have the **right to withdraw** they may remain in a study and continue to be harmed. This is especially problematic if they didn't provide informed consent in the first place.

Why is it an issue? It is an issue because there are various circumstances where participants do not feel they can withdraw.

For example... A number of American studies use college students as participants and the students receive course credits for their participation. This may make them feel they can't withdraw. Participants in other studies may feel they can't withdraw because it would spoil the study.

4. Protection from harm

Participants should not experience physical or **psychological harm**.

Why is it an issue? It isn't always possible to anticipate when participants will experience harm.

For example... In Milgram's study the extent of distress wasn't expected as the preliminary survey of opinion suggested that most people would stop before reaching the maximum level of shock.

5. Confidentiality and privacy

Confidentiality concerns the trust that personal information is protected. **Privacy** concerns a person's right to control the flow of information about themselves. Privacy and confidentiality are linked. If privacy is invaded, confidentiality should be protected.

Why is it an issue? It is difficult to establish what exactly counts as 'private'.

For example... In an observational study, some people might regard it as an invasion of their privacy to be watched in a supermarket, which is a public place.

You could be set either of the following essays related to the content on this spread:

• *Assess ethical issues in the use of human participants in research in psychology.* [15]

• *Assess ways of dealing with ethical issues when using human participants in research in psychology.* [15]

The key point is that students often answer the first question when they are set the second one, i.e. they describe issues when they should be explaining how they would *deal* with them.

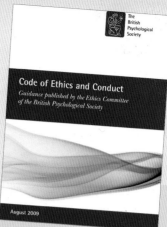

WAYS OF DEALING WITH ETHICAL ISSUES WITH HUMAN PARTICIPANTS

In many cases the way of dealing with an ethical issue is the same as the issue itself. For example, psychologists deal with the issue of informed consent by offering participants the opportunity to provide informed consent. Psychologists deal with confidentiality by ensuring, as far as possible, that the identity of all participants is not available. In addition there are some special methods, discussed below.

1. Debriefing

Once a study is completed, participants should be informed of the true aims of the study, offered the opportunity to discuss any concerns they may have and be given the opportunity to withdraw their data from the study – to compensate for the lack of opportunity for informed consent.

Problems … Debriefing can't turn back the clock– a participant may still feel embarrassed or have lowered **self-esteem**.

2. Presumptive consent

Presumptive consent is method of dealing with lack of informed consent or deception, by asking a group of people who are similar to the prospective participants in a study whether they would agree to take part in the study. If this group of people consent to the procedures in the proposed sudy, it is presumed that the real participants would agree as well.

Problems … In a sense Milgram (1963) sought presumptive consent when he surveyed 14 Yale Psychology students before his study took place. The fact they estimated that almost no one would go beyond 450 volts suggested that there was no potential for psychological harm and therefore participants would be 'happy' to take part.

3. Ethical committee

Every institution where research takes place has an ethical committee and the committee must approve any study before it begins. It looks at all possible ethical issues raised in any research proposal and at how the researcher suggests that the issues will be dealt with, weighing up the *benefits* of the research against the possible *costs* to the participants.

Problems … Cost–benefit decisions are flawed because they involve subjective judgements, and the costs are not always apparent until after the study. The cost–benefit approach may actually raise more problems than it solves.

4. Ethical guidelines

Professional bodies, such as the BPS (*British Psychological Society*) and APA (*American Psychological Association*), produce **ethical guidelines** and codes of conduct (see right). The intention of such guidelines is to tell psychologists what behaviours are not acceptable and tell them how to deal with ethical dilemmas.

Problems … This 'rules and sanctions' approach is inevitably rather general because of the virtual impossibility of covering every conceivable situation that a researcher may encounter. The CPA (*Canadian Psychological Association*) takes a slightly different approach – it presents a series of hypothetical dilemmas and invites psychologists to discuss these. The strength of this approach is that it encourages discussion whereas the BPS and APA approach tends to close off discussions about what is right and wrong because the answers are provided. Guidelines also absolve the individual researcher of any responsibility because the researcher can simply say 'I followed the guidelines so my research is acceptable'.

5. Punishment

If a psychologist does behave in an unethical manner, such as conducting unacceptable research, then the BPS reviews the research and may decide to bar the person from practising as a psychologist. It is not a legal matter (the researcher won't be sent to prison) but it could affect the researcher's livelihood.

BPS *Code of ethics and conduct*

The *British Psychological Society* (BPS) produces ethical guidance for research psychologists as well as practising psychologists (for example those who treat mental patients). There are a variety of documents that deal with specific issues faced, for example, when treating mental patients or conducting research with animals. However, one document applies to all psychologists – the *Code of Ethics and Conduct*. The code is based on four ethical principles:

1. Respect Psychologists must value the dignity and worth of all persons, with sensitivity to the dynamics of perceived authority or influence over clients, and with particular regard to people's rights including those of privacy and self-determination.

2. Competence Psychologists must value continuing development and maintenance of high standards of competence in their professional work. They should also recognise the limits of their knowledge, skill, training, education and experience.

3. Responsibility Psychologists must value their responsibilities to clients, to the general public, and to the profession and science of Psychology, including the avoidance of harm and the prevention of misuse or abuse of their contributions to society.

4. Integrity Psychologists must value honesty, accuracy, clarity and fairness in their interactions with all people, and seek to promote integrity in all facets of their scientific and professional endeavours (BPS, 2009, page 21).

CAN YOU...? No. 1B.2

1... For each of the **five** ethical issues and **five** ways of dealing with ethical issues select **two** key phrases or concepts.

2... For each key phrase/concept write **four or five** sentences explaining the phrase.

3... For each of the **five** issues and **five** ways of dealing with issues try to think of your own examples.

4... Use all of this material to write an answer to the following exam questions: (a) *Assess ethical issues in the use of human participants in research in psychology*. (b) *Assess ways of dealing with ethical issues when using human participants in research in psychology*. Your answers should be about 500 words.

Don't forget to read the essay-writing guidance on pages 8 and 9, as well as the notes for Section C of PY3 on page 52.

ETHICAL ISSUES AND NON-HUMAN ANIMALS

It is important to remember that an **ethical issue** is a *conflict*. When considering psychological research with non-human animals we are weighing up the conflict between the wider benefits for society and the potential harm to animals that are used.

There are two important points to bear in mind: (1) your focus must be on psychological research, rather than, for example, the use of animals for cosmetic testing, and (2) your focus must be on objective, evidence-based arguments rather than emotionally fuelled diatribes.

▶ *Photographs like the one on the right are frequently used to support arguments against the use of non-human animals in research. Not all psychological research with animals involves such physical interventions – although psychological treatments may be as damaging as physical ones. And, in fact, research rarely involves higher mammals.*

Examples of research with non-human animals

This is a short introduction to some examples of non-human animal research. You might investigate these examples in greater depth in order to be able to use them in your essays, and also find some others of your own.

The origins of love Harry Harlow (1959) placed infant rhesus monkeys in a cage with two wire mothers (see left) – one with a feeding bottle and one wrapped in soft cloth. The monkeys spent most time with the cloth-covered mother demonstrating the importance of contact comfort.

So where's the harm? The monkeys developed into emotionally maladjusted adults despite their contact comfort – they couldn't socialise with other monkeys and rejected their own infants. However, the research had an important influence on understanding of infant emotional development.

Sensory deprivation Our understanding of perceptual development has relied on studies where young animals were deprived of their sight. This research is described on page 70.

Naturalistic observations Ethologists seek to study animals in a way that does not affect their behaviour: for example, Dian Fossey's (1983) work observing gorillas in the natural habitat to reach a greater understanding of their social relationships, made famous through the film *Gorillas in the Mist*.

Drug and addiction research Psychologists and psychiatrists have a great interest in the safety of medication for mental disorders and, as such, the research testing of these drugs constitutes psychological research. Animals are also used in research on addiction. Both kinds of research inevitably result in some degree of pain and suffering for the animals involved. However, psychoactive drugs allow people with mental illnesses to lead relatively 'normal' lives (protecting them and protecting society), and **addiction** research offers important insights into the damaging process of addiction.

ETHICAL ISSUES WITH NON-HUMAN ANIMALS

Value of non-human animals

Although the vast majority of investigations in psychology involve the study of *humans*, there are several reasons why psychologists may choose to carry out research using non-human animals.

● Non-human animals may be studied simply because they are fascinating to study in their own right and such research may ultimately benefit non-human animals.
● Animals offer the opportunity for greater control and objectivity in research procedures.
● Human beings and non-human animals have sufficient of their physiology and evolutionary past in common to justify conclusions drawn from the one being applied to the other. Although it can be argued that animals tested under stressful conditions may provide very little useful information.

Wider benefits to society The bottom line is that we use animals when research procedures would not be possible with human beings, see for example the research described on the left. Animals are used because they 'cost' less and the benefits of such research outweigh the costs to the animals.

Moral justification

The question remains as to whether 'science at any cost' is justifiable.

Sentient beings Do animals experience pain and emotions, i.e. are they sentient? There is evidence that they respond to pain but this may not be the same as conscious awareness. There is evidence that animals other than primates have **self-awareness** (see page 149) and are therefore **sentient**. In fact, in December 2009 the Treaty of Lisbon, which governs the European Union, declared that 'all animals are sentient' so it appears that the argument is resolved.

A different line of argument, in relation to sentience, is that some humans lack sentience, such as brain-damaged individuals or infants, but we wouldn't use them in research without consent. The conclusion must be that lack of sentience does not provide moral justification for the use of animals.

Speciesism Peter Singer (1975) argued that discrimination on the basis of membership of a species is no different from racial or gender discrimination and thus suggested that the use of animals is an example of 'speciesism', similar to racism or sexism. However, Jeffrey Gray (1991) argues that we have a special duty of care to humans, and therefore speciesism is not equivalent to, for example, racism.

Animal rights Singer's view is a **utilitarian** one, i.e. whatever produces the greater good for the greater number of individuals is ethically acceptable. This means that, if animal research can alleviate pain and suffering for a large number of people, it is justifiable. Tom Regan (1984), however, argued that there are no circumstances under which animal research is acceptable (an **absolutist** position). Regan claimed that animals have a right to be treated with respect and should never be used in research.

The 'animal rights' argument can be challenged by examining the concept of rights – having rights is dependent on having responsibilities in society, i.e. as citizens. It can therefore be said that as animals do not have any responsibilities, they do not have any rights.

Empty Cages

Empty Cages is the title of Tom Regan's book, arguing his absolutist position – in contrast with Peter Singer's relativist utilitarian view. However, even Regan agrees that *some* animals could be used. Central to Regan's philosophy is the concept 'subject of a life'. He claims that any individual who is the 'subject of a life' has inherent value to that individual which is independent of any usefulness to others. Any individual (human or animal) who has inherent value has a right to be treated with respect and a right not to be used. It should be noted that Regan believes that all mature mammals are 'subject of a life' but it is not clear to what extent this applies to other animals. This means that all mature mammals should be treated the same as humans. In a sense, Regan's approach has been supported by legislation which bans the use of primates (chimpanzees, gorilla and orang-utans) in research.

Existing constraints

Legislation The UK *Animals (Scientific Procedures) Act* (1986) requires that animal research only takes place at licensed laboratories with licensed researchers on licensed projects. Thus, there are three 'levels' of regulation, all of which require a separate licence, which are only granted if:

- Potential results are important enough to justify the use of animals. When considering costs versus benefits, investigators must consider whether the knowledge to be gained from any investigation justifies harm or distress to animal participants.
- The research cannot be done using non-animal methods.
- The minimum number of animals will be used.
- Any discomfort or suffering is kept to a minimum by appropriate use of anaesthetics or painkillers.

The Act relates only to vertebrate animals and to those more than halfway through their gestation period. One invertebrate species (the octopus) was added in 1993. Primates, cats, dogs and horses have additional protection.

The principle of the 3Rs – Replace, Reduce, Refine In 2000, the Home Office issued further guidance on the operation of the 1986 Act. This introduced the guiding principle of the **3Rs**, first proposed by Russell and Birch in 1959. Researchers should seek, wherever possible, to *replace* animals with suitable alternatives (e.g. brain scanning), to *reduce* the number of animals used, and *refine* procedures so that they cause less suffering. A national group, *The National Centre for the Replacement, Refinement and Reduction of Animals* (NC3Rs), has been set up to encourage, research and support the use of the 3Rs.

BPS guidelines are published for research with animals. Psychologists are advised, for example, to conform to current legislation, heed the 3Rs, choose species that are suited to the research purpose, be aware of an animal's previous experience and remember that their responsibilities extend to the care of animals when not being studied, including the provision of companions (for social animals). In particular, any procedure that may cause pain should be carefully evaluated and alternatives considered. Regulation of food intake (e.g. for conditioning experiments) may be considered harmful and researchers should consider an animal's normal food intake and metabolic requirements.

Do these constraints work? Dunayer (2002) argues that animal legislation simply sets standards for the imprisonment, enslavement, hurting and killing of animals. Such laws are similar to the laws that codified norms of black enslavement in America. Dunayer argues that making it legal doesn't make it right.

The NC3Rs recently sponsored an analysis of 271 studies in the US and the UK that had used non-human animals (note that these are not all psychological studies). Only 59% of these studies mentioned the number of animals that were used, many of them reported different numbers of animals in the methods section and results sections of the report, and many studies were poorly designed. The NC3Rs analysis concluded that there are a number of issues that need to be addressed in non-human animal research, including using more careful design as required by the 3Rs and providing more accurate scientific reporting (Kilkenny *et al.*, 2009).

The facts

The data below are taken from the 'Understanding Animal Research' website, sponsored by a group that supports the importance of animal research for scientific understanding and medical progress. It isn't as simple as saying that all research should be stopped, for example British law requires that any new drug (such as antidepressants, for example) must be tested on at least two different species of live mammal.

The graph below shows a general reduction in animal experiments since 1975. Recent rises are due to the use of genetically altered animals (mostly mice and fish), now half of all animals used.

It is noteworthy that UK bioscience and medical research funding more than doubled in real terms between 1998 and 2008, but animal procedures rose by just one-third, which suggests that the principle of the 3Rs is having an effect.

But remember – most of this research is not psychological. Data about psychological research are not kept separately.

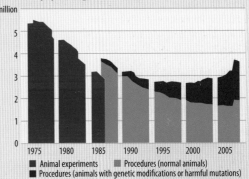

▲ *Animal experiments in the UK, 1975–2008*

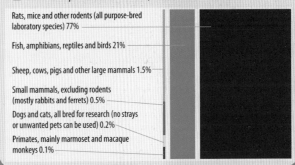

Rats, mice and other rodents (all purpose-bred laboratory species) 77%

Fish, amphibians, reptiles and birds 21%

Sheep, cows, pigs and other large mammals 1.5%

Small mammals, excluding rodents (mostly rabbits and ferrets) 0.5%

Dogs and cats, all bred for research (no strays or unwanted pets can be used) 0.2%

Primates, mainly marmoset and macaque monkeys 0.1%

CAN YOU...?　No. 1B.3

1... Identify at least **five** key arguments either for or against the use of non-human animals in psychological research.

2... For each argument write **four or five** sentences explaining the argument.

3... For each argument describe at least **one** example from psychological research.

4... Use all of this material to write an answer to the following exam question: *Discuss ethical issues in the use of non-human animals in research in psychology.* You might also compose some 'building block' essays: (a) *Discuss arguments for the use of non-human animals in research in psychology.* (b) *Discuss arguments against the use of non-human animals in research in psychology.* Your answers should be about 500 words.

Don't forget to read the essay-writing guidance on pages 8 and 9, as well as the notes for Section C of PY3 on page 52.

ETHICAL ISSUES IN APPLICATIONS OF PSYCHOLOGY

The *Code of Conduct* published by the *British Psychological Society* (BPS, 2009) is not just relevant to research psychology but also to practising psychologists. Many psychologists work in psychiatric hospitals, education systems, the military and other organisations. On this spread we consider some of the **ethical issues** that should concern psychologists in practice.

◀ *In 2003 Channel 4 broadcast a programme called* Inside the Mind of Paul Gascoigne. *Professor Kevin Gournay, a psychiatric nurse, offered a diagnosis of his mental condition without actually having met Gascoigne, concluding that he was suffering from attention deficit disorder, obsessive–compulsive disorder and Tourette's syndrome. Such labels are damaging because they alter the public perception of the person and are hard to shake off. If the diagnosis was based on real fact we still might object, but it is even worse that it was based on hearsay.*

▼ *The BBC series* A Child of our Time *is a 20-year project following the lives of 25 babies born in 2000. The aim of the series is to investigate systematically the effects of genes and environment on the development of these individuals. This includes conducting regular experiments to test their behaviour and abilities. Clearly, these children did not have the opportunity to provide their informed consent at the beginning, or even during, the study.*

PSYCHOLOGISTS AND THE MEDIA

There are many media examples where psychologists are in demand: newspaper advice columns, magazine self-improvement articles, psychology books, radio phone-in shows, talk-show appearances, experts on the TV news and consultants for films and television shows (Bouhoutsos *et al.*, 1986). People are interested in understanding the behaviour of other people and psychologists are the 'experts'.

The role of the BPS

The BPS recognises this demand for psychologists by the media and provides a free contact service, putting journalists in touch with over 1000 media-friendly psychologists. The BPS also recognises that talking to the media raises a number of ethical considerations, especially the increasing use of psychologists on TV (e.g. being a 'talking head' in a documentary or selecting participants for a reality TV programme). For that reason the BPS has produced a document *Ethical Implications for Psychologists Working on TV: A Guide for Production Companies* (BPS, 2010). The points below are drawn from this guide.

Informed consent

Psychologists should ensure that any TV programme participants are fully aware that they are losing the right to **privacy** and control over what may be used, especially as the behaviour they produce may later lead to embarrassment. This is particularly important when children are involved because they may be too young or not fully understand the situation they are being placed in.

For example… Participants of the BBC programme *Castaway 2000* were fully informed of the implications of taking part by the show's psychologist Dr Cynthia McVey. It subsequently became apparent that despite this, the participants didn't really understand the later repercussions, such as newspaper articles criticising their personal characters (BPS, 2010).

Manipulation

One of the major issues, especially for reality TV, is the extent to which participants' behaviour is manipulated. The BPS guide reminds psychologists that it is their duty to protect participants from any physical or mental harm that might be greater than that experienced in their normal lives. Psychologists also should not lie to participants or withhold information if the psychologist believes that participants are typically likely to object or show unease once debriefed.

For example… Professor David Wilson was employed by the reality TV programme *Big Brother* as the resident psychologist. He resigned when he realised that the programme makers wanted him to create psychological situations that would increase tension in the house and cause distress (Wilson, 2005).

Other issues

Duty of care The BPS guide reminds psychologists that their role, as professionals, is to ensure that all TV participants are treated with 'the highest standards of consideration and respect'.

Confidentiality Psychologists should ensure that confidential discussions can take place between psychologists and TV show participants, which will not be filmed.

Follow-up involvement It is not appropriate for psychologists to become intimately involved with TV participants and then withdraw as soon as the show ends. TV companies should therefore ensure continued involvement, even if this only involves reassurance.

Professional boundaries Psychologists should not offer advice on matters that are outside their area of expertise.

The reputation of psychology The general code of conduct published by the BPS states that 'In all their work psychologists shall conduct themselves in a manner that does not bring into disrepute the discipline and the profession of psychology'.

PSYCHOLOGISTS AND THE MILITARY

If you accept the need for an army then it makes sense to use all the resources at your disposal, including psychologists. The involvement of psychology with the military (sometimes referred to as 'PsyOps', which stands for psychological operations) raises a number of ethical issues.

Improving interrogation techniques

A key task for the military is eliciting information from the enemy. The development of effective interview techniques has drawn on various areas of psychological research.

For example ... Hebb *et al.* (1952) conducted a series of mind control experiments, sponsored by the American Central Intelligence Agency (CIA) (McCoy, 2007). In one study on **sensory deprivation** (SD) volunteer students were kept in physical and social isolation, wearing translucent goggles and long cuffs to restrict sensory experience. Within days many started to experience extreme visual and auditory hallucinations and after a while were unable to distinguish waking from sleeping. More important, from the sponsor's point of view, the volunteers were found to be much more susceptible to any type of propaganda while in SD.

Training animals for warfare

Animals have been trained (using **conditioning** techniques) to become agents of human warfare. Most recently sea lions have been trained to attach something like a handcuff to enemy divers (*Daily Mail*, 2009).

For example ... During World War II the **behaviourist** B.F. Skinner masterminded 'Project Pigeon' where pigeons were trained to accurately pilot a missile to seek out ships. They were able to distinguish different types of ships so that they would avoid Allied ships and dive onto enemy ones. In the end, the American military decided against using the pigeons.

Psychologists' stance on torture

The growing use of psychological techniques to enhance distress in places such as Guantánamo Bay, Abu Ghraib and Afghanistan has led to pressure on organisations such as the APA and BPS to make their position on torture clear (Patel, 2007). At the time of writing the BPS has not issued any explicit statements. Patel suggests that such a statement might include reference to obligations under international law, the health impact and ineffectiveness of torture as a method of interrogation, and clear mechanisms to support those who may face problems as a result of ethical compliance or wishing to report breaches by others.

Propaganda

Psychologists are employed to develop propaganda campaigns, i.e. media presentations of information that are designed to influence the attitude of a community toward some cause or position. Propaganda often presents facts selectively and is a form of political warfare.

For example ... During the Vietnam War in the 1960s American psychologists collected social information about the Vietnamese so they could work out how to influence them most effectively. One instance was related to the grieving practices of the Vietnamese, where people remember their dead relatives on anniversaries of their death, as well as 49 and 100 days after their relatives died. The Americans dropped propaganda leaflets on these dates after big battles in areas where people would have been likely to have lost relatives. The aim was to increase the misery of those days and further undermine the morale of the Vietnamese.

Positive influences

Psychologists can also have a positive influence, such as helping members of the military to cope with traumatic stress and injury. The concept of **post-traumatic stress disorder** has its origins in World War I 'battle fatigue'. Another positive approach is to prepare personnel for possible capture.

Peace and conflict studies draw on psychological theory and research, as well as other disciplines such as sociology and politics. Magazines such as the *Journal of Peace Research*, and organisations such as the *Peace Research Foundation* seek to encourage and disseminate research on promoting peace.

For example ... a classic study by Sherif *et al.* (1961) demonstrated how conflict resolution can be resolved by getting opposing sides to work together on a task involving superordinate goals, such as repairing a failed water supply that was used by both groups.

Real-world application

The APA has a military division, and the BPS is currently considering a proposal for one in the UK. The APA *Society for Military Psychology* encourages research and the application of psychological research to military problems. During World War II, half the pages of the *Psychological Bulletin* were devoted to topics of military psychology, and from 1943 to 1945 one in every four psychologists in the country was engaged in military psychology (Driskell and Olmstead, 1989).

The APA military division website (www.apadivision19.org) provides a small sample of the types of contributions that can be made by military psychologists: (a) working in mental health or family counselling clinics to improve the lives of service personnel and their families, (b) performing research to select recruits into the service and assign them to one of many possible jobs, and (c) analyses of humanitarian and peacekeeping missions to determine procedures that could save military and civilian lives.

CAN YOU...?   No. 1B.4

1... **Two** applications of research are covered on this spread. For each application, identify at least **five** key topics.

2... For each topic write **four or five** sentences explaining the topic.

3... For each topic describe at least **one** example from psychological research. (In some cases you will need to develop your own examples.)

4... Use all of this material to write an answer to the following exam question: *Discuss ethical issues arising from two applications of psychology in the real world.* You might also compose some 'building block' essays: (a) *Discuss ethical issues arising from the application of psychology to the media.* (b) *Discuss ethical issues arising from the application of psychology to the military.* Your answers should be about 500 words.

Don't forget to read the essay-writing guidance on pages 8–9, as well as the notes for Section C of PY3 on page 52.

ADVANTAGES OF THE USE OF THE SCIENTIFIC METHOD IN PSYCHOLOGY

1. The scientific method is empirical
- Empirical data comes from direct observation or experiment (rather than reasoned argument or beliefs).
- This provides evidence for the truth of a theory or the benefits of a treatment (e.g. whether a drug reduces anxiety).

2. The scientific method is objective
- Empirical data is objective (is not affected by the expectations of the researcher). For example, the strict criteria used by Gardner and Gardner to judge whether Washoe had learned new words.

3. The scientific method is falsifiable
- We cannot prove a hypothesis correct but the scientific method allows a hypothesis to be tested by falsification, i.e. by rejecting a null hypothesis.
- For example, Freud's theory of psychoanalysis is untestable because it is unfalsifiable, e.g. the idea 'all men have repressed homosexual tendencies' cannot be disproved – a man who seemed to contradict the view might just have very deeply repressed homosexual tendencies.

4. The scientific method is controlled
- In a lab experiment an independent variable is manipulated and the effect on a dependent variable observed. Possible extraneous variables are controlled (easiest in a lab) so causal relationships can be found.
- For example, in an experiment we can be sure that the drug, rather any other variable, reduced anxiety.
- Lab experiments are not the only research method used in the scientific method.

5. The scientific method permits replication
- Standardised procedures allow for replication and repeating a study helps to demonstrate validity.
- For example, Milgram's study has been replicated.

DISADVANTAGES OF THE USE OF THE SCIENTIFIC METHOD IN PSYCHOLOGY

1. The scientific method may lack internal validity
- Investigator effects and demand characteristics threaten internal validity.
- For example, a questionnaire with leading questions would lack validity.
- Investigator effects also occur in the 'hard' sciences, e.g. the uncertainty principle.

2. The scientific method may lack external validity
- If experimental findings don't match real-life observations they do not generalise beyond the setting in which they were conducted.
- For example, Milgram's findings about proximity did not explain obedience in the Nazi death camps.

3. The scientific method can be reductionist
- Operationalising variables is reductionist as we oversimplify behaviours.
- For example, Laing suggested we should consider each case of schizophrenia individually (idiographic approach) rather than describing them as in purely physical–chemical terms.

4. The scientific method tends to ignore individual differences
- Science is nomothetic, looking for similarities and making generalisations.

5. The scientific method raises ethical issues
- Good scientific research has ethical costs, e.g. psychological harm. A balance between scientific benefits and ethical costs is desirable but may ignore individual rights.

ETHICAL ISSUES AND HUMAN PARTICIPANTS

1. Informed consent
- Participants should be told about all aspects of the research before agreeing to take part (informed consent). This is an issue because the information may compromise the study but if there is a potential for harm participants should have the opportunity to decline to participate.
- For example, in Milgram's study.

2. Deception
- Honesty is important especially as without it participants cannot give informed consent.
- For example, Rosenhan deceived hospital staff so they may not trust patients afterwards.

3. Right to withdraw
- Without a right to withdraw participants may be exposed to unnecessary harm, especially if they didn't give informed consent. Right to withdraw may be difficult if participants offered incentives, e.g. course credits.

4. Confidentiality
- Confidentiality depends on the protection of personal information, although this may be an unobtainable ideal.
- For example, if the participant in a case study is so unusual they can be recognised from the data.

5. Privacy
- If privacy is invaded (e.g. we are watched when we wouldn't expect to be), confidentiality should be protected but what counts as 'private' may be hard to establish.
- For example, observing a shoplifter in a public place would be an invasion of privacy.

Socially sensitive research
- Socially sensitive research has potential negative implications for the participants or the people it applies to, e.g. drug addicts or homosexuals.
- Evidence on inter-racial differences in IQ may be flawed but is used to support discriminatory social policies.
- An issue arises when weighing the potential damage of such research against the potential loss if it is not conducted.

DEALING WITH ETHICAL ISSUES WITH HUMAN PARTICIPANTS

Ethical issues are often dealt with in the same way, e.g. lack of informed consent is dealt with by seeking informed consent and the issue of confidentiality is dealt with by protecting confidentiality.

1. Debriefing
- Straight after a study participants should be told the real aims, be able to discuss concerns and be allowed to withdraw their data – but this may not solve embarrassment or low self-esteem.

2. Presumptive consent
- A similar group of people to the prospective participants are asked whether they would agree to take part; if they would, this is presumptive consent.
- For example, Milgram would have presumed there was no potential for psychological harm as 14 students estimated that almost no one would go beyond 450 volts, therefore no psychological harm was expected.

3. Ethical committee
- Each institution's ethical committee considers the issues in proposed research, weighing the benefits of the research against possible costs to the participants.
- However, cost–benefit decisions are subjective and costs may not appear until it is too late.

4. Problems with ethical guidelines
- The BPS and APA guidelines offer a 'rules and sanctions' approach, but these may be too general and absolve a researcher of responsibility if they have 'followed the guidelines'.
- The Canadian Psychological Association presents hypothetical dilemmas for discussion instead. This is better as it encourages discussion about what is right and wrong.

5. Punishment
- The BPS reviews research it considers may be unethical and can stop psychologists from practising, although breaking the guidelines is not illegal.

BPS *Code of ethics and Conduct*
- The BPS *Code of Ethics and Conduct* provides ethical guidance for research and practising psychologists.
- The four ethical principles are: respect (valuing people's dignity and rights), competence (developing and maintaining professional standards and working within the limits of their ability), responsibility (to clients, the public and psychology), integrity (valuing honesty and accuracy).

ETHICAL ISSUES AND NON-HUMAN ANIMALS
NON-HUMAN ANIMALS

Examples of research with non-human animals

- Harlow studied infant monkeys with surrogate mothers. The monkeys became emotionally maladjusted adults but the research helped us to understand emotional development in human infants.
- Blakemore and Cooper raised kittens in an environment with vertical lines, which damaged their brain development but was useful as we know to treat children's visual defects early.
- Ethologists such as Fossey (with gorillas) use naturalistic observations to study animals in the natural habitat without affecting their behaviour.
- Psychological research investigates addiction and tests of drugs for mental disorders (but not other uses), which can cause pain and suffering to animals but potentially helps people with addiction and mental illnesses.

Value of non-human animals

- Most psychological research uses human participants but non-human animals may be used: as they are interesting in themselves, offer greater control and objectivity in research procedures and because we share physiology and evolutionary past justifying generalisation from animal research to humans.
- Mainly we use animals when research procedures would not be possible with human beings, because the benefits of such research outweigh the costs to the animals.

Moral justification

- If animals experience pain and emotions they are sentient so should not be subjected to pain (but just reacting to pain may not be the same). Some animals are self-aware so are sentient.
- Conversely, some humans (e.g. brain-damaged people and infants) are not sentient but wouldn't be used in research without consent, so a lack of sentience is not a moral justification for using animals.
- Singer argued that discrimination based on species (speciesism) is no different from racism or sexism but Gray argues that our responsibility for humans means that racism/sexism and speciesism are not equivalent.
- Singer's view is based on 'the greater good' (utilitarianism) so if animal research can alleviate suffering, it is justifiable. Regan argues that animal research is never acceptable (absolutism). He says that any individual who is the 'subject of a life' (mature mammals) has inherent value so should treated with respect and has a right not to be used.
- The 'animal rights' argument is challenged by the concept that having rights is dependent on having responsibilities. As animals have no responsibilities in society, they have no rights.

Existing constraints

- The UK *Animals (Scientific Procedures) Act* requires licensed laboratories, researchers and projects for research. It protects only vertebrates (when more than half way through their gestation) and the octopus.
- Licenses are granted if: potential benefits exceed costs (to animals), if research cannot be done using non-animal methods, minimum numbers are used and suffering is minimised (e.g. using anaesthetics).
- The Home Office recommends 'the 3Rs': replace animals with alternatives, reduce the number of animals used and refine procedures to alleviate suffering.
- The BPS guidelines suggest researchers: choose suitable species, consider the animal's previous experience, ensure good care of animals when not being studied and limit the potential harm of controlling food intake.
- Dunayer argues that animal legislation doesn't protect but instead sets standards for harm (like laws relating to slavery).
- Kilkenny *et al.* analysed studies using non-human animals (for psychological and other purposes) and found poor design and reporting, therefore standards should be improved.
- British law requires that any new drug (including antidepressants) must be tested on at least two different species of live mammal.

ETHICAL ISSUES IN APPLICATIONS OF PSYCHOLOGY

PSYCHOLOGISTS AND THE MEDIA

Psychologists appear as experts in the media, such as magazines, radio and TV, to help others to understand people's behaviour.

The role of the BPS
- The BPS provides a contact service for the media and recognises that media involvement raises ethical considerations (e.g. in reality TV programmes) so has produced *Ethical Implications for Psychologists Working on TV: A Guide for Production Companies*.

Informed consent
- Psychologists should ensure that TV programme participants know they are losing the right to privacy and control over what may be used (e.g. over embarrassing segments), especially children who may not fully understand the situation.

Manipulation
- When behaviour is manipulated, e.g. in reality TV, participants should be protected from physical or mental harm beyond any normal risk. Psychologists should not lie or withhold information if participants may object when debriefed.

Other issues
- Psychologists have a duty of care to ensure that TV participants are treated with consideration and respect.
- They should ensure that confidential (non-filmed) discussions can take place between psychologists and participants. TV companies should ensure the psychologist supports participants after the show. Psychologists should not offer advice outside their area of expertise.
- Psychologists should maintain the good reputation of psychology.

PSYCHOLOGISTS AND THE MILITARY

PsyOps apply psychological insights to military concerns.

Improving interrogation techniques
- One military task is to obtain information from the enemy. Psychological operations (PsyOps) help to develop effective interview techniques.
- For example, Hebb *et al.* conducted mind control experiments using sensory deprivation (e.g. physical and social isolation, wearing translucent goggles). Volunteers had hallucinations and didn't know if they were awake or asleep, and were more susceptible to propaganda.
- Although the APA and BPS have no specific statements about torture, Patel suggests they should make such statements and they might refer to obligations under international law, the health impact and ineffectiveness of torture for interrogation.

Training animals for warfare
- Animals can be conditioned for use in human warfare, e.g. sea lions being used to put handcuffs on enemy divers during the Iraq War.
- For example, Skinner's 'Project Pigeon' trained the birds to distinguish Allied and enemy ships for piloting missiles (although they were never used).

Propaganda
- Propaganda uses the media to influence attitudes but in political warfare facts are selectively presented.
- For example, in the Vietnam War psychologists found out about Vietnamese grieving practices so leaflets were dropped on particular dates following battles to increase misery and undermine morale in the Vietnamese people.

Positive influences
- Psychologists have positive influences, e.g. to cope with post-traumatic stress disorder and to prepare personnel for possible capture.
- Some magazines (e.g. the *Journal of Peace Research*) and organisations (e.g. *Peace Research Foundation*) focus on research promoting peace.
- For example, research by Sherif *et al.* explored conflict resolution through working on superordinate goals.

Question **Discuss ethical issues arising from *two* applications of psychology in the real world.** [15]

Student answer

Paragraph 1 Ethical issues can arise from the direct application of results to some real-world activity (e.g. in therapy or education) or from the use that research has been put to by others (e.g. for military or for political purposes). An example would be the use of operant conditioning in behaviour therapy and intended warfare (Skinner's rocket-guiding pigeons).

Paragraph 2 The most famous example is the intelligence test (IQ test). The original test was devised by Galton in the nineteenth century, and was general knowledge based. Galton intended to show the genetic superiority of white middle-class males, which is racist, class biased and sexist.

Paragraph 3 The modern test started with Binet at the beginning of the twentieth century, and was simply a way of identifying under-performing schoolchildren in order to give them extra tuition. Yerkes devised tests which were used on 1.7 million soldiers in the US Army in World War I. These were biased for the white population and discriminated against immigrants and the native black population, most of them being illiterate. Yerkes and others used the results to argue that Afro-Americans and immigrants were genetically inferior, and didn't need the education that white people got. Also the US government banned some groups from entering the US, and this even resulted in European Jews being returned to Germany to die in the death camps. Yerkes and many psychologists at the time believed that discrimination in favour of white males was a good thing, as breeding with others would 'weaken' the gene pool. IQ testing is still used in the UK in education and in business.

Paragraph 4 My second example is the media. Psychologists do lots of work in the media, e.g. *Big Brother*, *Castaway* and *Most Haunted*. Often they give opinions on public behaviour, especially if some celebrity has done something stupid or there is a mass killing like the recent one in Whitehaven. The BPS has provided guidelines for this which cover consent, manipulation, care and confidentiality.

Paragraph 5 Psychologists have to behave ethically, so the one on *Big Brother* resigned in 2005 when he was supposed to cause tension and distress. However it can't always be predicted. The people on *Castaway* were fully briefed by a psychologist but later they were caused distress by media stories about their private lives.

Paragraph 6 The worst examples are when psychologists give opinions outside their area of expertise. A professor gave an opinion on Paul Gascoigne in a programme, suggesting he had various mental problems including OCD, but he hadn't met Gascoigne and he wasn't even a psychiatrist. Some psychologists are always called upon by the media, e.g. if a celebrity has a gambling problem the media always get Professor Mark Griffiths on the TV. This can damage the reputation of psychology in the public's eyes.

Paragraph 7 My last example is from the military. Lots of work was carried out on sensory deprivation especially in the 1960s because people thought it would alter conscious states. Because it had lots of negative effects on people it became useful in interrogating prisoners and is used by the Americans in Guantanamo and other bases.

[512 words]

Examiner comments

Oh dear, the classic error! The question asks for two applications, and the candidate has given three. The examiner can either cross out the last one or, as WJEC advises examiners, give credit for the best two. In either case, the military example is the one to go. So the essay loses Paragraph 7.

The essay has a good opening which is creditworthy as 'scene setting'. It is clear that the example is just an example and not one of the applications (otherwise this might have counted as a fourth application!).

Paragraphs 2 and 3 concern intelligence testing which is not covered in this chapter but you can read about it on pages 122–123. The information in these paragraphs demonstrates a good understanding of intelligence testing but the candidate doesn't fully draw out the ethical issues. Protection from harm is implicit in the discussion but the candidate might have considered other ethical issues, for example whether it is appropriate to use such tests with other cultural groups, with the result that such groups may appear inferior. Or might have considered whether it is OK for psychologists to stand by and say nothing, or do psychologists have a responsibility about the uses of their work?

Paragraphs 4 to 6 present an informed commentary about psychology and the media; the information is reasonably accurate and shows awareness of the issues. However, these paragraphs could be considerably improved by putting the BPS information first and then showing how each part applies in the real world, using the examples provided already. This would show a better structure to the essay.

Paragraph 7 has been ignored because it is the third example, which was not required.

This essay has some identifiable relevant information but is not thorough or clear – a requirement of the top band. Therefore it is placed in the second band (8–11) and is awarded marks towards the top end of this band since the descriptors are met (see mark scheme on page 42).

10/15 places the essay as a clear grade C.

Improvement?

The writer has a lot of good information but hasn't really structured it well. Ethical issues are the basis of the question and should be clearly identified and then logically illustrated – too often here the examiner/reader has to mentally organise the material. Paragraph 3 is a good example where there is slightly jumbled material needing to be more clearly set out. The structure of the answer could also be improved. For example, in paragraph 4 it would be better to put the BPS Guidelines first and then to use these Guidelines to organise the following material.

Chapter 2
Controversies

Chapter contents

66   Introduction to the study of controversies
68   Psychology as a science
70   Science versus ethics
72   Genetic and environmental influences
74   Cultural bias in psychology
76   Gender bias in psychology
78   Free will and determinism

End-of-chapter review

80   Chapter summary
82   Exam question with student answer

Specification breakdown	
The status of psychology as a science	Science is the umbrella term for an agreed set of activities for investigating the physical world. This has been a successful method in the physical sciences, but psychology seems to have one foot in and one foot out! The question is whether psychology is a science, partly a science, or a set of activities, some of them being science.
The balance of scientific benefits measured against ethical costs in psychology	This topic is an extension of the material in the Chapter 1B, looking at the knowledge and benefits psychology has brought to humans and balancing these ethical costs, using examples from across the whole range of psychological activity.
The balance of genetic and environmental influences on human behaviour	Evolution represents the eternal dance between the partners 'gene' and 'environment'. Our biggest genetic influence is of course being a human, but what of the interplay between inheritance and environment from the moment of conception onwards? Using examples from across the range of psychology, this area discusses the gene–environment balancing act.
Issues of cultural bias in psychology	The 'environment' includes the social environment of people, which differs widely from place to place and time to time. Culture constrains the way we see, feel and think – yet psychological research is so often presented as representative of humans in general. There are many examples from psychology, textbooks, theories and practices that show how considerable this bias can be.
Issues of gender bias in psychology	In the 1980s the *American Psychological Association* declared women to be invisible in psychology! We are often unaware that the author of a research study is a woman, and psychological research regularly uses male participants and assumes females would think and behave the same.
The question of free will and determinism in respect of human behaviour	Can we decide, completely without influence, to do something? Are all our behaviours determined somehow? So much of our socialisation influences our mental life and our decisions, yet is there a possibility we can act independently in some way? In some respects it is like asking what it is to be a human.

WHAT IS A CONTROVERSY?

The Oxford Concise Dictionary (1996) defines a controversy as 'a disagreement on a matter of opinion'. Controversies come in all shapes and sizes and, if on television, are also frequently accompanied by some pretty heated arguments and a fair amount of mud-slinging. Academic debates involve a discussion of some topic, usually presenting both sides of the argument. Many of these are actually phrased as if there was a contest (e.g. nature *versus* nurture), although invariably (rather like the debates we witness on television) the truth lies somewhere in between. It is important to understand there is no clear answer to a controversy – that is why they remain controversies. Conclusions can be drawn but there will be no final resolution.

So, this section of the specification allows you to consider some of the disputed topics in psychology, such as science versus ethics, free will versus determinism and so on. The topics have been specifically chosen to provide an opportunity for synopsis – to draw on the knowledge you have gained throughout your psychology course. They also allow you to show knowledge about psychology's relationship with the real world.

In Chapters 3–12 you will find signposts (such as the one above) on each spread. We have included these to remind you that you can make reference to controversies as the AO2 element of your essay. For example, you might discuss the effect of cultural bias on the study of a particular topic area and the problems this has created.

The exam

Possible questions

The PY4 exam is divided into **three** sections. Sections B and C contain questions covered in Chapters 3–12. Section A relates to the contents of this chapter. You must answer **three** questions across Sections B and C, and one from Section A. Altogether you have 2½ hours to answer this paper – about 35 minutes for each of the four questions. Each question is worth a total of 25 marks.

You will always have a choice between two questions in Section A and the questions will always be parted.

Part (a) is a starter question where you are asked to define one of the terms used in the question, for example: *What is meant by the term science?* [3]

The possible terms are: science, scientific benefits, ethical costs, genetic influences, environmental influences, cultural bias, gender bias, free will and determinism.

In order to gain the full three marks you should present a basic definition, such as 'Science is the acquisition of knowledge, primarily of the physical world, using standardised methods of enquiry'. You then should expand this using your own examples.

Part (b) will be composed by using a command word (e.g. discuss, describe and evaluate, etc.) plus the specification entry:

- *Discuss the status of psychology as a science.* [22]
- *Discuss the balance of scientific benefits measured against ethical costs in psychology.* [22]
- *Discuss the balance of genetic and environmental influences on human behaviour.* [22]
- *Discuss issues of cultural bias in psychology.* [22]
- *Discuss issues of gender bias in psychology.* [22]
- *Discuss the question of free will and determinism in respect of human behaviour.* [22]

Writing Grade A answers

On pages 8–9 we have discussed how to write Grade A answers for essay questions. The advice offered there is appropriate for most of the exam questions on PY4; however section A questions are marked differently.

The driving force in the essay must be the argument. You have to construct a *logical exploration* of the exam question that will hopefully enable you to draw a conclusion at the end. In order to do that you must use evidence from psychology, and that evidence needs to be *evaluated* and/or you can evaluate the arguments with a *counter-argument*.

Your essay should look something like this:

Argument 1	Argument 2	Argument 3	etc.	Conclusion
+ evidence	+ evidence	+ evidence		
+ evaluation	+ evaluation	+ evaluation		

Here's an example from an average student essay on genetic and environmental influences, highlighted to show argument, evidence and evaluation:

> Sexual selection has been shown to have a major genetic influence. Buss's evolutionary psychology study (1989) showed that many characteristics we look for in a mate are universal such as men seeking a partner who is young and women seeking a partner who can provide. These characteristics have roots in evolution as young women are more likely to be fertile and therefore will produce babies that are more likely to survive and men who can provide would be better because women have to spend time caring for children and the survival of their children is assisted by having a provider. However, different cultures do look for different things in mate selection. In Spain and Columbia men all rated ambition as more important in women than the women did in men. In Zulu culture women do all physical tasks such as building the house, which Zulu men rate as important when choosing a mate. Many things seem universal but it is clear that culture also has an effect on mate selection.

In total your answer should be about 800 words long and if each 'chunk' is about 150 words (as in the answer above) then you need about five or six chunks like the one above, plus a conclusion.

STARTER ACTIVITIES

HOW FREE ARE YOU?

First: Write down all the things you did today, as John has done on the top right.

Second: Consider to what extent any of them were actually the product of your free will, as John has done in the second box.

John's list of what he did today

1. Got up at seven – I had to do this if I want to get to work and keep my job.
2. Went to the loo – my body demanded it!
3. Had a shower – I don't want to be smelly because people won't like me. Used a deodorant that I saw on the TV and fancied trying out.
4. Had fruit juice, cereal and a cup of coffee for breakfast.
5. Brushed my teeth – worried I might get dental decay, don't like going to the dentist.
6. Drove to work because I didn't have time to walk or cycle the five miles.
7. Stopped for a couple of minutes in the lay-by at the highest point, and took in the beautiful spring morning – it cheers me up!

Which of my seven actions were totally of my free will?

1. Partly determined by my social obligations to others and the need to make money.
2. Largely determined by bodily needs.
3. Socially determined, and the choice of deodorant determined by advertisers trying to make me identify with their product.
4. Well-established habits that don't vary much, though occasionally I may have a bacon sandwich. Still determined by my personal history and the fact I'm not religious, so I have no prohibitions about eating pork or meat in general.
5. Affected by dental scare stories and by my granny having false teeth.
6. Had to do it to keep from hassle with my job.
7. Nearest to free will? Yes, but the behaviour has a long positive reinforcement history and I'm often not conscious of making the decision until I'm almost at the lay-by.

The mark scheme

Essays in Section C are marked using the two assessment objectives: **AO3** and **AO2**.

- **AO3** rewards the main argument part of your essay. In total there are up to 15 marks for the arguments so you need to spend a reasonable amount of time demonstrating a clear and coherent understanding of the argument.
- **AO3** also rewards the evidence used to explain the arguments.
- **AO3** also rewards structure – the extent to which you have been able to present the arguments/evidence in a logical manner.
- **AO2** is for evaluation of theories, ideas or evidence. In total there are up to 7 marks for evaluation. The concept of evaluation is discussed on page 9 of the introduction. Remember, it does not mean simply giving strengths and weaknesses but generally commenting on the value of the argument. This can include alternative arguments as long as they have been juxtaposed, i.e. 'on the other hand…'

A summary of the mark scheme for PY4 Section A

AO3 Marks	Arguments and structure	Evidence	Range and depth of evidence	Conclusion	Terminology
12–15	Presented in a structured manner	Clearly interpreted and analysed	Displayed though not in equal measure	Reasoned conclusion	Appropriate terms used throughout
8–11	Presented effectively	Interpreted and analysed	Limitations in range or depth, or structure or overall conclusion		Some appropriate
4–7	Structure and conclusion limited	Basic			Few appropriate
1–3	Confused and/or severely limited	Little evidence related to the question			Not used or used incorrectly
0	No relevant evidence				

AO2 Marks	Evaluation	Elaboration	Depth and breadth
6–7	Relevant, clearly structured and thorough	Coherent	Displayed though not in equal measure
4–5	Relevant and structured	Some coherence	Depth or breadth
2–3	Some relevance but basic		
1	Some relevance but very limited		
0	No relevant evaluation presented		

Psychology is often defined as the 'science of behaviour and experience' which potentially puts an end to the question of whether psychology is a science! Nevertheless the *claim* to be a science is disputed. On this spread we examine the arguments on both sides of the controversy.

There is a discussion of the advantages and disadvantages of the use of the scientific method in psychology in Chapter 1B (see pages 54–55). The focus there is on the scientific method – the method used by scientists in their research. On this spread our interest is in the wider issue of whether psychology is a science.

What is 'science'

Science is defined as 'a branch of knowledge conducted on objective principles involving the systematised observation of and experiment with phenomena' (*Oxford Concise Dictionary*). The important points of this definition are that science aims to gain knowledge by being objective and systematic and science aims to discover natural laws in order to predict and control the world (e.g. build dams, create vaccines, treat schizophrenia). The method used to gain scientific knowledge is the scientific method (see pages 54–55).

Hard and soft science There is a division between what people regard as the 'hard sciences', such as physics, chemistry and astronomy, and the 'soft sciences', such as psychology, sociology and ecology. This is reflected in university departments which are either science or social science – which suggests there is one form of science that applies rigorous methods, whereas the other form is less rigorous. Psychology is not found in university science departments.

The history of psychology

Early thinking about human behaviour The Greeks considered questions about human behaviour. For example, Hippocrates (400BC) proposed that individual differences in personality were related to body 'humours' (fluids) – too much *black bile* (*melan coln*) led to depression (*melancholia*) and so on. Until the late-nineteenth century human behaviour was the province of philosophers and physiologists.

The birth of psychology

The origins of psychology are often traced to 1879 when Wilhelm Wundt, trained as a physiologist, set up the first psychology laboratory at Leipzig University, Germany. His aim was to make the study of mental processes more systematic using *introspection*. He trained psychology students to make objective observations of their thought processes, and used the results to develop a theory of conscious thought. Students from all over the world journeyed to Leipzig to learn about scientific psychology.

◄ *Wilhelm Wundt (centre) in his Leipzig psychological lab among his assistants.*

However, many scientists were not impressed by the methods of introspection. Psychology probably owes its true claim to scientific status to J.B. Watson (1913), an American who recognised that the work of Ivan Pavlov could be used to create a really objective and therefore scientific psychology which he called **behaviourism** (it is said that he suffered from 'physics envy'). Pavlov (1902), experimenting with salivation in dogs, developed the principles of **classical conditioning** which provided Watson with a simple observable behaviour – conditioned reflexes.

ARGUMENTS FOR PSYCHOLOGY AS A SCIENCE

Scientific research is desirable

We might claim that men are more aggressive than women or that **ECT** cures **depression**, but people will demand proof of these claims. For this reason, early psychologists in the nineteenth century sought to create a *science* of psychology in order to produce verifiable knowledge as distinct from commonsense or 'armchair psychology'. See 'The history of psychology' below for evidence to support this argument.

Psychology shares the goals of all science

Psychology is a science insofar as it shares the goals of all sciences and uses the **scientific method**. Most psychologists generate models which can be **falsified** and conduct well-controlled **experiments** to test these models.

However… There is the question of whether simply using the scientific method turns psychology into a science. Miller (1983) suggests that psychologists who attempt to be scientists are doing no more than 'dressing up'. They may take on the tools of sciences such as quantified measurements and statistical analysis but the essence of science has eluded them. Perhaps at best it is a **pseudoscience** – but it is a dangerous one because psychologists then can claim that their discoveries are fact.

At least some 'levels' of psychology are scientific

The concept of 'levels' of explanation comes from the idea of **reductionism** – complex phenomena may be best understood in terms of a simpler level of explanation. It could be argued that the lower 'levels' of psychology are scientific, such as physiological, **genetic** and **behaviourist** explanations. In contrast, the 'higher', more complex levels are arguably not scientific, for example psychological and social explanations that require a more **holistic** view of human behaviour.

The former may be considered 'hard' science, and the latter, 'higher' levels may be considered as 'soft' science.

Signing your name is often given as an illustration of different levels of explanation. At a high level your signature can be analysed in terms of social meaning – it signifies your agreement. At a lower level, the behaviour can be analysed in terms of the activity of muscles and nerves needed to perform the act.

However… If lower levels (e.g. physiological or behavioural explanations) are taken in isolation then the meaning of behaviour may be overlooked. This may lead to fundamental errors of understanding. For example, prescribing Ritalin to hyperactive children because their behaviour is considered biological in origin may miss the real causes of a child's problem (e.g. family or emotional problems).

The scientific approach is reductionist because complex phenomena are reduced to simple variables in order to study the causal relationships between them. It is also reductionist in the development of theories – the *canon of parsimony* or *Occam's razor* (a principle attributed to the mediaeval philosopher William of Occam) states that 'Of two competing theories or explanations, all other things being equal, the simpler one is to be preferred'.

Science is also determinist in its search for causal relationships, i.e. seeking to discover whether X determines Y. If we don't take a determinist view of behaviour, this rules out scientific research as a means of understanding behaviour.

Reductionism and determinism are mixed blessings. If we reduce complex behaviour to simple variables this may tell us little about 'real' behaviour, and yet without this reductionism it is difficult to pick out any patterns or reach conclusions. Determinism may also oversimplify the relationship between causes and effects, but provides insights into important factors, such as the influences of nature and nurture.

ARGUMENTS AGAINST PSYCHOLOGY AS A SCIENCE

Psychology has no paradigm

Thomas Kuhn (1962) claimed that psychology could not be a science because, unlike other sciences, there is no single **paradigm** (i.e. a shared set of assumptions). A science such as biology or physics has a unified set of assumptions whereas psychology has a *number* of paradigms or approaches – cognitive, physiological, behaviourist, **evolutionary**, **psychoanalytic** and so on – but there is no unifying paradigm. Therefore Kuhn suggested psychology was a 'pre-science'.

Why is this an issue? Psychologists might claim their discoveries are fact, but this would be dangerous if they are not facts. For example, if people are led to believe that **cognitive–behavioural therapies** work, they will use them. But such therapies may be no better than just having someone to talk to.

However… It may be that psychology has yet to identify its paradigm, i.e. it is a pre-science – however, this status need not detract from the use of the scientific method in some areas of research.

Psychology lacks objectivity and control

Some psychologists claim that human behaviour can be measured as objectively as the measurement of physical objects (objectivity is a key goal of science). But is this true? In psychology the object of study reacts to the researcher and this leads to problems such as **experimenter bias** and **demand characteristics**, which compromise **validity**. However, similar problems apply to the hard sciences. Heisenberg (1927) argued that it is not even possible to measure a subatomic particle without altering its 'behaviour' in doing the measurement. This **uncertainty principle** is a kind of **experimenter effect**: the presence of an experimenter changes the behaviour of what is observed even in physics.

Are the goals of science appropriate for psychology?

Some psychologists do not see the value of science for gaining psychological insights. For example, the psychiatrist R.D. Laing (1965) argued that 'scientific' explanations of **schizophrenia** (e.g. a physical–chemical system gone wrong) missed important elements of the disorder, such as the distress experienced by a patient. In addition, Laing claimed that the aim of the scientific approach is to make generalisations about behaviour (the **nomothetic** approach), whereas he felt that treatment could only succeed if each patient was treated as an individual case (the **idiographic** approach). This suggests that the scientific approach may not be suitable for at least some of the concerns of psychologists.

Perhaps the way to decide whether science is appropriate for psychology is to look at the results of research. For example, scientific approaches to treating mental illness (such as the use of psychoactive drugs) have had, at best, modest success, which suggests that the goals of science are not always appropriate.

Qualitative research Some psychologists advocate the use of more subjective, **qualitative** methods that are humanly rather than statistically significant. However, these methods are still 'scientific' insofar as they aim to produce systematic, valid observations. The results from various qualitative studies can be compared with each other as a means of verifying them and making them objective. This is called **triangulation**.

Paradigm shifts

Our understanding of science owes much to the writing of scientific philosopher Thomas Kuhn in his book *The Structure of Scientific Revolutions* (Kuhn, 1962). He proposed that scientific knowledge does not develop in the logical, objective way that is often described. Instead, he proposed that it advances through revolutions. This contrasts with Popper's theory of falsification (see page 54) whereby theories are fine-tuned by a successive series of experiments. Kuhn proposed that there are two main phases in science. One is called 'normal science', where one theory remains dominant despite occasional challenges by disconfirming studies. The disconfirming evidence gradually accumulates until the theory can no longer be maintained and it is then overthrown. This is the second phase – a revolutionary or paradigm shift. Kuhn didn't use the term 'theory', he spoke of a paradigm which he defined as 'a shared set of assumptions about the subject matter of a discipline and the methods appropriate to its study'.

An example of a paradigm shift in psychology was the move in the 1950s from behaviourism (the dominant paradigm for the previous 50 years) to cognitive psychology and, more recently, from cognitive psychology to biological and evolutionary psychology. This does suggest that psychology has yet to identify a final paradigm – or it could be argued that there have simply been successive paradigms.

CAN YOU...?   No. 2.1

1... Select **five** or **six** arguments (or issues) from this spread. Write about 50–100 words describing each of these, including evidence to support your argument.

2... For at least **four** of the arguments/issues present a counter-argument or counter-evidence. You should again write about 50–100 words explaining your point.

3... Use all of this material to write an answer to the following exam question: *Describe and evaluate the status of psychology as a science.* Your answer should contain about 500 words of description and 300 words of evaluation, and include an overall conclusion at the end.

4... You should also write a brief answer (about 100–150 words) to the following exam question: *What is meant by science?* Use examples to amplify your explanations.

Don't write an essay without reading the essay-writing notes on pages 8–9, as well as the notes for Section A of PY4 on page 66.

SCIENCE VERSUS ETHICS

Ethical issues are issues because there are conflicting values between the needs of a researcher to conduct scientifically valid, useful research and the concerns or rights of the participant. One way to evaluate this conflict is to consider the scientific benefits of the research versus the potential ethical costs, a **cost–benefit analysis**. The controversy is about striking the right balance.

The topics selected here are the tip of the iceberg. You could use any research that you have studied, for example any of your AS core studies, or studies covered during your A2 course. In particular you might also include research using non-human animals, such as the study discussed below.

Research using non-human animals

Blakemore and Cooper (1970) conducted a classic experiment raising kittens in a perceptually restricted world. The kittens were placed in a drum with either vertical or horizontal stripes and wore a cuff to prevent them seeing lines of any other orientation (see below). When they were released into the real world at the age of five months they appeared to be virtually blind to lines whose orientation was perpendicular to the lines they had experienced. For example, the kittens exposed to vertical lines tripped over ropes stretched in front of them.

The conclusion that the brain is affected by visual experience was further supported by testing the activity of cells in the kitten's visual cortex. The cells in the visual cortex that usually respond to horizontal lines were absent in the kittens reared with vertical lines (Hubel and Wiesel, 1970).

This research has had an important application in making decisions about remedial surgery in humans for problems such as squints (when both eyes don't look in the same direction and therefore visual input is not properly co-ordinated). Banks *et al.* (1975) found that children born with squint eyesight do not develop normal binocular vision (using both eyes, which is important for depth perception). The squint can be corrected by surgery, however there is a **critical period** for such surgery; after the age of four there is permanent damage to the cells of the visual cortex that deal with binocular vision.

SCIENTIFIC BENEFITS

Milgram's obedience study

Scientific benefits Milgram's research has had a lasting impact on psychology in many ways. First, it triggered a large number of subsequent studies. This is a desirable part of the **scientific method** because such replications refine and enhance our understanding of behaviour. Therefore a 'good' piece of research (theory or study) is one that encourages researchers to conduct further research.

The second main reason for its importance is the fact that the findings were counter-intuitive. Milgram's initial interviews indicated that people would not be willing to obey unjust orders – but the results showed just how important situational factors were.

However… These findings are not without criticism. For example, Mandel (1998) points to a real-life study of a group of German policemen during the Holocaust who behaved quite differently, for example being physically close to their victims didn't make them disobey. Mandel suggests that Milgram provided 'an obedience alibi' and in real life people obey for other reasons (such as, during the Holocaust, being prejudiced against Jews). This questions the scientific benefits of Milgram's study.

Zimbardo's prison study

Scientific benefits Zimbardo's prison study is briefly described on page 22. Like Milgram, Zimbardo showed that human behaviour could be explained in terms of situational factors (in this case conforming to social roles). Zimbardo hoped his findings would change the way American prisons are run.

However… There is little evidence that the study had any effect on American prisons – if anything, they became more impersonal over the years. This suggests that there is little scientific value to the study. There has been one attempt to replicate it, *The Experiment*, filmed by the BBC. Reicher and Haslam (2006) claimed that this 'experiment' showed that social identification was a better explanation for the behaviour of prisoners and guards rather than Zimbardo's view that conformity to roles was the explanation.

Case study of HM

Scientific benefits **Case studies** are often used in psychology to provide rich insights into unique circumstances, such as in the case of HM (see pages 71, 87 and 95). The testing and observation of HM's capabilities over a period of 40 years provided psychologists with important insights into human memory.

However… the same information has been gained from more anonymous studies of patients with amnesia and, more recently, **brain scans** of normal individuals performing different memory tasks.

Humphreys' tearoom trade study

Scientific benefits Humphreys (1970) sought to demonstrate that certain common prejudices about homosexuals were mistaken. To do this he pretended to be a 'watchqueen' in a 'tearoom' (a public toilet where homosexual men meet for sex). The main finding of this study was that most of the homosexuals in everyday life lived as heterosexuals, providing an important insight into the lives of men at the time.

However… The importance of this study is debateable! It did provide evidence to support existing research that the proportion of people who only had same-sex relationships was relatively small, but the proportion of people who sometimes had same-sex relationships was much larger (Kinsey *et al.*, 1948). However, this information was already known and may not have needed this extra support.

AO3 marks are gained by *describing* either the scientific benefits or *describing* the ethical costs or both. You do not need to do both but can.

AO3 marks are also gained from evidence used to support these descriptions.

AO2 marks are gained by evaluating the evidence and/or the arguments, for example by showing that the ethical costs were well dealt with or weren't really that serious.

AO2 marks can also be gained by considering the importance of the issues.

The cost–benefit approach

All research institutions have an ethical committee whose job it is to approve any study before it begins. They look at all possible ethical issues raised in any research proposal and at how the researcher suggests that the issues will be dealt with, weighing up the *benefits* of the research against the possible *costs* to the participants.

Ethical guidelines also tend to be based on a 'cost–benefit' approach in that scientific ends (the benefits) are seen as justifying the use of methods that sacrifice individual participants' welfare (the costs), particularly when the research promises 'the greatest good for the greatest number'.

Diana Baumrind (1975) argued that the cost–benefit approach solves nothing because the intention is to develop a means of solving ethical dilemmas but, in fact, one is left with another set of dilemmas, i.e. weighing up the potential benefits against the potential costs. Judging such potential benefits and costs prior to a study is impossible. Baumrind also argued that the cost–benefit approach in a way legitimises unethical practices. For example, it suggests that deception and harm *are* acceptable in many situations provided the benefits are worthwhile.

ETHICAL COSTS

Milgram's obedience study

Ethical costs Milgram's study is frequently criticised over the ethical issues raised, such as **psychological harm** to participants and lack of **right to withdraw**. The fact that the participants were observed to 'sweat, tremble, stutter, bite their lips, groan and dig their finger nails into their flesh' demonstrates the anxiety they must have been feeling. They were told that they could leave the experiment at any time, yet being told by the experimenter that 'the experiment requires that you must continue' made leaving very difficult.

However… Milgram defended himself in several ways. First, he did not know, prior to the study, that such high levels of distress would be caused. Second, he asked participants afterwards if they had found the experience distressing and interviewed them again a year later – 84% felt glad to have participated, and 74% felt they had learned something of personal importance. Milgram (1974) also claimed his research was criticised because of the findings rather than the procedures used. Milgram's findings appeared all the more shocking because they challenged Western assumptions about freedom and personal responsibility.

Zimbardo's prison study

Ethical costs Zimbardo's participants were fully informed about what was going to take place but nevertheless many of them found the experience more unpleasant than they ever would have imagined. Over the course of what should have been a two-week study the guards became increasingly tyrannical and required prisoners to perform demeaning tasks such as cleaning the toilets with their bare hands. Five prisoners had to be released early because of extreme depression and the study was stopped after six days.

However… Zimbardo could not have anticipated the distress that would be caused and he did conduct debriefing sessions for years afterwards. Furthermore, Aronson (1999) points out the humans are actually quite resilient and recover well from such studies and they are not permanently harmed. However, Savin (1973) believed that 'the ends did not justify the means'.

Case study of HM

Ethical costs The big issue concerns **informed consent**. HM could not remember anything new for more than about 90 seconds, so he was unable to give his consent to the prolonged testing he underwent. He did not know what was being done to him or even who was doing it. This could be seen as exploitation of a man who had no choice.

However… At the time of the operation that robbed HM of his memory, his parents were alive and may have provided consent, but they died many years ago. When HM died in 2008 his brain was sliced up into sections and is now kept at the University of California, San Diego. There was no one who could have given consent.

Humphreys' tearoom trade study

Ethical costs Humphreys' observations clearly involved **deception** in a place where individuals would expect their **privacy** to be protected. Furthermore, while apparently watching out for danger, Humphreys made a note of the license plate numbers of the visitors to the tearoom. He later was able to access the addresses of the car owners and interviewed them at home (which is how he found about their heterosexuality), claiming to be a health services worker. After this he destroyed the record of any individuals' names.

However… Humphreys might argue that he had protected the privacy of his participants by destroying the names. However, he had invaded their right to privacy by observing them and obtaining further information from them through the use of deception.

CAN YOU…? No. 2.2

1... Select **five** or **six** arguments (or issues) from this spread. Write about 50–100 words describing each of these, including evidence to support your argument.

2... For at least **four** of the arguments/issues present a counter-argument or counter-evidence. You should again write about 50–100 words explaining your point.

3... Use all of this material to write an answer to the following exam question: *Critically consider the balance of scientific benefits measured against ethical costs in psychology.* Your answer should contain about 500 words of description and 300 words of evaluation, and include an overall conclusion at the end.

4... You should also write a brief answer (about 100–150 words) to the following exam questions: (a) *What is meant by scientific benefits?* (b) *What is meant by ethical costs?* Use examples to amplify your explanations.

Don't write an essay without reading the essay-writing notes on pages 8–9, as well as the notes for Section A of PY4 on page 66.

You are either the product of your **genes** (nature) or of your **environment** (nurture). At one time nature and nurture were seen as largely independent and additive factors, however a more contemporary view is that the two processes do not just interact but are inextricably entwined. It is no longer really a debate at all but a new understanding of how genetics works.

What is meant by…

Genetic influences are referred to as 'nature'. This does not simply refer to abilities present at birth but to any ability determined by genes, including those that appear through maturation.

Environmental influence, or 'nurture', is learned through interactions with the environment, which includes both the physical and the social world, and may be more widely referred to as 'experience'.

Environmental effects are inherited

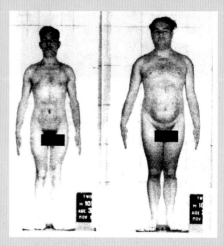

The picture above shows identical twins separated at birth; the one on the left was very malnourished through childhood. It's a clear demonstration of how the environment can modify the expression of our genes. Research has uncovered a new understanding of genes, called **epigenetics** (i.e. 'on top of' genes). This refers to the material in each cell of your body that acts like a set of 'switches' that turn genes on or off. Life experiences, like nutrition and stress, control these switches and, most importantly, these 'switches' are passed on to subsequent generations. Therefore the two men above might produce children who would differ in weight even though they had identical diets – because of the epigenetic material they inherited which was derived from an environmental effect.

This explains why cloning doesn't produce identical copies. Cloning involves placing the genetic material from one individual into an egg that has no nucleus. The egg should then grow into an identical copy of the cloned individual, but that doesn't happen, as you can see in the picture below. Genes from the parent cat, Rainbow, were cloned to produce the kitten CC (Carbon Copy). Except the clone isn't identical. The reason is that there is epigenetic material in the donor egg cell. This epigenetic material was produced by environmental effects in the donor's lifetime.

What does it all mean? It means that genetics and environment are much less separate than was previously thought.

GENETIC INFLUENCES

Intelligence

Twin and adoption studies (described on page 124) suggest that a large component of the variation in **IQ** is due to genetic factors. Other evidence comes from **gene mapping** studies (e.g. Chorney *et al.*, 1998) where individual genes associated with high IQ have been identified.

However… There is equally strong evidence for the effects of nurture, for example the *Flynn effect* is the observation that IQs all over the world have increased by as much as 20 points in 30 years (Flynn, 1987), which must be due to environmental enrichment.

Furthermore, a recent study illustrated a gene–environment interaction. Turkheimer *et al.* (2003) showed that the extent to which genetic factors mattered depended on the **socioeconomic status** of the children. In children from affluent families, about 60% of the **variance** in IQ scores could be accounted for by genes, but for children from impoverished families, genes accounted for hardly any of the variance (see page 125).

Mental illness

Twin and adoption studies again show that the closer two individuals are genetically, the more likely that both of them will develop the same mental disorder (see pages 232 and 236). For example, the **concordance rate** for **schizophrenia** is about 40% for **MZ twins** (who have the same genes) and 7% for **DZ twins** (who, on average, share 50% of their genes) (Joseph, 2004).

However… There is clearly a significant environmental component. This is well described by the **diathesis–stress model** which represents both nature and nurture: individuals who have a genetic vulnerability (diathesis) for a particular disorder only develop it under certain conditions (stress). For example, Tienari *et al.* (1994) found that adopted children who had schizophrenic biological parents were more likely to become ill themselves only if the adopted family was rated as disturbed. In other words, the illness only manifested itself under appropriate environmental conditions.

Evolutionary explanations

Any **evolutionary** explanation is based on the principle that a behaviour or characteristic which promotes survival and reproduction will be **naturally selected** because it is adaptive and thus the genes for that behaviour/characteristic will be passed on to subsequent generations.

Your AS core study by Buss (1989) illustrated evolutionary processes. He demonstrated that certain aspects of mate choice behaviour are universal, such as the tendency for women to value ambition and industriousness more than males. The fact that such behaviours are universal implies there must be a genetic basis.

However… Such genetic behaviours are modified by culture. Buss found exceptions to the general tendencies. For example, in 22% of the samples females did not value ambition and industriousness more than males. This is described as cultural relativism.

Phenylketonuria – genetic or environmental?

The classic example of blended nature and nurture is *phenylketonuria*, an inherited disorder that prevents the amino acid phenylalanine being metabolised resulting in brain damage. However, if the condition is detected at birth, an infant can be given a diet devoid of phenylalanine and thus brain damage is averted. If prevention can be achieved through environmental manipulation, is this condition due to nature or nurture?

Approaches to psychology

In your AS course you studied four psychological approaches to explaining behaviour: the biological, behaviourist, psychodynamic and cognitive approaches. In our AS book we recommended that one way to compare these approaches was in terms of their position on the nature/nurture debate, so you could use this information here.

Behaviourists support the environmental view. One of the early behaviourists was J.B. Watson, who famously said *'Give me a dozen healthy infants, well-formed, and my own specified world to bring them up in and I'll guarantee to take any one of them at random and train him to become any type of specialist I might select'* (Watson, 1925).

ENVIRONMENTAL INFLUENCES

Aggression

Bandura's view was that aggressive behaviour is mainly learned through observation and **vicarious reinforcement**, the key concepts of **social learning theory (SLT)**. Bandura suggested that this enables us to learn the specifics of aggressive behaviour (e.g. the forms it takes, how often it is enacted, the situations that produce it and the targets towards which it is directed). Bandura *et al.*'s (1961) classic study using the Bobo doll illustrates many of the important principles of this theory.

However... This is not to suggest that the role of biological factors is ignored in this theory, but rather that a person's biological make-up creates a potential for aggression and it is the actual *expression* of aggression that is learned.

There is certainly evidence to support the importance of biological factors, for example Coccaro *et al.* (1997) studied twin pairs and found that nearly 50% of the variance in aggressive behaviour could be attributed to genetic factors.

Neural plasticity

Blakemore and Cooper's work with kittens (previous spread) shows how experience affects **innate** systems. This is an example of *neural plasticity*, the ability of the brain both in development and adulthood to be changed by the environment and experience.

One study of London taxi drivers showed that the region of their brains associated with spatial memory was bigger than in controls – this is not because they were born this way but because their **hippocampi** had responded to increased use (Maguire *et al.*, 2000).

Another study found that the region of the brain that controls finger movement increased in size in participants required to play a piano finger exercise daily over the course of only five days, and a similar effect occurred when participants merely imagined doing the exercises (Pascual-Leone *et al.*, 1995). Studies with non-human animals have observed the way neurons shrink and grow in response to changing environmental conditions (e.g. when exposed to light and dark) (Edwards and Cline, 1999).

A political debate

Underlying the nature–nurture debate is a subtext relating to politics. The contrasting concepts of human nature have tended to correlate with contrasting political ideals. On the one side, 'nature' has been linked with twentieth-century *eugenics* (enforced selective breeding), as advocated by the Nazis. If nature determines behaviour then the human stock can be improved by selective breeding. Many other countries (particularly the US) sterilised thousands deemed 'inadequate'. On the other side, the 'environment is all' idea is popular with people who believe that any human trait can be altered with the appropriate changes in social institutions. This has led to equally brutal regimes such as Stalin (in the former Soviet Union) and Pol Pot (in Cambodia) who believed that you could engineer the behaviour of others through conditioning so that they behaved as you wished them to behave. Such political agendas may mean that arguments for or against nature (or nurture) may be as much founded on political beliefs as on scientific evidence (Pinker, 2003).

Genes modify the environment – indirect effects

Genes may affect behaviour directly (e.g. a gene for schizophrenia creates a vulnerability for the disorder). Plomin *et al.* (1977) suggested the following *indirect* effects of genes.

Reactive influence Genetic factors create an infant's **microenvironment**. For example, a child who is genetically more aggressive provokes an aggressive response in others. This response becomes part of the child's environment and affects the child's development.

Passive influence Parents' genes determine aspects of their behaviour. For example, a parent with a genetically determined mental illness creates an unsettled home environment. In this case the child's mental disorder may be due to indirect, passive effects.

Active influence, or what Scarr and McCartney (1983) call **niche picking**. As children grow older they seek out experiences and environments that suit their genes. This explains why the influence of genes increases and the influence of shared environment gradually disappears with age (see page 125). The importance of the term 'shared environment' is the understanding that what was once regarded as 'the environment' breaks down into surroundings that are *shared* with peers and siblings (such as teachers or parents or books) and those that are *unshared* (such as your particular friends or the age when your parents divorced). Some aspects of this unshared environment are actively selected (or 'picked') by an individual and, most importantly it is your genes that influence the kind of things you prefer – your selections.

CAN YOU...? No. 2.3

1... Select **five** or **six** arguments (or issues) from this spread. Write about 50–100 words describing each of these, including evidence to support your argument.

2... For at least **four** of the arguments/ issues present a counterargument or counterevidence. You should again write about 50–100 words explaining your point.

3... Use all of this material to write an answer to the following exam question: *Critically consider the balance of genetic and environmental influences on human behaviour.* Your answer should contain about 500 words of description and 300 words of evaluation, and include an overall conclusion at the end.

4... You should also write a brief answer (about 100–150 words) to the following exam questions: (a) *What is meant by genetic influence.* (b) *What is meant by environmental influence?* Use examples to amplify your explanations.

Don't write an essay without reading the essay-writing notes on pages 8–9, as well as the notes for Section A of PY4 on page 66.

Cultural bias occurs when people of one **culture** make assumptions about the behaviour of people from another culture based on their own cultural norms and practices. Traditional psychology is characterised by theoretical and research biases that reflect the culture of Europe and the US. Both researchers and participants have tended to come from within this cultural background, yet much of the psychology derived from this background is represented as a *universal* description of human behaviour.

▲ *A biased view is one that starts from a particular set of opinions. These opinions then shape the way the person views the world, like looking through a pair of rose-tinted glasses – they change the way the world looks. This wouldn't matter if you lived in a rose-tinted world (the world would look the same with or without the glasses) but in a different world the glasses would distort what is really there.*

Bias versus difference

Our concern is with bias rather than difference. Many studies have found *differences* between human cultural groups, for example some cultures are described as **individualist** and focus on independence and self-achievement, whereas other cultures are described as **collectivist** because of greater emphasis on group goals.

Cultural bias is not concerned with these differences; it is concerned with the distorted view that psychologists have because of their own cultural affiliations and how this bias affects their theories and studies.

If psychological theories and studies are culture-biased this may explain why differences are found between cultures. It may not be the cultures that differ, but the methods used to test or observe them are biased so some cultural groups appear different.

◀ *Supporting your own team is an example of ethnocentrism. The end result of ethnocentrism is that we feel better about ourselves. If you overestimate the value of the group you belong to and underestimate the value of all other groups, you increase your self-esteem. Ethnocentrism is a psychological inevitability.*

EXAMPLES OF CULTURAL BIAS

Why is cultural bias an issue?

Hare-Mustin and Maracek (1988) suggested that before being able to decide if there are cultural differences one must consider the extent to which any research (theory or study) is biased. Only then can the 'truth' be disentangled from the way psychological research has found it.

Alpha and beta bias

Hare-Mustin and Maracek proposed that there are two different ways that theories may be biased. **Alpha bias** refers to theories that assume there are real and enduring differences between cultural groups. **Beta biased** theories ignore or minimise cultural differences. They do this by assuming that all people are the same and therefore it is reasonable to use the same theories/methods with all cultural groups.

An example of alpha bias A distinction is often made between individualist and collectivist cultures (e.g. the US and Japan respectively). For instance, we would expect members of individualist cultures to be less conformist because they are less oriented towards group norms. To assess the validity of this view, Takano and Osaka (1999) reviewed 15 studies that compared the US and Japan in terms of individualism/collectivism. Surprisingly, 14 of the 15 studies did not support the common view.

An example of beta bias Psychologists are interested in comparing the intelligence of different groups of people and use IQ tests to do this. However, these tests are devised by Western psychologists who assume that their view of intelligence applies to all cultures equally. The result is that, when such tests are used on non-Western cultures, they may appear less intelligent (see page 122). Such tests are described as an **imposed etic**, which is discussed on the facing page.

Ethnocentrism

Ethnocentrism refers to the use of our own ethnic or cultural group as a basis for judgements about other groups. There is a tendency to view the beliefs, customs and behaviours of our own group as 'normal' and even superior, whereas those of other groups are 'strange' or deviant. The opposite of ethnocentrism in psychology is **cultural relativism** – the idea that all cultures are equally worthy of respect and that in studying another culture we need to try to understand the way that a particular culture sees the world.

For example ... Eurocentrism is a particular form of cultural bias whereby psychologists place more emphasis on European (or Western) theories and ideas, at the expense of other cultures.

Bias in studies

Most psychological research is carried out on Americans. One analysis of a British textbook found that 66% of the studies were American, 32% European and 2% came from the rest of the world (Smith and Bond, 1998). In addition, Sears (1986) reported that 82% of research studies used undergraduates as the participants in psychology studies and 51% were psychology students. This suggests that a considerable amount of psychology is based on middle-class, academic, young adults who incidentally are often male. Psychology findings are not only unrepresentative on a global scale, but also within Western culture.

The biological approach

You would think that there would be no cultural bias in research on the brain; however recent neuroscience research has found evidence that the cultural environment plays a role in shaping the way the human nervous system becomes organised (Ardila, 1995). This has led to the growing field of cultural neuropsychology.

This means that biological accounts of human behaviour are likely to be culture-biased because they assume all humans function in the same way. This is not true. One example of this is the development of self-awareness, an ability that develops in humans as they mature. However, the timing of its appearances varies from culture to culture depending on experiences (Liu et al., 2004). This shows that a biologically determined behaviour is modified by culture.

DEALING WITH CULTURAL BIAS

Indigenous psychologies

'Psychology' has traditionally meant Western psychology, with the assumption that psychological knowledge can be applied to the whole of humankind because it holds true in Western society. But psychology, as practised in other parts of the world, has created the need for an alternative view of human behaviour – i.e. one based on indigenous (native) cultures. Most of this type of research is done in Asia – there are more social psychologists in Asia than in Europe (Yamagishi, 2002), but it is almost absent in Africa. South Africa, with its largely Western individualist conception of psychology, fails to reflect the country's more collectivist indigenous culture. This is perhaps unsurprising for a country where 90% of the psychologists are white, yet only 13% of the population are white.

Afrocentrism is a movement whose central proposition is that all blacks have their roots in Africa and that psychological theories must, therefore, be African-centred and must express African values. Afrocentrism disputes the view that European values are universally appropriate descriptions of human behaviour that apply equally to Europeans and non-Europeans alike. It suggests that the values and culture of Europeans at worst devalue non-European people, and at best are irrelevant to the life and culture of Africans.

The emic–etic distinction

The terms *emic* and *etic* were originally used to distinguish between sounds whose meaning was unique to a particular language (*phonemics*) and those that were more universally used in human language (*phonetics*). In psychology and anthropology they are now used to indicate the different set of assumptions that may underlie **cross-cultural research**.

The emic approach emphasises the uniqueness of every culture by focusing on culturally specific phenomena. Cross-cultural comparisons that ignore these are seen as invalid. Emic approaches typically involve indigenous researchers studying their own cultural group, i.e. it is the study of behaviour from within a culture. The findings tend to be significant only to the understanding of behaviour within that culture.

The etic approach assumes that human behaviour is universal. In general etic approaches study behaviour from outside a culture and produce findings that are considered to have universal application in psychology. However, the **derived etic approach** does acknowledge the role of cultural factors and recognises that human behaviour differs from one culture to another and therefore the use of methods from other cultures is inappropriate. For example, American tests of intelligence or the use of Asch's technique to study conformity may not produce meaningful results.

At the other extreme is the imposed etic where cultural influences are ignored. Assessments are made using standard (usually Western) instruments, and interpretations made at face value.

It is difficult to achieve a balance between obtaining meaningful results and deriving universal understandings of human behaviour.

Cross-cultural research

In Chapter 1A we discussed cross-cultural research and some of the advantages and disadvantages (see page 23). The validity of cross-cultural research can be questioned on the basis that observations of behaviour in a foreign culture are prone to difficulties such as imposing one's own cultural standards. We might also argue that it is never possible to replicate studies exactly in different cultures, therefore it is impossible *not* to be culturally biased in the study of human behaviour. Smith and Bond (1998) outlined some of the problems of establishing equivalence in cross-cultural research. When reading their list below think about the AS core study by Buss (1989) and the extent to which his research might, or might not, be regarded as controversial.

- *Translation* Participants are instructed by spoken or written word and their verbal or written responses often constitute the main findings of the research. These instructions and responses must be faithfully translated for the purposes of comparison.

- *Manipulation of variables* The operationalisation of variables and the impact of any manipulation must be the same in each cultural group being studied. For example, the expression of happiness might be different in different groups, and the impact of a specific independent variable (such as an insult) is dramatically different depending on the way it is interpreted by those involved in the study.

- *Participants* Although these may be taken from similar social groups (university students, schoolchildren, etc.) they may have quite different social backgrounds and experiences in different cultural groups. For example, gaining access to a university in some cultures does not involve the same criteria as it does in the West.

- *The research tradition* In many cultures people grow up being used to the idea of scientific research and respond positively to participation in this tradition. Inherent in this positive attitude is the belief that their responses will remain confidential. This trust in the whole research process cannot be taken for granted in all other cultures where psychological research may be rare, if practised at all.

CAN YOU...? No. 2.4

1... Select **five** or **six** arguments (or issues) from this spread. Write about 50–100 words describing each of these, including evidence to support your argument.

2... For at least **four** of the arguments/issues present a counterargument or counterevidence. You should again write about 50–100 words explaining your point.

3... Use all of this material to write an answer to the following exam question: *Discuss issues of cultural bias in psychology.* Your answer should contain about 500 words of description and 300 words of evaluation, and include an overall conclusion at the end.

4... You should also write a brief answer (about 100–150 words) to the following exam question: *What is meant by cultural bias?* Use examples to amplify your explanations.

Don't write an essay without reading the essay-writing notes on pages 8–9, as well as the notes for Section A of PY4 on page 66.

Major theories of development are frequently characterised by a **gender bias** resulting from a 'male as norm' perspective. In recent years, however, there has been a surge of interest in women-centred psychology in order to counteract this male (**androcentric**) bias. The use of traditional research methods in psychology has also been biased towards males, and the development of feminist research methods has done much to redress the balance, and represent women in a technically more accurate and more favourable manner.

'Representation of the world, like the world itself, is the work of men; they describe it from their own point of view, which they confuse with absolute truth.'

(Simone de Beauvior, 1949)

Gilligan's research on moral development

The American psychologist Carol Gilligan took an interest in Lawrence Kohlberg's influential theory of moral development. Kohlberg (1969) developed his theory using a set of moral dilemmas, for example one about a man who wanted to steal a drug for his dying wife because the chemist would only sell it for a lot of money. (You can read this on page 159 of our AS book.) Kohlberg would ask participants what they thought the man should do and why, and then Kohlberg used the responses to construct a developmental scale of moral reasoning. The scale showed the kind of reasoning which was typical of people at different ages.

One of Gilligan's (1982) criticisms of Kohlberg's research was that his study involved boys and men only. He interviewed male participants and assumed that their responses represented *human* behaviour.

Gilligan made another important criticism of Kohlberg's work. She pointed out that the dilemmas used by Kohlberg had a male orientation because they were concerned with justice rather than being concerned with, for example, hurting someone else's feeling (a moral of care). When Kohlberg tested women he found that they were less morally developed than men but Gilligan claimed this was only because they were less concerned with dilemmas concerning justice. This was supported in a study by Gilligan and Attanucci (1988). They asked a group of men and women to produce accounts of their own moral dilemmas and found that overall men favoured a justice orientation and women favoured a care orientation.

Gilligan's approach was to show that men and women are different; neither kind of moral is better, they are just different.

However, Kohlberg's theory may not be as gender biased as claimed; Funk (1986) used Kohlberg's dilemmas and found that women scored higher than men.

EXAMPLES OF GENDER BIAS

Why is gender bias an issue?

When we discussed cultural bias (on the previous spread), we referred to Hare-Mustin and Maracek's paper on alpha and beta bias. In fact, their article focused on gender bias rather than cultural bias, so it is even more appropriate to use it here. As with cultural bias, gender bias may result in the erroneous identification of gender differences.

Alpha and beta bias

As we have seen on the previous spread, **alpha-biased** theories assume there are real and enduring differences; in the case of gender bias these are real differences between men and women. **Beta-biased** theories tend to ignore or minimise differences, in this case between men and women. Such theories tend either to ignore questions about the lives of women, or assume that insights derived from studies of men will apply equally well to women. There is an androcentric bias in psychology, i.e. theories and studies tend to be written by or conducted by men. Therefore beta-biased theories/studies tend to favour the male perspective.

An example of alpha bias Freud's theory of psychosexual development is an example of an alpha-biased theory because he viewed femininity as failed masculinity. In his discussion of female development, Freud claimed that 'we must not allow ourselves to … regard the two sexes as completely equal in position and worth' (Freud, 1925). As Josselson (1988) points out, 'Classical psychoanalytic theory is grounded in the genital inferiority of women and deduces their moral inferiority as well'. The 'deficiency' of women was, according to Freud, caused by the absence of a penis. In this theory, women are seen as being inferior to men because they are jealous of men's penises (**penis envy**) and because they cannot undergo the same **Oedipus conflict** as boys do (which involves castration anxiety). Because the **superego** develops from the Oedipus conflict, women must therefore be morally inferior.

An example of beta bias Kohlberg's theory of moral reasoning is discussed on the left. This theory had an androcentric bias for two reasons – the dilemmas used to assess moral reasoning were based on a male perspective (justice orientation) and the developmental scale was based on research with males. Nevertheless the theory was then applied to both men and women *assuming* that it had universal relevance. Unsurprisingly Kohlberg found females did not reason at the same higher level that males did. The beta bias in the theory produced evidence of a difference which may not be real and the end result is that the female perspective is devalued – the importance of care in moral judgements (a female perspective) is devalued compared with abstract principles of justice (a male perspective).

The biological approach

It is rather surprising to find examples of beta bias in biological research but they can be found. Early research on stress used male participants because females have regular hormone cycles (governing the production of eggs) and these interfere with assessing the levels of other hormones in their bodies. In the case of stress, hormones such as adrenaline are responsible for triggering the 'fight or flight response'.

However, this understanding of this 'fight or flight response' is based on research with males and it was assumed to apply equally to women. The value of the fight or flight response to male survival is to deal with emergency situations, such as attack by a predator, and therefore has been naturally selected. However, different considerations would apply to females who make a greater biological investment in pregnancy and nursing their offspring.

Real differences

There are real differences between men and women. There are obvious physical differences and there are also some fairly well documented psychological differences. For example, Maccoby and Jacklin (1974) reviewed a large number of gender studies and concluded that girls have a superior verbal ability, whereas boys are better at spatial tasks. It is possible that such differences are due to the effects of **hormones** on the developing prenatal brain. Hormones also may explain why men are more aggressive than women (the male hormone **testosterone** is associated with increased aggressiveness).

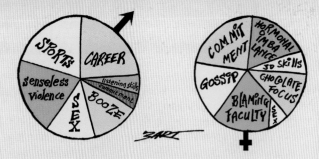

Brains as Pie Charts

▲ *Bias or difference?*

DEALING WITH GENDER BIAS

Feminist psychology

Traditional psychology has sought to explain behaviour in terms of internal causes, such as biological sex differences. This has led to inevitable gender biases in psychological theories. The alternative, **social constructionist** approach aims to understand behaviour in terms of social processes and thus find a way to greater equality. **Feminist psychologists** argue that there may be real biologically based sex differences, but socially determined stereotypes make a far greater contribution to perceived differences.

Feminist psychology takes the view that a prerequisite to any social change with respect to gender roles must be a revision of our 'facts' about gender. Whether such facts are true or not, they perpetuate our beliefs about women. Feminist psychology is a branch of psychology that aims to redress the imbalances in psychology.

One way to redress the balance is, perhaps surprisingly, to use evidence that women may be inferior to provide women with greater support. For example, Eagly (1978) acknowledged that women may be less effective leaders than men but this knowledge should be used to develop suitable training programmes and therefore create a future with more women as leaders.

Reverse alphas bias

Another approach is to develop theories which show the differences between men and women but that emphasise the value of women. This can be seen in feminist theories such as Gilligan's (facing page). In Gilligan's view, women are concerned with interpersonal relations (concerned with an ethic of care) whereas men are more concerned with justice and reason. Unlike Freud, Gilligan views gender differences in a positive light.

Avoiding a beta bias

Beta bias, or minimising differences, has consequences for women. On the positive side, equal treatment under the law has allowed women greater access to educational and occupational opportunities.

However, Hare-Mustin and Maracek point out that arguing for equality between men and women draws attention away from women's special needs and from differences in power between men and women. In a society where one group holds most of the power, seemingly neutral actions end up benefiting the group with the power. For example, equal parental leave ignores the biological demands of pregnancy, childbirth and breastfeeding, and the special needs of women, therefore disadvantaging women.

Research by Taylor *et al.* (2000) provided support for the contention that gender differences in the reaction to stress may be rooted in our evolutionary history. According to this view, and contrary to early research findings, biological mechanisms should evolve that inhibit the fight or flight response in females and shift their attention to *tending* (looking after children) and *befriending* (forming defensive networks of females) behaviour. Taylor *et al.*'s research found evidence that male and female sex hormones activate behaviours that conform to these predicted gender-related differences in stress reaction.

Aspects of gender bias in psychological research

Researcher bias may be evident in research because of a gender imbalance in research institutions (more men than women), or a marginalisation of female research interests.

Male researchers may propose hypotheses that promote stereotypical (rather than real) differences between men and women, or that show women to be 'prisoners of their own biology' (e.g. premenstrual syndrome research).

Gender bias may also be evident in the biased sampling of participants, with many influential studies in psychology (e.g. Kohlberg, Milgram, Asch) using only male participants and then generalising findings to women.

The use of some research methods, such as lab experiments, is criticised by feminists because it specifically disadvantages women. Findings created in the controlled world of the lab, it is claimed, tell us very little about the experiences of women outside of these settings. In a meta-analysis of the relationships between gender and leadership, for example, Eagly and Johnson (1990) noted that lab studies of differences between men and women as leaders contained findings that were contradictory to studies carried out in more applied settings. In studies of people in leadership positions in the 'real world' women and men were judged as more similar in styles of leadership than in lab settings.

CAN YOU...?   No. 2.5

1... Select **five** or **six** arguments (or issues) from this spread. Write about 50–100 words describing each of these, including evidence to support your argument.

2... For at least **four** of the arguments/issues present a counterargument or counterevidence. You should again write about 50–100 words explaining your point.

3... Use all of this material to write an answer to the following exam question: *Discuss issues of gender bias in psychology*. Your answer should contain about 500 words of description and 300 words of evaluation, and include an overall conclusion at the end.

4... You should also write a brief answer (about 100–150 words) to the following exam question: *What is meant by gender bias?* Use examples to amplify your explanations.

Don't write an essay without reading the essay-writing notes on pages 8–9, as well as the notes for Section A of PY4 on page 66.

FREE WILL AND DETERMINISM

Determinism is the view that an individual's behaviour is shaped or controlled by either internal or external forces as opposed to an individual's will to do something. This means that behaviour should be predictable. '**Free will**' is used to refer to the alternative end of the spectrum where an individual is seen as being capable of self-determination. According to this view, individuals have an active role in controlling their behaviour, i.e. they are free to choose and are not acting in response to any external or internal (biological) pressures. However, it is important to realise that free will does not mean randomness and determinism may not necessarily lead to predictability.

Approaches to psychology

In your AS course you studied four psychological approaches to explaining behaviour: the biological, behaviourist, psychodynamic and cognitive approaches. In our AS book we recommended that one way to compare these approaches was in terms of their position on the free will/ determinism debate, so you could use this information here.

◄ *The chaos effect – a butterfly flapping its wings in Bristol can, in theory, produce a tornado in Kansas. One small change may lead to a series of other unpredictable changes.*

So what?

Does it really matter whether we have free will or not?

There have been attempts in criminal cases for murderers to claim that their behaviour was *determined* by inherited aggressive tendencies and therefore they should not be punished with the death penalty. Stephen Mobley, who killed a pizza shop manager in 1981, claimed this happened because he was 'born to kill' as evidenced by a family history of violence. The argument was rejected, and Mobley was sentenced to death. In practice, therefore, a determinist position may be undesirable.

Determinism is also an issue in the treatment of mental disorder. If you take the view that disorders such as schizophrenia and depression are determined by an individual's biology (genes and neurotransmitters) then it follows that treatment should target their genes or neurotransmitters. However, such determinist treatment may then block the consideration of other treatments that might be beneficial, such as cognitive-behavioural therapy.

ARGUMENTS FOR DETERMINISM

Genetic determinism

Research into the human genome is producing increasing evidence of **genetic** influences on behaviour. The more we discover, the more it appears that our behaviours (not just our physical characteristics) are determined by our genes. For example, research on **Alzheimer's disease**, intelligence and on depression has identified specific genes (see pages 94, 124 and 236).

However… It is doubtful that 100% genetic determination will ever be found for any behaviour. For example, studies that compare identical twins (individuals who have an identical genetic make-up) find about 70–80% similarity on a range of characteristics such as intelligence and depression. In other words, if one twin has a high IQ or has developed depression there is only a 70% chance that the other twin will be the same. Therefore genes do not entirely determine behaviour.

Scientific determinism

Scientific research is based on the belief that events have a cause and effect. If we don't take a determinist view of behaviour then this rules out psychological research into explaining causes of behaviour. It also means that, at a personal level, you wouldn't be able to predict what anyone else is about to do – which would make social relationships quite difficult. An 'anti-determinist' view would suggest that the human world is totally unpredictable – and that is contrary to most people's experience.

However… It may be that psychology is not a science (as we have already considered on pages 68 and 69). Even if it were a science, Dennett (2003) argues that, in the physical sciences, it is now accepted that there is no such thing as total determinism. **Chaos theory** proposes that very small changes in initial conditions can subsequently result in major changes, sometimes called 'the butterfly effect'. The conclusion is that causal relationships are **probabilistic** rather than determinist.

Biological determinism

If free will is the product of conscious thinking and decision making, and we can explain such processes in terms of brain activities, then free will can be explained within a determinist framework. In other words, free will is another aspect of behaviour determined by the brain.

However… Determinist explanations tend to oversimplify human behaviour. They may be appropriate for non-human animals (e.g. mating behaviour in a peacock) but human behaviour is less rigid and influenced by many factors, including thinking. This means that the idea of ever finding a simple formula is unrealistic.

Reconciling free will and determinism

William James (1890) first suggested the idea of **soft determinism** – that we should separate behaviour into a physical and mental realm. The former is determined whereas the latter is subject to free will.

Other compromises have been proposed. Heather (1976) suggested that behaviour may be predictable but this doesn't make it inevitable. Individuals are free to choose their behaviour but this is usually from within a fairly limited repertoire.

Valentine (1992) claimed that behaviour is always determined, it just sometimes appears to be less determined: behaviour that is highly constrained by a situation appears involuntary (i.e. determined), whereas behaviour that is less constrained by a situation *appears* voluntary (i.e. free will). This was supported by a study by Westcott (1982) where university students were asked to indicate the extent to which they felt 'free' in 28 situations. They reported feeling most free when they were in situations with little responsibility or when their behaviour would result

Measuring free will

In the 1980s Benjamin Libet, an American physiologist, devised an ingenious way of testing free will. A participant is connected to a machine that records brain activity (an electroencephalogram (EEG) machine) and also to a machine that records movement (an electromyograph (EMG) machine). An *oscilloscope* displays a dot moving in a circular motion like the hand of a clock. It takes 43 milliseconds for the dot to travel between marked intervals.

The participant is asked to repeat a simple motor action such as lifting their finger or pressing a button. Each time the movement is made the participant is asked to note the position of the dot on the oscilloscope when he/she was first aware of the wish to act. The time between the wish to act and the actual action is measured using the EMG machine. On average this is approximately 200 milliseconds. But the astonishing piece of information is that brain activity is apparent 500 milliseconds before (Libet *et al.*, 1983). In fact recent research using fMRI has found activity in the prefrontal cortex (where decisions are made) up to 10 seconds before the participant was aware of their decision to act (Soon *et al.*, 2008). The implication is that free will plays no part in our wish to act – our sense of free will is simply a consciousness of our actions.

However, Trevana and Miller (2009) recently showed that brain changes may not indicate a *decision* to move but just a kind of readiness.

ARGUMENTS FOR FREE WILL

Subjective experience

Subjective experience supports the idea of free will. Most people believe they have free will, as Dr Johnson famously confirmed (see caption below right).

***However*…** Despite our subjective sense of having free will this is not proof of free will. We may think we are free but that is because the causes of our behaviour are hidden from us, e.g. unconscious forces or genetic factors.

People are self-determining

People do make decisions, i.e. they are self-determining. People are not bound to their desires and inclinations.

***However*…** Just being able to decide between courses of action is not free will but it may give us the *illusion* of having free will. The behaviourist B.F. Skinner argued that free will is an illusion. The idea of self-determination may also be a culturally relative concept, appropriate for **individualist** societies only. **Collectivist** cultures place greater value on behaviour determined by group needs.

Moral responsibility

The basis of moral responsibility is that an individual is responsible for his or her own actions, i.e. can exercise free will. The law states that children and those who are mentally ill do not have this responsibility but otherwise there is the assumption, in our society, that 'normal' adult behaviour is self-determined. In other words, humans are responsible for their actions, regardless of genetic factors or the influences of early experience.

***However*…** Most psychological theories of moral development present moral thinking and behaviour as being determined by internal and/or external forces. For example, cognitive developmental theorists such as Piaget suggest that moral development occurs as a result of biologically determined cognitive maturity, not free will. The behaviourist view is that we behave 'morally' because otherwise we are punished, i.e. moral behaviour is determined by punishment (or not). If this is true then there is no need for a concept of moral responsibility, as suggested by the free will argument. If an individual behaves in an antisocial way, according to this view, then it doesn't matter if they were responsible or not, they should simply be punished to prevent it happening again.

▲ *The eighteenth-century English author Dr Samuel Johnson dealt with the question of determinism versus free will by saying 'We know the will is free; and there's an end to it'. Nevertheless, philosophers and scientists continue to debate the question.*

What is it that does the willing? This has been a vexing question that challenges the concept of free will. Either one must suppose the existence of some non-physical 'will' or search for a physical embodiment. One possibility is the part of the brain associated with volition – the limbic system. If this is removed an animal ceases to initiate activity.

(Ridley, 2003)

in escape from an unpleasant situation, i.e. little constraint. They felt least free in situations when they recognised that there were limits on their behaviour, for example having to take their abilities into account when selecting course options, i.e. most constraint.

In Chapter 7 of this book we have examined some more recent attempts to reconcile free will and determinism (see page 148). Pinker (2008b) argues that our behaviour is determined by our biological system; however it cannot ever be predictable because the system is composed of billions of cells and trillions of connections between the cells. In Pinker's view we simply appear to have free will because our behaviour is not predictable.

Dennett (2003) suggests that, despite the determinist nature of our minds, the human brain is capable of anticipating future events, considering and evaluating consequences of our behaviour, and therefore deciding on a course of action. In this sense we do have free will.

CAN YOU...?   No. 2.6

1... Select **six** arguments or issues from this spread. Write about 50–100 words describing each of these, including evidence to support your argument.

2... For at least **four** of the arguments/issues present a counterargument or counterevidence. You should again write about 50–100 words explaining your point.

3... Use all of this material to write an answer to the following exam question: *Discuss the question of free will and determinism in respect of human behaviour.* Your answer should contain about 500 words of description and 300 words of evaluation, and include an overall conclusion at the end.

4... You should also write a brief answer (about 100–150 words) to the following exam questions: (a) *What is meant by free will?* (b) *What is meant by determinism?* Use examples to amplify your explanations.

Don't write an essay without reading the essay-writing notes on pages 8–9, as well as the notes for Section A of PY4 on page 66.

END-OF-CHAPTER REVIEW: CHAPTER SUMMARY

PSYCHOLOGY AS A SCIENCE

ARGUMENTS FOR PSYCHOLOGY AS A SCIENCE

Scientific research is desirable
- Early psychologists aimed for a *science* of psychology to verify their claims.
- The origins of scientific psychology can be traced to Wundt (German physiologist) who set up the first psychology lab in 1879, to study mental processes systematically using introspection.
- Watson used Pavlov's objective studies of classical conditioning as the basis of a truly scientific approach to psychology (behaviourism).

Psychology shares the goals of all science
- Psychology (largely) uses the scientific method, falsifiable models and well-controlled studies.
- However, if psychologists only 'dress up' the subject by using quantified measurements and statistical analysis they may falsely (and dangerously) claim discoveries to be fact when they are not.

At least some levels of psychology are scientific
- Physiological, genetic and behaviourist explanations are scientific ('lower' levels of explanation, 'hard' science). 'Higher' levels take a holistic view embracing the complexity of behaviour (e.g. the social approach, 'soft' science).
- However, if only lower levels are considered the fundamental causes of behaviour may be missed, e.g. seeing hyperactivity as purely biological and treating it with drugs.

Reductionism and determinism
- Science must be reductionist because complex phenomena are reduced to simple variables to study and explain them. Without reductionism it is hard to find patterns.
- Science has to be determinist (to show that X determines Y).

ARGUMENTS AGAINST PSYCHOLOGY AS A SCIENCE

Psychology has no paradigm
- Kuhn claimed psychology couldn't be a science because, unlike other sciences, there is no single paradigm so it is a 'pre-science'.
- Kuhn argues that science advances through revolutions (paradigm shifts), whereas Popper says theories are fine-tuned through a series of experiments.

Psychology lacks objectivity and control
- Objectivity is essential to science (for validity) but it may not be possible to measure human behaviour objectively (e.g. experimenter bias).
- However, even in physics the presence of an experimenter may affect the behaviour of what is being observed (Heisenberg's uncertainty principle).

Are the goals of science appropriate for psychology?
- Science may not provide psychological insights. For example, Laing argued that 'scientific' explanations of schizophrenia missed important elements (e.g. distress).
- Laing also suggested that scientific generalisations (nomothetic) were less appropriate than looking individually at each case (idiographic approach).
- Research shows that psychological approaches to treating mental illness are only moderately successful, so maybe a scientific approach isn't appropriate.
- Psychologists sometimes use subjective, qualitative methods (which are humanly rather than statistically significant). They produce systematic, valid observations.

SCIENCE VERSUS ETHICS

SCIENTIFIC BENEFITS

Milgram's obedience study
- Milgram's research triggered much further research, a scientific benefit because it refines and enhances understanding.
- The findings were counterintuitive, demonstrating the role of situational factors.
- However, Mandel's contrary evidence (police obedience in the Holocaust even when close to victims) suggests other reasons for obedience, e.g. prejudice against Jews.

Zimbardo's prison study
- Zimbardo hoped his findings on situational factors would improve prisons, however, if anything, prisons have become more impersonal suggesting the study had little scientific value.
- Reicher and Haslam's replication showed social identification was a better explanation.

Case study of HM
- The case of HM provided important insights into human memory.

- However, the same findings have been obtained anonymously from other amnesics and using brain scans of normal individuals doing memory tasks.

Humphreys' tearoom trade study
- Humphreys' (1970) covert observation of homosexual men found most led heterosexual lives, providing an insight into lives of men at the time.
- However, the study only supported existing evidence (e.g. Kinsey *et al.*) that exclusive homosexuals were relatively rare.

Research using non-human animals
- Blakemore and Cooper showed that early visual restriction damages brain development.
- Hubel and Wiesel supported this conclusion, showing that cells responding to horizontal lines were absent from the visual cortex in vertically reared kittens.
- This research is useful, e.g. Banks *et al.* found children born with squints develop impaired vision unless operated on before four years of age.

ETHICAL COSTS

Milgram's obedience study
- Milgram's study raised ethical issues, e.g. psychological harm and lack of right to withdraw.
- However, Milgram didn't know the study would cause such distress, and 84% of the participants were glad to have participated, and 74% felt they had learned something important.
- Milgram also argued criticisms were based on his findings (not procedures) because these challenged Western assumptions about personal responsibility.

Zimbardo's prison study
- Although Zimbardo's participants were fully informed the experience was much more unpleasant than expected. Five prisoners were released early because of depression.
- However, Zimbardo didn't know the study would cause such distress and participants had debriefing sessions for years after. Aronson says people are resilient and not permanently harmed by such studies, but Savin argued that 'the ends did not justify the means'.

Case study of HM
- HM could not remember anything new for more than 90 seconds, so couldn't give informed consent.
- However, when HM had his operation his parents were alive and may have given consent. When HM died his brain was sliced up and stored. There was no one to give consent.

Humphreys' tearoom trade study
- Humphreys' observations involved deception and invasion of privacy. He noted licence plate numbers, traced the owners' homes and interviewed them under false pretences.

The cost–benefit approach
- Ethical committees approve proposed research, weighing the benefits of the research against possible costs to participants.
- Ethical guidelines also use a 'cost–benefit' approach.
- Baumrind argued that cost–benefit simply replaces the original ethical dilemma with another dilemma. Cost–benefit decisions are subjective and can't assess costs until later.

GENETIC AND ENVIRONMENTAL INFLUENCES

GENETIC INFLUENCES

- Genetic influences (nature) includes abilities present at birth and those determined by genes which appear later through maturation.
- This is typified by the biological approach.

Intelligence
- Evidence from twin, adoption and gene mapping studies (e.g. Chorney *et al.*) suggests IQ has a large genetic component.
- However, also evidence for nurture, e.g. the Flynn effect.
- Turkheimer *et al.* showed a gene–environment interaction as genes determined a lot of the variance in IQ of children from affluent families but little in those from poor families.

Mental illness
- Twin and adoption studies support nature, e.g. concordance for schizophrenia is higher for MZs than DZs (Joseph).
- However, the diathesis–stress model suggests genetically vulnerable people only develop disorders under certain environmental conditions.
- For example, adopted children with schizophrenic biological parents are more likely to become ill if the adopted family was also disturbed (Tienari *et al.*).

Evolutionary explanations
- Behaviours promoting survival and reproduction will be naturally selected so genes for those behaviours/characteristics are passed on to later generations.

- For example, Buss found aspects of human mate choice are universal (implying genetics), e.g. women valuing ambition and industriousness more than males.
- However, this is modified by culture (cultural relativism), e.g. Buss found in 22% of the samples females did not value ambition and industriousness more than males.

Genes modify the environment – indirect effects
- Genes may affect behaviour indirectly as well as directly (Plomin *et al.*): reactive influence (microenvironment), passive influence and active influence ('niche picking' (Scarr and McCartney)).

Nature and nurture
- Phenylketonuria, an inherited disorder causing brain damage (nature), can be detected at birth and a phenylalanine-free diet (nurture) will prevent damage.

Nature–nurture: a political debate
- If nature determines behaviour then selective breeding would improve the human stock (e.g. eugenic approach of the Nazis) and enforced sterilisation of 'inadequates' (e.g. in the US).
- If the environment can change human traits, social institutions have the power to engineer behaviour, e.g. the brutal regimes of Stalin (former Soviet Union) and Pol Pot (Cambodia).

ENVIRONMENTAL INFLUENCES

- The environmental influence (nurture) view is that behaviours are learned through interactions with the physical and social environment, i.e. 'experience'.
- This is typified by the behaviourist approach.

Aggression
- Social learning theory suggests that specific aggressive acts (and targets) are learned through observation and vicarious reinforcement. Bandura *et al.*'s Bobo doll studies illustrate this theory.
- However, this theory doesn't ignore biological factors – our biology creates a potential for aggression (only the expression of aggression is learned). For example, Coccaro *et al.* found nearly 50% of variance in aggressive behaviour in twins was due to genetic factors.

Neural plasticity
- Blakemore and Cooper's kitten study illustrates how the brain is changed by experience.
- Maguire *et al.* showed that London taxi drivers develop brains with bigger hippocampi (spatial memory).
- Pascual-Leone *et al.* found that the brain region controlling finger movement grew larger when participants performed or thought about finger exercises.

Environmental effects are inherited
- The environment can affect genes in an individual. Epigenetic effects are caused by cellular 'switches' that turn genes on or off. These 'switches' can be controlled by life experiences (e.g. nutrition or stress) and can be passed on to subsequent generations.
- Epigenetics explain why cloning doesn't produce exact copies.

CULTURAL BIAS IN PSYCHOLOGY

EXAMPLES OF CULTURAL BIAS

Why is cultural bias an issue?
- Researchers and participants in psychology are mainly from Europe and the US but the conclusions are used as a universal description of human behaviour.
- Hare-Mustin and Maracek suggest that cultural bias in theories/studies may lead to the erroneous identification of cultural differences.

Alpha and beta bias
- An alpha bias assumes there are real and enduring differences between cultural groups.
- For example, people from individualist cultures (e.g. the US) are assumed to be less conformist than those from collectivist cultures (e.g. Japan) – an alpha bias. However Takano and Osaka found there was no difference.
- A beta bias ignores or minimises cultural differences (assumes all people are the same).
- For example, Western psychologists assumed their view of intelligence applies to all cultures, which could make non-Western cultures seem less intelligent (an imposed etic).

Ethnocentrism
- Ethnocentrism is the use of our own cultural group as a basis for judging other groups so our beliefs, customs and behaviours seem normal and better.
- Cultural relativism is the idea that all cultures are equally worthy of respect (and that we should try to understand different cultural perspectives).

Bias in studies
- Most psychological research is carried out by and on Americans. Smith and Bond showed that 66% of studies in a British textbook were American.
- Sears found that 82% of psychology studies used undergraduates as participants so psychology is based on middle-class, academic, young adults.

The biological approach
- The cultural environment shapes the development of the human nervous system so biological explanations of behaviour may also be culture-biased.

DEALING WITH CULTURAL BIAS

Indigenous psychologies
- Globally, the (culturally biased) Western approach is dominant but there are other views of human behaviour, based on indigenous (i.e. native) cultures.
- In some cultures, e.g. South Africa, Western individualist psychology isn't representative of the collectivist indigenous culture.
- Afrocentrism proposes that European values are not universally appropriate and are irrelevant to, and potentially devalue, non-European peoples.

The emic–etic distinction
- The emic approach stresses the uniqueness of each culture and typically relies on indigenous researchers studying their own cultural group.
- The etic approach assumes that human behaviour is universal and studies behaviour from outside the culture, claiming universal application.
- The derived etic approach acknowledges cultural factors and so recognises that psychological measures may not apply equally.
- In an imposed etic, cultural influences are ignored, e.g. tests are used that have been developed by other cultures.

Cross-cultural research
- Smith and Bond found problems establishing equivalence in cross-cultural research (e.g. Buss's core AS study); translation, operationalisation of variables, equivalence of participants and research tradition.

GENDER BIAS IN PSYCHOLOGY

EXAMPLES OF GENDER BIAS

Why is gender bias an issue?
- Hare-Mustin and Maracek suggest that gender bias in theories/studies may lead to the erroneous identification of gender differences.

Alpha and beta bias
- An alpha-biased theory would assume there were real and enduring differences between men and women.
- For example, Freud's psychosexual theory is alpha-biased because he viewed femininity as failed masculinity.
- A beta-biased theory would minimise differences between the genders, ignoring questions about women's lives.
- Psychology has an androcentric bias. Theories and studies tend to be written/conducted by men.
- For example, Kohlberg's research into moral reasoning was beta-biased because he assumed the findings from interviews with boys and men, using dilemmas based on a male perspective of morality, would apply equally to women. The result was female morality was devalued.
- Gilligan and Attanucci demonstrated that men favoured a justice orientation, whereas women favoured a care orientation, i.e. they were different (rather than better/worse).

The biological approach
- Research on stress is beta-biased; it is based on males (because women have fluctuating hormone levels) but assumes results apply to men and women.
- Males have evolved a 'fight or flight' response to stress, females respond with 'tend and befriend' (to look after children and form defensive networks) (Taylor et al.).

Real differences
- There are real physical and psychological differences. Maccoby and Jacklin found that women are better at verbal, and boys at spatial, tasks.
- Such differences may be due to hormones, e.g. prenatal effects on brain development.

Aspects of gender bias in psychological research
- Researcher bias may stem from gender imbalances of staff in institutions or in research topics.
- Hypotheses may promote stereotypical (rather than real) gender differences or suggest that women are 'prisoners of their own biology' (e.g. premenstrual syndrome research).
- Sampling may be biased (e.g. in Kohlberg, Milgram and Asch), generalising male findings to women.
- Feminists argue that lab experiments disadvantage women and say little about the real-life experiences of women, e.g. Eagly and Johnson compared findings from lab and applied settings.

DEALING WITH GENDER BIAS

Feminist psychology
- Social constructionism aims to understand behaviour in terms of social processes rather than biological differences, seeking greater gender equality.
- Feminist psychologists aim to redress the imbalances in psychology by challenging the perpetuation of 'facts' about gender.
- One surprising approach is to demonstrate that women may be inferior, so they can be given support.

Reverse alphas bias
- Other theories emphasise gender differences and stress the value of women.
- Gilligan's view of women having a 'care ethic' (rather than focusing on justice) represents differences more positively.

Avoiding a beta bias
- Beta bias (minimising differences) has led to equal treatment, e.g. in access to education and occupations.
- But Hare-Mustin and Maracek point out that a focus on the lack of gender differences detracts from real differences between men and women, e.g. in power.
- Arguing for equal parental leave ignores the biological demands of pregnancy, childbirth and breastfeeding, i.e. the special needs of women.

FREE WILL AND DETERMINISM

ARGUMENTS FOR DETERMINISM

- Determinism is the view that individuals' behaviour is shaped or controlled by internal or external forces, i.e. predictable.
- Free will suggests that individuals are capable of self-determination, i.e. actively choose and control their behaviour (not that behaviour is random).

Genetic determinism
- Research into genetic influences on behaviour has found specific genes, e.g. relating to intelligence and depression.
- However, it is unlikely that any behaviour is 100% genetically controlled. Even MZ twins are only about 70–80% alike.

Scientific determinism
- Science assumes that events have a cause and effect so must take a determinist view of behaviour.
- On a personal level we believe we can predict behaviour quite well.
- Dennett argues that even in the physical sciences determinism isn't absolute, so some lack of predictability would not prevent psychology being a science.
- Chaos theory proposes that very small changes in initial conditions can effect major changes (the butterfly effect).

Causal relationships are probabilistic rather than deterministic.

Biological determinism
- If free will is the product of conscious thought, and thinking can be explained by brain activities, this gives us a deterministic account of free will.
- However, determinist explanations oversimplify human behaviour, which is less rigid than that of animals and influenced by more factors, e.g. thinking.

Does it matter whether we have free will or not?
- If behaviour is determined then murderers who have inherited aggressive tendencies might be excused.
- If mental disorders are determined by genes and neurotransmitters then biological treatments should be possible but they may detract from other possibly beneficial treatments (e.g. CBT).

Reconciling free will and determinism
- James suggested soft determinism which separates behaviour into a physical (determined) realm and a mental one in which we have free will.

- Heather suggested that even if behaviour is predictable it isn't inevitable; an individual is free to choose from a limited repertoire.
- Valentine claimed behaviour is always determined, but sometimes seems less so.
- Westcott found participants felt most free in situations with little constraint or responsibility and least free when they recognised limits on their behaviour.
- Pinker argues that behaviour is determined by biological systems but it can't be predictable because the system is so complex. Free will is an illusion.
- Dennett suggests that, despite biological determinism, we can anticipate and evaluate possible courses of action so in this sense have free will.

Measuring
- Libet tested free will using an EEG, EMG and oscilloscope. Time between deciding to act and action was about 200 milliseconds, whereas brain activity preceded this, suggesting that free will is simply a consciousness of actions.

ARGUMENTS FOR FREE WILL

Subjective experience
- Subjective experience supports the idea of free will.
- However, this is not proof of free will. The causes of our behaviour may be hidden from us (e.g. unconscious or genetic).

People are self-determining
- People make decisions (are self-determining) rather than being bound by their desires and inclinations.
- However, just choosing between courses of action only gives the illusion of free will (Skinner).
- Self-determination may be culturally relative, appropriate for individualist societies.

Moral responsibility
- The basis of moral responsibility is that an individual is responsible for his/her own actions, i.e. can exercise free will.
- However, most moral development theories suggest moral behaviour is determined, e.g. by biological factors (Piaget) or punishment (behaviourists).
- If the behaviourist view is correct, anti-social acts should be punished to stop them, regardless of whether the individual is morally responsible or not.

Chapter ❷ Controversies   **81**

Question 2 **(a) What is meant by the term 'genetic influence'?** *[3]*
(b) Discuss the balance of genetic and environmental influences on human behaviour. *[22]*

Student answer

(a) These are factors that you inherit from your parents that affect your behaviour throughout your life.

(b)

Paragraph 1 ▶ Buss demonstrated that some mate choice behaviour is universal and is likely to be genetically determined (e.g. women wanting industrious men and men wanting younger women). However there was a lot of counter evidence in several cultures (e.g. where males and females rated industriousness equally) and religious cultures stressed chastity. These are environmental effects. Genes and environment interact!

Paragraph 2 ▶ A historical thread in psychology has been the nature–nurture debate, which asks to what extent are our individual characteristics inherited. Is intelligence inherited?

Paragraph 3 ▶ 'Intelligence' is extremely difficult to define and measure satisfactorily in a modern scientific sense. It has been historically measured by using some form of puzzle test, and the more formalised of these have been called IQ tests (named after the method of arriving at a single descriptive statistic). Measured IQ has been used in both twin and adoptive studies and the historical conclusion was that the major factor in intelligence (g) was inherited.

Paragraph 4 ▶ However in the last 40 years this idea has been robustly challenged. Flynn has noted the worldwide increase in IQ performance which must be an environmental effect, and Turkheimer showed that the gene–environment balance varied according to socioeconomic status in families. Psychology has been too simplistic, and genes and environment always interact.

Paragraph 5 ▶ Mental illness is another area where twin and adoption studies show high concordance rates for MZ twins and lower ones for DZ twins. Joseph estimated the rate to be 40% for MZ twins and 7% for DZ twins in schizophrenia. This suggests a large genetic component. However the diathesis–stress model suggests that it is vulnerability that is inherited and then environmental stress causes it to develop. In support, Tienari found that adopted children of schizophrenic parents only developed the illness if their adoptive family was a disturbed one.

Paragraph 6 ▶ Work on aggression suggests it is determined by genetic factors to some extent as Coccaro attributed 50% of variance in aggression in twins to genetics. In contrast Bandura has clearly shown that the form and expression of aggression is learnt, as in his Bobo Doll study.

Paragraph 7 ▶ If anything, modern work on the brain using scanning techniques has shown how the genetically determined brain structures constantly change when the environment changes. In support of this, Maguire's study of the London cab drivers showed the increased use of memory learning their routes had increased the size of the hippocampus. This has been shown to happen over a few days in people learning the piano.

Paragraph 8 ▶ It is a very complex business. Children can alter their environments due to genetic influences (e.g. having an aggressive temperament) which then feeds back into the behaviour as an environmental influence (Plomin). Also Scarr suggested that we increasingly seek out environments suited to our genetic tendencies, explaining why the influence of genes seems to grow with age.

Paragraph 9 ▶ In summary, some genes are selected by environments, some persist randomly, but they combine to express those characteristics that make us human. For humans culture is a massive influence. The limits of behaviour and potential are conditioned genetically by being a human and also by proximal genetic influences (e.g. musicality in the extended Mozart family). The actual course of behaviour is determined by the environment, especially the influence of other people.

[534 words]

Examiner comments

Part (a) This is correct but weak and incomplete. No mention is made of long-term operation (evolution), when or how these factors operate, nor is there an example to completely demonstrate understanding. **A01 = 1 out of 3 marks.**

A better answer would be:
The biological factors influencing behaviour that operate at a distance (evolution) or immediately (family) and emerge from the moment of conception. Genes operate together with the environment to determine all our behaviours. A good example is language where genes determine our language apparatus but the social environment determines the language we hear and use.

Part (b) This is a very good and well-structured essay, and would be highly rewarded under examination circumstances. There is a clear narrative (**A03**) drive here and a large range of material from several areas of psychology is used. The candidate has a good grasp of their topic and brings appropriate evidence into place in the argument.

Paragraphs 1 and 2 could better be swapped around so the general statement is followed by a specific example. There is a small amount of evaluation (**A02**) in Paragraph 1, highlighted in grey.

Paragraph 3 is fine, but needs an example or evidence (see Improvements below).

Paragraph 4 is a solid piece of evaluation using evidence. Paragraphs 5, 6 and 7 are short but sweet covering a range of topics, including argument, evidence and evaluation. They do need a little expansion.

Paragraph 8 is a little disjointed as if the student ran out of time when writing these good points.

Paragraph 9 contains a good conclusion.

As far as **A03** is concerned the mark scheme for the top band asks for range or depth (range is definitely present), the argument is presented in a structured manner, evidence is interpreted (but there is some shortage in places) and terminology is correctly used. This is therefore clearly in top band for **A03, 14 out of 15 marks.**

Evaluation (**A02**) is relevant and structured but is not thorough, and therefore does not get into the top band, **5 out of 7 marks.**

Overall total is 20/25 which places the essay as a firm Grade B.

Improvement? The mark could be improved simply by providing more detailed or extended evidence in both the argument itself and in the evaluation. The aggression material could be developed in this way in particular (other theories, different types of aggression, extra evidence), as could the evidence in Paragraph 1 with Buss (e.g. details of exactly which cultures differed and how). Paragraphs 1 and 2 need swapping to improve the structure. Paragraph 9 could be shortened considerably while Paragraph 8 needs expanding into two major points with evidence.

Chapter 3
Memory

Chapter contents

84   Introduction to the study of memory

86   The multi-store model of memory

88   Alternatives to the multi-store model

90   The role of emotion in memory

92   Explanations of forgetting

94   Explanations for disorders of memory

End-of-chapter review

96   Chapter summary

98   Exam question with student answer

Specification breakdown

The multi-store model of memory (e.g. Atkinson and Shiffrin).	The multi-store model is the most well-known early model of memory processes. It now appears simplistic, but was a necessary first step in the scientific testing of memory. It remains the dominant model in non-scientific ideas about memory and a central part of the study of memory.
Alternatives to the multi-store model of memory (e.g. levels of processing, Craik and Lockhart; working memory model, Baddeley).	Various alternative theories to the multi-store model have been proposed to account for contradictory research findings. You can study any alternative theories although the levels of processing approach and working memory model are the most well known. The levels of processing approach suggests that the way we process information affects the strength of a memory. The working memory model focuses only on short-term memory. For many years it was the central (or modal) model and is still very influential.
The role of emotion in memory (e.g. flashbulb memories, repression, depressive state).	Emotion is a profound aspect of our experience of the world, so it is not surprising that emotion is a fundamental aspect of our memory and may determine what is remembered and what is forgotten. You can study any aspect of the role of emotion in memory – the list provided in the specification provides examples only.
Explanations of forgetting (e.g. decay, displacement, context dependency, interference).	Many psychologists would contend that we are forgetting machines rather than remembering ones! The loss of memories is a set of natural processes, the most common of which are listed in the specification. Knowledge of a range of them is necessary, along with related evidence.
Explanations for disorders of memory (e.g. amnesia, Alzheimer's disease).	There are many disorders of memory, the most common of which occur when disease attacks the brain. One all-too-common example is Alzheimer's disease and the result is progressive loss of memories. Amnesia is another well-known disorder of memory where often only one type of memory is lost. The cause may be physical or psychological.

THE ORIGINS OF MEMORY

Have you ever been called 'bird-brained'? Well, that may not actually be as insulting as you might think. Scientists at the University of New Hampshire in the USA are trying to learn more about the **evolution** of human **memory** by studying the Clark's nutcracker, a bird regularly faced with a particularly challenging task – remembering where it buried its supply of food for winter. Like many animals preparing for the winter, every autumn the Clark's nutcracker spends several weeks gathering food stores. What makes it unique among foraging animals is that it harvests more than 30,000 pine nuts, buries them in thousands of different food 'stores' over a 15-mile area, and then relies almost solely on its memory of where those stores are located to survive through winter. Evolution appears to have solved this problem for Clark's nutcrackers as the birds have developed a particularly good memory for spatial information. Nutcrackers have a better developed spatial memory than other *corvidae* (such as crows) which are not as dependent upon the recovery of food during the winter for their survival.

► Clark's nutcracker – their memory skills are essential to survival during the long winter months.

Natural selection

Memory and learning abilities in animals are *adaptive specialisations* that have been shaped by **natural selection** to solve the specific problems posed by their environment. Darwin's theory of evolution by natural selection is based on three main assumptions. First, only a small proportion of each generation survives to reproduce. Second, offspring are not identical to their parents, and so each generation exhibits a degree of variation, and at least some of this variation is heritable. Third, some characteristics give the animal that possesses them an advantage over others in the 'survive and reproduce' stakes. Heritable differences in memory, therefore, will only evolve if these differences lead to survival and reproductive success for the individuals that possess them.

▼ A male olive baboon. Remembering whom you owe favours to and who owes you is essential in baboon society.

But exactly how *does* memory benefit animals in the struggle for survival? An ability to remember and adjust later behaviour in line with previous learning is evident in many different aspects of animal behaviour. The impressive behaviour of Clark's nutcrackers would not be possible without a very efficient spatial memory which permits exploitation of the available food resources. Animals must also compete over access to resources such as food, territory or mates, struggling against the same individuals on a regular basis. Retaining a memory for the outcome of previous contests, and being able to remember specific individuals would work to the advantage of both the winners and losers. Reducing the costs of fighting would have the major advantage of reducing the likelihood of injury, and make more time available for feeding and other activities. The same is true for social groups where animals rely on cooperation between individuals. Male olive baboons, for example, 'take turns' at keeping guard while the other mates with a willing female. Baboons must remember those with whom they have previously cooperated, so that the favour can be returned. By the same token, the ability to remember 'cheats' (who take but do not return the favour) is essential so that the same mistake is not made again.

What these examples do tell us is that memory comes in many forms, and serves an important **adaptive** function for all animals. For the Clark's nutcracker a good memory is essential if individuals are to survive a harsh winter where food is extremely scarce. For our own ancestors, also struggling to survive in a harsh environment, memory was an equally important adaptation. What is clear, however, is that the type of task we face today is not the same as memory first evolved to solve. Remembering lengthy passages of factual information, or trying to recall several different usernames and passwords or the birthdays of all those friends, was never a problem for our distant ancestors. As you embark on your study of memory, remember why it evolved in the first place. Now, if I could only remember where I left those pine nuts…?

STARTER ACTIVITIES

NOW THAT *IS* INTERESTING...

Clark's nutcrackers are not the only animal capable of impressive feats of memory. We humans are pretty good at it as well. It appears, however, that we need to be *interested* in something in order to remember it well – the more interested we are, the better motivated we are to remember it. For example, Chase and Simon (1973) showed that expert chess players were much better at recalling chess positions than were novice players. Similarly, Morris *et al.* (1981) found that football enthusiasts could recall scores better than people with little or no interest in football. This particular relationship is fairly easy to test – simply get some people, test their knowledge about football (and therefore interest in football) using the test below, then ask them to read through the football scores. These scores are randomly chosen from the 2002 season – you could choose a different day if you don't like the result for your team! Likewise, you may have to change some of the questions if Tottenham sack their manager or Chelsea's owner sells the club. About 30 minutes or so later, give your participants the same list of matches, but this time with the scores removed. Their task is to fill the scores in. You might give 2 marks for a completely correct score and just 1 mark if the result is right (e.g. Aston Villa winning) although the score was wrong (e.g. 0–2).

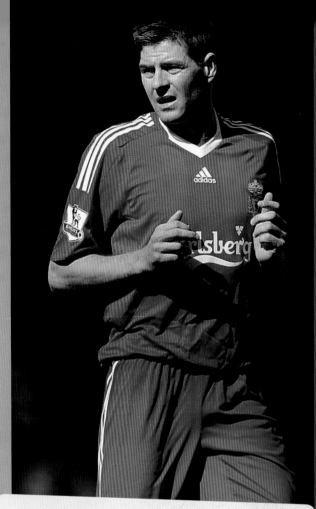

Football knowledge test

1. What country does Chelsea's owner come from?
2. Who is manager of Tottenham Hotspur?
3. Which British club plays at 'The Stadium of Light'?
4. What was the name of the Liverpool goalkeeper whose heroics helped them to win the Champions League final in 2005?
5. How many substitutes can be used by one team during a Premier League match?
6. What colour shirts do Everton wear?
7. For which Spanish club did David Beckham play until his transfer in 2007?
8. Which team has the nickname 'The Canaries'?
9. England's 1966 World Cup winning captain Bobby Moore played for which club side?
10. Who is 'Motty'?

Correct answers are 1. Russia 2. Harry Redknap 3. Sunderland 4. Jerzy Dudek 5. Three 6. Blue 7. Real Madrid 8. Norwich 9. West Ham United 10. John Motson

Premier League scores for 11 May 2002

Arsenal	4–3	Everton
Blackburn	3–0	Fulham
Chelsea	1–3	Aston Villa
Leeds Utd	1–0	Middlesbrough
Leicester	2–1	Tottenham
Liverpool	5–0	Ipswich
Man. Utd	0–0	Charlton
Southampton	3–1	Newcastle
Sunderland	1–1	Derby County
West Ham	2–1	Bolton

When you have tested a few people and worked out their scores for the two tests, you can **correlate** them (see pages 34–35) to see if people who score higher on the football knowledge test also score higher on their recall of the scores. There should be a lesson in this for your own study of psychology – if you haven't worked out what that is, maybe you just aren't interested enough...!

Try this

Briefly show the dots on the right to someone and then cover them up. Ask your 'participant' to say how many dots there were. The span of immediate memory is between about four and seven items, which means your participant probably didn't get the right answer. If you repeated the task with just five dots they should have got it right.

The term **memory** has a number of meanings in psychology, as we shall see in this chapter, but the essential definition is that it refers to the process by which we *retain information about events that have happened in the past*. Note that 'the past' does not simply refer to things that happened years ago, but also to things in our immediate past. If you can recall anything about the start of this paragraph, you must be using your memory.

On this spread and the next, we will be looking at three models – the **multi-store model** (MSM), **levels of processing** (LOP) and the **working memory model** (WMM).

Three memory stores

	Duration	Capacity	Encoding
SM	Milliseconds	Large, e.g. information at the eyes	Visual at the eyes, acoustic at the ears
STM	Seconds/minutes	Limited to around 4–7 chunks.	Usually acoustic
LTM	Potentially forever	Potentially unlimited	Usually semantic (meaning)

In psychology, a 'model' of something should never be taken as an exact copy of the thing being described, but rather as a representation of it. A map of the London Underground, for example, is a representation of the Underground layout that helps us appreciate how it works and where it goes. Of course direction, scale etc. must be distorted somewhat to make it all fit neatly on the page. A model of memory is also a representation. Based on the evidence available, a model provides us with what is essentially an analogy of how memory works. Describing memory in terms of 'stores' or 'loops' makes our understanding more concrete, and simply conveys to a reader an approximate idea of how a particular psychologist has attempted to understand and explain the available evidence. These models change as the available evidence changes, so should not be seen as permanent fixtures.

▼ *A model of the Tube*

DESCRIPTION OF THE MSM

The multi-store model was first described by Richard Atkinson and Richard Shiffrin in 1968. It is illustrated in the diagram below. The key feature of the model is the existence of three separate stores that differ in terms of **capacity**, **duration** and **encoding**.

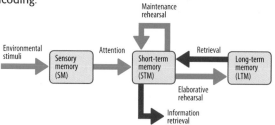

▲ *The essence of the multi-store model is shown above – three stores and an indication of the processes which enable transfer of information between the stores.*

Sensory memory (SM)

The **sensory store** (or sensory memory) is the information at the senses: information collected by your eyes, ears, nose, fingers and so on. The sensory stores are constantly receiving information but most of this gets no attention. This incoming data remains in the sensory store for a very brief period. If a person's *attention* is focused on the sensory store (for whatever reason) the data is then transferred to short-term memory. This explains the first step in remembering something – attention.

Short-term memory (STM)

Your memory for events in the present or immediate past (e.g. trying to remember an order of drinks at the bar) is referred to as your **short-term memory** (or STM). Information held in STM is in a 'fragile' state. It will disappear (**decay**) relatively quickly if it isn't rehearsed. This may well be familiar to you. When you try to remember things for a test, what do you do? You possibly repeat the things you want to remember over and over again – verbal (maintenance) rehearsal! This information will disappear if new information enters STM pushing out (or displacing) the original information. This happens because STM has a limited capacity (probably between four and seven **chunks** of information).

The next step in the memory process is moving information from STM to LTM. Atkinson and Shiffrin said that this also happens through rehearsal. Initially, rehearsal maintains information in STM but the more something is rehearsed the more lasting the memory. This kind of rehearsal is referred to as **maintenance rehearsal** which is largely verbal. In a later version of the model (Atkinson and Shiffrin, 1971), maintenance rehearsal was expanded to include **elaborative rehearsal**, as shown in the diagram above. We will explain elaborative rehearsal on the next spread.

Long-term memory (LTM)

Your memory for events that have happened in the more distant past (such as remembering this distinction between STM and LTM in an exam) is referred to as your **long-term memory** (or LTM).

Atkinson and Shiffrin proposed a direct relationship between rehearsal in STM and the strength of the long-term memory – the more the information is rehearsed the better it will be remembered.

So the multi-store model is what it says, a description of how memory works in terms of three 'stores': your senses (sensory memory), STM (limited capacity, short duration) and then LTM (potentially unlimited capacity and duration). The processes of attention and rehearsal explain how data is transferred.

The cognitive approach

You learned about the **cognitive** approach in psychology as part of your AS studies and the multi-store model is an excellent example of that approach. It was first proposed in the 1960s when psychology was dominated by the idea of the mind being like an information processing machine. It should not, therefore, come as a surprise that the model fails to acknowledge some key aspects of memory, such as the effects of emotion, because they do not fit the 'machine' analogy for human behaviour.

EVALUATION

Evidence for three separate stores

Duration Sperling (1960) demonstrated the very brief duration of SM, using a grid of digits and letters (see above right) exposed for 50 milliseconds (a blink of an eye). When asked to report the whole thing, recall was poorer (five items recalled, about 42%) than when asked to give one row only (three items recalled, 75%). This shows that information decays rapidly in the sensory store.

In another classic study, Peterson and Peterson (1959) tested the duration of STM using *consonant syllables* followed by a three-digit number (e.g. WRT 303 or SCX 591). Immediately after hearing the syllable and number the participant had to count backwards from the number in threes or fours until told to stop (after 3, 6, 9, 12, 15, or 18 seconds) and then was asked to recall the consonant syllable. The reason for counting backwards was to stop the participant *rehearsing* the syllable because rehearsal would aid recall. Participants remembered about 90% when there was only a three-second interval and about 2% when there was an 18-second interval. This suggests that, when rehearsal is prevented, STM lasts about 20 seconds at most. More recently, Nairne *et al.* (1999) have shown that STM may actually last as long as 100 seconds – but it is still a very limited duration.

Bahrick *et al.* (1975) conducted a natural experiment to test the duration of LTM. They asked people of various ages to put names to faces from their high school yearbook; 48 years later, people were about 70% accurate. In this case, the duration of memory was impressively long, presumably because the material to be remembered was meaningful to the participants.

Capacity Research on capacity has focused on STM. In one of the earliest psychology experiments, Jacobs (1887) used the **digit span technique** to assess the capacity of STM. He found the average span for digits was 9.3 items, whereas it was 7.3 for letters. It may be easier to recall digits because there are only ten possible digits (0–9).

Miller (1956) proposed that the capacity of STM was 7 ± 2 chunks (rather than just items) – a chunk is a meaningful collection of items such as BBC or FIFA. Simon (1974) found that the size of the 'chunk' does affect memory – we remember more short than long chunks. Cowan (2001) reviewed recent research and concluded that the number of chunks we remember is more likely to be four than seven.

Encoding We can compare the way that information is stored in STM and LTM in terms of the encoding of the memory trace. *Acoustic* coding involves coding information in terms of the way it sounds, and *semantic* coding involves coding information in terms of its meaning. Baddeley (1966a and 1966b) tested the effects of acoustic and semantic similarity on short- and long-term recall. He gave participants lists of words which were acoustically similar (e.g. mad, map) or dissimilar (e.g. pit, few) and words that were semantically similar (e.g. big, tall) or dissimilar (e.g. cold, top). He found that participants had more difficulty remembering acoustically similar words in STM but not in LTM, whereas semantically similar words posed little problem for STM but led to muddled long-term memories.

Brain scans One way to demonstrate the existence of separate stores in memory is to link STM and LTM to specific areas of the brain. For example, research has found that the **prefrontal cortex** is active when individuals are working on a STM task (Beardsley, 1997) whereas the **hippocampus** is involved when LTM is engaged (Squire *et al.*, 1992).

Case studies of individuals with brain damage One case involved HM (Scoville and Milner, 1957). His brain damage was caused by an operation to remove the hippocampus from both sides of his brain to reduce his severe epilepsy. HM's intellect and STM remained intact but he could not form new long-term memories, although he could remember things from a long time ago. This suggests that the hippocampus may actually function as a memory 'gateway' through which new memories must pass before entering permanent storage in the brain for anything that happened since.

Strengths and weaknesses of the MSM

Strengths The MSM was historically important in memory research as the first model that produced testable predictions, a factor that is important for the **scientific method** to enable theory verification. This 'testability' led to a wealth of research evidence to support the existence of three separate stores.

Weaknesses The main criticism is that the model oversimplifies memory processes. For example, the MSM model suggests that STM is just one store whereas research evidence indicates otherwise (as we will see on the next spread). Research evidence also shows that LTM can be divided into several different types, such as **semantic** (factual memory), **episodic** (events) and **procedural** (e.g. riding a bike) memory.

The original model suggested that memories are retained through verbal rehearsal only, which was an oversimplification – though elaboration rehearsal was added later, as shown in the diagram on the facing page.

Another more major criticism is that the idea of separate stores may misrepresent memory. STM may not be entirely separate from LTM. Logie (1999) pointed out that STM actually relies on LTM and therefore cannot come 'first', as suggested in the MSM. Consider the following list of letters: WJECBBCITVIBM. In order to 'chunk' this you need to recall the meaningful groups of letter and such meanings are stored in LTM, so STM and LTM are much more part of the same thing.

7	1	V	F	high tone
X	L	5	3	medium tone
B	4	W	7	low tone

▲ *Stimulus material used by Sperling.*

VALIDITY

An important criticism of the MSM is that the supporting evidence lacks **validity** for a number of reasons. First of all, tests of memory frequently involve word lists which are related to semantic memory (memory for words rather than events). This is relevant to understanding school work but generally not relevant to everyday memory.

The studies also have largely involved college students. It is quite likely that people aged 18–21 have rather different memories from people of other age groups, and students are probably (possibly) more than averagely intelligent!

You might think of some other limitations of the research, such as the problems with using case studies. But remember, there are advantages to consider as well.

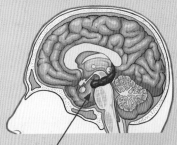

▲ *The hippocampus looks like a seahorse and that's what the word means literally (Greek: hippos = horse, kampi = curve). In Alzheimer's disease, the hippocampus is one of the first regions of the brain to suffer damage leading to memory problems and disorientation.*

CAN YOU...?　(No. 3.1)

1... Select **six** key concepts for the multi-store model.

2... For each key concept write **three or four** sentences explaining the concept.

3... Identify about **ten** points of evaluation (these can be positive or negative).

4... Elaborate each point (see page 9).

5... Use all of this material to write an answer to the following exam question: *Describe and evaluate the multi-store model of memory.* Your answer should contain about 300 words of description and 500 words of evaluation.

Don't forget to read the essay-writing guidance on pages 8–9.

The multi-store model of memory (MSM) was first described by Atkinson and Shiffrin more than 40 years ago. Since then research (theories and studies) have increased our understanding of the structure and processes of memory, showing that memory is much more complex than the MSM had suggested. Two such 'theories' are examined on this spread.

Processed peas

Why are processed peas called 'processed'? Because they are peas that have been put through some 'process'. Things have been done to them to change them slightly (for better or worse). Processing information is the same.

Question? What method of exam revision would be recommended by the multi-store model? What methods would be recommended by the levels of processing model?

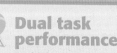

Dual task performance

Baddeley and Hitch felt that STM was not just one store but a number of different stores. Why did they think this?

Research (e.g. Hitch and Baddeley, 1976) shows that if you do two things at the same time and they are both visual tasks, you perform them less well than if you do them separately.

However, if you do two things at the same time and one is visual whereas the other involves sound (auditory), then there is no interference. You do them as well simultaneously as you would do them separately.

This suggests that there is one store for visual processing and one store for processing sounds, as portrayed by the WMM.

THE LEVELS OF PROCESSING (LOP) APPROACH

Craik and Lockhart (1972) proposed a view of memory that contrasted with the MSM. Their view focused particularly on the way long-term memories are made. They suggested that enduring memories are created by the processing that you do rather than through **maintenance rehearsal**. They recognised that we process experiences in different ways; some information is processed more *deeply* than other information and this leads to more lasting memories. Craik and Lockhart proposed that memory is an automatic by-product of processing.

This **levels of processing** approach does not propose that the idea of separate stores (the multi-store model) should be scrapped. Craik and Lockhart suggested that there is a *primary memory* (similar to STM) where information is 'recirculated' at a lower level of processing. And they suggested that there are more enduring memories which are created when deeper levels of processing are involved. In other words, they suggested that memory is explained better in terms of increasing depths of processing rather than separate 'stores'. The key is the 'meaningfulness extracted from the stimulus' (Craik, 1973). No rehearsal is needed. The more you 'work over' or process the information, the more it becomes memorable.

Craik and Lockhart observed that early stages of analysis use physical or sensory features (e.g. shape or volume) whereas later stages use semantic analysis and comparisons to past learning (e.g. of facts or rules). They suggest that this hierarchy of depths of processing doesn't just apply to verbal material but to visual and auditory information as well.

THE WORKING MEMORY MODEL (WMM)

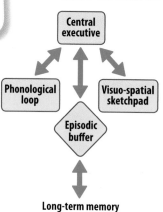

Central executive

Phonological loop

Visuo-spatial sketchpad

Episodic buffer

Long-term memory

Baddeley and Hitch (1974) used the term 'working memory' to refer to that bit of memory you are using while working on a complex task which requires you to store information as you go along; for example, when calculating a complex sum or reading a sentence to determine the meaning of the whole sentence.

The components of working memory

The **central executive** directs attention to particular tasks, determining at any time how 'resources' (or 'slave systems') are allocated to tasks. The central executive has no storage capacity.

Slave systems

- **Phonological loop** (PL) deals with auditory (sound) information and preserves the order of information. Baddeley (1986) further subdivided this loop into the **phonological store** and an **articulatory process**. The phonological store holds the words you hear, like an inner ear. The articulatory process is used for words that are heard or seen. These words are silently repeated (looped), like an inner voice, a form of maintenance rehearsal.
- **Visuo-spatial sketchpad** (VSSP) is used when you have to plan a spatial task (like counting the number of windows in your house). Visual and/or spatial information is temporarily stored here. Visual information is what things look like. Spatial information is the relationship between things. Logie (1995) suggested that the visuo-spatial sketchpad can be divided into a **visual cache** (store) and **inner scribe** which deals with spatial relations.
- **Episodic buffer** was added by Baddeley (2000) because he realised the model needed a *general* store which, like all components of WM, has limited capacity. It integrates information from the central executive, the phonological loop, the visuo-spatial sketchpad and also from long-term memory.

Real-world applications

The concept of working memory has been used in diagnosing mental illness. For example, Park *et al.* (1999) reviewed a number of studies and concluded that problems with working memory were a key distinction between normal individuals and patients with **schizophrenia**. In other words, the concept of working memory is one means by which one can diagnose schizophrenia.

It also has been used to test IQ – test yours at www.bbc.co.uk/science/humanbody/mind/surveys/memory/no_flash_version.shtml

EVALUATION OF THE LOP APPROACH

Research support

A range of studies has been conducted to support the value of processing for creating long-term, enduring memories. The classic study by Craik and Tulving, described on the right, demonstrates the importance of 'meaning'. Other studies have looked at organisation and elaboration as examples of processing 'depth'.

Organisation Mandler (1967) asked participants to sort 52 word cards into up to seven piles, based on any system of categories. Each participant was required to repeat this until the sort was 95% consistent. Recall was best for those who had used the most categories and poorest for those who had used the fewest. This suggests that the act of organising information makes it memorable without any conscious effort or rehearsal.

Elaboration Palmere et al. (1983) gave participants a description of a fictitious African nation – a description which was 32 paragraphs long! Some of the paragraphs were short and sweet whereas others had several sentences that elaborated the main idea. When tested later, recall was higher for the ideas that had been expressed in the elaborated paragraphs.

Criticisms

Performance depends on what you are required to recall Morris et al. (1977) conducted a similar experiment to the one by Craik and Tulving but they gave their participants a *rhyming recognition test*. In other words, the participants weren't asked simply to recall the words but to recall words that rhymed with stimulus words. This time, the words that were best remembered were not the ones that had been deeply processed – it was the ones that had been phonemically processed (i.e. what they sounded like). This is called **transfer-appropriate processing**. This shows that there are other explanations for memory, not just depth of processing. Lockhart and Craik (1990) recognised this problem and suggest that depth refers to greater processing *within the relevant domain*.

The definition is circular Many psychologists question the idea of 'depth'. Something is remembered if it is deeply processed. Deep processing leads to better memory. This is a *circular definition*. It is like saying 'I like ice cream because it is tasty. What is a tasty thing? It is something like ice cream'. This criticism may not be entirely fair as subsequent research (e.g. reviewed above) has tried extending what is meant by 'depth' to include organisation, distinctiveness, elaboration and effort. 'Depth', then, can be seen to be an increasingly complex interaction with information to be remembered.

Deep processing

The levels of processing approach was demonstrated by Craik and Tulving (1975). They gave participants a list of common nouns such as 'shark' and asked a question about the word. There were three kinds of question:

1. An analysis of the physical structure (*shallow processing*), a participant might be asked 'Is the word printed in capital letters?'

2. An analysis of sound (*phonemic processing*), for example 'Does the word rhyme with "train"?'

3. An analysis of meaning (*deeper processing*), such as 'Is the word a type of fruit?'

There were 60 sentences altogether. Afterwards, the participants were shown 180 words and asked to identify any of the original words. Participants remembered most words from question 3 and least from question 1. This suggests that deeper processing leads to enhanced memory.

EVALUATION OF THE WMM

Research support

Experiments Baddeley et al. (1975) demonstrated the existence of the visuo-spatial sketchpad. Participants were given a visual tracking task (they had to track a moving light with a pointer). At the same time they were given one of two other tasks: task 1 was to describe all the angles on the letter F, and task 2 was to perform a verbal task. Task 1 was very difficult but not task 2, presumably because the second task involved a different component (or 'slave' system).

Brainscans Dolcos et al. (2007) used **fMRI scans** to study the effects of dual task performance on brain activity. As predicted by the WMM, different areas of the **prefrontal cortex** were activated when performing two tasks affecting the same store than when performing two tasks affecting different stores.

Brain-damaged patients Shallice and Warrington (1970) studied KF, whose brain was injured in a motorcycle accident. This **case study** showed that STM works independently to LTM as he had no problem with long-term learning, but some aspects of his STM memory were impaired. His short-term forgetting for auditory information was much greater than for visual stimuli, and his auditory problems were limited to verbal material such as letters and digits but not to meaningful sounds (such as a phone ringing). Thus, his brain damage seemed to be restricted to the phonological loop.

Criticisms

There are two major criticisms. First, the WMM only concerns STM which means that, as a model of memory, it is limited. The second major criticism is that a number of the stores are poorly defined. For example, the concept of the central executive is too vague and doesn't really explain anything. Critics also feel that the notion of a single central executive is wrong and that there are probably several components (Eslinger and Damasio, 1985). In fact, in general working memory may not exist as a separate system, localised in a region of the brain. It may be better conceptualised as a property of many different areas of the brain (D'Esposito, 2007).

On the positive side, the WMM offers a better account of STM component than the MSM. This is because it moves from describing STM as a unitary store to one with a number of components. The WMM also accounts for a number of research findings not explained by the MSM, such as **dual-task performance** (see far left).

CAN YOU...? (No. **3.2**)

1... Select **three** key concepts for the LOP approach and **three** for the WMM.

2... Write **three or four** sentences explaining each concept.

3... Identify about **ten** points of evaluation (these can be positive or negative).

4... Elaborate each point (see page 9).

5... Use all of this material to write an answer to the following exam question: *Critically consider alternatives to the multi-store model of memory.* Your answer should contain about 300 words of description and 500 words of evaluation.

Don't forget to read the essay-writing guidance on pages 8–9.

THE ROLE OF EMOTION IN MEMORY

ETHICS

DETERMINIST

PSYCHOLOGY AS SCIENCE

Emotion can have a powerful effect on memory – for good or bad. Being emotionally aroused may lead you to have a very clear memory for events that occurred when in this state. Such enhanced memories may be explained in terms of **evolutionary** processes – events that are surprising and consequential may be important for survival and it would, therefore, be advantageous to have a good memory for these events. For example, it might be useful to recall the context of a life and death struggle with a lion so you could avoid this situation in the future. This might explain why **flashbulb memories** have evolved. However, emotion may also have the opposite effect. People consciously or unconsciously 'forget' things that are unpleasant – referred to as suppression or **repression** respectively. Mood states, such as **depression**, may also reduce the ability to remember things.

ENHANCED MEMORY

Flashbulb memories

Flashbulb memories (FBs) are a special kind of memory which differ from 'ordinary memories' because they involve an enduring imprint of events surrounding an important incident. An individual has a detailed and lasting recollection of the context in which they first heard about a personally important event. The definitive example of a flashbulb memory is the assassination of President John F. Kennedy in 1963. You might have a 'flashbulb' memory of the terrorist attack on the World Trade Center in New York in 2001. Note that the memory is not for the event itself but where you were when you heard about it. The analogy of a *flashbulb* describes the way we can often remember incidental details such as where we were, what we were doing and who we were with, as if somehow the whole scene had been illuminated by a giant flashbulb. This photographic analogy appears to suggest that FBs are like photographs in their accuracy and unchanging nature but, unlike photographs, FBs do not record every part of the scene.

Of course, we not only have FBs for important public events but we may also have them for a serious injury, the death of someone close or other significant personal events. The key ingredient of all FBs is a high level of emotional arousal at the time the event was committed to memory.

▲ *This is not an example of a flashbulb memory – however you might have a flashbulb memory of where you were and who you were talking to when you heard about the attack on the New York Twin Towers.*

IMPAIRED MEMORY

Repression

People may 'forget' experiences because of unpleasant associations. For example, you might have 'forgotten' to do your homework because you didn't want to do it, so you simply pushed it out of your mind. This is called suppression, which is a conscious or semi-conscious behaviour, as distinct from repression that occurs unconsciously.

The idea of repression was proposed by Freud over a century ago. In Freud's theory of personality (which you studied as part of your AS course), he used the term 'repression' to describe one method by which the **ego** protects itself from emotional conflicts. Traumatic events cause anxiety and to reduce this the memory of the event is banished. A repressed memory, therefore, is the memory of a traumatic event placed beyond conscious awareness – into the unconscious mind. This displacement makes one feel better, at least temporarily.

Freud further theorised that these repressed memories continue to affect conscious thought, desire and action even though there is no conscious memory of the traumatic event. The anxiety may be expressed through dreams or disordered behaviour, as in the case of Little Hans's phobia (described in the AS book on page 32).

Depressive state

Depression has been linked to impaired memory in a number of ways. First, depression creates a negative recall bias – depression leads people to recall mostly negative, unhappy experiences and this compounds their depression. This may be explained in terms of mood-dependent memory (see below).

A second link between depression and poor memory is that depression may lead people to be inattentive and fail to encode passing events in long-term memory. In this case, it isn't so much that the depressed person has forgotten, but that the memory was never stored in the first place (Lyketsos, 2001).

Third, the biochemical causes or effects of depression may affect memory processes. Evidence for this is explored on the facing page.

Mood-dependent memory (MDM)

When we encode a memory, we not only record the visual and other sensory data, we also store our mood and emotional state. This means that mood will later act as a cue to recall certain memories – when we are in a sad mood we are more likely to recall sad memories (and the same for happy mood and memories). This was demonstrated in a study by Eich *et al.* (1994). In the first part of the experiment participants were read a list of 16 neutral nouns and for each word asked to describe an associated event from their personal past. Two days later, participants were asked to return to the lab and were given each of the nouns and asked to recall the associated event they had described two days previously. The key factor was that some participants were asked to imagine they were in a sad mood during recall whereas others were asked to imagine they were in a happy mood. Participants in an induced happy mood were more likely to remember happy events from their past whereas those in a sad mood were more likely to remember the sad links.

Determinist

The explanations provided on this page represent a number of different approaches in psychology. The idea of repressed memories comes from Freud's psychodynamic approach and the idea that biological factors may explain enhanced and impaired memories represents the biological approach. Both of these approaches are determinist, as you should remember from your AS studies, which can be seen as both a strength and a weakness.

EVALUATION OF THE ROLE OF EMOTION IN MEMORY

Are flashbulb memories special?

Accuracy Wright (1993) interviewed people about their recall of events related to the Hillsborough football disaster in 1989 where 96 Liverpool supporters were crushed to death. After five months most people didn't report strong FBs, they only had rather vague memories. Wright concluded that most people reconstructed their memories, blending real experiences with accounts by other people and things they had read about.

On the other hand, Sheingold and Tenney (1982) asked participants about personal memories, such as the birth of a brother or sister. Most people had good memories for when they were told, who told them, and so on; and such accounts remained consistent over time (i.e. strong FBs). However, we have no way of checking the accuracy of these recollections.

Flashbulb memories are different from 'everyday' memories Conway et al. (1994) felt that the reason some studies do not support FBs is because the event was not important to the participants and therefore they hadn't formed accurate and enduring FBs. To demonstrate this, Conway et al. looked at personal memories surrounding Mrs Thatcher's resignation. They tested participants shortly after the resignation and re-interviewed them 11 months later. Of the UK participants interviewed, 86% still had memories surrounding the event, compared with 29% in other countries. This supports the idea that the UK participants had some kind of flashbulb memory for the event (although personally we – Cara and Julia – don't remember the event, let alone what we were doing at the time!).

Repressed memories

Natural experiment Williams (1994) used city hospital records detailing cases of 206 sexual assaults on girls from April 1973 to June 1975. About 20 years later, 129 of these girls (now women) were re-interviewed aged 18–31. They were told that the **interviews** were part of a follow-up study of the health of women who had received medical care from the city hospital during childhood (i.e. they were deceived). Over one-third (38%) did not show any recall for the earlier sexual abuse. Of those who did recall the abuse, 16% reported that they had, at one time, not been able to recall these incidents but had 'recovered' the memory. The results suggest that having no memory of child sexual abuse is relatively common and also that spontaneous recovery is possible.

Case studies There are also **case studies** of individuals who claim to have *event-specific amnesia*. For example, the man who killed Robert Kennedy, Sirhan Sirhan, claimed to have no recall of this event (Bower, 1981). Karon and Widener (1997) studied hundreds of cases of WWII veterans who experienced battlefield trauma and repressed these memories. The result was many years of mental illness finally alleviated when the traumas were remembered in therapy. This provides evidence of repressed memories and the effects they have.

Controversy The concept of repressed memory has led to the use of 'repressed memory therapy' (RMT) where therapists help patients to recover memories from their childhood. Critics of RMT maintain that many therapists are not helping patients recover repressed memories, but are (often unwittingly) suggesting and planting '**false memories**' of sexual abuse, alien abduction or even satanic rituals. Loftus and Pickrell (1995) demonstrated how such false memories can be created in a study referred to as 'lost in the mall'. They interviewed participants about childhood events, implanting a memory about having been lost in a shopping mall when younger (they were told a close relative had reported the incident). About 20% of the participants came to believe in their false memories to such an extent that they still clung to the false memories even after being debriefed.

Depressive state

The effect of depression on memory was demonstrated in a Finnish study, involving 174 adults with major depression who, when tested, performed poorly on memory tasks such as the ability to repeat short stories or lists from memory. After six months of treatment those patients whose depression had been reduced performed better on the memory tests and also reported fewer memory problems (Antikainen et al., 2001).

Flashbulb memories

Brown and Kulik (1977) coined the term 'flashbulb memory' and sought to identify what kind of events generate FBs. They questioned 40 white and 40 black Americans about their memories related to nine well-known American assassinations or attempted assassinations (such as of John F. Kennedy and Martin Luther King). They also asked participants about a personal, unexpected shock. Each FB account was scored using the following categories: place, ongoing event (e.g. 'I was washing the dishes'), informant who brought the news, effect on others, effect on self and immediate aftermath. By scoring each instance of these categories a measure of the complexity of the recall was obtained.

White people had greater recall for events concerning white individuals, and the same was true for black people. This *race effect* supports the view that people have FBs for events that are of personal consequence, presumably because they are more emotionally important.

The biology of emotional memories

Research has shown that **hormones** associated with emotional arousal, such as **adrenaline** and **cortisol**, affect memory. Cahill and McGaugh (1995) found that when rats were injected with a stimulant drug (like adrenaline) before a learning task, the rats showed better recall, and Buchanan and Lovallo (2001) demonstrated superior recall in humans when given cortisol.

Other research has found long-term negative effects from cortisol. For example Sheline et al. (1999) used **MRI scans** to measure the **hippocampuses** of 48 women aged 23 to 86, half of whom had a history of clinical depression. The women with depression had smaller hippocampuses and scored lower on memory tests than the non-depressed group, regardless of age. Sheline et al. propose that high cortisol in depressed patients may cause shrinkage of the hippocampus, thus leading to memory deficits.

CAN YOU...? (No. **3.3**)

1... **Three** examples of how emotion may affect recall are described on the facing page. Write about 100–150 words describing each of these.

2... Identify about **ten** points of evaluation (these can be positive or negative).

3... Elaborate each point (see page 9).

4... Use all of this material to write an answer to the following exam question: *Describe and evaluate the role of emotion in memory.* Your answer should contain about 300 words of description and 500 words of evaluation.

Don't write an essay without reading the essay-writing notes on pages 8–9.

The concept of forgetting something has a number of meanings in psychology, but generally is taken to refer to a person's loss of the ability to recall or recognise a thing that they have previously learned. Forgetting from **short-term memory** (STM) is usually explained in terms of the information simply being lost from a limited **capacity** and limited **duration** store. But what about forgetting from **long-term memory** (LTM)?

Earlier in this chapter you have read that the capacity and duration of LTM are effectively unlimited, so why do we appear to lose information once we have submitted it to LTM? Not being able to retrieve information from LTM may be due to it no longer being *available* (i.e. it is no longer there) or because over time it has become *inaccessible*, although it is still there. Forgetting, therefore, has a simple definition, but its explanation may be a little bit more complicated.

FORGETTING IN STM

Decay theory

One way to think about memory is in terms of a **memory trace** (or engram). This refers to the physical representation of information in the brain. It is suggested that this trace simply disappears or **decays** if it is not rehearsed (rehearsal may strengthen the connections between **neurons**). This would explain the results from the Peterson and Peterson experiment (described on page 87). No rehearsal was permitted and the information had disappeared from STM after 18 seconds at the most.

Displacement theory

The second, obvious explanation for forgetting in STM is that a new set of information physically overwrites the older set of information. This happens because STM is a limited **capacity** store. When it is full and more information is presented then all that can happen is **displacement** – by overwriting.

FORGETTING IN LTM

Decay theory

Do we forget things from years ago because the memory trace simply disappears, as in STM? Individuals who suffer brain damage where parts of their brain no longer function experience forgetting. In this case, it is the loss of a memory trace that causes forgetting.

Lashley (1931) conducted some famous experiments on rats. He trained them to learn mazes and then removed sections of their brains. He found that there was a relationship between the amount of material removed and the amount of forgetting that happened. This again suggests that LTM forgetting may be related to physical decay.

Interference theory

In the 1950s **interference theory** was the theory of forgetting. Consider the following: you are used to opening a particular drawer to get a knife. Your mother decides to re-organise the kitchen and puts the knives in a different drawer. However, every time you go to get a knife, you go to the old drawer. An old memory is continuing to interfere with new learning. After many months you have got used to the new arrangement. Your mother decides it was a bad idea and changes them back to the original scheme. Now what happens? You continue to go to the second location. The newer memory interferes with past learning.

- **Proactive interference** (PI) Past learning interferes with current attempts to learn something.
- **Retroactive interference** (RI) Current attempts to learn something interfere with past learning.

Psychologists have found evidence of both proactive and retroactive interference. A typical study on interference (e.g. Underwood, 1957) involves learning lists of word pairs, such as cat–tree and candle–whale from lists A and B shown on right. A participant is then required to learn a second list that interferes with the first list, such as the word pairs cat–stone, and candle–cloth from lists A and C. Finally, the participant is given the first word of the pair and asked to recall the word from List C (proactive interference) or List B (retroactive interference). A control condition is included to see what recall will occur when there is no interference.

Cue-dependent forgetting

Forgetting in LTM is mainly due to **retrieval failure** (lack of accessibility rather than availability). This is the failure to find an item of information because you have insufficient clues or cues. If someone gave you a hint then the memory might pop into your head but, in the meantime, you are faced with a blank. It is possible that you actually have a vast store of memories and could access them – if only someone could provide the right cues.

There are several different kinds of cue – external or internal.

External cues **Context-dependent learning** (or forgetting) – Abernethy (1940) arranged for a group of students to be tested before a certain course began. They were then tested each week. Some students were tested in their teaching room by their usual instructor, or by a different instructor. Others were tested in a different room either by their usual instructor or by a different one. Those tested by the same instructor in the same room performed best. Presumably, familiar things (room and instructor) acted as memory cues. Look at the wall in front of you. Does anything there trigger a memory? If so, it is acting as a cue.

Internal cues **State-dependent learning** (or forgetting) such as the mood dependent memories described on the previous spread – Goodwin *et al.* (1969) found that people who drank a lot often forgot where they had put things when they were sober but recalled the locations when they were drunk again! Miles and Hardman (1998) found that people who learned a list of words while exercising on a static bicycle remembered them better when exercising rather than at rest.

List A	List B	List C
Cat	Tree	Stone
Candle	Whale	Cloth
Book	Fork	Jail
Plant	Tank	Claw
Water	Market	Gold
Track	Lemon	Kettle
Dish	Cane	Swamp
Flask	Picture	Mast
Cigar	Jelly	Nail
Animal	Nurse	Pencil

◀ *Word lists like this are used to demonstrate interference as an explanation for forgetting.*

EVALUATION OF EXPLANATIONS OF FORGETTING

Decay or displacement?

Peterson and Peterson's experiment appears to show that information decays within 18 seconds from short-term memory if verbal rehearsal is prevented. However, it is possible that the information did not 'disappear' (decay) but that it was displaced by the numbers being used to count down.

Reitman (1974) tried to overcome this problem of displacement by giving participants a different task in the retention interval. She asked participants to listen for a tone. This meant that their attention was diverted elsewhere and should have prevented rehearsal of data. In a 15-second interval participants' recall for five words dropped by 24%, which is evidence for decay… except that we can't be *entirely* certain that new information had not entered STM.

Waugh and Norman (1965) used the **serial probe technique** to investigate whether decay or displacement is the explanation. This technique involves presenting a series of numbers to participants, such as 11, 23, 45, 31, 56, 32, 19, 23, 16, 12. Then the experimenter says the probe – in this case it might be 45, and the participant has to recall the number that came after the probe in the list (i.e. 31 for this list).

They presented 16 numbers to participants. If the probe was early in the list, recall was poor (less than 20%). If the probe came near the end of the list, recall was good (over 80%). This supports displacement theory because forgetting must be due to the fact that subsequent numbers increasingly displaced earlier numbers.

However, if the speed of presentation is altered there is some evidence for decay as well. In a second experiment the digits were presented at a rate of one per second (slower) or four per second (faster). This timing affected recall. If the numbers were presented faster, recall improved – which must be because the numbers had less time to decay. If displacement was the only explanation there should be no difference between the two conditions.

Shallice (1967) also found that forgetting was reduced if the numbers were presented faster, *but* found a stronger effect for moving the position of the probe. This suggests that displacement and decay explain forgetting in STM but that displacement is more important.

Decay or interference in LTM?

If something disappears from long-term memory, has it decayed or has interference from other information been the cause? Baddeley and Hitch (1977) conducted a **natural experiment** to investigate this. The **dependent variable** was recall of rugby fixtures played over a season. Some players played in all of the games in the season whereas others missed some games because of injury. The time interval from start to end of the season was the same for all players but the number of intervening games was different. If decay theory is correct then all players should recall a similar percentage of the games played because time alone should cause forgetting. If interference theory is correct then the players who played most games should forget proportionately more because of interference – which is what Baddeley and Hitch found, supporting interference theory.

▲ A 'Viking' couple prepare for dinner at the Jorvik Viking Centre in York, where smells are very much a feature of the display. Aggleton and Waskett (1999) used the different smells in the exhibit to show that smell was an effective retrieval cue when testing recall in people who had visited the museum.

Interference or cue-dependent forgetting?

Interference does cause forgetting but only when the same stimulus is paired with two different responses. These conditions are rare in everyday life and therefore interference only explains a limited range of forgetting. Furthermore, even in relevant situations, it seems that it is not the most important explanation for forgetting, as Tulving and Psotka (1971) demonstrated. Participants were given six different word lists to learn, each consisting of 24 words divided into six different categories (so over the six lists there were 36 categories, such as kinds of tree and names of precious stones). After each list was presented, participants were asked to write down as many words as they could remember (**free recall**). After all the lists were presented there was a final total free recall (of all the lists they had learned) and then the participants were given the category names and again asked to recall all the words from all the lists (**cued recall**).

Some participants only learned one list, others learned two and so on. According to interference theory, the more lists a participant had to learn the worse their performance should become. This was what Tulving and Pstoka found – evidence of retroactive interference.

However, when participants were given cued recall, the effects of interference disappeared – participants remembered about 70% of the words they were given regardless of how many lists they had been given. This shows that interference effects may mask what is actually in memory. The information is there (available) but cannot be retrieved.

Some psychologists believe that all forgetting is cue-dependent forgetting. Michael Eysenck (1998) says 'It is probable that this is the main reason for forgetting in LTM'. There is a considerable amount of research to show the importance of cues and how they trigger memory. The **encoding specificity principle** further states that a cue doesn't have to be exactly right but the closer the cue is to the thing you're looking for, the more useful it will be.

CAN YOU...? No. 3.4

1... Write **one** sentence describing each of the explanations of forgetting.

2... Now provide some further explanation/examples for each of these explanations.

3... Identify about **ten** points of evaluation (these can be positive or negative).

4... Elaborate each point (see page 9).

5... Use all of this material to write an answer to the following exam question: *Discuss explanations of forgetting*. As good practice you might also answer the following 'building block' essays: (a) *Discuss explanations of forgetting in short-term memory*. (b) *Discuss explanations of forgetting in long-term memory*. Your answers should contain about 300 words of description and 500 words of evaluation.

Remember that, when writing an essay, you can include material from other spreads – but only if it is made specifically relevant to the essay. For example, in an essay on forgetting you might include research on the role of emotional factors in memory, discussed on the previous spread.

Ecological validity

Many of the studies used to support cue-dependent forgetting are lab-based and not very like everyday memory. Therefore cue-dependent recall may not apply to all aspects of everyday memory. For example, procedural knowledge (knowing how) is not related to cue-dependent recall. Examples of this kind of memory include remembering how to play ping pong or to play the recorder. Such memories are rather resistant to forgetting, but not totally immune. If you haven't played ping pong in years, there is some relearning to do but even so, cues don't really explain this.

EXPLANATIONS FOR DISORDERS OF MEMORY

Memory helps to make us who we are. Imagine waking up and having no idea what you did the day before. The absence of continuity would rob you of your enduring sense of self. This is what happens to some people with **amnesia** who are also unable to recognise people's faces, name them or recall that they were ever familiar. Very dense amnesia leads to being unable to store any new information at all, so the people and places that surround amnesiacs continue to be strange.

Alzheimer's disease, which largely affects older adults, causes cognitive problems such as confusion, hallucinations, memory loss and other symptoms, e.g. **insomnia** and **depression**.

By studying such problems, psychologists can learn how memory functions, for example showing that memories are not distributed evenly over the brain but that some brain structures have specific roles in the formation of memories.

EXPLANATIONS OF AMNESIA

The loss of explicit memory

Some memories are explicit – the information can be deliberately and consciously recalled. Other kinds of memory are implicit – their recollection is independent of conscious awareness.

Explicit memory in amnesia Schacter (1987) suggested that the pattern of forgetting in amnesics could be explained by impaired **explicit memory**. Many amnesics perform better on tests of **implicit memory** (e.g. tasks where they demonstrate learning through a change in behaviour) than explicit memory. This is illustrated by the **case study** of HM and his responses on the **Gollin test** (see box on facing page).

Procedural and declarative memory There are different kinds of **long-term memories** (LTMs). **Procedural memory** is the acquisition of physical or 'motor' skills, i.e. 'knowing how', such as learning how to ride a bike. **Declarative memory** is fact-related, i.e. 'knowing what', such as remembering that you are able to ride a bike. As amnesics tend to have relatively poor explicit but unimpaired implicit memory, this can account for the near-normal performance of amnesics on tests of procedural memory compared with their loss of declarative memory. HM's mirror drawing skill illustrates this difference.

Inability to consolidate new memories

Anterograde amnesia is the inability to form new LTMs. Issac and Mayes (1999) suggested that **anterograde amnesia** might be due to problems with **consolidation** or retrieval of memories. Isaac and Hayes tested amnesics and controls and found that amnesics performed about as well as the controls on **cued recall** and recognition, suggesting that the problem is with consolidation rather than retrieval.

Retrograde amnesia is the loss of memory for past events. Some amnesics have **retrograde amnesia**, and usually their recall is worst for events occurring closest to the onset of amnesia. Recall of memories older than this improves as more time passes since they were formed. This change over time is called a **temporal gradient** and indicates that LTMs need to be consolidated otherwise they are 'lost'. Amnesic symptoms may be caused by disruption of the process of consolidation and is associated with damage to the **hippocampus**, suggesting that this part of the brain plays a key role in forming LTMs.

EXPLANATIONS OF ALZHEIMER'S DISEASE

β-amyloid and plaques

One of the proteins found in the brain is called amyloid precursor protein (APP). This is normally broken down to produce a smaller molecule *β-amyloid protein 40*. In patients with Alzheimer's disease (AD) a slightly different molecule, β-amyloid protein 42, is produced (referred to as **β-amyloid**). This builds up in the spaces between **neurons** forming **plaques**. These plaques cause problems in the communication between neurons.

The plaques start to form before the symptoms of AD appear (Selkoe, 2000) but their progressive damage causes the **cerebral cortex** to shrink. The surface of the cerebral cortex usually has tight folds, but the plaques cause the spaces between the folds to enlarge. Other areas, including the hippocampus, are also affected. One reason this change in brain tissue affects memory is because cells in the **basal forebrain** (which increases arousal in the cerebral cortex) are damaged, so people with AD are less alert and find attending to stimuli more difficult (Berntson *et al.*, 2002).

Another effect is more direct. Snyder *et al.* (2005) found that β-amyloid interferes with **NMDA**, a **neurotransmitter** involved in learning. NMDA normally helps to produce changes in the **synapses** that produce **long-term potentiation** – the posh name for the changes in neurons that are linked to behavioural changes when we learn.

Tangles

A second change in the brains of people with AD is the development of **tangles**. These are formed by a build-up of **tau protein** which normally provides support for the cell structure within a neuron. Tangles arise when the structure of the neuron's cell body degenerates. Although tangles are associated with other diseases, they are of a distinct form in AD.

Genes

The first genes associated with AD were identified in early-onset cases of AD. **Down's syndrome** is a type of mental retardation caused by having an additional copy of **chromosome** 21. Most people with Down's syndrome who reach middle age get early-onset AD (Lott, 1982). This led researchers to look for (and find) genes associated with AD on chromosome 21. Other genes for early-onset AD have been identified on chromosomes 1 (Levy-Lahad *et al.*, 1995) and 14 (Schellenberg *et al.*, 1992). Genes associated with later-onset AD, e.g. on chromosome 10 (Ertekin-Taner *et al.*, 2000), have also been found. One role these genes play is to produce more β-amyloid, therefore explaining why some people are more prone to develop AD.

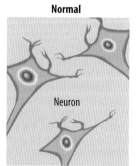

▲ *Plaques and tangles are found between and inside the neurons of patients with AD.*

Set 1 Set 2

Set 3 Set 4 Set 5

▲ The **Gollin test** – a participant is shown 20 incomplete drawings and asked to guess what they are of. They are progressively shown more complete versions. When retested, patients can identify the objects more quickly, showing that they have some memory of the sequence they have seen before even if they cannot recall having done it.

A famous amnesic

On pages 71 and 87 we mentioned the case of HM (Scoville and Milner, 1957), whose anterograde amnesia meant he could not acquire new declarative memories, such as learning to recognise new people or to remember where he was or how he had got there. HM did, however, have a normal STM and could access LTMs formed a year or so prior to the operation which caused his amnesia, i.e. he had little retrograde amnesia. HM's operation removed his hippocampus, amygdala and part of the temporal lobes bilaterally (from both sides). This suggests that these brain areas are involved in the specific memory problems he experienced.

Although HM's condition was described as global amnesia, he was better at some types of memorising than others. For example, he improved on the Gollin test with repetition, and still recognised the partial images four months later – even though he couldn't recall having done the test before (Warrington and Weiskrantz, 1968). He also learned to draw using only a reflection in a mirror (which is difficult!) but he was unable to remember that he could do so (Milner, 1962).

EVALUATION OF EXPLANATIONS OF AMNESIA

Explicit and implicit memory

No explicit memory Stickgold *et al.* (2000) used the video game 'Tetris', in which falling blocks are used to build a 'wall', to test memory. People with normal memory learn the skill in a few hours and can describe it. Amnesics improve at the task (though more slowly), but can neither recall playing nor describe it, i.e. they develop an implicit but not explicit memory of the game.

Some implicit memory Generally, amnesics find explicit tasks hard but can do implicit ones – but this is not always the case. Schacter *et al.* (1995) found that re-presenting learned word pairs in the same voices rather than different ones helped 'normal' participants but did not improve performance in amnesics.

Relational memory binding The implicit/explicit distinction identifies a key difference in memory function in amnesia but it does not indicate why this happens – it is descriptive rather than explanatory. However, it may be explained by *relational memory binding*, which suggests that amnesics lack the memory function that links pieces of information together (Ryan *et al.*, 2000). In other words, amnesics might be failing to recall the *relationship* between explicit and implicit aspects of events.

Consolidation

Anterograde and retrograde amnesia Many amnesics have both retrograde and anterograde amnesia, implying that both are caused by problems with the same brain area. However, Gabrieli (1998) found that damage to just part of the hippocampus (called CA1) caused anterograde amnesia alone.

Role of the temporal lobe Reed and Squire (1998) took **MRI scans** of four patients with retrograde amnesia. All had hippocampal damage but those with the worst symptoms also had lesions to the temporal lobe. This confirms the role of the hippocampus in memory but suggests other structures are also important.

Animal studies One problem with studies of human amnesics is that such studies are imprecise as both the symptoms and the extent of brain damage vary. An alternative approach, **lesioning** of animals' brains, offers more control. Remondes and Schman (2004) showed that rats with damage to the hippocampus could learn a maze but forgot it quickly, suggesting they could make new memories but could not consolidate them. This suggests that the hippocampus is associated with consolidation.

EVALUATION OF EXPLANATIONS OF ALZHEIMER'S DISEASE

Plaques and tangles

Role of β-amyloid The link between β-amyloid deposits and cognitive problems is rather weak, which makes it difficult to see how plaques can be the cause of AD. However, Murphy and LeVine (2010) suggest that this is because, early in the disease, β-amyloid triggers a chain of events that, once started, continues irrespective of β-amyloid levels. This explanation has yet to be tested and the exact consequences have not been identified, although the formation of tangles may be one important effect.

Animal studies Much of the work on the role of β-amyloid has been conducted using animals, although no single species has all the same symptoms or physiological consequences as human AD patients. For example, although other **primates** have the same β-amyloid as ours, unlike us, they develop little nerve damage and few cognitive symptoms in old age. In contrast, dogs do deposit more β-amyloid with age and this correlates with cognitive dysfunction (Cummings *et al.*, 1996a), but they do not lose neurons or produce plaques or tangles (Cummings *et al.*, 1996b). This means that generalisations from animals to humans may not be valid.

Genes

Minor influence Of all patients with AD, about half have no known relatives who are sufferers (St George-Hyslop, 2000), suggesting that the genetic influence is small. Therefore, although genes associated with late-onset AD have been found, they only account for a fraction of the risk.

Other factors In a cross-cultural comparison of the Yoruba people of Nigeria and Americans, Hendrie (2001) found that although the frequency of genes linked to AD was similar, the Yoruba suffered much less from the disorder. This tells us that other factors also affect the incidence of the disease. For example, it is possible that the Yoruba diet, which is low in calories, fat and salt, reduces the risk of AD developing.

Genes and β-amyloid Nevertheless, genes are important as they influence the production of β-amyloid and tau proteins. Cleary *et al.* (2005) found that injecting rats with β-amyloid disrupted memory. In an experimental treatment for AD, Hock *et al.* (2003) triggered an **immune response** to β-amyloid in patients. Those with the strongest immune responses (which would destroy most β-amyloid) stopped deteriorating in terms of memory.

CAN YOU...? (No. 3.5)

1... **Five** explanations for disorders of memory are described on this spread. For each explanation write a sentence summing up its essence.

2... For each explanation provide some further evidence/examples.

3... Identify about **ten** points of evaluation (these can be positive or negative).

4... Elaborate each point (see page 9).

5... Use all of this material to write an answer to the following exam question: *Describe and evaluate explanations of disorders of memory.* Your answer should contain about 300 words of description and 500 words of evaluation.

Don't write an essay without reading the essay-writing notes on pages 8–9.

MULTI-STORE MODEL OF MEMORY

DESCRIPTION OF THE MSM

Sensory memory
- Attended-to information retained in sensory memory for that sense (e.g. sight or hearing).
- Large capacity but very short duration (milliseconds).

Short-term memory
- Limited capacity memory (between four and seven chunks) that will decay unless maintained by rehearsal.
- New chunks cause displacement of earlier information unless it has been transferred to LTM.
- Duration seconds/minutes, encoded acoustically.

Long-term memory
- Elaborative rehearsal of information in STM causes transfer to LTM.
- Semantic encoding, potentially unlimited capacity and duration.

EVALUATION

Evidence for three separate stores
- Evidence shows the three stores differ in duration, capacity and encoding.
- Sperling showed brief duration of sensory memory using grids of letters and numbers displayed for 50 milliseconds. Peterson and Peterson showed STM of consonant syllables decays within 20 seconds. Bahrick et al. showed LTM lasts decades using faces in high school yearbook.
- Jacobs used the digit span technique to show the capacity of STM was 9.3 digits or 7.3 letters. Miller found STM capacity was 7 ± 2 meaningful chunks but Cowan suggests only four chunks.
- Baddeley showed that recall was muddled when similar sounding items were recalled from STM and similar meaning ones were recalled from LTM. This shows encoding is acoustic in STM but semantic in LTM.
- Brain scans show that the prefrontal cortex is active in STM tasks but the hippocampus is active in LTM tasks.
- HM had his hippocampus removed. Scoville and Milner's case study found his STM and old LTM were unharmed but he could not make new LTMs.

Strengths and weakness of MSM
- Historically important as first testable model of memory.
- MSM is an oversimplification – STM is not just one store (see WMM), LTM isn't one store either (semantic, episodic and procedural memories).
- STM and LTM are not entirely independent as STM uses meanings from LTM in chunking.
- Evidence for MSM lacks validity, e.g. limited samples and lacking everyday relevance.

ALTERNATIVES TO THE MULTI-STORE MODEL

THE LEVELS OF PROCESSING APPROACH

- Craik and Lockhart suggested that lasting memories were a by-product of processing.
- Processing information deeply (using meaning) results in better memory than shallow processing.

EVALUATION

Research support
- Craik and Tulving showed that shallow processing (structure) produced the worst recall, deep or 'semantic' processing (meaning) the best, with phonemic processing (sound) in between.
- Organising information causes deep processing so improves recall (Mandler)
- Elaborating information causes deep processing so improves recall (Palmere et al.).

Criticisms
- Morris et al. showed that the level of processing has to be transfer-appropriate, i.e. within the relevant domain to improve recall (e.g. phonemic processing only helps if recall is phonemic).
- 'Deep processing produces better memory' is circular, although defining depth using organisation, distinctiveness, elaboration and effort resolves this criticism.

THE WORKING MEMORY MODEL

- Baddeley and Hitch suggested that 'working memory' holds the information for dealing with a current task.
- The central executive is the part of WM that allocates resources.
- The phonological loop (PL) is for auditory information. It can store the order of information (phonological store) or the sound of words (articulatory process).
- The visuo-spatial sketchpad (VSSP) holds visual and spatial information. Can be divided into visual cache and inner scribe.
- The episodic buffer is a general store which holds and transfers information between the other stores and LTM.

EVALUATION

Research support
- Baddeley et al. showed that the VSSP and PL were separate because it was hard to track a light (visual) and describe angles (spatial) at the same time, i.e. WMM can explain dual task performance.
- Dolcos et al. used fMRI to show that different brain areas were active when using different stores.
- Shallice and Warrington found the amnesic KF's VSSP was better than his PL.

Criticisms
- WMM is limited to explaining STM.
- The subsystems describe but don't explain anything.
- The central executive may not be one structure; the functions may be spread over several brain areas.

THE ROLE OF EMOTION IN MEMORY

ENHANCED MEMORY – FLASHBULB MEMORIES

- Better memory for emotional events when remembering them could help survival so can be explained by evolutionary theory.
- A flashbulb memory (FB) is a lasting memory of the context in which the memory was made, e.g. who told you about the attack on the World Trade Centre.

EVALUATION

- Brown and Kulik found FBs of black and white Americans were stronger for famous assassinations/attempted assassinations of people of their own ethnicity. This suggests FBs are well recalled because they relate to personally relevant emotional events.
- Wright found that five months after a disaster at Hillsborough football stadium people's memories were vague even though it was an emotional event, so the memories had probably been reconstructed.
- Sheingold and Tenney found that people had good memories for details about the birth of a sibling (e.g. when they were told and by whom), but this is hard to check.
- Conway et al. showed that FBs differ from everyday memories as they are important to the individual. Participants from the UK, but not those from other countries, recalled details surrounding Mrs Thatcher's resignation 11 months after the event.

IMPAIRED MEMORY – REPRESSION

- Suppression is where memories are consciously or semi-consciously pushed from the mind.
- Repression is an unconscious mechanism which Freud said protects the ego by making us unaware of traumatic memories.
- These can affect conscious thinking, e.g. through disordered behaviour and the associated anxiety may emerge from the unconscious in dreams.

EVALUATION

- Mood can cue recall. Imagining a sad mood makes recall of sad events more likely than happy ones (Eich et al.).
- Williams interviewed women who had been sexually assaulted in childhood. 54% either could not recall, or had previously been unable to recall, the earlier abuse.
- Event-specific amnesia has been reported in murderers (Bower) and war veterans (Karon and Widener). Therapy alleviated the mental illnesses suffered by war veterans by helping them to recall repressed memories of their battlefield traumas.
- Repressed memory therapy may help people by recovering childhood memories of abuse but has been criticised for creating false memories.
- Loftus and Pickrell showed that childhood memories could be implanted in their 'lost in the mall' study.

IMPAIRED MEMORY – DEPRESSION

- In depression, the negative mood biases recall so unhappy memories are more likely to be recalled (making the depression worse).
- Lyketsos suggests that depressed people may be inattentive so are less likely to form long-term memories of events.
- Biochemical differences between depressed and non-depressed people may make memory processes less effective in depression.

EVALUATION

- Antikainen et al. found that people with untreated depression have poor memories. After treatment, those whose depression had lifted were better on memory tasks and day-to-day recall.

GENERAL EVALUATION

- Biological factors can affect memory directly.
- Stress hormones given before learning can improve performance, e.g. cortisol (Buchanan and Lovallo).
- Depressed women had small hippocampuses and poorer memory than non-depressed ones (Sheline et al.). High cortisol levels in depression may shrink the hippocampus causing poor memory.
- Both Freud's ideas and the biological explanations are determinist.

EXPLANATIONS OF FORGETTING

FORGETTING IN STM

Decay theory
- Stored information can be thought of as an engram (physical memory trace). If this trace is not rehearsed it decays (disappears).

Displacement theory
- STM has limited capacity so new information will displace (overwrite) old information if STM is full.

EVALUATION

- Peterson and Peterson found STM only lasts 20 seconds suggesting it decays but the consonant syllables might have been displaced by the counting used to prevent rehearsal.
- Reitman solved this by diverting attention to prevent rehearsal. This also caused forgetting, supporting decay theory but displacement could still have occurred.
- Waugh and Norman used the serial probe technique. Participants recalled the number following a probe best when it was near the end of a list with fewer numbers after it that could have displaced it.
- Recall was also better for numbers presented quickly, which can only be explained by decay. Displacement is more significant but decay occurs too.
- Many studies are lab-based and only related to some aspects of memory.

FORGETTING IN LTM

Decay theory
- Forgetting in brain-damaged people could be caused by loss of memory traces.
- Lashley damaged rats' brains after they had learned mazes. The more brain he removed, the more the rats forgot the maze, supporting physical decay of memory.

Interference theory
- Past learning can interfere with new memories and cause forgetting – proactive interference.
- Alternatively, new learning can interfere with old memories and cause forgetting – retroactive interference.
- Underwood compared recall of consecutively learned word lists. Old lists inhibited the recall of new ones (proactive interference) and new lists inhibited the recall of old ones (retroactive interference).

Cue dependent forgetting
- Memories may be available but inaccessible because of a lack of cues. This is cue-dependent forgetting.
- Context-dependent forgetting happens if external cues (e.g. people or places) that were present during learning are absent at recall.
- Abernethy found that students tested by the same instructor and in the same room as when they learned a course had better recall than if these cues were absent. Smell can act as a retrieval cue (Aggleton and Waskett).
- State-dependent forgetting happens if internal cues (e.g. mood) that were present during learning are different at recall.
- Goodwin et al. found that sober people forgot where they had put things when drunk but remembered when drunk again.
- Exercise acts as state cues for memory (Miles and Hardman).

EVALUATION

- Baddeley and Hitch's natural experiment supported the interference rather than decay theory as rugby players who had played more games forgot more about the games over the season.
- Tulving and Psotka found that learning more lists worsens free recall of all the lists (retroactive interference). However, if recall is cued, there is no difference suggesting the information is available but inaccessible so interference must occur during retrieval.

EXPLANATIONS FOR DISORDERS OF MEMORY

EXPLANATIONS OF AMNESIA

The loss of explicit memory
- Amnesics are better at implicit memory tasks (not requiring conscious recollection) than explicit ones (conscious recollection) (Schacter).
- This explains why amnesics can do procedural memory tasks but not ones testing declarative (fact-related) memory, and why HM could do the Gollin test and learned to mirror-draw but didn't know he could do it.

Inability to consolidate new memory
- Anterograde amnesia (like HM had) prevents new LTMs forming; retrograde amnesia prevents the recall of old LTMs.
- Issac and Mayes showed amnesics could retrieve memories but not consolidate them as they were as good as controls at cued recall and recognition.
- In retrograde amnesia, the temporal gradient describes how older memories are easier to recall than more recent ones. This suggests that consolidation has been disrupted. This can arise from hippocampal damage (e.g. in HM's case).

EVALUATION

Explicit and implicit memory
- Stickgold et al. used 'Tetris' to show that amnesics could learn a new task (implicit memory) but not recall doing so (explicit memory).
- Schacter et al. found that amnesics cannot always learn implicitly – they did not benefit from repetition of word pairs using the same voice as control participants did.
- The implicit/explicit memory distinction describes rather than explains memory function in amnesia.
- Ryan et al. offer an explanation – amnesics lack relational memory binding – which links related information – which is why they fail to connect the implicit and explicit aspects of a task.

Consolidation
- Gabrieli found that damage to one part of the hippocampus caused anterograde amnesia alone suggesting that the symptoms might be caused by damage in specific brain regions.
- Most amnesic patients have other lesions too, e.g. to the temporal lobe (Reed and Squire).
- Experimental studies of animals suggest that hippocampal damage causes forgetting by preventing consolidation rather than preventing the formation of memories (Remondes and Schman).

EXPLANATIONS OF ALZHEIMER'S DISEASE

β-amyloid and plaques
- A faulty protein (β-amyloid) is produced in the brains of people with Alzheimer's disease (AD).
- β-amyloid builds up between neurons forming plaques which prevent neurons communicating and which damage the cerebral cortex, causing it to shrink.
- Plaque damage affects memory possibly because AD patients are less alert (Berntson et al.) or because β-amyloid interferes with the NMDA neurotransmitter, which is involved in learning (Snyder et al.).

Tangles
- Tau protein builds up in the brains of people with AD.
- It normally supports the structure of neurons but in AD it forms tangles inside the cell bodies of neurons when they die.

Genes
- Several genes associated with AD have been found.
- People with Down's syndrome often have early-onset AD. They have three copies of chromosome 21 and genes for early-onset AD have been found there as well as on chromosomes 1 and 14.
- Genes associated with late-onset AD have been found on chromosome 10.
- These genes affect the production of β-amyloid explaining why some people are more likely to develop AD.

EVALUATION

Plaques and tangles
- The link between plaques and cognitive problems is weak so seems poor as an explanation.
- Murphy and LeVine suggest this is because β-amyloid triggers damage that continues regardless of β-amyloid levels.
- The role of β-amyloid has been studied using animals but they are different from human AD patients in many ways, e.g. loss of cognitive function not comparable and no formation of plaques and tangles.

Genes
- The effect of genes on AD must be small as about half of patients have no relatives who are sufferers (St George-Hyslop).
- Many cultures have similar frequencies of genes for AD but not the same incidence of the disorder (Hendrie). Other factors, such as diet, may be important.
- Injecting rats with β-amyloid disrupts memory (Cleary et al.) showing that it is important, and deterioration in memory is prevented when the immune system is triggered and destroys patients' β-amyloid (Hock et al.).

Question 3 Discuss the role of emotion in memory. *[25]*

Student answer

Paragraph 1 It appears that not only 'facts' or visual detail is saved in a memory but also the emotion aroused at the time the memory event happened. Numerous studies have shown that the most vivid memories are linked with highly emotional events.

Paragraph 2 'Evolution' may show why this is the case. Selye showed with his GAS model that response to events is at first only to do with survival. So we record the level of fear an event causes so we can respond correctly next time ('fight or flight'). Humans have a lot of behavioural flexibility to change or override our natural responses, but at the bottom it is a powerful survival link. Because we are social animals, emotional response when recognising others is important too ('friend or foe'). Cahill and McGaugh (1995) showed that surprising events increased hormone levels and this rise in hormones linked to better memories.

Paragraph 3 Brown and Kulik suggested there were special memories called 'flashbulb memories' that relate to very important moments — do you remember what you were doing when you heard about Princess Di's death? They asked people about the death of Martin Luther King, which was important to Americans like Princess Di's death was here. Black people were more likely to recall what they were doing at the time than white people (a race effect), but they all had strong memories for these emotional events.

Paragraph 4 There is evidence for and against flashbulb memory but Wright (1993) found that these memories were no more accurate than normal ones and subject to the same distortions, so weren't special after all. Anyway, why should Princess Di's death be any more important to you than the first day at school or your granny dying? Sheingold found that personal memories of important events remained consistent over time, but personal memories are likely to be rehearsed anyway when recalling them in conversation, which is the basis of Wright's criticism of FB memory.

Paragraph 5 Memory can be made worse by mood. People diagnosed with clinical depression in a Finnish experiment were worse at memory tests than after they had been treated. It's possible that depressed people don't actually make the memories, rather than simply forgetting them, they just haven't stored the memory. Links between mood and memory can be demonstrated. Eich (1994) did this using the usual lab techniques of recalling a word list. People recalling a word list while thinking they were in a sad mood recalled less words than someone who imagined they were in a good mood.

Paragraph 6 Freud suggested, from his case studies, that some painful memories from childhood were hidden away in the unconscious by the ego, in order to protect you from emotional damage. This is called repression. There is a lot of case study evidence for this but it is almost impossible to test scientifically, as there is no way to independently measure a person's thoughts or feelings, and if they were repressing they couldn't self-report. Williams followed up sexual assault victims 20 years later, showing that a small number of victims of childhood abuse didn't recall their early traumatic experiences till they were adults. 38% didn't recall it at all, 16% had recovered the memory when grown up. This was supporting repression. Loftus showed that these could be false memories however.

Paragraph 7 Neither FB memory or repression have been scientifically verified. It is really difficult to see how they could be.

[562 words]

Examiner comments

This answer is typical of what would be considered as a 'good' essay produced under examination conditions. The immediate impression on reading is that the candidate understands the subject. This is clearly demonstrated in paragraphs 1 and 3. The examiner will not be looking at the lowest mark bands as this response is definitely not muddled!

There is clearly an appropriate range of topics covered so breadth is present, but not a great amount of detail or depth (it is a relatively short essay).

The first question is about the quality of evidence (**A01**). Is the material accurate? Yes it is! While accuracy is present, the level of detail is variable. Some evidence is reported fully, some partly (e.g. Brown and Kulik), and some only vaguely (e.g. Loftus).

This would lead the examiner to consider the 6–7 mark band. While the level of detail might suggest 6 as an appropriate mark, the degree of understanding demonstrated in paragraph 3 sways the decision towards awarding **7 out of 10 marks for A01**.

The second question is about the relevance, structure and quality of the evaluation present (**A02**). The **A02** content is highlighted in grey. Is the evidence relevant? Yes! Is it structured? Yes! Is it limited in detail? Largely not. So immediately the examiner is not looking at the lowest mark bands.

Equally, evaluation is not thorough or elaborated. Some parts are anecdotal (Princess Di) and others are vague or limited (e.g. the final paragraph). So we are not looking at the top mark band either, then.

The examiner is left with the 8–11 mark band. This response is a little short but reasonably well developed, accurate and not far off a very good response. On that basis it is awarded **9 out of 15 marks for A02**.

16/25 places the essay as a low B grade.

Improvement? The candidate has not developed any osf the areas in detail and especially has not developed the evaluation. Specifically there could be more material relating to mood and memory beyond the limited material on depression and memory. So we are suggesting that improvements should be made to the depth of evaluation (more studies and summaries, development of the biology perhaps) and improvements to the detail – a small increase of detail in all areas. The candidate could look at restructuring the evaluation using better techniques (see page 9).

Chapter 4
Relationships

Chapter contents

100 Introduction to the study of relationships
102 The formation of relationships
104 The dissolution of relationships
106 Benefits of relationships on well-being
108 Understudied relationships
110 Cultural variations in relationships

End-of-chapter review

112 Chapter summary
114 Exam question with student answer

Specification breakdown

Explanations relating to the formation of relationships (e.g. sociobiological explanations, attraction, social exchange).	In a profoundly social species such as *Homo sapiens*, interpersonal relationships are perhaps one of the most important areas of study for psychologists. You start your study of relationships by looking at explanations of the formation of such relationships, ranging from the biological to the psychological.
Explanations relating to the dissolution of relationships (e.g. Lee's model, Duck's phase model, predisposing factors).	Psychologists try to detect patterns in human behaviour and in this section the focus is on the common features of relationship dissolution (breakdown). There are two approaches – one is to look at the stages in a relationship that ultimately result in dissolution (stages theories such as Duck's phase model) and the other approach is to consider the common factors that are likely to trigger breakdown (i.e. precipitating factors).
Benefits of relationships on psychological well-being (e.g. self-esteem, buffering effects from stress).	What are the benefits of relationships? There are many, such as playing sports, having a travelling companion or producing children together. However, the focus in this section is particularly on psychological *well-being*, for example how relationships affect the way people feel about themselves (self-esteem) and how relationships help us to cope with life's stresses (buffering effects).
Research relating to understudied relationships (e.g. homosexual relationships, mediated relationships).	The world is always changing and this includes the kind of relationships that are possible or acceptable. Psychologists take a while to catch up with new trends which means that some kinds of relationship are 'understudied'. Two obvious examples are homosexual (or same-sex) relationships and mediated relationships (i.e. relationships conducted through some medium such as the internet or mobile phone).
Cultural variations in relationships (e.g. intra- and inter-cultural variations).	Psychological research has been quite ethnocentric in its outlook and tended to ignore the wider cultural context of human behaviour. In particular there are significant variations in the kind of relationships that are the norm in different cultures. These cultural variations in relationships show both similarities to and differences from Western mainstream culture.

▲ *Your behaviour is determined by many factors – a bit like a layer cake.*

You may find it bewildering when you start this chapter and look at some of the theories of relationships. It might help to begin with a perspective on all the factors that influence our relationships, which are a sort of layer cake if you like. The different 'factors' are related to the different approaches and perspectives in psychology – you are already familiar with the idea of different approaches from your AS studies.

Factor 1 EVOLUTION We are social animals, a system that evolved because living in groups aids survival. Being social means we are primed to have relationships and these relationships have evolved to best fit the environment in which we live. One aspect of such adaptation is the different behaviours observed in men and women. At AS level you studied Buss's research and discovered that our choices in heterosexual mating were universal and predictable as a result of **natural selection**. This set of influences may partly determine our relationships today; men look for good reproductive health (hip–waist ratio, symmetrical looks) and women for good support systems (intelligence, strength, wealth) in men.

Factor 2 BIOLOGICAL INFLUENCES Some scientists (e.g. LeVay, 1991) argue that our sexual orientation, such as homosexuality and heterosexuality, are determined **genetically** (which helps explain evolutionary processes). **Neuroanatomy** and **neurotransmitters** predispose individuals to behave in particular ways and have particular interests. So these biological factors could have an influence on our relationships.

Factor 3 CULTURE The term **culture** refers to the rules, customs, morals and ways of interacting that bind together members of a society or some other collection of people. We acquire culture mostly through observation of those around us and **vicarious reinforcement** (i.e. **social learning**). Culture dictates the nature and limits of our relationships. In many religious groups, marriages are arranged for financial reasons or to unite families in alliances. This is possibly the norm historically, as it would be a way of mixing **gene** pools to avoid inbreeding defects and disorders. Romantic reasons may be a minority taste!

Culture also places boundaries, or even threats, to those whose preferred partners are of the same sex; gay/lesbian relationships are accepted in the Western world but punishable by death in some countries such as Iran.

Factor 4 FAMILY **Freudians** would argue that fathers set the template for their sons' relationships with males in later life, and the same is true for mothers and daughters (though this is an oversimplification of a complex theory). It is certain that most formative events that affect later relationships have their roots in the family experience (see Bowlby's theory of attachment, below).

Factor 5 PERSONAL EXPERIENCES These add a final layer to the factors affecting relationships, as we will see in detail in this chapter.

◄ *The layers of your 'relationship' cake – how you came to be what you are.*

Bowlby's theory of attachment

One view of relationships is that 'love' evolved because it was **adaptive**, i.e. increased the survival and reproduction of humans. Love is a bond between parents to ensure high-quality parental care. Love is also a bond between mother and infant to maintain proximity between them, thus promoting survival of the infant because he or she is protected and fed. Bowlby (1969) called this mother–infant relationship **'attachment'** and suggested that the quality of this early bond set a template for future relationships. He suggested that a mother (or mother substitute) who is sensitive to her child's needs and is reliable creates a *securely attached* child, who will base their own romantic style on this early relationship – a securely attached infant tends to form secure attachments later in life. Similarly, an *insecurely attached* child will tend towards insecure attachments later, for example being fearful of closeness or falling in and out of love easily.

This so-called *'continuity hypothesis'* (a continuity from infant to adult attachments) was tested by Hazan and Shaver (1987). They produced a 'love quiz' that appeared in the *Rocky Mountain News* – some examples are given on the facing page. The full questionnaire consisted of nearly 100 questions and 620 people sent in their answers. As expected, they found that those respondents classed as securely attached infants (on the basis of their quiz answers) had certain beliefs about relationships (e.g. that love is enduring) and tended to have adult relationships based on mutual trust. On the other hand, insecurely attached respondents often described love as 'rare' and tended to fall in and out of love easily. They found relationships less easy and were more likely to be divorced.

STARTER ACTIVITIES

Photo 1

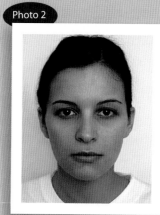

Photo 2

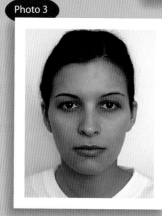

Photo 3

HERE'S LOOKING AT YOU

Which face would you select as the most attractive?

Psychologists have conducted studies using faces such as those on the left. They do this to investigate the babyface hypothesis. Have you ever noticed that most young mammals have the same distinctive facial features (big eyes, large forehead, squashed up nose)? We have been cooing over babies and 'aaahing' over young animals for thousands of years. If you haven't noticed this similarity, Walt Disney certainly did! These features act as a trigger for parenting behaviour and are necessary for a young animal's survival. They elicit our desire to look after and care for babies.

However, the effect doesn't end there. Since we have an innate tendency to find babyface features appealing, this spills over into the way we judge adult faces. This is the babyface hypothesis. People all over the world rate adult faces that have an element of 'babyfaceness' as the most attractive (Langlois and Roggmann, 1990) and also describe people with baby-like faces as being socially, physically and intellectual weak (Zebrowitz, 1997).

The faces on the left were created by 'morphing' an adult woman's face with an average child's face (formed by averaging four child photos). Photo 1 is 50% child 50% adult, photo 2 is 20% child 80% adult and photo 3 is 0% child 100% adult.

In a study using sets of faces similar to these only a few participants (9.5%) rated the totally adult face as being most attractive. Most of the participants preferred female faces that contained childlike proportions between 10 and 50% (Gründl, 2007).

THE LOVE QUIZ

1. **Which of the following best describes your parents' relationships with each other?**
   (a) My parents have a caring relationship and are affectionate with each other.
   (b) My parents appear to have a good enough relationship with each other but are not especially affectionate.

2. **Which of the following best describes your relationship with your mother/father (select the parent you feel closest to)?**
   (a) My mother/father treats me with respect and is accepting and not demanding.
   (b) My mother/father treats me with respect but is sometimes rejecting.

3. **Select the statement that best describes your experiences of intimacy:**
   (a) I don't often worry about being abandoned or about someone getting too close to me.
   (b) I am nervous when anyone gets too close, and often, romantic partners want me to be more intimate than I feel comfortable being.

4. **Select the statement that best describes your attitudes towards love:**
   (a) Romantic feelings wax and wane but at times they reach the intensity experienced at the start of a relationship.
   (b) Intense romantic love is common at the start of a relationship but rarely lasts.

See answers below.

The Love Quiz: Interpreting your answers

The first two questions assess your infant attachment type and the second two questions represent your adult attachment style. In each case choice (a) is secure attachment and choice (b) is insecure attachment.

THE FORMATION OF RELATIONSHIPS

GENETIC INFLUENCES

DETERMINISM

NATURE AND NURTURE

We may prefer to think of the development of relationships as being based on deep feelings and shared emotions rather than **genetic** factors or similarity. Social psychologists, however, are not usually known for such romanticised views of relationships. The scientific study of how relationships form has shown that, in the initial stages at least, this process may have little to do with shared emotions, and more to do with self-interest.

◀ *Red cheeks, rosy full lips and glossy hair are all signs of youth and reproductive fitness – evolutionarily significant characteristics.*

EXPLANATIONS OF RELATIONSHIP FORMATION

Sociobiological explanations

Sociobiology is the study of social behaviours in terms of **evolutionary** processes. Sociobiologists and evolutionary psychologists explain behaviour in terms of the **adaptive** pressures faced by our distant ancestors millions of years ago in the **environment of evolutionary adaptation** (EEA). These pressures shaped human behaviour at that time and are still active today, unconsciously guiding the mate choice of women and men. The pressures would have been different for men and women because of their different reproductive investments – described as **parental investment**.

Parental investment Human females invest a great deal in their offspring, being pregnant for nine months and providing intense care for their children. As a consequence, the best strategy for women, in evolutionary terms, is to have relatively few offspring over their lifetime and focus their energy on ensuring that any reproduction is successful. It is imperative, therefore, that a female should look for a partner who is able to provide resources for her and her offspring to enhance the likelihood of her reproductive success.

On the other hand, the parental investment of men is low because they can provide sperm at almost no physiological cost. Therefore male reproductive success should be concerned with mating as frequently as possible. However, this will be enhanced if men choose partners who are fertile.

Evolutionarily significant characteristics The facts of parental investment lead us to predict that women will seek signs of resource potential and men will seek signs of fertility. Resource potential is indicated by wealth and power, fertility is demonstrated by youthfulness and healthiness – individuals who are young and healthy are more likely to be fertile. One way to assess youthfulness is in terms of physical appearance, such as smooth skin, white teeth, shiny hair and good muscle tone, which all indicate youthfulness and healthiness.

Characteristics such as smooth skin and glossy hair are also signs of genetic quality, and such signs would be important to both men and women when selecting a mate in order to enhance successful reproduction.

Physical attractiveness As we have just seen, physical characteristics are important in attraction because of their evolutionary significance. People who are physically attractive generally possess characteristics that would in some way guarantee breeding success.

Physical attractiveness may affect initial attraction through a positive **stereotype** – if someone is physically attractive, we attribute other positive characteristics to them as well. They are, for example, perceived as sexually warmer, more sociable and more socially skilled (Feingold, 1992). This is called the **halo effect**. It follows, therefore, that we would be more attracted to physically attractive people, and that physical attractiveness is an important mediating factor in the initial stages of relationship formation.

Stages in the development of a relationship

Thibaut and Kelley believed that there were four stages in the development of a relationship:

Sampling – People consider the potential costs and rewards of a new relationship and compare it with other relationships.

Bargaining – As the relationship develops, partners give and receive rewards.

Commitment – As predictability increases in the relationship, each partner knows how to elicit rewards from the other and costs are lowered.

Institutionalisation – Norms are developed within the relationship of rewards and costs for each partner.

Social exchange theory (Thibaut and Kelley, 1959)

Profit and loss At the centre of this theory is the assumption that all social behaviour is a series of exchanges; individuals attempt to maximise their rewards and minimise their costs. In our society, people exchange resources with the expectation (or at least the hope) that they will earn a profit, i.e. that rewards will exceed the costs incurred. Rewards that we may receive from a relationship include being cared for, companionship and sex. Costs may include effort, financial investment and time wasted (i.e. missed opportunities with others because of being in that particular relationship). Rewards minus costs equal the outcome (a profit or a loss). Social exchange, in line with other 'economic' theories of human behaviour, stresses that commitment to a relationship is dependent on its profitability.

Comparison level In order to judge whether one person offers something better or worse than we might expect from another, Thibaut and Kelley proposed that we develop a **comparison level** (CL), a standard against which all our relationships are judged. Our CL is a product of our experiences in other relationships together with our general views of what we might expect from this particular exchange. If we judge that the potential profit in a new relationship exceeds our CL, the relationship will be judged as worthwhile and the other person will be seen as an attractive partner. If the final result is negative (profit is less than our CL), we will be dissatisfied with the relationship and the other person is thus less attractive. A related concept is the **comparison level for alternatives** (CLalt), where the person weighs up a potential increase in rewards from a different partner, less any costs associated with ending the current relationship. A new relationship can take the place of the current one if its profit level is significantly higher.

EVALUATION

Sociobiological explanations

Research support from personal ads We expect men to look for cues that signify fertility, and that is what was found in personal ads in US newspapers: 42% of males sought a youthful mate compared with 25% of females; 44% of males sought a physically attractive partner compared with 22% of women (Waynforth and Dunbar, 1995). In contrast, we expect women to seek resources, which again was what Waynforth and Dunbar found, and men were more likely to advertise their economic status and earning power.

Research support from cross-cultural studies If the predicted gender differences are genetically determined then we should find that people in different cultures have the same preferences. As you know from your AS studies, Buss (1989) questioned 10,000 people from 37 different cultures and found that more women than men desired mates who were 'good financial prospects', i.e. qualities that were linked to resource acquisition, such as ambition. In contrast, men placed more importance on physical attractiveness and men universally wanted mates who were younger than them – an indication that men valued increased fertility in potential mates.

Is it fertility? Research suggests that men universally seek characteristics in a mate that signify fertility. However, there is an alternative view – there are other features that are universally rated as physically attractive as put forward in the **babyface hypothesis** (see previous spread). Adults may have evolved a preference for 'baby' features because this ensures that we care for our young and, for this reason, such features elicit feelings of attraction.

Is physical attractiveness important? People who are physically attractive gain many advantages, for example research has shown that attractive people get lighter criminal sentences (Stewart, 1980). Other studies have compared essay grades given to attractive and unattractive students (the essays had a photograph attached). The same essay supposedly written by an attractive student got higher grades (Landy and Sigall, 1974). And students rate attractive teachers as nicer, happier and less punitive than unattractive ones (Hunsberger and Cavanagh, 1988).

However, not all research has found that physically attractive people are perceived better. Dermer and Thiel (1975) found that attractive women were judged as egoistic and materialistic. Sigall and Ostrove (1975) found that attractive female criminals whose crime was related to their attractiveness were judged more harshly.

Although you might think that everyone would seek out the most attractive partners on this basis, this may not necessarily be the case. The **matching hypothesis** (Walster *et al.*, 1966) suggests that we are attracted to those individuals who most closely match our perceptions of our own level of attractiveness. Thus, although we may be attracted to physically attractive individuals as potential partners, a compromise is necessary to avoid rejection by our more attractive choices.

Social exchange theory (SET)

Profit and loss The notion of exchange has been used to explain why some women stay in abusive relationships. Rusbult and Martz (1995) argue that when investments are high (e.g. children, financial security) and alternatives are low (e.g. nowhere else to live, no money) this would be considered a profit situation and a woman might choose to remain in such a relationship despite the 'cost' of abuse.

Comparison level Support can be found by looking at how people in a relationship deal with potential alternatives; one way of dealing with such potential threats is to reduce them as a means of protecting the relationship. Simpson *et al.* (2007) asked participants to rate members of the opposite sex in terms of attractiveness; those participants who were already involved in a relationship gave lower ratings. However, SET does not explain why some people leave relationships despite having no alternative, nor does it suggest how great the disparity in CL has to be to become unsatisfactory.

Limitations SET has been criticised for focusing too much on the individual's perspective and ignoring the social aspects of a relationship, such as how partners talk with each other and interpret shared events (Duck and Sants, 1983). The main criticism, however, focuses on the selfish nature of the theory. Are people only motivated to maintain relationships out of hedonistic (selfish) concerns? It is possible that such principles only apply in **individualist** cultures, if at all.

The evolutionary approach

The evolutionary approach is a biological one, suggesting that aspects of human behaviour have been coded into our **genes** because they were or are adaptive. The alternative view is that behaviour is affected by **nurture** – experience and environment, a view proposed by the social approach.

One criticism of the evolutionary approach is that it is **determinist**, i.e. that our genes specify exactly how people will behave. In the case of gender roles, for example, the argument is that genes specify that men have a natural inclination to seek younger women as partners.

However, this determinist criticism is mistaken; evolutionary psychologists suggest that genes only *predispose* us to behave in certain ways but this does not *dictate* what individuals choose to do. Other factors also determine behaviour, such as the **culture** in which we live, and ultimately our personal experiences and decisions. This is an example of **nature** interacting with nurture.

Sex, lies and social exchange

SET has been increasingly applied to exchanges between intimate partners, and several studies have demonstrated that sex is used as an exchange resource in intimate relationships. Such is the importance of sex in the maintenance of romantic relationships that deception becomes a strategic weapon in the exchange process. Marelich *et al.* (2008) surveyed 267 students in the US, finding that men were more likely to use blatant lies (e.g. about caring and/or commitment) to have sex, while women were more likely to have sex to avoid confrontation, gain partner approval and promote intimacy. Such findings show that sexual deception is an important part of the social exchange process, with sex for pleasure and positive relationship outcomes (e.g. approval, commitment) acting as rewards, and unwanted sex and deception consequences (e.g. guilt, lack of trust) as costs.

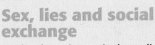

CAN YOU...?   No. **4.1**

1... For each of the **two** explanations presented on the facing page, select about **four** key concepts.

2... For each key concept write **two or three** sentences explaining the concept.

3... Identify about **ten** points of evaluation (these can be positive or negative).

4... Elaborate each point (see page 9).

5... Use all of this material to write an answer to the following exam question: *Describe and evaluate explanations relating to the formation of relationships.* Your answers should contain about 300 words of description and 500 words of evaluation.

Some relationships flourish, some survive in name alone and some fail completely, i.e. they 'dissolve' or break down. In our culture, relationships are considered 'successful' if partners stay together, and those relationships that end 'prematurely' are considered failures. This is despite the fact that ending an unhappy relationship may help each partner to find a new and happy life elsewhere with a new partner.

EXPLANATIONS OF THE DISSOLUTION OF RELATIONSHIPS

Precipitating factors

Duck (2007) suggests that the dissolution of relationships can be explained in terms of 'risk factors', i.e. certain characteristics that make failure more likely. Relationships, according to Duck, are a little like cars, in that both can have 'accidents' for many reasons. Sometimes it is the 'driver's' fault, sometimes it is a mechanical failure that causes the accident and sometimes it is the actions of other road users. Like a car, a poorly maintained relationship is more at risk of breakdown.

A few of these precipitating factors are explained below.

Lack of skills Sometimes, relationships are difficult because people lack the interpersonal skills to make the relationship mutually satisfying. Individuals lacking social skills may be poor conversationalists, poor at indicating their interest in other people, and are likely to be generally unrewarding in their interactions with other people (Duck, 1991). The lack of social skills, therefore, means that others perceive them as not being interested in a relationship, so a relationship tends to break down before it really gets going.

Lack of stimulation According to social exchange theory (see previous spread), people look for rewards in their relationships, one of which is 'stimulation'. We would expect, therefore, that lack of stimulation would be a reason why relationships break down. There is evidence (e.g. Baxter, 1994) that lack of stimulation (e.g. boredom or a belief that the relationship wasn't going anywhere) is often quoted when breaking off a relationship. People expect relationships to change and develop, and when they do not this is seen as sufficient justification to end the relationship or begin a new one (i.e. have an affair).

Maintenance difficulties There are clearly some circumstances where relationships become strained simply because partners cannot maintain close contact. Going away to university, for example, places a great strain on existing relationships, and is often responsible for their breakdown (Shaver *et al.*, 1985). Whilst enduring romantic relationships should be strong enough to survive the pressures of decreased daily contact, it is evident that for many this isn't the case.

Stage models of relationship dissolution

Lee's model (1984)

Loren Lee (1984) used a **questionnaire** to investigate personal experiences of the dissolution of premarital, romantic relationships. She collected data from over 100 students and concluded that there were five distinct stages in the process of break-up:

1. ***Dissatisfaction* (D)** One or both partners recognises problems.
2. ***Exposure* (E)** Problems brought out into the open.
3. ***Negotiating* (N)** Attempting to resolve problems by discussing issues raised in E stage.
4. ***Resolution* (R)** Partners try to resolve problems from N stage.
5. ***Termination* (T)**.

Lee found that stages E and N were the most intense and exhausting parts of this process. Not all couples went through all five stages. Those who went straight from D to T (i.e. just walked out) reported having felt less intimate with their partners even when the relationships were satisfactory. People whose journey from D to T was particularly protracted reported more attraction to their former partners and the greatest loneliness following the break-up.

Rollie and Duck's model (2006)

Keeping it personal The process begins when one of the partners becomes distressed with the way the relationship is conducted (*breakdown*). This leads to an *intrapsychic process* characterised by a brooding focus on the relationship. During this phase, nothing is said to the partner, although the dissatisfied partner may express dissatisfaction in other ways, e.g. in a personal diary entry.

Some people will end relationships without discussing their dissatisfaction with their partners. The promise of 'I'll call you' or 'Let's stay friends' often disguises a deeper dissatisfaction with the other person as a romantic partner. In the *dyadic process*, people confront their partners and begin to discuss their feelings and the future. At this stage, the relationship might be saved or partners begin to involve others in their dissatisfaction.

Going public Up to this point, partners might have kept their dissatisfaction fairly private, but it now spills over to a network of friends and family as it reaches the *social process*. Others may take sides, offer advice and support, or help in mending any disputes between the two sides. Alternatively, friends/family may speed the partners towards dissolution through revelations about one or other of the partners.

Once breakdown occurs, partners attempt to justify their actions. This *grave-dressing process* is important as each partner must present themselves to others as being trustworthy and loyal, key attributes for future relationships. In this phase, people may strategically reinterpret their views of their partners. For example, they may have been attracted to their partner's 'rebellious' nature, but now label that characteristic as 'irresponsibility'. In the *final resurrection process* each partner prepares themselves for new relationships by redefining themselves and building on past mistakes and experiences.

BREAKDOWN Dissatisfaction with relationship *Threshold: I can't stand this any more*
INTRAPSYCHIC PROCESSES Social withdrawal Brooding on partner's 'faults' and relational 'costs' Re-evaluation of alternatives to relationship *Threshold: I'd be justified in withdrawing*
DYADIC PROCESSES Uncertainty, anxiety, hostility, complaints Discuss dissatisfactions Talk about 'our relationship'; equity, roles Reassessment of goals, possibilities, commitments *Threshold: I mean it*
SOCIAL PROCESSES Going public; support seeking from third parties Speak badly of partner, alliance building Social commitment, outside forces create cohesion *Threshold: It's now inevitable*
GRAVE-DRESSING PROCESSES Tidying up memories; making relational histories Stories prepared for different audiences Saving face *Threshold: Time to get a new life*
RESURRECTION PROCESSES Recreating sense of own social value Defining what to get out of future relationships Preparation for a different sort of relational future *Reframing of past relational life: What I learned and how things will be different*

▲ *A summary of Rollie and Duck's model of relationship breakdown.*

EVALUATION

Precipitating factors

Extramarital affairs A major reason why relationships break down is that one or both partners have an extramarital affair. Boekhout *et al.* (1999) showed how such affairs might be a direct reaction to the perceived lack of skills and/or stimulation in the current relationship. They asked undergraduates to rate various sexual and emotional reasons for men and women to be unfaithful in a committed relationship. Participants judged that sexual reasons for infidelity (e.g. sexual excitement, boredom, variety) would be more likely to be used by men, whereas emotional reasons for infidelity (e.g. lack of attention, lack of commitment, emotional satisfaction) would be more likely to be used by women.

Maintenance difficulties Long-distance romantic relationships (LDRR) and long-distance friendships (LDF) are perhaps more common than we think. One study found that 70% of students sampled had experienced at least one LDRR and that 90% had experienced one LDF (Rohlfing, 1995). The fact that in our mobile society people do have to move and do become separated from family, friends and/or partners means that it is useful to understand the management strategies that people use. For example, Holt and Stone (1988) found that there was little decrease in relationship satisfaction as long as lovers are able to reunite regularly.

Lee's model

Research support The model is based on Lee's research though this was restricted to certain kinds of relationships (premarital) and a young participant base (students). Therefore it may not be relevant to marital break-ups where there is more invested – financially and socially.

Criticisms of stage models Both of the stage models described on the facing page are more descriptions than explanations of why relationships break down, whereas the 'precipitating factors' approach provides greater explanatory power. However, such descriptions can be useful, for example they can be used in marriage guidance to identify the stage of dissolution and develop appropriate repair strategies for that stage.

Rollie and Duck's model

Research support Rollie and Duck's model is supported by observations of real-life break-ups. Tashiro and Frazier (2003) surveyed undergraduates who had recently broken up with romantic partners. They typically reported that they had not only experienced emotional distress, but also personal growth. These students reported that breaking up with their partners had given them new insights into themselves and a clearer idea about future partners. Through grave-dressing and resurrection processes they were able to put the original relationships to rest and get on with their lives.

Implications for intervention Rollie and Duck's model stresses the importance of *communication* in relationship breakdown. By paying attention to the things that people say, the topics that they discuss and the ways in which they talk about their relationship, the model offers both an insight into their stage in the process and also suggests interventions appropriate to that stage.

   If the relationship was in the intrapsychic process for example, repair might involve re-establishing liking for the partner, perhaps by re-evaluating their behaviour in a more positive light. In the later stages, different strategies of repair are appropriate. For example, people outside the relationship may help the partners patch up their differences.

Comparing the stage models Lee's version focuses mainly on the various processes when there is still hope that the relationship can be saved, whereas Duck's model is more concerned with processes after it is clear the relationship has ended. It is possible that a combination of the two models would provide a more adequate account of relationship break-up than either model on its own.

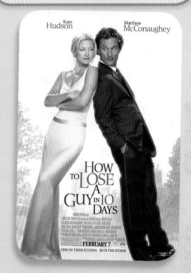

▲ *Most films are about the formation of relationships, but in this one Andie Anderson (Kate Hudson) tries all sorts of tactics to end her relationship with Benjamin Barry (Matthew McConaughey).*

CAN YOU...?   No. 4.2

1... **Three** explanations of the dissolution of relationships are provided on this spread. For each explanation write **one or two** sentences outlining the explanation (do not list the factors or stages because they're in Q2!).

2... Write a sentence or two explaining each factor/stage.

3... Identify about **ten** points of evaluation (these can be positive or negative).

4... Elaborate each point (see page 9).

5... Use all of this material to write an answer to the following exam question: *Discuss explanations relating to the dissolution of relationships*. Your answer should contain about 300 words of description and 500 words of evaluation.

Don't forget to read the essay-writing guidance on pages 8–9.

BENEFITS OF RELATIONSHIPS ON WELL-BEING

We invest a lot in a relationship, so what do we get back? It seems that we benefit in terms of mental and physical health. Two key ways in which relationships can influence our mental health are through the effect they have on our self-esteem and the extent to which they buffer (protect) us from the effects of stress.

There are a number of self-esteem tests (or 'scales') available, such as the Rosenberg Self-Esteem Scale used in the study by Krause (see below). You can use the scale yourself at www.wwnorton.com/college/psych/psychsci/media/rosenberg.htm.

Interviews and questionnaires

One of the studies on self-esteem used interviews to collect data while another used questionnaires.

In the study by Krause (1987) people were *interviewed* at the start of the study. The interviewers asked about emotional support (e.g. empathy, caring, love and trust), tangible help (e.g. financial, transport or household assistance) and informational support (knowledge about ways to cope better – or insights that may help). Support provided to others was also measured (as the individual may gain from helping). At the end of the study the *Rosenberg Self-Esteem* (RSE) scale was used, in which participants rate the relevance of statements such as 'I feel I do not have much to be proud of'.

Symister and Friend (2003) collected data about social support using *questionnaires*. The participants completed questionnaires at the start of the study and again three months later. These provided information about social support, problematic support ('help' which is viewed negatively by the recipient) and self-esteem. In addition, depression and optimism were measured to indicate how well adjusted the patient was.

Questionnaires feel more anonymous than interviews so may produce more honest responses. However, they are also easier to drop out of, as shown by the fact that Krause retained more of his sample than Symister and Friend.

Increased self-esteem

Self-esteem is the evaluation you have of yourself – whether you think highly of yourself or not. Research has generally shown that high self-esteem is associated with being successful at school, your job and so on. One source of self-esteem is the social support provided by relationships.

Social support and self-esteem The effects of social support on self-esteem were demonstrated in a study by Krause (1987), looking at retired participants aged 65–95 years (see details on the left). Krause also found that the increased social support led to a decrease in **depression**. This effect was largely due to the influence of emotional support and its effect on feelings of self-worth and, to a lesser extent, on informational support (e.g. being given advice about coping strategies). This shows how important it is to mobilise social support in the elderly.

Interaction with stress It seems that the beneficial effects of social support on self-esteem may only be found in people who are stressed. This was the conclusion reached by Druley and Townsend (1998) who studied both healthy and unhealthy people but found that self-esteem only improved in the unhealthy people. This may be because we rely on other people most when feeling stressed, due to the incapacity of illness. Symister and Friend (2003) further explored the effect of social support on self-esteem in unhealthy participants in a study of 86 patients with kidney failure. For these patients social support was found to increase self-esteem which, in turn, increased optimism and reduced depression.

Buffering from stress

Stress has a damaging effect on health, as you know from your AS studies of Selye's **general adaptation syndrome**. Research has shown that social support can act as a buffer against these damaging effects. For example, Kamark *et al.* (1990) gave participants a series of stressful tasks and assessed their physiological reactions. Some participants completed the tasks with a friend sitting next to them whereas others were alone. Those who were with a friend showed lower physiological responses, i.e. less stress.

The main (or direct) effect hypothesis suggests that psychological well-being is **correlated** with social support because our relationships with acquaintances, friends or partners are, in themselves, rewarding. This could provide a sense of belonging or boost our self-esteem so we benefit regardless of whether or not we are under stress. Conversely, an absence of social support is stressful so would be the cause (rather than consequence) of ill health. If so, relationships would benefit health regardless of stress level. The main effect hypothesis therefore predicts that people with stronger social networks should be healthier regardless of the stressors they encounter.

The buffering hypothesis suggests that psychological well-being is correlated with social support only because our relationships protect us from the negative effects of stress. People in our social network could boost our coping through emotional, tangible or informational support. According to this hypothesis, social support acts like a vaccination – you don't seem any different from someone without that advantage until there is a significant threat (an infection) when it protects you against the disease. Likewise, the buffering effects of social support only become apparent when the stressed individual's own resources are insufficient.

▶ *According to the main effect hypothesis, social support helps us at all levels of stress, as shown in diagram (a), whereas the buffering hypothesis predicts that social support helps to protect health most when stress levels are high, as shown in diagram (b).*

— Low social support
-- High social support

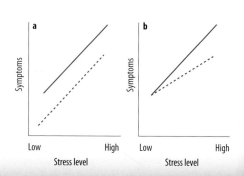

Measuring social support

Social support in itself can be difficult to measure. One technique is to look at the structure of an individual's social network, i.e. the number of people they can rely on for support. This indicates perceived support – the extent to which they could obtain help if they wanted it. When social support is assessed in this way, findings tend to support the main effect hypothesis. Alternatively, social support can be measured in functional terms, i.e. the extent to which support is actually received. When social support is assessed functionally, findings tend to support the buffering hypothesis.

EVALUATION

Increased self-esteem

Methodological issues Krause (1987) used an elderly sample. In such individuals we might expect that their ability to accurately recall events was poor, as recall declines with age. This might be a potential problem because the second interview required remembering stressful events from the past year. However, as there is little loss of memory for highly salient events (Brown and Harris, 1982), and these are the most important to psychological well-being, it is unlikely that forgetting threatened the **validity** of the study.

A further issue with Krause's study is that self-esteem was only measured at the end of the study. It is possible that older adults with high self-esteem are more likely to seek out and receive social support than those with lower self-esteem. This means that the reason high self-esteem was associated with social support was not because social support caused increased self-esteem but the other way round. This is a threat to the validity of the study.

Negative effects In some instances, social relationships can be disadvantageous. For example, Revenson et al. (1991) found that patients who reported social support that was more problematic (e.g. difficult relationships) also had higher rates of depression. Pagel et al. (1987) found that carers who experienced problems within their social network were also more depressed. The important point is that not all relationships provide beneficial support.

Buffering from stress

The main effect hypothesis Lin et al. (1979) asked participants about their interactions with friends, neighbours and their community. Individuals with higher levels of social contact had lower levels of psychiatric symptoms irrespective of their stress levels, supporting the main effect hypothesis. Importantly, social support was more closely linked to symptoms than **life events**, indicating the value of relationships across the spectrum of stress. However, this was a correlational study, so it is possible that individuals with worse psychiatric symptoms found it more difficult to establish or maintain social contacts.

Bell et al. (1982) also showed that a strong social network (being married, having friends and relatives nearby, attending church and belonging to clubs or organisations) was associated with better mental health (lower depression scores). This effect was irrespective of stress levels, so supported the main effect hypothesis.

The buffering hypothesis There is also research that supports the buffering hypothesis. For example, DeLongis et al. (1988) investigated the stress levels, self-esteem and the health of 75 married couples. Those individuals in unsupportive relationships (that is, with low social support and low self-esteem) became more ill in stressful situations than did the individuals in supportive relationships with high self-esteem. This supports the buffering hypothesis as it shows that social support matters most when stress levels are high.

In another study, Pearlin et al. (1981) investigated the stress of unemployment. They found that social support from a spouse or other confidant was related to lower symptoms of stress in unemployed individuals (who would be experiencing high stress). This again supports the buffering hypothesis. They also found that individuals who were well supported were less depressed and had higher self-esteem than those with only moderate or weak levels of support.

We can consider the benefits of relationships by looking at the flip side – what are the effects of a lack of relationships, such as divorce or the death of a partner. Such research also highlights the fact that relationships are not always beneficial. For example, Bradburn (1969) found that people who were separated, divorced or widowed were less happy (7%) than people who were never married (18%). This shows that the breakdown of relationships has a negative effect on happiness.

The effects go beyond 'mere' happiness. For example, Cochrane (1988) analysed data on admissions to UK mental hospitals and found the largest group was the divorced, with men being slightly more affected than women. In terms of physical health, Lynch (1977) found that unmarried people (single, divorced or widowed) were much more likely than married individuals of the same age to die from several kinds of physical conditions (e.g. diabetes, stroke, various cancers). People who are divorced or widowed have a particularly high risk of dying prematurely (Johnson et al., 2000). These results are widespread across the world.

It may be that the observed effects are not just due to the lack of a relationship but also the disruption and grief that goes along with divorce or death of a partner. Indeed, Kiecolt-Glaser and Glaser (1986) found poorer immune functions in people suffering marital disruption.

Effects on health are less likely if the individual was the instigator of the divorce, had high self-esteem, has a strong social network and tolerates change well (Buunk, 1996).

CAN YOU...?　　No. 4.3

1... Select **two** (or more) benefits of relationships and for each identify **three** studies/concepts.

2... For each study/concept write **two or three** sentences explaining the concept.

3... Identify about **ten** points of evaluation (these can be positive or negative).

4... Elaborate each point (see page 9).

5... Use all of this material to write an answer to the following exam question: *Describe and evaluate research relating to the benefits of relationships on psychological well-being.* Your answer should contain about 300 words of description and 500 words of evaluation.

Remember that, when writing an essay, you can include material from other spreads – but only if it is made specifically relevant to the essay. For example, in an essay on the benefits of relationships, you can consider any kind of relationship and any kind of benefit on well-being – as long as this can be linked to psychological research. In Chapter 6 we look at the benefits of marriage on health (see pages 8–9), research that could be used in an essay on the benefits of relationships.

UNDERSTUDIED RELATIONSHIPS

For many years mainstream social psychological research tended to concentrate on face-to-face, romantic love relationships among heterosexuals in contemporary Western cultures. The term 'understudied relationships', coined from Wood and Duck's 1995 book of the same name, concerns relationships that fall outside that relatively narrow focus of research. This includes same-sex relationships and the increasing phenomenon of relationships conducted through computer 'mediated' communications, such as the internet, email and mobile phones.

There are other 'understudied relationships' that you could consider, such as arranged marriages (see next spread).

Relationship quality in heterosexual and same-sex relationships

Kurdek and Schmitt (1987) surveyed heterosexual and same-sex couples (79 married or cohabiting heterosexual couples, 50 gay and 56 lesbian couples). Respondents were asked about demographic details (e.g. age, income, education and job prestige) to determine similarity. They were also asked about the quality of their relationships. For all groups partner age was correlated, i.e. couples tended to be of the same age. In fact, for gay couples this was the only significantly correlated variable. In all other groups, partner income and education were also correlated. Partner scores for all couple types also correlated for 'shared decision making' – which contributes to relationship maintenance. However, in terms of 'love for the partner' only gay and lesbian couples' results were correlated. Measures of relationship quality were higher for lesbian couples than any other group. So, in some respects same-sex relationships are similar to heterosexual ones, in others they are different, and gay couples are the least similar to each other whereas lesbian couples were the most similar.

RESEARCH RELATING TO SAME-SEX RELATIONSHIPS

Similarity

There is mixed support for similarity in same-sex couples. Kurdek's early study (Kurdek and Schmitt, 1987, see left) found that there was very little similarity in gay couples, except for age. On the other hand, a later study by Kurdek (2003) found that partners within gay and lesbian couples were similar in terms of age, education and income. This study involved 80 gay couples and 53 lesbian couples studied from 1986 to 2000.

Duration

In general there is an expectation that same-sex relationships have a shorter duration than heterosexual ones. Blumstein and Schwartz (1983) found that 48% of lesbian and 36% of gay couples broke up within two years of being interviewed, compared with 29% of heterosexual cohabitees and 14% of married couples. Gottman et al. (2003), however, found a similar rate of dissolution to heterosexual couples, of 20%, in a 12-year study of same-sex couples.

In the study by Blumstein and Schwartz (above) gay relationships were less stable than lesbian or heterosexual ones. We might expect this to be the case because men and women are socialised differently and men find sex without emotional commitment more acceptable than do women. However, a number of studies have found the reverse. Kurdek (2003) found that lesbian relationships were shorter than those of gay men (16 versus 18 years together) and Gottman et al. (2003) also found most dissolutions were between lesbians.

Relationship satisfaction

Kurdek and Schmitt found that gay and lesbian couples reported similar levels of love for each other, which was not true for heterosexual couples. Gottman et al. found that, as in heterosexual relationships, gay and lesbian couples were more satisfied when the partners identified more benefits (e.g. companionship) and fewer costs (e.g. conflict).

EXPLANATIONS OF MEDIATED RELATIONSHIPS

Most relationships include some 'mediated' communication, i.e. interaction that is not face to face (FtF), such as writing letters or more recent 'computer-mediated communication' (CMC) including text messages, instant messages, email and use of the internet such as chat rooms or social networking sites. CMC, it has been argued, is less 'complete' than FtF interaction – although Plato raised similar objections to writing taking the place of speech!

Reduced cues theory

As CMC is text-based, it lacks physical and social cues such as eye contact and the stress, tempo and volume of speech. The *reduced cues theory* of CMC (Culnan and Markus, 1987) suggests that this makes CMC less effective than FtF interaction in the development of relationships. This would make sense, as we have seen earlier in the chapter, that factors such as facial expressions, physical attractiveness and abilities, such as conversational skills, are important in relationship formation and maintenance.

Culnan and Markus (1987) also suggest that having fewer cues leads to **deindividuation** (a lack of individual identity) that fosters anti-normative and uninhibited behaviours. As CMC may lack shared social norms, users may be more aggressive and impulsive in their

communications. This, in addition to the difficulty of indicating emotions (because of reduced cues), makes CMC less effective for developing relationships than FtF interaction.

Social identity model of deindividuation effects (SIDE)

SIDE suggests that CMC is not impersonal. It proposes that a **social identity** is created when people belong to groups (i.e. your identity is influenced by the group identity). This can produce deindividuation because of the anonymity of belonging to a group. The anonymity and deindividuation in turn strengthen social identity. As reduced cues hide individual differences in CMC, the limited, stereotyped information that is available causes people to rely on perceived similarities, so a strong social identity develops. According to SIDE, therefore, CMC will *help* relationships to form within the group.

SIDE can also explain a problem with CMC relationships. As social identity becomes more important, people internalise group norms, e.g. believing that 'everyone is like this on the internet'. Mason (2008) suggests that this is why cyberbullies ignore the usual social controls on behaviour and become more impulsive and aggressive.

EVALUATION OF RESEARCH RELATING TO SAME-SEX RELATIONSHIPS

Sampling and matching

Kurdek and Schmitt (1987) used well-**matched** samples of different couple types with similar sample sizes, average ages and none had children living with them. Furthermore, the partners in each couple independently described themselves as **monogamous**. However, a mixture of **opportunity** and **volunteer sampling** was used. As a consequence, more of the married sample (93%) were from the American Midwest (the other groups were around 60%) and they had a higher income than all other groups. The married couples had also been living together the longest (52 months on average), the cohabitees the least (25 months) and the gay and lesbian couples an intermediate time (42 and 43 months respectively). The return rate of questionnaires for the different groups was unknown because many were distributed through friendship networks. These issues may have led to biases in the results.

Kurdek's (2003) study also used samples that were well matched. For example, all couples were cohabiting and none were living with children. All participants were recruited in the same way (through advertisements in the gay press). However, some couples were lost from the sample each year and this **attrition** might have biased the sample, for example if they were more likely to be those who were splitting up. The sample was also predominantly white and well educated, so was not representative of the diversity within the gay and lesbian community.

Snapshot versus longitudinal studies

The studies by Kurdek (2003) and Gottman et al. (2003) were both **longitudinal**, benefitting from being able to measure the course of relationships over time. In contrast, **snapshot studies** such as Kurdek and Schmitt (1987) can only assume that those relationships that are most satisfying will survive – which is not necessarily the case.

Subjectivity and objectivity

A key problem in relationship research is that a partner may not be objective in their reporting of their own, or their partner's, behaviour or feelings. For example, although Kurdek (2003) found that lesbians reported greater relationship satisfaction, they were no more likely to avoid dissolution. One explanation for this is that lesbians are more strongly motivated to report the positive aspects of their relationship than are gay men. To overcome subjectivity in reporting, Gottman et al. (2003) used direct observations of emotional behaviours between partners (coding of vocal tone, facial expression and speech content, e.g. stonewalling and whining) and measured physiological changes (pulse rate) during interactions, both of which are more objective measures.

CAN YOU...?   No. 4.4

1... On this spread **two** types of understudied relationships have been examined. For each type write about 200 words describing research studies/explanations.

2... Identify about **five** points of evaluation for each type of understudied relationship (these can be positive or negative).

3... Elaborate each point (see page 9).

4... Use all of this material to write an answer to the following exam question: *Critically consider research relating to understudied relationships.* As good practice you could also answer the following 'building block' essay:
(a) *Discuss research related to homosexual relationships.*
(b) *Discuss research related to mediated relationships.* Your answers should contain about 300 words of description and 500 words of evaluation.

Don't forget to read the essay-writing guidance on pages 8–9.

▲ *An example of mediated communication.*

EVALUATION OF EXPLANATIONS OF MEDIATED COMMUNICATION

Reduced cues theory

According to reduced cues theory, mediated relationships should be less effective than FtF ones. Early research supported this view, showing that CMC groups found it harder to reach a shared point of view (Kiesler and Sproull, 1992), and were more verbally aggressive and blunt (Dubrovsky et al., 1991).

However, users can enrich their communication. Whitty (2003) compared flirting in FtF situations and online. Flirting offline included giggling and facial expressions (e.g. smiling and eyebrow flashes) that cannot be used in CMC, but typing LOL ('laugh out loud'), BG ('big grin') and smiley or winking faces (emoticons) mimics these cues. Indeed, Whitty observed that men might use *more* facial signals in CMC (such as emoticons) than they would FtF.

The speed of a reply also communicates meaning: a quick response can indicate interest, whereas a slow one might feel like a snub. Walther and Tidwell (1995) found that a slow reply to a social message was seen as more intimate and affectionate than an immediate one. So clearly there are ways to express emotions via CMC. Indeed, if CMC were emotion-free, we would be unable to use it to hurt people, but bullying by text and email is increasingly common in schools (Mason, 2008).

If cues matter, differences between CMC and FtF groups should persist, but they do not. Walther (1993) found that experimentally set up groups did not initially form strong opinions about their co-workers when working through CMC, but by the third 'meeting' impressions were just as strong as those in FtF groups.

Social identity model of deindividuation effects (SIDE)

In support of the SIDE, Spears et al. (1990) found that anonymity does strengthen social identity, suggesting that deindividuation in CMC could promote relationship formation within the group. Certainly, CMC is used to enhance relationships, for example Ling (2001) described how young girls text their friends 'good night', consolidating their social network, and Lea and Spears (1995) found that people got to know the friends they had made in chat rooms better than FtF ones they had known for years.

CMC does, however, carry the threat of deception. Investigations of honesty in online environments have shown that women lie to protect their identity, especially in chat rooms. Men lie about their occupation, education and income, as predicted by **evolutionary** explanations of relationship formation (Whitty, 2002; Whitty and Gavin, 2001). Whilst some dishonesty is harmless, or may enhance safety, other examples of deception have led to fatal encounters.

CULTURAL VARIATIONS IN RELATIONSHIPS

CULTURAL BIAS

ENVIRONMENTAL INFLUENCE

NATURE AND NUTURE

In our experiences of relationships, we tend to view the whole process from the perspective of our own **culture**. In particular, our exposure to stories of love and friendship structure what we might expect and how we should act in our relationships with others. However, cultures are not all the same, therefore we might expect many differences in how relationships are viewed and how they are acted out. Psychologists have discovered important differences between Western cultures such as the USA and UK, and non-Western cultures such as India and China.

Culture and romance

Love and romance are viewed as being the stuff that long-term relationships are made of. Indeed, 'falling in love' is viewed as an important part of the process of growing up. Erikson (1968) believed that the establishment of an intimate relationship is an essential task of young adulthood which, if unsuccessful, will lead to social isolation.

Marrying for love is seen as a vital component of long-term relationships in the West, but for Chinese couples, romance and love are less important and are only considered in the light of responsibility towards parents and the family. Spontaneous expression of love, especially in terms of sex outside marriage, is not considered appropriate in Chinese society (Ho, 1986).

Moore and Leung (2001) tested this predicted cultural difference in an Australian study. They compared 212 Anglo-Australian (born in Australia, New Zealand or the UK) and 106 Chinese-Australian (born in Hong Kong or China) students to see if the 'romantic conservatism' of Chinese students would manifest itself in different attitudes toward romance and different romantic styles.

Of the two groups, 61% of the Anglo-Australian students were in a romantic relationship, compared with just 38% of Chinese students.

Chinese students reported significantly more loneliness than Anglo-Australian students.

Anglo-Australian males were less romantic (and more casual about relationships) than were females. However, Chinese males were no less romantic than Chinese females.

Contrary to the stereotypical view that romance is a characteristic only of Western cultures, positive attitudes to romantic love were endorsed by both groups.

WESTERN AND NON-WESTERN RELATIONSHIPS

Voluntary or non-voluntary relationships

A distinguishing feature of many Western cultures is that we live in predominantly urban settings, with relatively easy geographical and social mobility. This ensures that, on a daily basis, we voluntarily interact with a large number of people, many of whom are first acquaintances. Western cultures, therefore, are characterised by a greater 'pool' of potential relationships. Non-Western cultures, on the other hand, have fewer large urban centres and less geographical and social mobility, therefore people have less choice about those they interact with on a daily basis. Interactions with strangers are rare, and relationships are frequently tied to other factors, such as family or economic resources.

Individual or group-based relationships

Western cultures place great importance on the rights and freedom of the individual, with individual happiness and pleasure seen as fundamentally important. Such cultures are described as **individualist** because of their focus on the individual rather than the group. In non-Western cultures, the group tends to be the primary unit of concern. Members of such **collectivist** cultures are encouraged to be interdependent rather than independent. The cultural attitudes of individualist cultures, where individual interests are more highly regarded than group goals and interests, are consistent with the formation of relationships that are based on freedom of choice, whereas collectivism leads to relationships that may have more to do with the concerns of family or group (Moghaddam *et al.*, 1993).

Continuity and discontinuity

Using a comparison of Chinese and North American societies, Hsu (1983) described the Chinese regard for heritage and ancestry, and the suspicion with which change is generally viewed. American culture, on the other hand, emphasises progress, with change seen as inevitable and important. Things that are 'old-fashioned' are viewed with disdain. This cultural difference is consistent with the types of relationship typically found in Western and non-Western cultures. Non-Western cultures that emphasise continuity are therefore likely to be dominated by permanent relationships. Western cultures emphasise change and discontinuity, and therefore tend to favour more temporary relationships.

Norms and rules

Norms are general descriptions of what is considered appropriate behaviour within a particular relationship. These act as guidelines for behaviour and influence how we act out any given relationship. One such norm that plays a key part in personal relationships is the *norm of reciprocity*, i.e. for a benefit received, an equivalent benefit should be returned. Ting-Toomey (1986) found that, in individualist cultures, reciprocity in personal relationships tends to be voluntary, but in collectivist cultures it is more obligatory. In such cultures, failure to return a favour is seen as a failure of one's moral duty. In Japanese culture, for example, there are specific rules about gift-giving and reciprocity, whereas no such formal norms exist in Western cultures.

Rules within a relationship may be explicit (as in the case of a formal marriage) or implicit and difficult to define (as in the case of friendship). **Cross-cultural research** has demonstrated the important role of such rules in relationships in different cultures. Argyle *et al.* (1986) examined the presence and nature of relationship rules in the UK, Italy, Hong Kong and Japan. They found that different rules were seen as being relevant to relationships across the four cultures (e.g. the rules for close friendships), but there were also important similarities. All cultures acknowledged the importance of relationship rules, such as showing courtesy and respect and avoiding social intimacy.

▲ **What's love got to do with it?**
Romantic relationships in different cultures follow quite different patterns. In many Arab cultures men have more than one wife, as in the picture above left of a Rashaidan man with his three wives and children. In Rashadian culture men and women have few chances to meet on their own accord and marriages are usually arranged between families. Often only older men can afford a large dowry of jewelry, camels or cash.

In Ethiopia, Surma brides, above right, are exchanged for cattle. The number of cattle is determined by the size of the clay lip plate. This plate is inserted six months before marriage. Successive stretching is achieved by placing increasingly larger plates into the lip. The final size of the lip indicates how many cattle are required for her hand in marriage.

EVALUATION

Voluntary or non-voluntary relationships

In societies with reduced mobility 'non-voluntary' or arranged marriages make good sense and seem to work well. Divorce rates are low for such marriages, and, even more surprising, in perhaps about half of them the spouses report that they have fallen in love with each other (Epstein, 2002). Myers *et al*. (2005) studied individuals in India living in arranged marriages. No differences in marital satisfaction were found when compared with individuals in non-arranged marriages in the USA.

However, in some rapidly developing cultures, such as China, there has been a noticeable increase in 'love matches', i.e. a move away from traditional 'arranged' marriages. In China, instances in which parents dominate the process of partner choice have declined from 70% prior to 1949, to less than 10% in the 1990s. What effect has this had on marital satisfaction? A study of women in Chengdu, China found that women who had married for love felt better about their marriages (regardless of duration) than did women who experienced arranged marriages (Xiaohe and Whyte, 1990).

Individual or group-based relationships

Although we might expect relationships based on love to produce more compatible partners, this may not necessarily be the case. Parents may be in a better position to judge compatibility in the long term, whereas young people may be 'blinded by love' and overlook areas of personal incompatibility that will become apparent later. However, contrary to this view, in Xiaohe and Whyte's study, freedom of mate choice appeared to promote marital *stability* rather than instability.

Continuity and discontinuity

The Western shift to more discontinuous and non-permanent relationships is relatively recent. Fifty years ago, divorce was rare in the West and extended family groups more common (for example, according to the Statistical Office of the European Communities, divorce rates for British women were 2 per 1000 in 1960 rising to just over 12 per 1000 in 2007). This marks a shift within Western society that may again be related to greater urbanisation and mobility, indicating that the significant distinction may not be Western/non-Western or individualist/collectivist but an urban/non-urban one.

Norms and rules

Argyle *et al*.'s cross-cultural comparison of relationship rules in different cultures (Argyle *et al*., 1986) did find support for some predictions (e.g. rules concerning intimacy) but failed to support others (e.g. the claim that Japanese placed more importance on formalised gift exchange than the British). However, a problem with this research is that the list of rules was formulated in the UK, and may have failed to include rules that are specific to a particular culture, such as Japan.

Research on cross-cultural differences is valuable for understanding how to successfully conduct relationships that cross cultural boundaries. Knowledge of the norms and rules underlying relationships is an important aspect of any attempt to understand and improve relations between different cultural groups within a host country.

The importance of culture

One reason why social psychologists have traditionally ignored culture in their study of human relationships is because of their preoccupation with the experimental method and with US students as the unit of study. Lab experiments, through the manipulation of isolated variables, are seen as the most rigorous way of establishing cause and effect, and the best way of furthering our understanding of the processes involved in human relationships. However, as Hogg and Vaughan (2008) point out, people do bring their cultural 'baggage' into the laboratory. Although cultural background may be seen as a problematic extraneous variable to some researchers, it is clear that culture itself is an important variable that influences the relationship processes being studied.

Is love a universal evolutionary adaptation?

Pinker (2008) views romantic love as a 'human universal' that has evolved to promote survival and reproduction among human beings. Being in a long-term committed relationship offers lower mortality rates, increased happiness and decreased stress. As a result, there is a clear **adaptive** value to being in a long-term relationship, but how necessary is love? For romantic love to be an evolved adaptation, it should be experienced everywhere among human groups. Research has shown that romantic love is not exclusive to Western cultures, but is also found in many non-Western cultures. For example, Jankowiak and Fischer (1992) searched for evidence of romantic love in a sample of non-Western tribal societies. They found clear evidence of romantic love in 90% of the 166 cultures studied. Evidence for the universality of romantic love also comes from Bartels and Zeki (2000), who claim to have discovered a 'functionally specialised system' that lights up during **fMRI scans** of brains of people who claim to be in love.

CAN YOU...?   No. **4.5**

1... For each of the **four** cultural variations listed on the facing page, identify **two** key issues/concepts.

2... For each key issue/concept write **two** or **three** sentences explaining it.

3... Identify about **ten** points of evaluation (these can be positive or negative).

4... Elaborate each point (see page 9).

5... Use all of this material to write an answer to the following exam question: *Critically consider cultural variations in relationships.* Your answer should contain about 300 words of description and 500 words of evaluation.

Don't write an essay without reading the essay-writing notes on pages 8–9.

FORMATION OF RELATIONSHIPS

SOCIOBIOLOGICAL EXPLANATIONS

- Selection pressures acting in the EEA affected men and women differently because females invest more in each child than males.
- This difference in parental investment means females' reproductive success is maximised by having a few well looked after children but males increase their reproductive success by mating frequently with fertile partners.
- So the sexes have evolved to look for different characteristics in a mate, women seeking wealth and power, men seeking fertility (youth and health).
- Physical attractiveness also contributes through the halo effect: we attribute other positive characteristics to good-looking people.

EVALUATION

- Dunbar and Waynforth studied personal ads and found men look for young, attractive mates and advertise their wealth to attract women, supporting the sociobiological explanation.
- Buss found cross-cultural similarities in women's desire for wealthy men and men's desire for fertile (young, attractive) women.
- The babyface hypothesis suggests men are attracted to young-looking women not for their fertility but because evolutionary pressures have made adults like (and therefore care for) babies.
- Physical attractiveness is advantageous, e.g. leading to lighter criminal sentences (Stewart) and better marks for students (Landy and Sigall).
- But sometimes attractive people are disadvantaged, e.g. getting longer sentences if they used their looks to commit a crime (Sigall and Ostrove).
- Walster et al. proposed the matching hypothesis – that people seek the closest match to their own attractiveness level, rather than the most attractive person, thus avoiding rejection.
- Evolutionary explanations suggest genes predispose rather than determine. Genetic factors (nature) interact with our environment (nurture) to produce mate choice.

SOCIAL EXCHANGE THEORY

- Thibaut and Kelley suggest commitment to a relationship depends on 'profits' (e.g. care or sex) being greater than 'costs' (e.g. time or money wasted).
- The four stages of a relationship are: *sampling* (comparison), *bargaining* (exchange of rewards), *commitment* (lowered costs) and *institutionalisation* (cost norms develop).
- Experiences and beliefs lead us to have a 'comparison level' (CL) against which a relationship is judged.
- If our 'comparison level for alternatives' judges a potential new relationship to be more profitable than an existing one, we would change partners.

EVALUATION

- Rusbult and Martz used social exchange theory (SET) to explain why women stay in abusive relationships (needs of children or financial security outweigh costs).
- Marelich et al. found that sex has associated profits (e.g. pleasure, approval, intimacy) and costs (unwanted sex, guilt) so part of the social exchange process.
- Simpson et al. found people rated members of the opposite sex as less attractive if they themselves were in relationships already, which ensured their current partner still met their comparisons level.
- Comparison levels can't explain when a relationship is inadequate or why people leave relationships without an alternative.
- SET focuses on individuals but relationships are social, i.e. involve communication and shared events. The theory may be less relevant in collectivist cultures.

PRECIPITATING FACTORS

- Duck suggests some relationships fail (dissolve) because they have more 'risk factors'.
- A lack of interpersonal skills can prevent a relationship satisfying both partners, e.g. if one person appears not to be interested in the other.
- Stimulation is something we expect to exchange in a relationship, so if a person is boring or doesn't develop, their partner may be dissatisfied.
- Physical distance between partners can lead to maintenance difficulties if they cannot cope without close contact.

EVALUATION

- Affairs are a common cause of relationship breakdown, and may occur because of lack of skills or stimulation in a relationship (Boekhout et al.).
- There are gender differences in relationship breakdown. Men's reasons for infidelity might be boredom-related, whereas women's might relate to emotional satisfaction.
- Long-distance romantic relationships are quite common, 70% of students had experienced one (Rohlfing), and if the couple reunites regularly the relationship is still satisfying (Holt and Stone).

BENEFITS OF RELATIONSHIPS ON WELL-BEING

INCREASED SELF-ESTEEM

- High self-esteem is partly dependent on social support from our relationships.
- Krause showed that older adults with better emotional support (e.g. love, care, trust) were less depressed, mainly because they had higher self-esteem.
- Druely and Townsend found that social support only improved self-esteem in healthy people, suggesting that the effect of self-esteem is only important when people are stressed.
- Symister and Friend also found that social support improved the self-esteem of ill people and this made them more optimistic and less depressed.

EVALUATION

- There are methodological problems with research into the effect of social support on self-esteem.
- Krause used an elderly sample that may have had difficulty remembering stressful events when interviewed. Although Brown and Harris suggest memory for salient events is not affected.
- As Krause measured self-esteem only at the end of the study, the results could be explained by older adults with higher self-esteem seeking out more support.
- Relationships can also have negative effects. Revenson et al. found that patients who received problematic support were more depressed and carers who have problems within their social networks are also more depressed (Pagel et al.).

BUFFERING FROM STRESS

- Stress affects health and this is influenced by social support. Kamark et al. found that participants doing a stressful task alone had higher physiological responses (i.e. were more stressed) than if a friend was with them.
- The main effect hypothesis suggests that well-being is linked to social support because relationships are rewarding (e.g. giving a sense of belonging or boosting self-esteem).
- This means that having a better social network would improve health regardless of stress level.
- The buffering hypothesis suggests that well-being is linked to social support because people help us to cope by giving emotional, tangible or informational support.
- This means that the effect of having a better social network would only appear when we were stressed; so the worse the stressor, the more social support would help us.

EVALUATION

- The main effect hypothesis is supported by Bell et al. who found that people with more social contacts (e.g. a spouse, clubs) were less depressed regardless of their stress levels.
- Lin et al. also found that people with wider social networks had fewer psychiatric symptoms irrespective of their stress levels. However, as this is a correlation, it may be that people with worse psychiatric problems find relationships more difficult to build or keep.
- The buffering hypothesis is supported by DeLongis et al. who found that people with poor social support and low self-esteem were more likely to become ill when stressed and Pearlin et al. who found that unemployed people with social support had fewer symptoms of stress than those without a spouse or other confidant.
- When social support is measured structurally (the number of people perceived to be able to offer support), findings tend to fit the main effect hypothesis.
- When social support is measured functionally (the amount of support received), findings tend to fit the buffering hypothesis.

BREAKDOWN OF RELATIONSHIPS

- Unmarried people, (separated, divorced or widowed) were less happy than married ones (Bradburn). A similar pattern is seen for physical health, e.g. diabetes, stroke or cancer (Lynch).
- Divorced people are also more likely to be admitted to mental hospitals (Cochrane) and divorced or widowed people are likely to die earlier (Johnson et al.).
- Kielcott-Glaser and Glaser identified poor immune function in people experiencing marital disruption.

OF RELATIONSHIPS

STAGE MODELS OF RELATIONSHIP DISSOLUTION

Lee's model
- Lee identified five stages in the breakdown of student relationships: *dissatisfaction* (recognising problems), *exposure* (being open about problems), *negotiating* (trying to resolve problems), *resolution* and *termination*.
- The relationships of couples going straight from dissatisfaction to termination (walking out) tended to have been less intimate all along.
- When dissatisfaction to termination took a long time, individuals reported having been very attracted to their partners and were lonelier afterwards.

Rollie and Duck's model
- Rollie and Duck identified six stages in the breakdown of relationships.
- *Breakdown* – one partner reaches a threshold of dissatisfaction.
- *Intrapsychic processes* – social withdrawal, resentment and consideration of alternatives. The relationship may end here.
- *Dyadic processes* – problems are discussed amid uncertainty and hostility but the relationship may be saved.
- *Social processes* – involvement of other people, e.g. for support or advice. This may help resolution or speed dissolution (e.g. with revelations).
- *Grave-dressing processes* – mental preparation for life outside the relationship.
- *Resurrection processes* – active changes in self and future expectations.

EVALUATION

Lee's model
- Lee's model was based on a limited sample of premarital relationships and young participants so might not apply to marital breakdown.
- Stage models, unlike precipitating factors, are descriptive rather than explanatory, although they may guide reconciliation.

Rollie and Duck's model
- Tashiro and Frazier found post-relationship-breakdown students had gained insight into themselves and future relationships, supporting the ideas of grave-dressing and resurrection.
- The focus on communication in relationship breakdown suggests an approach for intervention.

- Rollie and Duck's model looks mainly at processes when the relationship has failed whereas Lee's model considers the possibility of saving the relationship. A combination may offer a more complete view.

UNDERSTUDIED RELATIONSHIPS

RESEARCH RELATING TO SAME-SEX RELATIONSHIPS

Similarity
- Early studies found partners in gay couples were dissimilar except in age but recent evidence (e.g. Kurdek) shows partners in lesbian and gay couples to be similar in age, income and education.
- Lesbian couples are the most similar and gay couples the least (Kurdek and Schmitt).

Duration
- Blumstein and Schwartz found that lesbian and gay relationships were shorter than married or cohabiting heterosexual ones. Kurdek found relationships between lesbians were *shorter* than between gay men.
- Gottman et al. found similar rates of relationship dissolution for same-sex couples as heterosexual ones although most dissolutions were between lesbians.

Relationship satisfaction
- Kurdek and Schmitt found that partners in gay and lesbian couples, unlike heterosexual ones, were similar in their love for their partners.
- Gottman et al. found that same-sex couples, like heterosexual ones, were more satisfied when relationship benefits (e.g. companionship) were high and costs (e.g. conflict) were low.

EVALUATION

- Kurdek and Schmitt used well-matched samples. However, the sample was biased as more married couples were from one geographical area, were wealthier and had been together the longest.
- Kurdek's sample was mainly white and well educated so were not representative.
- In longitudinal studies (e.g. Kurdek and Gottman et al.) the researchers can identify whether relationships in which partners are most satisfied are those that survive. In snapshot studies (e.g. Kurdek and Schmitt) this can only be assumed.
- Lesbians report being more satisfied in relationships but they are just as likely to break up as gay men (Kurdek). This may be because self-reports are subjective; lesbians may simply report more positive aspects of their relationships.
- Gottman et al. used physiological measures of communication between partners, which is more objective.

EXPLANATIONS OF MEDIATED RELATIONSHIPS

Reduced cues theory
- Computer-mediated communication (CMC) lacks direct social cues, such as eye contact. Culnan and Markus' (1987) reduced cues theory suggests this makes it less effective than face-to-face (FtF) communication.
- The lack of cues may lead to deindividuation fostering aggressive behaviour and making relationships more difficult.

Social identity model of deindividuation effects (SIDE)
- The SIDE suggests that CMC can lead to deindividuation but that this is because people feel anonymous within a group and adopt the group's social identity. Reduced cues hide differences, and stereotypes enhance similarities, strengthening social identity. This shared identity can help relationship formation within the group.
- As this social identity also causes the internalisation of group norms it can explain why people ignore normal social controls and become more aggressive. Mason suggests this is how cyberbullying operates.

EVALUATION

Reduced cues theory
- Early research found people were more aggressive and that it was harder to reach agreement using CMC than when FtF, supporting Culnan and Markus' theory.
- However, emoticons etc. make CMC effective, e.g. allowing people to flirt and maybe helping men to express emotions more easily (Whitty). Slower replies can indicate intimacy (Walther and Tidwell) and the existence of cyberbullying suggests CMC readily conveys emotion.
- Walther showed that reduced cues are unimportant as, although slower to form than when FtF, impressions of other people based on CMC were just as strong.

Social identity model of deindividuation effects (SIDE)
- Spears et al. supported SIDE by showing that anonymity strengthens social identity and CMC friends form strong relationships.
- CMC carries the risk of deception, which can be protective or dangerous. Lying is found along the lines predicted by evolutionary theory, e.g. men exaggerating their income.

CULTURAL VARIATIONS IN RELATIONSHIPS

WESTERN AND NON-WESTERN RELATIONSHIPS

Voluntary or non-voluntary relationships
- Western culture is typified by mobility offering many relationship possibilities.
- In non-Western cultures relationship choice may be limited by meeting fewer people and family ties.

Individual or group-based relationships
- Western individualist culture values each person's independent rights and freedom.
- Collectivist cultures (e.g. China) value *inter*dependence, i.e. group goals.
- Individualist cultures therefore stress the individual's choice in relationships. Collectivist cultures consider the needs of the family or group.
- Moore and Leung found that fewer Chinese-Australian students (with a collectivist responsibility to the family) were in romantic relationships than Anglo-Australians, as expected, but that both groups valued romantic love.

Continuity and discontinuity
- American culture emphasises progress, therefore change, (discontinuity) is acceptable whereas Chinese culture values continuity (e.g. heritage).
- Non-Western relationships therefore more permanent, Western ones more temporary.

Norms and rules
- Ting-Toomey found reciprocity in personal relationships was voluntary in individualist cultures but expected in collectivist ones, e.g. moral obligations to return favours.
- Rules may be explicit (e.g. in marriage) or implicit (e.g. in friendships).
- There are similarities between cultures, e.g. in rules about showing courtesy and respect, and differences, e.g. in rules about close friendships (Argyle et al.).

EVALUATION

Voluntary or non-voluntary relationships
- Non-voluntary (arranged) marriages make sense in societies with low mobility.
- Divorce rates are low in such marriages and Epstein reports that about half of the partners in such marriages are in love.
- Myers et al. found no difference in marital satisfaction between those in arranged marriages in India and non-arranged marriages in the USA.
- In China, the parental role in partner choice has declined. Xiaohe and White found that Chinese women who had married for love felt better about their relationship than women in arranged marriages.
- Jankowiak and Fischer identified romantic love in 90% of 166 cultures studied and Bartels and Zeki claim to have found an active brain area in people who are in love.

Individual or group-based relationships
- There may be relationship benefits to either choices based on love or on the objective position of parental judgements of long-term compatibility – although this isn't supported by Xiaohe and White's findings.

Continuity and discontinuity
- The rise in divorce rate and reduction in extended family groups in the West may be more closely linked to urbanisation than to individualism.

Norms and rules
- Argyle et al. failed to support some predictions about cultural differences (e.g. about formal gift exchange in Japan). However, as the list of rules used was formulated in the UK it may not have included culture-specific rules for Japan.
- Such research can help to promote effective relations between cultural groups.
- The differences in cultural expectations can bias research but culture itself is important to relationships in multicultural societies so is important to study.

Question 4 **Discuss explanations relating to the formation of relationships.** *[25]*

Student answer

Paragraph 1 There are many types of relationship that people experience in their lives. Everyone has parent or carer relationships and most people have friends and school friends and neighbours, as well as people in shops and at work. Most people also have romantic relationships at some time and many get married even if they are gay or lesbians. When we are older we become parents, grandparents and then we have less relationships as we get very old. There are also relationships over the internet which are very important today.

Paragraph 2 Most research is in romantic relationships. Psychologists don't look at actual romance because they are scientists and anyway they often take a sociobiological view. Buss tried to show this with his cross-cultural study as he thought there were basic things that everyone looked for in a partner and this was due to the EEA back in prehistoric times, and these were still present. Males will look for fertility signs like big hips, full lips, rosy cheeks and big breasts. Females will look for things that show ability to provide like a lot of money or a good job, or a powerful body that shows the man can protect her and the child. This is called 'parental investment'.

Paragraph 3 There is a lot of support for the sociobiology theory. Dunbar and Waynforth looked at personal adverts and found that men advertised their earning power but looked for youth and physical attraction in a female. This is exactly what Buss found, but his study was flawed because some of his samples were very small. Dunbar and Waynforth's study was also flawed because it just looked in the USA.

Paragraph 4 Evolutionary theory is supposed to be determinist because it says the preferences are fixed genetically and relate to the roles of men and women where men went hunting and women raised children. However it is not really because these genes have to interact with the environment so we all turn out differently. It is just a tendency. Also it's not the same for gays and lesbians. Also it might be influenced by the media where women are shown like stick insects and size zero is supposed to be attractive.

Paragraph 5 There is also attractiveness, which is partly genetic. Men tend to prefer women who have rosy cheeks, full lips and glossy hair as well as a sort of hourglass shape. Many cultures show men preferring women to have slightly baby face looks. Attractive people get a lot of extras in life including smaller prison sentences (Stewart 1980), better marks in exams and attractive teachers are rated better than ugly ones! This is due to the halo effect. Walster showed that we tend to be attracted to people who are similar to ourselves in attractiveness.

Paragraph 6 Another type of theory is social exchange theory (SET). Everything is down to profit and loss in a relationship where each partner tries to get the most rewards such as companionship and sex. The costs of getting these are weighed up and the relationship goes on if the rewards are greater. Costs are things like effort, spending and time wasted. We all develop a comparison level (Thibaut and Kelley) to judge our other relationships by and to work out if we should change our relationship to another one.

Paragraph 7 This is an 'economic' theory of human behaviour which means we do things sensibly weighing up the pros and cons. But we know from studies of thinking that people just don't behave rationally and have lots of biases. However it does make you think about abusive relationships where being out on the street is the alternative to being hit. SET focuses too much on individuals and ignores the quality of a relationship. Duck criticises SET because it does this and it is very selfish. However it does seem to be shown to be true in Marelich's study of deception in relationships. This study is very recent and shows that the students in the sample weighed up the rewards and costs, and often lied to keep them balanced. But this is only a small sample in one culture.

Paragraph 8 This is the big problem with such theories because they only look at romantic heterosexual love and only in Western cultures. There may be differences with gays and lesbians, and in many cultures around the world arranged marriages are normal so the relationship really is determined by money or other reasons, not love. This means the theories are ethnocentric.

Paragraph 9 I think the sociobiological ideas have most evidence for them, where people make a free choice.

[756 words]

Examiner comments

This essay shows clear understanding, a large amount of accurate data with a reasonable amount of detail and there is a very clear logical flow to the whole essay.

The first paragraph is the type many students write, showing a good grasp of the topic, however it is not actually more than a 'general studies' introduction. The examiner would note the understanding demonstrated, but the paragraph doesn't really contribute to the mark.

Paragraph 2 is reasonable and factual (**A01**). The details of the Buss research are accurate, although the reference to parental investment is incorrect.

Paragraphs 3 and 4 are evaluative (**A02**). The **A02** content is highlighted in grey. The content of these two paragraphs is correct and the student writes logically, although there are some untidy comments (such as 'however it is not really because these genes have to interact with the environment so we all turn out differently' – which could be written more clearly and precisely, demonstrating deeper understanding). This kind of 'untidy' writing is typical in the pressured exam situation (but would not be acceptable in a prepared homework, for instance).

Paragraphs 5 and 6 introduce new theoretical positions. This is followed by two paragraphs of well-detailed and logical criticism, both of the evidence and of more general matters.

If this essay was produced in an exam, the examiner would consider a mark in or near the top bands for both AO1 and AO2. **Therefore 7 out of 10 marks for AO1, and 13 out of 15 marks for AO2.**

20/25 makes this an A grade, and would represent a good piece under the time pressures of an exam.

Improvement? There is plenty of room for more detail in the studies quoted, and the development of points like the difficulties of evolutionary theory when applied to homosexual relationships.

Students can get 25 out of 25 and many have done in the past. Perfection does not occur in exams and examiners do not reserve full marks just for genius answers; but they are awarded for essays that fulfil the marking band criteria shown on page 7.

Chapter 5
Intelligence

Chapter contents

116 Introduction to the study of intelligence
118 Theories of cognitive development
120 Theories of the nature of intelligence
122 Issues relating to the measurement of intelligence
124 Role of genetic factors in intelligence
126 Role of environmental factors in intelligence

End-of-chapter review

128 Chapter summary
130 Exam question with student answer

Specification breakdown	
Theories of cognitive development (e.g. Piaget and Vygotsky's theories).	Cognition is the process of thinking, so 'cognitive development' is the study of the way our thinking (cognition) changes as we move from infant to child to adult. There are two dominant explanations for cognitive development, produced by two giants of twentieth-century cognitive science – Piaget and Vygotsky. Their theories have had a profound effect on research as well as on the way education has been conducted in the UK.
Theories of the nature of intelligence (e.g. Spearman's two-factor theory, Thurstone's multifactor theory, Gardner's multiple intelligences, Sternberg's triarchic theory).	An interest in intelligence stretches back to the very earliest days of psychology, which is not surprising since it is a key aspect of behaviour. Spearman's theory was one of the first theories and Sternberg's is one of the most recent. You need to study only two theories but we have covered all of the examples given in the specification to provide a fuller picture of what intelligence might be.
Issues relating to the measurement of intelligence (e.g. uses and limitations of IQ testing).	IQ testing is so embedded in our Western culture that it is important to stand back and consider just how valid attempts to measure it are, and the limitations of attempts to do this.
The role of genetic factors in the development of intelligence (e.g. twin studies, family studies, adoption studies, genome research).	Intelligence must have a genetic basis as it is a property of our evolved brain. The question has always been 'to what extent is it genetic?' You will be looking at the major sources of evidence, such as twin and family studies as well as recent gene mapping studies.
The role of environmental factors in the development of intelligence (e.g. prenatal and postnatal factors, cultural and sub-cultural factors).	If intelligence is not due to genetic factors then it must be due to environmental factors, but again the question is 'to what extent?' This is the nature–nurture question. In this section you will study the evidence for the nurture side of the debate, such as family and educational influences as well as cultural attitudes.

HOW INTELLIGENT ARE YOU?

You have taken several intelligence tests (**IQ tests**) during the course of your school life even though you may not have been aware that they were tests of your **intelligence**. Broadly speaking, such tests come in two forms: tests of *verbal intelligence* and tests of *non-verbal intelligence* – see examples below. There are many other tests of thinking, such as tests of creativity and tests of moral understanding. There are also tests of animal intelligence, illustrated by the *Birdbrain of Britain* feature on this page.

Items from a test of non-verbal intelligence

Raven matrices test

Find the missing peice of the pattern.

Items from a test of verbal intelligence

1 Which of the following five is least like the other four?
   Celery, lettuce, onion, grape, asparagus

2 What would be the next number in this series?
   15 ... 12 ... 13 ... 10 ... 11 ... 8 ... ?

3 Gina is faster than Jan, and Nora is slower then Gina.
   Which of the following statements would be most accurate?
   a) Nora is faster than Jan
   b) Nora is slower than Jan
   c) Nora is as fast as Jan
   d) It is impossible to tell whether Jan or Nora is faster

Taken from IQ test on www.queendom.com

What makes some people do well on such tests while other people do less well? The answer is not age. IQ tests are adjusted for age so that a person aged eight who gets 50% of the answers right on an IQ test will be given a higher IQ score than a person aged 12 who gets 50% correct on the same test. The letters IQ stand for *intelligence quotient* because the first intelligence tests calculated a person's score by dividing the number of correct items answered by the person's age (you may recall from primary school that a quotient is what you get when you divide one number by another). More recent tests don't do such a division but use norms to work out a person's IQ based on their score and age.

Scores are then converted to a standard scale so that a score of 100 means an average IQ. If you have a score of 115 that means you are more intelligent than 82% of the population, whereas a score of 85 means you are less intelligent than 82% of the population (15 IQ points is one standard deviation).

So what does make some people score higher on IQ tests than others: **heredity**, having good teachers, eating nutritious food, having parents who read lots of books – **nature** or **nurture**, **genetics** or **culture**? We discuss this towards the end of the chapter.

> WWW

Test your own intelligence (or other psychological attributes)

There are a large number of psychology tests on the web – tests of personality, self-esteem, creativity and intelligence. Psychometric testing (the measurement of psychological abilities) is big business and also endlessly fascinating.

Try these websites:

- BBC – Test the Nation, take the test or look at the results **www.bbc.co.uk/testthenation**

- Queendom, the land of tests – professional quality psychological tests, assessments and quizzes **www.queendom.com**

- Raven's matrices can be found at **www.clipsite.com.ar/HOME/Salud/Test/Raven** (fill in your name and age).

- Or look at **www.iqtest.com www.intelligencetest.com www.mensa.org.uk/iq-tests**

Birdbrain of Britain

Brooks-King and Hurrell (1958) showed that some birds are more intelligent than others by devising tests of bird intelligence. One was a perspex device with holes (top) which enabled peanuts to be suspended on matchsticks. If a bird removed the correct matchsticks, the peanut would fall to the bottom so that it could be eaten. Blue tits and coal tits were the only species that could solve this test, which involved up to five rows of matchsticks.

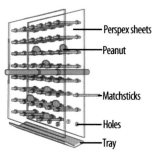

- Perspex sheets
- Peanut
- Matchsticks
- Holes
- Tray

History of intelligence tests

Binet and Simon Early in the twentieth century, the school authority in Paris was concerned about children who were not making progress. Alfred Binet was part of a movement who wished to find ways of identifying retarded children so they could be given the special education they deserved. Binet, working with Theodore Simon, piloted many tests to find ones that would differentiate between children of different ages who were or were not doing well according to their teachers. The result was a graded set of 30 assessments ranging from simple ones, such as tracking a moving object or naming objects in pictures, to difficult ones, such as putting three nouns in a sentence (e.g. Paris, river, fortune) or reversing the hands of a clock (Binet, 1905). Each child worked up through the graded items until they got to a point where they were consistently failing them. This point indicated the child's mental level or mental age – the age of a child typically able to reach that level. The test they created became known as the *Binet–Simon scale*.

The Stanford–Binet test At the same time as Binet and Simon were working in France, a number of Americans were seeking means to assess the mental abilities of the large immigrant population to ensure that only the best were identified for education, jobs and even reproduction. The **eugenics movement** advocated that the feeble-minded should be prevented from reproducing.

Lewis Terman, in the USA, extended Binet and Simon's test to 90 items. The **Stanford–Binet Intelligence Scale** included two types of item. Verbal tests relied on language, e.g. testing general knowledge and vocabulary. Performance or *non-verbal tests* assessed perceptual skills and non-verbal reasoning, e.g. copying an arrangement of coloured blocks or arranging pictures logically to make a story.

Link with Piaget In this chapter you will read about the work of Jean Piaget (see next spread as well as the activity on the facing page). He started out working with Theodore Simon in Paris on the design and administration of IQ tests. When analysing children's answers he was intrigued by the observation that children of the same age were tending to make the same logical mistakes. This was the beginning of his theory that the way children think matures as they get older.

FIRST, FIND A SMALL CHILD …

This chapter begins with the study of theories of **cognitive development**, including the highly influential theory developed by Jean Piaget. One of his key ideas was that the ability to conserve quantities develops with age (he called this ability '**conservation**'). On the right you'll see an illustration of this. The first pair of identical glasses contain the same volume of liquid. If I poured the liquid from one of these into a tall thin glass (as the picture shows), you would not be fooled by the appearance that there is now more liquid in the tall glass because you know that volume cannot change – it stays the same despite what it may look like, i.e. it is 'conserved'. Piaget observed out that children under the age of seven don't understand conservation. They would say there is now more liquid in the tall glass than the short one.

Piaget repeated this activity with other quantities. For example, he set out two rows of counters as below:

Then he changed the bottom row so the one row now looked like this:

● ● ● ● ● ● ●

Young children would now say there are more counters.

Naughty teddy

McGarrigle and Donaldson (1974) argued that Piaget's study 'fooled' young children and in fact they were quite capable of conserving quantities. McGarrigle and Donaldson argued that the deliberate transformation in the conservation experiment acted as a **demand characteristic**, demanding an alternative response. When a 'naughty teddy' toy accidentally messed up the counters making one row longer, younger children coped better because the change was 'explained' by naughty teddy's behaviour, eliminating demand characteristics (i.e. that the apparent change needed an explanation).

McGarrigle and Donaldson weren't the only psychologists to criticise Piaget's methods. Another criticism was that asking two questions may have confused younger children in particular and this may explain why they appeared to be less capable than slightly older children. In the conservation experiments the children were shown the two identical displays and asked 'Are these the same?'. Then the display was transformed and the children were again asked 'Are they the same?' Some children might find this confusing and think that asking the question again implies there must be a different answer. Samuel and Bryant (1984) showed that younger children did better when they were only asked once (after the transformation) if the two displays were the same, instead of Piaget's standard two questions (before and after).

Conservation involves recognising that quantities don't change even if they look different. Piaget believed that conservation was the single most important achievement of the concrete operational stage of cognitive development (which occurs between four and seven years old). Children at this stage are not capable of reversibility of thought. For example, they fail to understand that the physical properties of an object (e.g. its mass, volume, number, area and weight) remain the same despite changes in its appearance. The development of conservation is important because it provides evidence of the child's command of logical operations.

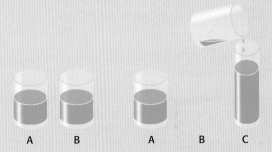

▲ *In this conservation task a child is shown two glasses of water (A and B) and asked if they contain the same amount of water. Then the researcher pours the contents of one glass into a taller glass and asks the child whether the quantity is the same in glass A and C. A young child is dominated by what they can see and the quantities look different so the child says no.*

WHAT YOU CAN DO?

Try some of these experiments yourself with a young child. However, you need to be especially careful about **ethical issues** – most particularly **informed consent** and **psychological harm**. It is not enough to ask consent from the child's parent, you should also discuss what you are doing with the child. Discuss these issues in class and decide how to approach a suitable participant. This should be a child who is a relative or a child of someone you know well.

Maynard the cat

This is one of my (Cara) all-time favourite psychology experiments. Three year olds were shown Maynard the cat and then the cat went behind a screen and a mask was placed over his head. Despite being aware of the transformation, the children, when asked what the second animal was, said that it was a dog (deVries, 1969).

This illustrates the appearance–reality distinction which underlies young children's inability to conserve – their logical reasoning is over-influenced by the appearance of things.

THEORIES OF COGNITIVE DEVELOPMENT

CULTURAL BIAS

NATURE AND NURTURE

Jean Piaget (1896–1980) and Lev Vygotsky (1896–1934) were born in the same year but worlds apart – Vygotsky was Russian whereas Piaget was Swiss. Both men produced highly influential theories about how our thinking develops in childhood.

Piaget's chief contribution was to show the *way* that children think changes qualitatively as they get older (rather than just gaining more knowledge). He also claimed that these changes are mainly driven by biological processes. Piaget's theory dominated Western views of cognitive development until the 1960s when Vygotsky's theory was first published in English.

Vygotsky's views were based on Russian **collectivism** – the social group rather than the individual is of prime importance. Therefore Vygotsky believed that **culture** is the prime determinant of individual development.

PIAGET'S THEORY

Piaget (1954) believed that our intellectual abilities develop as a result of two influences: (1) **maturation** (a biological process) and (2) the environment. As a child gets older (matures), certain mental operations become possible. This leads to distinct stages in development. However, maturity alone is not sufficient, interactions with the environment create pressure that leads to changes in the way the child thinks.

The mechanisms of cognitive development

Schema are 'programmes' that people construct for dealing with the world. A child is born with a few **innate** schema (such as grasping) that then increase (in number and sophistication) through experience.

Assimilation involves the incorporation of new information into an existing schema. For example, a baby who is given a new toy car to play with may grasp or suck that toy in the same way that they grasped or sucked a rattle.

Accommodation occurs when a child adapts existing schema in order to understand new information that doesn't appear to fit, resulting in the development of new schema.

Equilibration is achieved through assimilation or accommodation. When we encounter something that doesn't fit existing schema, an imbalance is created. The need for balance (equilibrium) is satisfied by assimilation or accommodation.

Stages in cognitive development

Stage 1 (0–2 years): **Sensori-motor** stage Children learn to co-ordinate sensory input (e.g. what they see) with motor actions (i.e. with their hand movements) through **circular reactions** where an infant repeats the same action to test sensori-motor relationships.

Stage 2 (2–7 years): **Pre-operational stage** Children's thought lacks consistent logic but becomes increasingly symbolic, as they begin to represent their world with words, images and drawings. Their thinking is based on what they see rather than any internally consistent rules, i.e. based on the appearance of a situation rather than reality (the **appearance–reality distinction**). Children at this stage are also **egocentric** in their thinking – they only see the world from their own position and are not aware of other perspectives.

Stage 3 (7–11 years): **Concrete operational stage** Children acquire the rudiments of logical reasoning, and display **decentration** (no longer focusing on just one aspect of a task). This means that they are now able to conserve quantities (see previous spread).

Stage 4 (11+ years): **Formal operational stage** Children can now solve abstract problems. They can solve problems using **hypothetico-deductive reasoning**, thinking like a scientist, developing hypotheses and testing them to determine causal relationships.

VYGOTSKY'S THEORY

The major theme of Vygotsky's theory is that social interaction plays a fundamental role in cognitive development.

Mental processes

Vygotsky (1962) proposed that children are born with **elementary mental functions**, such as perception and memory. These are transformed into **higher mental functions** (such as use of mathematical systems) by the influence of culture. Lower mental functions are biological and a form of natural development. Higher mental functions are exclusively human.

The process of cultural influence

Cultural influences affect cognitive development in several ways, for example:

The role of others: experts A child learns through problem-solving experiences shared with someone else, usually a parent or teacher but also more competent peers. All people with greater knowledge are called 'experts'. Initially, the person interacting with the child assumes most of the responsibility for guiding the problem-solving activity, but gradually this responsibility transfers to the child.

Semiotics and the role of language Vygotsky believed that culture is transmitted by experts using **semiotics**, i.e. the signs and symbols developed within a particular culture. Language is the semiotic system of foremost importance, but mathematical symbols are valuable too. Children begin using language to solve problems around the age of two or three, and frequently talk out loud when trying to solve problems, a type of speech known as *egocentric* speech. At around age of seven, this gives way to silent or *inner* speech. These inner dialogues continue throughout life to be used as a way of reflecting upon and solving problems.

The social and individual level Every function (e.g. counting) of the child's developing cognitive skills appear twice: first, on the social level (between people), and later on the individual level (inside the child).

The zone of proximal development (ZPD) A child's **zone of proximal development** (ZPD) is the region where cognitive development takes place. It is the distance between what a person can currently do unaided and their potential when aided. The learner is aided by cultural influences (e.g. experts and language). At first, learning is between people (social) and later it becomes internalised (individual) – a process called 'internalisation'; this mirrors the distinction between the social and individual level described above.

EVALUATION OF PIAGET'S THEORY

Research support

The mechanisms of development There is actually little research to support Piaget's ideas about the effects of disequilibrium. Inhelder *et al.* (1974) did show that children's learning was helped when there was a mild conflict between what they expected to happen and what did happen, but this wasn't really the sort of conflict that Piaget was talking about (Bryant, 1995).

Stages in development Research on **conservation** is described on the previous spread. Piaget also illustrated pre-operational thinking using the *three mountains task* (see illustration to the right). Children were shown a set of pictures and asked to choose the one which showed the doll's perspective. Children aged three to four years tended to choose their own perspective, rather than the perspective of the doll. However, Hughes (1975) showed that young children could cope with the task if it was more realistic, for example using a naughty boy doll who was hiding from a toy policeman.

▲ *The three mountains task.*

Strengths and limitations

Limitations Research suggests that Piaget underestimated children's abilities at younger ages, and may have overestimated the ability to use abstract logic in the formal operational stage. His theory is perhaps more relevant to academic, middle-class Western values. In other cultures and social classes greater value may be placed on, for example, a more basic level of concrete operations (i.e. making things rather than thinking about abstract ideas).

In general, his theory focuses too much on logic and generally ignores social factors, such as the benefit of cooperative group work. A further criticism is that the methods he used to research children's behaviour were flawed (see above and previous spread). However, the revised evidence still supports the view that there are qualitative changes in cognitive development as a child matures.

Strengths Despite the wealth of criticism, Piaget remains one of the most influential psychologists of the twentieth century. His theory has had an enormous influence on psychology and education. Bryant (1995) reminds us that Piaget's key contribution was to highlight the radical differences in the way young children and adults think. Before Piaget, the view was that children were just smaller adults with less knowledge about the world; now we know that it is more complex than that – a point which has had a major impact in schools on the way that children are taught to think rather than simply to acquire knowledge.

EVALUATION OF VYGOTSKY'S THEORY

Research support

Cultural influence Gredler (1992) pointed to the primitive counting system used in Papua New Guinea as an example of how culture can limit cognitive development. In Papua New Guinea counting is done by starting on the thumb of one hand and going up the arm and down to the other fingers, ending at 29. This system makes it very difficult to add and subtract large numbers, a limiting factor for cognitive development in this culture.

The role of the ZPD McNaughton and Leyland (1990) observed young children working with their mothers on jigsaw puzzles of increasing difficulty, and then a week later observed the children working on their own. The children reached a higher level of difficulty with their mothers (their potential ability) than when working on their own (their current ability), so defining their ZPD. Vygotsky predicted that 'experts' will put the greatest effort into teaching at the edge of the ZPD, the point at which the child can still cope but with difficulty. McNaughton and Leyland's observations supported this.

Strengths and limitations

Limitations There has been relatively little research related to Vygotsky's theory compared with the abundance of research on most aspects of Piaget's theory. This is partly because Vygotsky's theory doesn't lend itself as readily to experimentation because the concepts, such as the ZPD, are more difficult to **operationalise**.

A further issue is that Vygotsky may have overplayed the importance of the social environment – if social influence was all that was needed to advance cognitive development then learning would be a lot faster than it is.

Strengths From the point of view of the tutor, Vygotsky's approach is a more active one. Vygotsky offered advice about how others can take an active part in the learning process by leading a child through their ZPD, whereas Piaget believed it was fundamentally important for the learner to make their own discoveries, with minimal input from others.

Nature and nurture

Piaget's theory combines nature (biological maturation) with nurture (experience) to explain cognitive development. Piaget's conception of 'nurture' is more focused on the *physical* environment, whereas Vygotsky emphasised the *social* environment.

Comparing Piaget and Vygotsky

The differences between the two theories reflect differences between the two men. Vygotsky was a communist believing in the power of community and thus valued the role of society in the development of the individual (a **collectivist** approach); Piaget was a product of **individualist** European society. Apart from their different cultural backgrounds the two men may also represent rather different kinds of learner: Piaget's child is an **introvert** whereas Vygotsky's child is an **extrovert**, and this may be a reflection of the men themselves (Miller, 1994). Thus, the two views can be reconciled because they are talking about different styles of learning and different kinds of learner. It is also possible to reconcile the theories by taking the view that they are not that different at their central core (Glassman, 1999). If one contrasts these theories with others in psychology, such as those by Freud, Pavlov or Skinner, we can see there are similarities: they both place cognition at the centre of the theory, both emphasise the complex interactionist character of development, both see abstract scientific thought as the final stage of development, and both see the learner as active rather than passive.

Real-world application

Both theories have had an impact on teaching. You can read about this in Chapter 9 (see pages 184–185).

CAN YOU...? No. 5.1

1... For each theory, select about **five** key concepts.

2... For each key concept write **two or three** sentences explaining the concept.

3... Identify about **five** points of evaluation for each theory (these can be positive or negative).

4... Elaborate each point (see page 9).

5... Use all of this material to write an answer to the following exam question: *Critically consider theories of cognitive development.* Your answer should contain about 300 words of description and 500 words of evaluation.

THEORIES OF THE NATURE OF INTELLIGENCE

ETHICS VERSUS SCIENCE

GENETIC INFLUENCE

CULTURAL BIAS

GENDER BIAS

Intelligence can be defined as 'the ability to acquire information, to think and reason well, and to deal effectively and adaptively with the environment'. Over the past 100 years psychologists have produced many different theories to explain the nature of intelligence. Early theories were described as '**psychometric**' because they focused on its measurement (psycho = psychological, metric = measurement). Later theories have moved away from this narrow view of intelligence, and included the processes involved in intelligent behaviour and the importance of using intelligence in the real world (as opposed to using theoretical tests).

> WWW

Learn more about MI and assess your own intelligence profile at:

http://surfaquarium.com/MI

THEORIES BASED ON IQ TESTS

Spearman's two-factor theory

At the turn of the nineteenth century Charles Spearman developed the technique of **correlation** (Spearman's test of correlation on page 35 is named after him). He developed the technique to analyse correlations between different intelligence test results using a statistical technique called **factor analysis**.

Spearman (1927) used this technique to show that individuals who do well on one test of intelligence tended also to do well on other tests of intelligence, i.e. there was a **positive correlation**. He also found that individuals tended not to do equally well on all tasks on the tests. This led Spearman to propose two factors that together could explain these results:

- *General intelligence* ('*g*') which determines performance on all types of intelligence test (and thus would explain the positive correlation between performance on all tests).
- *Specific abilities* ('*s*'), such as vocabulary and mathematical abilities, which explain the unevenness in performance on different tasks.

Thurstone's multifactor theory

Louis Thurstone was another early psychologist with a major interest in measuring human abilities. Like Spearman, he factor analysed IQ tests but he concluded that there was not one single factor. He claimed there were a variety of key mental abilities (multifactors). Thurstone (1938) proposed a model of *primary mental abilities* (PMAs), listing seven of them: spatial ability, perceptual speed, numerical ability, verbal comprehension, word fluency, memory and inductive reasoning (generating rules from a set of observations). Thurstone regarded *g* as an average of these PMAs. He argued that PMAs are independent and not correlated; thus *g* will vary depending on which mental tests are used and which PMAs they tap.

Cultural bias

Although Gardner never actually claimed that each of the eight intelligences would be valued equally in different cultures, it is clear from research that some intelligences are valued more highly than others by members of different cultures. For example, Chan (2004) found that mathematical intelligence was most valued among parents and children in Hong Kong, while bodily–kinaesthetic and naturalist intelligences were rated the lowest.

MORE RECENT THEORIES

Gardner's theory of multiple intelligences (MI)

Howard Gardner (1983) claimed that the traditional view of intelligence as having one general underlying factor was far too limited. He suggested that, particularly in the West, educators tend to tailor their teaching around a view that ignores other 'less traditional' forms of intelligence, such as interpersonal intelligence.

Gardner initially identified seven types of intelligence, and later added an eighth – *natural* intelligence (Gardner, 1999).

- *Linguistic intelligence* (language and expression skills).
- *Logical–mathematical intelligence* (numerical, scientific skills).
- *Spatial intelligence* (understanding relationships in space).
- *Bodily–kinaesthetic intelligence* (using the body).
- *Musical intelligence* (playing an instrument or composing).
- *Interpersonal intelligence* (relating to others).
- *Intrapersonal intelligence* (understanding oneself).
- *Natural intelligence* (showing an expertise in the natural world).

Gardner believed many different abilities could count as 'intelligence' if they resolved genuine problems within a particular cultural setting. He believed that each of these intelligences are independent of each other and reside in separate parts of the brain. However, they can and do interact with each other when needed. For example, being able to sing and dance at the same time requires a certain level of both musical and bodily–kinaesthetic intelligence.

Sternberg's triarchic theory of intelligence

In 1985 Robert Sternberg published a booked called *Beyond IQ* which introduced his own theory of intelligence. As the title suggests, Sternberg's theory defines intelligence as a process rather than a measurable quantity. Individual differences in intelligence, therefore, reflect differences in the cognitive operations (information processing) that people use when solving problems.

Sternberg's theory is called 'triarchic' because he claims that there are three distinct aspects (or *sub-theories*) of intelligence as follows:

- *Analytical (componential) intelligence* is the ability to combine the most appropriate mental mechanisms, or 'components' when applying intelligence to a problem.
- *Practical (contextual) intelligence* is the ability to use your intelligence in the 'real' world rather than abstract problem solving. It means making a 'considered' response to a problem dependent on the context in which the problem occurs. It is a kind of streetwise intelligence.
- *Creative (experiential) intelligence* helps an individual identify when a problem is a novel one. Intelligence is being able to produce new ideas from previously unrelated information based on past experience, i.e. to be creative.

According to Sternberg, a complete explanation of intelligence must entail all of these three sub-theories. Conventional notions of intelligence miss this important interaction between components, context and experience. For example, faced with a puncture, we might use our analytical intelligence to work out what happened, use our practical intelligence to change the tyre, and use our creative intelligence to come up with an alternative solution, such as hitching a lift.

EVALUATION

Spearman's two-factor theory

Neurophysiological evidence Support for the idea of an underlying general intelligence (*g*) comes from a study by Duncan *et al.* (2000) using **PET scans**. Researchers presented participants with tasks that either correlated highly with tests of general intelligence or did not, using both verbal and visual stimuli. They then watched to see which areas of the brain 'lit up'. Regardless of whether the tasks were visual or verbal, tasks associated with general intelligence consistently led to activation of the same areas of the **frontal lobes**, whereas 'non-*g*' tasks did not, this supports the existence of *g*.

Criticisms Spearman's two-factor theory was never widely accepted and was replaced by the multifactor approach in the 1930s. Nevertheless the idea continues to have appeal and draw support. For example, Johnson and Bouchard (2005) analysed the performance of over 400 adults on a range of 40 different tests of mental ability, and claimed to have found evidence for a *g* factor, i.e. they found one factor running through all the tests that correlated positively with performance on the tests.

Thurstone's multifactor theory

An objective approach The factor analysis approach claims to produce objective statistical facts. However, the factors that are identified are not 'real' things, they are just arbitrary categories. Different theorists have used the same method and got different outcomes. For example, Spearman and Thurstone drew quite different conclusions. Therefore it is not as objective an approach as supporters claim.

Intelligence or cognitive style? A fundamental criticism of this theory (and also MI theory) is the belief by many critics that each ability or intelligence is nothing more than a **cognitive style** (i.e. a preferred way of using information to solve problems) rather than a stand-alone distinct form of intelligence (Morgan, 1996).

Gardner's theory of multiple intelligences

Research evidence Gardner used various criteria to identify whether a specific ability is sufficiently distinct to be regarded as an 'intelligence'. These include the following:

- *Neuropsychological evidence* – People with brain damage usually retain some intellectual skills, for example, a brain-damaged musician may have impaired speech, yet retains the ability to play music.
- *Individuals with exceptional talent* in one area such as autistic savants (see right).
- *Experimental evidence* shows that a person engaged in a crossword puzzle is less able to carry on a conversation effectively, because both tasks demand the attention of linguistic intelligence, which creates interference. Dancing and talking creates less interference, suggesting they rely on different types of underlying intelligence.

Research evidence To date there have been very few published studies that support MI theory. Gardner himself admits it is difficult to assess the theory objectively, which limits its acceptability as a 'scientific' theory of intelligence. Research support is, however, beginning to filter through. For example, Onika *et al.* (2008) found that compared with direct instruction, teaching methods that focused on the development of *multiple* intelligences produced significant increases in several areas of importance to a student's academic social and emotional well-being.

Sternberg's triarchic theory of intelligence

Research evidence Merrick (1992) developed a test of triarchic abilities – the *Cognitive Abilities Self-Evaluative Questionnaire* (CASE-Q). The responses from 268 Dutch high-school students were factor analysed and evidence for all three types of intelligence were found.

Real-life applications Sternberg's theory has been successfully applied to education at both school and university level. For example, Sternberg *et al.* (1999) have shown that teaching 'triarchically' tends to result in significant improvements in academic achievement. Williams *et al.* (2002) assessed the impact of the *Practical Intelligence for School* (PIFS) intervention, in which all three types of intelligence are emphasised. Where PIFS was used as a major part of the curriculum, significant improvements in practical intelligence were obtained.

Strengths and limitations A strength of Sternberg's approach is that it is concerned with *how* people actually solve complex problems, whereas the psychometric approach simply provides a description of the human intellect. However, critics, such as Gottfredson (2003), claim that Sternberg has failed to provide sufficient evidence to support his assertion that practical intelligence is distinct from general intelligence (*g*), or that traditional IQ tests do not measure practical intelligence.

▲ *The human camera? Autistic savant Stephen Wiltshire.*

Autistic savants

Stephen Wiltshire is an 'autistic savant', a term used to describe individuals with **autism** who have extraordinary skills not exhibited by most people. For example, many autistic savants possess calendar memory – they could be asked a question such as 'What day of the week was 7 October 1959?', and would be able to determine the answer in seconds. Stephen possesses one exceptional ability – being able to draw extremely complicated scenes (such as the London skyline) completely from memory.

Autistic savants like Stephen support Gardner's theory because they show exceptional ability in one area while showing deficits in others. For example, Stephen barely uttered a word as a child and has difficulty relating to other human beings. Stephen shows exceptional intelligence in one area (spatial intelligence) while showing deficits in others (linguistic interpersonal intelligences).

CAN YOU...? No. 5.2

1... Select **three** key concepts for each theory.

2... For each key concept write **three or four** sentences explaining the concept.

3... Identify about **ten** points of evaluation (these can be positive or negative).

4... Elaborate each point (see page 9).

5... Use all of this material to write an answer to the following exam question. *Discuss theories of the nature of intelligence.* As good practice you also might try to produce 'building block' essays on just one of the theories. Your answers should contain about 300 words of description and 500 words of evaluation.

Don't forget to read the essay-writing guidance on pages 8–9.

ISSUES RELATING TO THE MEASUREMENT OF INTELLIGENCE

ETHICS VERSUS SCIENCE

GENDER BIAS

CULTURAL BIAS

Intelligence is measured using **IQ tests**, which were described at the beginning of this chapter. Like any other measure of a psychological variable, an IQ test is only useful if it is accurate. That means it should produce consistent results, i.e. be **reliable**, and should measure something 'real', i.e. be **valid**. You will have gathered from the previous spread that these expectations may be a little hopeful as intelligence is not necessarily one single, simple thing.

EXAM TIP
The material on this spread should enable you to write a description of the issues relating to the measurement of IQ and an evaluation of these issues. However, there would still be some merit in including a *description* of IQ tests themselves (see page 9) – but be aware that the evaluation of these tests is actually part of the AO1 content. The AO2 content is an evaluation of the evaluation!

THE RELIABILITY OF IQ TESTS

Internal reliability
Internal reliability concerns whether items within the test are consistent, i.e. are all testing the same thing. If items on a test lack internal reliability then the whole of an individual's score would not reflect their intelligence but instead would partly be measuring some other variable.

External reliability
The second aspect of reliability, **external reliability**, relates to whether a test will produce a consistent measure of an individual's intelligence from one occasion to another. If an IQ test has external reliability that suggests we are measuring a stable characteristic. If, however, IQ tests vary with factors such as tiredness, motivation or practice, they might not fairly reflect an individual's potential. For example, highly motivated children achieve higher IQ scores than less well motivated ones (Zigler and Butterfield, 1968).

The effects of practice Basso et al. (2002) retested adults on a standard IQ test after either three- or six-month intervals and found their IQ scores increased by between 3 and 11 points on different **sub-scales**. These increases were similar regardless of the time interval, but there were no corresponding increases in **working memory**. This suggests that practice tends to inflate IQ scores so the findings of repeat performances should be treated with caution. For example, if an IQ test is being used to assess an educational intervention, the mere effect of retesting may produce an apparent improvement.

THE VALIDITY OF IQ TESTS

Internal validity
Internal validity concerns the extent to which an IQ test measures what it claims to measure.

Construct validity Any IQ test is based on a particular theoretical approach to intelligence, i.e. a 'construct'. For example, a test based on Sternberg's theory would suggest that people with higher practical intelligence scores should be better at 'real-world' problem solving. If they are then the test would have construct validity. But what if the theory were wrong? The test would still have construct validity but not be valid for other reasons. Similarly, if you believe that IQ tests measure an **innate** characteristic, the IQ shouldn't be affected by coaching – but it is (see box on facing page).

Criterion validity is assessed by comparing IQ test scores with some other criterion, such as exam results. If a test is measuring something 'real', these two measures should **correlate**. The issue is that, if they do not correlate, then using IQ tests as a means to select children (or adults) for different courses or jobs in the future may lead to flawed decisions. Some evidence suggests that IQ scores do predict academic success. For example, Petridies et al. (2005) found that verbal IQ predicted the performance of British school children at the end of Key Stage 3 and at GCSE.

Content validity is an indication of whether the items on a test are appropriate for measuring a particular attribute, in this case, intelligence. Obviously, we can look at whether they seem to measure intelligence (**face validity**) but to be more precise than this, **factor analysis** is used. If an IQ test has content validity, this should reveal just one factor (intelligence). However, as some theories suggest that there are several kinds of intelligence, valid tests can be examined for factors such as 'verbal ability' or 'non-verbal ability' separately.

External validity
External validity concerns the extent to which the findings of a study or test can be generalised beyond the setting in which they were measured. In the context of intelligence, testing is a matter of the meaningfulness of the result.

Culture bias Cultural differences in defining intelligence can cause **culture bias** in IQ tests. For example, Western societies see intelligence as something *within* the individual. In contrast, Ugandan society sees intelligence as a functional relationship depending on shared knowledge between the individual and society (Wober, 1974), and in Kenya an intelligent child is one who is obedient, respectful and trustworthy (Harkness and Super, 1992) with good practical and social skills (Grigorenko, 2001). Opinions about 'intelligent' responses to IQ test questions will therefore differ between cultures.

Another cause of culture bias is the reliance of some IQ tests on language; for example, the *Stanford–Binet* test (see page 116) has spoken instructions for the items testing non-verbal skills and many of the required responses are verbal. Thus, children with limited verbal ability, or working in an additional language, will be disadvantaged.

Gender bias Males have a higher mathematical IQ and females higher verbal IQ. However, the findings of Spencer et al. (1999) suggest this is, in part, because women are threatened by the perception that maths is stereotypically a male domain. Davies et al. (2002) supported this by showing that women underperformed on a maths test if they were first shown with gender stereotyped TV adverts. Furthermore, white males can be primed to do poorly on maths tests by telling them that Asian students are better at maths (a threatening stereotype) (Aronson et al., 1999).

The 'reification' of intelligence
Some critics of Spearman's theory of general intelligence (discussed on page 121) have pointed out that Spearman committed the logical error of *reification* (i.e. treated an abstract concept as a concrete 'thing') – a criticism which applies to all IQ tests. In Spearman's case, he took an abstract correlation and reified it as a 'thing' with a location in the brain. Once the error of reification is committed, it is easy to make another logical error, circular reasoning, where the only evidence for an explanation of some phenomenon is the phenomenon itself. In Spearman's case, the only evidence for *g* was the positive correlations between test performances on different tests, even though it was those correlations he was trying to explain in the first place.

Coaching students to pass IQ tests

For years, tests such as the 11 Plus have been used to select bright children for a grammar school education, yet a BBC survey carried out in 2008 found that half the children in grammar schools in the UK had been coached for the exam by private tutors. A further third had been prepared by their parents. Bunting and Mooney (2001) found that pupils coached for nine months improved their 11 Plus scores by 40%. Head teachers have warned that such coaching gives children an unfair edge, and that some artificially peak to get a place but then struggle to keep up with the academic demands of grammar school life.

EVALUATION

Consequences of lack of reliability

Internal reliability IQ tests may appear to lack internal reliability but that's because they consist of sub-scales, and these sub-scales generally are high in internal reliability. For example, WISC-V, a modern IQ test for children, has internal reliabilities of .76 for picture concepts, .92 for perceptual reasoning, .94 for arithmetic and .96 for verbal comprehension (Ryan *et al.*, 2009). This shows that each sub-scale consistently taps the target ability for that sub-scale.

The effects of practice suggest that IQ tests are not measuring a stable characteristic of an individual because practice leads to improved scores. This has important implications if, for example, the results were being used to select children for schools (see box on coaching above) or adults for jobs. Consider two job applicants; the less able applicants may have more experience taking IQ tests and therefore may do better on the day and – inappropriately – be given the job.

Consequences of lack of validity

Culture free One way to overcome the problem of culture bias is to use non-verbal tests such as *Raven's Progressive Matrices* (see page 116). However, culture can still affect performance. For example, children who are more familiar with pencils and paper are likely to do better on any test, even a non-verbal test.

Another example of how culture may affect performance is that the answers, even on a non-verbal task, are culturally determined. Consider a typical IQ test sorting task asking a child to sort a list of objects including, for instance, an orange; the 'intelligent' response from Western children would be to group orange and potato together (food) and knife and hoe together (tools), i.e. group things together in terms of 'type of object'. However, the 'intelligent' response for Kpelle farmers in West Africa would be to group by function – you hoe potatoes and cut oranges so they would group the objects 'wrongly' according to the test. When asked how an idiot would group the objects, the Kpelle response was to sort them by type (Glick, 1975).

Culture fair An alternative approach is to design tests so that they take cultural differences into account. In reality, however, it is very difficult to assess in advance how the knowledge and skills of different cultures will affect test performance.

The use of IQ data

Evidence relating to the reliability and validity of IQ tests suggests that traditional IQ tests are (a) not measuring a stable characteristic of individuals (i.e. they lack reliability); and (b) not equally fair to all people who take them.

The implication, therefore, is that IQ is only an indicator, and perhaps a questionable one, of our intelligence. However, proponents of **psychometric** tests have succeeded in persuading those with political power that such tests reliably measure intelligence, and these tests have accordingly been used to make important social decisions. For example, Herrnstein and Murray (1994) claimed, in their controversial book, *The Bell Curve*, that IQ tests were accurate and could predict future success (e.g. in a person's academic life or career). On the assumption that IQ was also **inherited**, they concluded that there would be racial differences in intelligence and suggested that IQ scores should be used to steer social policy. This is questionable for many reasons. One important reason is that, as we have seen, the lack of validity may make such decisions unfounded. It might be possible to eliminate cultural differences in IQ by removing items from IQ tests that indicate such differences. However, this could merely mask underlying causes of differences, such as social deprivation.

"We've given you a brain scan and we can't find anything."

The mismeasure of man

Gould (1981) wrote a book called *The Mismeasure of Man*, detailing the extent to which early IQ tests were culturally biased but the results were nevertheless taken to show that certain groups of people were inferior.

In 1915, Robert Yerkes persuaded the US army to test the intelligence of 1.75 million men using psychometric tests. Literate recruits were given the *Army Alpha* Test (a written examination), whereas illiterates were given the *Army Beta* Test, which was based on pictures. Army psychologists then graded each man from A to E. The tests showed that European immigrants fell slightly below white Americans in terms of IQ, and African-Americans were at the bottom of the scale with the lowest mental age. However, the European immigrants could not answer questions on the examination because they were about American food, sports, etc., and the African-Americans could not answer the questions because the objects in the test represented white middle-class American culture. Despite this, Yerkes never came to the conclusion that the poor scores were a result of the cultural bias of the tests used. Test results such as these have 'lent scientific credibility to the prevailing prejudice' and have led to popular stereotypes concerning race and IQ.

CAN YOU...? (No. 5.3)

1... Select **six** issues relating to the measurement of intelligence.

2... For each issue write **three or four** sentences explaining the issue.

3... Identify about **ten** points of evaluation (these can be positive or negative).

4... Elaborate each point (see page 9).

5... Use all of this material to write an answer to the following exam question: *Discuss issues relating to the measurement of intelligence*. Your answer should contain about 300 words of description and 500 words of evaluation.

Don't forget to read the essay-writing guidance on pages 8–9.

ROLE OF GENETIC FACTORS IN INTELLIGENCE

NATURE AND NURTURE

DETERMINISM

CULTURAL BIAS

ETHICAL ISSUES

Nowhere has the **nature versus nurture** argument been more keenly fought than in the study of intelligence. The notion that intelligence could be **genetically** influenced to any great extent goes against the fundamental belief that we are all born equal – if intelligence is genetically determined then some people must be more intelligent than others. It is clear that human intelligence must be the outcome of **natural selection** in the same way that all traits must be adaptive to be perpetuated. Therefore, it makes sense that we should find a major role for genetics in the development of this trait.

Although there are cultural differences in what might be described as 'intelligent behaviour', intelligence is, in the West, commonly equated to performance on **IQ tests**. In this section, intelligence and IQ are therefore used interchangeably.

THE HERITABILITY OF INTELLIGENCE

In explaining the origins of intelligence, there are only two dimensions that determine intelligence test performance. The first is genetics (i.e. characteristics inherited from parents) and the second is environment (e.g. family background, educational experiences, etc.). These two components will always add up to 100% of the variation in intelligence scores between two people, hence if researchers calculate that the genetic part is 40%, then that would mean 60% could be attributed to the environment. The extent to which a particular characteristic (such as eye colour, temperament or intelligence) is passed from parents to children purely by means of their genes is known as *genetic heritability*. Traditionally, psychologists have used studies of twins and adoption studies to assess the relative contributions of genetics and environment in intelligence test performance, i.e. to a person's IQ.

Twin and adoption studies

Twin studies There are two types of twin, **dizygotic** (DZ) twins who, on average, share 50% of their genes and are therefore genetically related by .50. **Monozygotic** (MZ) twins are genetically identical and therefore have a degree of genetic relatedness that is 1.0. It follows, therefore, that if genetic factors are important in intelligence, MZ twins will be more alike than DZ twins. This was demonstrated in the study by Malouff *et al.* (above right). However, it is difficult to disentangle the relative influences of genes and environment when twins are reared together. Therefore, the real indication of the importance of genetic factors in intelligence comes from studies which have assessed the degree of similarity in twins reared *apart*, i.e. in situations where, for one reason or another, twins have been separated at birth and brought up in entirely different environments. Research (e.g. Bouchard and McGue, 1981) has shown that closer IQ similarity of MZ twins is still evident even when they are reared apart. Bouchard and McGue estimated an average **concordance rate** of IQ (i.e. the degree to which intelligence level was the same for two individuals) for DZ twins reared together of 60% (or .60), yet for MZ twins reared *apart*, the concordance rate was much higher, at 72% (or .72).

Adoption studies Finding large numbers of MZ twins who have been reared apart is (thankfully) relatively difficult, but there is another important source of data for the assessment of the role of genetic factors. Adoption studies compare the IQs of adopted children with those of other members of their adoptive families *and* members of their biological families. If genetic factors influence intelligence, research should find a similarity between the IQ levels of adopted children and those of their biological families. The *Texas Adoption Project* (Horn *et al.*, 1979) tested members of 300 Texan families who had adopted children shortly after their births from a home for unwed mothers. When the children were first assessed, there were higher **correlations** between the children's IQs and those of their adoptive mothers than with their biological mothers. However, when the researchers tracked down many of the participants ten years later, the only correlations that remained above .20 were between the children and their biological relatives (Loehlin *et al.*, 1989). This finding has been evident in many other studies – the impact of family (environmental) influences tend to decrease with age, while genetic influences tend to increase.

A 'meta' meta-analysis

Malouff *et al.* (2008) aggregated the results of nine meta-analyses, covering over 400 separate studies, mostly involving comparisons of MZ and DZ twins. Although the study included many different aspects of human behaviour (including antisocial behaviour, smoking and anxiety disorders), the specific findings related to *intelligence* suggested that 48% of the variance in intelligence could be attributed to genes. Another factor associated with intelligence test performance, *mental chronometric performance* (how fast the brain processes information), appears to be 41% based on our genes.

Is there a gene for intelligence?

IGF2R Chorney *et al.* (1998) tested the IQs of a group of children between the ages of six and 15 years old. They then divided the children into two groups. The average IQ in one group (the 'super-bright' group) was 136 and in the other (the average-IQ group) it was 103. The researchers examined each child's **chromosome** 6, and discovered that a specific form of the gene IGF2R (insulin-like growth factor 2 receptor) occurred in twice as many children in the high-IQ group as in the average group – 32% versus 16%. They concluded that this form of the IGF2R gene (called **allele** 5) contributes to intelligence.

Genetic markers for intelligence In a more recent study, Butcher *et al.* (2008) took cheek swabs from about 7,000 children and scanned their genes with a device called a *microarray*, a small chip that can recognise half a million distinctive snippets of DNA. This device enabled the researchers to detect genes that only had a tiny effect on the variation in IQ scores. They found only six genetic markers (i.e. genes or fragments of DNA associated with particular traits) that showed any sign of having an influence on IQ test scores. However, when they ran stringent statistical tests, only one gene passed, accounting for just 0.4% of the variation in IQ scores.

▶ *A mother and child living in poor conditions in Tower Hamlets, London.*

EVALUATION

Are twins a representative group?

A criticism of twin studies is that twins, particularly those drawn from Western cultures, may not constitute a representative group and so may lead to an overestimation or underestimation of the heritability of intelligence, particularly with reference to a non-twin population. Voracek and Haubner (2008) addressed this issue through a meta-analysis of published studies, comparing twins and singletons (non-twins). This analysis compared more than 30,000 twins with nearly 1.6 million singletons across six different countries and a variety of intelligence tests. They found that, on average, twins score 4.2 IQ points less than singletons, although it is not clear whether this effect persists over their lifespan. Likely causes of the effect appear to be prenatal and perinatal factors (e.g. reduced foetal growth and shorter gestation for *twins*).

A gene for intelligence

IGF2R Although the IGF2R gene appears to be associated with high IQ, it is not sufficient on its own to account for high IQ. Of Plomin's high IQ group, a larger proportion of the high IQ children did *not* have the IGF2R gene compared with those who *did* have the gene. Similarly, some of the average IQ group did have the gene, but still had only average IQ. Presumably this is because intelligence, if it *is* influenced by genetic factors, requires a combination of many different genes, each of which is responsible for only a small variation in overall intelligence. A further problem is that others have failed to replicate Chorney *et al.*'s study, effectively rendering the results scientifically meaningless.

Genetic markers Not everybody is enthusiastic about the search for genetic markers of intelligence. Members of the *Campaign for Real Intelligence* argue that IQ is only one element of mental ability, and should not be taken as the sole measure of a person's intelligence. They warn that the discovery of any genes connected with IQ could divide society by marginalising people who lack these 'IQ genes'.

Gene–environment interactions

Breastfeeding and IQ Caspi *et al.* (2007) found that children with one version of the FADS2 gene scored seven points higher in IQ tests if they were breastfed, whereas children with another variant of this gene showed no such benefits associated with breastfeeding. This study is significant because it appears to show how genes can alter the effect that a particular environmental influence (in this case breastfeeding) has on intelligence.

Genes can mould the environment Genes may also influence behaviour in terms of how intelligence develops, by moulding the intellectual environment in particular ways. For example, genes may cause us to seek out some experiences rather than others (**niche picking**), which in turn affects our intelligence for better or worse. This might explain why the influence of genes on IQ performance becomes more pronounced as people get older. As people grow up and take control over their own lives, they are free to act in a way that is consistent with their psychological make-up. Thus, the influence of their genes becomes stronger, and the influence of family (environmental) background becomes weaker.

Subcultural bias

Turkheimer *et al.* (2003) highlight a potential bias in the reporting of genetic factors in IQ. It appears that the same gene can have different effects in different environments. This is particularly important where research has concentrated on children from one particular type of background. Researchers analysed the IQ test scores of hundreds of twins, taking into consideration their socioeconomic status (including family income and educational level of the parents). They found that the influence of genetic factors depended on the socioeconomic status of the children. In children from affluent families, about 60% of the variance in IQ scores could be accounted for by genes, but for children from impoverished families, genes accounted for almost none of the variance. Turkheimer suggests that poverty brings with it powerful environmental forces that may shape intelligence from the womb through school and beyond. However, when children grow up in the relative stability of an affluent home, only then do genetic influences begin to make themselves felt.

CAN YOU...?   No. 5.4

1... Explain the nature–nurture argument in the context of intelligence.

2... Identify **five** pieces of evidence for the role of genetic factors in intelligence.

3... Describe each piece of evidence in 50–100 words.

4... Identify about **ten** points of evaluation (these can be positive or negative).

5... Elaborate each point (see page 9).

6... Use all of this material to write an answer to the following exam question: *Describe and evaluate the role of genetic factors in intelligence.* Your answer should contain about 300 words of description and 500 words of evaluation.

Remember that, when writing an essay, you can include material from other spreads – but only if it is made specifically relevant to the essay. For example, in an essay on the genetic factors in intelligence you might include evidence related to environmental factors, discussed on the next spread. But do be very careful to use it effectively.

ROLE OF ENVIRONMENTAL FACTORS IN INTELLIGENCE

SOCIALLY SENSITIVE RESEARC

NATURE AND NURTURE

CULTURAL BIAS

The list of potential environmental factors that might influence intelligence is endless. It includes family factors, such as parental occupation and birth order, educational opportunities, and wider cultural influences, such as peer groups and media. We can also throw into the pot such immeasurables as environmental luck, e.g. who you sit next to at school, or even a chance comment from a teacher.

The *High Scope/Perry Preschool Project*

The *High Scope/Perry Preschool Project*, carried out from 1962 to 1967, provided high-quality preschool education to three- and four-year-old African-American children living in poverty and assessed to be at high risk of school failure. The study randomly allocated a group of 128 children to either a programme group (who received high-quality preschool education for 2½ hours each weekday morning) or a control group that did not receive the programme. For the programme group, teachers also provided a weekly home visit to each mother and child, designed to involve the mother in the educational process. Initial improvements were encouraging, with 67% of the programme group having IQ levels in excess of 90 when they began school (100 is considered 'average'), compared with just 28% of the non-programme group.

The children were followed up at age 27 (Schweinhart *et al.*, 1993), at which point, compared with the control group, the programme group:

- Completed an average of almost one full year more of schooling (11.9 years versus 11 years).

- Spent an average of 1.3 fewer years in special education for mental or learning impairment (3.9 years versus 5.2 years).

- Had a much higher rate of high-school graduation (65% versus 45%).

ENVIRONMENTAL FACTORS IN INTELLIGENCE

Family environment

Socioeconomic status A family's **socioeconomic status** (SES) is based on many things, including parental occupations and income, status, educational level of the parents and so on. In the UK, SES is based on parental occupation, and is graded from Class I (professional occupations) to Class V (unskilled occupations). Mackintosh (1998) provides evidence from the *British National Child Development Study* (NCDS), showing that even when factors such as birth weight, financial hardship and area of residence were taken into consideration, children with fathers in Class I occupations scored 10 points higher on **IQ tests** than did children of Class V fathers.

Birth order and family size An early Dutch study (Belmont and Marolla, 1973) looked at the relationship between family size, birth order and IQ in a sample of 386 19-year-old Dutch men. They found that, even when SES was controlled, children from larger families had lower IQ levels than children from smaller families, and first-born children typically had higher IQ levels than later-born children. A recent Norwegian study (Bjerkedal *et al.*, 2007) also found that first-born children had higher IQ levels than later-born children and also that if the first-born child had died, the second child 'moved up a place', scoring closer to the IQ level of an average first-born child.

Education

School effects The relationship between formal education and IQ test scores is often taken for granted, but is there evidence that school boosts intelligence? There have been many studies testing this claim, and Ceci's (1991) **meta-analysis** of such studies concluded that children who attend school regularly score higher than those who attend less regularly, that IQ scores decrease over the long summer holidays, and that there is a rise of 2.7 IQ points for each year of formal schooling.

Compensatory education Early attempts to boost the IQs of disadvantaged children by a period of preschool education were somewhat disappointing. The most famous of these programmes, *Head Start*, began in the 1960s. Although there were some initial gains in IQ scores, its effectiveness has been questioned in the longer term, with some studies showing positive gains from participation, whereas others have reported no significant gains. However, the findings from another major US study (see left) have been far more encouraging.

Culture

Group socialisation theory Harris (1995) claims that experiences outside the home may be more important in developing people's intelligence than experiences within it. As children get older, they become less influenced by their families, and more influenced by life outside the home. Children identify with a number of different groups, and the shared norms within these groups dictate much of their subsequent development (e.g. the degree to which they engage in 'intellectual' pastimes such as reading books or going on to university).

Ethnicity and IQ Herrnstein and Murray (see far right) compared IQ test scores for different groups in the US. Among their findings was that immigrants coming into the USA had IQ levels that were significantly lower than resident Americans. Controversially, they argued that as more and more immigrants came into the country, this caused a downward pressure on intelligence levels and an increase in the social problems associated with people with low IQ.

Statistical fallacies

Maltby *et al.* (2007) argue that much research in this area is misleading because the statistics themselves are misleading. Research on the relationship between birth order and IQ, for example, must also take into account family size, education, region of the country and so on. It would be inappropriate to draw conclusions concerning birth order and IQ by comparing a first-born child raised in a small, professional family in an affluent area of Surrey and a second-born from the large family of an unskilled migrant worker in South Wales. It would be impossible to determine which, if any, of these environmental factors was responsible for any differences in IQ. Such erroneous conclusions based on simple comparisons are known as 'statistical fallacies'.

◄ *Research suggests that environmental factors such as socioeconomic status and family size can have a significant influence on measured intelligence.*

EVALUATION

Family environment

Socioeconomic status undoubtedly affects measured intelligence, but why? One reason is that families with high SES are better able to prepare their children for school because they have better access to resources and information that enhance children's cognitive and intellectual development. For example, the *National Statistics Omnibus Survey* found that in 2000, 71% of Class I households in the UK had Internet access compared with just 26% of Class V households.

Birth order and family size In the Bjerkedal *et al*. study (facing page), one finding was that first-born children typically had IQ scores three points higher than second-born children. In societies where such a discrepancy could make a huge difference to a child's life (e.g. the difference between an elite university and a less prestigious institution) such a finding is bound to provoke anxiety. But is there any evidence that such differences persist? A study of more than 100,000 people, found that in small- and medium-sized families, birth order had no effect on how far children progressed in education (Blake, 1989).

Education

Herrnstein and Murray (see right) and Ceci (see facing page) reach sharply contrasting conclusions about the potential for education to increase the intelligence of individuals. Herrnstein and Murray's conclusion is that 'the story of attempts to raise intelligence is one of high hopes, flamboyant claims and disappointing results'. In contrast, Ceci concludes that 'schooling exerts a substantial influence on IQ formation and maintenance'.

How do we explain such different conclusions from the same research studies? There are, perhaps, two main reasons. The first is a failure to define what constitutes an *improvement*. All of them would presumably agree that education has some effect, but the issue appears to be more to do with the size of the effect and the circumstances in which it manifests itself. The second reason concerns the generally accepted belief that *g* (see pages 120–121) is both a meaningful concept and can be accurately measured by traditional IQ tests. This position has been challenged by theorists such as Howard Gardner and Robert Sternberg (see page 120) who both argue that intelligence is multidimensional, and that any attempts to measure it using a simple **psychometric** test, or to assess the success of an educational programme in the same way is a meaningless exercise.

Culture

Group socialisation theory Pinker (2002) rejects Harris's claim that intelligence, like many other characteristics, is more a product of peer group than family influences. Pinker sees the interaction between genes and peers as a possible explanation for some behaviours, such as smoking, but not for intelligence.

Culture bias in IQ tests Greenfield (1997) argues that assessing the IQ of people from cultures other than the one in which the test was developed represents a **cultural bias** that will inevitably influence any results. In societies where formal schooling is common, for example, students gain an early familiarity with organising items into rows and columns, which gives them an advantage over test takers in cultures where formal schooling is rare. Likewise, media technologies such as television and video games give test takers from cultures where such media are commonplace an advantage on visual IQ tests.

THEORIES OF COGNITIVE DEVELOPMENT

PIAGET'S THEORY

- With maturation, new mental operations become possible so there are stages in development but interaction with the environment is also needed.

The mechanisms of cognitive development
- Schema are programmes we construct to understand the world.
- Assimilation adds new information to an existing schema.
- Accommodation changes an existing schema so as to understand new and very different information.
- Equilibration overcomes the imbalance caused by new information. Cognitive development is driven by the need for equilibrium.

Stages in cognitive development
- Stage 1: Sensori-motor – learning to coordinate sensory input and motor actions through repetition.
- Stage 2: Pre-operations – thought lacks internally consistent logic but becomes more symbolic. Thought is based on what is seen rather than rules (the appearance–reality distinction). Children are also egocentric.
- Stage 3: Concrete operations – children acquire basic logical reasoning and can decentre (so can conserve).
- Stage 4: Formal operations – abstract thinking used to solve problems (hypothetico-deductive reasoning).

EVALUATION

Research support
- Little research supports the idea of disequilibrium, although Inhelder et al. found that mild conflict did help learning.
- Piaget's conservation research (e.g. with beakers and buttons) showed that children couldn't conserve until the concrete operational stage but later research showed children could conserve earlier, e.g. McGarrigle and Donaldson with naughty teddy.
- Piaget's three mountains test showed that pre-operational children were egocentric but Hughes found that younger children could decentre with a more realistic task using a toy policeman.

Strengths and limitations
- Piaget underestimated young children's abilities and overestimated the abilities of older ones (in their use of abstract logic).
- The theory applies to academic, middle-class Western culture.
- The focus on logic tends to ignore other important factors, e.g. social ones.
- Although Piaget's research was flawed, evidence still shows qualitative changes in cognition with maturation.
- Piaget's ideas, especially that children think differently from adults, have been influential, e.g. in teaching.
- Piaget's explanation of cognitive development combines nature (biological maturation) with nurture (experience).
- Piaget, an introvert, from an individualist society, produced a theory relating to individual learning.

VYGOTSKY'S THEORY

- Vygotsky believed that social interaction was crucial for cognitive development.

Mental processes
- Children have innate elementary mental functions (e.g. perception and memory). In humans, culture (i.e. other people) develops these elementary functions into higher functions.

The process of cultural influence
- Children learn through sharing problem solving with experts, e.g. parents, teachers or peers.
- Cultures have specific signs and symbols (semiotics), e.g. language, and mathematical symbols are also important.
- Two- and three-year-olds talk aloud to solve problems (egocentric speech). This becomes inner speech at about seven years.
- Functions appear twice in cognitive development; first at a social level and then at an individual level (internalisation).
- The zone of proximal development (ZPD) is the region of ongoing development.

EVALUATION

Research support
- Gredler identified how culture limits cognitive development as the primitive counting system (up to 29) used in Papua New Guinea makes adding and subtracting difficult.
- Young children working with their mothers cope with more difficult jigsaws than when working alone (confined by ZPD), so most teaching input occurs at the edge of the ZPD (McNaughton and Leyland).

Strengths and limitations
- There is less research relating to Vygotsky's theory than Piaget's as the concepts are harder to operationalise.
- Vygotsky may have overstressed social roles. Cognitive development would be much quicker if all that was needed was social input.
- Vygotsky's approach offers ways to involve others actively to assist learning, which is therefore a more practical approach than Piaget's.
- Vygotsky, an extrovert from a communist, collectivist society, produced a theory relating to learning within a social context.

THEORIES OF THE NATURE OF INTELLIGENCE

THEORIES BASED ON IQ TESTS

Spearman's two-factor theory
- The psychometric approach focuses on measuring intelligence (using IQ tests).
- Spearman developed a correlational technique to analyse relationships between different intelligence test scores to look for patterns (factor analysis).
- Spearman proposed two factors: general intelligence ('g') causes a positive correlation between performance on different tests. Specific abilities ('s') cause individuals to perform consistently on similar subtasks.

Thurstone's multifactor theory
- Thurstone used factor analysis to identify many different mental abilities (multifactors) and proposed seven primary mental abilities (PMAs) (spatial ability, perceptual speed, numerical ability, verbal comprehension, word fluency, memory and inductive reasoning).
- Thurstone saw g as an average of the PMAs.

EVALUATION

Spearman's two-factor theory
- Duncan et al. used PET scans to show that visual or verbal tasks associated with general intelligence (g) activated the same frontal lobe areas, whereas 'non-g' tasks did not.
- Johnson and Bouchard analysed performance on 40 different tests and claimed to find evidence for a g factor.

Thurstone's multifactor theory
- Factor analysis claims to be objective but the identified factors are only arbitrary categories.
- A criticism of the multifactor (and MI) approach is that each 'intelligence' is only a cognitive style (Morgan).

MORE RECENT THEORIES

Gardner's theory of multiple intelligences (MI)
- Gardner suggested that teaching ignores less 'traditional' forms of intelligence. He identified seven types of intelligence (and later added the eighth): linguistic, logical–mathematical, spatial, bodily–kinaesthetic, musical intelligence, interpersonal, intrapersonal (understanding oneself) and natural (expertise in the natural world).
- Gardner believed many abilities could count as 'intelligence' if they resolved problems in real (cultural) settings.
- Gardner thought each form of intelligence was located separately in the brain but that they could interact.

Sternberg's triarchic theory of intelligence
- Sternberg defined intelligence as a process rather than a measurable quantity so individual differences reflect differences in cognitive operations (information processing).
- Sternberg's triarchic theory has three aspects of intelligence: analytical (componential: combining thinking strategies to solve a problem), practical (contextual: solving real-world rather than abstract problems) and creative (experiential: developing novel ideas based on experience).

Gardner's theory of multiple intelligences
- Gardner provided evidence from three sources: (1) Neuropsychological evidence from people with brain damage; although they lose some intellectual skills, they retain others; (2) Individuals with exceptional talent in one area (such as autistic savants); (3) Experiments showing that some tasks interfere with each other, but others don't.
- Few studies support MI theory although Onika et al. found that teaching which focused on developing MI increased students' academic, social, and emotional well-being more than direct instruction.
- Gardner's approach can help us to understand how cultures differ. Chan found that in Hong Kong mathematical intelligence was most important, and bodily–kinaesthetic and naturalist intelligences least important.

Sternberg's triarchic theory of intelligence
- Merrick found Sternberg's three abilities using the Cognitive Abilities Self-Evaluative Questionnaire.
- Teaching 'triarchically' improves academic achievement (Sternberg et al.) and Practical Intelligence for Schools (PIFS), an intervention to improve practical intelligence, is effective (Williams et al.).
- Sternberg's approach is more practical as it looks at how people solve problems rather than just describing intelligence as the psychometric approach does.
- Gottfredson claims that there is insufficient evidence to distinguish practical from general intelligence.

ISSUES RELATING TO THE MEASUREMENT OF INTELLIGENCE

THE RELIABILITY OF IQ TESTS

- To be useful, tests need to be reliable, i.e. should produce consistent results.

Internal reliability
- Internal reliability is whether all test items are measuring the same thing. If an IQ test lacks internal reliability only part of the IQ score reflects intelligence.

External reliability
- External reliability is about the stability of IQ between testings, but results may be affected by motivation or practice making the results unreliable.
- Zigler and Butterfield found highly motivated children achieved higher IQ scores, suggesting the test lacked external reliability.
- Adults doing an IQ test twice improved their IQ scores, suggesting that practice reduces external reliability (Basso et al.).

THE VALIDITY OF IQ TESTS

- An IQ test needs to be valid, i.e. it should measure something 'real'.

Internal validity
- Internal validity is whether an IQ test measures what it claims to measure.
- The construct validity of an IQ test is determined by whether the test can be shown to measure a particular theory/construct. A test may have construct validity but if the theory is wrong then the IQ test lacks validity.
- Spearman's theory, and IQ tests in general, can be criticised on the basis of reification. Spearman's only evidence for g was the correlation between different test performances – the thing he was trying to explain.
- Criterion validity is judged by correlating IQ test scores with another measure, e.g. exam results. Petridies et al. (2005) found that verbal IQ predicted academic success at Key Stage 3 and GCSE.
- Content validity indicates whether items on a test are appropriate for measuring intelligence.
- Content validity can be measured using factor analysis.

External validity
- External validity is whether the test findings will generalise.
- Cultural differences in the constructs of intelligence can cause culture bias.
- Western societies see intelligence as within the individual, whereas in Uganda it is seen as depending on shared knowledge between the individual and society, and in Kenya as relating to practical and social skills, and obedience.
- Culture bias also stems from the use of language in IQ tests.
- Gould described the early use of culturally biased IQ tests and the consequent treatment of certain groups of people as inferior.
- Gender differences are found in that males have a higher mathematical IQ and females higher verbal IQ.
- Such differences may partly be due to gender bias because men and women expect to do less well on certain tasks, e.g. Davies et al. found that women underperformed on a maths test if they were primed with gender-stereotyped TV adverts.

EVALUATION

Co Consequences of lack of validity
Consequences of a lack of reliability
- Modern IQ tests for children typically have high internal reliability for different subscales, ranging from 0.76 to 0.96 (Ryan et al.).
- If IQ test scores improve with practice this suggests IQ tests are not measuring a stable characteristic and are not reliable. This would have implications for the use of tests to select children for schools or adults for jobs.
- Half of grammar school children are coached for the 11 Plus exam. Coaching improves 11 Plus scores by 40% (Bunting and Mooney).

Consequences of lack of validity
- Non-verbal tests (e.g. Raven's Progressive Matrices) aim to be culture-free as they don't use spoken instructions or responses. Performance on Raven's Matrices correlates well with other tests suggesting that it is valid.
- However, some children may be less familiar with pencils and paper, leading to culture bias.
- Glick found that Westerners grouped objects by 'type' (e.g. foods, tools) but the Kpelle of West Africa grouped by function (e.g. linking the food with the tool used).
- Tests may be designed to take cultural differences into account but it is difficult to determine how cultural knowledge and skills will affect test performance.

The use of IQ data
- Evidence suggests that traditional IQ tests lack reliability and are biased against some people so IQ is a questionable indicator of intelligence.
- If unreliable or invalid tests are used to make important social decisions, these are unfounded. Cultural differences in IQ scores could be eliminated by changing the tests, but this could mask

ROLE OF GENETIC FACTORS IN INTELLIGENCE

THE HERITABILITY OF INTELLIGENCE

- Two factors determine intelligence test performance: genetics and the environment. These must add up to 100% of the variation in intelligence scores (e.g. if genes account for 40%, the environment accounts for 60%).

Twin and adoption studies
- Dizygotic (DZ) twins share 50% of their genes on average, whereas monozygotic (MZ) twins are genetically identical. If genes affect intelligence, then MZs should be more alike than DZs.
- Malouff et al. combined the findings of nine meta-analyses, mostly involving comparisons of MZ and DZ twins, and concluded that 48% of the variance in intelligence was due to genes.
- Disentangling the influence of genes and environment is difficult when twins are reared together. Bouchard and McGue found that MZs have similar IQ scores even when reared apart. DZs reared

together have a concordance rate of 60% but for MZ twins reared apart, it is higher (72%).
- Adoption studies compare the IQs of adopted children with those of their adoptive and biological families. Horn et al. found that the IQs of adoptees correlated initially most highly with their adoptive mothers' IQs but most highly with their biological mothers' IQs ten years later.
- Environmental influences decrease with age while genetic influences increase.

Is there a gene for intelligence?
- Chorney et al. used IQ to divide children into 'super-bright' and 'average' IQ. They found that a form of the IGF2R gene occurred in more of the high-IQ group.
- By analysing snippets of DNA in detail, Butcher et al. found six genetic markers with an influence on IQ test scores but only one had a significant effect, accounting for just 0.4% of the variation.

EVALUATION

Twins
- Twins (especially when from Western cultures) may not be representative of intelligence in the non-twin population.
- Voracek and Haubner compared twins and singletons and found that twins scored 4.2 IQ points less than singletons, possibly because of factors which reduced foetal growth.
- Kamin and Goldberger suggest twin studies overestimate the heritability of intelligence. MZs tend to be treated more similarly than same-sex DZs and share more time and friends so their environmental experience is more alike. Therefore, some of the similarity between MZ twins may be due to more similar environment rather than greater genetic similarity.

A gene for intelligence
- Although the IGF2R gene may be linked to high IQ, it is insufficient as an explanation. More of Chorney et al.'s high IQ group did not have the IGF2R gene than did and some of the average group did have the gene.
- Others researchers have failed to replicate Chorney et al.'s findings.
- The Campaign for Real Intelligence suggests IQ is only one aspect of mental ability and that finding genes linked to IQ could marginalise people who lack them.

Gene–environment interactions
- Breastfeeding produces higher IQ in children with one version of the FADS2 gene but not those without this variant (Caspi et al.), suggesting that genes can influence the effect of the environment on intelligence.
- If some genes make us seek out experiences that affect our intelligence (niche picking) it could explain why genes affect IQ more as we get older (as we gain control over our lives).
- The same gene can differ in its effects in different environments, potentially biasing studies exploring genetic factors in IQ. Turkheimer et al. found that in affluent families, about 60% of the variance was due to genes. In low SES families, genes accounted for little variance, suggesting that in higher SES homes, genetic influences have 'room' to take effect.

Ethical issues
- The (distant) possibility of using genetic engineering to increase intelligence raises ethical issues.
- US researchers have genetically modified mice to be better at learning (Tang et al.).

ROLE OF ENVIRONMENTAL FACTORS IN INTELLIGENCE

ENVIRONMENTAL FACTORS IN INTELLIGENCE

Family environment
- Socioeconomic status is determined by parental occupation in the UK but also may include income and educational level.
- Mackintosh found that, even after excluding factors like birth weight, financial hardship and residential area, children with fathers in high SES occupations scored ten points higher on IQ tests than children of low SES fathers.
- Belmont and Marolla found that, even when SES was controlled for, children from larger families had lower IQs and first-borns had higher IQs than later children.
- Bjerkedal et al. found that if a first-born child died, the IQ of the second child increased to the average for first-borns.

Education
- In a meta-analysis, Ceci found that children who attend school regularly score higher than poor attenders and that IQ rises for each year of formal schooling.

- Compensatory education to boost the IQ of disadvantaged children is not always effective, e.g. Head Start.
- In the High Scope/Perry Preschool Project, 67% made early gains compared with 28% of the control group.
- At age 27, the programme group was more successful than the controls and was more likely to have graduated from high school (65% versus 45%) (Schweinhart et al.).

Culture
- Harris suggests that children identify with different groups and the norms within those groups affect development (group socialisation theory).
- Herrnstein and Murray compared the IQs of US immigrants and residents and found the immigrants' IQs were lower. Controversially, they argued that increasing immigration was causing lower national IQ levels and increasing social problems. They have been criticised for promoting a racist view (of the inferiority of disadvantaged groups).

EVALUATION

Family environment
- Wahlsten described adoption studies that showed infants moved from low to high SES families improve in IQ.
- SES affects measured intelligence in part because high SES families (with good access to resources) can better prepare children for school, e.g. in the UK in 2000, 71% of high SES households had internet access but only 26% of low SES households.
- Although Bjerkedal et al. found first-borns had an IQ advantage, Blake found that in small- and medium-sized families, birth order did not affect educational progression.

Education
- The findings of Herrnstein and Murray and Ceci about the role of education in increasing intelligence are contradictory.
- Two reasons for this are that there are different ways to define 'improvement' and that intelligence is multidimensional,

so trying to measure it using simple psychometric tests is meaningless.

Culture
- Pinker contradicts Harris's view that intelligence is a product of group socialisation, claiming that the interaction between genes and peers may explain some behaviours, e.g. smoking, but not intelligence.
- Greenfield argues that using IQ tests developed in another culture will produce a bias. Children from societies where formal schooling is common are advantaged compared with those in cultures where it is rare. Technologies like television and video games also help test takers on visual IQ tests.
- Maltby et al. suggest research into IQ is misleading as many variables are involved. Studies which could lead to social consequences for the participants or those people represented by the research are described as socially sensitive (Sieber and Stanley).

Question 5 Describe and evaluate theories of cognitive development. *[25]*

Student answer

Paragraph 1 This essay will examine two theories of cognitive development. The first theory will be Piaget's theory of cognitive development and the second theory will be Vygotsky's theory of cognitive development. These are the most famous theories of cognitive development from two men who were actually born in the same year. One was Swiss and the other was Russian. They never met and Vygotsky died when he was very young.

Paragraph 2 Piaget wrote a stage theory of cognitive development. He thought there were four stages in cognitive development. Each of the stages is briefly described below.

* Sensorimotor stage where children learn to put what they see together with what they do. This stage occurs at 0–18 months.

* Pre-operational stage where children start to use symbols to describe the world. A typical aspect of this stage is that they are egocentric which means they only see the world from their view. In other words they are selfish. This stage starts at 18 months and continues up until the child is about 7 years.

* Concrete operational stage is when children can do conservation tasks and think properly. It starts at seven years and finishes about 11 years.

* Formal stage is the final stage, where children are able to think in an adult way.

Paragraph 3 Piaget thought that children were born with simple schema about the world. As the child gets older, the maturation process leads to more complex schema. This happens through the two processes of assimilation and accommodation.

Paragraph 4 However Piaget was wrong about the ages he identified in his theory. This was shown by Hughes with his study that used policeman. It was also shown by another psychologist called Donaldson who used a naughty teddy. Hughes showed that children were in fact not as egocentric as Piaget had found if the task was familiar, like when they had to do the same task that Piaget got them to do, only this time they did it with a policeman.

Paragraph 5 It is important to realise that Piaget had a lot of influence on schools in the UK although he was Swiss. Piaget pointed out that children didn't just know less than adults, they actually thought differently to adults and his theory made schools change their teaching methods so children found it easier to learn. He also believed play was important.

Paragraph 6 Vygotsky was a Russian who was dead before his work was translated into English. He lived in communist Russia and so he looked at community influences on development. In particular he looked at social influences on cognitive development.

Paragraph 7 His theory is very similar to Piaget as in his theory children have elementary mental functions at birth that become more complex. But Vygotsky said that the change happens from the influence of other people. Parents are the first experts in a child's life, then teachers. Their teaching becomes internal to the child, the child stops talking out loud. Social interaction becomes a silent internal action. Culture affects learning, sometimes holding it up.

Paragraph 8 Gredler did a study where he showed that the type of counting can restrict maths development. Other research has shown that the ZPD exists and can explain learning. There isn't much research on Vygotsky.

Paragraph 9 It's all ethnocentric as they are both European and not relevant to other countries. They are really the same except Piaget doesn't use social learning.

[560 words]

Examiner comments

This is a very typical essay from a candidate who has definitely learnt some of the material, but whose understanding of both the subject matter and the demands of the exam are limited. A small amount of extra work and understanding could easily have turned this essay into a much better answer.

Paragraph 1 is typical of candidate introductions, it scores nothing because it is not relevant to the question asked – there are no marks for general background and no marks for definitions. This is also true of rephrasing of the question, often taught by English teachers as a useful essay technique. This too, alas, scores nothing in a Psychology exam answer.

Paragraphs 2 and 3 demonstrate relevant knowledge (**AO1**) about Piaget's theory including the use of technical terms but there are many missed opportunities for demonstrating knowledge, such as explaining the terms 'assimilation and accommodation'.

The description (**AO1**) of Vygotsky's theory in paragraphs 6 and 7 is less detailed.

The lack of detail throughout means that, while largely accurate, the detail is basic. The examiner has to decide whether to put it in the 4–5 or 6–7 bands for **AO1**. Because the material is accurate and logically structured, but less detailed, the examiner **awarded 6 out of 10 for AO1**.

The **AO2** content is highlighted in grey. Overall, there is less **AO2** than **AO1** although there should be more as there are more marks for **AO2**. In total there are four separate paragraphs, each with accurate information and presented in a logical order, but all the points are undeveloped. For example, more information is needed to understand Hughes' study and how it contrasted with Piaget's.

When determining the **AO2** mark, the examiner looked at the 4–7 band (basic analysis, limited in terms of development of argument) and **awarded it 4 out of 15 marks for AO2** as it is near the bottom of this band.

10/25 makes this essay typical of someone who will gain a D/E grade.

| **Improvement?** | The most important thing to understand is the crucial role of **AO2**. You should expect just over half of your essay to consist of **AO2**, and you should plan it with that in mind. You should also become familiar with the techniques of indicating A**O2** to the examiner. (See 'Writing effective essays for A2' on pages 8–9.) | Elaboration is important, especially when writing **AO2**, but to make an **AO2** point using studies you do not need to describe studies in any great detail other than a sentence on 'what was done', a sentence on 'what was found' and then you should focus on the relevance of the **AO2** to the topic. | For example: 'In support of Vygotsky, Gredler (1992) showed that the method of counting in Papua New Guinea, ending at 29, made it very difficult to do large calculations. Culture was restricting cognitive development as predicted.' |

Chapter 6

Adolescence and adulthood

Chapter contents

132 Introduction to the study of adolescence and adulthood

134 Lifespan theories of development

136 Explanations of adolescent identity

138 Conflict during adolescence

140 Effects of events during middle adulthood

142 Effects of events during late adulthood

End-of-chapter review

144 Chapter summary

146 Exam question with student answer

▶ Our society has stereotypes about 'typical' adolescents and 'typical' older people – we picture the typical teenager as experiencing 'storm and stress' and the typical older person as worried and dependent. Insights provided in this chapter may change your mind.

Specification breakdown

Lifespan theories of development (e.g. Erikson's 'eight ages of man'; Levinson's 'seasons of a man's life'; Gould's 'evolution of adult consciousness').	The core of this chapter is the idea of a statistically predictable life cycle. There have been several attempts to formulate such theories and here you will examine the more well-known ones, as well as the criticism they have attracted.
Explanations of adolescent identity (e.g. Blos's psychoanalytic theory; Erikson's theory of psychosocial development; Marcia's theory).	Adolescence will be a topic close to students' hearts as most students will be classed as adolescent! Mature students will presumably remember what it was like! Here you examine theories about identity during adolescence, i.e. how you find out and develop who you really are or will become. You can judge whether these theories ring true.
Conflict during adolescence including storm and stress and alternative views.	It is standard movie fare – the difficult adolescent, moody and unstable, and the strange world of 'youth' culture which no adult understands. So do these theories of conflict illuminate our understanding or do they miss the point?
Effects of events during middle adulthood (e.g. marriage, parenthood, divorce).	Now for the boring bit, reading about what happens to your parents and may happen to you in the future. Probably the most profound event for anyone will be becoming a parent for the first time. Some readers will have experienced the effects of divorce on their families. You will see if psychology has something informative to say about this period of life.
Effects of events during late adulthood (e.g. retirement, adjustment to old age, bereavement).	This is probably the most distant period of life for many readers, the last quarter of life. However, some of the events may be experienced at any time, such as bereavement. Does the evidence accord with readers' experiences? Are there important cultural differences?

DEVELOPMENTAL PSYCHOLOGY

Developmental psychology is concerned with how children and adults change as they get older. One of the obvious issues for developmental psychologists is why. What is the cause of such change – is it **nature** or is it **nurture**? Do changes happen because of **genetic** or **environmental** factors? For example adolescence begins with the onset of *puberty*, signalled by the appearance of secondary sexual characteristics, such as pubic hair. Each person's individual timetable for puberty (a biological event) is influenced primarily by **heredity** (nature) but environmental factors, such as diet and exercise (nurture), also exert some influence. This illustrates that change, or development, is generally driven by both nature and nurture.

For many years people thought of development as something that stopped as soon as a person reached adulthood. People certainly stop growing in height around the beginning of adulthood, but other changes happen after that time. There are obvious physical changes to hair and body shape and, more importantly, people continue to change and develop psychologically – various life experiences, such as becoming a parent or facing retirement, trigger emotional, cognitive and social changes.

Lifespan psychology

In the early years of psychology, developmental theories focused only on childhood and adolescence. For example, Freud's theory of the development of personality ended in adolescence, suggesting that personality was thereafter fixed. Piaget's very influential theory of the development of thinking (described on pages 118–120) described how children don't simply know less, they actually think differently. Piaget suggested that the qualitative changes in the way we think end around the age of 11 – from there on people are thinking in an adult manner.

These theories were both proposed in the first half of the twentieth century. By the 1960s psychologists began to acknowledge that there were continuing psychological and social changes throughout the lifespan, giving rise to *lifespan psychology* which is concerned with physical, psychological and social development from conception to death.

One of the best examples of this approach is Erik Erikson's (1963) 'eight ages of man', a theory of personality development that spans a man's (and woman's) life. This stage theory is outlined in the table below. Erikson was originally a trained Freudian **psychoanalyst** and therefore subscribed to Freud's personality stages which end with adolescence (e.g. the **oral** and **genital stages** – which you studied in your AS course). However, Erikson's own experiences with patients and research participants led him to formulate a more comprehensive theory (see table below). Like Freud, Erikson felt that at particular ages an individual is faced with specific dilemmas which need to be resolved in order to move on and continue to grow and develop – this is a *positive outcome*. Failure to deal with an age-specific crisis leads to a *negative outcome* and prevents healthy personality development. For example, in the first year of life the crisis relates to learning to trust a mother figure, which forms the basis of trust in all future relationships. If this crisis is not resolved, however, the individual will be untrusting, suspicious and insecure as an adult.

Erikson's theory is a true lifespan theory but in this chapter we will only be concerned with the stages after childhood – adolescence and adulthood.

▼ *Erikson's eight ages of man*

Age	Life crisis	Social focus	Positive outcome	Negative outcome
1st year	Trust vs mistrust	Maternal figure	Trust	Suspicion, insecurity
2nd year	Autonomy vs shame	Parents	Sense of autonomy, self-esteem	Shame and self-doubt
3–6 years	Initiative vs guilt	Family	Initiates activities	Fear of punishment, guilt feelings
To puberty	Industry vs inferiority	Neighbourhood	Competence and achievement	Inadequacy and inferiority
Adolescence	Identity vs role confusion	Peers	Strong personal identity	Confusion
Early adulthood	Intimacy vs isolation	Friendships, lovers	Ability to experience love	Isolation
Middle age	Generativity vs stagnation	The household	Wider outlook	Boredom, self-involvement
Old age	Integrity vs despair	Humankind	Satisfaction, self-acceptance	Regrets, fear of death

WHAT IS YOUR IDENTITY TYPE?

Erikson described adolescence as one of eight life stages (see facing page). He proposed that there is a crisis at every life stage. In adolescence the crisis is *identity formation*, which must be resolved to continue healthy development. Marcia (1966) sought to **operationalise** the concept of identity formation, i.e. he developed a means of measuring it by interviewing adolescents. The data he collected suggested that there were four different **identity statuses**: *identity diffusion, identity foreclosure, identity moratorium* and *identity achievement* (these are described on page 137).

What is your identity status? Marcia interviewed adolescents to find out the answer but you can use a questionnaire developed by Adams *et al.* (1979), called the *Objective Measure of Ego Identity Status* (OMEIS). This is reproduced on the right and provides respondents with a score for each of the four identity statuses. There is an extended version of this scale (64 items) by Bennion and Adams (1986) which can be found at www.uoguelph.ca/%7Egadams/OMEIS_manual.pdf

For each question below circle the figure that best represents yourself.	Strongly agree	Moderately agree	Agree	Disagree	Moderately disagree	Strongly disagree
1. I haven't really considered politics. They just don't excite me much.	1	2	3	4	5	6
2. I might have thought about a lot of different things but there has never really been a decision since my parents said what they wanted.	1	2	3	4	5	6
3. When it comes to religion I just haven't found any that I'm really into myself.	1	2	3	4	5	6
4. My parents decided a long time ago what I should go and do and I'm following their plans.	1	2	3	4	5	6
5. There are so many different political parties and ideals. I can't decide which to follow until I figure it all out.	1	2	3	4	5	6
6. I don't give religion much thought and it doesn't bother me one way or the other.	1	2	3	4	5	6
7. I guess I'm pretty much like my folks when it comes to politics. I follow what they do in terms of voting and such.	1	2	3	4	5	6
8. I haven't chosen the occupation I really want to get into, but I'm working towards becoming a _____ until something better comes along.	1	2	3	4	5	6
9. A person's faith is unique to each individual. I've considered and reconsidered it myself and know what I can believe.	1	2	3	4	5	6
10. It took me a long time to decide but now I know for sure what direction to move in for a career.	1	2	3	4	5	6
11. I was never really involved in politics enough to have to make a firm stand one way or another.	1	2	3	4	5	6
12. I'm not so sure what religion means to me. I'd like to make up my mind but I'm not done looking yet.	1	2	3	4	5	6
13. I've thought my political beliefs through and realise that I may or may not agree with many of my parents' beliefs.	1	2	3	4	5	6
14. It took me a while to figure it out, but now I really know what I want for a career.	1	2	3	4	5	6
15. Religion is confusing to me right now. I keep changing my views on what is right and wrong to me.	1	2	3	4	5	6
16. I'm sure it will be pretty easy for me to change my occupational goals when something better comes along.	1	2	3	4	5	6
17. My folks had their own political and moral beliefs about issues like abortion and mercy killing and I've always gone along accepting what they have.	1	2	3	4	5	6
18. I've gone through a period of serious questioning about faith and can now say I understand what I believe in as an individual.	1	2	3	4	5	6
19. I'm not sure about my political beliefs, but I'm trying to figure out what I truly believe in.	1	2	3	4	5	6
20. I just can't decide how capable I am as a person and what jobs I'll be right for.	1	2	3	4	5	6
21. I attend the same church as my family have always attended. I've never really questioned why.	1	2	3	4	5	6
22. I just can't decide what to do for an occupation. There are so many possibilities.	1	2	3	4	5	6
23. I've never really questioned my religion. If it's right for my parents it must be right for me.	1	2	3	4	5	6
24. Politics are something that I can never be too sure about because things change so fast. But I do think it's important to know what I believe in.	1	2	3	4	5	6

Adams, G.R., Shea, J.A. and Fitch, S.A. (1979) Toward the development of an objective assessment of ego-identity status. *Journal of Adolescence*, 8, 223–237.

Scoring ⟶

Scoring: Calculate the totals for each identity status by adding the scores for the following answers together:

Diffusion questions 1, 3, 6, 8, 11, 16
Moratorium questions 5, 12, 15, 19, 20, 22
Foreclosure questions 2, 4, 7, 17, 21, 23
Achievement questions 9, 10, 13, 14, 18, 24

LIFESPAN THEORIES OF DEVELOPMENT

NATURE VERSUS NUTURE

GENDER BIAS

CULTURAL BIAS

Lifespan theories aim to describe the typical pattern of psychological change from conception to death. The changes during childhood are the focus of particular theories, such as Freud's theory of personality development (in your AS studies) or Piaget's theory of cognitive development (see pages 119–120). Other theories, such as Levinson's theory below, focus on the older end of the human lifespan. We start with Erikson's theory, which we outlined on the previous spread. This theory covers the whole lifespan but here we are only concerned with adulthood.

Erikson's lifespan theory

Erik Erikson (1963) proposed that development proceeds through 'eight ages of man' (see previous spread). Erikson is described as a neo-Freudian because his theory is a 'newer' development of Freud's theory. Erikson's theory extended development into old age and also incorporated social influences. Each stage of personality development is characterised by a specific developmental 'task' or psychosocial 'crisis'.

Crises are resolved through interactions with others (thus 'social'), for example in early adulthood the crisis is *intimacy versus isolation* (see table on previous page). Individuals resolve this in their relationships with friends and lovers, learning how to conduct intimate relationships and respect the other person in the relationship. If it is not possible to do this, the negative outcome is a lifetime of isolation. The two other stages of adulthood are middle age and old age, each with their own crisis – *generativity versus stagnation and integrity versus despair*.

The outcome of each crisis is a mixture of positive and negative traits. Having too many negative traits is unhealthy; they make successful resolution of the developmental crisis of the next stage more difficult and will lead to difficulties later in life. However, problems not resolved earlier can be worked through later in life leading to a more positive outcome.

Gould's consciousness theory

Roger Gould (1980), like Erikson, also derived his theory from Freud, calling it the 'evolution of adult consciousness'. Gould believed that growing up involves a progressive casting aside of various false assumptions. Such assumptions exist to protect one from anxiety but they prevent evolution (development) of adult consciousness.

On the basis of his dialogues with patients as a psychiatrist, Gould devised a **questionnaire** consisting of 160 statements about ten different areas of life. The statements were beliefs that need to be challenged during each phase of adult development for continuing healthy development. The questionnaire was answered by 524 white, middle-class men and women between 16 and 50 years old. He used the answers to develop his 'stage' theory below.

Levinson's transitions theory

Daniel Levinson (1978) described adulthood as a series of 'seasons' rather than stages: the 'seasons of man's life'. This theory is outlined below. 'Seasons' implies that the next step is not 'better' or more advanced but just different.

Levinson conducted extensive **interviews** with 40 men aged 35–45 (ten novelists, ten biologists, ten factory workers, ten business executives). The men were interviewed for 10–20 hours and re-interviewed two years later. Levinson concluded that everyone proceeded through the same seasons (eras) at about the same ages.

Life structure is the underlying pattern of a person's life at any given time. It changes with age and is mainly built around relationships and work. 'Eras' consist of:

- Stable periods when life structures are built, these are shown in dark grey in the table.
- Transitional phases when life structures are changing and there may be a crisis, shown in light grey in the table.

Transitions occur where eras overlap and may last for five years. Transitions are necessary for healthy adjustment because they allow the individual to reassess what has gone before.

▼ *Levinson's transitions theory – the seasons of a man's life*
The ages given below are approximate. Dark grey shows stable periods and light grey is transitional phases.

Era of pre-adulthood		
17–22	Early adult transition	Moving from childhood dependence to independence and forming one's 'Dream' to guide and motivate. Unrealistic dreams block development.
Era of early adulthood (17–45 years)		
Becoming one's own man (BOOM), settling down, starting a career, having a family. For some there is an 'age 30 transition' – recognising that life is beginning to pass by.		
41–45	Midlife transition	Time to take stock, can be an unhappy time if Dream not realised (midlife crisis).
Era of middle adulthood (40–65 years)		
May involve a modified or new life structure, e.g. new job or new attitudes. Starting to be more inward looking.		
61–65	Late adult transition	
Era of late adulthood (60+ years)		
An acceptance of the inevitability of physical decline, and of what life has been.		

▼ *Gould's evolution of adult consciousness theory*

Age	False assumption	Factors which may lead to unhealthy 'evolution'
18–21	'I will always belong to my parents and believe in their world.'	Marriage at this age is an attempt to gain independence but may fail because such marriages are too dependent.
22–28	'Doing things my parents' way, with willpower and perseverance, will bring results. But if I become too frustrated, confused or tired or am simply unable to cope, they will step in and show me the right way.'	This dependence on parents (or a loved one) prevents independence and ultimately leads to feelings of hostility.
28–34	'Life is simple and controllable. There are no significant coexisting contradictory forces within me.'	An inability to recognise the contradictory pressures from within and without will block development.
35–45	'There is no evil in me or death in the world. The sinister has been destroyed'.	One must come to terms with mortality. Men have to recognise that success and hard work cannot protect them from dying, women may strike out on their own as a means of challenging man as the protector and coping with their own mortality.

EVALUATION

Erikson's lifespan theory

Research evidence The evidence for Erikson's lifespan theory came from several sources. First, Erikson was trained as a **psychoanalyst** (with Freud) and, working with patients first in Europe and later in America (after he emigrated), had the opportunity to observe human behaviour and draw conclusions about possible causes of development. He also conducted interviews with, for example, the Dakota Indians. This means that his theory was grounded in a wealth of knowledge about human behaviour, though this was mostly related to abnormal individuals.

Strengths and limitations Erikson's theory made an important contribution in establishing that development is a lifelong process rather than ending in adolescence as Freud suggested. Furthermore he incorporated social influences into the theory and thus de-emphasised the importance of biological (**genetic**) influences.

However, the theory is biased in many ways. The theory is **gender-biased** because it is based on male values, such as independence, whereas women tend to emphasise interdependence and the importance of relationships (Gilligan, 1982). The theory is also **culture-biased** because it focuses on self-identity which is more relevant to **individualist** cultures. Furthermore it is historically biased because today, very few things last a lifetime – people get divorced and change jobs which makes it harder to achieve intimacy through marriage or identity through work. There is also an increasing tendency for adults to delay commitment to an intimate relationship and to delay having children. A possible consequence of this is that they may well be dealing with all three adult goals simultaneously. This doesn't mean that Erikson's central ideas are wrong, just that the details probably need updating.

Levinson's transitions theory

Research evidence Levinson produced evidence to support his theory, as described on the facing page. For example, he found that 80% of his original male sample had experienced a moderate or severe crisis in midlife.

Levinson conducted a similar study with 45 randomly selected women (businesswomen, academics and homemakers) and found a similar pattern of life seasons. However, Roberts and Newton (1987) found that men and women did differ significantly, in terms of the 'Dream' and their major goals. The fact that more women today have full-time jobs may mean this is now less true.

Midlife crisis The concept of a midlife crisis is not supported by all research. For example, Farrell and Rosenberg (1981) found that in fact only about 12% of adults experienced a midlife crisis, and that if there was a crisis this was related to whether the individual was experiencing a number of changes all at the same time (e.g. children leaving home, lack of promotion, etc.). If such events were spread out there was no crisis.

Strengths and limitations The research evidence is limited but is rich in detail and can therefore provide useful insights. One issue is that the data may suffer from a **cohort effect** (behaviours may be specific to a particular generation who had unique experiences). As we have already noted, modern adult life is quite different today. There is also more tolerance for unusual lifestyles so people feel less forced to follow a conventional pattern.

The theory is also culturally biased as it is clearly an account of adulthood based firmly in individualist, Western culture.

Gould's consciousness theory

Research evidence The theory was derived from Gould's own research as described on the facing page. This research involved the analysis of answers to a questionnaire. However, there were no attempts to assess the **reliability** of the questionnaire (for example retesting some of the participants to see if they gave consistent answers). This in turn questions the **validity** of the data.

Strengths and limitations Like the other two theories reviewed on this spread, Gould's theory is a culture-biased account. This is because the sample consisted of white, middle-class Americans, and therefore cannot be generalised to people all over the world.

A further issue is that, according to this theory, development ends at age 45, which is at odds with the other two theories.

In terms of strengths, Gould's theory has provided a real-world application. Gould has translated his theory into a computer-based therapy (TLP, *Therapeutic Learning Programme*), which has been compared favourably with traditional, individual psychotherapy (Jacobs *et al.*, 2001).

Stage theories

All three theories on this spread are essentially 'stage theories', i.e. theories that represent development in terms of a set of qualitative steps or 'seasons'. The question of continuity versus stages is a significant issue in the field of developmental psychology – does an individual's development occur in a gradual and progressive (continuous) fashion, or in a distinct series of 'steps'?

Later in this chapter you will study the effect of key **life events**, such as marriage and retirement. The life events approach is a more 'continuous' one which doesn't look at stages but instead at how particular *events* influence development.

The life events approach also highlights how apparent 'stages' in adult development may not be stages at all – it is just that certain events tend to occur in most people at key ages (such as starting one's career or becoming a parent) rather than being a 'stage' in development.

Questionnaires

Both Levinson and Gould collected data using self-report techniques (interviews and questionnaires). The validity of such data is threatened by the fact that respondents may present themselves in socially desirable light (social desirability bias).

▲ **A man's view** *It seems extraordinary today that these theories were all about male development and even called the 'eight ages of* **man**' *and the 'season's of a* **man's** *life'.*

CAN YOU...? (No. **6.1**)

1... For each theory on this spread identify **two** or **three** key concepts.

2... For each key concept write a few sentences explaining the concept.

3... Identify about **three** or **four** points of evaluation for each theory (these can be positive or negative).

4... Elaborate each point (see page 9).

5... Use all of this material to write an answer to the following exam question: *Critically consider lifespan theories of development.* You could also prepare 'building block' essays on the different theories. Your answers should contain about 300 words of description and 500 words of evaluation.

Don't forget to read the essay-writing guidance on pages 8–9.

On this spread we look specifically at one stage of lifespan development – adolescence. Adolescence is a transitional period between childhood and adulthood. *Biologically* this period begins when an individual enters puberty and ends on reaching sexual maturity. *Psychologically* there are a number of levels on which the individual makes the transition to adulthood (e.g. social, emotional and cognitive).

Our focus is on the development of identity during adolescence. A person's identity is the view a person has of themselves, their individuality and personality.

If you haven't already done so, you might like to revisit your AS notes on Freud's personality theory to remind yourself of some of the concepts in this chapter.

BusinessName
COMPANY SLOGAN HERE

▲ *Brand identity is crucial for high selling power. A company must identify what it is they are trying to sell and create a symbol to represent this. For product retailing the question is 'What am I?' For us the question is 'Who am I?'*

Erikson's psychosocial theory

Erik Erikson's (1963) lifespan theory is described on the previous two spreads. It is a **psychoanalytic** theory proposing that, at each stage of life, there is a crisis or conflict which is resolved through social interactions. In adolescence the crisis relates to the formation of adult identity. Before puberty a child has an identity but this is challenged by the major physical changes at puberty, resulting in role confusion.

The task for adolescents is to resolve the conflict between *identity* and *role confusion*. To achieve this, according to Erikson, adolescents need to develop relationships with friends and romantic partners, establish autonomy from parents, take initiative in terms of future plans and be industrious. *During* the stage of adolescence role confusion is healthy but if unresolved will ultimately lead to *identity diffusion* (a lack of personal identity), which may lead to:

- *Negative identity*, e.g. becoming delinquent which permits some sense of control.
- *Lack of intimacy*, avoiding close relationships because of a fear of loss of identity if one commits to others, but may worship a pop star.
- *Time perspective*, avoiding making future plans because the idea of adulthood creates anxiety.
- *Diffusion of industry*, difficulty concentrating.

Successful resolution results in a new and unified sense of identity or self. Adult identity has many facets (e.g. occupational, religious, political) and is redefined throughout life.

Blos's psychoanalytic theory

Freud identified puberty and adolescence as the **genital stage**, a time when a child focuses again on genitals (as they did during the **phallic stage**) and also focuses on the development of independence. Blos (1967) took up these ideas and suggested that adolescence was like a second period of **individuation**. The first period of individuation took place when the infant became a self-reliant toddler. In adolescence the individual is again achieving independence ('re-individuation'). Adolescents may typically overreact to parental authority and be at pains to assert their individuality.

This separation from parents, according to Blos, results in an emotional emptiness that is satisfied by group experiences. The striving for independence may also lead to **regression** to more child-like behaviour, which Blos regarded as a healthy and necessary response. Regression may be to a more infantile state in order to receive substitute parenting, or may take the form of hero worship that can act as a substitute parent. Blos also believed that rebellion was important as a means of **ego defence** in order for the adolescent to prevent him/herself becoming dependent on their parents again.

Marcia's theory

James Marcia (1966) further developed Erikson's ideas because Erikson's theory consisted of abstract ideas that could not be tested **empirically**. Marcia **operationalised** Erikson's concepts by creating **behavioural categories** that could be measured. He did this by interviewing adolescents, and asking them about their 'identity status' in areas such as occupation, religion, politics and attitudes about sex. He focused particularly on *crisis* and *commitment*, asking the adolescents whether they were considering alternatives (i.e. were in crisis) or they had made a firm decision about their views (i.e. showed commitment). Marcia concluded from his research that adolescents were in one of four possible categories or **identity statuses**:

- *Identity diffusion* Identity crisis not yet experienced (crisis is low, commitment is low).
- *Identity foreclosure* Uncertainties avoided by committing self to safe, conventional goals (e.g. determined by parents) without exploring alternatives (crisis is low, commitment is high).
- *Identity moratorium* Decisions about identity put on hold while various roles explored (crisis is high, commitment is low).
- *Identity achievement* Individual emerges with firm goals, ideology, commitments (crisis is high, commitment is high).

These categories have then been used to conduct research on identity development. This is not a stage model as it is not necessary for an adolescent to go through all four statuses. Marcia found that only moratorium appears to be necessary for a successful resolution of the adolescent identity crisis.

▼ *Table showing levels of crisis and commitment for all four identity statuses*

	Crisis low	Crisis high
Commitment low	Identity diffusion	Identity moratorium
Commitment high	Identity foreclosure	Identity achievement

See page 133 for questionnaire assessing identity status.

EVALUATION

Blos's psychoanalytic theory

Connectedness rather than independence The notion that independence is part of healthy adolescent development may be an oversimplification. More recent research suggests autonomy develops best when it is accompanied by continuing attachment to parents – independence and connectedness lead to healthy development (Coleman and Hendry, 1990). 'Connectedness' does not mean 'dependence' but describes how independence can occur only when an individual continues to have a **secure base**, in the same way that infants are only confident about exploring their environment if they have a secure base and are **securely attached** to their parents (Ainsworth *et al.*, 1978). Adolescents who are securely attached to their parents have greater **self-esteem**, better emotional adjustment, are less likely to engage in problem behaviours, and are physically healthier (Cooper *et al.*, 1998).

Erikson's psychosocial theory

Research evidence On page 135 we discussed the research evidence for Erikson's theory, drawn from his clinical practice and interviews with Dakota Indians.

Resolution of adolescent crisis Erikson suggested that one consequence of identity formation was being able to form intimate relationships, a link supported by Kahn *et al.* (1985) who found that those students who had been assessed as low in identity development later had less success in relationships (e.g. men likely to remain unmarried, women more likely to be separated). There may, however, be a gender difference in the link between intimacy and identity. Erikson suggested that female identity development depends on finding a partner first, whereas for males intimacy comes after identity. This may be a **gender bias** or a real difference.

Strengths and weaknesses Erikson's theory has been influential particularly because it introduced the idea of lifespan development. However, it is difficult to test this theory because some concepts are vague, such as how a crisis is resolved and how to precisely define 'identity'. In terms of adolescence, the theory actually focuses only on one aspect of adolescence – transition to adulthood rather than, for example, the earlier biological changes.

Marcia's theory

Research evidence Marcia's theory is grounded in his own research with adolescents. There is further research support for the developmental sequence of these stages. For example, Waterman (1985) found an increase of identity achievement with age and a decrease in diffusion status. There is also support for the description of the statuses, e.g. Kroger (1996) reports that identity achievers are found to function well under stress, whereas those in moratorium are consistently more anxious, avoid intimate relationships and express more scepticism.

The myth of identity achievement Research also shows that identity achievement comes later than predicted and may not be permanent. Meilman (1979) interviewed men aged 24 and found that only 50% had reached identity achievement (i.e. it is not a part of adolescence). Marcia (1976) found that six years after his initial interviews some of those who had achieved a stable identity had returned to identity foreclosure or diffusion.

Oversimplified Marcia's categorisation may be oversimplified. Archer (1982) found that only 5% of those interviewed were classed in the same identity status for all concerns, 90% were in two or three different statuses (e.g. in identity confusion for sexual attitudes, but identity achievement for occupational choice).

Strengths The importance of Marcia's research is that it provides a tool for categorising adolescents into one of four types which facilitates empirical research. However, it is possible that the original participants may have provided socially desirable answers and the fact that the original sample was American boys creates a possible gender/**cultural bias**.

The concept of identity moratorium can be usefully applied. Erikson (1968) used the example of a young girl from a 'good' family who was arrested for prostitution. He argues that she may have been trying out a potential role but, if prosecuted, might have been prematurely assigned a final identity. The concept of identity moratorium promotes the view that role experimentation is good and should not be seen as final.

Is adolescence a time of crisis? Both Erikson and Marcia suggest that adolescence is a time of crisis. This is an issue we will examine on the next spread, presenting some research that supports the ideas of Erikson and Marcia and some research that challenges their notion of crisis.

Biases

The research described on this spread is biased in a number of ways. First it is culturally biased. Identity development is important in individualist societies but may be unimportant in collectivist groups where personal identity is less important than group identity. In addition, Kroger (1996) suggests that identity and role choice only occur in industrialised societies where there are choices and therefore only applies to such societies.

Second is the issue of gender bias. Both Erikson and Marcias's theories were based largely on data from boys. It may be that identity development is different or less important in the future development of girls.

Finally, historical bias is an issue. The theories described here (and on the previous spread) were researched more than 40 years ago; today people often change jobs through their lives and thus identity may be more flexible.

▲ *Who am I? That is the question at the core of adolescence.*

CAN YOU...?   No. 6.2

1... For each theory identify **two** or **three** key concepts.

2... For each key concept write a few sentences explaining the concept.

3... Identify about **ten** points of evaluation (these can be positive or negative).

4... Elaborate each point (see page 9).

5... Use all of this material to write an answer to the exam following question: *Describe and evaluate explanations of adolescent identity.* You might also try writing three 'building block' essays on each separate theory. Your answers should contain about 300 words of description and 500 words of evaluation.

Don't forget to read the essay-writing guidance on pages 8–9.

On this spread we continue our look at adolescent development, this time focusing on crisis rather than identity. For many theorists, adolescence is characterised by a 'crisis' which is regarded as necessary in order to achieve identity. Erik Erikson and James Marcia (see previous spread) in particular have emphasised that this period of crisis (or conflict) is crucial for the achievement of a mature adult identity. However, some research suggests that adolescence is not especially stressful, at least no more so than other times of life. On this spread we will examine explanations of conflict as well as possible alternative views.

► The view of adolescent crisis originates from nineteenth-century German writers, such as Goethe, who referred to adolescent 'Sturm und Drang' (storm and stress).

Evolutionary approach

The **evolutionary approach** suggests that the changes associated with adolescence are adaptive, i.e. essential to human survival. Adolescence appears to be uniquely human and one suggestion is that it is required for the development of the complex social skills needed for adulthood and reproductive success.

Support for focal theory

Coleman and Hendry (1990) confirmed the basis of *focal theory* in a study of 800 boys and girls aged between 11 and 17. The participants were questioned about topics which were anxiety-provoking, such as self-image, occupational choice and peer, sexual and parental relationships.

The results are shown in the graph below, illustrating different issues peaking at different ages, as suggested by focal theory. For example, young boys are concerned about heterosexual relationship but later become concerned about conflicts with parents. Concerns about peer relations tended to peak earlier than occupational choice.

The fact that the various 'crises' were spread out meant that the individuals could cope without becoming too stressed. Stress would only be experienced if more than one crisis was present at any one time – which is the same at any age.

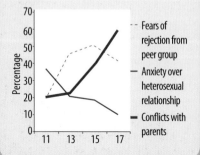

EXPLANATION OF CONFLICT: STORM AND STRESS

As we saw on the previous spread, a number of psychologists have suggested that conflict is inevitable during adolescence. Blos (1967) suggested this was because adolescents seek to gain independence from their parents, which causes conflict.

Erikson (1963) suggested that adolescence was one of several periods of conflict or crisis, each of which must be resolved in order for continuing healthy development. According to Erikson, the adolescent crisis is related to the development of identity which involves gaining autonomy from parents.

Marcia (1966) further developed Erikson's theory, identifying crisis and commitment as the cornerstones of adolescent development. Adolescents resolve their various crises by becoming committed to particular viewpoints or remaining in crisis. Unhealthy identity formation (*identity foreclosure*) occurs when adolescents take on parents' attitudes rather than developing their own.

ALTERNATIVE VIEWS

Connectedness

The concept of '**connectedness**' was also discussed on the previous spread. Adolescent conflict may be avoided when adolescents continue to have a warm and close relationship with their parents – independence and *connectedness* lead to healthy development, a contrast with the views above which focused on just the importance of conflict in developing independence (Coleman and Hendry, 1990).

Coleman's focal theory

Coleman's (1980) **focal theory** suggests that crisis is not inevitable. It only occurs when issues accumulate according to this view. 'Normal' adolescent development is conflict free because individuals *focus* on one issue at a time.

Focal issues and development From his research with adolescent boys and girls, Coleman (1974) discovered that concerns about different issues peaked at different points during adolescence. This was confirmed in a later study by Coleman and Hendry (see left). Coleman argued that an issue, such as fear of peer group rejection, comes into focus at a particular stage of development and, in time, comes to be replaced with another focal issue. Once finished with one challenge or problem individuals can cope with another one, such as conflict with parents. Because the process of adaptation is spread over a relatively long period, the stresses of adolescence rarely lead to crisis (Coleman, 1990).

Stress and adaptation An important implication of this theory is that adolescents who have to deal with more than one issue at a time might be considered to be more at risk than those for whom issues are well spaced out. A young person who has to cope, for example, with family breakdown as well as having to adjust to a change of school and to a new peer group, may be particularly vulnerable. Similarly, those whose onset of puberty and growth spurt occurs at the normal time can adjust to this *before* dealing with the pressures of parental conflict later on. However, should these two problems be forced upon the adolescent at the same time, as may be the case for late maturers, then they experience an increase in stress, which may lead to 'storm and stress'.

EVALUATION OF EXPLANATIONS OF CONFLICT

Supporting research evidence There is some supporting evidence for adolescent conflict. For example, Smith and Crawford (1986) found that over 60% of secondary school pupils reported at least one instance of suicidal thinking and 10% had attempted suicide. Montemayor (1982) found that, on average, adolescents had one argument every three days lasting 11 minutes. The fact that adolescent–parent rows were mainly 'mild' supports the notion that these conflicts are a 'healthy' means of achieving individuation.

Challenging research evidence Siddique and D'Arcy (1984), for example, found that about one-third of adolescents interviewed reported no psychological distress, a similar number reported mild distress and a further third reported higher levels. Rutter *et al.* (1976) studied over 2000 14–15-year-olds on the Isle of Wight. The teenagers reported a higher frequency of conflict, but rarely reported serious disagreements or criticised their parents.

It may be that the 'storm and stress' view of adolescence is a consequence of early research based on abnormal populations. 'Normal' adolescence is relatively stress free.

Cultural differences Most research has been conducted in the US and Europe and may not apply universally. In other cultures, such as in India, adolescents continue to have closer and more subordinate relationships with parents (Larson and Verma, 1999).

EVALUATION OF ALTERNATIVE VIEWS

Connectedness

Attachment Allen and Land (1998) found that adolescents with secure attachments to parents had fewer problems and greater confidence in themselves. Ryan and Lynch (1989) point out that securely attached adolescents, e.g. infants, find it easier to become independent, supporting the view that attachment not separation is important for independence.

Autonomy and connectedness Larson *et al.* (1996) used pagers to find out what 10–18-year-old participants were doing at random times during the day. They found that time spent with family decreased sharply in early adolescence. However, time spent alone with each parent individually was fairly consistent. This shows that both autonomy and connectedness occur.

Gender differences Parental relationships have been found to be more important for boys than girls (Frey and Rothlisberger, 1996) although girls are more affectionate and helpful towards parents (Eberly and Montemayor, 1999).

Focal theory

Research evidence Coleman and Hendry's research support is described on the facing page. These findings were further supported in a study by Simmons and Blyth (1987). In this study it was found that **self-esteem** and school performance were unaffected in adolescents experiencing just one crisis, but self-esteem and performance scores dropped significantly in those adolescents who experienced over three life transitions in a short space of time (e.g. parental divorce, starting new school, onset of puberty).

Practical application A strength of this theory is that it provides a suggestion for how adolescents who are experiencing a sense of crisis might deal with this. Troubled adolescents might be advised to reduce the number of issues they are currently coping with and to focus on one or two at a time.

Life events approach In your AS course you studied research by Rahe, Mahan and Arthur (1970) concerning the effect of **life events** on health. Some people have suggested that Coleman's theory is nothing more than a theory of life events applied to adolescence – the more events, the more stress. Coleman and Hendry (1990) claim it is more than this because focal theory suggests that the adolescent plays an active role, which further explains why some adolescents cope and others fail to adapt despite having a similar number of crises. This person–context approach (a) emphasises the lack of disordered behaviour in adolescence, and (b) highlights the circumstances under which an adolescent may become vulnerable.

If Coleman is right, then why is the 'storm and stress' view perpetuated? One reason may be 'media amplification'. Certain adolescent behaviours, such as vandalism and drug taking, are often reported sensationally in the media and this creates an exaggerated picture of the problem in the eyes of the general public.

Alternative explanation Eccles *et al.* (1993) suggested that the reason many adolescents experience stress is because of the mismatch between their developing needs and the opportunities afforded to them by their social environments. Indeed, in some Western cultures, adolescents would appear to be held in a state of moratorium by laws that block access to the adult world, such as the minimum school-leaving age and minimum voting age (see 'Origins of adolescence' top right).

The origins of adolescence

Shaffer (1993) claims that adolescence is an 'invention' of the twentieth century; in the past older children went to work alongside adults so there was no in-between period which we now regard as adolescence. Children simply went straight to adulthood. The same continues to be true in many non-Western cultures.

In addition, in many non-Western cultures, children undergo a 'rite of passage' where they are then regarded as adults. Entry to adulthood is made easier because young people have clear roles.

In our culture there are no clear roles at the end of childhood, nor is there a clear demarcation between childhood and adulthood (is it age 16 when you can smoke, 17 when you can drive, 18 when you can vote...?).

CAN YOU...?　　　No. 6.3

1... **Two** views of adolescent conflict are represented on this spread – for and against. For each of these select about **five** key points.

2... For each key point write a few sentences explaining the point.

3... Identify about **ten** points of evaluation (these can be positive or negative).

4... Elaborate each point (see page 9).

5... Use all of this material to write an answer to the following question: *Discuss conflict during adolescence, including storm and stress and alternative views.* You might also try writing two 'building blocks' essays, one on adolescence as a time of storm and stress, and the other on the alternative views. Your answers should contain about 300 words of description and 500 words of evaluation.

Remember that, when writing an essay, you can include material from other spreads – but only if it is made specifically relevant to the essay. For example, in an essay on adolescent conflict you might include research on adolescent identity development – as long as it is made relevant.

The final two spreads of this chapter take a different developmental approach – rather than looking at lifespan development in terms of stages, we now take a **life events** approach. You are familiar with the idea of 'life events' from your AS core study by Rahe, Mahan and Arthur (1970), who used a version of the **SRRS** to demonstrate a relationship between health and life events, such as marriage and divorce. 'Life events' create stress and this may have a negative effect on health.

The Social Readjustment Rating Scale (SRRS)

The SRRS (Holmes and Rahe, 1967) was developed by asking 400 people to score a range of life events in terms of how much readjustment would be required by the average person. Scores were totalled and averaged to produce *life change units* (LCUs) – a measure of the stressfulness of each life event. Each life event was placed in rank order, e.g. death of a spouse came highest.

MARRIAGE

Negative effects

Holmes and Rahe (1967) rated marriage as 7th on their list of most stressful life events. This would suggest it could have a negative impact on physical health, although this might be related to other events associated with marriage, such as buying a house or having a baby.

Positive effects

Happiness Bradburn (1969) found that married people were happier than never-marrieds (about 35% as compared with 18%). The separated, divorced or widowed were even less happy (7%).

Why might marriage be linked to increased happiness? Wilson and Oswald (2005) suggest the following reasons:
- *Financial* – married couples gain financially.
- *Protective* – marriage brings emotional support.
- *Guardian* – the emotional support provided in marriage reduces stress (see research on pages 106–107), which reduces risky behaviours (e.g. smoking, less sleep), which brings health benefits.
- *Selection* – individuals who are mentally/physically healthier are more likely to be selected as partners. Thus health may be a cause rather than an effect of marriage.

Wilson and Oswald concluded from a review of studies that protection is the prime factor but not the sole one.

Mental health Cochrane (1988) found that the rate of admission to mental hospital was only 0.26% for married people, whereas it was 0.77% for single individuals, 0.98% for widowed individuals and 1.4% for the divorced.

Physical health Lynch (1977) found that married people were much less likely than single, divorced, or widowed individuals of the same age to die from several kinds of physical conditions (e.g. a stroke or cancer).

PARENTHOOD

Negative effects

Parenthood is not all positive, it may cause marital problems because of conflicts over child-rearing practices and jealousy.

Pregnancy scores 12th on the Holmes and Rahe scale, a new family member scores 14th and a child leaving home scores 23rd. Hultsch and Deutsch (1981) found that 50–80% of adults described the birth of their first child as a moderate to severe crisis.

Positive effects

Turner and Helms (1983) suggested that parenthood is positive because (1) children provide a sense of achievement (Erikson's notion of *generativity*, see page 135), (2) they allow parents to give and to receive love, (3) having children is a cultural expectation in many societies, and (4) children can give their parents a sense of importance.

DIVORCE

Some of the evidence related to marriage can be manipulated to indicate the negative effects of divorce, e.g. marriage provides social support, so divorce involves a reduction in social support.

Negative effects

Stress Divorce scores 73 LCUs (2nd) on the Holmes and Rahe scale, separation is 3rd and reconciliation 9th.

Clulow (1990) argued that divorce is similar to bereavement, both for the couple and their children. It involves grief, sorrow and anger (see Bereavement on the next spread).

Mental health Cochrane's study (see above left) showed that admission rates to mental hospitals were highest for the divorced.

Physical health Kiecolt-Glaser and Glaser (1986) found poorer immune functions where persons were suffering marital disruption. Carter and Glick (1970) found increased rates of various illnesses in women who were divorced. People who are divorced or widowed have a particularly high risk of dying prematurely (Johnson *et al.*, 2000). These results are widespread across the world.

Positive effects

It seems plausible that the ending of an *unhappy* marriage would result in positive effects and increased opportunities for partners to find a new and happy life. Kalmijn and Monden (2006) found less depression in divorcees who 'escaped' from an unhappy marriage, supporting the 'escape' hypothesis.

"I'M SURE THAT MISTER RIGHT WILL COME ALONG SOMEDAY... UNTIL THEN, I GUESS I'LL JUST STAY MARRIED."

General evaluation

The life events approach assumes that certain events have the same meaning for everyone but there are important individual differences related to age, personality, childhood experiences and so on. There is also the issue of the *quality* of the relationship. Many of the studies do not consider the *kind* of relationship – for example, 'poor' marriages would probably not provide the same health benefits as good marriages, and the effects of divorce depend on the length of the marriage, the age of the partners, the quality of the relationship, the number and age of any children, and who ended it.

EXAM TIP

Notice that the title of this spread and the associated exam question are about the effects of life events not the events themselves. So your essay answers must address the *effects* and not describe the events.

EVALUATION

Marriage

Length of marriage Glenn and McLanahan (1982) found a U-shaped relationship between marital satisfaction and the length of the marriage. Marital satisfaction declined sharply with the birth of the first child, and only rose again when the last-born child left home.

Marriage vs partnering Horwitz and White (1998) found that cohabitors do not rank as highly as married couples in terms of health benefits. This is possibly because such relationships are, on average, of lower 'quality'.

Gender differences In term of mental health, Cochrane (1988) found that married women are much more likely to be admitted to mental hospital than married men, although married women are still less likely to be admitted to mental hospital than single women. So, marriage is clearly protective of mental health for all genders but among the married, men are protected far more than women.

In terms of physical health, Lillard and Waite (1995) found that married men have a significantly lower mortality risk than single men; the difference is greater than between married and single women.

Explaining gender differences One possibility is that men get more protection than women from being married, i.e. they gain more emotional support. Women have more developed social networks than men outside their marriage and already gain support from these (Shumaker and Hill, 1991). This would also explain why males suffer more than women when widowed or divorced. A second possibility is that marriage leads men to cut back on risky behaviours (such as smoking and drinking) more than women (the 'guardian' explanation) and this ceases when marriage ends.

Cultural differences In some cultures marriage is arranged rather than freely determined by the couple. However, when Yelsma and Athappily (1988) compared American marriages with Indian arranged marriages, they found few differences and similar levels of happiness.

Parenthood

Gender difference You are familiar with **parental investment** theory from your AS core study by Buss (1989). This theory predicts that females will have a greater interest in parenting because their physiological 'investment' is greater from the very beginning. However, in humans, the extended period of care of the young means that males also have an interest in caring for offspring to protect their investment.

Social class differences Russell (1974) found that middle-class parents were more dissatisfied than working-class parents. This may because they start with higher ideals and the mother is more likely to have to give up a career.

Cultural differences In **collectivist** societies there appears to be greater satisfaction which may be because the extended family takes a greater role in child rearing. For example, Mexicans practice a family ritual, *la cuarentena*, where the first 40 days after birth involve considerable support for mothers (Wadeley, 2000).

Divorce

Genetic predisposition Plomin *et al.* (1997) reported that an identical twin whose co-twin had divorced was rather more likely to become divorced than an identical twin whose co-twin had not divorced, even when twins had been reared apart. This would suggest that some aspect of relationship maintenance is inherited.

Cause or effect? Some of the negative findings related to divorce (e.g. poor mental or physical health) may be the cause of marital breakdown rather than the effect.

Gender differences Although women have more practical difficulty coping, men experience more stress because of fewer social support networks (see Cochrane, 1988, left).

Cultural differences Divorce rates are related to culture, e.g. in the UK the rate is 2.8 per 1,000 whereas it is 0.11 per 1,000 in India (United Nations 2004). People in **individualist** societies are more likely to divorce because of the belief that one should seek the best for oneself. Brodbar-Nemzer (1986) compared traditional (collectivist) Jewish families in New York with those who had become more individualist, finding more divorces in the latter.

Methodology

Many studies use questionnaires/interviews. Social desirability bias can be a problem, and it is also true that only certain kinds of people answer questionnaires (e.g. literate, highly motivated) so the sample may be biased.

CAN YOU...? (No. **6.4**)

1... **Three** life events have been described on this spread. For each life event identify at least **one** negative and **one** positive effect.

2... Write about 50–100 words describing each of these effects.

3... Identify about **ten** points of evaluation.

4... Elaborate each point (see page 9).

5... Use all of this material to write an answer to the following question: *Describe and evaluate effects of events during middle adulthood*. It might be good practice to write separate 'building block' essays about each of the three life events. Your answers should contain about 300 words of description and 500 words of evaluation.

Remember that, when writing an essay, you can include material from other spreads – but only if it is made specifically relevant to the essay. In Chapter 4 (pages 106–107) we have discussed the benefits of relationships on psychological well-being and some of this material might be useful here.

On this final spread we consider a further three **life events**. These are typical of late adulthood but are by no means exclusive to this age group – many people take early retirement, and bereavement is something that can occur at any age.

RETIREMENT

Positive effects
Many studies indicate that retirement is good for you. Dave *et al.* (2006) reported an 11% improvement in mental health after retirement.

Schellenberg *et al.* (2005) found that about half of retirees reported taking more pleasure in life after retirement. They found that meaningful relationships, good health and financial well-being were the key ingredients to enjoying life in retirement, as well as being involved in physical activities, hobbies or volunteer work.

Negative effects
Other research suggests that retirement is quite stressful. It is scored 10th on the Holmes and Rahe SRRS scale.

Psychological and physical effects A recent study found that self-esteem declined around the time of retirement (Orth *et al.*, 2010). Tsai *et al.* (2005), in a study of 3,500 Texans, found that people who retired aged 55 were twice as likely to die before those who continued to work.

Moderating factors A number of factors may reduce the possible negative effects, such as being married, having friends or having high **self-esteem** (Reitzes and Mutran, 2004).

A phase model
Atchley (1982) identified the effects in terms of five typical phases:
- *Honeymoon phase* – period of relative enjoyment and euphoria.
- *Disenchantment phase* – special activities fail to measure up to expectations. Failing health may mean less is possible.
- *Reorientation phase* – a more realistic approach develops, seek new roles.
- *Stability phase* – life takes on an orderly routine again.
- *Termination phase* – poor health requires significant lifestyle changes.

ADJUSTMENT TO OLD AGE
The key question appears to be whether people cope with the effects of old age better if they remain active or if they withdraw from society.

Activity theory
Havighurst (1961) proposed that psychological health in old age is promoted by continued or new interests, i.e. the best way to cope with ageing is to stay active and involved. Any loss of roles should be replaced by new roles or activities to maintain a 'role count'.

Research evidence Activity and control have been shown to promote mental and physical health. This was vividly demonstrated in your AS core study by Langer and Rodin (1976) which showed that those elderly nursing home residents who had a greater sense of control lived longer than those who had less control.

Rubin (1973) showed the effect of activity on mental health by comparing elderly living in their own homes with those in nursing homes. The former remained mentally more able.

Social disengagement theory
Cumming and Henry (1961) proposed that a gradual withdrawal from personal contacts and world affairs is the route to adjustment in old age. This withdrawal may be instigated by the individual who feels less active and less able, or may be imposed on him/her by external events, such as retirement or the death of a spouse. Disengagement is mutually beneficial for the individual and for society.

Cumming and Henry described three phases:
1. *Shrinkage of life space* – less interaction with others and fewer social roles.
2. *Increased individuality* – due to decreased social pressure.
3. *Acceptance of life changes* – becoming more inward focused.

Longitudinal study Cumming and Henry's theory was based on a five-year study of nearly 700 individuals aged between 40 and 90. They observed that older people gradually lost contact with others, had fewer roles and then were freed to play the roles they wished.

BEREAVEMENT

Coping
Kübler-Ross (1969) constructed a classic stage account of the process of accepting one's own death, which applies to bereavement generally (dealing with one's own impending death is a form of bereavement). The stages were derived from interviews she had with over 200 dying patients. These stages may not follow in a sequence, and may also come and go:
- *Denial and isolation* – others often avoid the dying or bereaved individual.
- *Anger* – the beginning of acceptance.
- *Bargaining* – trying to find a little extra time or some way out.
- *Depression* – it is important to allow individuals to express their sorrow in order to reach a final acceptance.
- *Acceptance*.

Negative effects
Death of spouse scores 1st on the Holmes and Rahe SRRS scale, the death of a close family member is 5th and a close friend is 17th.

Hinton (1967) found a higher incidence of death in recent widows than a sample of married women of the same age. Parkes (1987) found that 75% of widows sought medical advice within six months. However, Mor *et al.* (1986) suggested that this may be because an illness had been ignored in the period leading up to a spouse's death.

Abnormal grief may occur as a response to extreme circumstances. Lindemann (1944) described reactions after the Coconut Grove fire (nearly 500 people died in a fire at a night club): somatic distress, guilt, hostility, sense of unreality and preoccupation with the deceased.

Moderating influences
Kahn and Attanucci (1980) investigated the effects of the 'convoy' on coping with bereavement. The 'convoy' are friends, family and others who offer social support. People who lack such support are more prone to illness, emotional upset and death. Littlewood (1992) studied the Aberfan disaster where nearly 150 children and adults were killed; the closeness of the community helped villagers to cope.

The life events approach

At the beginning of this chapter we compared the stage theory approach to the life events approach (see page 136). Both have their problems. In particular, the life events approach assumes that key events have the same effect on all people but, as we have noted below, there are many important individual differences.

(see page 136)

Real-World applications

The research described on this spread has many useful applications. Understanding the factors that moderate successful retirement can be used in pre-retirement courses and understanding bereavement processes helps counsellors to provide more effective support.

The issue of activity versus disengagement has very important implications for social policies. The 'activity' perspective encourages the development of recreational facilities for the elderly. The 'disengagement' perspective implies a policy of segregation for the elderly and condones rejection of the elderly (Blau, 1973).

EVALUATION

Retirement

Research evidence Research has not found a consistent pattern in the phases people go through when retiring, for example Ekerdt *et al.* (1985) found a decline in satisfaction after one year (as suggested by Atchley) whereas Richardson and Kilty (1991) found the decline occurred in the first six months.

Individual differences The experience and effects of retirement depends on whether it is voluntary and looked forward to, how much the individual enjoyed work and the company of co-workers, physical health, money, friends and so on.

Adjustment to old age

Individual differences The disengagement approach to old age may suit some personality types – people who have always preferred to disengage but had to remain active members of society for work/family. Havighurst *et al.* (1968) re-analysed the original data and found different types of people, e.g. some were *disengagers*, individuals who have always been rather reclusive and tend to disengage in their later years. But others were not disengagers.

Correlation or cause? Research only shows that activity or disengagement is *linked* to certain outcomes. There may be important **intervening variables**, e.g. people with more money may be more active; being better off might be the key factor rather than activity.

Is old age any different from other times of life? Atchley (1977) proposed '*continuity theory*', that the people who age most successfully are those who *continue* to do the same things in old age that they were doing before. However, Erikson (1963) suggested that old age was different from other times of life. He proposed that there is a particular crisis to be resolved at this time: *integrity versus despair*. The individual reviews and evaluates their life, which results in either feeling satisfied and accepting the inevitability of death, or feeling regret and fearing death.

Socioemotional selectivity theory (SST) Cartenson *et al.* (1999) suggested that as people age they become increasingly selective in order to conserve energy and promote emotionally rewarding experiences. This is a slightly more positive approach than disengagement and suggests that the individual is in control rather than being controlled by society.

Bereavement

Individual differences Bereavement varies with a person's own feelings about death and their emotional type, the type of death, the age of the deceased, relationship with the deceased (closeness, dependency, duration) and so on. The grieving is much harder where interpersonal problems were unresolved.

Gender differences Barrett (1978) found that widowers (men whose spouse has died) had a lower morale, expressed greater dissatisfaction and required more help than widows (women whose spouse has died). Many men rely on their wives domestically and for friendship, and therefore experience greater loss. Some women experience a greater sense of loss than others, depending on how much they defined themselves in terms of their husbands (Lopata, 1979).

Cultural bias Most accounts of bereavement are based on Western practices. Collectivist cultures have extended families that provide support at times of bereavement. Religions all have different practices, e.g. Buddhists pray weekly during the 49-day funeral period. Certain rites may help the bereavement process more than others. Burgoine (1988) compared widows in the Bahamas with those in London and found that the former culture encouraged overt expressions of grief and the widows had fewer psychological problems.

Use it or lose it

A recent study (Chen *et al.*, 2010) has shown the importance of learning in maintaining an active brain. The study showed that learning stimulates a brain substance that facilitates the growth and differentiation of synapses, responsible for communication between neurons. This substance is called *brain-derived neurotrophic factor* (BDNF). If a person stops learning, this substance declines and therefore the brain also stops developing.

Historical bias

Today the elderly have more money, greater leisure opportunities, healthier lifestyles and often remain in employment, so research from the twentieth century may be misleading.

The UK Office of Statistics (2010) reports that in 2009 16% of the population was over the age of 65. They expect this to rise to 23% by 2034. Understanding old age is therefore going to be increasingly important, and people aged over 65 are going to progressively exert their so-called 'grey power'.

CAN YOU...? No. 6.5

1... **Three** life events have been described on this spread. For each life event identify at least **one** negative and **one** positive effect.

2... Write about 50–100 words describing each of these effects.

3... Identify about **ten** points of evaluation.

4... Elaborate each point (see page 9).

5... Use all of this material to write an answer to the following question: *Describe and evaluate effects of events during late adulthood.* It might be good practice to write separate 'building block' essays about each of the three life events. Your answers should contain about 300 words of description and 500 words of evaluation.

Don't write an essay without reading the essay-writing notes on pages 8–9.

LIFESPAN THEORIES OF DEVELOPMENT

ERIKSON'S LIFESPAN THEORY

- Erik Erikson's 'eight ages of man' extends Freud's psychoanalytic theory into old age and incorporates social influences. Each stage has a specific psychosocial 'crisis' with a positive or negative outcome, but outcomes might mix positive and negative traits. Problems that are not resolved can be worked through later in life.
- The stages in adulthood are: *intimacy vs isolation* (early adulthood), *generativity vs stagnation* (middle age), *integrity vs despair* (old age).

EVALUATION

- Erikson's theory was grounded in his work as a psychiatrist (with European and American patients) and interviews, e.g. with Dakota Indians.
- Established development as a lifelong process linked to biological and social factors.
- The theory is gender-biased (based on male values, e.g. independence rather than interdependence), culture-biased (emphasises self-identity which is more relevant to individualist cultures) and historically biased (e.g. modern people often divorce), so Erikson's ideas need updating.

LEVINSON'S TRANSITIONS THEORY

- Levinson 'seasons of man's life' implies each step is 'different' rather than 'better'. It is based on interviews with 40 men aged 35–45. He suggests life alternates between stable periods when life structures are built and transitional phases when life structures are changing, and there might also be a crisis.
- The eras are:
  - Pre-adulthood – *early adulthood transition* (childhood dependence to independence).
  - Early adulthood – becoming one's own man.
  - *Midlife transition* (taking stock).
  - Middle adulthood – modified life structures.
  - *Late adult transition.*
  - Late adulthood (accepting own life and physical decline).

EVALUATION

- Levinson found that 80% of his original male sample had experienced a moderate or severe crisis in midlife, but Farrell and Rosenberg found only 12% of adults experience a midlife crisis (which was related to an accumulation of life events).
- Levinson found that women had similar life seasons, but Roberts and Newton found that men and women differed, e.g. in their 'Dream'. This may be less true today as more women have full-time jobs.
- Although Levinson's extensive interview technique provided detailed data, there may be a cohort effect and the data may be affected by social desirability bias.
- The theory is culturally biased as it is based on adulthood in individualist, Western cultures.

GOULD'S EVOLUTION OF ADULT CONSCIOUSNESS THEORY

- Gould's theory, derived from Freud, suggests a progressive casting aside of various false assumptions which protect us from anxiety. These must be challenged for continuing healthy development.
- For example, false assumption: *belonging to one's parents and their world* (age 18–21). Marriage at this time may fail because based on dependence since independence not established.
- Other false assumptions that must be challenged: *that the parents' way will work* (age 22–28), *that life is controllable* (age 28–34), *that there is no evil in me or death in the world* (age 35–45).

EVALUATION

- Gould's research used a questionnaire which wasn't assessed for reliability, and may have been subject to a social desirability bias.
- Gould's theory is a culture-biased account as it was based on white, middle-class Americans.
- It also suggests that development ends at age 45.
- Gould's theory produced a computer-based therapy (TLP, Therapeutic Learning Programme) which is as successful as individual psychotherapy (Jacobs et al.).

- Blos suggested that adolescents inevitably conflict with their parents as they seek independence.
- Erikson suggested each age of life has a conflict which, in adolescence, relates to becoming autonomous from parents to develop an identity.
- Marcia developed this idea, with crisis and commitment as the keys to adolescent development.

EVALUATION

- Evidence for conflict includes Smith and Crawford who found that over 60% of 11–16-year-olds had had suicidal thoughts, and 10% had attempted suicide. Montemayor (1982) found that adolescents averaged one argument every three days. Such conflicts were mild and thus a healthy means to achieve individuation.
- However, Siddique and D'Arcy found that about one-third of adolescents experienced no psychological distress and, although Rutter et al. found that teenagers reported frequent conflict, this was rarely serious.
- It may be that the 'storm and stress' theory of adolescence is a consequence of early research based on abnormal populations.
- As most research has been conducted in the US and Europe, it may not apply to other cultures in which adolescents have closer and more subordinate relationships with parents (Larsen).

EXPLANATIONS OF ADOLESCENT IDENTITY

BLOS'S PSYCHOANALYTIC THEORY

- According to Freud, independence first develops in early childhood. Blos suggested that adolescence is a time of 'reindividuation'.
- Independence creates emotional emptiness which leads to a desire for group experience, and/or a desire for substitute parenting (gained though infantile regression or hero worship). Rebellion is an ego defence to prevent becoming dependent again.

EVALUATION

- Independence may have been overstressed as continuing attachment to parents (connectedness) is also key to healthy development – like securely attached children use a secure base.
- Adolescents who are securely attached to their parents are healthier, better behaved, and have higher self-esteem (Cooper et al.).

ERIKSON'S PSYCHOSOCIAL THEORY

- The adolescent crisis in Erikson's lifespan theory relates to identity formation. The child's established identity is challenged by physical changes at puberty, causing role confusion.
- Adolescents must resolve the conflict between identity and role confusion, by developing relationships, autonomy from parents and making future plans.
- If this remains unresolved it leads to identity diffusion – negative identity (e.g. delinquency), lack of intimacy, avoidance of future plans or difficulty being industrious.
- Successful resolution leads to a new, unified sense of self, which may be further redefined.

EVALUATION

- Research evidence drawn from clinical practice and Dakota Indians.
- Kahn et al. supported the idea that identity matters to intimate relationships as low identity students had less success in relationships, although there were gender differences. Erikson suggested that, in females, identity developed *after* finding a partner, whereas identity comes *before* intimacy in males.
- Although Erikson's theory is supported by his interviews it is difficult to test as some concepts are vague, e.g. how to define 'identity'.

MARCIA'S THEORY

- Marcia developed Erikson's ideas so they could be tested empirically. Interviews with adolescents asked about their identity status relating to occupation, religion, politics, attitudes to sex, etc. to find out if they were in crisis (considering alternatives) or commitment (had made a firm decision).
- Four possible statuses appeared: *identity diffusion* (no crisis or commitment yet), *identity foreclosure* (crisis avoided by committing to conventional goals), *identity moratorium* (crisis while roles explored so low commitment), *identity achievement* (crisis results in commitment). An individual doesn't have to go through all four statuses.

EVALUATION

- Support from Waterman showed an increase of identity achievement and a decrease in diffusion status with age. Kroger found that identity achievers coped better under stress than those in moratorium.
- Identity achievement may happen later than predicted. Meilman found only half of young men had reached identity achievement.
- Identity achievement may not be permanent. Marcia found that some people regressed from a stable identity to foreclosure or diffusion.
- The identity statuses may oversimplify reality. According to Archer, few people have the same identity status for all concerns (e.g. in identity confusion for sexual attitudes, but identity achievement for occupational choice).
- Marcia's theory provides a way to group adolescents together that is helpful for research. However, his participants (American boys) may have provided socially desirable answers and produced potentially gender- and culture-biased results.
- Erikson showed that identity moratorium is a useful concept, e.g. rebellious behaviour in young people may be them trying out possible roles and overreaction to this might prematurely determine identity.
- It is possible that only some adolescents experience crisis, which challenges Marcia's and Erikson's ideas.

ALTERNATIVE VIEWS

Connectedness
- Adolescents may become independent without conflict if they have a close relationship with their parents (connectedness).

Coleman's focal theory
- Crisis is not inevitable but happens because issues build up.
- Coleman and Hendry asked 800 boys and girls aged 11–17 about anxiety-provoking topics. The peaks for each issue were spread out, which gives time to cope with challenges one by one, so avoiding crisis.
- Adolescents are at risk if issues arise at the same time, e.g. family breakdown.

EVALUATION
- Allen and Land found that adolescents with secure attachments to parents had fewer problems.
- Larson *et al.* found that time spent with family decreased in early adolescence but time spent alone with each parent did not, showing both autonomy and connectedness.
- Parental relationships are more important for boys than girls (Frey and Rothlisberger), but girls are more affectionate and helpful towards parents (Eberly and Montemayor).
- Simmons and Blyth found that self-esteem and school performance were unaffected when adolescents had only one crisis.
- A useful application is to cope by focusing on fewer problems at a time.
- Coleman's theory might simply be a life events theory of adolescence – but Coleman claims it is more than this because adolescents play an active role.
- 'Media amplification' may perpetuate the conflict view, e.g. through sensationalist reporting of minority vandalism and drug use.
- Eccles *et al.* suggested adolescents stressed by mismatch between needs and (lack of) opportunities in their social environments, e.g. minimum age laws, creates a moratorium.

EFFECTS OF EVENTS DURING MIDDLE ADULTHOOD

MARRIAGE

Negative effects
- Holmes and Rahe rated marriage as the 7th most stressful life event.

Positive effects
- Bradburn found that marrieds were happier than never-marrieds (who were happier than those separated, divorced or widowed).
- Wilson and Oswald suggest reasons why marriage is linked to happiness: *financial*, *protective* (emotional support), *guardian* (fewer risky behaviours), *selection* (healthier people more likely to get married).
- Admissions to mental hospital are higher for single than married people, and higher still for those widowed or divorced (Cochrane).
- Lynch found that marrieds were less likely than single, divorced, or widowed individuals to die from diabetes, strokes or cancer.

EVALUATION
- Glenn and McLanahan found a U-shaped relationship between marital satisfaction and length of marriage which falls when the first child is born and rises again when the last leaves home.
- Horwitz and White found cohabiting couples did not gain as many health benefits as married ones, perhaps lower 'quality'.
- Cochrane found that more married women than men are admitted to mental hospital (though still less likely to than single women).
- Married people have a lower mortality risk than single people, and this is most pronounced for men (Lillard and Waite).
- Gender differences may be because men gain more from being married, e.g. emotional support, or fewer risks (e.g. drinking).
- Cultural differences – Yelsma and Athappily found few differences between American marriages and Indian arranged marriages.
- Individual differences – 'poor' marriages provide fewer health benefits.

PARENTHOOD

Negative effects
- Parenthood is not all positive, it may cause marital problems because of conflicts over childrearing practices and jealousy.
- Pregnancy scores 12th on the Holmes and Rahe scale. A new family member scores 14th and a child leaving home is 23rd.
- Hultsch and Deutsch found that 50–80% of adults described the birth of their first child as a moderate to severe crisis.

Positive effects
- Turner and Helms suggested that parenthood is positive because:
  (1) sense of achievement;
  (2) can give and receive love;
  (3) cultural expectation;
  (4) sense of importance.

EVALUATION
- Parental investment theory predicts that females have a greater interest in parenting because of greater physiological investment. In humans, the long-term need for care of children means males also wish to protect their investment.
- Russell found that middle-class parents were more dissatisfied than working-class ones, possibly as they have higher ideals.
- In collectivist societies satisfaction may be higher because the extended family helps.

DIVORCE

Negative effects
- Divorce scores 2nd on the Holmes and Rahe scale, separation 3rd and reconciliation 9th.
- Clulow argued the grief, sorrow and anger of divorce are like bereavement for the couple and their children.
- Kiecolt-Glaser and Glaser found poorer immune function during marital disruption. Carter and Glick found increased illness rates in divorced women.

Positive effects
- Kalmijn and Monden found less depression in divorcees who 'escaped' from an unhappy marriage.

EVALUATION
- Plomin found that identical twins with a divorced co-twin were also more likely to become divorced.
- Some negative findings about divorce may be causes of marital breakdown rather than effects.
- Although women have more practical difficulties, men experience more stress because of lack of support.
- Related to culture, e.g. 0.28% in the UK but 0.011% in India. Brodbar-Nemzer found fewer divorces in collectivist Jewish families in New York than individualist ones.
- There are individual differences, the effects depending on length of marriage, age of children, etc.
- The use of self-report methods means that social desirability can bias findings.

EFFECTS OF EVENTS DURING LATE ADULTHOOD

RETIREMENT

Positive effects
- Some evidence shows that mental health improves at retirement (Dave *et al.*).
- Schellenberg found about half of retirees found more pleasure in life, though good health and financial well-being were important to enjoying retirement, as well as physical activities, hobbies and volunteer work.

Negative effects
- Retirement is 10th on the Holmes and Rahe scale.
- Orth *et al.* found that self-esteem declines. Patterson found people who retired at 55 died earlier than those who continued to work.
- Many factors limit negative effects, e.g. being married, having friends and having high self-esteem (Reitzes and Mutran).

A phase model
- Atchley identified five phases of adjustment: *honeymoon* (enjoyment), *disenchantment* (failure to reach expectations), *reorientation* (more realistic approach), *stability* (routine develops), *termination* (poor health requires lifestyle changes).

EVALUATION
- Research findings are inconsistent, e.g. Ekerdt *et al.* found satisfaction fell after one year but Richardson and Kilty found the decline occurred sooner.
- It is important whether retirement is voluntary and looked forward to and how much the individual enjoyed work and the company of co-workers, physical health, money, friends, etc.

ADJUSTMENT TO OLD AGE

Activity theory
- Havighurst suggested that people cope better with the effects of old age if they remain active in society. New interests benefit psychological health, important to maintain 'role count'.
- Langer and Rodin found that elderly people with a greater sense of control lived longer, and Rubin found elderly people in their own homes were more mentally healthy than those in nursing homes.

Social disengagement theory
- Cumming and Henry proposed that older people adjust best when they withdraw from personal contacts and world affairs, and that this is beneficial for the individual and society.
- They described three phases: *shrinkage of life space* (less interaction), *increased individuality* (due to decreased social pressure), *acceptance of life changes* (more inwardly focused).
- This was based on study of 40–90-year-olds which showed that people gradually lose contact and roles, freeing them to play only chosen roles.

EVALUATION
- Havighurst *et al.* found some types of people are *disengagers* (always been reclusive and tended to disengage in later years) but others were not.
- Intervening variables, e.g. wealth, may be more important.
- Atchley proposed *continuity theory* – successful agers are those who continue to do the same things in old age as they did before.
- Erikson suggested *integrity versus despair* crisis means the individual must evaluate their life.
- Socioemotional selectivity theory (Cartenson) suggests that, with age, people become more selective (to maximise energy and emotional reward).
- Chen *et al.* showed that learning helps to maintain an active brain – if a person stops learning, *brain-derived neurotrophic factors* decline and the brain stops developing.

BEREAVEMENT

Coping
- Kübler-Ross's stage account of accepting one's own death (or bereavement) was based on interviews with dying patients.
- The stages: *denial and isolation* (avoidance by others), *anger* (acceptance begins), *bargaining* (trying to find a way out), *depression* (sorrow), *acceptance*.

Negative effects
- Death of spouse is 1st on Holmes and Rahe's scale, close family member 5th, close friend 17th.
- Hinton found recent widows were more likely to die than married women. Parkes found widows sought more medical advice but this may be because illnesses are ignored leading up to a spouse's death (Mor *et al.*).
- Abnormal grief may occur in extreme circumstances, e.g. following a night-club fire, somatic distress, guilt and hostility occurred (Lindemann).

Moderating influences
- The 'convoy' are friends, family, etc. who offer social support reducing risk of illness, emotional upset and death (Kahn and Attanucci).

EVALUATION
- There are individual differences in bereavement, e.g. emotional type, type of death and age of and relationship to the deceased.
- Barrett found gender differences; men had lower morale and required more help than women. When women define themselves in terms of their husbands they experience greater loss (Lopata).
- Collectivist cultures provide extended support, religions help bereavement to differing extents.

Question 6 Discuss the effects of events during late adulthood. [25]

Student answer

Paragraph 1 Late adulthood is the time after people have retired. This is usually after 65 in Western societies but since things are different in other cultures such as collectivist ones this shows we should be very careful about being ethnocentric. In some societies people don't retire or old age means different things.

Paragraph 2 Retirement is reported as being psychologically good for people. Mental health improves by over 10% (Dave et al. 2006) and another researcher found that half of the retiring people reported a more pleasurable life.

Paragraph 3 However this means that half didn't, of course. On the negative side there are studies that report higher levels of stress after retirement and it is 10th on the SRRS scale of stress impact on health. One Texan study found that people retiring at 55 were twice as likely to die earlier than those who carried on working. This suggests there are other factors involved in happiness after retirement, such as a happy marriage, having networks of friends or having interesting hobbies. Atchley's phase model mentions lifestyle changes and this is going to be really important especially when there isn't a lot of money, state pensions aren't much in this country and in many other countries you starve if you don't work. There are big individual differences of course.

Paragraph 4 One of the theories about late adulthood is Havighurst. He suggested that coping in old age means staying active and involved. Langer and Rodin showed that in their nursing home study having more control over little details in your life meant better health prospects. Going into a home is not a good idea anyway, Rubin showed the elderly at home stayed more mentally stable.

Paragraph 5 Lots of theories like Cumming and Henry say that elderly people withdraw from personal contact and world affairs. This is called disengagement theory and is based on a longitudinal study of 700 older people. Disengagement is speeded up when your partner dies or you become less active.

Paragraph 6 However, Havighurst noticed big individual differences based on personality; some people were 'disengagers' and had always shown that tendency. This links to having lots of friends — social networks are psychologically healthy as I've said before. Atchley even goes as far as to suggest there isn't a change at all — people who always did things will continue to be very active but those who were more isolated will become more and more isolated. These maybe are Havinghurst's 'disengagers'.

Paragraph 7 Cartenson also suggests that this is due to control being used to conserve energy and select important experiences. All these ideas are a lot more positive, and in Britain the elderly are doing lots more. You often see on the news about 70 year olds doing sky-diving, climbing, expeditions, mountain biking and all sorts. Perhaps many of the theories are culture-biased — they were true years ago but not now as much.

Paragraph 8 Everybody dies in the end and in late adulthood people will have coped with other people's deaths and suffered bereavement. People also have to think about their own death. Death of a partner is 1st on the SRRS and all studies find that widowhood means worse health or even early death.

Paragraph 9 However there are gender differences — widowers suffer greater morale loss and need more help than widows, perhaps because of gender roles in Western society. Also there are huge cultural differences because collectivist societies tend to have rituals after someone's death that support the bereaved. Burgoine found that women in the West Indies were allowed to show more grief and this resulted in fewer psychological problems than in British women.

Paragraph 10 Finally, Kübler–Ross identified five stages in contemplating your own death. These go from denial through anger to acceptance. The stages aren't in strict order, but a general tendency.

Paragraph 11 Once again there will be differences across cultures and also I think it will depend on religious belief as well. This is always a problem in making general theories because cultures differ, and there are even differences in this country especially where there are close extended families. There are also big differences across time. Modern science has shown that activity promotes brain growth even in the elderly (Chen, 2010) and many of the theories were formed at times when the elderly were expected to fade away and die. Twenty-first-century elderly people in Britain are far less likely to do this, in line with scientific recommendation. Therefore we should question the validity of these theories for modern times.

[739 words]

Examiner comments

This is a good essay. There is a clear structure where theories are described and facts established and then substantial evaluation is presented, using both research findings or established critical themes (such as ethnocentrism and validity). The examiner will be fairly sure on reading this essay that the marks will be in the top half of the mark range for both **AO1** and **AO2** (the latter highlighted in grey). One of the ways to indicate evaluative content is to use phrases such as 'however', as has been done in this essay (see page 9 for other ways to indicate evaluative material).

Paragraph 1 immediately introduces a critical theme (culture differences) that is picked up in paragraphs 7, 9 and 11. Remember that culture can mean the same society at different times as well as different societies. Paragraph 2 is a short piece of description that sets up the evaluation of paragraph 3. This paragraph is largely accurate and very telling, although there are statements that aren't expanded on until later (e.g. 'There are big individual differences of course').

Paragraphs 4 and 5 again state the effects of events clearly and simply, based on theories and research studies. This is followed by another two evaluative paragraphs (paragraphs 6 and 7) which are perhaps a little fragmented but on the whole express clear arguments.

Paragraphs 8 and 9 repeat the **AO1/AO2** pattern, picking up the culture theme again. Paragraph 10 is too brief on Kübler-Ross, and really it isn't more than a filler before the very strong finish of paragraph 11, which offers a wealth of evaluative material and criticism.

The **AO1** material deserves a mark of **9 out of 10 marks** rather than full marks because some of the descriptive material is too vague. The evaluation (**AO2**) is spot on for **15 out of 15 marks**.

24/25 makes this a very good A* standard of essay.

Improvement?

There isn't much to improve but researchers' names and the dates of their research would enhance the detail. Generally more precise details would be better.

Chapter 7
Levels of consciousness

Chapter contents

148 Introduction to the study of levels of consciousness

150 Theories of hypnosis

152 The nature of dreams

154 Theories of sleep

156 The role of endogenous and exogenous factors in bodily rhythms

158 Explanations for disorders of sleep

End-of-chapter review

160 Chapter summary

162 Exam question with student answer

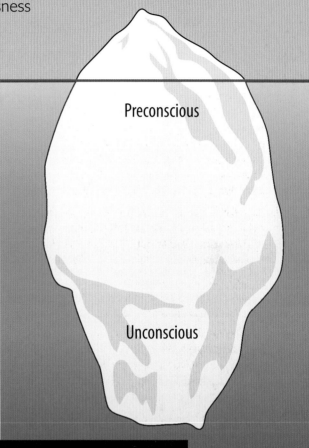

Conscious

Preconscious

Unconscious

▶ *In your AS course you studied Freud's psychoanalytic theory of personality, where he suggested that the conscious mind was like the tip of the iceberg. Other theorists have distinguished between different levels of consciousness rather than just separating consciousness from unconsciousness.*

Specification breakdown	
Theories of hypnosis including state and non-state explanations.	With an image that varies from sinister manipulation to the hilarity of stage hypnosis, the question asked in this section is whether hypnosis is a special state of consciousness, or a variant of normal behaviour.
The nature of dreams (e.g. Freud's psychoanalytic theory, lucid dreaming, nightmares).	We have covered the two main theories of dreaming as a way to answer the question of 'what is the nature of dreams' – is it the *royal road to the unconscious* (as Freud claimed) or a meaningless jumble caused by overnight memory processing?
Theories of sleep (e.g. restoration and ecological/evolutionary explanations).	The specification gives the two main perspectives as examples of theories of sleep. We have followed this by looking at restoration and evolutionary approaches. Sleep remains one of the mysteries of animal behaviour.
The role of endogenous and exogenous factors in bodily rhythms (e.g. circadian, infradian, ultradian rhythms and disruption of these rhythms).	Like previous sections, the specification provides examples of what you might study. This does not mean you are required to study these examples nor that you would be required to refer to them in an exam question. We have been selective in our coverage so that you have the required amount of information – not too much or too little for a 25-mark question.
Explanations for disorders of sleep (e.g. narcolepsy, insomnia, hypersomnia).	Sleep is never so important to us than when it is disturbed or disrupted. In this section the more serious disturbances are examined through explanations and research evidence. Note that the specification is about 'explanations', which means that answers must always focus on describing and evaluating explanations – not describing research evidence; such evidence is used to develop and support your explanations.

The term 'consciousness' has a variety of meanings, such as being awake or just being aware. Consciousness may be one of the factors that distinguishes humans from non-humans, or at least distinguishes higher mammals from others, as self-awareness appears to be unique to higher mammals (see the 'mirror test' at the bottom of the facing page).

The traditional view is that there are three states of consciousness in humans – you're either awake or asleep, and if you are asleep then you are either in an REM or an NREM state (REM stands for rapid eye movement, as discussed below. NREM is non-REM sleep). Recent brain research suggests that there are more than these three states of consciousness. For example, during sleepwalking the brain is half awake and half asleep – the parts of the brain involved in consciousness are offline but other areas of the brain are active. Patients in a coma state have usually been regarded as unconscious, yet recent research shows brain activity when they are asked to imagine certain scenes.

THE MYSTERY OF CONSCIOUSNESS

It is very difficult to specify what consciousness is, though all of us know what it feels like. One view (described as determinist) proposes that consciousness, like all behaviour, is determined by the physical matter of which we are made and can be explained solely in terms of chemical and physical processes. The philosopher Daniel Dennett (2003) suggests that consciousness is like a conjuring trick – such tricks fool you into thinking that something extraordinary is happening whereas in reality it is a totally mechanical process.

Consciousness and free will

If our behaviour is determined by the physical matter of our brain and body, then this means our behaviour is entirely predictable and implies that we have no free will. However, there is plenty of evidence that human behaviour is not predictable which would suggest that there is such a thing as free will – but this unpredictability can be explained within a determinist framework. The psychologist Steven Pinker (2008b) argues that lack of predictability is inevitable in a determinist system composed of billions of cells and trillions of connections between the cells. In Pinker's view our behaviour is unpredictable but we do not have free will.

Dennett offers a different solution to reconciling determinism and free will. He suggests that, despite the determinist nature of our minds, the human brain is capable of anticipating future events, considering and evaluating consequences of our behaviour, and therefore deciding on a course of action. In this sense we do have free will.

THE MYSTERY OF SLEEP

Sleep usually involves being very still, though dolphins and other marine mammals are not still. They come up to the surface regularly to breathe and, to do this, only one hemisphere (half of the brain) sleeps at a time.

Sleepers are usually quite unresponsive, though they are not unconscious. Most animals are woken by significant noises. For example, most parents will wake if they hear their babies crying.

Animals usually sleep in a quiet, private, secure place and they usually do it lying down in the dark, though it is possible to sleep on a busy underground train sitting up. Cows sleep standing up (except during REM sleep) and cats snooze in bright light.

What does this tell us? There are no certain features of sleep. It also shows us that, although all animals sleep, they all do it differently.

NREM and REM sleep

The most distinctive thing about sleep is that it is accompanied by characteristic patterns of electrical activity in the brain (see EEG recordings on the right). That's how you know that an animal is sleeping. One of these characteristic patterns is called REM (rapid eye movement) sleep. At various times during sleep an individual's eyes dart back and forth under closed eyelids and the body may twitch slightly, though in fact the individual is in a state of paralysis. Unlike sleep, not all animals have REM activity; for example reptiles don't.

If you wake a person up during REM sleep they often (but not always) report that they have been dreaming. However people also sometimes report dreams if woken from NREM (non-rapid eye movement sleep). We don't know whether all animals dream. People like to think, when they watch their dog twitching in its sleep, that their pet is in some delicious reverie involving a stick. But we will never know. No dog has yet reported what might have been going on in its mind.

In humans, the different patterns of sleep (REM and NREM) alternate throughout the night. This is one example of a biological rhythm. The sleep–wake cycle is another kind of biological rhythm. The disruption of such rhythms has important effects (for example, most road accidents occur when drivers are sleepy) which makes the whole area of sleep research of important practical consequence.

▼ *The illustration shows EEG (electroencephalograph) recordings of characteristic brain waves. As a person goes to sleep their brain waves increase in amplitude (the height of the wave) and the wave frequency also increases (the distance between the crest of one wave and the next).*

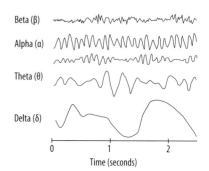

▼ *An illustration of the changing ultradian rhythm of sleep during the night. The sleep–wake cycle is a circadian rhythm.*

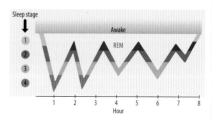

▼ *The stages of sleep.*

NREM sleep	
Stages 1 & 2	Relaxed state, easily woken. Alpha and theta waves, heart rate slows, temperature drops.
Stages 3 & 4 Slow wave sleep (SWS)	Delta waves, metabolic rate slowest, growth hormone produced.

REM sleep	
Rapid eye movement (REM) sleep	Called 'paradoxical sleep' because brain and eyes are active but body is paralysed.

A SLEEP AND DREAM SURVEY

We all are well aware of the individual differences in sleep habits and dream experiences – some people seem content with six hours of sleep per night whereas others want ten hours; some people experience sleep disorders such as **insomnia**, *night terrors*, sleepwalking, whereas others having uninterrupted sleep; some people have vivid, memorable dreams whereas other remember almost nothing. Try collecting some data about these individual differences.

Develop a questionnaire which can be handed out by all members of your class to family and friends (see example below for some ideas). Once the data is collected divide your class into groups and let each group produce a summary of different parts of the questionnaire. Each group should present their summary to the class.

An alternative approach is to ask individuals to keep a sleep diary (see right) for a few weeks where they record when they went to sleep and woke up, and also record information about their dreams. You could also ask them to record other information, such as what kind of activities they had been doing in the day (to see if there is a link between hours asleep and daily activities).

Individual sleep and dream record

You might construct a form like the one below so individuals can record details of their sleep and/or dreams each night.

1. Who features in your dreams?	Known (e.g. family, friends)	Generic (e.g. a teacher rather than a specific teacher)	Animals	Other
2. What is the dream about?	Emotional	Not emotional	Positive	Negative
3. Meaningfulness	Could you describe the dream well?	Was it just fragments?	Was it related to specific daytime events?	

Sleep and dream survey

1. How old are you?
2. How many hours of sleep do you usually have per night?
3. Do you have difficulty going to sleep?
4. Do you have difficulty waking up?
5. Are your dreams long or just fragmentary?
6. Do you remember a lot of detail in your dreams?
7. Describe what your dreams tend to be like.

Add some more questions of your own.

Is it best to use open or closed questions, or a mixture? Also think about social desirability bias… check information about the design of questionnaires and interviews on page 27.

> **WWW**

Read more about the content analysis of dreams at www.insomnium.co.uk/dream-theory/dreams-schneider-domhoff/

The mirror test

Gallup (1970) and Amsterdam (1972) independently developed a test of self-awareness which may be a clue to consciousness. The test involves placing a smudge of rouge or red colouring on an individual's nose and then seeing what they do when shown their reflection in a mirror. If they possess self-awareness they will touch their own nose, otherwise they will touch the mirror. To this day the '**mirror test**' (also called the 'rouge test' or 'mark test') is regarded as the best way to assess self-awareness.

Gallup (1970) demonstrated that chimpanzees were able to recognise themselves in a mirror. After becoming accustomed to the mirrors, the chimpanzees were anaesthetised and a red mark placed on their foreheads and ears. After recovering from the anaesthetic, none of the animals showed any interest in the marks until seeing their reflections in the mirror. This caused them to touch the marks on their faces, using the mirror to direct their responses.

Amsterdam (1972) tested 88 babies, obtaining reliable data from 16 of them (many didn't want to play). She found that babies aged 6–12 months behaved as if the baby in the mirror was someone else. Between 13 and 24 months babies looked warily at the image in the mirror, possibly displaying some self-awareness. By 24 months babies clearly recognised themselves.

Various other studies have used the mirror test to demonstrate self-awareness in great apes (except for gorillas), bottlenose dolphins, killer whales, pigeons, elephants and magpies (the only non-mammal that appears to pass the mirror test). The big question is – does this mean they have consciousness, and if so, what kind of consciousness?

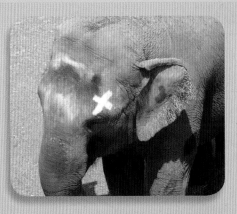

▲ *Happy the elephant had a white cross on her forehead and was filmed using a mirror to try to touch the mark, see www.empathogens.com/empathy/happy-elephant.html*

Hypnosis is regarded as a 'level of consciousness' because it appears to be a special state of awakeness. When hypnotised, people report feeling relaxed, awake but inwardly focused (rather than unaware) and responsive to the hypnotist (rather than self-motivated). An observer can also see changes in hypnotic subjects, such as suggestibility to ideas from the hypnotist, increased imagination and ability to enact a role.

One possible explanation of these features is that hypnosis is a special 'state', i.e. an altered level of consciousness induced by the hypnotic procedure. Alternatively, the effects experienced by a hypnotised individual might be explained by other psychological processes, such as social factors. This is the 'state' versus 'non-state' argument.

Suggestibility, susceptibility and compliance The terms suggestibility and susceptibility are almost the same; **suggestibility** is the extent to which an individual responds to the hypnotist's suggestions. In general this is measured on a susceptibility scale – indicating how responsive a person is to suggestions. Non-state theorists think in terms of compliance rather than suggestibility or susceptibility.

STATE EXPLANATIONS

A hypnotic subject may appear to be in a trance. State theorists argue that this is an altered state of consciousness, differing from our normal state as, for example, sleeping does from wakefulness.

The neodissociationist view

The state view held by Ernest Hilgard (1977) suggests that hypnotic experiences happen because of a **dissociation** of cognitive systems. The influence of the hypnotist separates (dissociates) levels of cognitive processing so that we are aware of some aspects of our thinking but not others. The ones we are aware of cause hypnotic experiences such as hallucinations, and the suppressed levels account for **amnesia**, **analgesia**, etc.

'Reals' versus 'fakers' If hypnosis is a different state, it should be possible to tell the difference between someone who is truly hypnotised ('real') and a 'simulator' who is just 'faking'. In an observation of behaviour when the hypnotist left the room, Evans and Orne (1971) found that hypnotised subjects continued to respond for longer than the simulators. Hypnotised individuals also show a stronger 'post-hypnotic' response (Evans and Orne *et al.*, 1968).

Hidden observer Hilgard (1977) suggests that the **hidden observer** (see facing page) provides access to an otherwise unavailable level of consciousness, i.e. the level that has become dissociated from conscious experience. For example, hypnotic analgesia can be used to mask the pain normally felt when holding a hand in very cold water. When asked if they feel pain, a hypnotised subject says 'no' but the hidden observer reports pain.

Remarkable physical feats have been claimed under hypnosis, such as the response of a hypnotic subject to the suggestion that they are as stiff as a board; they can be placed with only their head and ankles supported and hold themselves still for a long time.

Unique brain states Some aspects of the hypnotic experience are not seen in any other situation, suggesting that hypnosis is a special state. For example, Kosslyn *et al.* (2000) found distinctive brain activity patterns associated with hypnosis and not with other waking states.

A neo-state view

A newer theory has focused on particular structures in the brain. Oakley (1999) has suggested that, during 'normal' consciousness, the *executive control system* (in the **frontal cortex**) monitors incoming information and then makes a decision about what to do. In addition the executive control system separately monitors behaviour and this gives us a sense of self-awareness. During hypnosis, the hypnotist 'hacks into' the executive control system so the hypnotist's suggestions influence decision making by the executive control system and are seen as the cause of behaviour. Thus the hypnotised subject doesn't have their usual sense of self-awareness because the decisions were under the hypnotist's influence and not their own.

NON-STATE EXPLANATIONS

This view suggests that hypnotic induction affects behaviours such as relaxation, imagination and compliance, thus making 'hypnotised' individuals behave differently from 'waking' ones.

Socio-cognitive theory of hypnosis (SCT)

According to Graham Wagstaff (1986), hypnotic induction does not result in a different state but it changes two processes: compliance and belief.

Compliance The processes of obedience and conformity are familiar to you from your AS studies by Milgram and Asch. These processes are related to compliance, which describes the behaviour of someone who is conforming/obeying. Compliance refers to situations where a person changes their behaviour (but not their attitudes) to go along with others. In hypnosis the subject complies with the expectations of the hypnotist. For example, a hypnotic subject who is offered the suggestion that 'you can feel your arm rising on its own' is likely to oblige (comply) by creating that feeling. Subjects are motivated to comply with such a suggestion to avoid the embarrassment of 'failing' to be hypnotised, or to avoid appearing 'disobedient' or implying that the hypnotist is inadequate.

Belief Compliance is volitional, i.e. a person consciously decides on what to do. The key point, however, is that a hypnotised person *believes* their responses are not volitional, i.e. they can't help themselves. It is this belief that leads them to regard the hypnotism as 'real', i.e. being in a separate state.

Why do they label their behaviour as 'non-volitional'? A study by Valins (1966) offers some insight. In this study male participants were required to rate images of semi-nude females. When viewing some of the photos the men were given 'false feedback' about their heart rate, i.e. they thought it was faster than it was. The men rated these photos as more attractive presumably because they thought their increased heart rate meant they were more attracted to the photo. When interviewed later they tried to 'excuse' their judgements by using strategies such as noticing previously unidentified features or a resemblance to an ex-girlfriend. Like hypnotic subjects, these participants misinterpreted information and subsequently tried to offer rational explanations for their behaviour. In the case of hypnosis, subjects explain their compliance in terms of being hypnotised and not in control of their own behaviour.

The ESC process Hypnotic subjects may seek experiences which confirm the hypnotist's suggestion, for example when the hypnotist says 'your hand will feel lighter and float upwards' they may interpret a twitch in one hand within this framework. The 'task' for a hypnotic subject therefore has three components: they must decide what the hypnotist 'wants', employ cognitive strategies to produce congruent experiences and, if this fails, resort to behavioural compliance. Wagstaff calls this the *ESC process* (Expectation, Strategy, Compliance). For example in hypnotic amnesia, ESC suggests that the subject judges that forgetting is a requirement of the situation (expectation) then they either employ inattention to block memory (strategy), or is unable to generate the required response and therefore fakes it (compliance).

MAGNÉTISME HYPNOTISME

PARIS, DELARUE ÉDITEUR 5, R. des GRANDS AUGUSTINS

The 'hidden observer'

During a demonstration of hypnosis to a class of students, Hilgard suggested that the subject would be unable to hear but this deafness would cease when his shoulder was touched. As expected the hypnotised subject became unresponsive to noises or voices. Then, Hilgard quietly asked the subject if there was any part of his brain that was fully aware and if so to raise a finger. To the surprise of Hilgard, his class and the unsuspecting subject, he raised a finger. Hilgard reinstated the student's hearing by touching the subject's shoulder and asked him what he could recall. The subject reported that everything had become still and boring, so he'd resorted to thinking about statistics until he became aware that his finger had moved and he wanted to know why. When Hilgard asked 'the part of his brain which had listened before and made your finger rise' to answer, the subject reported accurately all that had happened (Hilgard, 1977). Hilgard used the term 'hidden observer' to refer to this monitor of all the events during hypnosis, even those of which the subject is not consciously aware.

EVALUATION

State explanations: The neodissociationist view

'Reals' versus 'fakers' The difference between 'reals' and 'fakers' may not be a product of the presence or absence of a hypnotic state but of an underlying difference in the abilities of the individuals. For example, simulators have been found to be poorer at imagining and acting ability, which would make their simulation more transparent to observers.

Remarkable physical feats may not be exclusive to hypnotised subjects. Druckman and Bjork (1994) report that without hypnosis, highly motivated people demonstrate strength, stamina, learning and perceptual abilities comparable to hypnotised ones.

Evidence from the brain There is physiological evidence suggesting that hypnosis produces a distinct state. Using **PET scans**, Rainville et al. (1997) showed that hypnotic analgesia produced a reduction in brain activity relating to attending to painful stimuli without affecting the processing of the sensory information itself. This fits with the idea of dissociation.

Further evidence shows distinct differences between hypnotised and non-hypnotised states. For example, Williams and Gruzelier (2001) have shown that brain activity is different in hypnosis (with more alpha waves) and relaxation (with more theta waves). Egner et al. (2005) reported consistent differences in anterior *cingulated gyrus function* between hypnotised and non-hypnotised participants.

Finally, there is also evidence to show brain differences in terms of susceptibility to hypnosis. Naish (2006) reported that hemispheric asymmetry in brain efficiency was related to hypnotic susceptibility. Those with the larger imbalances were more easy to hypnotise, those with lowest imbalances were the most difficult.

Non-state explanations: Socio-cognitive theory of hypnosis

Compliance This theory explains hypnosis in terms of familiar **socio-cognitive processes** such as compliance. But is this a sufficient explanation? If subjects are merely compliant then we would expect at least some of them to admit that they are pretending. However they don't, even when appeals are made to their honesty (Kihlstrom et al., 1980). However Spanos (1986) suggests that hypnotised subjects fail to admit to pretending because they have invested heavily in the role of being hypnotised and this causes them to reinterpret their experiences (for instance by ignoring memories that they were told to forget).

Compliance and susceptibility If hypnosis is simply compliance, then highly susceptible subjects should be generally more compliant, and this is not the case. Orne (1970) tested participants' hypnotic susceptibility and asked them to return a stack of postcards – the more postcards returned, the more compliant a person was judged to be. Orne found that highly susceptible subjects were not more compliant; if anything the low susceptibility subjects were more compliant (perhaps because they felt they had 'failed' by being unhypnotisable).

The ESC process A key strength of the non-state view over the 'state' approach is that it attempts to explain, rather than just describe, the experience of the subject. For example, in the case of hypnotic amnesia, state theory suggests that the subject is unable to recall 'lost' items because the state prevents recall; this is a circular argument.

Susceptibility

State theorists would argue that some individuals achieve the state of dissociation between cognitive subsystems controlling behaviour and awareness more readily than others, and thus it is a special state. Hilgard (1965) found 20% of people are highly susceptible and Piccione et al. (1989) showed this was a stable trait.

If highly hypnotisable people are special then it should not be possible to acquire this capacity. However, Wickless and Kirsch (1989) found that hypnotisability depended on expectation. All participants were hypnotised but one group were 'tricked' by being exposed to fake lights and sounds which they believed were the effects of hypnosis. When later tested for susceptibility, most of 'tricked' participants scored as highly hypnotisable. This appears to suggest that hypnotisability can be induced but subsequent studies, for example Benham et al. (1998) have failed to replicate the effect.

The non-state view is further supported by Spanos et al. (1985) who found that the responses of highly susceptible subjects differed depending on their expectations. If they were led to believe that 'deeply hypnotised' subjects had no voluntary control (such as 'you cannot bend your arm') they followed the hypnotist's suggestions. However, if they were led to believe that countering instructions was a sign of deep hypnosis, then they tended to maintain voluntary control. This suggests that highly susceptible subjects are simply more compliant.

CAN YOU...? No. 7.1

1... Select **four** key concepts for both state and non-state theory.

2... For each key concept write **three or four** sentences explaining the concept.

3... Identify about **ten** points of evaluation (these can be positive or negative).

4... Elaborate each point (see page 9).

5... Use all of this material to write an answer to the following exam question: *Discuss theories of hypnosis*. As good practice you might also write answers to the following 'building block' essays: (a) *Discuss state theories of hypnosis*. (b) *Discuss non-state theories of hypnosis*. Each answer should contain about 300 words of description and 500 words of evaluation.

Don't forget to read the essay-writing guidance on pages 8–9.

Dreams are mental activities occurring during sleep. There are a number of theories about *why* we dream. These can be broadly divided into psychological theories and **neurobiological** theories. Psychological theories offer an explanation of the *meaning* of dreams. Neurobiological theories regard the dream experience itself as an epiphenomenon – simply a by-product of neurobiological processes in the brain. However, there is one common thread – in both approaches a dream involves the activation of memory.

You studied the psychodynamic approach to psychology as part of your AS course and some of you will have studied Freud's dream analysis as an example of a psychodynamic therapy. The description of Freud's psychoanalytic theory of dreams below is a brief summary of the material in the AS book.

▲ *Freud believed it was necessary to consider dreams in the context of a person's life. For example, a fish could represent a person's friend who is a fisherman or another friend who has a Piscean star sign. Freud did not support the idea of dream dictionaries. Freud also recognised that not everything in a dream is symbolic; 'sometimes a cigar is just a cigar'.*

PSYCHOLOGICAL THEORY: FREUD'S PSYCHOANALYTIC THEORY

Sigmund Freud (1900) proposed that the **unconscious** mind expresses itself through dreams and, therefore, the content of a person's dreams can reveal what is in their unconscious.

Dreams as primary-process thought (repression) The **id** is associated with irrational, instinct-driven unconscious thought called **primary-process thought**. This form of thought is unacceptable to the adult conscious mind so is relegated to our dreams, i.e. **repressed**. If we do not dream, the energy invested in these desires would build up to intolerable levels and so threaten our sanity.

Dreams as wish fulfilment Freud believed that all dreams were the unconscious fulfilment of wishes that could not be satisfied in the conscious mind. Dreams, therefore, protect the sleeper (primary-process thought) but also allow some expression to these buried urges (wish fulfilment).

The symbolic nature of dreams According to Freud, the contents of dreams are expressed *symbolically*. The real meaning of a dream (**latent content**) is transformed into a more innocuous form (**manifest content**), through the process of **dreamwork**. Dreamwork consists of various processes such as **condensation** (rich, complex dream thoughts are condensed to the brief images) and **symbolism** (a symbol replaces an action, person, or idea).

NEUROBIOLOGICAL THEORY: THE ACTIVATION-SYNTHESIS HYPOTHESIS

Most dreams occur in conjunction with rapid eye movements; hence, they are said to occur during **REM sleep**, a period typically taking up 20–25% of sleep time. Allan Hobson and Robert McCarley (1977) suggested that the characteristic neurobiological activity associated with REM sleep can explain what we experience as dreams.

Activation

There is clear evidence from **EEG** measurements that the cerebral cortex (see diagram on right) is highly active during REM sleep, although few external stimuli are being received. Likewise, although the motor cortex (the part of the brain that initiates impulses to promote movement) is active, impulses do not reach the muscles that control the limbs – we are effectively paralysed during REM sleep. The only muscles that are allowed to express themselves are those that control the eyes. This is why REM sleep is accompanied by rapid eye movement. Hobson and McCarley (1977) suggested that during REM sleep, the brainstem generates random signals that are essentially indistinguishable from external stimuli.

Synthesis

It is during the synthesis part of this process that dreams are created. When the activation (random electrical signals from the brainstem) reaches the areas of the brain that normally process internal and external sensations (e.g. the prefrontal cortex), these areas of the brain essentially do the same job that they do when we are awake – they try to make sense of the stimuli being received.

The synthesis portion of the model proposes that the often bizarre nature of dreams is due to the mixing of the electrical signals from the brainstem with stored images in memory. The output is built into a coherent narrative with no inherent meaning but it may have meaning for the individual since it is derived from the dreamer's memories (Hobson, 1988). The activation-synthesis hypothesis assumes, therefore, that dreams are as meaningful as they can be given the fact they are generated by random nervous impulses.

Revisions

Hobson has continued to revise the activation-synthesis hypothesis in response to criticisms and new evidence. For example, Hobson (1994) suggested that lower levels of the **noradrenaline** and **serotonin** distinguish the REM state from other states. These lower levels create the bizarre nature of dreams and also create attentional problems, explaining why we don't remember dreams.

▼ *The diagram below shows the main parts involved in the activation-synthesis model. In mammals, the brain is covered with a thin layer of cells which is just a few millimetres thick – like a tea cosy. This is called the **cerebral cortex**, or sometimes just the cortex. The anterior (front) part of the **frontal lobe** is called the **prefrontal cortex**. The brainstem is part of the **hindbrain**.*

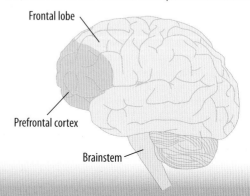

Frontal lobe

Prefrontal cortex

Brainstem

EVALUATION OF FREUD'S PSYCHOANALYTIC THEORY

Arguments against Freud's dream theory

Falsification One issue is that Freud's theory is difficult to **falsify** (prove wrong). We do not have a way of demonstrating that Freud's interpretation of a dream is correct because Freud argued that support for his interpretation of the dream could be given in two ways – either the dreamer accepted his interpretation or the dreamer rejected it, but such rejection was a form of confirmation because, Freud would argue, the patient is repressing unacceptable thoughts. This means it is impossible to prove his theory wrong (i.e. falsify it).

Are dreams wish fulfilments? It is difficult to see how nightmares would be wish fulfilments or how they might protect the sleeper (because they wake you up rather than enable you to sleep unworried). Freud did suggest that there is a class of dreams that do not seem to be fulfilments of wishes. He gave the example of one of his own dreams of a time when he was working in a chemistry lab, work that he was not good at. He regarded this dream as a 'sensible warning' rather than wish fulfilment.

Research evidence

Irrational and rational thinking Modern methods of brain imaging have provided evidence to support Freud's theory – see Solms' research on the right. On the other hand, the same evidence can be used against Freud's theory. Braun (1999) points out that if the rational, thinking part of the brain is not active during REM sleep, then how do we explain the processing that is taking place to turn latent into manifest content? This complex interpretation of meaning would seem to require high level processing.

Dreamwork Freud's concept of 'condensation' is supported by research on neural networks in the brain. This research involves computer simulations that aim to mimic the action of the brain. Such computer simulations show that **neural networks** deal with an overloaded memory by conflating or condensing 'memories' (Hopfield *et al.*, 1983).

EVALUATION OF THE ACTIVATION-SYNTHESIS HYPOTHESIS

Supporting evidence

There is some neurophysiological evidence that supports the activation-synthesis hypothesis. For example Braun *et al.* (1997) used PET scans to show that the brainstem is indeed active during REM sleep, as predicted by the *activation* portion of the activation-synthesis hypothesis.

There is also neurophysiological evidence to support the lack of coherence in dreams suggested by the activation-synthesis hypothesis. Solms' evidence (see top right) shows that activity in the prefrontal cortex is suppressed during dreaming which would explain the bizarre nature of dreams – but at the same time this evidence challenges the *synthesis* portion of the theory because this part of the brain should be active for synthesis to take place.

Challenging evidence

REM activity The activation-synthesis hypothesis predicts an association between dreams and REM activity, yet Solm's research indicates that dreams are not necessarily linked with REM activity (see above right). There is also evidence that people do dream during **NREM sleep** and these dreams are the same as those during REM sleep (Antrobus *et al.*, 1995). Hobson's (2000) answer is that REM activity may be more omnipresent than once thought, i.e. present during apparently NREM sleep.

Furthermore, research shows that children under the age of seven dream less than adults, although they do have REM activity (Foulkes, 1997). This challenges the activation-synthesis principle that REM activity is the basis of dreams.

Dream content Evidence from studies of dream content undermine the activation-synthesis hypothesis prediction that dreams will be fragmentary and bizarre (see research study at top right).

Some support for Freud, challenge for Hobson and McCarley

Mark Solms, a neuro-psychoanalyst, has produced research evidence to support Freud's theory of dreams. Solms (1999) first of all described case studies of some brain-damaged patients who no longer had REM brain activity and yet still reported having dreams. Conversely there were also patients with forebrain damage who had intact REM activity but reported no dreams. This suggests that the activation-synthesis hypothesis is wrong and Freud might be right.

In further research Solms (2000) used PET scans to examine brain activity in 'normal' individuals. Freud had predicted that the rational part of the brain is inactive during REM sleep whereas the centres concerned with memory and motivation are very active. In Freud's language, the ego (rational and conscious thought) becomes suspended while the id (the more primitive, unconscious 'driven' parts of the mind) is given free reign. Solms' brain scans indeed showed that the cortical areas to do with rational conscious thought (primarily the prefrontal cortex) are inactive during REM sleep while the limbic areas in the forebrain which are to do with memory and motivation are very active. Therefore Solms proposes that dreams are activated by the forebrain not by the brain stem – supporting Freud and challenging Hobson and McCarley.

However, both theoretical approaches have a problem. Both Freud and Hobson and McCarley portray dreams as bizarre. This is not supported by detailed studies of dream content. For example Snyder (1970) analysed over 600 dreams of young adults and concluded that dreams are 'a remarkably faithful replica of waking life'. Only 5% were categorised as exotic, and about 70% were rated as highly coherent on a three-point scale, as compared with less than 5% that were rated as low on coherence.

Combining the theories

Zhang (2005) has proposed the *continual-activation theory of dreaming* which offers a kind of bridge between both approaches. According to Zhang the brain must remain continually active. During sleep, activity levels drop and when this happens the continual-activation mechanism is triggered to generate a stream of data. This is similar to the activation part of the activation-synthesis approach.

At the same time there are other activities occurring during sleep (both REM and NREM sleep). One of these involves transferring data from temporary memory to the long-term memory (consolidation). The unconscious part of a brain is busy processing memory. This aspect of continual-activation theory may fit Freud's theory of dreams.

CAN YOU...? (No. 7.2)

1... For each explanation of dreaming select about **four** key concepts.

2... For each key concept write about 50 words explaining the concept.

3... Identify about **ten** points of evaluation (these can be positive or negative).

4... Elaborate each point (see page 9).

5... Use all of this material to write an answer to the following exam question: *Discuss the nature of dreams*. You could also write separate 'building block' essays for each theory. Your answer should contain about 300 words of description and 500 words of evaluation.

Don't forget to read the essay-writing guidance on pages 8–9.

Sleeping must have some benefit, otherwise why would humans and other animals spend so much time asleep? There are two alternative explanations. Restoration theory suggests that sleep provides some vital biological function whereas the **evolutionary approach** focuses more on its protective value e.g. saving energy or avoiding predators by staying still.

RESTORATION THEORY

Sleep is divided into several different stages, as we have seen on page 149. Two of the stages – **slow-wave sleep** (**SWS**) and **REM sleep** – are associated with particular benefits. Oswald (1980) proposed that these each had different functions – that SWS enables *body* repair and REM sleep enables *brain* recovery.

Slow-wave sleep (SWS)

Growth hormone is secreted during SWS Growth **hormone** (GH) stimulates growth but also enables protein synthesis, cell growth and tissue regeneration. This is vital because proteins are fragile and must be constantly renewed. GH is secreted in pulses throughout the day, but a significant amount is released at night and mainly during SWS. Sassin *et al.* (1969) found that, when sleep–waking cycles are reversed by 12 hours (i.e. a person goes to sleep in the morning and gets up at night), the release of GH is also reversed. This shows that GH release is controlled by neural mechanisms related to SWS. Further evidence comes from research that found that the amount of GH released correlates with the amount of SWS (van Cauter and Plat, 1996).

The immune system Lack of SWS has also been associated with reduced functioning of the immune system, the body's system of defence against viruses and bacteria (Krueger *et al.*, 1985). The **immune system** consists of various protein molecules – *antibodies* – which are regenerated during cell growth and protein synthesis in SWS.

REM sleep

Brain growth The percentage of REM sleep is far higher in babies than adults, and even higher in premature babies. This has been explained in terms of their rapid brain growth. It has been suggested that the amount of REM sleep in any species is proportional to the immaturity of the offspring at birth; for example the platypus is immature at birth and has about eight hours of REM sleep per day, whereas the dolphin, which can swim from birth, has almost no REM sleep (Siegel, 2003). This suggests a relationship between neural development and REM sleep.

Neurotransmitters Siegel and Rogawki (1988) suggest that REM sleep allows for a break in **neurotransmitter** release which in turn permits neurons to regain their sensitivity and function properly. Support for this comes from the action of some **antidepressant** drugs such as **MAOIs**. These drugs aim to increase the levels of monoamine neurotransmitters (such as **dopamine** and **serotonin**) (Siegel, 2003). A side effect is that MAOIs abolish REM activity which may be due to the two being linked – the increase in monoamines means that the monoamine receptors don't need to be revitalised and therefore there is no need for REM sleep.

REM sleep and memory Research on dreams (see previous spread) suggests a link between dreaming and memory. The evidence currently suggests that REM may be important in the consolidation of **procedural memory** (related to skills such as riding a bicycle) whereas SWS sleep is important for the consolidation of **semantic memory** (related to knowledge and the meaning of things) and **episodic memory** (memory for events) (Stickgold, 2005).

EVOLUTIONARY THEORY

The evolutionary approach to explaining behaviour is outlined on page 12.

Energy conservation

Warm-blooded animals (like ourselves) need to expend a lot of energy to maintain a constant body temperature. This is particularly problematic for small animals who tend to have high **metabolic rates**, such as mice. All activities use energy and animals with high metabolic rates use even more energy. Sleep, however, serves the purpose of providing a period of enforced *inactivity* (therefore using less energy) much like hibernation is a means of conserving energy. Webb (1982) described this as the **hibernation theory** of sleep.

Foraging requirements

If sleep is a necessity for energy conservation, the time spent sleeping may be constrained by food requirements. Animals have to gather food – herbivores, such as cows and horses, spend their time eating plants (such as grass) that are relatively poor in nutrients; as a result they must spend a great deal of time eating and consequently cannot 'afford' to spend time sleeping. Carnivores, such as cats and dogs, eat food that is high in nutrients, and so do not need to eat continuously. Therefore they can 'afford' to rest, and by resting they can conserve energy.

Predator avoidance

A further likelihood is that sleep is constrained by predation risk. If an animal is a predator, then it can 'afford' to sleep for longer. Whereas for prey species, their sleep time is reduced as they must remain vigilant to avoid predators. Logically, to be safe they shouldn't sleep at all but if sleep is a vital function then they are best to sleep when least vulnerable.

Waste of time

Meddis (1975) was the first to propose the 'waste of time' hypothesis. He suggested that sleep helps animals to stay out of the way of predators during the parts of the day when they are most vulnerable. For most animals, this means sleeping during the hours of darkness. It also means sleeping in places where they will be hidden. According to Meddis, sleep may simply ensure that animals stay still when they have nothing better to do with their time (i.e. 'wasting' their time).

Siegel (in Young, 2008) concurs with this view and points out that in fact being awake is riskier than sleeping because an animal is more likely to be injured. Siegel's view, based on what we currently know about sleep patterns, is that the only possible explanation for sleep is that it enables both energy conservation and keeping an individual out of danger: 'in the wild the best strategy for passing on your genes is to be asleep for as long as you can get away with … and that is exactly what you see' (Young, 2008). For example, the little brown bat is awake for just a few hours each day, only when the insects that it eats are awake. This is an adaptive behaviour – the bat is a small mammal with a high metabolic rate and should therefore eat as much of the time as it can and sleep for only a short time. However, the brown bat doesn't need to do this because it can get enough food in a few hours. In fact, being awake at any other time would have no value and therefore the bat can afford to sleep a lot.

▲ Peter Tripp – awake for 201 hours.

EVALUATION OF RESTORATION THEORY

Sleep deprivation

Total sleep deprivation Various **case studies** (see above) suggest that lack of sleep doesn't result in long-term damage. However, closely-monitored participants who have been deprived of sleep for more than 72 hours display short episodes of **microsleep** while they are awake. EEG recordings show that microsleep is the same as sleep (Williams *et al.*, 1959). It could be that apparent 'non-sleepers' are in fact getting the benefits of sleep while appearing to be awake.

Partial sleep deprivation may led to 'rebound'. For example, people awoken during REM sleep show up to 50% increases in REM activity (Empson, 2002). The same has been observed when SWS sleep is prevented (Ferrara *et al.*, 1999). This rebound effect appears to be solely related to REM and SWS which suggests that these are the two kinds of sleep which are vital.

Exercise and the need for sleep

If the restoration theory is correct physical exercise should lead to increased sleep in order to restore proteins and biochemicals. Shapiro *et al.* (1981) found that marathon runners slept for about an hour more than usual on the nights after the race. However, Horne and Minard (1985) found that participants who were given numerous exhausting tasks didn't sleep more than usual. The participants went to sleep faster than usual but not for longer.

Comparative studies

Even though sleep is universal in animals with a **central nervous system**, sleep needs vary considerably. For example, EEG studies of dolphins have found no evidence of REM sleep (Klinowska, 1994); if REM sleep is vital to restoration, then why don't dolphins need it as well?

EVALUATION OF EVOLUTIONARY THEORY

Energy, foraging or predation?

Energy Zepelin and Rechtschaffen (1974) found that smaller animals, with higher metabolic rates, sleep more than larger animals. This supports the view that energy conservation might be the main reason for sleep. However there are many exceptions, for example sloths are very large yet they sleep for 20 hours per day.

Foraging and predation Recent research by Capellini *et al.* (2008) focused on well-controlled studies of animals, whereas previous research had relied on flawed observations. Capalllini *et al.* found a negative relationship between metabolic rate and sleep, which doesn't support the energy conservation hypothesis. They also found that the relationship between predation risk and sleep is a complex one. Animals that sleep in exposed positions sleep less but sleep time was also reduced in species that sleep socially – and they ought to be able to sleep longer because of safety in numbers.

REM and NREM sleep

It may be that only **NREM sleep** evolved for energy conservation because that is the only time that brain energy consumption drops; during REM sleep the brain is still relatively active. This would lead us to expect that the relationship between body size and amount of sleep would only be in terms of NREM sleep and not REM sleep. However, the data from Capellini *et al.* found no correlation between body size and NREM sleep. So, as yet, we don't have a clear answer.

There is a further argument for the REM/NREM distinction. Animals that are more 'primitive', such as most reptiles, only have NREM sleep. REM sleep evolved about 50 million years ago in birds and mammals. It might be that NREM sleep evolved first, for energy conservation, whereas REM sleep may have evolved later to maintain brain activity. This is supported by the greater need for REM sleep in infants whose brains are developing. However, again this hypothesis is not supported by Capellini *et al.*.

Phylogenetic signal

Perhaps the key piece of evidence for the evolutionary approach is the existence of a strong **phylogenetic signal** for sleep among mammals. Research has found that mammalian species that are genetically close have more similar sleep patterns than one would expect by chance (Capellini *et al.*, 2008), which would indicate that sleep patterns have an evolutionary basis.

A combined approach

Neither approach quite fits the facts. Perhaps the resolution lies in a combined approach which recognises that some elements of sleep are for restoration whereas other aspects of sleep behaviour are related to the function of occupying unproductive hours, e.g. conserving energy.

Horne (1988) proposed a theory that combines elements from both restoration and evolutionary theories. He suggested a distinction between **core** and **optional sleep**. Core sleep is equivalent to SWS and is the vital portion of sleep that an organism requires for essential body and brain processes. Optional sleep (REM sleep and some portions of NREM sleep) is dispensable. Horne believes that optional sleep has the function of occupying unproductive hours and, in the case of small mammals, conserving energy.

CAN YOU...? (No. 7.3)

1... For each of the **two** theories presented select about **five** key concepts.

2... Write about 40 words describing each of these key concepts.

3... Identify about **ten** points of evaluation (these can be positive or negative).

4... Elaborate each point (see page 9).

5... Use all of this material to write an answer to the following exam question: *Discuss theories of sleep*. As good practice you could also write separate 'building block' essays for each theory. Each answer should contain about 300 words of description and 500 words of evaluation.

Don't forget that you can use material from other spreads (such as the previous spread on dreaming) – as long as you make it relevant.

Biological rhythms are cyclical changes in the way biological systems behave. The most obvious rhythm is the sleep–wake cycle (a **circadian rhythm**, one that spans one day) – people and many animals go to sleep when it is dark and wake up when it is light. There are other rhythms, such as the seasonal patterns of activity in hibernating animals (an **infradian rhythm**, one that is longer than a day) or the stages of sleep (an **ultradian rhythm**, one that is shorter than a day). What controls these rhythms?

- Internal biological 'clocks', also called **endogenous pacemakers**.

- External cues from the environment, also called **exogenous zeitgebers**. These include sunlight, food, noise or social interaction.

'Endogenous' means 'inside', whereas 'exogenous' means 'outside'.

The word 'zeitgeber' is from the German meaning 'time-giver'.

The ticking of the biological clock

The basis of the circadian rhythm lies in interactions between certain proteins, creating the 'tick' of the biological clock; it is an ingenious negative feedback loop. Darlington *et al.* (1998) first identified such proteins in the fruit fly *drospholia*.

In the morning two proteins, called CLOCK and CYCLE (CLK–CYC) bind together.

- CLK–CYC produces two other proteins, PERIOD and TIME which combine to make PER–TIM.

- PER-TIM has the effect of making CLK–CYC inactive, so as PER-TIM increases CLK–CYC decreases and therefore PER-TIM starts to decrease too (negative feedback).

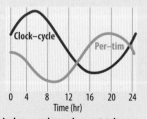

This loop takes about 24 hours and, hey presto, you have the biological clock! The actual proteins vary from animal to animal. In humans the main protein pairs are CLOCK–BMAL1 and PER–CRY.

This protein mechanism is present in the SCN (the *central oscillator*) and is also present in cells throughout the body (*peripheral oscillators*). The presence of peripheral oscillators explains why there are different rhythms for different functions such as hormone secretion, urine production, blood circulation and so on.

ENDOGENOUS PACEMAKERS

The suprachiasmatic nucleus

In mammals, the main endogenous pacemaker is a tiny cluster of nerve cells called the **suprachiasmatic nucleus (SCN)**, which lies in the **hypothalamus**. It is located just above the place where the optic nerves from each eye cross over (called the *optic chiasm* – thus 'supra', which means 'above' – chiasm). The SCN obtains information about light from the eye via the optic nerve. This happens even when our eyes are shut because light penetrates the eyelids. If our endogenous clock is running slow (e.g. the sun rises earlier than it did the day before), morning light automatically shifts the clock ahead, putting the rhythm in tune with the world.

In fact, each SCN is actually a pair of structures, one in each **hemisphere** of the brain, and each of these is divided into a ventral and dorsal SCN. The *ventral* (forward) SCN is relatively quickly reset by external cues whereas the *dorsal* (rear) SCN is much less affected by light and therefore more resistant to being reset (Albus *et al.*, 2005).

The pineal gland and melatonin

The SCN sends signals to the **pineal gland**, directing it to increase production of the **hormone melatonin** at night. Melatonin induces sleep by inhibiting the brain mechanisms that promote wakefulness. In birds and reptiles the pineal gland lies just beneath the bone of the skull and is directly regulated by light; light inhibits the production of melatonin. In fact many lizards have a 'third eye' near the pineal gland which actually protrudes through a small opening in the skull and receives information about light.

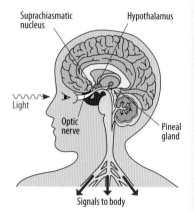

▲ *Diagram of the brain showing the position of the suprachiasmatic nucleus and pineal gland.*

EXOGENOUS ZEITGEBERS

The process of resetting the biological clock with exogenous zeitgebers is known as **entrainment**. The opposite of entrainment is 'free-running' – the biological clock operates in the absence of any exogenous cues.

Light

Light is the dominant zeitgeber in humans. As we have seen, light can reset the body's main pacemaker, the SCN. It also can reset the other **oscillators** located throughout the body because one of the proteins in the biological clock (see left) is CRY (cryptochrome), which is light sensitive. This may explain why Campbell and Murphy (1998) found that shining light on the back of participants' knees shifted their circadian rhythms.

Social cues

Until fairly recently, biologists thought that social cues were the main zeitgebers for human circadian rhythms – we eat meals at socially determined meal times, we go to bed and wake up at times designated as appropriate for our age, and so on. Our daily rhythms appeared to be entrained by social convention, not internal biology. Today we know that light, not social cues, is the dominant zeitgeber. However, it is also now understood that all parts of the body produce their own oscillating rhythms and some of these are not primarily reset by light. For example, the zeitgeber for cells in the liver is likely to be meal times because they are reset by eating (Davidson, 2006).

Temperature

Biological rhythms can also be entrained by temperature. For example, leaves on deciduous trees change colour and drop off because of changes in temperature as well as day length. Temperature is also a factor in the onset of hibernation. In the absence of light, temperature may be the dominant zeitgeber (López-Olmeda *et al.*, 2006).

EVALUATION

Research evidence

The endogenous clock has been demonstrated in many studies. For example, Aschoff and Wever (1976) placed participants in an underground WWII bunker and excluded any environmental or social time cues. They found that most people displayed circadian rhythms of 24–25 hours, though some rhythms were as long as 29 hours. This suggests that the rhythm must be controlled endogenously. However, this research also shows that external cues are important because the clock was not perfectly accurate; it lost a few minutes every day.

The role of the SCN has been demonstrated in non-human animal studies. For example, Morgan (1995) bred 'mutant' hamsters so they had circadian rhythms of 20 instead of 24 hours and then transplanted their SCNs into normal hamsters. The normal hamster then displayed the mutant rhythms. This shows that the SCN controlled the circadian rhythm.

Separate rhythms Under normal conditions the central oscillator (the SCN) coordinates all other body rhythms, but in certain circumstances the body's separate oscillators will desynchronise. For example, a young woman, Kate Aldcroft, spent some time in a cave. After 25 days her temperature rhythm was a 24-hour one, yet her sleep rhythm was on a 30-hour cycle (Folkard, 1996). Such desynchronisation leads to symptoms similar to **jet lag** – which is essentially a state of desynchronised biological rhythms.

The power of artificial lighting

The question is whether even low levels of lighting can act as a zeitgeber or whether bright daylight is needed. In the early studies of biological rhythms (e.g. Aschoff and Wever, above) participants were exposed to artificial lighting, but it was assumed this would not be bright enough to entrain rhythms. On the other hand, Campbell and Murphy (see left) shifted circadian rhythms just by shining a light on the back of someone's knees. Recent research has shown that, in general, artificial lighting does have an effect. For example, Boivin *et al.* (1996) found that circadian rhythms can be entrained by ordinary dim lighting, though bright lighting was more effective.

If dim lighting does reset the biological clock then the fact that we live in an artificially lit world may have some negative consequences. For example, Stevens (2006) suggests that exposure to artificial lighting disrupts circadian rhythms and thus disrupts melatonin production. Decreased melatonin levels are a cause of cancer and therefore the reduced melatonin production linked to artificial lighting might explain why women in industrialised (and well-lit) societies are more likely to develop breast cancer.

When the biological system fails

The down side of a biologically determined system is that, when it fails, it can't be easily 'fixed'. One example of this is when there are mutations in the genes which contribute to the ticking of the biological clock. *Familial advanced sleep-phase syndrome* (FASPS) has been linked to an inherited defect in one of the PER genes (Chicurel, 2001). This syndrome causes sleep onset around 7pm, and spontaneous awakening around 2am in affected family members, who have great difficulty leading a normal life. There are many other sleep phase disorders; in fact some research suggests that brain changes during adolescence lead to a form of **delayed sleep phase disorder**, which would explain why adolescents often have unusual sleep patterns.

The blended system

It sounds as if we are talking about two systems – one that is endogenous and the other that is exogenous but such neat divisions do not exist. Apart from total isolation experiments, the running of the biological clock is a combined endogenous–exogenous exercise. Biological rhythms have evolved for two reasons. First, the metabolic processes in our body need a rhythm so they are coordinated. The endogenous pacemaker acts like a conductor of an orchestra, coordinating the separate physiological processes in our bodies. Second, these rhythms also need to be fine tuned by external cues (exogenous zeitgebers) in order to remain in time with the external world which fluctuates in its rhythms (e.g. day and night, shorter days in winter).

A chipmunk's tale of survival

On this page we have argued that biological rhythms have adaptive value (an evolutionary approach to understanding behaviour). They are adaptive in part because the circadian clock enables tight temporal scheduling of physiological and behavioural programmes (Anton *et al.*, 2005). The other adaptive advantage would be that biological rhythms allow an animal (or plant) to anticipate daily environmental events, such as the patterns of light and dark. Patricia DeCoursey investigated this by functionally removing the SCN in 30 chipmunks (a lesion was made so the SCN was no longer connected). The chipmunks were returned to their natural habitat and observed alongside two other groups of chipmunk – 24 surgical controls and 20 intact controls. After 80 days significantly more of the SCN-lesioned chipmunks had been killed by weasels, presumably because these chipmunks remained awake in their burrows and the weasels could hear the noise and were able to locate the chipmunks (DeCoursey *et al.*, 2000).

Non-human animal research

A lot of data reported in this chapter is derived from research with non-human animals. There are two issues to consider: first, the issue of harm to animals involved in the research (such as the chipmunks above), and second, the issue of generalisability to humans.

In terms of the first issue, if we accept that such research does have important applications to human behaviour then the harm to animals may be considered acceptable as long as the key principles of non-human animal research are adhered to (see page 59).

As regards the second issue, we do know that biological systems differ from one animal to the next (for example reptilian biological rhythms have direct input to the pineal gland). Therefore it cannot be assumed that research findings generalise to human behaviour.

CAN YOU...?   No. **7.4**

1... Identify **six or more** key points related to the role of endogenous and exogenous factors in bodily rhythms.

2... Write about 50–100 words describing each of these points.

3... Identify about **ten** points of evaluation (these can be positive or negative).

4... Elaborate each point (see page 9).

5... Use all of this material to write an answer to the following exam question: *Discuss the role of endogenous pacemakers and exogenous zeitgebers in bodily rhythms.* As good practice you might also write 'building block' answers to the following essays: (a) *Discuss the role of endogenous pacemakers in bodily rhythms.* (b) *Discuss the role of exogenous zeitgebers in bodily rhythms.* Your answer should contain about 300 words of description and 500 words of evaluation.

Don't forget to read the essay-writing guidance on pages 8–9.

A sleep disorder is any condition that involves difficulty experienced when sleeping. Such disorders often result in daytime fatigue causing severe distress and impairment to work, social or personal functioning. Sleep disorders can be classified as:

- Problems with falling asleep or staying asleep despite the opportunity to do so, i.e. **insomnia**.

- Problems staying awake, such as **narcolepsy**, restless leg syndrome, snoring or sleep apnoea.

- Problems adhering to a regular sleep schedule due to, for example, **shift work** or jet travel.

- Sleep disruptive behaviours, called **parasomnias** (behaviours that occur during or around sleep) such as **sleepwalking**, **night terrors** and *bruxism* (teeth grinding).

◄ *The classic image of a sleepwalker is eyes closed, arms outstretched and walking. In fact a sleepwalker's eyes are invariably open and sleepwalking is a term that covers any activity characteristic of the awake state, such as sitting up in bed, getting dressed, looking out of a window and so on – in other words it doesn't just involve walking.*

INSOMNIA

Insomnia is not defined in terms of number of hours of sleep a person has because there are large individual differences in the amount of sleep that is 'normal' for each person. Insomnia may involve problems falling asleep (initial insomnia), remaining asleep (middle insomnia) or waking up too early (terminal insomnia). Insomnia is classified as either transient (short term), intermittent (occasional) or chronic when it is constant and long term (having occurred for one month or more).

Explanations of insomnia

Secondary insomnia is where there is a single, underlying medical, psychiatric or environmental cause. In such cases insomnia is a symptom of the main disorder, i.e. it is secondary. For example, insomnia is a characteristic symptom of illnesses such as **depression** or heart disease. It is also typical of people who do shift work or who have **circadian rhythm** disorders such as **delayed sleep phase disorder**. Insomnia may also be the result of environmental factors, such as too much caffeine (coffee, tea or even chocolate) or alcohol.

Primary insomnia describes cases where insomnia simply occurs on its own, with no known physical cause, for more than one month (**DSM** definition). In such cases insomnia is the person's primary problem. The individual may be feeling stressed or depressed, but such psychological states are not the problem – the insomnia is the problem. It may be that the individual has developed bad sleep habits (e.g. staying up late, sleeping in a room that is too light) and this has created insomnia, but insomnia is the problem. Sometimes insomnia may have had an identifiable cause but this has disappeared, yet the insomnia persists because of an expectation of sleep difficulty (see 'Real-world application' on the facing page).

SLEEPWALKING

Sleepwalking (SW) is a disorder which is most common in childhood, affecting about 20% of children and less than 3% of adults (Hublin *et al.*, 1997). SW occurs only during **NREM/SWS sleep** and is related to night terrors, which are also only found in NREM sleep. A sleepwalker is not conscious and later has no memory for events during SW.

Explanations of sleepwalking

Incomplete arousal EEG recordings made during SW show a mixture of the delta waves which are typical of SWS plus the higher frequency beta waves which are characteristic of the awake state. It looks as if SW occurs when a person in deep sleep is awakened but the arousal of the brain is incomplete. It is likely that this abnormal arousal is **genetic**.

Why is it common in childhood? One possibility is that it happens because children have more SWS than adults. Alternatively, Oliviero (2008) suggests that the **GABA** system that normally inhibits motor activity in SWS is not sufficiently developed in some children, and it also may be underdeveloped in some adults. Insufficient amounts of GABA leave the motor neurons capable of commanding the body to move even during sleep. Oliviero *et al.* (2007) indeed found that adult sleepwalkers had signs of immaturity in the relevant neural circuits when compared with normal controls.

NARCOLEPSY

The two main symptoms of narcolepsy are feeling sleepy all the time and episodes of **cataplexy** (loss of muscular control) during the day. Such episodes seem to be triggered by various forms of emotional arousal such as anger, fear, amusement or stress. Other symptoms include hallucinations and sleep paralysis, both experienced when falling sleep or waking up, and interruption of night-time sleep by frequent waking.

Explanations of narcolepsy

REM Over the past 50 years a variety of explanations have been put forward. In the 1960s the view was that narcolepsy was linked to a malfunction in the system that regulates REM sleep, which explained some of the classic symptoms of the disorder, such as the lack of muscle tone (cataplexy), which typically accompanies REM sleep, and the intrusion of REM-type sleep (hallucinations) into daytime wakefulness.

HLA In the 1980s research appeared to indicate that narcolepsy was linked to a mutation of the **immune system**. Honda *et al.* (1983) found increased frequency of one type of **HLA** (*human leukocyte antigen*) in narcoleptic patients. HLA molecules are found on the surface of white blood cells and coordinate the immune response.

Hypocretin More recently, research has uncovered a link between the **neurotransmitter hypocretin** (also called *orexin*) and narcolepsy. Hypocretins appear to play an important role in maintaining wakefulness. The first evidence came from narcoleptic dogs who had a mutation in a gene on chromosome 12, which disrupted the processing of the hypocretin (Lin *et al.*, 1999).

Real-world application

One of the causes of primary insomnia is a person's belief that they are going to have difficulty sleeping. Such an expectation becomes self-fulfilling because the person is tense when trying to sleep, causing insomnia. One clever way to treat this is a method based on **attribution theory** (which you studied in your AS course). The insomniac has learned to *attribute* their sleep difficulties to 'insomnia', but if they can be convinced that the source of their difficulty lies elsewhere this will end their maladaptive attribution. In one study insomniacs were given a pill and told either that the pill would stimulate them or act as a sedative. Those who expected arousal actually went to sleep faster because they attributed their arousal to the pill and therefore actually relaxed (Storms and Nisbett, 1970).

EVALUATION

Explanations of insomnia

The importance of diagnosis It is important to distinguish between primary and **secondary insomnia** because of the implications for treatment. If insomnia is a symptom of another disorder then it is important to treat the disorder rather than the insomnia. For example, if insomnia is the result of chronic depression it would be unhelpful to treat the insomnia. However, it may not be that simple to work out the cause – does depression cause insomnia or does insomnia cause depression? A study of almost 15,000 Europeans found that insomnia more often *preceded* rather than followed cases of mood disorder (Ohayon and Roth, 2003). This means that, in some cases, it might in fact be helpful to treat insomnia regardless of whether it is a primary or secondary effect.

Risk factors influencing insomnia When discussing risk factors, Spielman and Glovinsky (1991) distinguished between predisposing, precipitating and perpetuating components. Predisposing factors include a genetic vulnerability, for example twin studies indicate that 50% of the variance in the risk for insomnia could be attributed to **genetic** factors (Watson *et al.*, 2006). Research also suggests that physiological factors may predispose a person to develop insomnia. For example, it has been found that insomniacs are more likely to experience *hyperarousal* (high physiological arousal) (e.g. Bonnet and Arand, 1995). Hyperarousal would make it more difficult to get to sleep.

However, predisposing factors alone are unlikely to explain chronic primary insomnia – the **diathesis–stress model** of mental disorders proposes that environmental stressors are needed to precipitate the disorder. In the case of insomnia, stress or environmental change may trigger episodes of insomnia.

Explanations of sleepwalking

The explanation of sleepwalking (SW) can also neatly fit the diathesis–stress model. The diathesis (vulnerability) comes from a genetic predisposition for the disorder. Unlike narcolepsy there is strong evidence that SW has a genetic basis. For example, Broughton (1968) found that the prevalence of SW in first-degree relatives of an affected subject is at least ten times greater than that in the general population. Twin studies have also been used; Lecendreux *et al.* (2003) reported about 50% **concordance** in **MZ twins** compared with 10–15% in **DZ twins**, and also have identified a gene which may be critical in SW as well as night terrors (the DQB1*05 gene).

The stress part of the diathesis–stress model might be represented by environmental factors such as frequent nightly awakenings.

Explanations of narcolepsy

The REM hypothesis was first proposed after Vogel (1960) observed REM sleep at the onset of sleep in a narcoleptic patient rather than later in the cycle, as normal. This explanation was further supported by recordings of **neuron** activity in the **brainstem** of narcoleptic dogs showing that cataplexy is linked to the activation of cells that are only active during REM sleep in normal animals (Siegel *et al.*, 1999). However, the research in general has not been convincing.

The narcolepsy–HLA link continues to be researched; however the specific HLA variant (HLA–DQB1*0602) found most commonly in narcoleptics is not found in all narcoleptics and is also reasonably common in the general population (Mignot *et al.*, 1997). This means HLA cannot be the sole explanation.

Hypocretins are the most promising lead. The findings from narcoleptic dogs have been confirmed in human studies; for example it was found that human narcoleptics had lower levels of hypocretin in their **cerebrospinal fluid** (Nishino *et al.*, 2000). However, low levels of hypocretin are unlikely to be due to inherited factors because human narcolepsy doesn't run in families and it has not been found to be concurrent in twins where one has the disorder (Mignot, 1998). The reduction in hypocretin may be due to brain injury, infection, diet, stress or possibly it is the result of an *autoimmune* attack (where the body's immune system turns on itself rather than fighting external infection). This could explain the HLA link with narcolepsy because of the role of HLA in the immune response (Mignot, 2001).

Teenage insomnia

Rachel is in high school. She feels exhausted all day and goes to bed at 10pm to try to get some much-needed sleep. She reads, she writes, she gets back up. Finally around 1am she goes to sleep. Rachel is a typical example of a teenage insomniac (Kalb, 2008). Her sleep patterns suggest that her insomnia may be due to the shift in circadian rhythms which is typical of the teenage years – delayed sleep phase disorder.

A recent study by Roberts *et al.* (2008) found that teenage insomnia is a major problem, as much a problem in adolescence as either substance abuse or depression, but given less publicity. They analysed data from over 4,000 people aged 11–17 from Houston, Texas and found that 25% of the young people had symptoms of insomnia and 5% reported that their lack of sleep interfered with their ability to function during the day. In a follow-up study of those teenagers with symptoms of insomnia, 41% were found to still have symptoms one year later.

CAN YOU...?   (No. 7.5)

1... **Three** sleep disorders are described on this page. For each of them identify at least **two** possible explanations.

2... Write about 50–100 words describing each of these explanations.

3... Identify about **ten** points of evaluation (these can be positive or negative).

4... Elaborate each point (see page 9).

5... Use all of this material to write an answer to the following exam question: *Critically consider explanations of disorders of sleep.* You could also write separate 'building block' essays for each disorder. Your answer should contain about 300 words of description and 500 words of evaluation.

Don't write an essay without reading the essay-writing notes on pages 8–9.

THEORIES OF HYPNOSIS

STATE EXPLANATIONS

The neodissociationist view
- Hilgard suggests hypnotic experiences result from a *dissociation* caused by the hypnotist separating our cognitive processes so that we are only aware of some aspects of our thinking.
- Real hypnotised subjects can be distinguished from 'fakers' as they respond for longer (Evans and Orne) and have a stronger 'post-hypnotic' response (Orne *et al.*).
- Hilgard demonstrated the 'hidden observer', which allows access to the dissociated level of consciousness, e.g. reports feeling pain when the hypnotised subject says they feel none.
- Hypnotised subjects demonstrate remarkable physical feats, e.g. being 'as stiff as a board' when placed across two chairs.
- Kosslyn *et al.* found that the brain activity in hypnosis was different from normal wakefulness, i.e. a special state.

A neo-state view
- The hypnotist directs the executive control system. Behaviours then seem to just 'happen' rather being deliberate and this alters a subject's sense of self-awareness (Oakley).

EVALUATION

The neodissociationist view
- The difference between 'reals' and 'fakers' may be due to underlying differences (e.g. poorer imagination).
- No more exceptional feats of strength, etc. are possible under hypnosis than without (Druckman and Bjork).
- PET scanning supports dissociation by showing that hypnotic analgesia reduces brain activity relating to the pain but not the sensory information (Rainville *et al.*).
- Brain scanning, e.g. Williams and Gruzelier, found more alpha waves during hypnosis and more theta waves in relaxed state. Egner *et al.* reported consistent differences in anterior cingulated gyrus function.
- Brain differences related to susceptibility, e.g. more asymmetrical brain hemispheres (Naish).
- State theorists argue that some people can dissociate behaviour and awareness more easily.
- If hypnotisability is special then susceptibility should be a stable characteristic but Wickless and Kirsch found it depended on expectation. Students primed using trick lights and colours were more likely to be hypnotisable when tested later.

NON-STATE EXPLANATIONS

Socio-cognitive theory of hypnosis
- Wagstaff suggests compliance and belief are affected in hypnosis.
- A hypnotised person *complies* to suggestions from the hypnotist in the same way that we comply to obedience and conformity. Avoids the embarrassment of not being hypnotised or of appearing disobedient.
- A hypnotised person believes their behaviour is not volitional and this belief leads them to regard the state as 'real', same as, e.g. Valins, who found male participants provided rational explanations for non-volitional behaviour.
- The ESC (Expectation, Strategy, Compliance) process (Wagstaff, 1986) suggests that hypnotic subjects decide what the hypnotist wants then use cognitive strategies to achieve this. If this fails, they comply.

EVALUATION

Socio-cognitive theory of hypnosis
- Spanos *et al.* found highly susceptible subjects appeared more compliant; if expectations were manipulated their responses differed.
- If subjects are merely compliant some might admit to pretending but they don't (Kihlstrom *et al.*).
- Investment in the hypnotic role causes subjects to, e.g. ignore memories they were told to forget (Spanos).
- Hypnosis cannot be mere compliance as highly susceptible subjects are not *generally* compliant; Orne asked participants to return postcards.
- The non-state theory aims to explain whereas the 'state' approach is more descriptive.

FREUD'S PSYCHOANALYTIC THEORY

- Freud proposed that dreams express unconscious thoughts.
- Dreams protect us by allowing repressed primary process thinking (unacceptable id urges) to happen and by fulfilling unconscious wishes.
- Dreams are symbolic. The real meaning (latent content) is changed into a less threatening form (the manifest content) through dreamwork.
- Processes in dreamwork include condensation (complex thoughts are simplified) and symbolism (a symbol replaces an action, person or idea).
- Not all dream content is symbolic: 'sometimes a cigar is just a cigar'.

EVALUATION

- Freud's theory is difficult to falsify as Freud claimed interpretations were correct either if the dreamer accepted them or if they rejected them.
- Nightmares are unlikely to represent wish fulfilments or protect the sleeper although Freud did suggest that some dreams are not wish fulfilments, e.g. ones that are 'sensible warnings'.
- According to Freud, dreams should be bizarre but Snyder found that only 5% of dreams are described as 'exotic' and 70% are 'highly coherent'.

Research evidence
- Solms described brain-damaged patients who had no REM activity but still reported dreams and ones with REM activity who reported no dreams.
- Solms used PET scans to show that the rational part of the brain is inactive (e.g. prefrontal cortex) during REM sleep whereas memory and motivation (e.g. the limbic areas) are active. Fits with Freud's idea of inactive, rational ego and active id (linked to limbic area).
- However, same evidence could contradict Freud's theory as the rational part of the mind is needed for dreamwork (Braun).
- Computer simulations of the brain support condensation because neural networks condense 'memories' when overloaded (Hopfield *et al.*).
- Zhang proposed continual-activation theory – memory processing occurs during sleep involving the unconscious which fits with Freud's theory.

THE ROLE OF ENDOGENOUS AND EXOGENOUS FACTORS IN BODILY RHYTHMS

ENDOGENOUS PACEMAKERS

The suprachiasmatic nucleus
- The main internal biological clock (endogenous pacemaker) in mammals is the suprachiasmatic nucleus (SCN) in the hypothalamus.
- The SCN receives information about light from the eye so the morning light 'sets' the clock to a circadian rhythm.
- There are two SCNs each divided: ventral SCN (quickly reset by external cues) and dorsal SCN (less affected by light so harder to reset).

The pineal gland and melatonin
- SCN directs the pineal gland to secrete melatonin at night, induces sleep. Light inhibits the production of melatonin.
- In birds and reptiles the pineal gland receives direct light through the skull.

The ticking of the biological clock
- Two proteins, CLOCK and CYCLE bind together (CLK–CYC), in the morning producing two other proteins, PERIOD and TIME (PER–TIM). PER–TIM makes CLK–CYC inactive: as PER–TIM increases CLK–CYC decreases so PER–TIM decreases too by negative feedback. The whole loop takes about 24 hours.
- In humans the main protein pairs are CLOCK–BMAL1 and PER–CRY.
- This mechanism is found in the SCN and peripheral oscillators throughout the body (explaining why different functions, e.g. hormone secretion and blood circulation, can have different rhythms).

EXOGENOUS ZEITGEBERS

- Exogenous zeitgebers (external cues), including light, food, noise and social interaction, reset (entrain) the biological clock; in the absence of exogenous cues the biological clock free runs.

Light
- Main zeitgeber for humans, entrains the SCN and peripheral oscillators because they contain a light-sensitive protein CRY (cryptochrome). Campbell and Murphy reset circadian rhythm by shining a light on participants' knees.

Social cues
- Some peripheral oscillators *are* reset by other zeitgebers, e.g. liver cells reset by eating (Davidson).

Temperature
- Temperature is a zeitgeber for hibernation and may be the dominant factor in the absence of light (López-Olmeda *et al.*).

EVALUATION

Research evidence
- Participants without environmental or social time cues typically maintain circadian rhythms of 24 to 25 hours, though sometimes 29 hours (Aschoff and Wever). This shows both endogenous and exogenous control.
- Biological rhythms have evolved because it is beneficial to anticipate changes and respond to them.
- De Coursey *et al.* lesioned SCN in chipmunks who were then more likely to be killed; perhaps they were noisy at night so predators could hear them.
- Morgan bred 'mutant' hamsters and transplanted SCNs into normal hamsters; they too displayed the mutant rhythms.
- After 25 days in a cave, Kate Aldcroft's temperature varied on a 24-hour cycle but she slept on a 30-hour cycle (Folkard), showing that the central and peripheral oscillators can desynchronise. This leads to symptoms like jet lag.

The power of artificial lighting
- Stevens suggests artificial lighting may decrease melatonin production explaining why women in industrialised societies have a higher incidence of breast cancer (cancer linked to low levels).
- Circadian rhythms can be entrained by ordinary lighting even though it is dim, but bright lights are more effective (Boivin *et al.*).

When the biological system fails
- Circadian rhythms are biologically constrained so hard to 'fix'.
- Familial advanced sleep-phase syndrome is linked to an inherited defect in a PER genes (Chicurel) and brain changes during adolescence may lead to delayed sleep phase disorder.

The blended system
- Endogenous and exogenous factors coordinate metabolic processes and tune our behaviour to coincide with rhythmical changes in the external world.

Non-human animal research
- Biological systems differ between species so findings may not generalise.

THEORIES OF SLEEP

DREAMS

HOBSON AND McCARLEY'S ACTIVATION-SYNTHESIS

Activation
- EEGs show the cerebral cortex is active in REM sleep even though there are few external stimuli and we are paralysed (except the eye muscles).
- During REM sleep, the brainstem generates random signals like those from external stimuli.

Synthesis
- The prefrontal cortex combines random signals from brainstem with existing memories, making into a coherent sequence.
- Although the sequence has no inherent meaning, the dream may have meaning because it is contains the dreamer's memories (Hobson).

Revisions
- Hobson (1994) suggested that low levels of noradrenaline and serotonin explain the bizarre nature of dreams and loss of attention.

EVALUATION

Supporting evidence
- PET scanning shows that the brainstem is active in REM sleep (Braun et al.).
- Solms showed that the prefrontal cortex is inactive during dreaming, could explain bizarre nature of dreams – but doesn't explain synthesis.

Challenging evidence
- Activation-synthesis predicts that dreams and REM activity are linked but brain damage can affect the two independently (Solms), people can dream during NREM sleep (Antrobus et al.), and children dream less than adults though they have REM activity (Foulkes).
- Hobson suggests that REM activity may be present during apparently NREM sleep.
- Snyder's evidence suggests that dreams are coherent.
- Zhang's theory also fits with activation-synthesis hypothesis because drop in levels of brain activity trigger the continual-activation mechanism.

RESTORATION THEORY

- SWS for bodily repair and REM sleep is for brain recovery (Oswald).

Slow wave sleep (SWS)
- Growth hormone (GH) is secreted during SWS.
- Amount of GH correlates with amount of SWS (van Cauter and Plat) and if sleep–wake cycle is reversed, GH release swaps to the daytime (Sassin et al.).
- SWS helps defence against disease. A lack of SWS impairs the immune system as it uses proteins (antibodies) to fight viruses and bacteria (Krueger et al.).

REM sleep
- Babies have relatively more REM sleep than adults because their brains are growing quickly.
- Animal species born with immature brains need more REM sleep, e.g. platypus (immature at birth) has about eight hours per day whereas the dolphin (more developed at birth) has almost none (Siegel).
- Siegel and Rogawki suggest REM sleep allows neurons to regenerate neurotransmitters.
- MAOIs increase monoamine levels, less need for REM sleep because neurotransmitter levels already increased.
- REM consolidates procedural memories (motor) whereas SWS consolidates semantic (meaning-related) and episodic memories (events) (Stickgold).

EVALUATION

- Total sleep deprivation may cause problems, e.g. DJ Peter Tripp (hallucinations and paranoia); however this isn't always true, e.g. Randy Gardner and Hai Ngoc.
- Sleep deprivation for more than 72 hours causes microsleep (Williams et al.) so 'non-sleepers' might be benefitting from sleep but appear to be awake.
- Partial sleep deprivation causes a 'rebound', REM (Empson) and SWS (Ferrara et al.).

Exercise and the need for sleep
- Shapiro et al. did find that marathon runners slept for an hour longer than usual following a race. However Horne and Minard found participants given exhausting tasks fell asleep faster but didn't sleep for longer.

Comparative studies
- Some species of dolphin have no REM sleep suggesting REM sleep is not vital to restoration.

EVOLUTIONARY THEORY

Energy conservation
- Warm-blooded animals use energy to maintain a temperature, difficult for small animals because of high metabolic rates.
- The hibernation theory (Webb) suggests that sleep conserves energy because it reduces activity.

Foraging requirements
- Species which eat low energy food like grass (e.g. cows) must spend more time eating so sleep less than ones that eat high energy food like meat (e.g. cats).

Predator avoidance
- A sleeping animal risks being eaten. Predatory species sleep for longer as they are at less risk than prey species.
- For safety's sake prey species shouldn't sleep at all but sleep when least vulnerable.

Waste of time
- Sleep ensures that animals stay still and safe when they have nothing better to do (Meddis).
- Siegel adds that being awake has the risk of being injured, so animals should sleep for as long as possible – and that is the pattern we see, e.g. little brown bats.

EVALUATION

Energy, foraging or predation?
- Smaller species (higher metabolic rates) do sleep more (Zepelin and Rechtschaffen) but there are exceptions.
- Capellini et al. found a negative relationship between metabolic rate and sleep, and species sleeping in risky places sleep less but species sleeping in groups ('safety in numbers') also slept less – but shouldn't if predation view is correct.

REM and NREM sleep
- Brain energy use falls in NREM but not REM sleep suggesting only NREM is used for energy conservation.
- Allison and Cicchetti found that less NREM but not REM sleep in big animals, fitting this prediction, but Capellini et al. found no correlation between body size and NREM sleep.
- NREM sleep evolved first, for energy conservation, and REM sleep later.

Phylogenetic signal
- Genetically similar mammalian species have similar sleep patterns (Capellini et al.).

A combined approach
- Horne: core sleep (SWS) is for restoring body and brain and optional sleep (REM and some NREM) occupies unproductive hours and, for small animals, conserves energy.

EXPLANATIONS FOR DISORDERS OF SLEEP

INSOMNIA

- Secondary insomnia has a medical, psychiatric or environmental cause. It is a symptom of the main problem, e.g. depression, shift work or caffeine.
- Primary insomnia occurs on its own with no known physical cause, though the individual may feel stressed or depressed too. It may arise from bad sleep habits (e.g. sleeping with a light on) or the cause may have gone away but the insomnia persists because sleep problems are anticipated.
- The expectation of insomnia is self-fulfilling because trying to sleep is stressful.
- A treatment based on attribution theory shifts the insomniac's attribution of their problem from 'insomnia' to another cause (Storms and Nisbett).

EVALUATION

- Insomnia more often precedes than follows mood disorder (Ohayon and Roth) so treating as cause or consequence is important.
- Predisposing factors shown in twin studies as 50% of the variance in risk for insomnia appears to be genetic (Watson et al.).
- Predisposition may be linked to physiological factors, as insomniacs more likely to have hyperarousal (Bonnet and Arand), making getting to sleep harder.
- Predisposing factors alone cannot explain chronic primary insomnia. The diathesis–stress model suggests environmental stressors are also needed to precipitate episodes of insomnia.

SLEEPWALKING

- During SW, the EEG shows delta waves (typical of SWS) and beta waves (like being awake).
- SW may happen when someone is woken from deep sleep but arousal of the brain is incomplete. This abnormal arousal is probably genetic.
- Children have more SWS than adults, explaining why SW is more common when young.
- Oliviero suggests that insufficient amounts of GABA (due to underdeveloped system) mean that motor activity is not inhibited during SWS. Adult sleepwalkers do appear to have less mature neural circuits that control motor excitability when awake than controls (Oliviero et al.).

EVALUATION

- Diathesis–stress can explain SW. Genetic predisposition provides the 'diathesis' (vulnerability) as first-degree relatives of sufferers are ten times more likely to SW than the population (Broughton). Also, concordance is 50% in MZs but only 10–15% in DZs, and a gene which is important in SW (DQB1*05) has been found (Lecendreux et al.).
- The 'stress' is represented by environmental factors, such as frequent nightly awakenings.

NARCOLEPSY

- Regulation of REM sleep was an early suggestion. This would explain symptoms such as cataplexy (like paralysis in REM) and hallucinations.
- A mutation of the immune system may be a cause, leading to an increase of human leukocyte antigen (HLA) found in narcoleptic patients (Honda et al.).
- Disrupted processing of the neurotransmitter hypocretin (orexin) may be a cause, which normally helps keep us awake. Narcoleptic dogs with a mutation on chromosome 12 have disrupted hypocretin processing (Lin et al.).

EVALUATION

- The REM hypothesis was suggested because normal sleepers enter stage 1 sleep first whereas narcoleptics fall straight into REM (Vogel).
- Recordings from the brainstems of narcoleptic dogs show that cataplexy is linked to the activation of cells normally only active during REM sleep (Siegel et al.).
- HLA explanation isn't sufficient because not all narcoleptics have HLA variant (HLA-DQB1*0602) and it is fairly common in non-narcoleptics (Mignot et al.).
- Hypocretins have been found to be low in human narcoleptics (Nishino et al.).
- There is no evidence that low hyocretin levels are inherited (Mignot). Low levels may be due to brain injury, infection, diet, stress or an autoimmune attack. An autoimmune attack would also explain the HLA–narcolepsy link as HLA is important in the immune response (Mignot).

Question 7 Describe and evaluate theories of sleep. *[25]*

Student answer

Paragraph 1 We spend over a quarter of our lives asleep so it is important for psychology to have theories about what is going on and why. Most people would think it was for recovery – the restoration theory. This theory proposes that REM enables brain recovery and NREM sleep is important for body processes to recover.

Paragraph 2 REM sleep is the most famous part of sleep because most of our dreaming takes place in it. Since babies require more REM sleep than adults, and animals that are more mature at birth than us have less, the main theory (Seigel, 2003) suggests there is a direct link between neural development and need for REM. Seigel suggests that the main effect is to enable neuro-transmitters to recover. Antidepressant MAOI drugs have the side effect of getting rid of REM sleep. Seigel says this is because monoamine receptors don't need to recover, so REM isn't needed.

Paragraph 3 Slow-wave sleep (SWS) contains a lot of the release of growth hormone, which renews proteins and stimulates growth. If the sleep–wake cycle is reversed then growth hormone cycles reverse too, and also the amount of growth hormone correlates with level of SWS. This is important for the maintenance of the immune system and good health.

Paragraph 4 Support for the restoration theory comes from sleep deprivation studies where interrupted REM sleep increases the amount of REM sleep later (Empson, 2002) and this is also seen in SWS. This is called 'rebound'. However there is some evidence against this. People deprived of sleep don't actually need much extra sleep for recovery, although they could be having periods of microsleep. There is possibly no need for extra sleep when you do extra physical exercise as energy supplies are fed with food not sleep. Horne found that sleep was deeper but not longer when people took lots of exercise. Another finding that questions restoration theory is that mammals like dolphins can recover one hemisphere at a time so there is no need for total unconsciousness. So although restoration is a good theory it doesn't cover all the facts.

Paragraph 5 The theory suggests that avoiding predators is a good explanation for sleep since animals are likely to sleep under cover to avoid predators and be awake when they feed. It also conserves energy. However size of animal does not always relate to sleep needs and Capellini found that there is no relationship between risk from predators and sleep and the energy conservation idea isn't correct either.

Paragraph 6 Alison found that there is a relationship between body size and NREM sleep, but Capallini didn't. REM sleep seems only to exist in birds and mammals so it appears that REM evolved later perhaps for brain needs. This is supported by the fact that babies need more REM sleep.

Paragraph 7 What does this mean? There seems to be a lot of evidence that REM sleep is important for mammals, and the closer mammals are genetically the more similar their sleep patterns. Perhaps REM is linked to having a cerebral cortex sort of brain. Taken altogether, the evolutionary evidence is complicated and difficult to untangle.

Paragraph 8 Horne thinks that the reason is that there are two parts to sleep and these have different jobs. He thinks that there is core sleep (SWS) that is needed for restoration of body processes. He sees REM and some NREM sleep as optional, and it has evolved to occupy down time and conserve energy. This doesn't account for the variations in REM sleep very well though.

Paragraph 9 Sleep is a very complex behaviour and there doesn't yet appear to be agreement about what it actually does. There isn't as much interest as there should be in something we do for a big chunk of our lives.

[622 words]

Improvement?

This essay would be improved by better organisation for the second theory – a lengthy paragraph with a clear description of the theory and then several paragraphs containing positive and negative evaluations. This student doesn't seem to have been prepared to write an essay on the two theories – but should have been prepared since the essay titles are entirely predictable.

Examiner comments

This essay contains accurate information and evaluation but is a bit on the short side, especially in terms of evaluation.

The opening sentence is welcoming but attracts no credit. The rest of paragraph 1 and paragraphs 2 and 3 contain a lot of solid description that is reasonably detailed. However there are missed opportunities for evaluation – for example, look how they could re-write paragraph 2 in order to increase the **AO2** content of the essay:

REM sleep is the most famous part of sleep because most of our dreaming takes place in it. Since babies require more REM sleep than adults, and animals that are more mature at birth than us have less, this suggests there is a direct link between neural development and need for REM. In support of this theory, Seigel (2003) suggests that the main effect is to enable neurotransmitters to recover and support for this comes from the action of antidepressant MAOI drugs which as a side effect get rid of REM sleep. Seigel says this is because monoamine receptors don't need to recover, so REM isn't needed.

The underlined text turns **AO1** into **AO2** because it is now an explicit evaluation, which would give a better **AO2** mark. Read the guidance on essay writing (pages 8–9) which shows you how to use language to maximise your **AO2** mark.

Paragraph 4 contains good evaluation. It is based on research evidence and contains a balanced evaluation.

Paragraph 5 introduces a second theory of sleep, as required in this essay. The description of evolutionary theory is brief and does not display a clear understanding of evolutionary theory. However there are further elements of description in later paragraphs.

Paragraphs 6, 7 and 8 contain a reasonable range of evidence though important details are thin (for example 'Capellini didn't' and 'the evolutionary evidence is complicated and difficult to untangle').

Paragraph 9 is a short summary (rather than a conclusion), which does not attract much credit.

Taken altogether the **AO1** descriptive material for restoration theory fits the criteria for the 8–10 mark band but the material on evolutionary theory is weaker. Therefore **7 out of 10 marks** for **AO1**. The evaluation is not provided in sufficient breadth or depth for the top band but there are elements of both, therefore **9 out of 15 marks** for **AO2**.

16/25 makes this a weak Grade B.

Chapter 8
Health psychology

Chapter contents

164   Introduction to the study of health psychology

166   Theories of addiction

168   Treatment of addiction

170   Management of stress

172   Issues in health promotion

174   Factors affecting health behaviour

Chapter summary

176   End-of-chapter review

178   Exam question with student answer

Specification breakdown	
Theories of addiction, including biological and social/psychological explanations.	Theories of addiction offer explanations about the development of addictions. No one theory can explain all the different kinds of addictions that people develop, so it is valuable to have a range of possible explanations to apply as appropriate.
Treatment of addiction (e.g. biological and social/ psychological treatments).	What can be done to break an addiction? The different kinds of treatment are linked with the various theories, as each theory implies certain types of treatment. Remember, the results of treatment must be judged scientifically and not by media headlines!
Management of stress, including physiologically based and psychologically based techniques.	We know from the AS core study by Rahe, Mahan and Arthur (1970) that stress affects future health. Therefore, we seek ways to reduce the effects of stress through stress management techniques. Physiological and psychological techniques are described and evaluated.
Issues in health promotion (e.g. the health belief model, theory of reasoned action, health education programmes).	How can health be promoted? Can a person's health behaviour be changed? Perhaps the most important question relates to whether health behaviour should be changed. There are various theories or models of how health behaviour can be changed. These are described and evaluated in terms of their worth in explaining and predicting the results of health promotion programmes.
Factors affecting health behaviour (e.g. personality type, age, social class).	You know it's bad for you, so why do you do it? This section looks at some of the factors that determine whether or not people engage in healthy behaviours and evaluates the evidence supporting their importance.

WHY DO PSYCHOLOGISTS STUDY HEALTH?

One of the key aims of psychology is to improve people's quality of life. An obvious way to do this is to help us to behave in healthier ways. At a theoretical level, psychologists can play a role in trying to try to predict what causes us to adopt healthy or unhealthy behaviours and suggest ways to improve our health behaviours. At a practical level, psychological research aims to find out what factors affect our health and the behaviours that contribute to maintaining (or impairing) health. Many psychologists are also engaged in testing whether their predictions and suggestions actually work.

Cycle safety

Teenagers rarely wear helmets when cycling, even though helmets protect against serious injury and death. Why?

Lajunen and Rasanen (2004) looked at possible explanations which relate to ideas you will encounter in this chapter.

Of the teenagers surveyed, 44% said they had a cycle helmet but only 15% said they used it 'always or often', and 42% said they never wore it. Providing teenagers with free helmets to overcome the barrier of cost is unlikely, therefore, to be an effective health strategy. What else could be done?

Beliefs and attitudes, as well as behaviours, need to change. Three possible models were explored by Lanjunen and Rasanen: the health belief model, the theory of planned behaviour and the locus of control model.

Lanjunen and Rasanen found that the theory of planned behaviour and the locus of control model fitted the data well, but the health belief model less so. From these findings they offered ideas for health education strategies. For example, they suggested that the way to change attitudes to cycle helmet wearing should be to target parents and teenagers differently. Parents should be encouraged to promote the benefits (such as emphasising that cycle helmets have the same status as moped helmets). For teenagers, the focus should be on reducing the obstacles to wearing helmets (such as having bikes with a built in lock to hold the cycle helmet so it's always available).

> WWW

Health issues in the UK

Every ten years a general survey is conducted in the UK which samples thousands of UK households asking about many aspects of people's lives. Each year there are also specific health surveys looking at key issues. You can explore the findings of these surveys, based on data from England and Wales, via the following government websites:

www.statistics.gov.uk/ssd/surveys/general_household_survey.asp

www.statistics.gov.uk/default.asp

How do psychologists contribute to the study of health?

You may find it helpful to start this topic by thinking back to some of the material you studied in your AS course that relates to the topic of health. The biological approach is used to understand health behaviour.

The biological approach: how neurons work All our cognition and behaviour is, essentially, the product of neural activity. This is particularly important when considering the action of drugs.

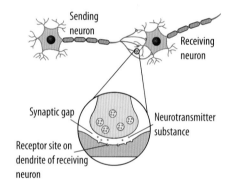

▲ *Neurons communicate by sending chemical signals across the synaptic gap, a space between one neuron and the next.*

At AS you learned about the way that **neurons** convey messages across the **synaptic cleft** using molecules called **neurotransmitters**. These neurotransmitters attach to specific receptors on the next neuron and can stimulate or inhibit its activity. Many drugs work on the body in the same way. They attach to receptor sites on neurons and either affect the neuron by stimulating or inhibiting it, as a neurotransmitter would, or by blocking access to the receptors and prevent neurotransmitter activity. Other drugs work by preventing the 'recycling' of neurotransmitters in the synaptic cleft. This applies to both drugs of abuse and those used therapeutically.

The biological approach: research on stress Selye (1936) discovered that the underlying process of adapting to stressors was a biological one, as you know from your AS studies. Selye studied the **stress** response in animals, but humans share the same neural and **hormonal** processes that determine the stress response. However, if these were the only factors that determined our response to stressors, all people should respond to stress in similar ways. In fact, some of us withstand stress better than others. More recent research into stress has explored some of these factors. One factor which psychologists have found to be important is our **locus of control** (LoC) – the extent to which we feel in control of our lives. The quiz on the facing page will allow you to test your own LoC.

Other approaches The biological approach is not the only useful approach. In the course of this chapter we will also see how the **behaviourist** and **cognitive approaches** are also usefully applied to health issues.

Answer the two questionnaires below, and mark them using the instructions at the bottom of the page. Discuss the results with your class, particularly with reference to the discussion about locus of control at the bottom of the facing page.

TEST YOUR LOCUS OF CONTROL

This test of locus of control was devised by Rotter (1966).
Choose the response to each question which best fits how you feel.

1a	Children get into trouble because their parents punish them too much.
1b	The trouble with most children nowadays is that their parents are too easy with them.
2a	Many of the unhappy things in people's lives are partly due to bad luck.
2b	People's misfortunes result from the mistakes they make.
3a	One of the major reasons why we have wars is because people don't take enough interest in politics.
3b	There will always be wars, no matter how hard people try to prevent them.
4a	In the long run, people get the respect they deserve in this world.
4b	Unfortunately, an individual's worth often passes unrecognised no matter how hard he tries.
5a	The idea that teachers are unfair to students is nonsense.
5b	Most students don't realise the extent to which their grades are influenced by accidental happenings.
6a	Without the right breaks, one cannot be an effective leader.
6b	Capable people who fail to become leaders have not taken advantage of their opportunities.
7a	No matter how hard you try, some people just don't like you.
7b	People who can't get people to like them don't understand how to get along with others.
8a	Heredity plays a major role in determining one's personality.
8b	It is someone's experiences in life that determine what they're like.
9a	I have often found that what is going to happen will happen.
9b	Trusting fate has never turned out as well for me as making a decision to take a definite course of action.
10a	In case of the well-prepared student there is rarely, if ever, such a thing as an unfair test.
10b	Many times, exam questions tend to be so unrelated to coursework that studying is really useless.
11a	Becoming a success is a matter of hard work, luck has little or nothing to do with it.
11b	Getting a good job depends mainly on being in the right place at the right time.
12a	The average citizen can have an influence on government decisions.
12b	This world is run by the few people in power, and there is not much the little guy can do about it.
13a	When I make plans, I am almost certain that I can make them work.
13b	It is not always wise to make plans too far ahead because many things turn out to be a matter of good or bad fortune anyway.
14a	There are certain people who are just no good.
14b	There is some good in everybody.
15a	In my case, getting what I want has little or nothing to do with luck.
15b	Many times we might just as well decide what to do by flipping a coin.
16a	Who gets to be the boss often depends on who was lucky enough to be in the right place first.
16b	Getting people to do the right thing depends on ability – luck has little or nothing to do with it.
17a	As far as world affairs are concerned, most of us are victims of forces we can neither understand, nor control.
17b	By taking an active part in political and social affairs, people can control world events.
18a	Most people don't realise the extent to which their lives are controlled by accidental happenings.
18b	There really is no such thing as 'luck'.
19a	One should always be willing to admit mistakes.
19b	It is usually best to cover up one's mistakes.
20a	It is hard to know whether or not a person really likes you.
20b	How many friends you have depends upon how nice a person you are.
21a	In the long run, the bad things that happen to us are balanced by the good ones.
21b	Most misfortunes are the result of lack of ability, ignorance, laziness or all three.
22a	With enough effort we can wipe out political corruption.
22b	It is difficult for people to have much control over the things politicians do in office.
23a	Sometimes I can't understand how teachers arrive at the grades they give.
23b	There is a direct connection between how hard I study and the grades I get.
24a	A good leader expects people to decide for themselves what they should do.
24b	A good leader makes it clear to everybody what their plans are.
25a	Many times I feel that I have little influence over the things that happen to me.
25b	It is impossible for me to believe that chance or luck plays an important role in my life.
26a	People are lonely because they don't try to be friendly.
26b	There's not much use in trying too hard to please people; if they like you, they like you.
27a	There's too much emphasis on athletics in school.
27b	Team sports are an excellent way to build character.
28a	What happens to me is my own doing.
28b	Sometimes I feel I don't have enough control over the direction my life is taking.
29a	Most of the time I can't understand why politicians behave the way they do.
29b	In the long run, people are responsible for bad government on a national as well as a local level.

A high score = External locus of control   A low score = Internal locus of control

Scoring the locus of control test

Score one point for each of the following:

2a, 3b, 4b, 5b, 6a, 7a, 9a, 10b, 11b, 12b, 13b, 15b, 16a, 17a, 18a, 20a, 21a, 22b, 23a, 25a, 26b, 28b, 29a.

HEALTH QUESTIONS

1. Do you think smoking is a risky behaviour?

2. Why don't teenagers use condoms? Is it because they don't know that unprotected sex is dangerous or because they don't like to ask their partner?

3. Which is more likely to trigger a visit to the doctor: a persistent mild chest pain or a neighbour dying of a heart attack?

4. Late adolescents who are still part of the 'student' group are less likely to smoke but more likely to drink than those who have left education. True or false?

5. Only younger people benefit from exercise, it is too dangerous and difficult for elderly people. True or false?

6. One way to treat addiction is to give users addictive drugs. Yes or no?

7. If someone believes their destiny is out of their hands, would they wear a cycle helmet if they didn't want to? Yes or no?

What are the questions above about?

Question 1: Perceived vulnerability – we will only act healthily if we believe there is a genuine risk. *Question 2: Perceived barriers* – we may be prevented from behaving healthily by some physical or psychological sticking point. *Question 3: Cue to action* – we often know we should take protective action for our health but it takes a 'jolt' to get us to do it. *Question 4: True. Question 5: False. Question 6: Yes* – heroin addiction is treated with methadone, which is also addictive. *Question 7: No* – because they have an external LoC.

THEORIES OF ADDICTION

NATURE VERSUS NUTURE

DETERMINISM

People can become addicted to many things, such as food, sex or gambling. Most **addiction** research focuses on drugs and this has led to an understanding of some general factors that underlie addictions of many kinds. The term 'addiction' itself can mean several things, including **physiological dependence** – when the individual suffers unpleasant physical withdrawal symptoms in the absence of the drug – and **psychological dependence** – when the individual has a compelling belief that they need the drug in order to function normally.

▶ *Twin addicts – genetics or environment?*

BIOLOGICAL EXPLANATIONS

It seems likely that there is some **genetic** component to addiction in humans as animal studies show that there are genetic differences in both the acquisition of drug-related behaviours (e.g. Cunningham *et al.*, 1999) and in the experience of withdrawal (e.g. Klein *et al.*, 2008).

Genetic patterns in addiction

If genes play a part in the development of addictions, then closely related people should be similar in this respect. Studies typically show that such patterns exist, for example McGue (1999) estimated the **heritability** of alcohol dependence at 50–60% for both men and women. In a review of studies on illicit drug abuse and dependence, Agrawal *et al.* (2004) found heritability estimates at 45–79%.

Gene action and addiction

The DRD₂ gene Research has linked the D_2 **dopamine** receptor gene (DRD_2) to severe alcoholism. Noble *et al.* (1991) found the A1 variant of this gene in more than two-thirds of deceased alcoholics, but only one-fifth of deceased non-alcoholics. Blum *et al.* (1991) found that the A1 variant was also more common among the children of alcoholics.

Dopamine and the A1 variant Individuals with the A1 variant have fewer dopamine receptors in an area of the brain described as the '**pleasure centre**', a region that provides us with positive sensations in response to normally **adaptive** behaviours, such as eating and sex. This led Noble *et al.* to refer to DRD_2 as the 'reward gene'. People who inherit the A1 variant are more likely to become addicted to drugs that increase dopamine levels as this compensates for the deficiency by stimulating what few dopamine receptors they do possess. Their addiction is then maintained because it is only with the drug that they feel okay. The A1 variant of the DRD_2 gene is implicated in many addictions including cocaine, heroin and nicotine.

Drug use: an element of choice?

Julien (1998) suggests that people specifically select drugs to help treat differing forms of psychological distress. This means that addicts are not using drugs randomly or simply taking those they happen upon, but are making a choice based on the ability of the drug to counter their symptoms.

● *Nicotine* acts as an antidepressant.

● *Alcohol* reduces anxiety, sensitivity and inhibitions so increases socialisation, helping the individual to cope.

● *Cocaine* and *amphetamine* elevate mood and temporarily avert feelings of worthlessness.

● *Heroin* reduces physical and psychological pain, enabling the individual to deal with otherwise intolerable situations.

● *Cannabis* has a calming effect and produces a feeling of well-being, so could relieve anxiety, depression or the effects of social isolation.

SOCIAL/PSYCHOLOGICAL EXPLANATIONS

The self-medication model

Non-random drugs Gelkopf *et al.* (2002) proposed that individuals *intentionally* use drugs to treat psychological symptoms from which they suffer. This seems plausible as, according to Horner and Scheibe (1997), most individuals with substance abuse problems have psychiatric disorders in addition to their drug dependence. The drug that an addict uses is not selected at random, but is one that is perceived as helping with their particular problem (see examples in the box below left). The drug may not actually make things better, it is simply *thought* to do so by the individual.

Smoking and drinking Many smokers cite 'stress relief' as a reason why they persist with their habit. However, smokers actually report *higher* levels of stress than non-smokers, and their levels of stress *decrease* when they stop smoking. When they relapse and continue to smoke, their stress levels rise again (Cohen and Lichtenstein, 1990). Parrott (1998) suggests this apparent paradox exists because each cigarette has an immediate effect on stress by relieving the withdrawal symptoms that arise when a smoker can't smoke. However, the long-term effect of smoking is increased stress. Similarly with alcohol, the 'rush' of intoxication may help people forget their fears, but alcohol addiction ultimately creates even more problems.

Rational choice theory

Rational choice theory suggests that people decide to engage in an activity as a result of weighing up the costs and benefits. They only feel that the activity is out of control, i.e. has become an addiction, when it is unusually frequent or the costs are very high (West, 2006).

Economic model Becker and Murphy (1988) proposed an economic model which identifies a person as potentially addicted to a drug or activity if an increase in their current behaviour (e.g. drug use) increases their future 'consumption'. According to this model, users balance satisfaction (e.g. a child having a cigarette and feeling 'cool') against costs (e.g. the risk of getting caught) as if addictive behaviours were goods or services. Thus, the 'utility' of the activity is calculated by considering the negatives (such as 'budget restraints') against the potential positives. These can include considerations for the present and the future. From this perspective, addiction is experienced as a consumption of 'goods' (e.g. drugs or alcohol) and the addict is seen as a rational consumer who is maximising some benefit (e.g. euphoria or reduction of anxiety) which they value more highly than the costs they recognise (such as damage to health or a criminal conviction). As some of these consequences have more certain outcomes (I will get high, I might get caught) they differ in their relative importance to the addict.

EVALUATION OF BIOLOGICAL EXPLANATIONS

Genetic patterns in addiction

Individual differences Having a genetic predisposition which makes an individual more vulnerable to developing an addiction can explain why some people become addicted when others with the same experiences do not. This is the basis of the **diathesis–stress model**. Genetic vulnerability may also explain why some people with addictions are more resistant to treatment or more likely to relapse.

Supporting research evidence Twin studies have shown that addictive behaviours tend to co-occur, suggesting that addictiveness in general (rather than simply specific addictions) is influenced by genetic factors. For example, Button *et al.* (2007) found a **correlation** between dependence on alcohol and illicit drugs. A link has also been demonstrated between addictions to drugs and to gambling (Kessler *et al.*, 2008).

Gene action and addiction

Supporting research evidence Comings *et al.* (1996) found that significantly more smokers and ex-smokers had the DRD_2 A1 variant (48.7%) than the general population (25.9%) and that men with this variant also started smoking earlier and were abstinent for less time. The gene may also play a role in addictive behaviours other than drug taking. For example, Noble (2000) found a link between DRD_2 and obesity.

Are dopamine sensitivity and addiction inevitably linked? Grant *et al.* (1998) showed that, at least in monkeys, the dopamine system is influenced by social interactions. Animals that lost social status also lost D_2 receptors. This has implications for humans too, especially those experiencing poverty and stress. Volkow *et al.* (2001) claims that growing up in stimulating, engaging surroundings protects against addiction. She argues that, even for people with an unresponsive dopamine system, opportunities to get excited about natural stimuli reduce the need for an artificial dopamine boost from drugs.

Inconsistent research findings Although some research demonstrates a link between the DRD_2 A1 variant and alcoholism, other studies have failed to find any relationship or have found only a very weak one. Fowler *et al.* (2007) found that, while genes were one causal factor for problem drinking in adolescent twins, environmental factors (e.g. best friends' alcohol use) mattered too.

Limitations of neurochemical explanations A problem for neurochemical explanations of addiction is that they neglect other factors, such as social ones, which affect behaviours. However, regarding drug addiction as a disease creates the possibility of pharmacological treatment. This is a more progressive approach than treating drug addicts as delinquents who must be punished.

EVALUATION OF SOCIAL/ PSYCHOLOGICAL EXPLANATIONS

The self-medication model

Research support Using a **meta-analysis**, Gottdiener *et al.* (2008) tested a key feature of the self-medication model, that substance abuse disorders are linked to failures of **ego control** – the ability to resist impulses to self-medicate through drugs and alcohol. Gottdiener *et al.* found that participants with substance abuse disorders had weaker ego control than a non-alcoholic **control group**.

Problems of cause and effect The self-medication model argues that some form of psychological distress must precede drug use. There is some evidence to support this, for example, Sanjuan *et al.* (2009) found that sexually abused women are more likely to turn to alcohol and other drugs to remove sexual inhibitions than non-abused women. However, the self-medication model cannot explain the many cases of addiction where there are no psychological problems to be overcome.

Rational choice theory

Explaining restraint This theory can explain why, contrary to the 'out of control' view of addiction, some addicts can simply stop. The utility for the individual must reach a point where things are so unpleasant that the prospect of life without the addictive behaviour is better and the rational decision is to stop – so they do. For example, an addicted smoker may decide the harmful effects or increased price of cigarettes outweigh the pleasure gained from smoking, so they quit. Smokers who continue are also being rational as they perceive the costs of stopping as greater than the benefits (West, 2006).

Research support Sloan and Wang (2008) reviewed studies of smoking and found that anticipated future cigarette prices influence current smoking habits, supporting an 'economic' view. They also found that smokers see the costs of quitting as high, are tolerant of financial risk and value good health *less* than non-smokers, all of which contribute to the rational decision to continue.

Implications for treatment West (2006) suggests that the economic view of addiction has implications for intervention. Drugs can be treated in much the same way as any other consumer product, i.e. by changing their utility for the individual (e.g. making them more expensive, harder to get or illegal). In this way, the costs of continuation become higher than the benefits. However, many drugs already carry high price tags and risk of imprisonment but are still frequently abused, so this argument could be flawed.

CAN YOU...? No. **8.1**

1... Select *at least* **one** biological and **one** social/ psychological explanation.

2... For each explanation, select **two or more** key concepts and explain these concepts.

3... Identify about **ten** points of evaluation (these can be positive or negative).

4... Elaborate each point (see page 9).

5... Use all of this material to write an answer to the following exam question: *Discuss theories of addiction, including biological and social/psychological explanations.* As good practice you might also write 'building block' essays about just biological explanations and just social/psychological explanations. Each answer should contain about 300 words of description and 500 words of evaluation.

Don't forget to read the essay-writing guidance on pages 8–9.

TREATMENT OF ADDICTION

Addiction causes much personal distress and can create social problems such as crime and poverty; so psychologists have tried to find effective ways to intervene in the cycle of addictive behaviour. Some of these interventions are biological, e.g. drug treatments, and others involve psychological techniques. Drug treatments can provide the drug of addiction under controlled settings, to help the user to reduce their intake or at least regain some control and use the drug more safely. Alternatively, other, less harmful, drugs can be given to enable the individual to break their addiction. Psychological interventions work in a range of ways. Some, such as those based on **reinforcement**, aim to change the pattern of the addictive behaviour itself while others, such as **cognitive–behavioural therapy**, aim to resolve the faulty thinking associated with the addictive behaviour.

▲ *Cognitive therapy attempts to correct errors in thinking, thus reducing addictive behaviour.*

Approaches to treatment

Three different approaches are considered on this spread: biological, **cognitive** and **behaviourist**. Their very different perspectives on the treatment of addiction illustrate some of the key aspects of each approach. The biological approach takes the view that addiction has underlying *physiological* causes (e.g. **tolerance** to a drug) so drug treatment is an appropriate solution as it will rectify the problem, allowing the user to abstain. The cognitive approach also takes the view that that the underlying cause must be tackled. In this case the problem is seen as relating to the individual's faulty thinking, so therapy aims to correct this to allow the individual to cope without their addictive behaviour. In contrast to the other two perspectives, the behaviourist approach focuses on the individual's overt responses so aims to reduce the addictive behaviours by altering their *consequences*, e.g. by providing alternative reinforcers.

BIOLOGICAL TREATMENTS

Heroin addiction and methadone

Methadone is a synthetic drug, widely used for the treatment of heroin addiction. By mimicking some of the effects of heroin, it produces a lifting of mood and, importantly, reduces withdrawal symptoms and cravings. Methadone can be taken orally, so reduces the dangers associated with injecting and, as it is prescribed and (at least at first) administered at a clinic, the user can be monitored regularly. For *maintenance treatment*, the user simply uses methadone to prevent relapse. During *detoxification*, the dose of methadone is slowly decreased until the addict needs neither methadone or heroin.

Nicotine addiction

As many of the health problems linked to smoking are caused by components in cigarettes other than the nicotine to which smokers are addicted, one solution is to provide an alternative, safer, source of nicotine. This is the idea behind *nicotine replacement therapy*, which supplies nicotine from patches or gum. Once nicotine levels can be maintained, the habit of cigarette smoking can be broken. Thereafter it is easier to reduce the amount of nicotine and break that addiction. Sources of nicotine, such as patches, provide nicotine at a constant rate, avoiding the dips in nicotine level that arise during short periods of abstinence and which make the addictive behaviour of smoking so rewarding because they relieve withdrawal symptoms.

Gambling addiction

Another serious addiction that causes personal and social problems is problem gambling. No drug has yet been approved for use in the UK to treat pathological gambling, but research suggests that drug treatments can have beneficial effects. There is, for example, evidence to support **serotonin** dysfunction in pathological gambling (George and Murali, 2005), and in a study by Hollander *et al.* (2000), gamblers treated with **SSRIs** to increase serotonin levels showed significant improvements compared with a **control group**. Alternatively, administration of *naltrexone* (a **dopamine antagonist**) works by blocking the reinforcing properties of gambling behaviour so reducing the urge to gamble.

SOCIAL/PSYCHOLOGICAL TREATMENTS

Reinforcement

One way to reduce addictive behaviour is to give people rewards for not engaging in the activity in question. This is the basis of a **token economy** (see pages 206–207). Sindelar *et al.* (2007) investigated whether monetary rewards would improve patient outcomes for people on methadone treatment programmes. Participants were **randomly allocated** to either a reward or no reward condition, in addition to both groups receiving their usual care (i.e. a methadone dose daily and individual and group counselling). Participants in the rewards condition drew for prizes of various monetary value each time they tested negative for drugs. Drug use dropped significantly for participants in the rewards condition, with the number of negative urine samples being 60% higher than in the **control condition**.

Cognitive–behavioural therapy (CBT)

Cognitive–behavioural therapy is based on the idea that addictive behaviours are maintained by the person's thoughts about these behaviours (CBT was introduced in your AS studies and is discussed on the next spread and also in Chapter 12). The main goal of CBT is to help people change the way they think about their addiction, and to learn new ways of coping more effectively with the circumstances that led to these behaviours in the past (e.g. dealing with difficult situations or when exposed to peer pressure). In practice this means identifying triggers that cause craving (e.g. passing an off-licence or betting shop), rehearsing ways to control the cravings (e.g. by imagining walking past the shop door) and confronting and changing false beliefs. For example, with a gambling addiction the individual makes cognitive errors, such as the belief that they can predict and control outcomes (e.g. of card games). CBT attempts to correct these errors in thinking, thus reducing the urge to gamble.

EVALUATION OF BIOLOGICAL TREATMENTS

Heroin addiction and methadone

Multiple action Not only does methadone reduce cravings and withdrawal but also partially blocks the euphoria caused by heroin itself – so if users do relapse, they find the experience less rewarding. The risk of overdose on methadone is lower as it is of known strength and its effects last longer than those of heroin, up to 24 hours, which helps to maintain abstinence. As users attend a clinic to receive their daily dose, psychological support can be readily provided. This improves the chance of rehabilitation and breaks the user's links with the drug culture, so the risk of relapse is reduced further.

Maintenance minefield Relapse to heroin use can arise as there may still be some withdrawal symptoms (although these can be treated with other drugs such as *clonidine*) and the user may still crave the euphoria that heroin provides. Users often become as reliant on methadone as they were on heroin, thereby substituting one addiction for another rather than detoxifying. The use of methadone remains controversial, with *UK Statistics Authority* figures showing that methadone was responsible for the deaths of over 300 people in the UK in 2007. For the majority of users, methadone consumption is in fact unsupervised (because they earn the right to take doses home), which has created a black market for methadone.

Research evidence In a **meta-analysis**, Brink and Haasen (2006) found that methadone treatment reduced illicit heroin use, but some evidence (such as Michels *et al.*, 2007) casts doubt on long-term success as they report that, in Germany, 50% of patients are still on maintenance programmes after seven years. This is perhaps because a lack of supportive friends hinders the move from maintenance to detoxification (Gyarmathy and Latkin, 2008). However, methadone treatment does have the added benefit of reducing the risk of contracting HIV (Hartel and Schoenbaum, 1998).

Drug treatments for gambling addiction

In the Hollander study described on the facing page, the sample size was very small ($N = 10$), and was of relatively short duration (16 weeks). A larger and longer study (Blanco *et al.*, 2002), involving 32 gamblers over six months, failed to demonstrate any superiority for the drug treatment over a **placebo**. However, there is some support for the effectiveness of naltrexone, for example a study that found significant decreases in gambling thoughts and behaviours after six weeks of treatment (Kim and Grant, 2001).

Social desirability bias

One problem with studying the effectiveness of drug interventions is the unreliability of users' self-reports of their addictive behaviour – they tend to fail to report relapses. This has the effect of inflating the apparent success rate of the treatment. To overcome this, researchers typically conduct urine tests to check for the presence of drugs. On some treatment programmes it is a requirement to remain drug free, so this testing does not have any additional ethical implications regarding invasion of privacy by the psychologists.

EVALUATION OF SOCIAL/ PSYCHOLOGICAL TREATMENTS

Reinforcement

Research support *Contingency management* is an example of a reinforcement-based treatment that is effective with users of a range of drugs such as amphetamine, methamphetamine and cocaine (Olmstead *et al.*, 2007) and heroin and cocaine and alcohol (Olmstead and Petry, 2009). This supports reinforcement as a method of treatment.

Ignoring the problem? Although research, such as the Sindelar *et al.*, study has shown the effectiveness of reinforcement therapies for reducing addictive behaviour, such interventions do nothing to address the problem that led to the addiction in the first place. This means that although a specific addictive behaviour might have been reduced, there is the possibility that the person may simply engage in a different addictive behaviour instead. A drug addict might, for example, turn to alcohol, but in most cases new addictions tend to be subtle and therefore unrecognised, including compulsive spending or even developing dependent relationships.

Cognitive–behavioural therapy (CBT)

Research support Ladouceur *et al.* (2001) randomly allocated 66 pathological gamblers either to a cognitive therapy group or to a waiting list **control group**. Of those who completed treatment, 86% no longer fulfilled the **DSM** (Diagnostic and Statistical Manual) criteria for pathological gambling. They also found that after treatment, gamblers had a better perception of control over their gambling problem and increased **self-efficacy**, improvements that were maintained at a one-year follow-up.

A mixed approach Some interventions have combined cognitive *and* behavioural aspects of gambling, attempting to alter gamblers' cognitions and behaviours. Sylvain *et al.* (1997) evaluated the effectiveness of cognitive–behavioural treatments in a sample of male pathological gamblers. They found significant improvements after treatment, with these gains maintained at a one-year follow-up.

Crits-Christoph *et al.* (2003) looked at the effectiveness of *group drug counselling* (GDC) alone and when it was combined with either individual drug counselling or CBT. After six months, those receiving GDC+CBT relapsed the most (57%), compared with 52% relapse in those receiving GDC alone, or 37% in those receiving GDC++individual drug counselling. This suggests that CBT may not be the most useful treatment.

Rawson *et al.* (2002) compared participants on methadone maintenance alone (MM) or in combination with either a *reinforcement procedure* (MM+R) or CBT (MM+CBT). During the 16 weeks of the programme the MM+R participants showed the greatest improvement, although at the end of one year's follow-up, the MM+CBT group had made equally good progress (as indicated by self-report and urine analysis). This provides some positive support for CBT.

CAN YOU...? (No. **8.2**)

1... Select *at least* **four** treatments for addiction.

2... For each treatment, select **two or more** key concepts and explain these concepts.

3... Identify about **ten** points of evaluation (these can be positive or negative).

4... Elaborate each point (see page 9).

5... Use all of this material to write an answer to the following exam question: *Outline and evaluate treatments of addiction (e.g. biological and social/psychological treatments).* As good practice you might also write 'building block' essays about each treatment. Your answers should contain about 300 words of description and 500 words of evaluation.

Don't forget that you can use material from other spreads (such as material elsewhere in this book or from your AS studies on cognitive–behavioural therapy) – as long as you make it relevant.

MANAGEMENT OF STRESS

You learned about **stress** at AS, including the biological mechanisms underlying the response (Selye) and the effect of life events (Rahe, Mahan and Arthur, 1970). One practical application of research in psychology is to help people to manage the effects of stress. On this spread we will consider two types of stress management technique. The first is a physiologically based technique: the use of drugs to reduce symptoms, and the second is a psychologically based technique: stress inoculation training, which is an example of **cognitive–behavioural therapy** (CBT).

PHYSIOLOGICAL TECHNIQUE: DRUGS

The group of drugs most commonly used to treat anxiety and stress are **benzodiazepines** (BZs), which are sold under trade names such as *Librium* and *Valium*.

GABA BZs slow down the activity of the **central nervous system** in general. They do this by enhancing the activity of **GABA** (*gamma-amino-butyric acid*), a **neurotransmitter** that is the body's natural form of anxiety relief. About 40% of the **neurons** in the brain respond to GABA which, when released, quietens the activity of these neurons. It does this by attaching to the GABA receptors on the outside of the receiving neurons. This opens channels that increase the flow of *chloride ions* into the neuron. Chloride ions make it harder for the neuron to be stimulated by other neurotransmitters, and, in this way, GABA slows down activity in the central nervous system.

The action of BZs enhance the action of GABA by binding to special sites on the GABA receptor. This boosts the actions of GABA, allowing *more* chloride ions to enter the neuron, making it even *more* resistant to excitation. As a result, the brain's output of excitatory neurotransmitters is reduced and the person feels calmer.

BZs and serotonin BZs also reduce serotonin activity. Serotonin is a neurotransmitter that has an arousing effect, i.e. it stimulates some neurons, including those involved in the brain's 'punishment system'. When these neurons are stimulated, the individual may become more fearful of punishment. Anxiety in chronic stress conditions is a consequence of increased serotonin activity within this punishment system. BZs reduce this increased serotonin activity, which then reduces anxiety.

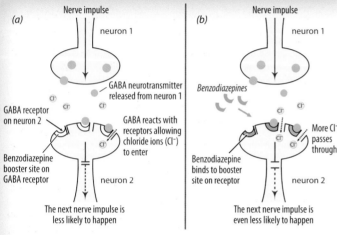

(a) Nerve impulse — neuron 1 — GABA neurotransmitter released from neuron 1 — GABA receptor on neuron 2 — GABA reacts with receptors allowing chloride ions (Cl⁻) to enter — Benzodiazepine booster site on GABA receptor — neuron 2 — The next nerve impulse is less likely to happen

(b) Nerve impulse — neuron 1 — Benzodiazepines — More Cl⁻ passes through — Benzodiazepine binds to booster site on receptor — neuron 2 — The next nerve impulse is even less likely to happen

▲ *(a) Normally, GABA is released and reduces the likelihood of subsequent nerve impulses in the next neuron.*
(b) Benzodiazepines attach to special sites on the GABA receptor neuron and enhance the effect of GABA so nerve impulses are even less likely.

PSYCHOLOGICAL TECHNIQUE: STRESS INOCULATION TRAINING (SIT)

Meichenbaum (1985) believed that although we cannot (usually) change the causes of stress in our life (e.g. a stressful job is still a stressful job), we can change the way that we *think* about the stressors. As negative thinking (e.g. 'I failed to hit the deadline, people must think I'm hopeless') may lead to negative outcomes such as anxiety and **depression**, positive thinking (e.g. 'Okay, so I missed the deadline, but my boss will still be impressed with what I've achieved') should lead to more positive attitudes and feelings. These reduce the stress response and enable us to cope better in the future.

Meichenbaum's therapy, called **stress inoculation training** (SIT), is a form of CBT developed specifically to deal with stress by enabling the individual to develop a form of coping before the problem arises. The person *inoculates* themselves against the 'disease' of stress in the same way that they would receive an inoculation against an infectious disease such as measles. Meichenbaum proposed three main phases to the process.

1. Conceptualisation The therapist (trainer) and client establish a relationship and the client is educated about the nature and impact of stress. For example, they are being taught to view threats as problems to be solved, breaking them down into components that can be coped with. This enables the client to think differently (i.e. reconceptualise) about their problem.

2. Skills acquisition (and rehearsal) Coping skills are taught and practised, first in the clinic and later in real life. The skills are both **cognitive** and **behavioural**: cognitive because they encourage the client to think differently, and behavioural because they involve learning new, more adaptive behaviours.

The skills are tailored to the individual's specific problems and can include positive thinking, relaxation, social skills, methods of attention diversion, using social support systems and time management. Clients might be taught to use coping self-statements, such as those on the right.

3. Application (and follow-through) Clients apply the newly learned coping skills in increasingly stressful situations, during which time other coping techniques might be used. These can include *imagery* (imagining how to deal with the event), **modelling** (watching someone else cope then imitating their behaviour), and role playing (acting out scenes involving stressors). Booster sessions are offered later on and clients could even be asked to help train others.

Examples of coping self-statements

Preparing for a stressful situation 'You can develop a plan and deal with it.'

Confronting a stressful situation 'Relax, you're in control. Take a deep breath.'

Reinforcing self-statements 'It wasn't as bad as you expected.'

Cognitive–behavioural therapy (CBT)

CBT is a combination of two approaches. The **cognitive** approach is based on the idea that the key influence on behaviour is how an individual thinks about a situation. Therefore, cognitive therapy aims to change maladaptive thoughts and beliefs. The **behavioural** approach is based on the idea that undesirable behaviours have been learned, so behavioural therapy aims to reverse this learning and to produce more adaptive responses.

EVALUATION OF DRUG THERAPY FOR STRESS

Effectiveness When used to combat the effects of stress, drugs can be very effective. This can be assessed by comparing outcomes – one group of stressed patients is given a drug and another group is given a **placebo** – a substance that has no *pharmacological* effects (i.e. it has no effect on the body). Patients are given medication but do not know whether it is the real thing or the placebo. This enables us to determine whether the effectiveness of the drug is due its pharmacological properties or something psychological (e.g. simply believing that taking the drug will make you better).

Kahn *et al.* (1986) followed nearly 250 patients over eight weeks and found that BZs were significantly superior to a placebo. A **meta-analysis** of studies focusing on the treatment of social anxiety (Hildalgo *et al.*, 2001) found that BZs were more effective at reducing this anxiety than other drugs, e.g. **antidepressants**.

However, BZs are not effective in treating all types of stress. Gelpin *et al.* (1996) compared **post-traumatic stress disorder** (PTSD) sufferers treated with BZs and a control group matched for gender and symptom severity. After six months, symptoms experienced by the patients in the BZ group were not significantly reduced compared with the control group.

Ease of use One of the appeals of using drugs for stress (or any other problem) is that the therapy requires little effort from the user. You just have to remember to take the pills. This is much easier than psychological methods. For example, stress inoculation therapy requires a lot of time, effort and motivation from the client if it is to be effective.

Addiction BZs were first introduced over 40 years ago and replaced *barbiturates*, which tended to be addictive, i.e. patients exhibited withdrawal symptoms when they stopped taking the drug, indicating a physiological dependence. Recently, however, problems with **addiction** to BZs have been recognised. Even patients taking low doses of BZs have shown marked withdrawal symptoms. As a consequence, it is recommended that BZs use is limited to a maximum of four weeks (Ashton, 1997).

Side effects BZ use produces 'paradoxical' symptoms (so-called because they are the opposite of what might be expected), such as increased aggressiveness and cognitive side effects. These cognitive side effects include impairment of memory, especially the ability to store acquired knowledge in long-term memory.

Treating the symptoms not the problem Drugs can be very effective at treating symptoms, but this only lasts as long as a person takes the drugs. As soon as they stop taking them, the effectiveness ceases. In cases of chronic stress, it may not be appropriate to employ a temporary solution, especially if the treatment produces further problems of its own (such as addiction). It may, therefore, be preferable to seek a treatment that addresses the problem itself (i.e. a *psychologically* based method) rather than only tackling the symptoms. Drugs may be used in conjunction with a psychological method to reduce anxiety so the problem can be tackled.

▲ *Being stressed affects our health, so it is important for psychology to offer ways to manage the effects of stress.*

EVALUATION OF STRESS INOCULATION TRAINING

Effectiveness Meichenbaum (1977) compared SIT with another form of psychological treatment called **systematic desensitisation** (which you might have learned about at AS). This involves presenting clients with a hierarchy of fearful stimuli, starting with the least fearful. When a client can relax and cope with the least fearful stimulus, the therapist introduces the next fearful situation. For example, patients used SIT or desensitisation to deal with their snake phobia. Meichenbaum found that although both forms of therapy reduced the phobia, SIT was better because it helped clients deal with a second, non-treated phobia. This shows that SIT can inoculate against other stressful situations as well as offering help to cope with current problems.

Sheehy and Horan (2004) examined the effects of SIT on the anxiety, stress and academic performance of first-year law students. Participants received four weekly sessions of SIT, each lasting 90 minutes. The participants receiving SIT displayed lower levels of anxiety and stress over time. The participants predicted to finish in the bottom 20% of their class also improved after SIT. More than half of these significantly raised their expected class rank.

Virtual reality training Wiederhold and Wiederhold (2008) have conducted and reviewed studies using *virtual reality* (VR) to enhance the realism of SIT. One study with military personnel used a 'virtual Baghdad' environment, aimed at reducing PTSD when they returned from active service. Participants either experienced a VR simulation of being shot at (i.e. stressed), or not. Those participants who trained in stress conditions performed better on a test task where they had to tend the wounded, i.e. they stayed focused so made fewer mistakes. Combat situations are highly stressful yet require calm, effective behaviour, so SIT was likely to inoculate against future stress.

Preparation for future stressors A major advantage of this method of stress management is that it doesn't just deal with current stressors, but also gives the client the skills and confidence to cope with future problems. The focus on skills acquisition provides long-lasting effectiveness so that the individual is less adversely affected by stressors in the future.

Time consuming and requires high motivation SIT requires a lot of time, effort, motivation and money. Its strength is also its weakness – it is effective because it involves learning and practising many new skills, but this complexity makes it a lengthy therapy which would suit only a limited range of determined individuals.

Relaxation may be all that is needed It may be that the effectiveness of SIT is due to key elements of the training rather than all of it. This means that the range of activities (and time) could be reduced without losing much of the effectiveness. For example, it might be equally effective to learn simply to talk more positively and relax more.

CAN YOU...?   No. 8.3

1... Select *at least* **one** physiologically based technique and **one** psychologically based technique.

2... For each technique, select **four or more** key concepts and explain these concepts.

3... Identify about **ten** points of evaluation (these can be positive or negative).

4... Elaborate each point (see page 9).

5... Use all of this material to write an answer to the following exam question: *Discuss management of stress including physiologically based and psychologically based techniques*. As good practice you might also write a 'building block' essay about each technique. Each answer should contain about 300 words of description and 500 words of evaluation.

Don't forget to read the essay-writing guidance on pages 8–9.

ISSUES IN HEALTH PROMOTION

Being unhealthy is unpleasant and sometimes quite expensive – but people persist in unhealthy behaviours. Models of health behaviour aim to help us understand the conditions under which people do or don't make healthy choices, and, ultimately, such models suggest ways to promote healthier habits.

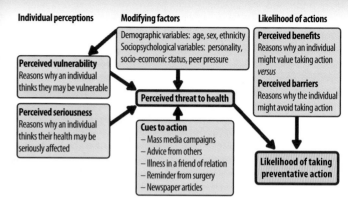

▲ *The health belief model (based on Becker and Maiman, 1975).*

THE HEALTH BELIEF MODEL

The **health belief model** (HBM) (Hochbaum, 1958) explains how health behaviours are influenced by the individual's beliefs about their health and the factors that affect it. Demographic and socio-psychological factors are important (see page 174) because they affect health beliefs (see diagram above right).

Key variables

The model suggests that we hold two beliefs about our level of risk for any health issue, such as a disease, drug abuse or dangerous driving. *Perceived vulnerability* is a judgement of the likelihood that we will be affected, and *perceived seriousness* is a judgement about how bad it could be if we are affected.

Together these determine the threat posed by the health issue. If a threat exists, the individual considers whether taking action will protect them on the basis of a balance between *perceived barriers* (aspects of the situation that prevent action, such as cost or effort) and *perceived benefits* (possible gains, such as reducing pain or anxiety).

Together the barriers and benefits provide the individual with a cost–benefit analysis. To behave in a healthy manner, even when the threat is acknowledged and the cost–benefit analysis suggests it is worthwhile, the individual may still need a *cue to action* – an immediate trigger to initiate a positive health behaviour. This could be internal, such as a sudden, severe bout of pain, or external, such as a friend dying from the same condition. These five factors (perceived vulnerability, seriousness, barriers, benefits and cue to action) predict whether a particular individual will perform a health behaviour in a given situation.

Consider a man with high cholesterol who believes that changing his eating habits will reduce his risk of dying of a heart attack (perceived benefit) even though the diet will be less tasty (perceived barrier). He is more likely to stick to the diet than someone who believes that the fuss about cholesterol levels is all hype (low perceived seriousness) or that has no one in their family with a heart problem so they are not at risk (low vulnerability). A friend dying of a heart attack might encourage him to stick to the diet (cue to action).

Implications for health education

The HBM suggests several ideas for educational interventions to improve health. People in high-risk groups need to be informed that the health issue is serious *and* that they are potentially vulnerable. In addition, they need to be aware of the benefits of changing their behaviour, and of any perceived barriers that need to be reduced. Importantly, just providing information is not enough; any new knowledge must also change *beliefs* otherwise it will not alter behaviour.

Recent research supports the importance of information aimed at reducing barriers and promoting benefits. Gardener *et al.* (2010) found that, following the scare about the MMR vaccine, parents were still worried about the risks of the vaccination and were relatively unaware of the advantages of having their children vaccinated.

THE THEORY OF REASONED ACTION

The **theory of reasoned action** (TRA) (Ajzen and Fishbein, 1980) proposes that people make rational decisions about their health behaviour, rather than this being the inevitable consequence of a set of factors, as the HBM suggests. A person's intention to act and the factors that influence that intention therefore determine health behaviours (see diagram on facing page).

Key variables

Two factors affect behavioural intention. An individual's *attitudes* – their feelings and beliefs about health behaviour – are affected by their beliefs about the outcomes of their behaviour (e.g. that exercise is good for the heart) and their *evaluation* of these beliefs (whether having a healthy heart matters). *Subjective norms* are our beliefs about what is expected of us. Expectations come from both **social norms** and people who are important to us. Our motivation to comply with these expectations influences the extent to which they affect us.

When attitudes and subjective norms are pro-healthy, positive health behaviour is more likely. This is because *behavioural intention* – whether we decide to engage in a health behaviour or not – is a product of attitudes and norms.

Implications for health education

According to the TRA, health campaigns should focus not on giving information but on changing attitudes and subjective norms. This requires interventions acting at a social as well as individual level.

In order to change attitudes, Taylor (1995) suggests that information should be vivid, virtually statistic-free, use case histories, come from expert sources, discuss both sides of the issue (with the strongest arguments at the start and end of the message), be short and clear, have explicit rather than implicit conclusions and not be too extreme.

Recent research supports the view about extreme messages. Hansen *et al.* (2010) showed cigarette packets with either death-related warnings (e.g. 'Smokers die earlier') or death-neutral warnings (e.g. 'Smoking makes you unattractive') to students. For students whose smoking was linked to their **self-esteem**, exposure to the extreme messages produced increased *positive* attitudes to smoking.

EVALUATION OF THE HEALTH BELIEF MODEL

Evidence for the importance of health beliefs Rimer *et al.* (1991) found that women with more knowledge about breast cancer (who were aware of their vulnerability, the severity of the disease and the benefits of early detection) were more likely to have *mammograms* to test for breast cancer. This shows that beliefs do affect health behaviours.

However, Abraham *et al.* (1992) studied teenagers' beliefs about condom use and found that belief was not enough, as predicted by the HBM. Although aware of the benefits of using condoms, the seriousness of HIV and their vulnerability to it, condom use was prevented by perceived barriers, including loss of pleasure, awkwardness of use and anticipated conflict with their partner. Such evidence has **external validity** as it is based on people's beliefs about real illnesses in the context of actual opportunities for action (screening, treatment and self-care).

Health education based on the HBM To help improve health, information must change *beliefs* and this must alter *behaviour*. O'Brien and Lee (1990) showed that manipulating women's knowledge about cervical smear tests (using a video) increased both knowledge and healthy behaviour.

Problems with the HBM Health education is only as good as the information provided. Matthews *et al.* (2003) surveyed Internet sites about alternative therapies for cancer and found that over 90% of the websites contained incorrect information.

However, just providing accurate information might not be the answer because it can sometimes increase anxiety which decreases a move to healthy behaviour. For example, Nestler and Egloff (2010) manipulated the apparent seriousness of a fictitious disease and participants' beliefs about their vulnerability to it. When told it was serious and that they were susceptible, some participants were less likely to say that they would change their behaviour to reduce the risk than when the information was more moderate.

People do not always behave as the HBM predicts, e.g. continuing to smoke despite cues to action from lung cancer deaths and knowledge about risks. In addition, our behaviour is affected by factors that the HBM does not take into account, such as **self-efficacy** (see top right) and intention.

EVALUATION OF THE THEORY OF REASONED ACTION

Evidence for TRA variables Health behaviour is affected as the TRA predicts. Povey *et al.* (2000) found that attitudes (e.g. to low fat diet), subjective norms (e.g. eating fruit and vegetables) and intention (for both dietary changes) were all important. Similarly, Michie *et al.* (1992) found that intention affected behaviour (in attendance at health information classes), and Braubaker and Wickersham (1990) showed that testicular self-examination was predicted by attitude, subjective norms and others' influence.
As the TRA includes variables not taken into account by the HBM, such as the influence of attitudes of others, it can account for a wider variety of factors affecting health behaviour.

Health education based on the TRA Bachman *et al.* (1988) used health interventions to teach young people to say 'no' to drugs. Students were encouraged to talk to each other about drugs, to state their disapproval of drug taking and to say that they did not take drugs. By successfully creating a new anti-drug social norm, this changed attitudes to drugs and reduced cannabis use.

The HBM and cancer screening

Murray and McMillan (1993) tested the HBM in relation to breast self-examination (BSE). They asked women about health beliefs such as: 'My chances of getting cancer are great' (vulnerability), 'I am afraid to even think about cancer' (seriousness), 'If cancer is detected early it can be successfully treated' (benefits) and 'I just don't like doctors or hospitals' (barriers). They also questioned the women's knowledge of cancer and confidence with BSE.

They found that BSE was related to knowledge and perceived benefits, and demographic variables (e.g. age and SES) were important too. The best predictor, however, was self-efficacy: confidence in their ability to carry out BSE. So, health education should aim to improve self-belief.

Murray and McMillan also investigated the HBM in relation to cervical cancer screening. Although attendance was related to knowledge and benefits, the best predictor was 'barriers'. Women who perceived little threat from the procedure or result were more likely to attend, suggesting that education should aim to reduce anxiety.

Ethical issues

There are a number of ethical issues related to health promotion. For example, how far do we consent to having our behaviour manipulated by governments and other agencies? Have we actually agreed to be made to stop smoking, drinking what we want, behaving in ways we want to, and so on? Is voting once every five years or so actually 'consent'? Can we refuse to take part?

CAN YOU...? (No. 8.4)

1... For each theory identify **four or more** key concepts.

2... For each key concept write a few sentences explaining the concept.

3... Identify about **ten** points of evaluation (these can be positive or negative).

4... Elaborate each point (see page 9).

5... Use all of this material to write an answer to the following exam question: *Describe and evaluate issues in health promotion.* As good practice you might also write 'building block' essays about each theory. Your answers should contain about 300 words of description and 500 words of evaluation.

Don't forget to read the essay-writing guidance on pages 8–9.

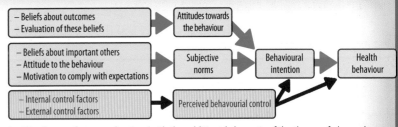

▲ *The theory of reasoned action (with the additional elements of the theory of planned behaviour in red).*

Problems with the TRA Intention does not, however, always predict action suggesting that the TRA is incomplete. For example, Armitage and Conner (1998) showed that *perceived behavioural control* (an individual's belief about whether they can perform a behaviour) is also important. This variable was added to the model by Ajzen (1985) in a revision called the **theory of planned behaviour** (TPB), which is shown in the diagram above. Perceived behavioural control is affected by internal factors (e.g. knowing that you can make yourself go to the gym) and external factors (e.g. living near a gym).

ENVIRONMENTAL INFLUENCES

GENETIC INFLUENCES

People's health statuses vary, even when they share similarities, such as genes, jobs or smoking. This suggests that many factors affect our health. On this spread we will consider three such factors: our personality, age and social class.

Prospective and retrospective studies

At AS level you learned about the study by Rahe, Mahan and Arthur (1970) on stress. This was a prospective study – taking a *current* measure (life events) and looking for links to *subsequent* events (health). Although such relationships are still only correlational, a prospective design eliminates some confounding variables, such as biases in recall or reporting based on current health.

The study by Greendale *et al.* (see right) is an example of a retrospective study. One problem with collecting data about the past is that it may not be remembered accurately. Importantly, there may be *biases* in recall. For example, a healthy 73-year-old man might remember his earlier years more favourably than an unhealthy 73-year-old man and so report having been more active. This would produce an apparent but invalid impression that early exercise is related to later well-being.

▲ *Feeling in control is especially important for older adults because they are more likely to actively manage their health, such as exercising and eating healthily.*

Personality type

Locus of control Models of health behaviour (discussed on the previous spread) suggest that our health behaviour depends, at least in part, on our beliefs and attitudes, including those relating to whether we feel we are able to control our health choices. Rotter (1966) described the personality variable of **locus of control** (LoC), a concept introduced in your AS core study by Langer and Rodin (1976). People with an **external LoC** ('externals') attribute control to factors they cannot govern, such as chance or the behaviour of other people. People who believe that they are responsible for themselves have an **internal LoC** ('internals'). Strickland (1978) suggested that this dimension is important in health behaviour as internals would engage in more preventative measures, such as avoiding accidents and being informed about their own health.

Measuring locus of control Wallston *et al.* (1978) developed a *Health Locus of Control* (HLC) scale (Rotter's LoC scale is shown on page 165) which measures three dimensions of beliefs about factors determining health:

- *Internal HLC* – the extent to which a person feels responsible for their own health, e.g. believing that 'The main thing that affects my health is what I, myself, do'.
- *'Powerful others' HLC* – a person's belief in the role that important people (such as doctors, nurses, family and friends) play in their health, e.g. holding views such as 'Whenever I don't feel well, I should consult a trained professional'.
- *Chance HLC* – the role a person assigns to 'pure luck' (or otherwise) and indicated by beliefs such as 'No matter what I do, if I am going to get sick, I will get sick'.

People with more internal HLCs and a low chance HLC are most likely to engage in healthy behaviours and to be most well.

Age

Age is a factor in health because there are different issues and risks associated with separate age groups, which require changing focus in order to promote healthy behaviour.

Childhood A major factor in children's health is parental attitudes and behaviour. Children copy eating behaviours from parents, which can be explained in terms of **social learning theory**. For example, a child's weight is affected by their parents' exercise habits, especially if they exercise together (Ross *et al.*, 1987).

Parents are also significant sources of reward or punishment for children (**operant conditioning**), and copied behaviours can be reinforced by approval or disapproval ('You're a good girl for eating all your food!'). Coercive strategies used by parents may be counterproductive (Striegel-Moore *et al.*, 1986). In the case of healthy eating, a child may be put off by 'Eat all your sprouts and you can have some pudding', reasoning that sprouts must be truly dreadful if bribery is required to eat them!

Adolescence As an individual takes greater responsibility for their health, their lifestyle choices become more important. Eiser (1997) estimated that 50% of adolescent illnesses and deaths are preventable and are due to negative health behaviours, including poor eating, substance abuse and risky sexual behaviour. Adolescents are highly affected by **social norms** within their peer groups and also those created by the media – for example, images that 'thin is good' and the view that everyone is having sex.

Adulthood Health during adulthood is affected not only by the biological process of ageing but also by factors such as taking exercise, having a strong social network and healthy lifestyle (e.g. eating well, not smoking and having few stressors).

Adult health behaviours are important for old age. In a retrospective study, Greendale *et al.* (1995) asked 1700 men and women with an average age of 73 to rate their exercise levels as teenagers, at age 30 and at age 50. Adults of both sexes with the highest activity levels had significantly higher bone mineral density in their hips than less active adults.

Old age As in adulthood, physical activity in old age is important, as is the maintenance of social and cognitive activity (see page 142). These help to stave off health problems, such as loss of strength, bone fractures, heart disease and memory loss. At this age, positive health behaviours make a very big difference to health (Belloc, 1973).

Social class

Socio-economic status (SES) can be defined by occupation, education or income. In general, people of higher SES enjoy better health than those who are less wealthy. White and Edgar (2010) demonstrated a clear pattern of greater *healthy life expectancy* (years of good health) with higher SES for England. According to UK statistics for smoking, people in routine and manual households were more likely to smoke than those in managerial and professional households (31% compared with 18%).

Educational level Winkleby *et al.* (1999) suggest that people spending more time in education are less likely to smoke. However, the reverse is true for alcohol; more schooling is linked to greater alcohol consumption (USDHHS, 1998).

Health education People from higher socio-economic groups are also more likely to benefit from health education. For example, Janssen *et al.* (2001) found that gay men with a lower SES were more likely to engage in high-risk sexual behaviours. As there were differences in health knowledge and beliefs between the groups, it was suggested that this could be resolved using health interventions that match recipients' educational level.

EVALUATION

Personality type

Locus of control Evidence suggests that the way individuals appraise their sense of control does affect their health. Not only do internals seek out more information (Seeman and Evans, 1962) but they are also more like to change their behaviour on the basis of this knowledge.

Contradictory evidence Although some studies have found differences in health behaviours between internals and externals, these are generally quite small (e.g. Calnan, 1989), and others have found no differences (e.g. McLarnon and Kaloupek, 1988). This inconsistency could arise from the importance of factors other than LoC (such as careers) or because the effects of LoC depends on context. Parkes (1984) found that, for nursing students, internals were more likely than externals to engage in direct coping when they believed they could control the situation; but where they felt the situation was one they must accept, they behaved no differently (although overall, internals did cope better).

Age

Childhood Children do make some of their own choices. For example, TV viewing is at least partly controlled by children themselves, and is an important factor in their weight. It is not just because they are not outside exercising, or that they are being exposed to adverts for calorie-rich foods; TV viewing itself is relaxing so lowers metabolic rate. This effect is greater in obese children (Klesges *et al.*, 1993), so they burn even fewer calories.

Adolescence Eiser (1997) suggests that one of the reasons for negative health behaviours in adolescence is the typical teenage **invincibility fable** – the belief that 'it won't happen to me'. Eiser also suggests that risky behaviour can be explained in terms of **hormonal** changes (early puberty leads to physical but not emotional maturity), *sociodemographic* causes (e.g. having alcoholic parents – as the child is more likely to also drink excessively) and peer-group pressure.

For health interventions to be successful, adolescents need accurate information, but it is also vital that educational programmes tackle **social norms** and emotional issues.

Adulthood Research has found that, for some people, increasing age is related to a decreasing willingness to exercise and to the belief that exercise is not enjoyable or beneficial (Wilcox and Storandt, 1996). Such attitudes clearly reduce the likelihood of exercising.

Research also supports the benefits of exercise. For example, one study found that women aged over 50 who regularly did resistance training could carry grocery bags with 36% less effort than those who did not, and they put much less stress on their leg muscles when getting up from a chair (Mayo Health, 2001).

Old age Research has demonstrated the benefits of exercise for the elderly. Frail nursing home residents aged 72–98 participated in resistance training three times a week. After 10 weeks the active participants were walking faster, had doubled their muscle strength and had increased their stair-climbing power by 28% (Fiatarone *et al.*, 1994).

Lack of information stops many older adults from exercising, as they believe that exercise is too difficult, useless or unsafe. So, apart from providing information about the benefits of exercise, older adults also need to be reassured that exercising is possible and safe.

Social class

Health education and SES One reason that people with higher SES benefit more from health education is because it is typically designed by, and therefore for, people who are well educated. It may be less accessible or less convincing for people of lower SES.

Talking about health Blair (1993) suggests that language is important to accessing healthcare. The language used by doctors (high SES) may be incomprehensible and alienating to patients of lower SES, especially as doctors tend to consider health from a mental perspective rather than a purely physical stance, as is typical of lower SES groups.

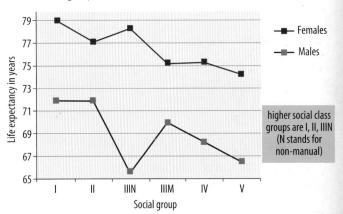

higher social class groups are I, II, IIIN (N stands for non-manual)

▲ *The graph above shows the relationship between life expectancy and SES in England and Wales (ONS, 2007). In general, research has found a negative class gradient for most fatal conditions, except skin cancer which is more likely to occur in higher social classes. People of lower social classes are more likely to develop diseases or die from them than people from higher social classes (Banyard, 2001).*

CAN YOU...? No. 8.5

1... **Three** factors affecting health behaviour are described on the facing page. For each factor identify **two or more** key points.

2... For each point, write a few sentences explaining it.

3... Identify about **ten** points of evaluation (these can be positive or negative).

4... Elaborate each point (see page 9).

5... Use all of this material to write an answer to the exam following exam question: *Describe and evaluate factors affecting health behaviour (e.g. personality type, age, social class).* As good practice you might also write 'building block' essays about each one of the factors. Your answers should contain about 300 words of description and 500 words of evaluation.

Don't forget to read the essay-writing guidance on pages 8–9.

THEORIES OF ADDICTION

BIOLOGICAL EXPLANATIONS

- McGue estimated 50–60% heritability for alcohol dependence, implying a genetic component, and Agrawal *et al.* found a similar pattern for illicit drug dependence.
- The A1 variant of the D_2 dopamine receptor gene (DRD_2) is found in more alcoholics than non-alcoholics (Noble *et al.*) and is more common in the children of alcoholics (Blum *et al.*). It is also implicated in cocaine, heroin and nicotine addiction.
- People with the A1 variant have fewer dopamine receptors in the brain's 'pleasure centre'. Drugs of addiction tend to increase dopamine levels and thus make up for dopamine insufficiency.

EVALUATION

- A genetic predisposition to addiction could explain individual differences (a diathesis–stress model).
- This could also explain individual differences in response to treatment or risk of relapse.
- Twin studies show that addictive behaviours (e.g. to drugs and gambling) co-occur, supporting role of genetic factors (Kessler *et al.*).
- Comings *et al.* found that significantly more smokers and ex-smokers had the DRD_2 A1 variant than the general population.
- Other addictive behaviours are linked to DRD_2, e.g. obesity (Noble).
- Grant *et al.* found that, in monkeys, social status falls with D_2 receptor loss – supporting the view that poverty and stress could increase risk.
- Some research fails to demonstrate a relationship between genes and addiction. Fowler *et al.* found environmental factors were also important (e.g. best friends' alcohol use).

Determinist
- Biological explanations are determinist, and offer pharmacological solutions to addiction, which is more progressive than considering addicts as delinquents to be punished.
- However, they ignore other potential influences, e.g. thought processes or social context.
- Individuals might take less responsibility for their recovery if they think addiction is inevitable because of their genes.

SOCIAL/PSYCHOLOGICAL EXPLANATIONS

The self-medication model
- Gelkopf *et al.* suggest that people intentionally choose a drug to treat their specific psychological symptoms, and most addicts do have additional psychiatric disorders (Horner and Scheibe).
- The drug is not selected at random, but is one *perceived* to alleviate a problem (e.g. anxiety) though it may actually make it worse, e.g. smokers claim to use nicotine for 'stress relief' but report *higher* levels of stress than non-smokers (Cohen and Lichtenstein).
- This paradox may arise because the short- and long-term effects of smoking are different (Parrott).

Rational choice theory
- Becker and Murphy proposed an economic model showing how users balance benefits (e.g. euphoria) against costs (e.g. health risks) as if addictive behaviour are goods or services, i.e. a rational choice.
- Present and future negatives (e.g. increasing price) act against potential positives. Some outcomes are more certain than others (e.g. 'I *will* get high' versus 'I *might* get caught').

EVALUATION

The self-medication model
- Gottdiener *et al.* supported the self-medication model, showing that substance abuse disorders are linked to the inability to resist drug use (low ego control).
- For self-medication to explain addiction, drug use must follow psychological distress. Sanjuan *et al.* found women who had been sexually abused more likely to abuse drugs.
- This model cannot account for addictions in the absence of psychological problems.

Rational choice theory
- This theory can explain why addicts can quit if they want to – they reach the point where costs exceed benefits. Continuation is also rational – the costs of stopping are perceived as greater than the benefits (West).
- In support of rational choice, Sloan and Wang found that increased cigarette price reduces smoking and that current smokers rate quitting as high-cost and health as low-benefit.
- West suggests that making cigarettes more expensive, more difficult to buy or illegal changes 'utility'.
- Drugs are expensive and users risk imprisonment, but drugs are still abused so the economic argument seems flawed.

THE MANAGEMENT

PHYSIOLOGICAL TECHNIQUE: DRUGS

- Benzodiazepines (BZs) are used to treat anxiety and stress. They act on the neurotransmitter GABA.
- GABA is the body's natural anxiety reliever. It reduces activity of many neurons in the brain by making it harder for other neurotransmitters to stimulate them.
- BZs enhance GABA's action by attaching to special sites on the GABA receptor so neurons become even harder to stimulate so the person feels calmer.
- The neurotransmitter serotonin is involved in the brain's 'punishment system', which becomes more active in chronic stress, causing anxiety. BZs lower serotonin activity, so reduce stress-induced anxiety.

EVALUATION

- Kahn *et al.* found that BZs were better at treating stress than a placebo and Hildalgo *et al.* found they treated social anxiety better than antidepressants.
- BZs are not always effective. Gelpin *et al.* found post-traumatic stress disorder sufferers treated with BZs were not significantly better than controls.
- Drugs are a quick and easy way to treat stress unlike psychological methods which take time, effort and motivation.
- BZs were better than the barbiturates they replaced as these were addictive but it seems patients taking BZs also experience withdrawal when they stop.
- BZs also produce paradoxical side effects, e.g. increased aggressiveness and memory impairment.
- Drugs treat symptoms only while the drug is used, they don't solve the underlying problem. For short-term stressors, this is effective but for chronic stress psychological methods may be better.

TREATMENT OF ADDICTION

BIOLOGICAL TREATMENTS

Heroin addiction and methadone
- Methadone mimics the mood-lifting effect of heroin and reduces withdrawal and craving.
- It is drunk in liquid form at a clinic so allows monitoring and avoids dangers of injecting.
- It is used either as a maintenance treatment or for detoxification.

Nicotine addiction
- The health problems linked to cigarettes rather than nicotine addiction can be overcome using nicotine replacement therapy, e.g. patches.

These provide nicotine at a constant rate, which reduces withdrawal problems.

Gambling addiction
- Gambling addiction causes personal and social problems. Research suggests that drug treatments can help, e.g. Hollander *et al.* found improvements with SSRIs.
- The dopamine antagonist naltrexone might also help by blocking the reinforcement of gambling.

EVALUATION

Heroin addiction and methadone
- Methadone reduces craving and withdrawal *and* partially blocks the euphoria caused by heroin so it is less rewarding for users who relapse.
- The risk of overdose on methadone is lower than for heroin and its effects last longer, helping abstinence.
- Attending the clinic means addicts receive psychological support and break links with the drug culture.
- Relapse can arise as some withdrawal symptoms experienced.
- Reliance on methadone rather than detoxifying is a risk and it does cause deaths (300 in the UK in 2007).
- When users progress to unsupervised methadone use, some sell it on the black market.

- Brink and Haasen found treatment reduced illicit heroin use, but Michels *et al.* doubt the long-term success because many patients remain on a maintenance dose for years.
- Methadone treatment also reduces the risk of contracting HIV (Hartel and Schoenbaum).

Gambling addiction
- Studies looking at drug treatment of gambling are typically short-term and use small groups (e.g. Hollander). A longer, larger study (Blanco *et al.*) found no benefit from SSRIs.
- Kim and Grant found that naltrexone helped to reduce gambling thoughts and behaviours.

SOCIAL/PSYCHOLOGICAL TREATMENTS

Reinforcement
- A token economy works by reinforcing abstinent behaviour.
- Sindelar *et al.* found that monetary rewards reduced illicit drug use by addicts on methadone treatment.
- This is a behaviourist approach so focuses on the individual's *responses* and aims to reduce the addictive behaviours by altering their consequences (by providing alternative reinforcers).

Cognitive–behavioural therapy (CBT)
- CBT aims to help people change their thinking patterns about addictive behaviours and to learn new ways to cope with the problems that led to them, e.g. by identifying the cause of craving and changing false beliefs.
- Combined with the cognitive approach, this tries to tackle the cause of addiction (faulty thinking) rather than just changing behaviour.

EVALUATION

Reinforcement
- Contingency management is based on reinforcement and helps reduce drug use, e.g. for amphetamine and cocaine (Olmstead) and heroin and alcohol (Olmstead and Petry).
- Although reinforcement therapies reduce addictive behaviour, they do not solve the initial problem so alternative addictions could arise, e.g. compulsive spending.

Cognitive–behavioural therapy (CBT)
- Ladouceur *et al.* found that cognitive therapy was effective for pathological gamblers.
- Sylvain *et al.* used combined cognitive *and* behavioural strategies and found long-term improvements with gamblers.

- However, Crits-Christoph *et al.* found that group drug counselling (GDC) was less effective when combined with CBT than when combined with individual drug counselling or GDC alone.
- When CBT or reinforcement were combined with methadone maintenance, the CBT group made slower initial progress but were as good after one year, judged by self-report and urine analysis (Rawson *et al.*).
- Using self-reports to measure addictive behaviour might be unreliable as users could fail to report relapses due to a social desirability bias, which would inflate the treatment success rate.

OF STRESS

PSYCHOLOGICAL TECHNIQUE: STRESS INOCULATION TRAINING (SIT)

- Meichenbaum believes we cannot (usually) remove stressors from our lives, but can change the way that we think about them.
- Stress inoculation training (SIT) is a form of CBT so helps change thinking and behaviour (coping skills).
- Phase 1 (conceptualisation): trainer and client build a relationship and the client is educated, e.g. to see threats as made up of solvable components.
- Phase 2 (skills acquisition): cognitive and behavioural coping skills (e.g. positive self-statements, relaxation, social skills and time management).
- Phase 3 (application): clients apply the new skills in more stressful situations and other coping techniques (e.g. imagery and role play) may be used. Booster sessions later and clients sometimes help to train others.

EVALUATION

- Meichenbaum found that both SIT and systematic desensitisation reduced snake phobia, but SIT also helped clients deal with a second, non-treated phobia.
- Sheehy and Horan found that SIT reduced stress and anxiety in students and helped to raise academic performance.
- Use of a virtual reality (VR) Baghdad environment formed part of a SIT programme for military personnel. Trainees who experienced stress during the VR task performed better on difficult tasks later.
- The skills acquired last, so the individual is less adversely affected by later stressors.
- The strength of SIT (its effectiveness based on learning an practice) is also its weakness (requires time, effort, motivation and money).
- Every element is not always necessary for it to be effective – talking positively and relaxing may be enough.

THE HEALTH BELIEF MODEL

- The health belief model (HBM) (Hochbaum, 1958) says that beliefs about health affect health behaviour. Demographic and socio-psychological factors also affect health beliefs.

Key variables
- For any health issue we hold two beliefs about risk: *perceived vulnerability* (our chance of being affected) and *perceived seriousness* (how bad it would be). These determine the threat posed.
- If a threat exists, action is determined by the balance between *perceived barriers* (e.g. cost or effort) and *perceived benefits* (e.g. reducing pain or anxiety).
- Even if the cost–benefit analysis based on barriers and benefits suggest a healthier behaviour is necessary, a *cue to action* may be needed. This could be internal (e.g. sudden pain) or external (e.g. a friend dying).

Implications for health education
- The HBM suggests high-risk groups need education about seriousness and vulnerability and about the benefits of changing behaviour and ways to reduce perceived barriers.
- But providing information is not enough; beliefs must change in order to alter behaviour.
- Huettig and Hartsuiker found that, following the MMR scare, worries continued and parents were relatively unaware of the benefits of childhood vaccinations.

EVALUATION

- Rimer *et al.* found that women with pro-healthy beliefs about breast cancer screening were more likely to have mammograms.
- Abraham *et al.* found that teenagers with pro-healthy beliefs about the benefits of using condoms still don't use them because of perceived barriers (e.g. loss of pleasure).
- Evidence supporting the HBM typically has external validity as research uses real illnesses.
- O'Brien and Lee found that knowledge about cervical smear tests increased healthy behaviour showing that changing beliefs can alter behaviour.
- Nestler and Egloff found that when participants' beliefs were changed so they thought they were vulnerable to a serious (fictitious) disease, some were *less* likely to say they would change their behaviour suggesting that anxiety also affects health behaviour.
- People do not always behave as the HBM predicts, e.g. continuing to smoke despite cues to action.
- Murray and McMillan found that for breast self-examination knowledge of perceived benefits and demographic variables mattered but self-efficacy was more important, the best predictor was barriers so education should aim to reduce anxiety.
- There are important ethical issues about manipulating people's behaviour even if it is done 'for their own good'.

THE THEORY OF REASONED ACTION

- The theory of reasoned action (TRA) (Ajzen and Fishbein, 1980) says we make rational decisions about health behaviour: our intention to act and the factors that influence that intention determine our behaviour.

Key variables
- Two factors affect behavioural intention: *attitudes* (which are affected by beliefs about the outcomes and an evaluation of the beliefs) and *subjective norms* (from social norms and our motivation to comply with the expectations of important others).
- When attitudes and subjective norms are pro-healthy, so is our *behavioural intention*.

Implications for health education
- The TRA says that health education should focus on changing attitudes and subjective norms so groups as well as individuals should be targeted.
- Taylor says that health education should be short, vivid, clear, balanced, personal, from experts and not too extreme.
- Hansen *et al.* found extreme messages made students whose smoking was linked to their self-esteem *more* positive about smoking.

EVALUATION

- Povey *et al.* found that for dietary changes attitudes, subjective norms and intention were all important. Michie *et al.* found that intention affected attendance at health information classes.
- Bachman *et al.* created a new anti-drug social norm in a group of young people, which changed attitudes to drugs and reduced cannabis use.
- However, intention does not always predict action, suggesting the TRA is incomplete, e.g. Armitage and Conner showed that *perceived behavioural control* (believing one can perform a behaviour) matters too.
- The theory of planned behaviour (Ajzen, 1985) adds perceived behavioural control to the TRA. This is affected by internal and external factors.

FACTORS AFFECTING HEALTH BEHAVIOUR

PERSONALITY TYPE

- Rotter's (1966) locus of control (LoC) suggests 'externals' attribute control to factors they cannot govern (e.g. chance or other people); 'internals' believe they are responsible for themselves.
- Strickland found internals take more preventative measures and are more informed about their own health.
- Wallston *et al.* developed a Health Locus of Control (HLC) scale which measures: *internal HLC* (how responsible someone feels for their health), *'powerful others' HLC* (belief in the role of important people) and *chance HLC* (the role assigned to 'luck').
- A high internal HLC and low chance HLC are associated with healthy behaviours and well-being.

EVALUATION

- People with an internal LoC do seek out more information (Seeman and Evans) and are more likely to change their behaviour because of this.
- However, differences between internals and externals are generally quite small (e.g. Calnan) and some studies show no differences (e.g. McLarnon and Kaloupek).
- Parkes found that nursing students who were internals engaged in more direct coping when they believed they had control. Overall, internals coped better.
- The link between attitudes and health behaviour assumes that people think rationally but we are more likely to be influenced by prejudices and stereotypes (Kahneman and Tversky).

AGE

- Health issues change with age, so the needs of health promotion does too.
- In childhood, parental attitudes and behaviour affect health, e.g. children copy behaviours (social learning), e.g. a child's weight is affected by their parents' exercise habits (Ross *et al.*).
- Parents also reward and punish behaviour (operant conditioning), e.g. to influence eating habits, but coercion may be counterproductive (Striegel-Moore *et al.*).
- Adolescents take more responsibility for their health so their lifestyle choices matter more. Eiser estimates that half of adolescent illness and death is due to poor health behaviours (bad diets, substance abuse).
- Adult health is affected by ageing and lifestyle factors (e.g. eating well, not smoking) and these have long-term effects, e.g. Greendale *et al.* found that the most active adults had the highest bone mineral density in their hips.
- Physical activity in old age is important too, as is maintaining social and cognitive activity.

EVALUATION

- Children do make some health choices, e.g. TV viewing influences exercise because of food adverts and it lowers metabolic rate. This is greatest in obese children so they burn even fewer calories (Klesges *et al.*).
- Eiser suggests that negative health behaviours in adolescence are due to an invincibility fable and hormonal changes at puberty which lead to risky behaviour. Sociodemographic causes (e.g. alcoholic parents) and peer pressure also matter.
- Health interventions for adolescents need to offer accurate information but also tackle social norms and emotional issues.
- In adulthood, attitudes also affect health. Wilcox and Storandt found that increasing age is related to a decreasing willingness to exercise and a belief that exercise is not enjoyable or beneficial.
- For older adults, exercise can also improve health, e.g. muscle strength (Fiatarone *et al.*). However, the fear that exercise is too difficult, useless or unsafe counters the potential benefits of exercise for older adults, so reassurance is important.

SOCIAL CLASS

- A higher socio-economic status (SES), as defined by occupation, education or income, is generally linked to better health, e.g. smoking is more common is lower SES households.
- White and Edgar found a higher healthy life expectancy with higher SES.
- However, whilst people with more education are less likely to smoke, the reverse is true for alcohol.
- Higher SES is also linked to greater benefit from health education. Janssen *et al.* found that gay men with lower SES engaged in more high-risk sexual behaviour.

EVALUATION

- People with higher SES may benefit more from health education because it is typically designed by, and therefore for, people who are well educated.
- Health professionals (high SES) use language that is incomprehensible and alienates lower SES patients (Blair).
- There is a negative class gradient for most fatal conditions, except skin cancer (Banyard).

Question 8 **Describe and evaluate factors affecting health behaviour.** *[25]*

Student answer

Paragraph 1 People vary a lot in the health of their lifestyles and also in the way they can carry on with unhealthy behaviours like smoking even when there is a lot of evidence to show how harmful it is. There are clearly lots of factors involved including how people think or what they believe, how old they are, what kind of personality they are and how rich they are.

Paragraph 2 Langer and Rodin's study showed how important feeling in control is for your health. This is called 'locus of control' (LoC). If you have an external LoC you always blame outside events and the environment for anything ('I can't exercise because there isn't a gym near me'). Internal LoC is thought to mean a person will look after themselves more as they take responsibility for anything that happens to them ('I can take up walking in the countryside to keep fit').

Paragraph 3 In support of this, Wallston made up a Health LoC test which measures internal LoC as well as their beliefs about both luck and the role of medical staff. People who selected lots of internal LoC items and did not believe in chance were most likely to be healthy and involved in healthy lifestyles. Internal LoCs look up information about health and practise healthy lifestyles. However many studies have found little or no difference between types of LoC (e.g. Calnan, 1989). Parkes found that that internal LoCs (in a student nurse sample) were generally better at coping and practising healthy behaviours when they could control events, but not in situations where they had no control.

Paragraph 4 Age is a factor because generally health behaviours can be deeply affected by childhood learning. If children see their parents behaving in a healthy manner, they will learn these behaviours via social learning (Bandura), and the parents could also reinforce behaviours by rewards and punishments (operant conditioning).

Paragraph 5 Supporting evidence is that parental exercise habits can be a factor in children's obesity (Ross, 1987). However it has been noted that attempted rewards can be off-putting to a child ('If you eat your vegetables you can have a chocolate bar').

Paragraph 6 Adolescents are notorious for poor health behaviours, often trying out such behaviours following the social norms in their peer groups about poor eating, substance abuse and risky sex behaviour (Eiser, 1997). The media has a big influence with TV and print media presenting distorted images of health (e.g. very thin models) and advertising using classical conditioning to make people feel good about unhealthy behaviours (e.g. vodka adverts and drinking). Eiser suggests that teenagers have an 'invincibility fable'; they don't think anything will harm them.

Paragraph 7 These behaviours have long-term effects on health and often attitudes persist into adulthood (e.g. normality of drinking excessive alcohol). Wilcox (1996) found that increasing age was related to decreasing willingness to exercise and to negative attitudes despite exercise being shown conclusively to improve both health and mental state, especially in the elderly (e.g. Fiatarone, 1994).

Paragraph 8 Another problem is that people just don't think rationally. Kahnemann and Tversky (1973) have shown that we don't use statistical information or logic in making decisions, but often use stereotypes and irrational thinking, especially affected by emotions. That is why advertisers try to condition positive emotions to their products by funny adverts on TV.

Paragraph 9 Something that does definitely affect health behaviour is socio-economic status (SES) or social class as it's better known. Most fatal diseases have a class gradient, in that people who are poorer are more likely to die from them. The only disease with the opposite gradient is skin cancer, as richer people get more holidays in the sun. There is a link with psychology, as the higher your educational level, the higher social class tends to be, and the more likely you are to behave rationally when presented with scientific evidence.

Paragraph 10 Evidence shows that people with higher SES are more likely to benefit from health education. Janssen (2001) found that low SES gay men were more likely to indulge in high-risk sex behaviours. Winkleby (1999) found that higher education level correlated with lower smoking behaviour but other studies have found that higher alcohol consumption correlates positively with higher SES.

Paragraph 11 Factors influencing health behaviours are many and complex and it is difficult to come to big generalisations even about SES and health.

[715 words]

Examiner comments

This is a good essay with a reasonable balance of description (**AO1**) and evaluation (**AO2**, highlighted in grey). It is a difficult essay to structure well and this candidate manages to do this very well indeed; many candidates are tempted to write what we call 'internet advice' essays (e.g. 'You will be healthier if you give up smoking...') but this essay is strong on psychology – as it should be.

In fact, the first paragraph is not a good example of the rest of the essay. It demonstrates understanding but doesn't contribute to the overall mark because it is too general.

Paragraph 2 is a good link to previous work at AS level and introduces the topic well. If it was used as an introduction then it could be better written with the first sentence 'Psychological factors are very important in healthy behaviours and health outcomes. A good example is...'.

Paragraph 3 offers good support for paragraph 2 and provides solid **AO2**, demonstrating depth in the analysis.

In paragraph 4 the topic of age is introduced with some description of the effects associated with childhood. Paragraphs 6 and 7 move on to adolescence as another aspect of age.

In paragraph 8 the issue of rationality is briefly introduced and evaluated.

The final three paragraphs look at the factor of social class, providing description and evaluation.

Overall the description (**AO1**) demonstrates breadth of knowledge and in most places depth too, so **9 out of 10 marks**. The breadth of evaluative points is good but often it is too brief (not 'sustained'), so **12 out of 15 marks**.

21/25 makes this a Grade A essay but not an A* standard.

Improvement?

Remove paragraph 1 to make the essay more psychologically focused.

Provide more evidence and particularly explain the evaluative points in more detail.

The paragraph structure could be improved by separating **AO1** and **AO2** material rather than placing it together as in paragraph 9.

Chapter 9

Educational psychology

Chapter contents

180 Introduction to the study of educational psychology
182 Behaviourist learning theory applied to education
184 Cognitive developmental theories
186 Individual differences in learning styles
188 Motivating factors in the classroom
190 Special educational needs

End-of-chapter review

192 Chapter summary
194 Exam question with student answer

Specification breakdown	
Behaviourist learning theory applied to education including classical and operant conditioning.	This section examines the role of association and reinforcement in teaching – classical and operant conditioning respectively. You first encountered both of these techniques in your AS psychology course. Teachers often reward and punish students, but is a *Smiley Face* sticker really effective?
Cognitive developmental theories applied to education (e.g. Piaget, Vygotsky and Bruner).	Cognitive developmental theory has had a massive impact on British education, especially in primary school classrooms. Here we look at how the main theories have been applied and evaluate their worth. You can read more details of some of the theories in Chapter 5.
Individual differences in learning styles (e.g. Curry's onion model and Grasha's six learning styles and gender and cultural differences).	It has become popular to use the concept of learning styles to inform and direct teaching, and many students 'know' their individual learning style. Here we examine two of the main theoretical frameworks and we also explore gender and cultural differences.
Motivating factors in the classroom (e.g. teaching styles, attribution theory, Maslow's hierarchy of needs).	Apart from the immediate effect of behavioural measures (see first section above) there are many other factors at work in the classroom that influence learning. This section explores and evaluates a selection of them.
Special educational needs including the assessment, categorisation and strategies for education of at least one special educational need (e.g. dyslexia, autism).	We are all different but 'some are more different than others' and such differences require special educational strategies. We focus on two of the more common 'differences' and look at the stages leading from assessment to teaching strategies.

EDUCATION

The word 'education' comes from the Latin 'to lead out', and refers to the relationship between the leader ('teacher') and the led (student).

Humans learn from others all the time, as do most animals. For example, some birds learn to imitate the song of other birds or even to imitate the sound of a chainsaw (listen to the lyre bird at www.youtube.com/watch?v=VjE0Kdfos4Y). Primates demonstrate even more complex and impressive learning skills, for example you can see an orangutan on YouTube washing socks, imitating what she has seen humans doing (see www.youtube.com/watch?v=IFACrlx5SZ0).

Formal education

One respect where we are quite different from animals is in formal education. Humans set out to teach other humans (and sometimes may also formally teach animals such as circus animals). Such formal education is immensely important to the development of individual humans and the advancement of any society. Therefore it is not surprising that, in the last 2,500 years of recorded history, teaching and learning have been extensively talked about, written about, and practised. In the 4th century BC the Greek philosopher Plato wrote about education, proposing ways to produce an educated ruling class through direct instruction. Plato believed that intelligence was gained through **nurture** and not inherited. In the 18th century the French philosopher Jean-Jacques Rousseau argued that learning was most effective when it was produced through experience rather than book learning. He also emphasised the importance of emotions rather than just knowledge.

Psychology and education

Until the development of psychology, education was in the realm of philosophy. The advent of psychology as a separate discipline provided the opportunity for **empirical** evidence which could demonstrate what techniques work best in educational settings. Thus, educational psychology was born – the application of psychological knowledge to the business of education. It is concerned with such things as how teachers can teach effectively, the factors related to successful learning and even the social psychology of the school.

▲ *Informal and formal education.*
Educational psychology is concerned with the process of formal education.

Teaching and learning

People often assume that teaching and learning are the same – if someone teaches you, you learn. But it doesn't necessarily follow. Teaching might lack effectiveness because teachers fail to take characteristics of the learner into account. On the facing page we look at one example of individual differences – how learners differ in terms of their **learning styles** (their characteristic pattern of tackling a learning problem).

Another aspect of the teaching–learning mismatch is that many educational practices might not actually be effective. For example, on the next spread we consider the use of rewards and punishment in teaching and discover that both could actually be counterproductive. Such research underlines the importance of educational psychology – taking a scientific approach to understanding how to maximise the effectiveness of teaching.

There are many areas of educational research that are outside the scope of this chapter, but the topics covered should give you a glimmer of understanding into the complexities of the educational business and the valuable contribution made by psychology.

What is an educational psychologist?

Educational psychologists are individuals trained in psychology who focus on problems that arise in educational settings. In particular they work with schools and young people to help individuals overcome learning difficulties and other problems which slow down educational progress. You can read more about educational psychology on the BPS website, see www.bps.org.uk/careers/advisor/advisor_home.cfm

▲ *'Gladly would he learn and gladly teach'. Geoffrey's Chaucer's description of the Clerk of Oxford; the educational ideal.*

Think like a psychologist!

you are an expert in education, having by now spent at least 12 years receiving formal education. You have a huge amount of experience to draw on both as an individual and in discussion with your classmates, but remember that these memories need to be carefully and thoughtfully analysed in a *psychological and scientific way* to help you to understand the psychology of education.

You might find it difficult to resist complaining about the maths teacher who used to shout at you from close range or fondly recall the PE teacher who praised every little thing you did. As a psychologist you will have to split off your emotional memories (such as your fear or pride) and consider questions like 'What forms of punishment are most effective immediately and in the longer term?', 'How can learning style be used to enhance education?', 'Where is the evidence to support my views?'

STARTER ACTIVITIES

WHAT SORT OF LEARNER ARE YOU?

It is fairly likely that, during your time at school, you will have been given at least one test that assesses your style of learning. The most common form of assessment concerns VAK – whether you are a visual, auditory or kinaesthetic learner. But learning styles don't end with VAK – there are tests that determine whether you are an activist or a theorist, a sequential or a global thinker, a participator or avoidant learner, collaborative or competitive and so on.

For all the different styles of learning there are specific tests (also called 'inventories'). Such tests are usually quite lengthy – too long to include here, but you can access many examples online. Not all of them are free but there are many that are – and we have provided some weblinks on the right.

Doing your own research

In the spirit of good psychological research you might try to relate the different styles to other characteristics. For example, are boys less likely to be visual learners than girls? Are people who do well academically more likely to be field dependent?

The value of learning styles

On page 186 we look at the value of learning styles. A number of recent studies have concluded that the concept is fairly meaningless because, in reality, everyone uses each style. Before you complain to your teachers that these learning styles are nonsense, there actually is some value in the concept. Simply using a variety of different styles when teaching is more exciting (and less boring) than the old 'chalk and talk' method, and that might make multi-method lessons more effective.

Understanding different styles could also help you to reflect on the fact that you can use different media when you learn – such as colourful mindmaps, podcasts or acting out certain concepts to create a 'muscle memory'.

Another idea for research

A recent review of research by Pashler *et al.* (2009) (see page 187) described the ideal piece of research that could be conducted to demonstrate whether learning styles mattered. First, you would identify whether individuals were visual, auditory or kinaesthetic learners. Then you would give each individual a task to do but randomly assign them to the visual, auditory or kinaesthetic version. For example, you could ask all students to learn about a particular study or concept and some students would do this visually (V group), some do it auditorily (A) and some do it kinaesthetically (K). Participants should be randomly assigned to the V, A or K group. If learning styles do matter, we would expect the visual learners to do better in the V group than if they were in the A or K group.

> WWW

Online tests

If you haven't got a VAK test in school, try:

www.personal.psu.edu/bxb11/LSI/LSI.htm or

www.howtolearn.com/lsinventory_teacher.html

Honey and Mumford's Learning Style Questionnaire (LSQ) tells you whether you are an activist, theorist, reflector or pragmatist. You can find it here:

www.nwlink.com/~donclark/hrd/styles/learn_style_survey.html

Felder and Silverman's Index of Learning Styles (ILS) distinguishes four dimensions: active–reflective, sensing–intuitive, visual–verbal, sequential–global. Visit:

www.engr.ncsu.edu/learningstyles/ilsweb.html

Go to www.learning-styles-online.com/inventory – it will classify you as: visual–spatial, aural–auditory, verbal–linguistic, physical–bodily–kinesthetic, logical–mathematical, social–interpersonal, and solitary–intrapersonal.

Remember that websites do come and go, so don't be disappointed if these links turn out to be non-existent – they were working at the time of writing.

Embedded figures test (EFT)

The EFT is used to assess field dependence – the extent to which a learner is dependent on the context in which a problem is presented. There is evidence that field-dependent learners could benefit from being taught by field-independent teachers. There is also evidence of gender and cultural differences in field dependence (see page 186).

You could test field dependence/ independence using the figures on the right. These are not from the EFT (which is often used but not available for free). Ask each participant to find the figure in the left-hand column in one of the more complex designs on the right. You could time how long it takes them; the shorter the time taken the more field independent they are.

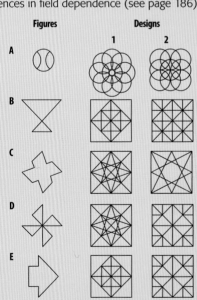

Answers:
Figure A is found in Design 1, B is in 1, C is in 2, D is in 2 and E is in 1.
From www.brainwaves.com/Puzzles_Tests.html

BEHAVIOURIST LEARNING THEORY APPLIED TO EDUCATION

Behaviourists believe that all of our behaviour can be explained in terms of classical and operant conditioning, concepts first introduced to you in your AS course. Behaviourists believe that we acquire or learn new responses through one of these two processes. Education in the first half of the 20th century was based on behaviourist principles – students were rewarded for doing well and punished if they didn't learn. Educationalists assumed that the learning process was a passive one, where teachers taught and students took in the knowledge. In some ways these practices continue despite large changes in educational philosophy.

What is learning?

Learning refers to all relatively permanent changes in what you know as well as acquiring new skills, habits, beliefs and attitudes – brought about through experience rather than maturation, drugs, fatigue, injury or disease.

Classical conditioning

The key principles New behaviours are acquired through *association*.

- Before conditioning an **unconditioned stimulus** (**UCS**) produces an **unconditioned response** (**UCR**), for example someone shouting at you elicits a fear response.
- During conditioning a **neutral stimulus** (**NS**) occurs at the same time as the UCS and therefore acquires its properties, for example in maths lessons (a neutral stimulus) a teacher shouts at you.
- After conditioning the NS is now a **conditioned stimulus** (**CS**) which produces a **conditioned response** (**CR**). In our example just thinking about maths makes you fearful.

Examples of classical conditioning in education The main importance of classical conditioning in the context of education is that students acquire positive or negative emotional associations which either enhance or discourage their readiness to learn. In the example above (and shown again on the right) a student may have acquired a conditioned fear of maths because of a bad experience with a teacher who shouted a lot, or a conditioned fear of maths might develop because maths lessons become associated with failure. In severe cases some children acquire school **phobias** and refuse to attend school at all.

Behaviourism and biology

Learning theory is a behaviourist explanation for behaviour, yet biology (the antithesis of behaviourism) can be used to understand the processes underlying learning. What is happening when you learn something? The **neurons** in your brain are forming new connections – but this doesn't happen all at once. Each time you go over something the connections become stronger and easier to access. This might explain the observation by Ebbinghaus (1885) that the first time you try to learn something it often seems to be forgotten but if you try to learn the same thing a week later it appears easier.

▼ *Acquiring a maths phobia*

UCS produces UCR
Teacher shouting produces anxiety
NS
Maths lessons
NS paired with UCS
Maths lessons + teacher shouting
CS now produces CR
Maths lessons create anxiety

Operant conditioning

The key principles New behaviours are learned through **reinforcement**. At any time an organism *operates* on the environment, resulting in positive consequences (rewards) or negative consequences (**punishments**).

Rewards (**reinforcers**) increase the probability that a behaviour will be repeated, punishers decrease the probability. Reinforcers can be *negative* (escape from an unpleasant situation) or *positive* (something pleasant).

Shaping explains how specific behaviours are learned – by reinforcing successively closer approximations to a desired performance.

Examples of operant conditioning in education Teachers intuitively reward students for desired behaviours (e.g. putting stars on your work) and punish inappropriate behaviours (e.g. giving a low grade for poor work). These are all conscious behaviours from teachers; there are also unconscious rewards and punishments, such as smiling or frowning or tone of voice.

In the examples given so far we have focused on *positive* reinforcement or *positive* punishment. **Negative reinforcement** also increases the repetition of a behaviour but this time it isn't because you experience something rewarding, but because you can escape from something unpleasant, which results in relief. For example, your teacher might get angry with you every time you hand in your work late – when you do manage to hand it in on time and your teacher isn't angry this is a relief and therefore reinforces that behaviour (handing in work on time). This is negative reinforcement. **Negative punishment** is the removal of something, for example detention is the removal of your normal privilege of going home on time.

Vicarious reinforcement refers to indirect reinforcement. We learn by watching someone else and modelling their behaviour if their behaviour was rewarded. This is the essence of **social learning theory**. Modelling can provide a faster, more efficient means for teaching a new behaviour rather than gradual shaping through reinforcement. One example might be teaching students how to produce well structured essays by showing them some good examples.

Self-efficacy, your belief in your own competence, is an important aspect of observational learning. The learner must believe that they are capable of doing the task to be modelled, otherwise they will not attempt to reproduce it. In other words, they might have learned the new behaviour but will not produce it unless they have a good sense of self-efficacy.

Reinforcement schedules

Rewards (reinforcements) can be delivered consistently or inconsistently, for example you could get a gold star every time you produce an excellent answer or just sometimes when you do excellent work. It appears that, in the early stages of learning, consistent reinforcement is most effective, but in the long term intermittent reinforcement leads to more durable learning. This was the conclusion drawn by Kollins *et al.* (1997) in a meta-analysis of 25 studies that looked at the effects of reinforcement schedules on human behaviour. In fact Bandura and Walters (1963) suggested that the attention-seeking behaviours of young children are so persistent precisely because they are rewarded intermittently.

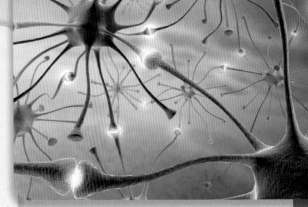

▲ *This is what learning looks like in the brain (see facing page for an explanation of behaviourism and biology).*

EVALUATION

Classical conditioning

How can teachers benefit? LeFrançois (2000) suggests that the implications from classical conditioning are that teachers should try, as far as possible, to maximise pleasant stimuli in their classrooms (e.g. attractive posters, pleasant smells, laughing during lessons) and minimise unpleasant unconditioned stimuli (e.g. shouting). He suggests teachers should also be aware of what is being paired with what in their classrooms, for example shouting paired with class discussions, and avoid such pairings.

Reducing unpleasant associations Another useful application of classical conditioning is **systematic desensitisation**, which you may have studied in your AS year as a method of treating phobias. It is a form of **counterconditioning** where a person is taught to associate something *pleasant* with the feared object, thus unlearning the phobia. This method could be used as a way to eliminate, for example a maths phobia.

Operant conditioning

Shaping in the classroom The technique of shaping has been usefully applied to a number of different teaching strategies. One of them is a form of **behaviour modification treatment** called **applied behaviour analysis** which is used with **autistic** children. This is described later in this chapter (see page 190).

Another application of shaping is *programmed instruction*, a computer or book-based instructional device. Each time you get an answer correct you are rewarded; each time you make an incorrect response you are directed to another question or some advice to enhance your understanding. Such programmes may include diagnostics and a record of progress.

Effectiveness of rewards We assume that being rewarded encourages desirable behaviours but there is evidence against this. One example relates to the distinction made between external and internal motivations. Lepper *et al.* (1973) showed that rewards may destroy **intrinsic motivations**. In this study nursery children were asked to draw some nice pictures. Some were told they would get a reward if their pictures were good. At the end all the children actually received a reward. When the children were observed a few days later, those children who had been promised a reward spent half as much time drawing as the other children, suggesting that their intrinsic motivation had been destroyed by the expectation of extrinsic rewards.

Another area of research has looked at how rewards create a form of **learned helplessness**. Dweck (1975) conducted a study looking at the effect of feedback on the performance of school students. In one group the students were persistently told that the reason they hadn't done well in their school work was because they were lazy and should try harder, whereas students in the other group were always praised, for example they were told 'Your work is very good, but you might just include a bit more evaluation'. At the end of the month the second group showed low task persistence on a difficult test – they were much more ready to give up when they didn't do well, whereas the first group met poor performance by increasing their efforts. This shows that rewards don't always lead to better performance.

Effectiveness of punishment Many people are aware of the fact that punishment often doesn't work and there is evidence to support this. For example, Hickmon (2008) found that children performed worse academically in US schools which still used corporal punishment than in schools which didn't use corporal punishment.

There are a number of reasons why punishment doesn't work. For example, punishment informs the recipient that what they have done is undesirable but often doesn't provide information about what behaviour is preferable. Punishment also may result in avoidance, for instance a child who is regularly punished at school may just avoid going to school. Punishment may also ultimately be rewarding (see 'Behaviour management' at top of page). Therefore, overall, it may be preferable to focus on reinforcing desirable behaviour.

Behaviour management

Behaviour management is a form of operant conditioning; it refers to the use of rewards and punishment to control pupils' undesirable behaviour. Such undesirable behaviours affect the learning process because unruly students prevent learning taking place in the classroom, both for themselves and their classmates.

The most obvious solution is to punish offenders, but as we have shown on the left punishment is not always effective and may in fact be counterproductive.

A further issue is that punishment may actually be rewarding. For example, a difficult pupil is given extra attention when a teacher is angry (even though it is negative) and this attention could encourage the student to behave in the same way again. The key is to reward desirable behaviours only.

Ethical issues

Behaviour management and behaviour modification raise ethical issues because they are essentially methods of engineering other people's behaviour. The question is, who decides which behaviours are desirable or not desirable?

CAN YOU...? (No. 9.1)

1... Select **three or more** key points for both types of conditioning described on this spread.

2... For each key point write **three or four** sentences explaining the concept.

3... Identify about **ten** points of evaluation (these can be positive or negative).

4... Elaborate each point (see page 9).

5... Use all of this material to write an answer to the following exam question: *Critically consider behaviourist learning theory applied to education including classical and operant conditioning.* As good practice you might also write 'building block' essays about the two different kinds of conditioning. Your answers should contain about 300 words of description and 500 words of evaluation.

Don't forget to read the essay-writing guidance on pages 8–9. And don't forget that you can use material from other spreads, such as material on behaviour modification techniques discussed on page 190. However, if you do introduce such material you must ensure that you make it relevant.

COGNITIVE DEVELOPMENTAL THEORIES

ENVIRONMENTAL INFLUENCES

GENETIC INFLUENCES

Cognitive development refers to how your thinking develops as you get older. Jean Piaget and Lev Vygotsky's theories are discussed on pages 132–133. You don't need to know these theories – you just need to apply them to education – but it may enhance your understanding to read about them.

The cognitive developmental approach differs from the **behaviourist** approach (covered on the previous spread) in two main ways. First, their focus is on what is going on inside your head; behaviourists are not interested in mental activity. Second, cognitive developmental theories advocate an active approach to education, emphasising the necessity for the learner to be actively involved, in contrast with the behaviourist approach which sees the learner as a passive recipient of knowledge and conditioning.

▲ *Vygotsky suggested that collaborative learning and working with more knowledgeable others (MKOs) enables students to move through their ZPD whereas, in Piaget's view, learning should be a more independent process and personal discovery is vital for complete understanding.*

APPLYING PIAGET'S THEORY TO EDUCATION

Readiness According to Piaget each stage of cognitive development appears through the natural process of ageing. Therefore you cannot teach a child to perform certain activities before they are biologically 'ready'; for example trying to teach a **pre-operational** child to perform abstract mathematical calculations will be difficult if not impossible because they lack the ability to think symbolically. For real learning to take place, activities should be at the appropriate level for a child's age. If a child is not mature enough, they may acquire skills superficially but in order to understand truly and become competent it is important to wait until they are ready.

Stages of development The concept of readiness means that educational programmes should be designed along the lines of Piaget's stages of development. For example, children in the **concrete operational stage** should be given concrete materials to manipulate (e.g. an abacus to develop numerical skills).

Motivation to learn Piaget suggested that cognitive growth comes from the desire to resolve the disequilibrium caused by cognitive conflict. A teacher's task is to create an environment where the learner is challenged to adapt current **schemas** to cope with new information. The teacher's role is not to impart knowledge but to ask questions and in this way a child's knowledge develops through **discovery learning**.

Logical thinking Piaget argued that logical thinking needs to be taught, therefore it is important to have maths and science subjects on the curriculum to facilitate cognitive development.

APPLYING VYGOTSKY'S THEORY TO EDUCATION

Collaborative learning refers to a method of learning in which students at various performance levels work together in small groups toward a common goal. Group members are responsible for one another's learning as well as their own, so the success of one student helps other students to be successful. When people work collaboratively, they bring their own perspectives to the activity, and so are better able to generate a solution through shared understanding.

The more knowledgeable other (MKO) refers to someone who has a better understanding, with respect to a particular task or concept, than the learner. Although the MKO is often a teacher or older adult, this is not necessarily the case. A child's peers may be the individuals with more knowledge or experience, and therefore may act as the MKOs (**peer tutoring**).

The ZPD and the motivation to learn A learner is motivated to move through their **zone of proximal development** (ZPD) by MKOs. Tutoring consists of encouraging a learner to tackle increasingly difficult tasks, the tutor takes control when necessary and handing over responsibility to the learner whenever they are ready. Through these supportive interactions, learners are guided through the development of their cognitive abilities – a process described as **scaffolding** (a term coined by Bruner, see below).

BRUNER'S PROCESS OF EDUCATION

Bruner's book *The Process of Education* (1960) had a profound effect on classroom practice in the US and beyond. The book triggered the move away from the passive approach of the time towards a more active approach which he also called 'discovery learning'.

Scaffolding is a 'process that enables a … novice to solve a problem, carry out a task, or achieve a goal which would be beyond his unassisted efforts' (Wood *et al.,* 1976). The expert or tutor creates a 'scaffold' (i.e. temporary support) which is gradually withdrawn as the child is more able to work independently.

Spiral curriculum Educators steer away from teaching 'difficult' concepts to young children, but Bruner believed this was mistaken. He argued that the solution is to start early and then repeatedly revisit such concepts. Children may not fully understand or remember initial experiences but will take in some of the information and this acts as a basis for later learning.

Modes of thinking A teacher's task is to explain the world in a way that is appropriate to the child's mode of thinking, such as working *enactively* (action based) with very young children. For example, one national health and body awareness programme starts by encouraging very young children to eat healthy foods and involve them in food preparation, all enactive (Tonkin *et al.,* 2008). Educators have to 'translate' topics into appropriate modes of thinking (*iconic/visual* and *symbolic* for older children) and thus are creating a **spiral curriculum**.

Motivation to learn Bruner believed that the best stimulus for learning lies in the material to be learned, thus making the learning active rather than passive. The growing child should be presented with problems that tempt him into the next stages of development. Bruner also believed that academic subjects have intrinsic attraction. Thus, educators do not need to present topics in real-life settings of children's daily experience to make them more interesting – they are intrinsically interesting.

EVALUATION

Readiness The notion of readiness implies that practice on a task should *not* lead to improved performance until a child is sufficiently mature. There is support for and against this. Bryant and Trabasso (1971) showed that pre-operational children could be trained to solve certain logical tasks. They argued that children's failure was due to memory restrictions rather than a lack of operational (logical) thinking. When pre-operational children practised solving simple problems they could cope with more complex tasks if they gradually built up to them, showing that practice rather than readiness mattered.

In contrast, Danner and Day (1977) found that practice made no difference. Students aged 10 and 13 were tutored on three **formal operational** tasks and showed no improvement, whereas the performance of 17-year-olds was improved, as we would expect, because they should be sufficiently mature. However, even when practice does improve performance this doesn't mean the child has understood the principles of the operation – they may be just repeating certain actions and will not be able to transfer this knowledge to a novel situation.

Limitations Sylva (1987) suggests that the criticisms of Piaget's theory (see page 120) undermine its educational application. Other critics feel that Piagetian discovery activities are often at the expense of content knowledge and may lead to backwardness in reading and writing because students spend too little time practising these skills (Modgil *et al.,* 1983). Furthermore, the Piagetian view may be culture biased. It suggests that the child is the sole agent of his learning which is an **individualist** approach.

EVALUATION

Collaborative learning Research has found support for the value of collaborative learning. For example, Gokhale (1995) found that students who participated in collaborative learning subsequently performed better on an individual critical-thinking test than students who studied individually.

Many studies have shown that peer tutoring leads to improvements in both tutees' and peer tutors' academic and social development (e.g. Cohen *et al.,* 1982). However, a consistent finding is that it is most effective for peer tutors (Cloward, 1967), which makes sense because the best way to understand something better is to teach it. One note of caution with these studies is that it is often the case that experimental groups receive peer tutoring in *addition* to normal lessons, and having extra lessons could be the reason for greater success (Slavin, 1991).

Limitations Vygotsky's approach may be more appropriate in **collectivist** settings because true sharing is the basis of such cultures. This is not to say that group work is not possible in individualist societies but in settings where children are encouraged to be more competitive and self-reliant, group work may be less effective. For example, Stigler and Perry (1990) compared American and Asian schools and found in the latter that maths was more effectively taught by group work than in individualist American schools.

EVALUATION

Scaffolding is a tricky strategy to test as it happens over a period of many years, which makes it difficult to control **extraneous variables** and decide on appropriate outcome measures, but there is some research support. For example, Wood and Middleton (1975) observed mothers helping their three–four-year-old children assembling a 3D pyramid puzzle, a task that was beyond the children's current abilities. They found a **positive correlation** between children's ability to master the task and the quality of scaffolding provided – a high-quality 'scaffolder' responds to the child's failure by providing *more* explicit instructions (e.g. identifying what particular piece needs to be moved) and responds to success by providing less explicit instructions (e.g. offering general practise for the strategy that has just been used).

The spiral curriculum The value of the spiral curriculum is demonstrated by the fact that it is widely used in all areas of education from nursery schools (as mentioned on the left) to GP training (e.g. Harden and Stamper, 1999).

Assessing teaching methods

It is difficult to assess outcomes partly because learning is so complex. It is also difficult to select suitable outcome measures (i.e. ways of measuring whether learning has taken place) because the goals of one teaching method are different to the goals of another method and therefore each would select different outcome measures. Furthermore two teachers may ostensibly be using the same method but there may be significant differences in what they do in practice.

GENERAL EVALUATION

Discovery learning All three approaches emphasise the active role of the learner and have had a major influence on education. For example, the British *Plowden Report* (1967) drew extensively on Piaget's theory and led to major changes in primary school education in the UK. This active approach is by no means new. The psychologist John Dewey advocated child-centred education in the 1920s as did the Greek philosopher Plato in the 4th century BC. Walkerdine (1984) suggests that theories of cognitive development are used simply to provide 'after the fact' justifications rather than being the original driving force.

Comparison with 'traditional' methods A classic study that compared the more formal, teacher-oriented approach with active learning methods (Bennett, 1976) found that, in general, children taught via formal (more passive) methods were better at reading, maths and English. However the best results of all were produced by *some* of the teachers who used more informal, active and child-centred methods. The general lack of success for active learning may be due to the fact that teachers in formal classrooms spend more time on the core topics and that is why children do better. A further reason could be that active learning requires greater sensitivity and experience from teachers in knowing how and when to guide pupils. Therefore it is not the method but the application of it that is the problem.

Emotion All three theories are mainly concerned with the development of problem-solving abilities and ignore the importance emotional intelligence. Projects such as SEAL (social and emotional aspects of learning) have been developed in English schools to redress the balance.

'Each time one prematurely teaches a child something he could have discovered for himself, that child is kept from inventing it and consequently from understanding it completely'. (Piaget, 1970)

'What the child is able to do in collaboration today he will be able to do independently tomorrow'. (Vygotsky, 1987)

CAN YOU...? No. 9.2

1... Three applications are described on this spread. For each of them select at least **two** key concepts.

2... For each key concept write **three or four** sentences explaining the concept.

3... Identify about **ten** points of evaluation (these can be positive or negative).

4... Elaborate each point (see page 9).

5... Use all of this material to write an answer to the following exam question: *Describe and evaluate cognitive developmental theories applied to education*. You could also prepare 'building block' essays on each of the theories. Your answers should contain about 300 words of description and 500 words of evaluation.

ENVIRONMENTAL INFLUENCES

GENETIC INFLUENCES

Learning styles are concerned with how learners learn. The previous two spreads were focused on how teachers organise the learning environment and we are now going to focus on education from the learner's viewpoint.

A person's learning style refers to the relatively consistent methods that they use on learning tasks. On page 181 we saw that this could be visual or kinaesthetic, sensing or intuitive and so on. Such styles might be **innate** or they might be learned through **reinforcement** from previous successes and failures. There is a huge number of learning style theories as well as tests to assess these. A number of people have tried to produce overarching theories to unify the different styles in some way. On this spread we will look at two of these – Curry's *onion model* and Grasha's *six learning styles*.

Individual differences

The whole 'learning style' approach focuses on individual differences, i.e. in what way we are all different in our preferred styles of learning. However, there are two key individual differences that interact with learning style: gender and culture.

Gender differences

Severiens and ten Darn (1994) conducted a **meta-analysis** of 22 studies and concluded that there were some key gender differences in learning style. For example they found that female students were more dependent on teachers and had a greater fear of failure, but were also more highly motivated to learn in comparison with male students.

Other research has also found that males tend more towards field independence (as measured by the *embedded figures test*, see page 181) (Huss and Kayson, 1985). However, more recent studies (e.g. Riding and Grimley, 2002) have found that these gender differences in cognitive style no longer exist or are at least much diminished. This may be due to reduced gender differences and suggests that the origins of cognitive style are cultural and thus modifiable.

Cultural differences

Asian students are often **stereotyped** as rote learners, yet a study by Sadler-Smith and Tsang (1998) found that British students showed greater reliance on memorisation than students from Hong Kong. Other research looking at Filipino and Nepalese students found no support for the stereotype (Watkins *et al.*, 1991).

However, there are important issues related to any **cross-cultural research**. Assessments of learning style rely on Western tests which might not be applicable to non-Western students (an example of an **imposed etic**), so any findings should be treated with caution.

INTEGRATIVE MODELS OF LEARNING STYLES

Curry's onion model

People differ in terms of **cognitive style**, personality traits (e.g. **field dependence**) and the way they approach learning tasks (e.g. preference for collaborative work). Curry's onion model aims to combine these various aspects of individual difference in one model. Lynn Curry (1983) developed the metaphor of layers of an onion to provide a framework for understanding how the different *kinds* of learning style relate to each other. She looked at nine of the major learning style tests and what they measured. She then categorised the styles identified into three broad levels, or layers:

- Innermost layer = *cognitive personality style* (or just **'cognitive style'**) a student's underlying approach to thinking as measured by the *Myers–Briggs Type Indicator* (MBTI) or *embedded figures test* (EFT) of field dependence. Curry suggested this layer was the least changeable and had the strongest effect on learning style.
- Middle layer = *information processing style*. This concerns the various strategies a student uses to process information, such as a preference for concrete learning, for example, which is tested by Kolb's *Learning Style Inventory* (LSI).
- Outermost layer = *instructional preferences*, e.g. the extent to which a learner prefers working at their own pace versus having a teacher set the pace, or how much structure the learner prefers. The student has little control at this level.

Each of these layers contributes to each person's overall unique learning style.

▲ *Don't make the mistake of calling this Onion's curry model – we know because we made that mistake! It's an onion model because it consists of layers.*

Grasha's six learning styles

Anthony Grasha (1996) was interested in teaching styles and learning styles. In his earliest research he interviewed about 60 students on their reactions to traditional classroom procedures and identified a group of negative reactions: avoidant, competitive and dependent. He later termed these reactions 'styles' and suggested that for each negative reaction there was an opposite positive reaction: participative, **collaborative** and independent. Thus there are six learning styles (see table on the left) and he suggested that most learners possess all of these learning styles to a greater or lesser extent.

The *Grasha–Riechmann Student Learning Style Scale* (GRSLSS) has been developed to test these six styles and aims to optimise the learning environment for all students by providing insight for teachers and students about their style preferences. It focuses on student attitudes towards learning, classroom activities, and the influence of teachers and peers.

▼ *Grasha's six learning styles*

Style	Typical behaviours associated with style
Avoidant	Organises work poorly, takes little responsibility for learning, often absent.
Participative	Willing to accept responsibility for self-learning, interested in work, eager.
Competitive	Motivated by desire to be best, likes to get recognition for academic achievement.
Collaborative	Enjoys working harmoniously with peers, prefers small group discussions and projects.
Dependent	Becomes frustrated when facing new challenges, prefers to be told what to do.
Independent	Prefers to work alone and requires little direction.

Learning style vs learning strategy vs cognitive style

All three of the above terms are used somewhat imprecisely and sometimes used to mean the same thing so it may be helpful to clarify them. Most people use *learning style* as an umbrella term which includes *cognitive style* (or cognitive personality style). Cognitive style refers to a person's characteristic way of thinking, perceiving, problem solving, etc., whereas *learning style* is the application of *cognitive style* to the learning situation. **Learning strategy** differs from learning style; it is something that changes from one situation to another (i.e. you use a different strategy when dealing with different kinds of task), whereas *learning style* is relatively stable across situations.

Psychometrics

'Psychometrics' refers to the measurement ('metric') of psychological traits. The study of 'learning styles' relies very much on the use of such measurements – psychological tests (or 'inventories') to assess learning style. As with any questionnaire, we are concerned (and should check) that such instruments are both valid and reliable (see page 19).

There are two special issues worth considering. First, according to Curry's model we would expect low test–retest scores on certain measures because they are assessing unstable traits. Thus low reliability scores may not reflect problems with the test.

Second, Jarvis (2005) argues that a test that is low in validity/reliability can still be used as an important aid to personal understanding of what strategies do or do not work, e.g. discovering whether you are a visualiser or verbaliser and considering the potential implications for studying.

EVALUATION

Curry's onion model

Extension of the original model Curry (1987) studied further learning style tests (21 in total), and extended her onion metaphor to include a fourth layer called 'social interaction'. This layer comes between the middle and outermost layer and relates to the extent to which people enjoy social interaction as a part of learning (e.g. **collaborative group work**).

Research support The model predicts that each learning style test within the same layer should assess the same thing. Ingham (1989) did find that significant positive **correlations** among styles within each layer were higher than across layers.

The model also predicts that when individuals are retested on traits in the innermost layers there should be less change than when **test–retests** relate to the outer layers. This was confirmed by Sewall (1986) who found the lowest change (highest correlations) for MBTI scales (cognitive personality layer) and most change (lowest correlations) for the *Canfield Scales* (instructional preference layer).

Strengths and weaknesses Curry's work pioneered the effort to bring together all the different learning styles identified by other research, but as yet there is little actual **empirical** evidence to test the predictions of the model (Zhang and Sternberg, 2009).

Grasha's six learning styles

Research evidence In various studies Grasha (1996) has used the GRSLSS to look at the relationship between learning style and other individual differences. He has found that female learners tend to score higher on collaborative style, that students over 25 score higher on independent and participant learning, and that students who achieve lower grades tend (not surprisingly) to have avoidant styles. He has not found any association between individual styles and students' academic major (e.g. maths or languages).

Strengths The strength of this approach is that the scale can be used to assess student preferences before and after certain learning experiences, for example to determine whether collaborative group work leads to more or less competitiveness. Such feedback can help a teacher decide what strategies work best.

The GRSLSS is popular because it is reliable and user friendly. Riechmann and Grasha (1974) reported test–retest reliabilities of about .80. It is also one of the few tests designed specifically for college/university students.

An evaluation of the learning style approach

The importance of the concept of learning styles lies in the educational benefits it might produce. It has been assumed that teaching and learning would be more effective if teaching matched the differing individual needs of the learner. Indeed some research supports this, for example Joyce and Hudson (1968) found when the learning style of medical students matched the teaching style of his or her instructor higher examination results were achieved.

However, in general there has been little evidence that compatible learning and teaching styles enhance learning. A recent review by Pashler *et al.* (2009), on behalf of the *Association for Psychological Science*, concluded that very few rigorous studies have been conducted to test the basic premise of the learning styles approach. They suggest that the obvious test would be to categorise a set of students into specific styles (e.g. visual learners, verbal learners, etc.) and then randomly assign them to groups receiving the different methods (e.g. give verbal instruction for visual learners). If the learning style hypothesis is correct we would expect to find that those learners taught in a way that matches their learning style should do better. Pashler *et al.* note that such research has not yet been conducted.

Other critics have focused on different issues. For example, Coffield *et al.* (2004) identified 71 different theories of learning style, finding very little empirical support for any of them. In fact, just the sheer range of different styles makes the concept unworkable – though it could be argued that the models described on the facing page have attempted to provide a framework.

The prominent UK scientist Susan Greenfield (2007) questioned the neuroscientific base for learning styles and concluded that this approach was basically 'nonsense'.

CAN YOU...? No. 9.3

1... On this spread we have discussed several ways in which learning styles differ from individual to individual: gender differences, cultural differences, Curry's onion model and Grasha's learning styles. For each of these identify **two or more** key points.

2... Write about 50–100 words describing each of these key points.

3... Identify about **ten** points of evaluation (these can be positive or negative).

4... Elaborate each point (see page 9).

5... Use all of this material to write an answer to the following exam question: *Discuss individual differences in learning styles.* Your answer should contain about 300 words of description and 500 words of evaluation.

Don't forget that you can use material from other spreads. For example, the concept of multiple intelligence has been associated with different learning styles (see page 120). However, if you do introduce this you must ensure that you make it relevant.

MOTIVATING FACTORS IN THE CLASSROOM

ENVIRONMENTAL INFLUENCES

DETERMINISM

The topic of motivation is of great interest to psychologists because it is probably one of the key aspects of individual differences in behaviour – why are some people driven to succeed at sport or school or being the best at anything, whereas others aren't? In education these questions are particularly important because there are many disaffected students who simply have no motivation – we want to understand this so we can do something about it.

Motivation refers to the sum of all the influences that make us choose to behave in certain ways. There are **extrinsic motives** – things outside us that motivate us, such as rewards. And there are **intrinsic motives** – those that come from within. On page 183 we looked at the research by Lepper *et al.* which suggests that extrinsic motives may destroy intrinsic motives. On this spread we are focusing on intrinsic motives.

ATTRIBUTION THEORY

Attribution theory was a required element of your AS course. Attribution is the process of explaining the causes of behaviour – other people's behaviour and your own behaviour. As you should remember, people do this by making **internal** or **external attributions**.

How does this apply to motivation? Weiner (1992) pointed out that every time learners succeed or fail on a task they attribute this success or failure to a cause. The term for this process is **causal inference**. Often we do not have sufficient information to make completely logical causal inferences, but instead rely on general beliefs about the situation and ourselves. Our attributions of success and failure can have a profound effect on motivation to tackle future tasks.

Factors that affect attributions Weiner identified three dimensions that determine the attributions made by learners regarding success and failure.

- **Locus of control** (LoC) refers to the extent to which the individual believes they can control events. (This is another concept you met at AS level in the core study by Langer and Rodin, 1976.) People with an internal LoC believe they can alter events and thus tend to be more motivated to tackle them positively.

- *Stability.* Causes of success and failure may be stable, i.e. they remain constant across situations (e.g. effort, task difficulty), or they may be unstable, i.e. they change from one situation to another (e.g. luck, mood).

- *Controllability* refers to how much control we think we have. For example, you can control the effort you put into revising but cannot control how easy or difficult an exam paper will be.

How does this apply to education? The box on the right shows some examples of how the three factors may be combined to produce attributions. These attributions then affect subsequent motivation.

Some examples of causal inferences

If you did well on an exam you might make one of the following attributions to explain your success:

…because I always work hard (internal LoC, stable, controllable)

…because it was an easy exam (external LoC, unstable, uncontrollable)

…because I have a great teacher who always inspires me to work hard (external LoC, stable, controllable)

Think of some further examples yourself.

MASLOW'S HIERARCHY OF NEEDS

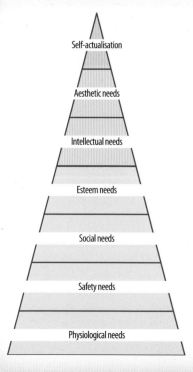

Maslow (1954) developed a theory of human motivation that aimed to explain all human needs and place them in a hierarchy representing the order of priority in which people seek to satisfy them. He made a fundamental distinction between D-needs (*deficiency* needs), which result from requirements for food, rest, safety, etc. and B-needs (*being* needs), which derive from our drive to fulfil our potential. We cannot strive towards our B-needs until our D-needs have been met. Maslow's hierarchy of needs is shown on the left.

The idea behind the model is that we ascend the hierarchy, satisfying each motive in turn. Our first priority is to satisfy our *physiological needs* such for as food and warmth. Only when these needs have been satisfied do we seek out safety. Once satisfied of our safety, we turn to *social needs*, i.e. to belong to a group and relate to others. *Esteem needs* then become paramount, being satisfied by achievement, competence and recognition. Once this has been achieved our focus will shift to satisfying our *intellectual needs*, including understanding and knowledge. Next are *aesthetic needs*, reflecting the need for beauty, order and balance. The final human need identified by Maslow is for **self-actualisation**, i.e. to find personal fulfilment and achieve one's potential.

How does this apply to education? The major application of Maslow's ideas has been in helping educators appreciate the sheer range of factors affecting the motivation of the learner. This can be useful in designing lessons with the needs of all learners in mind – until learners feel safe and part of a group they will not have satisfied more basic needs and therefore cannot be expected to focus on higher intellectual interests (Snowman and Biehler, 2000).

In addition, Maslow has focused our attention on the close relationship between intellectual motivation and our need for **self-esteem**. If self-esteem is a more basic need than intellectual interest, it follows logically that teachers have an opportunity to stimulate the motivation to learn by first of all boosting self-esteem.

Approaches

Attribution theory is an example of the cognitive approach because it emphasises the role of thinking, and in particular maladaptive thinking, on behaviour.

Maslow's theory is an example of the humanistic approach. In the first half of the 20th century the dominant approaches in psychology were behaviourism and psychoanalysis, both of which are reductionist and determinist. During the 1950s some psychologists, including Abraham Maslow, believed that a third 'force' was needed which would portray individuals as being in control of their own lives rather than being controlled by external forces, and which would be focused on a more subjective viewpoint (on how the experience feels for the individual).

EVALUATION

Learner's attributions If teachers can identify learners who make unhelpful attributions of their successes and failures, and work with them to alter these to more positive attributions, they should in principle be able to improve their students' motivation. Students who get poor grades tend to attribute their success to forces outside their control, for example 'I passed because I was lucky'. This leads to a kind of **learned helplessness** ('Why bother because my efforts don't matter') which in turn reduces their motivation. The road to improvement lies in learning to attribute both success and failure to one's own efforts, as in Dweck's concept of *mastery-oriented learning* (see right). Such methods have been formalised in **attribution training** programmes where individuals are taught to become more mastery oriented.

Using attribution training in practice Weiner's theory gives teachers a good basis for understanding how and when to challenge a learner's beliefs. However, it is only helpful for learners to attribute failure to lack of effort *provided* they did not actually make sufficient effort. It is quite possible for learners to make considerable effort and to fall foul of bad luck in exam questions or poor marking, and nothing could be more demotivating than to be told it was a result of lack of effort (Marshall, 1990). In such cases it might be more helpful to agree that the learner was unlucky and focus on the likelihood that next time they will probably have better luck.

Teacher attributions Teachers may be able to alter a learner's attributions but also need to be aware that they are a source of some attributions in the first place. Teachers put across distinct and perhaps unhealthy attributional messages whenever they talk in terms of learners' ability or intelligence. Giving excessive help, expressing surprise at success and offering praise for blatantly easy tasks can all reinforce a message that the learner lacks ability (Good and Brophy, 1991).

Research evidence There is evidence that working with teachers to improve attributional messages is associated with improved educational outcome. In a recent Spanish study Ramirez and Avila (2002) worked on attributions with 50 teachers and 150 children, taken from a mix of primary and secondary schools. Results showed that both teacher and learner attributions were successfully modified and that such modification was associated with reduced teacher **burnout** and improved school results.

EVALUATION

Empirical support Coleman (1961) asked high-school students how they would like to be remembered. More of them rated popularity as important rather than academic success, which fits Maslow's hierarchy – social needs are deficiency needs whereas intellectual needs come later.

Application of the theory Whilst Maslow has been helpful in moulding the way teachers think about learners, the motivational techniques deriving from his work are limited. Nevertheless, while applications may not be specifically derived from his theory, the concepts can be used to explain the success of certain techniques. For example, Bleach and Smith (1998) assessed a project to enhance motivation in English. They found that boys' motivation was reduced because, in order to remain 'cool' and popular, they felt they had to appear not to care about an unpopular topic such as English; social and esteem needs were more important than achievement. Therefore, enhancing social and esteem needs in other ways could motivate students.

Culture bias Maslow's view of people as striving for personal achievement is extremely culture bound, being firmly located in the **individualist** culture of the USA (Engler, 1999). Cross-cultural research by Kitayama and Markus (1992) has shown that, whilst positive feelings in American students were associated with personal achievements, Japanese students (**collectivist**) tended to associate positive feelings with good relations with others.

▲ *David Beckham is a good example of someone who is mastery oriented – he deals with setbacks and criticism by increasing his efforts rather than giving up.*

Mastery-oriented learning

We described research by Carol Dweck (1975) on page 183, discussing the effects of rewards on performance. We can now explain this research in terms of attribution. The group who were given critical feedback (e.g. being told 'you need to make more effort') were being taught to *attribute* their failure to a lack of their own effort, i.e. to make an internal attribution. Later, when given a difficult maths test, they dealt with a challenging situation by increasing their efforts rather than giving up.

Dweck calls this *mastery-oriented learning* as distinct from a *helpless response*. She suggests that mastery oriented people are motivated to master new things and embrace challenges rather than giving up when things are not going well.

CAN YOU...? No. **9.4**

1... Select **four or more** key points for both theories described on this spread.

2... For each key point write **three or four** sentences explaining the concept.

3... Identify about **ten** points of evaluation (these can be positive or negative).

4... Elaborate each point (see page 9).

5... Use all of this material to write an answer to the following exam question: *Critically consider motivating factors in the classroom.* As good practice you might also write 'building block' essays about the two different theories of motivation as applied to education. Your answers should contain about 300 words of description and 500 words of evaluation.

Don't forget to read the essay-writing guidance on pages 8–9.

EXAM TIP

When answering questions about motivating factors in the classroom, ensure that you do not simply describe the theories presented on this page but make your descriptions relevant to education.

SPECIAL EDUCATIONAL NEEDS

The term *special educational needs* (SENs) refers to children who have learning difficulties (or strengths) that make it harder for them to learn or access appropriate education than most children of the same age. Two of the best known and most common SENs are dyslexia and autism, which are considered on this spread.

DYSLEXIA

Dyslexia literally means 'difficulty with words'. Such problems arise despite 'conventional instruction, adequate intelligence and sociocultural opportunity' (Critchley, 1970). There is no single pattern of difficulty that affects all dyslexics – for some dyslexics text may appear to jump around, whereas others have an inability to distinguish between some letters such as b and d, and others have no problems reading but have problems making sense of what they read.

Assessment
Screening tests Non-verbal **intelligence tests** are used to establish that low intelligence is not the cause of the reading problems (see page 116). Perception tests are also used to rule out perceptual abnormalities. There are also reading and writing tests as well as specific tests related to dyslexia, such as tests to assess phonemic segmentation (the ability to break words down into constituent sounds), reading nonsense passages (testing ability to read unfamiliar words) and bead threading (assessing motor skills).

Full diagnostic assessments Screening tests are not 100% accurate, therefore an indication of dyslexia is followed up with a fuller assessment by an **educational psychologist** or specialist assessor.

Categorisation
There are various distinctions made between types of dyslexia. For example, distinguishing between 'pure' dyslexia and dyslexia with a tendency towards other learning difficulties. Another distinction that is made is between visual and auditory dyslexia – difficulty with sounds or difficulty with what the letters look like.

Another way to approach differences is in terms of the cause of dyslexia – *trauma dyslexia* occurs after some kind of brain injury, *primary dyslexia* has a **genetic** basis and tends to be passed on in families, and *secondary* or *developmental dyslexia* is caused during prenatal development and diminishes with age.

Strategies for education
There are many considerations, such as whether small groups or one-to-one teaching is best, whether it is best to teach to strengths and/or give remedial help for weaknesses, and whether to target phonetic skills or other areas of deficit, such as organisational skills.

Structured language programmes, such as the *Bangor Teaching Programme* or *Alpha to Omega Programme*. The 'structured' aspect of such programmes is that the skills taught are cumulative; the student starts with basic skills (sounds) and once these are mastered more complex skills (words) can be taught. The sequence might consist of letters, sound/symbol correspondence, blends (combinations of sounds), regular words, polysyllabic words and syllabic divisions.

Multi-sensory teaching combines the teaching of phonics with sensory modalities, linking visual modalities (tracing letter shapes in sand), auditory modalities (watching one's mouth in the mirror for auditory discrimination), kinaesthetic modalities (walking around large letter shapes) and tactile modalities (feeling letters with eyes shut).

AUTISM

Autism is a condition that is apparent very early in life. People with autism usually have a 'triad of impairment': affecting social interaction (indifference to other people), social communication (e.g. difficulty understanding social gestures) and imagination (e.g. lack of imaginative play). These can combine with challenging behaviour and/or repetitive behaviours.

Assessment
Diagnosis is generally made by a health professional using a checklist such as CHAT (*Checklist for Autism in Toddlers*) which lists behaviours, for example 'Does your child take an interest in other children?', 'Does your child ever pretend, for example, to make a cup of tea?', or 'Does your child use his/her index finger to point?'

A very recent development is the use of **MRI scans** to detect autism. Ecker *et al.* (2010) have identified key differences between the brains of 'normal' individuals and those with autism, and used their 'autism map' to diagnose autism with 90% accuracy.

Categorisation
The term *autistic spectrum disorder* (ASD) is used to refer to the range of associated disorders including autism, as defined above, and **Asperger's syndrome** (where individuals have the characteristics of autism but no significant language deficit; they also have normal intelligence and sometimes have exceptional skills, see autistic savants on page 121). There is also *pervasive developmental disorder not otherwise specified* (PDD-NOS) when children have some but not all of the classic symptoms of autism.

Strategies for education
Applied behaviour analysis (ABA), also called the **Lovaas method**, was developed by Ivar Lovaas (1987). It is a form of **behaviour modification treatment** which uses techniques such as **shaping** and **token economy**. The Lovaas programme identifies a range of target behaviours that are causing difficulties, such as language problems, self-care skills and self-damaging behaviour. These behaviours are then changed through **shaping**. Initially, almost any behaviour is rewarded but gradually rewards are given for behaviours that are closer and closer to the target behaviour. In a 'token economy' autistic people are given tokens for achieving target behaviours. The tokens can be exchanged for rewards such as sweets or special activities.

Communication programmes One of the key areas of difficulty for autistics is communication, which may lead to other behavioural problems. Autistics find visual information easier to process than verbal information so a communication system such as *Makaton* is based on the use of eyes, body, symbols and sometimes words. Thus, Makaton is more than just a sign language and was developed specifically for autistics in the 1970s.

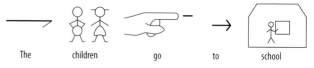

The   children   go   to   school

▲ *An example of Makaton*

Facilitated communication (FC) is also used with autistics. A facilitator supports the autistic's hand or arm while the autistic uses a communicator (a keyboard, or a chart of alphabetic letters and numbers) to spell out words.

Parental involvement Special home programmes have been devised, such as the TEACCH (Treatment and Education of Autistic and related Communication Handicapped Children)model, where parents are advised about their children's particular cognitive strengths and needs, and encouraged to work with their children at home.

To diagnose or not?

The point of diagnosing dyslexia or autism (or any other disorder) is to then be able to provide some successful treatment. So one of the important questions concerns the success of specific treatments (see 'Strategies for education').

However, there are other reasons. A diagnosis also means that people with disorders and their families can better understand why the individual is behaving as they do, and may feel relieved that it can be explained in terms of a recognisable disorder.

But, at the same time, labels (such as dyslexic or autistic) have negative consequences. They may lead the individual (and others) to have reduced expectations about what they will be able to do and such expectations may be self-fulfilling. Labels are also 'sticky', as described by Rosenhan (1973) in your AS core study about insanity.

Gifted children

Giftedness can be seen as another example of SEN and reminds us to emphasise the notion of 'difference' rather than better or worse. The issue of separate schooling also applies to the education of gifted children, but such separation could lead to difficulties later in life because of social isolation. Another possibility is acceleration, where gifted children move up through the school more rapidly, though this too may have a negative effect on social relationships because such children are more immature than their classmates. The final strategy is enrichment – offering gifted children special activities.

EVALUATION

Dyslexia

Research evidence Dyslexia is not something that can be cured but improvement is possible with the use of specialist programmes. Research suggests such programmes can be successful. For example, Scammacca *et al.* (2007) conducted a **meta-analysis** of 31 studies that assessed the effectiveness of reading interventions and found a highly significant effect from a range of programmes.

An interesting study compared success rates in poor readers who either had special help with reading or counselling or both. Those who received only counselling were the ones who improved most, which suggests that low **self-esteem** might be a barrier to success (Lawrence, 1971).

Individual differences One of the difficulties in evaluating educational strategies for dyslexia is that there is such a wide range of different kinds of dyslexia that any failure may be due to a mismatch between strategy and individual difference. What works for one child doesn't always work for another child because of unique disabilities.

The myth of dyslexia Elliott (2005) argued that dyslexia is no different from just having difficulty reading. He points out, for example, that many of the characteristics claimed to cause reading difficulties (such as clumsiness and letter reversals) are found in many people who can read. Therefore the signs used to identify dyslexia may actually have nothing to do with the individual's reading difficulties.

Autism

Mainstream or specialist education? One of the questions about educational strategies for autistic children is whether they will succeed better if educated in mainstream schools or not. Since autistic children have difficulties in social situations they might be expected to fare better at specialist schools. However learning to share experiences with others is an important part of social development and this may only be possible in mainstream education when mixing with socially adept children.

Applied behaviour analysis Behavioural techniques may not provide cures; once rewards are withdrawn, behaviours could relapse. The method relies on intensive interaction (Lovaas recommended 40 hours a week) which means high costs. However, there is considerable evidence of the success of the technique, even with limited hours. For example, Anderson *et al.* (1987) found that even an average of 20 hours a week of one-to-one support over a period of a year brought about significant improvement in cognitive functioning in half the sample of children treated.

However, the research evidence has been criticised because of selective sampling (some autistic children were rejected as unsuitable) and also because the studies tend to be conducted by supporters of the technique and, therefore, lack objectivity.

Communication programmes Various problems have been identified with the use of *Makaton*. One difficulty is that it is not used consistently from group to group which means that very few people outside a specific group of users can actually understand what a person is trying to communicate. It is also often taught as a last ditch method so may be doomed to failure because of negative expectations (Jordan, 1985).

There have been some strong claims for *facilitated communication*. For example, Crossley and Remington-Gurley (1992) suggest that many users can subsequently produce language of great complexity. However, Howlin (1997) reviewed 45 controlled trials and found independent communication in only 6% and, in more than 90% of cases, responses were found to be unwittingly influenced by facilitators.

"That one's dyslexic."

CAN YOU...? (No. **9.5**)

1... Two SENs are described on this spread. For each one select **two** key points relating to each of the following: assessment, categorisation and strategies for education.

2... For each key point write **two or three** sentences explaining the concept.

3... Identify about **ten** points of evaluation (these can be positive or negative).

4... Elaborate each point (see page 9).

5... Use all of this material to write an answer to the following exam question: *Critically consider special educational needs including the assessment, categorisation and strategies for education of at least one special educational need.* As good practice you might also write 'building block' essays about the two different SENs on this spread. Your answers should contain about 300 words of description and 500 words of evaluation.

Don't forget to read the essay-writing guidance on pages 8–9.

BEHAVIOURIST LEARNING THEORIES

CLASSICAL CONDITIONING

- Classical conditioning is learning through association.
- Before conditioning the UCS produces a UCR. During conditioning NS occurs at the same time as the UCS. After conditioning, the NS (now CS) produces a CR.
- Students acquire emotional associations, e.g. to teachers, which can enhance or discourage learning.
- Some children acquire school phobias and refuse to attend.

EVALUATION

- LeFrançois suggests teachers should maximise nice UCSs, e.g. posters, and minimise unpleasant ones, e.g. shouting.
- Systematic desensitisation uses counterconditioning to associate something pleasant with a feared object to unlearn a phobia, e.g. for maths.

OPERANT CONDITIONING

- New behaviours are learned through reinforcement (good consequences increase the probability of repeating a behaviour) and punishments (bad consequences decrease the probability of repetition).
- Reinforcers can be negative (escape from unpleasantness) or positive (something pleasant).
- Shaping reinforces successively closer approximations to a desired behaviour.
- Teachers consciously reward and punish students and may do this unconsciously, e.g. a smile or a harsh tone, can also reward or punish students. These examples are all *positive* reinforcement or punishment.
- Handing in your homework on time and *not* getting told off removes something unpleasant (negative reinforcement). Detention removes something good – going home on time (negative punishment).
- In social learning new behaviours are acquired by observing, vicarious reinforcement and modelling, e.g. learning to write good essays by seeing examples with good marks.
- The learner must also believe they can do the task being modelled, i.e. have self-efficacy.
- Consistent reinforcement is most effective in the short term but intermittent reinforcement leads to more durable learning (Kollins *et al.*).
- Bandura and Walters suggested that attention seeking by children persists because the behaviours are rewarded intermittently.

EVALUATION

- Shaping can help teachers, e.g. using behaviour modification in applied behaviour analysis with autistic children.
- Programmed instruction uses a computer- or book-based instructional device. This rewards you for each correct answer and directs you to another question for help if you make an incorrect response.
- Rewards are not always effective. Lepper *et al.* found that promising children extrinsic rewards destroyed their intrinsic motivations (to draw).
- Rewards can also create a form of learned helplessness. Dweck found praising students produced lower task persistence than those told to work harder.
- Punishment doesn't always work. Hickman found performance was worse in US schools when corporal punishment was used. Punishment only tells the learner what they have done wrong, not what is preferable; may lead to avoidance (e.g. truancy) and gives extra attention so may encourage the student to continue disruptive behaviour.
- Because operant conditioning techniques change another person's behaviour, such techniques raise ethical issues about who should decide which behaviours are 'desirable'.

MOTIVATING FACTORS

ATTRIBUTION THEORY

- Attribution is the process of explaining causes of behaviour, internal or external.
- When learners succeed or fail they make a causal inference which can affect motivation (Weiner).
- When there is insufficient information to make logical inferences, we use general beliefs.
- Weiner identified three dimensions determining attributions.
  - *Locus of control (LoC)* is our belief about control of events. People with internal LoCs are more motivated as they believe they can make a difference.
  - *Stability* is whether causes of success/failure are constant across situations (e.g. effort, task difficulty) or change (e.g. luck, mood).
  - *Controllability* refers to how much we can actually determine outcome, e.g. we have more control over revision than the difficulty of an exam paper).

EVALUATION

- If teachers can identify and alter unhelpful attributions they should be able to improve motivation. Unsuccessful students often attribute their success to forces beyond their control leading to learned helplessness that reduces motivation.
- Dweck's research suggests that critical feedback causes learners to make internal attributions (failure is due to lack of effort) so when challenged they try harder. This is mastery-oriented learning.
- Weiner's theory helps teachers to know how and when to challenge learners (attribution training) but they must be sure that learners who attribute failure to lack of effort really *didn't* try hard enough (to avoid demotivation when lack of success has another cause).
- Teachers can alter learner's attributions but are also a *source* of attributions, e.g. sending attributional messages by giving excessive help or praising easy tasks (Good and Brophy).
- Ramirez and Avila found that improving teacher attributions changed learner attributions. This reduced teacher burnout and raised achievement.

INDIVIDUAL DIFFERENCES IN LEARNING STYLES

INDIVIDUAL DIFFERENCES

Gender differences
- Female students depend on teachers more and have a greater fear of failure but are more motivated than males (Severiens and ten Dam). Males tended towards field independence (Huss and Kayson).
- However, Riding and Grimley suggest that gender differences in cognitive style are diminishing, implying that cognitive style is cultural so modifiable.

Cultural differences
- Asian students are often stereotyped as rote learners, but Sadler-Smith and Tsang found British students used memorisation more than those from Hong Kong, and Watkins *et al.* found no support for the stereotype in Filipino or Nepalese students.
- Learning style tests are Western so may not apply to non-Western students (imposed etic).

CURRY'S ONION MODEL

- Curry used the metaphor of layers of an onion to show how different *kinds* of learning style relate to each other.
- She identified three 'layers' (from looking at nine learning style tests):
  - Inner = *cognitive personality style*, underlying approach to thinking.
  - Middle = *information processing style*, strategies to process information.
  - Outer = *instructional preferences*, working at own or teacher-set pace.

EVALUATION

- Curry studied further learning style tests (total of 21) and added a layer (social interaction) between the middle and outer layers, which relates to enjoyment of social interaction within learning.
- The model predicts that each test within a layer should assess the same thing. Ingham found better correlations within than between layers.
- The model predicts that retest scores should also be more consistent on traits from inner layers and Sewall found the lowest change (highest correlations) for MBTI (cognitive personality style) and most change for the Canfield Scales (instructional preference layer).
- Although the model has united the different learning styles, Zhang and Sternberg observe there is little evidence testing its predictions.

GRASHA'S SIX LEARNING STYLES

- Grasha identified negative reactions to traditional classrooms and suggested corresponding positive ones = six learning styles: avoidant vs participative, competitive vs collaborative, dependent vs independent.
- The GRSLSS tests these styles and aims to help teachers and students optimise learning.

EVALUATION

- Grasha used the GRSLSS to test links between learning style and other individual differences. Female learners are more collaborative, students over 25 more independent and participant, and students with lower grades tend to be avoidant.
- Students can be assessed before and after learning experiences, e.g. to test whether collaborative work affects competitiveness, and to help planning.
- The GRSLSS is reliable and user-friendly and is designed specifically for college/university students.

GENERAL EVALUATION

Psychometrics
- Psychometric tests (or 'inventories') should be checked for validity and reliability. However, low test–retest scores would be expected on unstable traits.
- A test with low validity/reliability can still be useful to help individuals to decide which strategies work for them (Jarvis).

AN EVALUATION OF THE LEARNING STYLE APPROACH

- Learning should be best when teaching matches the needs of the learner. Joyce and Hudson found that if medical students' learning style matched their instructor's teaching style, exam results were better.
- However, Pashler *et al.* have identified few rigorous tests of the approach, e.g. randomly assigning learners to teaching styles.
- Coffield *et al.* identified 71 theories of learning style, each with little empirical support and suggested the sheer range makes the concept unworkable.
- Greenfield questioned the neuroscientific basis for learning styles and concluded that the approach was 'nonsense'.

COGNITIVE DEVELOPMENTAL THEORIES

APPLYING PIAGET'S THEORY TO EDUCATION

- You cannot teach a child to perform certain activities until they are biologically 'ready'.
- The concept of readiness means that educational activities should be appropriate to a child's stage of cognitive development.
- Cognitive development is motivated by the need to resolve disequilibrium. Teachers can facilitate this by asking questions.
- Piaget argued that logical thinking, which needs to be taught, facilitates cognitive development so we need maths and sciences on the curriculum.

EVALUATION

- Bryant and Trabasso contradicted the readiness approach as young children could be trained to solve logical tasks.
- But Danner and Day found practice made no difference to formal operational tasks in 10- or 13-year-olds but helped 17-year-olds, supporting readiness.
- Discovery learning can limit progress in reading and writing as children have too little practice (Modgil et al.).
- Seeing the child as sole agent of his learning is culture biased (individualist).

APPLYING VYGOTSKY'S THEORY TO EDUCATION

- In collaborative learning students at various levels work in small groups sharing understanding, successes and responsibility for each other's learning.
- A more knowledgeable other (MKO) understands a task or concept better than the learner.
- MKOs motivate learners to move through their zone of proximal development, giving them responsibility but helping too, i.e. scaffolding.

EVALUATION

- Gokhale showed that collaborative learning produced better performance on individual critical-thinking tests.
- Many studies, e.g. Cohen et al., show that both tutees and peer tutors benefit from peer tutoring socially and academically but peer tutors gain most (Cloward). However, experimental groups often have peer tutoring and normal lessons, lowering validity (Slavin).
- Vygotsky's approach may apply best to collectivist settings as children in individualist societies are more competitive and self-reliant. Stigler and Perry found groupwork was more effective for maths teaching in Asian (collectivist) schools than American (individualist) schools.

BRUNER'S PROCESS OF EDUCATION

- Scaffolding by 'experts' helps novices to reach goals they could not achieve alone. This help is gradually withdrawn as the child works more independently.
- In a spiral curriculum 'difficult' concepts are started early to provide a basis for later learning, and are revisited.
- A child's mode of thinking changes so teachers should start with enactive (action-based) mode and later use iconic (visual) and symbolic modes.
- Motivation to learn should come from active encounters with problems which tempt the learner, i.e. educators do not need to make topics accessible.

EVALUATION

- The effects of scaffolding are difficult to measure because programmes take years.
- Wood and Middleton found that task mastery (with a 3D puzzle) was positively associated with scaffolding – failure requires explicit instructions but success requires stepping back.
- The spiral curriculum is widely used, from nursery schools to GP training.

GENERAL EVALUATION

- The cognitive approaches stress the active role of the learner (e.g. in discovery learning) and have influenced education, e.g. the *Plowden Report* (1967). However, child-centred education is not new, e.g. Dewey (1920s) and Plato (4th century BC).
- Bennett found that children taught formally (passive approach) were better at reading, maths and English but the best results were produced by *some* teachers using active, child-centred methods.

- Comparisons are difficult as formal teaching spends more time on core topics and effective active learning requires more sensitive and experienced teachers.
- These theories focus on the development of cognitive abilities so ignore emotions, unlike projects such as SEAL.
- There are methodological issues related to how educational success can be measured.

THE CLASSROOM

MASLOW'S HIERARCHY OF NEEDS

- We are motivated to satisfy D-needs (deficiency) first, then B-needs (being): physiological, safety, social, esteem, intellectual, aesthetic and self-actualisation.
- Maslow's ideas help educators to appreciate the range of factors affecting motivation so the needs of all learners can be considered in designing lessons, e.g. feeling safe in a group needs to be satisfied before an individual will be motivated towards intellectual interests (Snowman and Biehler). Teachers must boost students' self-esteem before motivating them intellectually.

EVALUATION

- Coleman found that students rated being remembered as popular (a D-need) was more important than being academic (a B-need), which fits Maslow's hierarchy.
- Maslow's theory is hard to apply to *improving* motivation but it can explain why some techniques work. Bleach and Smith found that boys didn't try in English as they wanted to be 'cool' and popular, i.e. social and esteem needs mattered more than achievement.
- Maslow's view of striving for personal achievement is culture bound. Cross-cultural research shows that American students (individualist) felt good about personal achievements but Japanese students (collectivist) associated positive feelings with good relations with others (Kitayama and Markus).

SPECIAL EDUCATIONAL NEEDS

DYSLEXIA

- Dyslexia causes problems with words (reading and writing) even in individuals with adequate intelligence and education.

Assessment
- Screening tests (e.g. non-verbal intelligence and perception tests) eliminate other possible causes of reading difficulties.
- Reading and writing tests are used, or specific tests, e.g. phonemic segmentation (breaking words into sounds), motor skills (e.g. bead threading).
- Full diagnostic assessments are carried out by educational psychologists.

Categorisation
- Different types of dyslexia include 'pure' dyslexia, dyslexia with other learning difficulties and visual/auditory dyslexia.
- Classification by cause, e.g. trauma, primary dyslexia (genetic) and secondary or developmental (caused during prenatal development).

Strategies for education
- Small group versus one-to-one teaching; teaching to strengths versus remedial help and targeting phonetics versus organisational skills.
- Structured language programmes (e.g. Bangor Teaching) build up skills from basic to complex.
- Multi-sensory teaching links visual, auditory, tactile and kinaesthetic modalities.

AUTISM

- Autism appears early in life. The 'triad of impairment' affects: social interaction, social communication and imagination. Challenging and/or repetitive behaviour may also occur.

Assessment
- Checklists are used such as CHAT which asks questions (e.g. 'Does your child take an interest in other children?').
- MRI scans can detect differences between the brains of 'normal' individuals and those with autism with 90% accuracy (Ecker et al.).

Categorisation
- Autistic spectrum disorder includes autism, Asperger's syndrome and PDD-NOS.

Strategies for education
- Applied Behaviour Analysis (Lovaas), a behaviour modification therapy using shaping and a token economy to change behaviours causing problems.
- Makaton (using eyes, body, symbols and some words) was developed for autistics as they find processing visual information easier than verbal information.
- In facilitated communication, the autistic's hand or arm is supported while they use a communicator to spell out words.
- Programmes like TEACCH advise parents about how to work with their children at home.

EVALUATION

- Dyslexia cannot be cured. However, Scammacca et al. found many reading interventions worked well.
- Lawrence found that counselling alone benefitted poor readers more than special reading help on its own or with counselling; low self-esteem may hinder reading improvement.
- Evaluating interventions for dyslexia is difficult as there are many kinds of dyslexia; strategies may fail because they don't match particular problems.

- Elliott argued that dyslexia is just a difficulty with reading because characteristics claimed to cause reading difficulties (e.g. clumsiness and letter reversals) are also found in people who *can* read.
- Diagnosis aims to direct successful treatment but also allows people with disorders and their families to understand the problem, so can relieve stress.
- However, labels (e.g. 'dyslexic' or 'autistic'), which 'stick', may lead to low, self-fulfilling expectations.

EVALUATION

- As autistic children find social situations difficult, specialist schools seem a good idea but sharing experiences with others is important to social development.
- Behavioural techniques are intensive and rely on continuous rewards to avoid relapse.
- However, Anderson et al. found that a year of ABA improved cognitive functioning in half of the children treated even with only 20 hours a week.

- Evidence has been criticised because sampling is selective (rejection of some autistic children) and researchers lack objectivity.
- Makaton is not used consistently so people from one group of users might not understand what a person from another group is trying to communicate.
- Crossley and Remington-Gurley suggest that facilitated communication leads to effective later language but Howlin found very little evidence of independent communication and that facilitators often unwittingly influenced responses.

Question 9 **Discuss behaviourist theory applied to education including classical and operant conditioning** [25]

Student answer

Paragraph 1 ▶ In school there are two parts to look at. The first one is controlling bad behaviour and the second is getting people to learn.

Paragraph 2 ▶ Bad behaviour is a big problem for teachers and other kids because it stops other kids learning. Teachers used to be able to hit kids but now this has stopped because it was abuse. This is behaviourist because it was punishment. Punishment stops people doing things and fear of punishment is supposed to stop you before you do it.

Paragraph 3 ▶ This isn't true because when you get punished you just get upset and angry. Punishment doesn't work and it is useless for education. Using positive reinforcement is much better. Teachers shouldn't punish but should use positive reinforcement because it works better. Teachers can reinforce good behaviour and also when young children aren't being naughty, so they do more good behaviour. Some people like my gran think the cane should be brought back to teach kids how to behave but psychology says that's wrong.

Paragraph 4 ▶ Rewards can be done using stars or charts, this is called token economy. It is useful at primary school, but really only with the nice kids at secondary, since the bad kids will laugh at it. However kids will do things because they like them, so they don't need to have reinforcement when they're doing some interesting stuff. Teachers need to be trained how to teach properly.

Paragraph 5 ▶ Another behaviourist thing is classical conditioning. This is where you get emotional connections learnt, such as fear of a teacher or not liking a subject. This happens a lot with maths and with some kids can happen with school so they refuse to attend or throw up in fear. A teacher punishes them or there is bullying and the fear caused by this is the response which then gets attached to the school itself so the fear becomes about school. This can be a school phobia which is very difficult to change, unless the kid changes school. Some kids get bullied at lots of different schools anyway. A lot of young teachers think that shouting is OK and also putting kids down in a nasty way. Some older teachers do it too, but in my school some of the older teachers keep respect and good behaviour without being nasty.

Paragraph 6 ▶ Other behaviourist theories include social learning theory (SLT). SLT means you learn from watching others such as Bandura showed with aggression in his nursery study where small children imitated adults. At school you have lots of role models such as young teachers as well as big children in the years above. You can also have bad kids in your year.

Paragraph 7 ▶ If you get SLT and reinforcement then a behaviour becomes fixed. A kid who does what the bad kids do gets respect from the bad kids and also lots of teacher attention which is a big reward. We can all remember the kids that did this lower in school. It seems silly that they should get lots of attention, but there isn't anything else anyone can do if someone sets out to be bad.

Paragraph 8 ▶ Some of the bad kids come from bad homes where they have SLT from bad parents, and where their parents think it's OK to behave badly. This reinforces their bad behaviour and is stronger than teachers in getting kids to behave. People like that have to be taken to court and fined, but that might not work as it is punishment.

Paragraph 9 ▶ The best way is to make all the lessons interesting and for teachers to be trained not to shout or make people feel stupid. Punishment shouldn't be used unless it's going to work, there should be lots of rewards though.

[619 words]

Examiner comments

This candidate has absorbed a lot of basic psychology but has failed to express their understanding in the proper scientific style expected for A2 level and has not structured their essay well.

In paragraph 1 the categorisation of 'two parts' is crude and short.

Paragraphs 2 and 3 offer a description and evaluation (shaded in grey) of how bad behaviour can be controlled. There are occasional references to psychological knowledge though much of it is repetitive and non-academic (also called anecdotal).

Paragraph 4 contains a brief description followed by some basic evaluation but with no scientific evidence.

In paragraph 5 there are some good points about classical conditioning, but there is no evidence. Paragraph 6 introduces SLT, but there is no detailed consideration of Bandura other than a short mention.

Paragraphs 7 and 8 are again more anecdotal than psychological, and often not clearly related to education.

Paragraph 9 contains a brief summary which repeats points already made.

Overall there is very little evaluation (**AO2**) so that will only score in the 1–3 band (**2 out of 15 marks**). The descriptive content of the essay lacks clear psychology and is therefore 'basic' and closer to 'superficial' so **4 out of 10 marks** for AO1.

Total 6/25 which is a U grade.

Improvement?

A better structure and only a few pieces of identifiable evidence would elevate this answer to a much higher grade.

In terms of structure, the candidate could have begun by identifying the three main learning processes: classical conditioning, operant conditioning and social learning and then systematically covered each of these in the context of education. This helps to set up a structured essay.

Identifiable evidence is important for good evaluation. For example, paragraph 3 would gain more credit if rewritten as 'Hickmon (2008) showed that children in schools that had corporal punishment were academically worse than those in schools that had got rid of it. This implies that the negative consequences of punishment as a reinforcer led to less efficient learning'.

Additional evaluation would further improve the mark, for example when considering classical conditioning;

Our understanding of the role of classical conditioning in education has useful applications. LeFrançois (2000) has suggested that teachers maximise the pleasant stimuli in the classroom and minimise the negative. In practice this means having lots of posters and interesting displays in a nice clean colourful classroom, and for the teacher to avoid emotionally arousing unpleasant behaviour like shouting'.

</>

Chapter 10

Forensic psychology

Chapter contents

196 Introduction to the study of forensic psychology

198 Approaches to profiling

200 Decision making of juries

202 Theories of crime

204 Factors affecting the accuracy of eyewitness testimony

206 Treatment and punishment of crime

End-of-chapter review

208 Chapter summary

210 Exam question with student answer

Specification breakdown

Approaches to profiling (e.g. the US 'top-down' approach, the British 'bottom-up' approach and geographical profiling).	Immortalised in Hollywood films and subsequently distorted beyond any semblance of reality in TV shows such as *Cracker* and *Wire in the Blood*, criminal profiling has a complex and interesting psychological history. This section looks at the main approaches and their critical evaluation.
Decision making of juries (e.g. minority influence, majority influence and characteristics of the defendant).	One of the major social dramas in the legal system, and one that has literally been fought over, the decision making of juries is difficult to investigate as it is generally secret. Here we examine scientific attempts to understand the factors involved.
Theories of crime (biological, social and psychological).	Are criminals born or made? Is it nature or nurture? This is as much a political as a scientific question. We look at a selection of the many theories of criminal behaviour, along with some critical evaluation of the research and concepts involved.
Factors affecting the accuracy of eyewitness testimony (e.g. reconstructive memory, face recognition, attributional biases, the role of emotion).	'I know what I saw!' But we now know, through careful scientific research, that we do not accurately remember what we saw! This section looks at the nature of such memories and the factors that distort them.
Treatment and punishment of crime (e.g. cognitive therapies, behavioural therapies and zero tolerance).	This is another topic where science and politics are intertwined. If crime is to be reduced then science points largely in one direction – punishment doesn't work. However, this doesn't suit many political agendas. We examine what psychology tells us and also note how this knowledge is applied in practice.

WHAT IS FORENSIC PSYCHOLOGY?

Psychologists can help in the legal process in many ways. In terms of understanding criminal behaviour, psychologists have developed a range of explanations for how criminal behaviour arises. Different approaches to psychology have also contributed in many ways to policing and the judicial process – for example, tracking down suspects, recognising the problems with **eyewitness testimonies** and suggesting improvements, studying courtroom procedures and identifying problems with jury decision making, and devising ways to improve the rehabilitation of offenders.

Criminal heads and bodies

The earliest theories of criminality suggested that facial features or body shape were related to criminal behaviour. For example, Lombroso (1876) suggested that criminals typically had a narrow, sloping forehead, prominent eye ridges, large ears and a protruding chin.

1. Trococéphale violateur, de Ravenne.   2. Voleur milanais, condamné 13 fois.

▲ *Cesare Lombroso believed criminals had particular facial features.*

Many years later, Sheldon (1942) proposed the idea of *somatotypes* – classifying people according to their body types. He linked body type to criminality, suggesting that muscular aggressive mesomorphs were most likely to have criminal tendencies unlike thin, introverted endomorphs and fat, sociable ectomorphs.

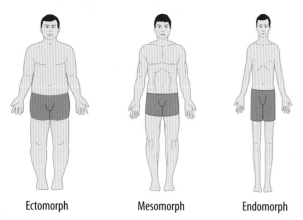

Ectomorph   Mesomorph   Endomorph

Both of these were biological theories in that they suggested the existence of some underlying biological trait that in some way led to criminal behaviour. Some modern biological theories consider personality traits rather than appearance, such as *impulsivity* or **psychoticism** – both of which have been linked to criminality. Others investigate the biological processes (**genetic, neural** or **hormonal**) which underlie differences between us. In the test on the facing page you can measure your own psychoticism score.

Crime in the UK

In the UK crime statistics are compiled in two ways.

1. *Recorded crime* is crime reported to the police, providing information about trends in well-reported crimes and local crime patterns.

2. *The British Crime Survey* (BCS) is based on interviews. It is able to provide a better reflection of the real extent of crime as it includes crimes that are not reported to the police.

The BCS is also a better indication of trends in crime as it is unaffected by changes in levels of reporting to the police or police recording practices. The BCS aims to take a nationally representative sample (now of more than 45,000 respondents) from households in England and Wales.

The graph below illustrates the trends in overall crime rates and the difference between recorded crime and the findings of the BCS.

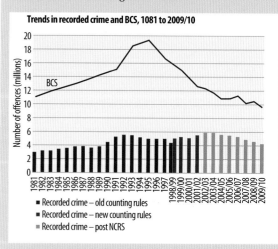

Trends in recorded crime and BCS, 1081 to 2009/10

- Recorded crime – old counting rules
- Recorded crime – new counting rules
- Recorded crime – post NCRS

▲ *Trends in recorded crime and BCS, 1981–2010.*

At the time of writing, the most recent BCS and police record crime statistics are from 2009/10. These show consistent falls in overall crime compared with the previous year. According to the BCS, crime decreased by 9% (to 9.6 million crimes) and recorded crime by 8% (to 4.3 million crimes). This is surprising against the background of a recession (although the full effects did not appear until 2011). There have also been some key falls, for example vehicle crime and domestic burglary.

STARTER ACTIVITIES

PERSONALITY TEST

The test below measures three personality factors: psychoticism (P), extraversion (E) and neuroticism (N). We are only interested in the P score because higher psychoticism relates to a greater likelihood of criminality. Eysenck and Eysenck (1977) proposed that criminals would be extravert (outgoing) rather than introvert and neurotic (i.e. emotionally unstable) and would have a high score on the psychoticism scale. However, support for the importance of extraversion and instability is inconsistent. Support for the importance of psychoticism is somewhat better. You can try to measure your own, but, bear in mind that this is only a short test and it won't be administered in a standard way, so don't read too much into your findings! When you have finished, try to use the nature of the P scale questions to work out how to define 'psychoticism'.

EPQR-S The Eysenck Personality Questionnaire (revised short form, Eysenck *et al.*, 1985)

Circle 'yes' or 'no' beside each of the 48 questions below.

1	Does your mood often go up and down.	YES	NO
2	Do you take much notice of what people think?	YES	NO
3	Are you a talkative person?	YES	NO
4	If you say you will do something, do you always keep your promise no matter how inconvenient it might be?	YES	NO
5	Do you ever feel 'just miserable' for no reason?	YES	NO
6	Would being in debt worry you?	YES	NO
7	Are you rather lively?	YES	NO
8	Were you ever greedy by helping yourself to more than your share of anything?	YES	NO
9	Are you an irritable person?	YES	NO
10	Would you take drugs which may have strange or dangerous effects?	YES	NO
11	Do you enjoy meeting new people?	YES	NO
12	Have you ever blamed someone for doing something you knew was really your fault?	YES	NO
13	Are your feelings easily hurt?	YES	NO
14	Do you prefer to go your own way rather than act by the rules?	YES	NO
15	Can you usually let yourself go and enjoy yourself at a lively party?	YES	NO
16	Are all your habits good and desirable ones?	YES	NO
17	Do you often feel 'fed up'?	YES	NO
18	Do good manners and cleanliness matter much to you?	YES	NO
19	Do you usually take the initiative in making new friends?	YES	NO
20	Have you ever taken anything (even a pin or button) that belonged to someone else?	YES	NO
21	Would you call yourself a nervous person?	YES	NO
22	Do you think marriage is old-fashioned and should be done away with?	YES	NO
23	Can you easily get some life into a rather dull party?	YES	NO
24	Have you ever broken or lost something belonging to someone else?	YES	NO
25	Are you a worrier?	YES	NO
26	Do you enjoy co-operating with others?	YES	NO
27	Do you tend to keep in the background on social occasions?	YES	NO
28	Does it worry you if you know there are mistakes in your work?	YES	NO
29	Have you ever said anything bad or nasty about anyone?	YES	NO
30	Would you call yourself tense or 'highly-strung'?	YES	NO
31	Do you think people spend too much time safeguarding their future with savings and insurances?	YES	NO
32	Do you like mixing with people?	YES	NO
33	As a child were you ever cheeky to your parents?	YES	NO
34	Do you worry too long after an embarrassing experience?	YES	NO
35	Do you try not to be rude to people?	YES	NO
36	Do you like plenty of bustle and excitement around you?	YES	NO
37	Have you ever cheated at a game?	YES	NO
38	Do you suffer from 'nerves'?	YES	NO
39	Would you like other people to be afraid of you?	YES	NO
40	Have you ever taken advantage of someone?	YES	NO
41	Are you mostly quiet when you are with other people?	YES	NO
42	Do you often feel lonely?	YES	NO
43	Is it better to follow society's rules than go your own way?	YES	NO
44	Do other people think of you as being very lively?	YES	NO
45	Do you always practise what you preach?	YES	NO
46	Are you often troubled about feelings of guilt?	YES	NO
47	Do you sometimes put off until tomorrow what you ought to do today?	YES	NO
48	Can you get a party going?	YES	NO

HOW MANY SMARTIES IN THE JAR?

In your AS course, one of your core studies was by Asch (1955), looking at **conformity**. You may recall that, in some ways, it was quite an unethical study. The following activity illustrates the phenomenon in an ethical way. Conformity is important in forensic psychology as the decision about the guilt or innocence of a suspect is made by a jury – a group of people who can be influenced by the opinion of a majority. If most people on a jury believe that a suspect is innocent, the individual is likely to be acquitted (even if they are guilty). Jurors also conform to a majority view about guilt. This behaviour can lead to miscarriages of justice, so forensic psychologists are interested in understanding the dynamics of majority influence.

Here's the study for you to try: Jenness (1932) asked individual students to guess privately the number of beans in a sealed bottle. In groups of three or four, the students then discussed their estimates before being asked to provide individual estimates again. Following the discussion, the individuals' opinions tended to conform to the group's estimate.

Using a group of students who are unaware of what is likely to happen, conduct a similar test, for example using sweets or pieces of pasta in a jar. Ensure that you make the **right to withdraw** clear and **debrief** your participants at the end of your investigation. When asking for consent, you might to tell potential participants that the investigation is about estimating. Although this is true, you will be withholding some information about the aim of the study. Why is this essential?

You also need to think about how you will analyse your results. For each participant you will have two estimates – before and after the discussion.

Scoring your personality

There are four scales altogether: P, E and N plus a lie scale (L). The lie scale questions assess the extent the respondent is actually being untruthful.

On each scale you score one point for any question to which you answered 'yes' if it appears in the 'yes' row and one point for any question to which you answered 'no' if it appears in the 'no' row. Ignore all other answers.

P scale
YES 10, 14, 22, 31, 39
NO 2, 6, 18, 26, 28, 35, 43

E scale
YES 3, 7, 11, 15, 19, 23, 32, 36, 44, 48
NO 27, 41

N scale
YES 1, 5, 9, 13, 17, 21, 25, 30, 34, 38, 42, 46

L scale
YES 4, 16, 45
NO 8, 12, 20, 24, 29, 33, 37, 40, 47

Profiling helps the police to identify the perpetrators of serious crime. It includes a range of techniques that aim to produce descriptions of suspects that can be used in the search for criminals such as **serial killers** (people who kill three or more victims, and not at the same time), serial rapists and arsonists. Different techniques can provide different kinds of information about the suspect, such as using behavioural assessments or finding out where suspects live or work and the belongings they may have (including 'souvenirs' of the crime).

Profiling does not *solve* crimes, but it can provide the police with useful information in the search for evidence and narrow down potential suspects.

An FBI profile

The case of the serial killer Arthur Shawcross typifies the US approach. The profile, based on evidence from 11 murders of women in New York state, was of a lone male, aged at least 35, with a menial job. It suggested he would own a functional vehicle, have a police record and, importantly, would return to the scene (to re-experience the pleasure of killing). The police set up surveillance around the body of the 11th victim and caught Shawcross on a nearby bridge. He was a 44-year-old who cut salads for a living, owned an ex-police car and was on parole for earlier child murders.

The US (top-down) approach

Modern offender profiling began with the Federal Bureau of Investigation (FBI) in the US. In the 1970s their *Behavioral Science Unit* began researching the family backgrounds, personalities, behaviours, crimes and motives of serial killers with sexual aspects to their crimes. This included in-depth interviews with 36 convicted murderers. Using their experience, and intuition, the FBI team developed a classification system for several serious crimes, including murder and rape. Each 'type' of criminal displayed a different set of characteristics (see table of murderer types, below right). Importantly, the analysis of the crime scene indicates the type of offender so the classification can be used to determine the characteristics they might have. This process is therefore called **crime scene analysis**.

A top-down approach As the FBI system is based on the crime types it is a **top-down process** – crime reconstruction and profile generation are driven from 'above' by the crime scene classification (e.g. into organised or disorganised).

The British (bottom-up) approach

This approach assumes that individuals are consistent, for example, in their personalities. This **interpersonal coherence** suggests that evidence about the offender's behaviour at the crime scene will reflect the way they act in day-to-day life. For example, some rapists are controlling and abusive, others are far less violent; this may indicate how the offender responds to women in his non-criminal life. The victim group may also reveal something about the criminal. For example, Theodore Bundy killed over 30 students while he, himself, was a student.

Data analysis Statistical techniques are used in the UK approach. So, although it is rare for a rapist to apologise to their victim, a series of assaults with this in common might suggest they were committed by the same person.

Forensic awareness Patterns in precautions that the offenders take to avoid detection are useful. Davies *et al.* (1997) found that rapists who attempt to conceal their fingerprints are likely to have a conviction for burglary.

A bottom-up approach As the UK system builds a profile from crime scene information, it is a **bottom-up** process – it is driven from 'below'.

Stages in US profiling

Data assimilation Available data are collected from many sources, e.g. photos of the crime scene, victim autopsy, witness reports.

Crime scene classification The evidence is used to place the crime into a typology, e.g. two types of murder and four types of rape (power–reassurance, power–assertive, anger–retaliatory and anger–excitement).

Crime reconstruction Hypotheses are developed about what the offender and victim did and the sequence of events based on a reconstruction of events.

Profile generation A profile is developed which can include the offender's age, ethnicity, social class, type of work, habits, personality, etc.

▼ *FBI murderer types*

Organised murderers	Disorganised murderers
High intelligence	Lower intelligence
Socially competent	Socially incompetent
Plans murders	Little, if any, preplanning of murder
Uses restraints on victim	Minimal use of restraints and body is often displayed in open view
Brings weapon to commit murder and takes it away from crime scene	Crime scene evidence may include blood, semen, fingerprints and murder weapon

UK profiling methods

Facet theory This non-statistical approach explores all the 'facets' or 'sides' of crime scene evidence. For example, multiple stabbings might be considered in terms of bloodiness, depth, range of weapons used, etc.

Smallest space analysis (SSA) Based on data from many incidents, this can identify the most useful crime scene evidence. For example, removing clothing is very common in rape so would not be helpful in narrowing down a search, but less frequent characteristics, such as theft, could be useful and as this rarely co-occurs with torture; the two together would be particularly unusual.

Geographical profiling

Used alongside other techniques, **geographical profiling** analyses the locations of a series of crimes to indicate where the offender might live, work, socialise or travel. It is typically used in serial murder or rape cases but also for arson, bombing and robbery. Geographical information can also indicate personality and habits.

Cognitive maps We each have a mental map of the places we often visit and the routes we take. This is our **cognitive map**. This relates to our 'activity space', the locations we range over in our residential, work and social life and how we move about in that area. A criminal, therefore, must know an area before he or she begins committing crimes there, and this knowledge will largely determine where the crime takes place. Geographical profiling aims to reconstruct and interpret the offender's cognitive map.

Criminal geographic targeting is a computerised system which uses data about the time, distance and movement between crime scenes to generate a 3D model called a **jeopardy surface**. This looks like a coloured mountain range and indicates likely locations for the offender's home, place of work, etc. Although only indicating probabilities for these places, this can direct the police to focus their investigative efforts, geographically prioritise suspects by their current or past locations and focus patrols in the most probable zones.

EVALUATION

The US approach

Limited use The US approach, like any profiling technique, is limited to crimes which leave significant evidence and are multiple offences such as serial murder, rape, arson, satanic crimes and paedophilia. While such offences are relatively rare, they are horrific crimes so it is worthwhile if profiling contributes to solving them. However, the very rarity of the crimes also means there are few examples on which to base the technique.

Does it work? It is often argued that profiling far from guarantees a conviction. However, Douglas (1981) reviewed the costs and benefits of profiling for the FBI. The findings showed that, indeed, profiling rarely led directly to the offender (only 15 of 192 cases), but in 77% of the cases it helped to focus the investigation.

Poor methodology The sample of murderers originally used by the FBI was neither large nor random. The FBI agents simply interviewed an **opportunity sample** of 36 serial murderers who agreed to talk to them (who were known to be manipulative and so were probably unreliable sources). The **interviews** were not standardised and the typologies were developed in an informal way. Finally, the classification was based on offenders who had been caught, who may differ in important ways from those who are still at large.

Too simplistic The **validity** of the organised/disorganised typology has been questioned. Canter et al. (2004) analysed evidence from 100 murders and found no such distinct subsets of characteristics. This basic model has been amended, for example a five-fold classification by Holmes and Holmes (1998). This amended classification in some ways reflects the original continuum – it has the disorganised 'visionary killer' (who is suffering a break with reality, e.g. seeing visions/hearing voices telling him to kill particular individuals) at one end, and the organised 'power/control killer' (who derives pleasure from dominating the victim) at the other. The remaining types being 'mission', 'hedonistic' and 'lust'. Even this model, however, has been criticised, for example Canter (2004) used SSA on evidence from 100 US serial murderers and found that the features of 'power/control' killings, for example, were found in over half the sample, and therefore typical of most murders and not a distinct type.

The British approach

Supporting evidence Unlike the US approach, there is methodologically rigorous evidence to support UK profiling methods and the data on which the technique is based is in the public domain. For example, using SSA, House (1997) showed that different types of rape could be identified by characteristics from the crime, and Santtila et al. (2003) found consistent patterns among juvenile fire-setters.

Does it work? Paul Britton, a key UK profiler, sent **questionnaires** to CID chiefs who reported that profiles were neither accurate nor contributed to arrests (Britton, 1992). However, Copson (1995), also using questionnaires, asked police officers who had used profiling whether they felt it was useful. More than half felt it had provided something extra and over 80% said the information had been useful. However, only 14% said it had assisted in solving a case and less than 3% said it resulted in the identification of the suspect. The value of profiling seems to be to offer reassurance that an investigation was on track.

How predictable are offenders? Mokros and Alison (2002) used data from 100 UK stranger rapes to see whether offenders who had similar demographic characteristics were also alike in their crime scene behaviour – as is generally assumed in profiling. They found no significant **correlations** between characteristics such as age, educational level or previous convictions in offenders with similar crime scene behaviour, i.e. more similar crime scene evidence was not related to more similar offender characteristics. Instead, they found other important variables, such as whether crimes were committed in the day or at night. So, although they showed that assumptions about crime scene actions and offender background were flawed, their research suggested other useful information for developing predictions.

Geographical profiling

Supporting evidence Canter and Larkin (1993) tested models of offender movement using data from 45 UK rapes. They found a pattern of 'marauder' rather than 'commuter' behaviour, i.e. most rapists (87%) moved in a region around their homes to carry out attacks. Similarly, Snook et al. (2005) found that 63% of serial murderers kill less than 10 km from their homes. Furthermore, Lundrigan and Canter (2001) found body disposal patterns for serial murderers ranged around the home base, showing that geographical patterns exist.

Wider applications Goodwill and Alison (2006) developed a *filter model* to prioritise burglary suspects. Of four sources of information tested, geographical was the most useful (closely followed by temporal, i.e. when crimes were committed) with behavioural data and dwelling types being least helpful. They found that if crimes were committed geographically close together this was most likely to indicate one offender (internal consistency) and also suggested that the crimes were separate from those committed by other individuals (external consistency).

The railway rapist

David Canter's profiling of the 'railway rapist' typifies the UK approach. Canter (1994) profiled the perpetrator of 24 sexual assaults on women over four years which had not initially been linked. He identified patterns in: what was said to the victim, how the victim's clothes were removed, the kinds of threats made, the sort of sexual activity and how the victim was treated after the attack. The rapist talked to his victim, forming a 'relationship' with them, showed some consideration and used the minimum necessary force. Canter's profile was of a sexually experienced man in his mid to late 20s, with a wife or girlfriend, in a semi-skilled job, had little contact with women, and who had been arrested before. The profile also suggested where he lived and that he had knowledge of the railway. John Duffy, who had not been a prominent suspect, was arrested after surveillance was triggered by his close match to the profile. He was a 27-year-old railway worker, separated and had a criminal record. He lived in the identified area.

▼ *John Duffy, the 'railway rapist'.*

CAN YOU...?   No. **10.1**

1... **Three** approaches to profiling are described on this spread. For each of them select *at least* **two** key points to describe them.

2... For each point, write 50–100 words.

3... Identify about **ten** points of evaluation (these can be positive or negative).

4... Elaborate each point (see page 9).

5... Use all of this material to write an answer to the following exam question: *Discuss approaches to profiling.* As good practice you might also write 'building block' essays about each separate approach. Each answer should contain about 300 words of description and 500 words of evaluation.

Don't forget to read the essay-writing guidance on pages 8–9.

DECISION MAKING OF JURIES

ETHICAL ISSUES

GENDER BIAS

CULTURAL BIAS

In the UK, a jury (of 12 jurors) is selected from individuals summoned to the Crown Court for jury service. Those summoned are a **random sample** chosen from people aged 18 to 70 who are on the electoral register. The role of the jury is to decide on a verdict: whether a defendant is guilty or innocent. This is based on the evidence they have heard in court and may be a unanimous or majority decision, depending on the situation. On this spread we will explore two key features that can influence the decision reached: the effects of the opinions of other jurors (social influence) and the personal characteristics of the defendant.

SOCIAL INFLUENCE

Majority influence

At AS you learned about Asch's (1955) study of **conformity**. His work showed that a single participant in a group of confederates would conform to the majority view, i.e. **majority influence**. This idea is central to understanding the behaviour of juries. Hastie *et al.* (1983) found that a jury's final verdict reflected the view held by the majority of jurors prior to deliberation (86% if the final decision was innocent, 90% if it was guilty). This effect arises because an individual whose opinion differs from the majority's tends to conform. Pressure to conform may come from either *normative influences* (e.g. wanting to be accepted or respected by the group) or *informational influences* (e.g. being affected by believing that others know more than you do).

Smith and Mackie (1995) suggest several reasons why the majority view is so influential:

- *Varied opinions* – The majority, being more numerous, can express their opinion in a variety of ways, producing deeper processing.
- *Deeper discussions* – Shared ideas are discussed for longer than those held by single individuals.
- *Greater confidence* – Knowing most people share their view allows members of the majority to sound more forceful and convincing so are more likely to convert others.

Minority influence

Contrary to the idea of conforming to a majority, a minority can sometimes change the opinions of the group. **Minority influence** may be even more effective than majority influence because it makes members of the majority question their own opinion (Nemeth, 1977), i.e. it undermines the consensus.

What colour is it? Moscovici *et al.* (1969) demonstrated the power of the minority in a similar procedure to Asch's. Each individual in a group consisting of four participants plus two **confederates** judged the colours of blue and green slides. If the confederates (a minority) incorrectly said 'green' most of the time, the participants also answered wrongly on 1.25% of trials. However, if both confederates *consistently* incorrectly said 'green', the error rate of the real participants rose to 8.42% showing that a consistent minority can influence the wider group. Moscovici suggests that individuals in juries can change the majority view when they have a long deliberation period. However, they need to be consistent in their opinions between themselves and over time and willing to discuss why they disagree with the majority rather than being rigid.

▶ *The halo effect is a cognitive bias which causes us to make a total judgement of a person based on one outstanding trait.*

CHARACTERISTICS OF THE DEFENDANT

A juror's beliefs about the defendant will affect their decision making. This is appropriate when those beliefs are based on the evidence they have heard, but not if they are the product of stereotypes. **Stereotypes** are simplistic generalisations about a group which can relate to defendant characteristics such as ethnicity, attractiveness, gender, age and even regional accent. For example, Dixon *et al.* (2002) asked participants to judge guilt from a recorded exchange between a suspect and a policeman. If suspect's accent was 'standard British', they were rarely identified as guilty, but with a Birmingham accent guilt was significantly more likely.

Ethnicity

Stereotypes based on ethnicity affect jurors' decisions. Duncan (1976) varied the ethnic group of the perpetrator and victim in a videotape of a potentially violent situation. Participants judged an ambiguous shove as more violent when performed by a black than a white individual. In a mock jury situation, Pfeifer and Ogloff (1991) found that white participants were more likely to judge a black than a white defendant guilty in a rape case, especially when the victim was white. Interestingly, when asked to justify the guilty verdict, the effect of ethnic group on the verdict disappeared. This suggests that the differences were due to stereotyping.

Judgements of ethic minorities are similarly biased in real trials. Baldwin and McConville (1979) found that black defendants were more likely to be wrongly convicted than wrongly acquitted, and this was the case even if the members of the jury were black.

Physical attractiveness

Being attractive helps in court because we tend to link positive characteristics together, associating beauty with innocence. For example, Saladin *et al.* (1988) showed participants photos of men and asked them to judge how capable they considered the men to be of committing murder and armed robbery. Attractive men were considered less likely to have committed either crime than unattractive ones. The same pattern is seen with sentencing. DeSantis and Kayson (1997) found that mock jurors recommended harsher sentence for burglary for unattractive defendants. This **halo effect** is strongest for women accused of serious but non-fatal crimes (Quigley *et al.*, 1995). However, if attractive individuals appear to be abusing their good looks, e.g. to con people, the advantage is lost.

In a **meta-analysis** of mock jury studies, Mazzella and Feingold (1994) found advantages in terms of conviction and sentencing for attractive defendants and this effect has been replicated outside the laboratory. Downs and Lyons (1991) demonstrated a **negative correlation** between independent ratings of defendant attractiveness and fines or bail payments even when the seriousness of the crime was controlled. However, attractiveness seems to be irrelevant when imposing fines or setting bail payments for more serious crimes (McKelvie and Coley, 1993).

EVALUATION OF SOCIAL INFLUENCE

Majority influence

Varied opinions In an experimental study, Hinsz and Davis (1984) presented groups with differing numbers of arguments. The more varied the opinions (as would be the case from exposure to the majority position in a jury) the greater the shift in opinion.

Deeper discussions Stasser and Stewart (1992) devised a situation in which some information was shared within the majority of a group and some given only to a single individual. Even when instructed to discuss all the information, the participants focused almost entirely on the shared information and virtually excluded all the non-shared information.

Greater confidence Knowing most people are on your side allows majority group members to be more forthright and argumentative, so their views are more compelling (Kerr *et al.*, 1987). This may also explain why majority groupd members seem more confident, logical and intelligent than those in a minority (McLachlan, 1986).

Dangers of discussion Myers and Kaplan (1976) tested **group polarisation** in mock juries using hypothetical traffic cases that were either high or low guilt. After discussing low-guilt cases the juries erred towards innocence and recommended more lenient punishment. In the high-guilt cases they became more harsh. These differences did not arise if the cases were not discussed (i.e. when there was no opportunity for majority influence).

Minority influence

An attribution effect Attribution theory (which should be familiar to you from your AS studies) can be used to understand why minorities may be able to influence the majority. Their behaviour is seen to be motivated by a deep conviction since they are defending and maintaining an unpopular stand and therefore we attribute their beliefs to internal, dispositional causes rather than external ones. This means they have a more powerful effect on us.

Minority size Larger minorities are more effective than lone dissenters in mock juries (Tindale *et al.*, 1990) and increasing numbers have a greater effect (Wood *et al.*, 1994). A minority of one can be dismissed as an eccentric but increasing numbers mean that their views cannot be easily dismissed.

Flexibility There is research support for the importance of flexibility rather than just consistency. Nemeth and Brilmayer (1987) found that a minority of one who refused to change his position (when arguing in a mock jury situation for the amount of compensation to be paid to someone in a ski accident) had no effect on others, whereas a minority member who changed his opinion and moved in the direction of the majority did exert an influence on majority opinion.

EVALUATION OF CHARACTERISTICS OF THE DEFENDANT

Ethnicity

Contradictory evidence Not all studies have found that ethnicity affects jury decisions. For example, Mazzella and Feingold (1994) found no overall effect of ethnicity on mock jury decisions of guilt or innocence, although punishment was affected by ethnic group.

The effect of the crime The effect of ethnic group varies with the crime. Gordon *et al.* (1988) found that longer sentences were given to black than to white defendants convicted of burglary, but the reverse was true for fraud.

Attributional bias Johnson *et al.* (2002) manipulated the ethnic group of the defendant. The participants, who were all white, made more **situational attributions** about the white defendant and suggested more lenient punishments than for black defendants, which could explain ethnic differences.

Physical attractivess

The effect of the crime The effect of physical attractiveness also varies with the crime. Sigall and Ostrove (1975) asked participants to suggest prison terms for defendants based on photographs. Unattractive defendants were given longer sentences for burglary than attractive ones, but the reverse was true for fraud, supporting the idea that the attractiveness effect ceases to operate if we believe that good looks have been used for criminal gain.

Gender bias Abwender and Hough (2001) studied both attractiveness and gender in an experiment in which participants rated guilt in a scenario of a fatal road accident. Female jurors treated attractive defendants significantly more leniently than unattractive ones, but the reverse was true for male jurors. However, such evidence can be criticised because in court the judgement of guilt or innocence is absolute rather than rated, so the situation was not entirely realistic.

Publication bias Most studies report a relationship between defendant features and jury decisions. Bull and McAlpine (1998) suggest this might reflect a **publication bias**; studies finding no effect on judgements tend not to be published.

Studying juries

For reasons of confidentiality, real juries cannot be observed. Research therefore uses:

Mock juries – groups of participants are given evidence (e.g. on paper) and asked to reach a verdict. Variables such as characteristics of the defendant can be controlled, but the group may not be representative of a randomly selected jury, the scenarios are less complex and less life-like than real cases and lack the consequences and hence motivation and arousal of real cases (so they lack ecological validity).

Real trial outcomes (i.e. convictions or acquittals) – this information can be related to observations, e.g. about the defendant's characteristics and the composition of the jury (e.g. gender ratio). This is more valid as it relates to real juries but the process leading to the decisions is unknown.

Cultural bias

Sommers and Ellsworth (2003) reviewed studies exploring the effect of race on juries. Many used only white participants, so we know how white jurors are affected by race but not whether black and white jurors respond differently. What little evidence there is suggests that black jurors are influenced by ethnicity regardless of the salience of racial issues at the trial. Sommers and Ellsworth also observed that, contrary to the common assumption, the major problem with racial bias is not with racially charged cases (such as that of OJ Simpson) but 'ordinary' ones.

CAN YOU...?　　No. 10.2

1... For each topic (social influence and characteristics of the defendant) select *at least* **three** key points.

2... For each point, write about 50 words.

3... Identify about **ten** points of evaluation (these can be positive or negative).

4... Elaborate each point (see page 9).

5... Use all of this material to write an answer to the following exam question: *Discuss decision making of juries.* As good practice you might also write 'building block' essays about each of the topics on this spread. Each answer should contain about 300 words of description and 500 words of evaluation.

Don't forget to read the essay-writing guidance on pages 8–9.

THEORIES OF CRIME

Psychologists have attempted to explain criminal behaviour in many different ways. On this spread we will look at three of these. The biological approach suggests that behavioural tendencies, including criminal ones, are the product of our **genes**. Genes can affect the way we behave by altering, for example, our **hormone** and/ or **neurotransmitter** levels. Psychological approaches take many different perspectives including ones that suggest that crime is the product of a self-fulfilling prophecy. Social approaches to crime suggest that our behaviour is affected by society – the behaviour of people around us.

Biological theory of crime

Family patterns It is likely that biological factors play a role in criminality as this tends to run in families. Osborn and West (1979) found that only 13% of sons of non-criminal fathers had convictions, but 20% of sons with criminal fathers did. Adoption studies allow psychologists to check whether such patterns are the product of the child's genes or their home environment. If a child's behaviour resembles that of their biological parents, the effect is genetic. If it is more like that of their adoptive parents this suggests that criminal behaviour stems from the environment. Mednick *et al.* (1987) studied convictions in over 14,000 adoptees and found more support for biological influence (see table above).

Parents with criminal record	% of sons with criminal record
Neither	13.5
Biological only	20.0
Adoptive only	14.7
Biological and adoptive	24.5

▲ *The table above shows that criminality tends to run in families, based on Mednick et al.'s (1987) evidence from 14,000 adoptees.*

Criminal genes? Research has investigated how specific genes relate to criminality. For example, Retz *et al.* (2004) found an association between one variant of the 5-HTTLPR gene and violent behaviour. Another gene, the NOS1 gene, has been linked to aggression in animals which led Reif *et al.* (2009) to investigate links between impulsivity (which could be a factor in criminality) and variants of the NOS1 gene in humans. One gene variant was more frequent in adults with high levels of aggressive behaviour to the self and other people. When they explored the brain activity of these individuals they found reduced activity in the **anterior cingulate cortex** – an area involved in emotion and reward, so the gene variant may affect the control of impulsive behaviour.

The role of hormones The hormone **testosterone** is found in both sexes, but adult males produce about ten times more than adult females. Dabbs *et al.* (1995) found that male prisoners who had committed violent crimes had higher testosterone levels than those committing non-violent crimes and Dabbs and Hargrove (1997) found the same relationship in female prisoners suggesting that hormone level is a key factor in criminal behaviour.

The role of neurotransmitters Animal research has shown that low **serotonin** turnover (how quickly the neurotransmitter is recycled after use) is linked to aggressiveness (Valzelli, 1973). Virkkunen *et al.* (1987) found that violent offenders also had a low serotonin turnover. They were also more likely to commit further violent crimes after their release from prison (Virkkunen *et al.*, 1989).

Psychological theory of crime

Self-fulfilling prophecy Suppose we believe that every skateboarding young person is a thug. This would lead us to respond negatively towards any youngster with a skateboard: avoiding them, shouting at them or jumping to conclusions about their activities. As a consequence of this **stereotype**, I would be falsely labelling some young people. How would it make them feel and behave? The **self-fulfilling prophecy** (SFP) suggests that an observer's stereotypes can affect the observed. If an observer holds **false beliefs** about another person or social group, these beliefs change how the observer behaves, specifically making them respond in ways that are likely to elicit the expected behaviour from the observed individual. This would, in turn, confirm their expectations and reinforce the stereotype.

Applied to crime In terms of crime, the SFP suggests that negative expectations cause individuals to behave towards others in ways that elicit criminal behaviour because their stereotypes change their social interactions. For example, a new student arrives at a university hall of residence. She looks sly and the other students treat her with suspicion – they hide their milk at the back of the fridge and won't share. She can tell she is being treated differently, so responds by not caring what they think, and takes whatever she likes from the fridge. The students' initial response thus triggered her theft and confirms their initial expectations.

Recidivism SFP also explains **recidivism**. Once labelled as a 'criminal' the image is hard to shift as other people reinforce it with their behaviour towards the criminal. It thus becomes part of the individual's **self-concept**, producing further deviant behaviour.

Social theory of crime

Social learning theory When you learned about the **behaviourist approach** in your AS studies, you considered **social learning theory**. This suggests that learning occurs when one individual, the learner, observes and imitates another, the model. According to Bandura (1977) the observer must pay attention, be able to remember and also reproduce what they have observed and be motivated to do so.

The motivation may be external or internal. External motivation comes from direct **reinforcement**, such as the gains from theft, or from **vicarious reinforcement**, that is, seeing a model benefit from their behaviour. Internal motivation may be generated by identification with a model, for example Bandura *et al.* (1961) found children were more likely to imitate same-sex models.

Applied to crime Children whose parents are criminals or who are surrounded by other role models who are criminals are likely to be externally and internally motivated to imitate this behaviour. If they see the adults benefitting from their crimes (e.g. spending stolen money or enjoying aggressive behaviour) they will be vicariously reinforced to imitate. If they identify with the models because they are high status this will increase the likelihood that they will imitate the criminal behaviour.

Individual differences Learner characteristics also matter. Individuals with low **self-esteem** are more likely to imitate. This is important as low self-esteem is also associated with criminal behaviour.

EVALUATION

Biological theory of crime

Are family patterns biological? Mednick *et al.*'s findings, supporting the biological theory, have been replicated by Bohman (1996) who found 12% of sons with a criminal record had a biological parent who was a criminal, compared with 7% who had an adoptive parent with a criminal record. Even when the adoptive parents *knew* about the child's family history of criminality this had no effect on their later behaviour, this suggests that genetic factors mattered more than any SFP.

Links between biological factors For genes to influence any behaviour they must work through a mechanism, such as brain structure or function. The gene which Retz *et al.* identified controls aspects of serotonin processing, so such a link could exist for aggressive and impulsive behaviours.

Useful applications Serotonin level is affected by diet as it is made in the body from the amino acid *tryptophan*, but high levels of another amino acid, *phenylalanine*, make production of serotonin difficult. Moeller *et al.* (1996) showed that men on an unbalanced diet became more aggressive soon after eating. The artificial sweetener *aspartame* (Nutrasweet) is particularly high in phenylalanine and low in tryptophan so should be avoided by people with aggressive tendencies.

Contradictory evidence Brunner *et al.* (1993) studied a Dutch family, many of whom were aggressive. Their behaviour was linked to a mutation of the gene for monoamine oxidase type-A, which helps to recycle serotonin. Since the mutation was associated with a lack of this enzyme, logically it should have produced a reduction rather than an increase in aggression as serotonin would not be broken down.

Just biology? Much evidence supporting the biological theory (such as the work of Dabbs on hormones) offers only relatively weak patterns, which suggests that other factors (such as the environment) also matter. So, although there does appear to be a genetic influence on criminal behaviour, it is not a complete explanation. However, it is also possible that there are more 'criminal' genes yet to be discovered, which would strengthen the biological case.

Nature and nurture Twin studies provide evidence of both nature and nurture. Lyons *et al.* (1995) found that **monozygotic** (MZ) twins were more similar in terms of juvenile crime than **dizygotic** (DZ) twins (but not much). However, the latter became much less similar in adulthood, suggesting that once the environmental impact of parenting was removed (which had made them more similar), genetic factors had a greater influence.

Psychological theory of crime

Self-fulfilling names Jahoda (1954) studied the Ashanti people who give boys birthday 'soul names' as this, it is believed, affects their character: 'Monday' boys (called 'Kwadowo') are expected to be mild-mannered and peace-loving whilst 'Wednesday' boys (called 'Kwaku') are expected to be aggressive and violent. Jahoda found that 13.5% of boys referred to the courts had 'Wednesday' names but they were responsible for much more (22%) of the violent crime. Only 6.9% of juvenile delinquents were Monday boys. This suggests that expectations about the boys' natures and the explicit labels (their names) resulted in differential treatment and, as a result, they fulfilled the expectations generated by their names.

Problem parents? Madon *et al.* (2003) assessed mothers' expectations of their teenage children's underage drinking. When mothers' believed their children would drink more, this expectation was likely to be fulfilled. Of course, it is possible that the mothers were simply very good judges of their offspring's future behaviour rather than being the cause of it.

Useful applications As negative expectations affect an individual's self-concept, this can increase deviancy. We should therefore resist labelling a child as a 'problem' as this may worsen their behaviour.

The effects of TV on antisocial behaviour

Natural experiments provide a real-world test of social learning theory. Such studies have observed levels of antisocial behaviour before and after the introduction of transmitted television to remote communities (which provides aggressive models not previously present in the indigenous society). Williams (1981) found that the level of physical and verbal aggression of children in a Canadian town almost doubled following the introduction of TV. Although levels of aggression in other towns also increased over the target period, this was less marked, suggesting the difference was due to the TV models.

By contrast, Charlton *et al.* (2000) found no increase in antisocial behaviour following the introduction of TV to St Helena island. This suggests that opportunities for social learning do not necessarily lead to negative behaviours. However, St Helena is a community with particularly prosocial norms which may explain why the children were less affected by the TV.

Social theory of crime

Real-world evidence Lab experiments such as Bandura's may not represent the acquisition of criminal behaviour in real life. An alternative approach is to use correlational data about exposure to media models and criminal behaviour. Eron *et al.* (1972) found a **positive correlation** between the level of violence in TV programmes watched by seven–eight-year-olds and their aggressiveness. By their teenage years, this was even stronger in boys (though not girls). By adulthood, the more violence the boys had watched on television as children, the more likely they were to be violent criminals (Eron and Huesmann, 1986).

TV censorship One application of the findings on social learning is the importance of regulating children's exposure to models. This has been implemented through the television watershed (limiting of 'adult' programmes to later than 9pm) and in the use of film and TV game classifications.

More than models The boys in Bandura *et al.* (1961) were more aggressive than girls, and girls were more likely to imitate verbal aggression, and boys physical aggression. This suggests that there are factors other than models that determine which specific acts will be imitated.

CAN YOU...? (No. **10.3**)

1... For each of the **three** theories on the facing page select *at least* **two** points.

2... For each point, write about 50 words.

3... Identify about **ten** points of evaluation (these can be positive or negative).

4... Elaborate each point (see page 9).

5... Use all of this material to write an answer to the following exam question: *Discuss theories of crime.* As good practice you might also write 'building block' essays about each of the three theories. Each answer should contain about 300 words of description and 500 words of evaluation.

Don't forget to read the essay-writing guidance on pages 8–9.

One of your AS studies concerned **eyewitness testimony** (EWT) – the study by Loftus and Palmer (1974) in which participants were shown film clips of car crashes. The use of different verbs (such as 'hit' or 'smashed') in questions about speed affected the participants' answers. This study demonstrated the unreliability of EWT, in particular that **leading questions** alter what people remember. However, leading questions are not the only explanation for the unreliability of EWT. On this spread we look at several other explanations for the unreliability of EWT (and memory generally).

Reconstructive memory

We often think of memory as being like a photograph or video – a stored copy that can be 'opened' and viewed. The idea of **reconstructive memory** was first proposed by Sir Frederick Bartlett in his book *Remembering* (1932). Bartlett proposed that we store fragments of information and when we need to recall something we reconstruct these fragments into a meaningful whole. This reconstruction leads to inaccuracy because our past experience, beliefs and expectations shape the way we reconstruct memory.

Consider the following example. Roswell, New Mexico, 1947, some debris from space was discovered and alleged to be a UFO crash, or was it a US military surveillance balloon? Whatever the true details of the event, we will never know what really happened because *people's memories are shaped by their own beliefs*. There are no accurate memories of the event.

Schema The core of Bartlett's theory is that our beliefs generate expectations and these expectations reconstruct memory. This can be seen in a classic study by Carmichael *et al.* (1932). Participants were shown a set of drawings (see middle column of illustration). There were two groups of participants. Each group saw the drawings but was given a different set of descriptions. When the participants were asked to recall the drawings, the 'label' they had been given affected the drawing they subsequently produced. This shows that the language used affected their memory. In essence, a phrase conjures up a set of expectations about an object, and this expectation affects the memory. So, in Carmichael's study, we might say that memory was affected by the **schema** provided. Such schema alter our recollection, for example, of a crime scene.

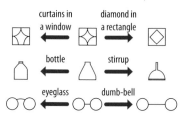

Stereotypes are (usually) simplistic schema that we have about a particular group of people. Such stereotypes often affect our recall of events. A classic study by Allport and Postman (1947) showed two men (one white and one black) arguing on a subway train (see left). Participants invariably remembered the open razor (the preferred mugging weapon in those days) as being in the hand of the black man, whereas in fact it had been held by the white man.

Face recognition

Eyewitnesses are often required to identify individuals at a crime scene; in particular their faces are important.

Ethnicity We are poor at recognising faces from races other than our own (Buckhout and Regan, 1988). This is called the **cross-race effect**.

Recognising unfamiliar faces Ellis *et al.* (1979) found that hair style and the outline of the face were more important for unfamiliar faces – whereas internal features such as eyes mattered more for the recognition of familiar ones. This is probably because features such as hair and outline of the face are relatively invariant whereas our eyes are constantly changing.

Noses and eyebrows Criminals might wear balaclavas for good reason. In studies looking at the ability to judge gender, masking the nose made decision making more difficult than if the eyes or mouth were masked (Roberts and Bruce, 1988).

Configural processing Research suggests that we recognise faces in terms of the configuration of features rather than feature by feature (e.g. Young *et al.*, 1987). This is also shown in the *Thatcher effect* on the facing page.

Attributional biases

Fundamental attribution error At AS you learned about **attribution theory**, which predicts that people use **dispositional** or **situational attributions** to explain the causes of another person's behaviour. This is important in EWT in several ways. For example, eyewitnesses will tend to commit **fundamental attribution errors**, i.e. to overestimate dispositional (internal) factors, tending to assume that a person is 'criminal' in nature rather than their behaviour being a consequence of circumstances. An everyday illustration of this would be assuming that someone who triggers an alarm on leaving a shop is a thief rather than having paid for an item that has had the security tag left on.

Actor–observer effect We tend to make situational attributions for our own behaviour but dispositional ones for others. This is called the **actor–observer effect** and also leads to dispositional judgements of criminals so we assume, for example, that someone who leaves a restaurant without paying has done so intentionally rather than accidentally.

These attributional biases mean that witnesses' recall will not be objective because they tend towards dispositional attributions and these may influence the way the event is recalled.

The role of emotion

Crimes are often frightening to witness, especially if the perpetrator has a weapon. How does this affect the accuracy of testimonies? It could either improve recall (perhaps by focusing attention) or reduce recall (for example, by distracting the witness or interfering with encoding). The effect of emotion on memory is discussed on page 90, including an explanation of flashbulb memories (detailed and lasting recall of the context in which you experienced something personally significant, such as witnessing a crime).

Optimum arousal The Yerkes–Dodson law says that performance (e.g. recall) improves with arousal up to a point (the 'optimum') but higher arousal then reduces performance. This would suggest that crimes that are moderately frightening would produce the best recall but very scary incidents would lead to poor recall.

Weapon effect Loftus *et al.* (1987) proposed the **weapon effect** which suggests that when a weapon is seen, the witness tends to focus on it (rather than, say, on the face of the criminal) because it is frightening.

EVALUATION

Reconstructive memory

Schema Do schema alter our initial perceptions or do they alter subsequent recall? Bartlett assumed that it was the retrieval process that was affected by schema but subsequent research has shown that initial comprehension and storage are also affected. For example, In the study by Loftus and Palmer the second experiment demonstrated that the **post-event information** (leading question) changed the original memory held for the event rather than creating a response bias.

Stereotypes Bartlett's results suggest that we tend to recall in stereotyped ways. Tuckey and Brewer (2003) found that people shown a video of a bank robbery recalled features fitting their stereotypes the best, for example that robbers are male. However, counter-stereotyped information was also well remembered, for example when the belief that 'robbers carry guns' was contradicted.

Face recognition

Poor face recognition Research has certainly found that eyewitnesses are poor at identifying possible criminals. Buckhout (1974) staged a purse-theft and conducted two line-ups to test the recall of 52 witnesses. Only seven correctly identified the thief on both occasions.

Mistaken identity Although we might recognise that we have seen an unfamiliar face before, we are less likely to know where we saw it (Brown et al., 1977). Thus witnesses may, for example, identify faces resembling ones they have seen on the TV. In one ironic case a psychologist was accused of rape by a victim who had seen the psychologist on television and confused the source of familiarity (Thompson, 1988).

Configural processing This has important implications for the use of Identikit pictures to aid recognition because such pictures are based on individual features more than configuration, and so could hinder identification. Research by Ellis et al. (1975) supports this. They found only 12.5% accuracy in choosing the target face from a set of reconstructions. One problem arising from the configural processing of Identikit faces is that, even if some of the individual features are a good likeness to the criminal, the composite face will have a different configural identity. Because faces are recognised as 'wholes' this reduces the likelihood of correct identification when using such composites.

Attributional biases

Fundamental attribution error Evidence typically supports the effect of the fundamental attribution error. For example, Barjonet (1980) found that people tended to believe car accidents were caused by driver error (a dispositional attribution) rather than situational factors, such as driving conditions.

Actor–observer effect Evidence also supports the actor–observer effect, which is particularly important when the witness is involved in the scene themselves, e.g. as a victim. The greater the personal impact on the witness (e.g. injury or fear) the greater the tendency to make dispositional attributions. For example, Walster (1966) gave participants a story about a car rolling down a hill. When little damage arose the participants suggested situational explanations such as handbrake failure. With greater damage they made dispositional judgements suggesting the driver was at fault.

The role of emotion

Optimum arousal Deffenbacher et al. (2004) **meta-analysed** studies of eyewitness recall and found that high stress has a negative impact on accuracy. However, Christianson and Hubinette (1993) found that witnesses to real bank robberies who had been threatened had better recall than onlookers who were not involved.

Weapon effect Evidence also supports the weapon effect. This was demonstrated in a study by Johnson and Scott (1978) where participants, while waiting for an experiment to begin, were witness to a man carrying a knife covered in blood. Other participants saw a man carrying a pen covered in grease. Participants in the first condition were less accurate in identifying the 'criminal'.

The Thatcher effect

People find it more difficult to recognise a person's face when it is upside down (inverted) rather than viewed the right way up, despite the same features being present. In fact, we process upside-down features in a strange way. An amusing example of this is the Thatcher effect (Thompson, 1980). The picture of the former Prime Minister Margaret Thatcher below looks fine, until you view it upside down. The explanation is that when a face is upside down, *configural processing* cannot take place (processing where features are viewed as related to each other rather than by *feature by feature* detection). This means that minor feature differences are more difficult to detect and supports the role of configural processing in face recognition.

Lab, field and natural experiments

Studies such as Loftus and Palmer (1974) and Young et al. (1987) are laboratory experiments, offering high levels of control but which compromise on the extent to which they represent the behaviour of real witnesses, in part because the 'crime' scenes are less realistic (e.g. are filmed) and less arousing and the consequences of the individual's testimony are less important (as they don't affect the conviction or acquittal of a suspect). The study by Johnson and Scott (1976) was a field experiment. As the participants were unaware that they were in a study, their responses should have been more representative of those of real eyewitnesses even though the situation was in fact artificial. Christianson and Hubinette's study was a natural experiment. Here the levels of arousal were higher as the threats were genuine. However, many other factors, such as how well the witnesses could see the robbers, could have affected the results.

CAN YOU...? No. 10.4

1... For each of the **four** explanations on the facing page select *at least* **two** points.

2... For each point, write about 50 words.

3... Identify about **ten** points of evaluation (these can be positive or negative).

4... Elaborate each point (see page 9).

5... Use all of this material to write an answer to the following exam question: *Discuss factors affecting the accuracy of eyewitness testimony*. As good practice you might also write 'building block' essays about each of the four explanations. Each answer should contain about 300 words of description and 500 words of evaluation.

Remember that, when writing an essay, you can include material from other spreads – but only if it is made specifically relevant to the essay. For example, in an essay on the accuracy of eyewitness testimony you might use material from the spread in Chapter 3 on memory and emotion, or you might use material from your AS study of Loftus and Palmer.

For many decades the prison service held a 'nothing works' attitude to the treatment of prisoners. Prisoners were simply detained and then released. More modern prison practice, however, utilises a range of techniques informed by psychological research. Some are based on the **cognitive** principles, for example **cognitive–behavioural therapy** (CBT) and others are based on a **behaviourist** approach, e.g. **token economy**. Psychologists have contributed in other ways, such as programmes to reduce anger.

CBT and token econo my are also discussed on pages 168, 170, 190, 234 and 238.

Cognitive deficits in prisoners

Below are some examples of the kinds of irrational thinking that is typical of criminals:

- *Self-control* – Problems with impulsive behaviour.
- *Cognitive style* – Individuals may lack empathy or have difficulty with abstract social concepts so it is hard for them to achieve social harmony or understand principles of justice.
- *Social perspective taking* – Egocentric prisoners may be unable to see other people's perspective or fail to understand that they should consider other people.
- *Values* – Prisoners typically have poor moral reasoning skills, e.g. they may be unable to see there is a mismatch between their actions and their beliefs.
- *Critical reasoning* – Prisoners' thinking is often irrational and illogical and they avoid self-analysis. This allows them to justify what they do by blaming others rather than accepting that they are responsible for their own behaviour.

▲ *Should prisoners be punished or should they be given psychotherapy? Which is best to reduce recidivism?*

Zero-tolerance (ZT) approach

According to Kelling and Wilson (1982) a neighbourhood could degenerate if just one broken window is left unrepaired because it creates a **social norm**. Once that is established other windows are broken and gradually there is a downward spiral into vandalism and street crime. A **zero-tolerance policy** suggests that this downward spiral of criminal behaviour can be avoided by tackling minor crime (social norms) at the outset to prevent escalation of crime rates and the seriousness of offences.

William Bratton, Police Commissioner for New York City in 1990, dealt with endemic serious crime with a ZT policy which targeted minor crimes (e.g. public drinking) using 7,000 extra police officers. In three years, the crime rate dropped by 37% and homicides by over 50%.

Cognitive therapy

Cognitive skills programmes are based on CBT, i.e. they aim to identify and correct cognitive deficits which lead to criminal behaviour. Some of the key deficits are listed in the box on the left.

The first task is to help the offender to recognise their cognitive deficits and then to help them change their thinking and behaviour through the acquisition of cognitive skills. Two programmes used by the prison service in England and Wales are the *Enhanced Thinking Skills* (ETS) and *Reasoning and Rehabilitation* (R&R) programmes.

ETS Inmates or offenders on probation typically attend 20 two-hour ETS groupwork sessions that are made compulsory. Skills include learning to think before acting, for example using the techniques of 'consider all factors' and 'plusses, minuses, interest'. Group exercises and role play demonstrate the value of stopping and thinking to help with understanding consequences.

R&R In groups of about six, offenders attend sequential modules – each session teaches sub-skills building on previous learning. This is based on the premise that offenders are typically under-socialised, lacking the values, attitudes, reasoning and social skills required for appropriate social behaviour. The modules cover areas such as: problem solving, social skills, negotiation skills, management of emotions, creative thinking, values enhancement (increasing pride and self-belief) and critical reasoning.

Behavioural therapy

Operant conditioning underlies token economy, a treatment used to improve the behaviour of people in prison. The behaviour of inmates can be changed by positively reinforcing desirable (e.g. non-aggressive) behaviours with tokens. These should be given immediately and consistently for clearly defined behaviours. The tokens may be coin-like or punches on a card, and are saved and exchange for goods or privileges such as cigarettes or watching TV. Punishment, such as isolation, is also used to reduce the frequency of non-desired behaviour. So, reinforcement leads to an increase in frequency of the acceptable behaviours, punishment decreases unacceptable ones.

Shaping is the reinforcement of successive approximations to the desired behaviour. In a token economy tailored to each individual, an inmate might initially receive tokens for being polite to other prisoners and later only for being helpful – moving their behaviour in an increasingly prosocial direction. When tokens are given by prison staff they are accompanied by praise. The intention is that this will eventually replace the tokens as a source of reinforcement. This aims to assist rehabilitation so that offenders do not expect rewards simply for behaving in acceptable ways.

Ethical issues

Various ethical issues are raised by token economies. Although the rewards for which tokens are exchanged are identified as privileges (prisoners do not use tokens for food or the right to exercise for example) it has been argued that the need to 'earn' them at all is infantilising. Although this may be seen as demeaning and counter to the needs of rehabilitation, in reality it reflects accurately the nature of the social world – people work to earn money for luxuries like holidays.

Another line of thinking suggests that positive reinforcement is preferable to purely punishment-based methods as it indicates what to do rather than just what not to do so is a more ethical option.

EVALUATION

Cognitive therapy

Strengths Unlike simply punishing offenders by imprisoning them, cognitive approaches can change thinking patterns and therefore should have lasting effects on reducing **recidivism**. This has been demonstrated in a review of their use by the probation service in England and Wales – male offenders in treatment groups reoffend less than controls (Hollin *et al.*, 2004). Some studies find both ETS and R&R are effective (e.g. Friendship *et al.*, 2002), others find a greater benefit with one approach; for example Cann *et al.* (2003) found that ETS was effective but R&R was not.

Who benefits? It is worth noting that reduced reconviction applies only to those who complete the courses; non-completers are not only more likely to be reconvicted than completers but also more so than controls (Palmer *et al.*, 2007). One possible explanation is that those who fail to complete the course have the most deviant thinking so are those most in need of help but perhaps least able to benefit.

Another group who appear to gain little from cognitive treatments are low-risk offenders (Palmer *et al.*, 2008). Such courses work best with medium- and high-risk offenders, whose problems may be related to their thinking patterns whilst problems of low-risk offenders may have other causes. Finally, the benefits may not be very long term. Cann *et al.* (2003) found that although reconviction rates were lower for higher-risk male offenders after one year, this advantage had been lost by two years post-release.

Gender bias The programmes were developed for use with male prisoners; ETS and R&R programmes with women have not reduced recidivism (Cann *et al.*, 2003). This may be because the courses are gender biased as, although the wording of the materials was changed, the content itself remained the same. However, Cann *et al.* suggest that the findings may alternatively be due to the absence of cognitive deficits related to the crimes committed by the women or because the samples were predominantly low-risk individuals.

Behavioural therapy

Immediate and consistent Immediate and consistent use of tokens is important for reinforcement to take place (which is not the case with prison sentences which are far removed from the original crime and thus may not act as effective punishment). The importance of consistency was illustrated by Bassett and Blanchard (1977). They observed one three-month programme which failed. This was attributed to staff misuse of the token system, which is further supported by improvements in prisoner behaviour when consistency was re-established.

Is it successful? Some evidence suggests that token economies do improve behaviour. Jenkins *et al.* (1974) followed up young male offenders for 18 months post-release. Differences between a **control group** and those on cognitive training programmes or a token economy were largely non-significant. However, the token economy group consistently had the lowest percentage of post-release offences for the last nine months of the study. However, in a **meta-analysis**, Garrido and Morales (2007) found that for juvenile offenders who had committed serious crimes (e.g. murder or armed robbery) recidivism was highest when they received no intervention but that cognitive programmes were more effective than behavioural ones (e.g. token economies).

Limitations The token economy approach has been largely replaced by cognitive treatments because it treats only overt behaviour, such as aggression, rather than the causes of that behaviour, as is the intention with cognitive treatments.

Another problem with token economies is that they only work if the inmates are motivated to collect tokens. In reality, powerful prisoners may control much more effective reinforcers (such as offering higher status to fellow prisoners) and punishers (such as bullying) than warders.

Zero-tolerance (ZT) approach

Other explanations The zero-tolerance (ZT) policy implemented in New York was clearly successful, but it is questionable whether the results were due to the policy itself or simply to the massive increase in the numbers of police on the beat. It is also possible that the changes would have occurred anyway. For example, a reduction in drug use might have accounted for the fall in criminality, as could economic growth (as crime rates fell in other American cities over the same period). Alternatively, the criminal activity could simply have shifted from the city to outlying areas. Furthermore, Pollard (1998) criticised the New York policy for being too harsh, for example harassing citizens by cracking down on non-criminal activities such as drinking. This could potentially alienate the community and be detrimental to long-term policing.

Support for ZT However, other studies do support the effectiveness of the policy. Ulmer *et al.* (2000) assessed the effect of a ZT policy towards road traffic offences by young drivers in Florida. The 9% decrease in accidents is convincing as pre-ZT rates provided a baseline and rates in an adjacent state (without a ZT policy) did not change over same period. Similarly, Bachman (1999) found that drug use in the US army fell following the implementation of a ZT policy but did not fall in civilians. This comparison over the same time period helps to exclude cultural influences, for example social norms that could have affected rates of drug use.

Earning release

Hobbs and Holt (1976) studied the effect of a token economy used with boys detained in a correctional institution for offences ranging from truancy to arson and homicide. The boys lived in cottages, three of which were on the token economy programme and one of which was not (the control). Behaviours such as rule-following, co-operation, being non-violent and not destroying property were rewarded with tokens which could be exchanged for drinks, sweets, toys and cigarettes (or saved up for recreational activities, trips and four-day passes to go home). Release from the facility also depended on the total number of tokens earned. The system improved the targeted behaviours compared with boys in the control cottage whose behaviour remained fairly constant.

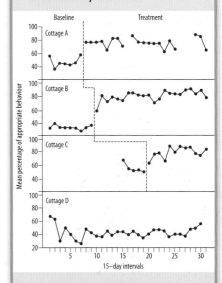

▲ *Changes in behaviour of boys on a token economy (cottages A, B and C) compared with a control (cottage D).*

CAN YOU...? (No. 10.5)

1... For each of the **three** explanations on the facing page select *at least* **two** points.

2... For each point, write about 50 words.

3... Identify about **ten** points of evaluation (these can be positive or negative).

4... Elaborate each point (see page 9).

5... Use all of this material to write an answer to the following exam question: *Discuss treatment and punishment of crime.* As good practice you might also write 'building block' essays about each of the three explanations. Each answer should contain about 300 words of description and 500 words of evaluation.

APPROACHES TO PROFILING

THE US (TOP-DOWN) APPROACH

- The FBI researched background, personality, behaviours, crimes and motives of 36 serial murderers.
- Crime scene analysis indicates type of offender and the classification indicates possible characteristics.
- Stages in US profiling: data assimilation (e.g. from scene), crime scene classification (e.g. organised or disorganised), crime reconstruction (hypotheses about events), profile generation (e.g. offender's age, habits).
- The apprehension of Arthur Shawcross was a successful example.
- A top-down process as crime *type* drives crime reconstruction and profile generation.

EVALUATION

- The US approach doesn't *solve* crimes and it can only be used with multiple offences where there is significant evidence (e.g. serial murder, rape, arson).
- Douglas found that profiling rarely led directly to an arrest but often focused the investigation.
- The FBI interviews with murderers were not standardised and used a small (possibly biased) opportunity sample.
- The organised/disorganised typology may not be valid. Canter et al. analysed 100 murders but found no such distinction.
- Holmes and Holmes extended the classification, giving five types, from disorganised 'visionary killers' to organised 'power/control killers'. Canter found these were typical of most murders, so were not distinctive 'types'.

THE BRITISH (BOTTOM-UP) APPROACH

- The UK approach assumes interpersonal coherence, e.g. in social competence, use of violence or the victim group (e.g. Bundy killed students).
- Information comes from: data analysis (e.g. link crimes with rare behaviours) and forensic awareness (e.g. offenders' precautions to avoid detection).
- Methods used: facet theory (explore all 'sides' of crime scene evidence) and smallest space analysis, SSA (look for infrequent combinations).
- The apprehension of the 'railway rapist' was a successful example.
- A bottom-up process because builds profile from crime scene information.

EVALUATION

- UK profiling methods, unlike US methods, are based on statistical data rather than informal intuition. House used SSA to show that different types of rape could be identified by characteristics from the crime and Santtila et al. found consistent patterns in fire-setters.
- Although Britton reported that CID chiefs felt profiles were not helpful, Copson found that over 80% of police officers felt they contributed to investigations even if they rarely identified suspects.
- However, Mokros and Alison found rapists who were demographically similar (e.g. in age or previous convictions) did not commit more similar crimes.

GEOGRAPHICAL PROFILING

- Indicates where an offender lives, works, socialises or travels.
- Aims to construct an offender's cognitive map of their 'activity space' (where they live, work and socialise).
- Criminal geographic targeting uses the time, distance and movement between crimes to generate a 3D jeopardy surface.

EVALUATION

- Canter and Larkin found 87% of rapists attacked in a region around their homes, Snook et al. found 63% of serial murderers kill less than 10km from their homes and Lundrigan and Canter found murderers disposed of bodies in shifting directions around the home base.
- Goodwill and Alison's filter model prioritises burglary suspects using geographical, temporal, behavioural and dwelling-type data. Geographical closeness best indicates a single offender.

BIOLOGICAL THEORY OF CRIME

- As criminality runs in families, biology is likely to be involved e.g. Osborn and West found 13% of sons of non-criminal fathers had convictions, but 40% had criminal fathers.
- The role of genes versus environment can be checked with adoption studies: Mednick et al. showed that adoptees resembled their (criminal) biological parents more than adoptive ones.
- Some specific genes have been related to criminality. Retz et al. found a 5-HTTLPR gene variant is associated with violent behaviour. The NOS1 gene is linked to aggression in animals and impulsivity in humans (Reif et al.).
- Higher testosterone levels found in male prisoners who committed violent crimes (Dabbs et al.) and same pattern in female prisoners (Dabbs and Hargrove).
- Low serotonin turnover is linked to aggressiveness in animals (Valzelli) and in humans (Virkkunen et al.).

EVALUATION

- Bohman replicated Mednick et al.'s support for biological theory. Environmental factors (e.g. adoptive parents' awareness of the criminal history) didn't affect the adoptees, suggesting genes mattered more than environment.
- Genes control biological processes so could affect aggressive or impulsive behaviours through serotonin processing.
- The body makes serotonin but a high phenylalanine, low tryptophan diet hinders this. Such diets increase aggression (Moeller et al.).
- However, Brunner et al. described a rare, very aggressive family, who lacked the gene for recycling serotonin. Logically this should have reduced aggression by preventing serotonin breakdown.
- Much evidence for the biological theory provides only limited support so other (environmental) factors must be important.
- Twin studies show that both nature and nurture matter. Lyons et al. found MZ twins were more similar than DZs twins. By adulthood, DZs were even less similar, underlining the importance of genetic factors.

DECISION MAKING OF JURIES

SOCIAL INFLUENCE

Majority influence
- Asch's conformity studies showed the power of majority influence. Hastie found jury verdicts reflected the pre-deliberation majority view in over 86% of trials.
- Pressure to conform may be normative (wanting respect from the group) or informational (believing others know more).
- Smith and Mackie suggest the majority is influential because greater number means more varied opinions, deeper discussions and greater confidence.

Minority influence
- A minority can sometimes change group opinions (minority influence), e.g. making individuals question their own opinions (Nemeth).
- Moscovici et al. showed that a consistent minority (of confederates) influenced the majority. In juries this could be effective during long deliberations but the minority would need to be: consistent (between themselves and over time) and willing to discuss.

EVALUATION

Majority influence
- Hinsz and Davis found that opinions did change more when arguments were expressed in a wider variety of ways.
- Strasser and Stewart found that even when instructed to discuss all the information, non-shared information was largely ignored.
- Majority group members more forthright (Kerr et al.) and seem more logical and intelligent (McLachlan).
- Myers and Kaplan showed group polarisation to the majority view after discussion, but none if there was no discussion (no majority influence).

Minority influence
- Minorities are seen to have a deep conviction (as they are maintaining an unpopular opinion) so we make internal rather than external attributions about the causes of their behaviour.
- Larger minorities are more effective in mock juries (Tindale et al.) and the larger the better (Wood et al.).
- Nemeth and Brilmayer showed that a minority member who changed his opinion slightly had a greater effect than one who refused to sway.

CHARACTERISTICS OF THE DEFENDANT

- Stereotyped beliefs affect jurors' decisions about a defendant. Dixon et al. found that suspects with a standard British accent were less often judged guilty than those with a Birmingham accent.

Ethnicity
- Participants judged a shove by a black individual as more violent than by a white individual (Duncan). Pfeifer and Ogloff found white participants were more likely to judge a black than a white defendant guilty of rape.
- In real trials, Baldwin and McConville found that more black defendants were wrongly convicted than wrongly acquitted (even by a black jury).

Physical attractiveness
- We link positive characteristics (halo effect), associating attractiveness with innocence. Saladin et al. found attractive men were thought less likely to have committed murder or armed robbery and DeSantis and Kayson found mock jurors recommended lighter sentences for attractive defendants.
- This effect is strongest for women accused of serious but non-fatal crimes (Quigley et al.) but weaker if good looks are misused, e.g. to con people.
- Downs and Lyons found a negative correlation between defendant attractiveness and fines or bail payments (regardless of seriousness of crime) although McKelvie and Coley found no effect of attractiveness.

EVALUATION

Ethnicity
- Mazzella and Feingold found no effect of ethnicity on mock jury decisions of guilt or innocence (but recommended punishment was affected).
- Gordon et al. found black burglars were given longer sentences than white ones but the reverse was true for fraud.
- Johnson et al. found white participants made more situational attributions and suggested lesser punishments for white than black defendants.
- Sommers and Kent suggest studies are culturally biased as many use only white participants, so we don't know whether black jurors respond differently.

Physical attractiveness
- Sigall and Ostrove found unattractive defendants were given longer sentences for burglary than attractive ones but the reverse was true for fraud.
- Abwender and Hough found that female jurors were more lenient to attractive defendants but the reverse was found for male jurors.
- Studies reporting an effect of defendant features on juries are common but Bull and McAlpine suggest this is a publication bias.

THEORIES OF CRIME

PSYCHOLOGICAL THEORY OF CRIME

- An observer's false beliefs about an individual (e.g. based on stereotypes) affect the observer's behaviour towards the observed individual leading to a self-fulfilling prophecy (SFP).
- The label 'criminal' can reinforce stereotyped responses in observers and lower self-esteem in the individual, producing further deviant behaviour (recidivism).

EVALUATION

- Jahoda found that Ashanti boys behaved as expected according to beliefs about their names. More 'Wednesday' than 'Monday' boys committed violent crime, supporting the SFP.
- Madon et al. found that mothers' expectations of their teenage children's drinking were fulfilled.
- We should not label 'problem' children as this could worsen their behaviour.

SOCIAL THEORY OF CRIME

- Social learning theory (SLT) proposes that behaviour is learned through observation and imitation of models, which creates motivation.
- External motivation comes from direct reinforcement (e.g. property from theft) or vicarious reinforcement (seeing a model benefit).
- Internal motivation comes from identification with, e.g., same sex or high status models.
- Low self-esteem leads to greater imitation and is associated with criminal behaviour.

EVALUATION

- Lab experiments (e.g. Bandura) may be unrepresentative, but real-life correlational data link TV viewing to aggressiveness (Eron et al.) and to adult violent criminality (Eron and Huesmann).
- Research findings suggest children's exposure to models should be regulated, e.g. through the watershed and film classifications.
- Bandura et al. found differences between imitated aggression by boys and girls suggesting factors other than models are important.
- Williams' natural experiment showed that children's aggression doubled following introduction of TV. However, Charlton et al. found no increase in a similar study, possibly because local norms were more prosocial.

FACTORS AFFECTING THE ACCURACY OF EYEWITNESS TESTIMONY

RECONSTRUCTIVE MEMORY

- Recall is an active rebuilding of information based on expectations (Bartlett). This can lead to inaccuracy, e.g. Loftus and Palmer.
- Carmichael et al. showed that verbal labels (schema) affected the way drawings were reproduced.
- Stereotypes affect our recall, e.g. Allport and Postman showed that participants mistakenly recalled a black man holding a weapon.

EVALUATION

- Schema could alter our initial storage or recall. Loftus and Palmer's second experiment showed that post-event information changed the original memory.
- Tuckey and Brewer showed that stereotyped facts about a bank robbery were recalled well but *counter*-stereotyped facts were too.

FACE RECOGNITION

- Cross-race effect means ethnicity of witnesses matters (Buckhout and Regan).
- Differences in recognition of familiar and unfamiliar faces, e.g. hair style and outline of face is important for unfamiliar faces (Ellis et al.).
- Nose shape is more helpful in identifying gender than the eyes or mouth (Roberts and Bruce). Eyebrows help more than hair style (Bruce et al.).
- Faces are recognised using the whole configuration not individual features (Young et al.) – explains the Thatcher effect.

EVALUATION

- Face recognition is poor, Buckhout staged a theft where only 7/52 witnesses correctly identified the thief both times in two line-ups.
- We may know we have seen a face before but not know where (Brown et al.). Witnesses might therefore mistakenly identify faces seen elsewhere, e.g. on TV (Thompson).
- Greater importance of configuration means Identikit pictures may not work. Ellis et al. found only 12.5% accuracy in recognition of reconstructed faces.

ATTRIBUTIONAL BIASES

- People make dispositional (internal) or situational attributions.
- Eyewitnesses often commit fundamental attribution errors, emphasising disposition (e.g. a 'criminal nature') over circumstances.
- The actor–observer effect means we assume an observed criminal act is intentional not accidental.

EVALUATION

- Barjonet supported the fundamental attribution error as people believed accidents were caused by driver error (disposition) rather than driving conditions (situation).
- Walster supported the actor–observer effect by showing that increased personal damage led to dispositional attributions about why a car rolled down a hill.

THE ROLE OF EMOTION

- The frightening nature of crimes could improve recall (focusing the witness's attention, flashbulb memory) or reduce recall (distracting them or interfering with encoding).
- The Yerkes–Dodson law suggests that moderately frightening crimes should produce the best recall.
- The weapon effect (Loftus et al.) suggests a weapon draws attention, so less is paid to the criminal.

EVALUATION

- Deffenbacher et al. found high stress in eyewitnesses reduced accuracy, whereas Christianson and Hubinette showed that real witnesses recalled better if they had been threatened.
- The weapon effect was demonstrated by Johnson and Scott, as recall was worse for a man holding a bloodied knife than one with a grease-covered pen.

TREATMENT AND PUNISHMENT OF CRIME

COGNITIVE THERAPY

- Cognitive skills programmes (based on CBT) aim to identify and correct cognitive deficits (e.g. impulsivity, lack of empathy, egocentricity).
- Enhanced Thinking Skills (ETS), 20 two-hour groupwork sessions. Offenders acquire skills (e.g. 'think before acting') using role-play to learn about consequences of their actions.
- Reasoning and Rehabilitation (R&R), group sessions teach sequential sub-skills, including problem solving, negotiation skills and managing emotions.

EVALUATION

- Cognitive approaches should have longer lasting effects on recidivism than simple punishment as they change thinking patterns.
- Male offenders in EST and R&R treatment groups reoffend less than controls (Hollin et al. and Friendship et al.); Cann et al. found only EST was effective.
- Reduced recidivism relies on completing the course (Palmer et al.) though offenders who don't complete may have the most deviant thinking so benefit less.
- Low-risk offenders also gain little from cognitive treatments (Palmer et al.), perhaps criminality in lower-risk offenders is not related to thinking patterns.
- Cann et al. found the benefits were short term. Reconviction was lower after one year but not by two years post-release.
- EST and R&R courses for women don't reduce recidivism (Cann et al.), possibly because the programmes are gender biased, or women may be predominantly low-risk (Cann et al.).

BEHAVIOURAL THERAPY

- Token economies (operant conditioning) improve behaviour by positively reinforcing desirable responses with tokens which are swapped for goods or privileges.
- Punishment (e.g. isolation) reduces non-desired behaviour.
- Shaping is used to move prisoners from a token economy to more 'normal' rewards such as praise, as well as escalating the behaviours that are rewarded.

EVALUATION

- Tokens must be given immediately and consistently to work (Bassett and Blanchard) so good staff supervision is vital.
- Jenkins et al. found that 18 months post-release, young male offenders from a token economy group committed consistently fewer offences than controls.
- Hobbs and Holt showed that a token economy improved behaviour of boys detained for offences from truancy to homicide compared with a control group.
- However, Garrido and Morales found that for juvenile offenders (convicted of serious crimes) a token economy reduced recidivism more than no intervention but not as much as cognitive programmes.
- A token economy only treats problem behaviour rather than its causes (unlike cognitive treatments).
- To work, a token economy must motivate inmates to collect tokens but powerful prisoners may employ more effective reinforcers and punishers than staff.
- Behavioural therapies raise ethical issues.

ZERO-TOLERANCE (ZT) APPROACH

- Kelling and Wilson described the 'broken windows' problem (one left unrepaired leads to vandalism and ultimately serious crime).
- A zero-tolerance policy breaks this downward spiral, e.g. Bratton in New York City targeted specific minor crimes and crime rate dropped by 37% in three years.

EVALUATION

- The success of the New York ZT policy may be due to other factors, e.g. more police officers, reduced drug use or economic growth.
- Pollard suggests the policy is too harsh, cracking down on non-criminal activities might alienate the community.
- Ulmer et al. found that a ZT policy for traffic offences by young drivers decreased accidents by 9%.
- Bachman et al. found that an army ZT policy reduced drug use by personnel (but not by civilians).

Question 10 Discuss approaches to profiling [25]

Student answer

Paragraph 1 ▶ Profiling is a technique used to help the police identify serious criminals, originally from the USA where they have lots of serial killers.

Paragraph 2 ▶ Profiling was created by the FBI where face-to-face interviews were carried out with 36 convicted killers. This led to a 'top-down' classification of offenders according to crime scene characteristics — crime scenes were categorised as 'organised' or 'disorganised'. Organised killers were described as people who were generally tidy and left no evidence after committing a crime, whereas disorganised killers were described as people who were likely to be white males with a history of poor employment and were likely to have low-level convictions for things like sex offences and violence.

Paragraph 3 ▶ The FBI had several special successes such as the Arthur Shawcross case, where the FBI predicted he would return to the scenes of crime and when he did return they caught him as they had predicted. The 36 killers they used in working out their profiling scheme were an opportunity sample. Also the interviews weren't standardised.

Paragraph 4 ▶ The British approach has been more scientific. Canter was asked in the 1980s to compose a profile of a rapist, and knowing nothing about police work, Canter looked for behavioural patterns in the rapist's behaviour. Canter suggested that the rapist knew the railways around London. This turned out to be accurate and was a good clue and detectives identified John Duffy. Duffy was just like the profile but had been way down the suspect list and so never would have been caught except Canter's profile led the police to him.

Paragraph 5 ▶ A major criticism of British profiling is that it isn't used much. Britton found that CID chiefs weren't interested and this was supported by Copson who found it helped to solve only 14% of the cases where it was used.

Paragraph 6 ▶ There is a lot of evidence that criminals are consistent in their criminal behaviour, Santilla showed this for firesetters and House showed this for rapists. There isn't much evidence for consistency between criminal and non-criminal behaviour and there isn't any evidence that types of criminal exist like in the FBI profiling. This was found by Alison.

Paragraph 7 ▶ Geographical profiling has been more successful and relates to people's cognitive maps. Offenders initially offend in their home area. Where there is more than one offence the sites of the offences can tell where the criminal is likely to live, which helps to focus the investigation. Canter has shown that rapists have distinct geographical movements and Snook showed that serial killers tend to kill within a 10 km radius of their home. This form of profiling has been computerised and is used in UK police forces to focus investigations. Alison has shown that for burglary this is the most useful form of profiling and the behavioural form of profiling is far less useful.

Paragraph 8 ▶ Overall I have to question how useful profiling is. You can see that for some cases like Duffy it could be useful, and also geographical profiling seems helpful, but when you have Copson's estimate that only 14% of profiling predictions are helpful it does make me question the amount of time and effort spent on it.

[522 words]

Examiner comments

This is a reasonable essay which demonstrates a fair amount of psychological knowledge. The student who wrote this clearly knows the topic reasonably well and is able to make some fair evaluative (**AO2**) points (highlighted in grey).

Paragraph 1 is a nice introduction to the essay but does not attract much, if any, credit. It would have been perfectly acceptable to start with paragraph 2.

The knowledge in paragraph 2 is accurate and appropriate but illustrates one of the key problems with the essay – the description is not as detailed as it could be.

Paragraph 3 presents evaluation of FBI profiling but it lacks coherence. A number of separate points are made but further details are not given. A better version of this paragraph is given in the 'improvements' below.

Paragraph 4 again lacks detail. The British approach is not actually explained. The main outline regards the capture of John Duffy, which is almost anecdotal (i.e. lacking psychological knowledge).

This is also the problem with paragraphs 5 and 6. These paragraphs are good because specific references are cited but to earn top marks there must be detail, for example how did Britton find this out, what did Copson do, and when?

Paragraph 7 is the best paragraph in the whole essay as it includes description of an assumption plus supporting evidence which acts as an evaluation.

Paragraph 8 doesn't attract any marks as it is a summary of previous points.

Throughout the essay **AO1** is reasonably accurate but lacks detail, placing it towards the bottom of Band 6–7, **6 out of 10 marks**. **AO2** is relevant and structured, but not as coherent nor detailed as it could be, fitting the descriptors of Band 8–11, **9 out of 15 marks**.

15/25 makes this essay as a solid Grade C.

Improvement?

Clearly detail needs to be improved both for **AO1** and **AO2**, as well as coherence. An example of this can be shown in an improved version of paragraph 3 which is both more detailed and coherent (additions are underlined):

The FBI had several special successes such as the Arthur Shawcross case, where the FBI predicted he would return to the scenes of crime and when he did return they caught him as they had predicted. However this does not mean that the system is scientific. A further issue is that the 36 killers they used in working out their profiling scheme were an opportunity sample. The problem with this is that the killers selected may not have been representative of all killers or indeed of criminals generally. Another methodological issue is that the interviews weren't standardised. This suggests that the data collected may lack validity because different killers were asked different questions and it might even be that the interviewers asked leading questions and thus got the answers they were expecting.

Coherence can be improved by identifying each separate evaluative point – which helps the examiner to understand what points you are trying to make.

Chapter 11
Sport psychology

Chapter contents

212   Introduction to the study of sport psychology
214   Improving motivation in sport
216   Internal factors affecting sporting performance
218   External factors affecting sporting performance
220   Effects of exercise on well-being
222   Theories of aggression in sport

End-of-chapter review

224   Chapter summary
226   Exam question with student answer

Specification breakdown	
Improving motivation in sport (e.g. explanations of motivation and ways of improving motivation).	Good coaches know what motivates their players and how each player is different. We examine some theories of motivation and how they lead to strategies for improving motivation.
Internal factors affecting sporting performance (e.g. arousal, anxiety, attribution theory).	'When the going gets tough, the tough get going.' Good performers are fully aroused yet manage to control anxiety. They also attribute success to internal factors. Here we examine the psychology of these factors.
External factors affecting sporting performance (e.g. team membership, audience effects).	Sportspeople often claim there is a significant home advantage for teams. This section looks at how social forces affect performance including all types of audience effect and the dynamics of teams and their coaches.
Effects of exercise on well-being (e.g. effects of physical and mental health).	The past 20 years have brought scientific proof that exercise is good for you, not least for your brain! Effects of different levels of exercise on psychophysical health are examined in this section.
Theories of aggression in sport (e.g. frustration–aggression hypothesis, ethological theory, social learning theory).	All sports involve some degree of interpersonal aggression, even chess. Does this mean that playing or watching sports makes people more aggressive? We look at some explanations for aggression to see if they suggest a link between sports and aggressive behaviour.

What separates a winner from the rest of the pack is not raw talent or physical ability; instead, it is the drive and dedication to work hard every single day, and the heart to go after your dream, no matter how unattainable others think it is.

Paralympian Linda Mastandrea

To the uninitiated, the idea of sport psychology may seem hard to grasp – surely the secret to sporting success lies in specific physical abilities not psychological strengths. People at the top of their game are successful because of their natural talent – you might think that but it isn't so. Success is as much in the head as in the body.

This is where sports psychology comes in. It is the study of the psychological and mental factors that enhance sporting performance. Some American sport psychologists make a distinction between academic sport psychology, which looks at more theoretical issues (like who chooses what sport), and applied sport psychology, which focuses purely on applying psychology to improve performance. However, most European sport psychologists do not make this distinction (Jarvis, 2006).

THE ORIGINS OF SPORT PSYCHOLOGY

Sport psychology is a relatively new field of psychology; the division of *sports and exercise psychology* of the *British Psychological Society* was founded in 2004, but psychologists have been conducting research related to sports psychology for a long time. In fact, some of the earliest studies in psychology are related to sports performance. We examine three of them here.

Faster cycling

Norman Triplett (1897) conducted what is often described as the first experiment in social psychology and it was related to sports. In his day, cycling was a relatively new sport and he was intrigued by the observation that cyclists performed better when in a race or with a pacemaker than when they practised on their own. One possible explanation was that improved performance was due to the fact that other cyclists provided shelter from wind and therefore they all went faster. Triplett, however, wondered if there might be a psychological explanation.

Triplett designed an experiment to test this. He arranged for participants to turn fishing reels. Each participant had to turn a reel as fast as possible so that a flag sewn to a thread made four circuits of a four-metre course. First, each participant practised until they became proficient. Next, in the actual experiment, participants did this on their own or sitting across from another person completing the same task (this is called **coacting**). Each participant performed six trials, alternating between the two conditions – alone and coacting. In total he tested 225 people of a range of ages.

Triplett found that the participants who were coacting did perform faster than those working alone, supporting his belief that the presence of others is stimulating. Triplett suggested that the presence of others might be psychologically stimulating because of the sense of competition; this stimulation would release energy not previously available. Another reason might be that seeing another person working apparently faster could increase a person's self-expectations. Research on **coaction effects** as well as **audience effects** are discussed on the right.

Anxiety in moderation is a good thing

Psychological research in the early 20th century was largely concerned with learning (**behaviourism** dominated psychology) and experiments frequently used animals as subjects. In one classic study of learning, Robert Yerkes and John Dodson (1908) used the *dancing mouse* to study to what extent learning was affected by anxiety. They used a mild electric shock to create varying levels of anxiety in their 'dancers'. The dancing mice were placed in a box with two exits (A and B), one marked with a white card and the other a black card – the cards were regularly swapped so sometimes exit A had a white card and sometimes it had a black card. If the dancer went towards the black card they received a shock. The aim was to see how many trials would be required before they learned to select the white route on a regular basis (the dancers were given ten tests every morning and success was achieved when they choose the white route correctly on three consecutive days, that is for 30 tests). Yerkes and Dodson found that using a weak or a strong electric shock was less favourable to the acquirement of the habit than the intermediate stimulus, i.e. too little or too much anxiety is not good for learning but a moderate amount is desirable. This has become known as the **Yerkes–Dodson effect** (see pages 204 and 216).

Social loafing

The presence of others doesn't always have a positive effect; in some cases group members become progressively less productive as the size of the group increases – an effect referred to as **social loafing**. This was first noted by Maximilien Ringlemann in 1913. Ringlemann, a French agricultural engineer, believed that when tug-of-war teams pulled on a rope, the addition of more people didn't result in a steady increase of pressure. He demonstrated this by attaching a rope to a strain gauge and measuring the pull exerted by people alone and in groups. The total of the group pulls did not equal the sum of individual efforts. Three people pulled at only 2.5 times the average performance for the person, and eight pulled at about four times the individual pull (should be eight times the individual pull). The **Ringlemann effect** refers to the **negative correlation** between the amount of pull per person and the size of a team.

COACTION AND AUDIENCE EFFECTS

The topics described on the facing page and throughout this chapter offer lots of opportunity for your own research – with the exception of the study delivering electric shocks to dancer mice! You could start this topic by trying out a few studies yourself, some of which are described below.

Schmitt et al. (1986) asked participants to perform two tasks: a simple, well-learned task (typing their name into a computer) and a difficult, novel task (type their name backwards with ascending numbers placed between each letter). This task was performed in one of three conditions: (1) alone (no audience), (2) mere presence (experimenter wore a blindfold and earphones) and (3) evaluation apprehension (the experimenter assessed the participant's performance).

They found that participants performed the simple task faster under both audience conditions than when alone. Participants performed the difficult task more slowly under both audience conditions. When the audience created 'evaluation apprehension' the participants were faster still on the simple task but performance was poor on the difficult task.

Michaels et al. (1982) watched pool players and recorded the number of successful shots and compared this with when they were playing alone. Players who are 'watched' should do better.

Geisler and Leith (1997) assessed audience effects by observing footballers taking football penalties. They found that the number of goals scored was the same whether there was or wasn't an audience present.

LOCUS OF CONTROL

Locus of control is related to sports performance. There is some research which suggests that people with an internal locus of control do better in terms of sport performance (see pages 174–175). Test your own locus of control with the quiz on page 165, you could correlate this with success on a sports-related task.

EFFECTS OF AROUSAL

You could also do some research on the effects of anxiety – without using shocks. Anxiety is often associated with general levels of physical arousal. Physical arousal can be created through physical activity.

1. Create three levels of arousal – low, medium and high – by asking participants to run on the spot for 10 seconds, 30 seconds and 50 seconds. You can check arousal levels by measuring their pulse.

2. Then ask each participant to perform a task. You could look at well-learned versus novel tasks (as in Schmitt et al.'s study), or you could ask them to perform a physical task such as potting pool balls or throwing darts.

ANOTHER QUIZ

Carol Dweck believes that having a growth mindset is more important than natural talent (see left). This is not to say that natural talent means nothing and cannot take a person far, but it is to say that the growth mindset, and the motivation and dedication that come with it, can take a person further. The growth mindset is important to any achievement – school work, exams or sporting. She characterises people with a growth mindset as

- Finding success in doing their best, in learning and improving.
- Finding setbacks motivating because they're informative and are a wake-up call.
- Taking charge of the processes that bring success and maintain it.
- Test your own mindset at http://mindsetonline.com/testyourmindset/step1.php

◄ **Mindset**
The psychologist Carol Dweck (2007) writes about the importance of 'mindset'. She claims that success on any kind of task depends on whether you have a 'natural ability' mindset or a 'growth' mindset. She claims that only those with an growth mindset maintain enduring success. One of the examples of a growth mindset that she gives is Muhammed Ali, widely considered one of the greatest heavyweight championship boxers of all time. Dweck claims Ali was not a 'natural'. He had the wrong body proportions for a fighter. He punched and rallied like an amateur, and while he was quick, he lacked strength and he lacked the classic moves. What he did have was motivation and, more than that, he had the ability to recover from defeat by becoming even more determined.

Motivation concerns goal-oriented behaviour and is what pushes a person towards a particular goal. Although most people participate in sport and exercise for pleasure, when we consider sport at competition level we get into the realm of achievement, and we need to consider people's motives to achieve.

EXPLANATIONS OF MOTIVATION AND IMPLICATIONS FOR IMPROVING MOTIVATION

Achievement motivation theory (McClelland *et al.*, 1953)

In his classic theory of motivation, David McClelland proposed that two factors are important: (1) the desire to succeed and (2) the desire to avoid failure. A person's decision to pursue a goal happens when motivation to succeed is greater than fear of failure. This has been called a mathematical model because performance can be formulated as *participation = intrinsic motivation – fear of failure*.

Motivation to succeed As you can see, in this model, motivation is related to **intrinsic motives**, an individual's own desire to find success, as contrasted with **extrinsic motives**, such as a desire to become famous, win prizes or some other reward.

Approach–avoidance Achievement motivation theory can be related to an approach–avoidance model of motivation. Whenever we enter a sporting situation we experience an *approach–avoidance conflict*. We want to approach the situation in order to enjoy taking part. At the same time we also want to avoid it to escape the anxiety that taking part will produce. 'Approach' is related to intrinsic motivation, 'avoidance' is related to fear of failure.

Individuals who are high in intrinsic motivation and low in anxiety are likely to be motivated to succeed at high levels (high 'approach', low 'avoidance'). Those who are low in intrinsic motivation and high in fear of failure are likely to experience considerable difficulty in competitive sport (more 'avoidance' than 'approach'). Those who have moderate intrinsic motivation but high anxiety (fear of failure) levels might enjoy sport but find it very difficult to compete at a high level where competitive anxiety is likely to be greater.

Need to achieve McClelland (1961) extended his theory further to explain individual differences in the *need to achieve* (nAch). For example, people with a high nAch avoid both low-risk and high-risk situations because in low-risk situations, easily won success is not a sign of true achievement, and in high-risk situations success might be as much due to luck as ability.

Self-efficacy (Bandura, 1982)

A number of approaches to understanding motivation concern the importance of self-confidence. Albert Bandura introduced the concept of **self-efficacy** to explain self-confidence in psychological terms.

Understanding self-efficacy Self-efficacy is often confused with **self-esteem**, but actually the two concepts are quite distinct. Whereas self-esteem is the emotional experience of how we feel about ourselves, *self-efficacy* refers to our beliefs about our abilities. As well as being a **cognitive** rather than emotional phenomenon, self-efficacy differs further from self-esteem in being situation specific. Our self-esteem is fairly constant and generalises across quite different situations, we can have different self-efficacy in different situations. For example, you might have low self-efficacy for academic success but high self-efficacy for sports. High self-efficacy generally has a positive impact on our motivation.

Sources of self-efficacy We get the information about our sporting abilities from several sources (Schunk, 1991).

- *Successful performance* is a direct source of information. If you succeed in a task this increases your self-efficacy for that task. A good coach will aid this by increasing the difficulty of tasks slowly to ensure success at every stage.
- *Vicarious experience* is an indirect source. Witnessing other people of similar ability succeed increases our own self-confidence.
- *Verbal persuasion* – other people encourage you through positive statements about your performance.
- *Emotional and physiological arousal* provides clues about success. If, for example, we are in a relaxed state we might interpret this as meaning we can cope with the task at hand. On the other hand, if we are tense, for whatever reason, we may interpret this as anxiety about being able to succeed, reducing our self-efficacy.

Goal perspective theory (Nicholls, 1984)

Goal orientation People are either *task* (*mastery*) or *ego* (*competitive*) in their orientation. **Task-oriented** individuals are concerned with the mastery of a particular skill whereas **ego-oriented** individuals aim to outperform others.

Motivational climate The environment in which an individual is undergoing training might be a *mastery* climate or a *competitive* climate. Mastery-oriented environments reward effort and emphasise cooperation. They also encourage self-confidence and intrinsic motivation. A competitive climate punishes mistakes and competition is encouraged.

Fostering a mastery climate Epstein (1989) coined the term TARGET to represent the environmental conditions that lead to a mastery climate:

T = Tasks to facilitate interest.

A = Authority yields to students who monitor their own progress and make decisions.

R = Rewards focus on individual improvement rather than social comparisons.

G = Grouping of students within cooperative units.

E = Evaluation using tests that focus on effort and self-improvement.

T = Timing of tasks and pace generally.

Increasing self-efficacy in weightlifters

In a classic demonstration of the impact of self-efficacy, Wells *et al.* (1993) randomly divided student participants into three groups and gave them weightlifting tasks. In one condition the participants were given accurate feedback about how much they were lifting. In another condition they were misled into believing they were lifting heavier weights, and in the final condition they were misled into thinking they were lifting lighter weights. The three groups were then compared on how much they could lift in the final session. The group who believed that they had lifted heavier weights than they really had were able to lift the most. This demonstrates both the power of self-efficacy and the ease with which a good coach can improve it. It doesn't necessarily have to be done by lying to athletes but by emphasising the positive aspects of their performance.

EVALUATION

Achievement motivation theory

Strengths Many of the concepts of achievement motivation theory are supported by evidence. For example, intrinsic motivation has been shown to be more important than extrinsic motivation (see page 188). Furthermore the model is helpful in understanding why athletes respond differently to different levels of competition.

Limitations The main problem is that it cannot be used to predict successful performance. Research has found that those high in achievement motivation, as calculated from intrinsic motivation and anxiety, do not consistently do better in competition than those low in achievement motivation (Russell and Jarvis, 2003). The model has largely been abandoned by sports psychologists in favour of more situation-specific theories, such as self-efficacy (Cox, 2007).

An alternative development is the trait-oriented view of achievement motivation (Schuler and Prochaska, 2000) and the associated *Achievement Motivation Inventory* (AMI) which lists 17 achievement orientations such as competitiveness, eagerness to learn, internality and fearlessness. An individual's score is given on each of the traits and can thus be used to increase motivation in particular areas.

Self-efficacy

There is no suggestion that self-efficacy is a complete explanation of sporting motivation, but it does appear to be an important influence. One of the reasons it is important is because it is an influence that can be harnessed by coaches to improve motivation.

Research evidence There is a wealth of evidence to show that motivation and performance can be improved by increasing an individual's sense of self-efficacy, for example the study on weightlifting described at the top of the page. This shows that performance can be improved through increased self-confidence.

Other research has demonstrated the effects of self-efficacy. Chalabaev *et al.* (2009) observed girls playing football in a French secondary school and questioned the girls on their beliefs concerning boys' and girls' footballing abilities. The researchers found that those girls who believed that boys were always better footballers than girls played worse, presumably because they did not believe in the competence of girls and this affected their performance.

Collective self-efficacy The concept of self-efficacy can also be applied to the performance of a whole team. Myers *et al.* (2004) examined the relationship between collective efficacy in women's ice hockey teams and their team performance. Efficacy scores collected on Saturdays were strongly predictive of performance later that day (correlation was +.56). There was a much weaker relationship between efficacy and performance on the previous day. This suggests that performance had a modest effect on collective efficacy but that collective efficacy had a very powerful effect on performance.

Goal perspective theory

Value of the mastery climate It might be expected that there would be a match between goal orientation and motivational climate, i.e. that task-oriented individuals thrive in a mastery climate but ego-oriented individuals thrive in a competitive climate. This is referred to as the **matching hypothesis**. However, research has found that the mastery climate is best for all orientation types (Newton and Duda, 1999), which would appear to underline the importance of effort and intrinsic motivation in success.

Intrinsic and extrinsic motivation Task- and ego-orientation appear to be related to intrinsic and extrinsic motivation. Zahariadis and Biddle (2000) questioned about 400 11–16-year-olds regarding their reasons for taking part in sport. A clear relationship emerged between reasons and orientations. Task-oriented young people spoke of team spirit and skill development as their main reasons for taking part in sport, whereas those classified as ego-oriented were more concerned with extrinsic rewards such as their social status.

Complex relationship A number of studies have found quite complex relationships between orientation and performance. For example, Sarrazin *et al.* (2002) found that goal orientation interacted with perceived ability (self-efficacy) and task difficulty when determining amount of effort exerted and final performance. Male participants aged 12–16 had to scale a rock-climbing wall. Effort was assessed in terms of heart rate reserve. When task difficulty was low there was little difference between the boys. As task difficulty increased the boys with low ego-orientation and high self-efficacy did best and those with high ego-orientation and low self-efficacy did worst.

EXAM TIP

We have presented theories of motivation on the facing page and evaluated these theories here. As far as possible we have tried to emphasise how these theories and the associated evaluations might be used to suggest how motivation can be improved – but there hasn't always been space to do this. In your essays you must remember to use your knowledge effectively when answering a question on *improving* motivation in sport.

CAN YOU...? No. 11.1

1... For each explanation on the facing page select **two or more** key points relating to how motivation could be improved.

2... For each key point write about 50 words explaining the point.

3... Identify about **ten** points of evaluation (these can be positive or negative).

4... Elaborate each point (see page 9).

5... Use all of this material to write an answer to the following exam question: *Discuss improving motivation in sport.* As good practice you might also write 'building block' essays about the different theories of motivation as applied to improving motivation in sport. Your answers should contain about 300 words of description and 500 words of evaluation.

Remember that, when writing an essay, you can include material from other spreads – but only if it is made specifically relevant to the essay. For example, in an essay on improving motivation in sport you might use material from the next spread on attribution theory (internal and external attributions) as well as evidence from in Chapter 9 on motivation.

INTERNAL FACTORS AFFECTING SPORTING PERFORMANCE

If you have taken part in any sporting contest – or indeed any physical activity where you are being assessed, such as a driving test – you will be familiar with the negative effect of anxiety on your performance. On the other hand, psychologists know that a certain amount of anxiety (or arousal) is good for performance – if you are too relaxed you don't do your best. Good performers are aroused yet manage to control anxiety. They also show an internal locus of control. Here we examine the psychology of these factors.

▶ Anxiety – good or bad for performance?

PHYSIOLOGICAL AND COGNITIVE FACTORS

At the top level of sporting competition there is relatively little difference in skill, fitness or motivation. Perhaps the most important factor separating winners from losers at this level is the ability to cope with arousal and anxiety (Jones, 1991).

Effects of arousal

'Arousal' refers to our general level of physical and psychological activation. It is related to the **sympathetic nervous system** which releases **adrenaline**, creating physiological arousal or 'readiness', preparing an organism for *fight or flight* (in your AS course you learned about this in relation to the stress response).

We are low in arousal when we are tired, bored or sleeping, and we are high in arousal when we are excited, anxious or angry.

Inverted U hypothesis Yerkes and Dodson (1908, see pages 204 and 212) first described the relationship between arousal and performance as an inverted U (see graph on right). Performance is best at the optimum level and drops off when arousal rises above or falls below this 'optimum'.

The optimum level of arousal for a task depends on the complexity of the motor skills used to perform that task. For a complex task involving fine motor skill, such as placing a dart in the bullseye, low levels of arousal are preferable. For gross tasks such as weightlifting, the optimum arousal level is much higher (see graph on page 219).

Effects of anxiety

Anxiety is a negative emotional state in which we experience high arousal accompanied by worrying, i.e. it is a mixture of physiological and **cognitive** factors. The physiological arousal is called *somatic anxiety* and the cognitive 'worry' state is called *state anxiety*.

Multidimensional anxiety theory Martens *et al.* (1990) proposed that the relationship between somatic anxiety (physiological arousal) and performance follows the inverted-U shape, whereas state anxiety shows a **negative correlation** with performance, i.e. as anxiety increases performance decreases.

The catastrophe model Fazey and Hardy (1988) suggested a more complex relationship. If somatic anxiety (arousal) increases beyond the optimum level, the inverted-U hypothesis predicts a gradual decrease in performance. However, Fazey and Hardy observed that in fact there is sometimes a catastrophic decline, which they suggest is due to increased state anxiety (worry) – the inverted U only describes increases in somatic anxiety (see diagram on left).

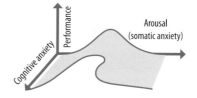

▲ At the back of the graph you can see the inverted U (Yerkes–Dodson law) – as arousal increases performance rises to an optimal point then decreases. However, as cognitive anxiety increases (closer to the reader), performance falls off a cliff after the optimal point and even arousal drops slightly. This is catastrophe theory.

Individual zone of optimal functioning There is also *trait anxiety* which is a personality variable – the extent to which people vary in their ability to cope with anxiety. Hanin (1986) suggested that any full account of the relationship between anxiety and performance needs to include the influence of trait anxiety as well. Hanin suggested that each person has an *individual zone of optimal functioning* (IZOF) and that performance is only affected in an individual if anxiety goes above or below this zone.

COGNITIVE FACTORS

As we have seen some aspects of anxiety are cognitive but cognitive influences also come from attributions – the way sports people think about the causes of their behaviour.

Attribution theory

In your AS course you studied **attribution theory** (Heider, 1958) and should be familiar with the concepts of **internal** and **external attributions** – people explain the behaviour of others and themselves either in terms of **dispositional** (internal) characteristics or **situational** (external) ones. These concepts can be applied to sports behaviour in many ways.

Self-serving bias It is more likely that we will attribute success to ability (internal attribution) and failure to task difficulty (external). This means that we do not own responsibility for failure and cannot improve because the

reasons for failure are not under personal control. A successful sports person learns to attribute failure to his or her own efforts.

Stability of attributions Weiner (1992) extended attribution theory. He suggested that self-attribution is based on two factors: whether an internal or external attribution is made, and whether the attribution is stable over time or varies from one situation to another. A person who makes stable attributions assumes that past success predicts future success or past failure suggests failure in the future. However, some people make unstable predictions – expecting that the next outcome will be different. An unstable approach may be a desirable way to deal with failure because the person believes it is only temporary and success can still happen.

Learned helplessness Seligman (1995) described the effects of lack of control. If a person (or animal) learns that their efforts have no effect they give up trying. When later placed in a similar situation they have learned not to bother to make an effort. Seligman tested this with dogs who were given shocks that they could not avoid. The dogs learned to passively accept the pain.

Locus of control People who prefer to make internal attributions about their own behaviour are said to have an internal locus of control (you can test yours on page 165 and read more about it on page 174). This means that they have the potential for change and may well learn from failure, whereas 'externals' don't.

EVALUATION

Effects of arousal

Research support There is considerable support for the inverted-U hypothesis from studies that have looked at all kinds of sports. For example, Sonstroem and Bernado (1982) studied basketball players and found that poorest performance occurred in those players who were at either high or low levels of arousal. It is worth, however, noting that arousal was not assessed in a particularly valid way – using a questionnaire related to state anxiety, administered one hour before the event.

Other support for the inverted-U hypothesis comes from studies of athletes' perceptions of what factors affect performance. Thelwell and Maynard (2000) asked approximately 200 county-level English cricketers what they considered to be the most important variables affecting their performance. Optimum level of arousal emerged in the top four factors affecting both batsmen and bowlers.

Real-life application Understanding optimum levels of arousal has an important application in mental preparation for different kinds of competition. In sports that involve fine motor skills, such as darts or snooker, a low level of arousal will be desirable – which might explain why drinking alcohol or the use of **beta-blockers** is more common in these sports (because both substances reduce activity in the sympathetic nervous system). On the other hand a sport involving gross motor skills requires a process of 'psyching up' to raise arousal levels. Some athletes have rituals to help them do this, a classic example being the Maori display used by the New Zealand 'All-Blacks' prior to rugby matches.

Effects of anxiety

The emphasis in modern sports psychology is more on state anxiety (worry) than arousal (somatic anxiety) as a predictor of performance. However, a **meta-analysis** of studies that investigated the relationship between state anxiety (measured by the standard psychometric test, the *Competitive State Anxiety Inventory-2*, or CSAI-2) and sporting performance found only a weak correlation (Craft *et al.*, 2003).

The catastrophe model has proved difficult to test directly because of its complexity. However, Hardy *et al.* (1994) designed a study (see box on right) which showed that performance does drop off when state anxiety is high as predicted by the model.

One strength of this model is that it does suggest that cognitive anxiety can be a positive factor in some circumstances (low or optimum arousal) so shouldn't necessarily be seen as a negative factor. In fact many athletes report they perform best when worried (Jones *et al.*, 1993).

Individual zone of optimal functioning Studies have found modest support for the IZOF. For example, Russell and Cox (2000) measured the positive and negative emotions experienced by American football and basketball players during a game, and also assessed performance levels. Those sportsmen who reported positive emotions (and thus must have been in their IZOF) performed better than those reporting negative emotions, but the difference was only moderate. A study by Randle and Weinburg (1997) actually found no difference in performance when players were in or out of the IZOF.

Attribution theory

Self-serving bias Gill (1980) studied female basketball players. After winning or losing a game, the players were asked whether their outcome was due to their own team or the other team. As predicted by the self-serving bias the players gave primary responsibility for the outcome to their own team if they were successful but to the other team if they failed. However, when asked about personal versus team responsibility, members of losing teams blamed themselves for the failure whereas members of winning teams attributed success to the team effort, failing to support the self-serving bias.

Stability of attributions The effect of stability may be positive or negative. One study looked at response to failure in 100 novice golfers undertaking a putting task. Generally those who made unstable attributions (e.g. suggested that their failure was due to luck) showed better task persistence, suggesting these are healthy attributions (Le Foll *et al.*, 2006). In contrast, in situations where a person is successful, stable attributions may be preferable because performance will increase self-confidence and future expectations.

Real-life application: Attribution training

All of this evidence can be applied to training programmes to help sports people change the ways in which they think about their performance. Orbach *et al.* (1999) investigated the effectiveness of **attribution training** with 35 inexperienced tennis players. The players were given false feedback over four training sessions, in order to lead them to attribute successes to internal rather than external factors. As hoped the players changed their attributions in response to the feedback, and these changes led to improved **self-esteem** and performance.

Testing the catastrophe model

Hardy *et al.* (1994) worked with eight experienced crown green bowlers who were tested twice: first under low state anxiety (neutral instructions were given) and second under high state anxiety (they were told that their scores would be compared with elite crown green bowlers and they needed to do well).

Physiological arousal (somatic anxiety) was created by getting the bowlers to do shuttle runs and was assessed using heart rate (increasing heart rate meant higher arousal). Anxiety was also assessed using a state anxiety questionnaire.

The researchers found, as predicted, that as arousal increased performance remained steady in the low state anxiety group, i.e. arousal had no effect on performance. In the high state anxiety group performance increased as arousal increased but dropped off sharply when a high level of arousal was reached, as predicted by the catastrophe model.

CAN YOU...?   (No. **11.2**)

1... Select **two or more** key points for each of the explanations described on this spread.

2... For each key point write about 50 words explaining the point.

3... Identify about **ten** points of evaluation (these can be positive or negative).

4... Elaborate each point (see page 9).

5... Use all of this material to write an answer to the following exam question: *Describe and evaluate internal factors affecting sporting performance.* As good practice you might also write 'building block' essays about the different internal factors. Your answers should contain about 300 words of description and 500 words of evaluation.

Don't forget to read the essay-writing guidance on pages 8–9.

The main external factor that affects sporting performance is other people – your team mates and opposing team members. This section looks at how social forces affect performance – for good or bad.

Home advantage

It is a well-known fact that teams are more likely to win when playing at home than away. This is called the **home advantage effect** (HAE) (also called home team/court/field advantage effect). One explanation for this is that a supportive home crowd will energise the home team, a form of **social facilitation**, and inhibit the performance of the away team. Another explanation relates to confidence – people (and animals) feel more confident in their own territory. Davies and Houston (1984) demonstrated this with the speckled wood butterfly. When an intruder lost a contest with the butterfly owning a particular 'territory' (a sunspot underneath a bit of wood), the researchers replaced the owner with the intruder. In the next contest the old owner backed down to the new owner.

There is also a *home disadvantage effect* (HDE) where the opposite effect occurs (teams do better playing away). Wright *et al.* (1995) analysed ice hockey games and found that teams played low-pressure matches better at home, but scored more highly in high-pressure games when they were away. It may be that, when teams are lacking confidence (e.g. in a high-pressure game or during a losing streak) they feel the home crowd is being critical of them and this causes players to become overly self-aware and make increased errors. In low-pressure situations the fans are supportive and this facilitates performance (Baumeister and Steinhilber, 1984).

Team membership

A team is not simply a collection of people. A team is committed to a common purpose and often has complementary skills. Members hold themselves mutually responsible for their success or failure. (Note that a team need not work together, as with the British Olympic team.)

Group cohesion A team with several brilliant individual members may underperform because of poor integration. Holt and Sparkes (2001) interviewed and observed university football teams over a season and concluded that there were four factors that enhanced group cohesion:

1. A clear role for each member.
2. Willingness to make personal sacrifices for the team.
3. Good communication between team members.
4. Shared goals for the team as a whole.

Coaching style has also been identified as important. A negative style (using ridicule and inequity) reduces cohesiveness, though this can be reversed through team building exercises (Turman, 2003).

Social loafing Underperformance of a team may also be explained in terms of the **Ringlemann effect** (described on page 212). Latané *et al.* (1979) called this **social loafing**. In their own experiment, Latané *et al.* asked participants to shout loudly, falsely explaining that the study was on sensory feedback. Participants wore blindfolds and headsets and heard a loud stream of noise to mask other supposed group members. When they thought they were alone they averaged 9 dynes/cm^2, when they thought they were in pairs this dropped to 66% of capacity and in a six-person group it dropped to 36%, demonstrating social loafing.

In a **meta-analysis** of 78 studies, Karau and Williams (1993) confirmed that social loafing is a robust finding across different kinds of task and participant groups.

Social facilitation

Coaction effects On page 212 we described the classic study by Norman Triplett, the first demonstration that the mere presence of others enhances sporting performance. Since Triplett's research such **coaction effects** have been shown in many different situation and not just with humans. Zajonc *et al.* (1969) placed a bright light at the start of a maze (see diagram at the bottom of the page). If cockroaches were in pairs they ran away faster (cockroaches have a natural tendency to run from the light to darker areas).

Audience effects take place when the others present are actually watching your performance. The effect could be positive or negative depending on certain other factors. For example, Zajonc (1965) recognised that there was a difference between tasks requiring dominant responses or tasks requiring non-dominant responses. *Dominant responses* are shown on well-learned, instinctive, often simple motor tasks. *Non-dominant responses* are shown on conceptual, novel or complicated tasks. Performance on dominant tasks is improved by the presence of an audience.

This can be seen in the home disadvantage effect (see left). It also can be seen in the study by Schmitt *et al.* (1986) described on page 213 and in a sporting-related study by Michaels *et al.* (1982) of pool players. Players were initially identified as below average (so playing was a non-dominant response) or above average (dominant response). Those below average played worse (in terms of number of successful shots) in the presence of an audience whereas the better players did better (dominant response enhanced by an audience).

Zajonc *et al.* (1969) also tested audience effects with their cockroaches. They found that performance increased when an audience of four cockroaches watched! They also found that in a simple maze condition (dominant response), cockroaches found the darkened area faster when there were other cockroaches observing. In the complex maze condition (non-dominant), however, the cockroaches completed the task slower when other cockroaches were observing.

▲ *Mazes used in the studies by Zajonc et al.*

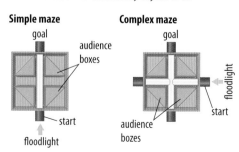

Simple maze   Complex maze

▶ On page 216 we looked at the relationship between arousal and performance and noted that for tasks involving gross motor skills (such as rugby), the optimal level of arousal is higher than for tasks involving fine motor skills (such as snooker). This can be related to dominant and non-dominant skills, where dominant skills, as with gross motor skills, are less affected by arousal than non-dominant skills/fine motor skills – as illustrated on the right.

Fine motor skills, non-dominant response   Gross motor skills, dominant response

Performance (y-axis) · Arousal (x-axis)

EVALUATION

Team membership

Group cohesion There is evidence to support a **positive correlation** between group cohesion and performance, for example Gould *et al.* (1999) found that poor cohesiveness was associated with underperformance in a study of US Olympic teams. However, the question is whether poor cohesiveness *caused* the underperformance or whether it was the other way round. Grieve *et al.* (2000) studied basketball teams and found that cohesiveness didn't affect performance but performance led to great cohesiveness. But in yet another study, this time looking at university hockey teams, there was evidence for both directions of causality. At the beginning of the season those teams assessed as high in cohesion did perform best. However as the season went on success became a determining factor in cohesion (Slater and Sewell, 1994).

Social loafing There are circumstances when social loafing doesn't occur, for example when people regard a task as important. There are also important individual differences. Swain (1996) conducted a study with about 100 adolescent boys who were timed when running a 30-metre sprint. First they ran individually, second they ran in teams but each individual boy's time was recorded, and third they again ran in teams but the boys thought only the team time was recorded. In the third condition some boys did run more slowly (as the Ringlemann effect would predict) but this wasn't true for all boys – those boys who were 'task-oriented' (see goal orientation on pages 214–215) ran equally fast in all conditions.

Social facilitation

Criticisms Not all research has been supportive. For example, Geisler and Leith (1997) looked at taking football penalties in 40 Canadian ex-university football players. They found that the number of goals scored was the same whether there was or wasn't an audience present.

A further issue is whether the audience effect is actually relevant to sports performance. In social facilitation research the audience is just watching and not interacting with the performers. Certainly in some sporting contests this is not true. However in situations where it is true, it is obviously an important consideration when ensuring fairness. For example, it is important to make certain that the presence of any audience and/or other competitors is the same for all participants. The same is true when conducting research on sporting performance – for conditions to be equal the presence of others needs to be constant.

Individual differences Other research has found that personality may be an important variable – **extraverts** perform better in front of an audience than **introverts** when they had to serve a tennis ball into a grid (Grayden and Murphy, 1995).

Explanations Zajonc (1965) suggested that social facilitation effects can be explained in terms of *drive theory*; the presence of other people creates arousal, resulting in an inverted-U relationship. When the task is not complicated (i.e. a dominant task or a skilled performance) the inverted U is 'higher' than when performing a complicated, non-dominant task where a person is unskilled (see graph at the top of the page). This explains, for example, why you need to be well practised at a skill in order to perform it in public.

Cottrell (1972) suggested that arousal is experienced not just from the presence of other people but because they are evaluating you (**evaluation apprehension**). Cottrell *et al.* (1968) tested participants on a task where the audience was blindfolded so they could not judge performance and found the audience effect disappeared. However, Schmitt *et al.* (1986) found the effect did not disappear with a blindfolded observer, which suggests that there is possibly a more complex relationship between evaluation apprehension and performance because it does not always have an effect.

A third possibility is distraction–conflict. Sanders (1981) suggested that the mere presence of others causes a distraction and this interferes with attention available for a task, which creates conflict over whether to attend to the task or to the people. The conflict produces arousal. Sanders *et al.* (1978) gave participants the same or a different task to others who were coacting – there should be less distraction from those who were doing a different task. Participants in the high-distraction condition (performing the same task with a co-actor) performed better on the simple task but worse on the complex one, supporting distraction–conflict. This explanation could account for the fact that social facilitation has been demonstrated in animals (for example, ants and cockroaches) since it is difficult to believe that animals experience evaluation apprehension.

HAE and other factors

Research has also found an interaction between the HAE and team quality. Bray (1999) used data from American hockey games spanning a period of 20 years and found that high-quality teams won 70% of their home games compared with 32% for low-quality teams. Conversely, in away games, high-quality teams won 52% of their games compared with 17% wins for low-quality teams. This is related to dominant/skilled responses – high-quality teams are more skilled and thus we expect arousal to have a less detrimental effect on their performance.

Furthermore the size of the audience has an effect on the HAE. Schwartz and Barksy (1977) found that the percentage of home wins increased as the size of the home crowd increased. This may also explain why the HAE is more prevalent in sports with large audiences (e.g. football) compared with sports with small audiences (e.g. basketball).

CAN YOU...? (No. **11.3**)

1... Select **two or more** key points for each of the effects described on the facing page.

2... For each key point write about 50 words explaining the point.

3... Identify about **ten** points of evaluation (these can be positive or negative).

4... Elaborate each point (see page 9).

5... Use all of this material to write an answer to the following exam question: *Describe and evaluate external factors affecting sporting performance.* As good practice you might also write 'building block' essays about the different effects. Your answers should contain about 300 words of description and 500 words of evaluation.

It may seem fairly obvious that exercise has a beneficial effect on physical fitness, but less obvious that it also benefits general physical health as well as mental health.

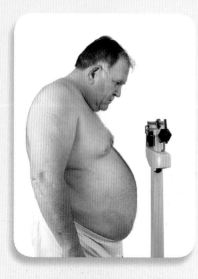

▲ *Exercise combats obesity which is a risk factor for many illnesses, such as diabetes (discussed below) and heart disease (and cardiovascular disease generally, such as stroke). There are also increased risks for fatty liver disease, breathing problems, arthritis, cancer – in other words, just about everything. Exercise is especially important because weight loss alone is not enough to remove the problems – fitness is important too.*

Effects on mental health

Depression Research has shown that exercise improves mood. In fact exercise has been shown to be as effective as either **psychotherapy** or **antidepressants**. For example, Babyak *et al.* (2000) compared the effects of either exercise or antidepressants on about 150 adults with **clinical depression**. After four months all patients showed significant improvement. After ten months there was much lower relapse in the exercise group. Nicoloff and Schwenk (1995) found greater reduction in depressive symptoms in **postpartum** women when they took part in an exercise plus therapy group rather than therapy alone.

Anxiety Exercise may also have a beneficial effect on anxiety. A recent **meta-analysis** by Herring *et al.* (2010) that included almost 3,000 people with various medical conditions (such as multiple sclerosis, cancer, arthritis and chronic pain) found that regular exercise reduced the associated anxiety symptoms by up to 20%.

Stress High levels of stress are associated with illness, as you know from your AS study by Rahe, Mahan and Arthur (1970), but it seems exercise can protect against these negative effects of stress. Brown (1991) measured stress, fitness and illness in college students and found that exercise reduced illness (as measured by visits to a health centre) in those who were stressed.

Self-esteem is an important factor in mental health. Carl Rogers, the 'father' of the counselling movement, argued that without high **self-esteem** a person is constantly striving for social acceptance, which prevents healthy adjustment (Rogers, 1959). Exercise increases confidence and esteem through increasing your sense of your own competence (**self-efficacy**). Research shows that people who are physically active have higher self-esteem scores (e.g. Frost and McKelvie, 2005).

Cognitive functioning Exercise enhances blood flow and glucose to the brain which improves mental activity. This is particularly important in older age when cardiovascular decline may have a negative effect on mental activity (Rogers *et al.*, 1990). Molley *et al.* (1988) found improvements in logical memory in older adults after a single 45-minute span of exercise. Labounty (2007) found improvements in short-term memory in college students after 15 minutes of walking.

Effects on physical health

Heart disease Early research found that London bus conductors suffered fewer cardiovascular problems than bus drivers (Morris *et al.*, 1953). This may be because conductors are more active, though it might also be because they are less stressed.

The importance of exercise in avoiding heart disease is underlined by the American Heart Association (1999) who list lack of exercise as the fourth highest risk factor in heart disease. Regular exercise lowers cholesterol levels and lowers blood pressure thus reducing the incidence of heart disease (Paffenbarger, 1994).

Diabetes is a condition where the amount of glucose in your body becomes dangerously high, either because insufficient insulin is produced or it is ineffective (insulin regulates glucose metabolism). People with Type 2 diabetes (those who do not need to take medication) benefit from regular exercise because blood sugar levels are better controlled and this reduces the risk of cardiovascular problems. For example, one study of obese boys (a risk factor for Type 2 diabetes) showed that a three-month programme of exercise reduced abdominal fat and increased their insulin sensitivity (Lee *et al.*, 2010).

Sleep Many people believe that exercise can encourage longer and better quality sleep, and sleep is important for physical health. Cappuccio *et al.* (2010) found that sleeping less than 6–8 hours a night is associated with a 12% increase in the risk of dying early.

The question is whether exercise increases the amount of sleep or whether it just helps us to get to sleep more easily. Shapiro *et al.* (1981) found that marathon runners slept for about an hour more than usual on the nights after a race.

On the other hand, Horne and Minard (1985) found that participants who were given numerous exhausting tasks didn't sleep more than usual but they went to sleep faster than usual. This may be especially important for insomniacs who have difficulty getting to sleep. Stanford sleep lab studies people with sleep complaints and found that exercise is related to improvements in sleep quality and ease of going to sleep (e.g. King *et al.*, 2008).

Ageing Many of the symptoms and conditions usually associated with ageing may in fact be the result of lack of exercise. Studies show that older people taking regular exercise experience none of the functional declines normally seen. For example, in one study following up a group of men 30 years after they were first assessed, it was found that the 50-year-olds returned to earlier cardiovascular fitness within six months of about five hours of exercise per week (McGuire *et al.*, 2001).

EVALUATION

Confounding variables

Type of exercise Exercise may be gentle or vigorous, it may be prolonged or brief, regular or sporadic. All of these factors are important in determining the benefits from the exercise. There is a wide range of research findings. In terms of duration, Craft and Landers (1998) found that long exercise programmes were better than short ones for depression, and North *et al.* (1990) argued that it is difficult to see how substantial cardiovascular changes could take place in short duration exercise programmes. Some research suggests that moderate exercise (e.g. brisk walking) for half an hour five times a week has benefits (Tully *et al.*, 2007), but other research suggests that exercise needs to be vigorous for benefits to be felt (Chomistek and Rimm, 2010).

Individual differences Individuals who engage in exercise have different characteristics from non-exercisers. For example, research has found that well-educated people are more likely to exercise (Dishman *et al.*, 1985) and exercisers are typically more reserved, serious, intelligent, imaginative, forthright and self-sufficient than non-exercisers (Hartung and Farge, 1977). Such individual differences might mean that the benefits of exercise are due to these differences rather than the exercise. However, it is worth noting that most of the studies cited on the facing page use randomised trials where participants are randomly assigned to the control or exercise groups thus eliminating individual differences as a **confounding variable**.

Psychological explanations for the benefits

The cognitive–behavioural hypothesis Exercise encourages positive thoughts and feelings. Bandura (1997) suggested that self-efficacy is increased when people tackle difficult tasks – an exerciser experiences a sense of achievement and increased sense of control.

Social interaction hypothesis Exercise may have beneficial effects because it enables contact with other people and social support is good for health (see pages 106–107). However, North *et al.* (1990) conducted a **meta-analysis** of other studies and concluded that there were actually greater reductions in depression when people were exercising at home alone than at other locations usually with others.

Distraction hypothesis The exerciser may feel better because during exercise they are distracted from their worries. Bahrke and Morgan (1978) found that meditation was as effective as exercise in reducing anxiety, implying that it is the mental state associated with exercise which may be important in its beneficial effects.

Physiological explanations for the benefits

Both physical and psychological effects may be explained in terms of physiological changes associated with exercise and fitness.

- Improved metabolic processes which relate to the production of proteins, breaking down of food and utilising energy. Being fitter means these processes become more efficient.
- Improved delivery of oxygen throughout the body.
- Enhanced production of *human growth hormone* (HGH) which helps maintain muscles, stamina and strength.
- Increased production of nerve cells which is especially important in the brain.
- Increased secretions of neurotransmitters such as **serotonin**, **dopamine** and **adrenaline** enhance neural activity and mood.
- Production of **endorphins** increases, which creates a feeling of euphoria – though research evidence is meagre; Kraemer *et al.* (1990) actually found a negative relationship between endorphin levels and positive mood.
- De-activation of **sympathetic arousal** because vigorous physical activity may send a message to the brain that a threat, or demand, has been dealt with so the 'fight-or-flight' response (sympathetic arousal) can now be 'switched off'. This lowers stress levels and the associated negative effects.
- The immune system may be protected. Fleshner (2000) found that stressed rats that had been regularly running on a wheel recovered more quickly when exposed to an infection compared with non-exercising rats.

Why don't people exercise?

Given the enormous benefits of regular, moderate exercise the question is why more people don't exercise. Health psychologists provide explanations of why people don't engage in health behaviours even when they know it's good for them. For example, the **health belief model** (described on pages 172–173) suggests that individuals consider perceived barriers (such as cost or effort) and perceived benefits before deciding whether to take action – but even before that they have to consider whether they are in any way threatened by possible illness.

When exercise isn't a good thing

Exercise is good for you. The United States Surgeon General recommends at least 30 minutes of moderate exercise, such as brisk walking, nearly every day. However, not all exercise is good. Vigorous exercise carries risks, such as a strain on your heart or muscles, and too much exercise could be damaging. For example, there is evidence that the immune system is suppressed for several hours after heavy exercise (Nieman, 2000).

Furthermore, some people become addicted to exercise. It becomes an **addiction** when it interferes with everyday life and becomes harmful to health and social relationships. The person cannot reduce participation despite attempts to do so. Addicts may have a rigid fitness schedule and experience feelings of anxiety when they cannot exercise. Compulsive exercise is a feature of eating disorders, such as **anorexia nervosa** or **bulimia nervosa**, as a means of restricting weight gain.

CAN YOU...? No. 11.4

1... Select **six or more** effects on mental health and/or effects on physical health.

2... For each effect write about 50 words explaining the point.

3... Identify about **ten** points of evaluation (these can be positive or negative).

4... Elaborate each point (see page 9).

5... Use all of this material to write an answer to the following exam question: *Discuss effects of exercise on well-being*. As good practice you might also write 'building block' essays about the effects on mental health and the effects on physical health separately. Your answers should contain about 300 words of description and 500 words of evaluation.

Remember that, when writing an essay, you can include material from other spreads – but only if it is made specifically relevant to the essay. For example, in an essay on the effects of exercise on well-being you might use material from the spread on Theories of addiction or the spread on Issues in health promotion in Chapter 8.

THEORIES OF AGGRESSION IN SPORT

Sport is associated with aggressive behaviour – in both players and spectators. It is perhaps useful to distinguish between different kinds of aggression. *Assertiveness* refers to the legitimate use of force, physical or otherwise. *Instrumental aggression* is the use of aggression in order to obtain a goal. There is no anger involved though harm is intended, as in a rugby tackle. Finally there is *hostile aggression* which involves anger plus the deliberate intention to harm another person. Such behaviour is outside the rules of sport but often arises from instrumental aggression. On this spread we will consider why sporting activities sometimes spill over into aggression.

Aggression is explained on this spread in terms of both psychological and biological factors. SLT and frustration aggression theory are psychological explanations, whereas ethological theory is biologically oriented because it is related to **innate** factors. There are other biological explanations not covered here, such as the influence of **hormones** on aggression.

Social learning theory (SLT)

One possible explanation is that sports players and fans learn to behave aggressively by modeling their behaviour on people they admire (e.g. famous sports people). The principles of **social learning theory** are familiar to you from your AS studies. Albert Bandura and colleagues (1961) famously demonstrated that young children will imitate specific acts of aggression and their general aggressiveness will increase when exposed to aggressive role models. Bandura explained this imitation in terms of **observational learning**. In subsequent research Bandura and Walters (1963) showed that imitation depends on **vicarious reinforcement** – a person not only needs to observe the aggressive behaviour but also needs to see the behaviour rewarded if they are later going to imitate it. The third key element is direct **reinforcement** – when a person does imitate a behaviour they have observed it may not succeed and thus they are not directly reinforced. Lack of reinforcement means that it is less likely that the behaviour will be repeated in the future.

Frustration–aggression theory

A second possible explanation for aggression in sports is that frustration arising from, for example, lack of success, creates aggression. Dollard *et al.* (1939) suggested that frustration always leads to some form of aggression and all aggression is the result of frustration. Frustration is anything that blocks or delays us as we strive to achieve something (a goal). In this theory aggression is triggered by external social factors rather than internal biological ones. Such social factors include people and any characteristics of the situation. These social factors create a state of frustration or physiological arousal, which motivates the organism to act.

Reformulated theory Berkowitz (1978) reformulated the initial frustration–aggression theory, proposing that frustration leads to negative feelings (e.g. anger or anxiety) rather than directly to aggression. This is called the *cognitive–neoassociation model*. Negative feelings may lead to aggression but can be controlled by higher cognitive functions (e.g. how you perceive the situation), so frustration doesn't automatically lead to aggression.

▲ *Does frustration always lead to aggression? This frustrated golfer is just getting angry with his golf club – to count as aggression it must involve the deliberate intention to harm another person.*

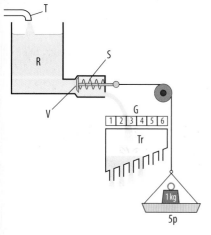

▲ *Lorenz proposed the hydraulic model of aggression. Aggressive energies increase like water in a reservoir (R) until they are released by stimulus (S) or until the pressure becomes too great on the valve (V). The aggressive energy then floods out. In particular Lorenz pointed to the need for release, and thus the benefit of providing humans with an acceptable means of 'emptying their reservoir' to avoid outbursts of harmful aggression, i.e. catharsis through sport (see facing page).*

Ethological theory

Ethological theory is based on the study of animal behaviour in the natural environment. Konrad Lorenz (1966) argued that the same laws applied to all animals because they are all governed by the same laws of **natural selection**. His observations of non-human animal behaviour led him to suggest that aggression has three key characteristics:

- *An innate tendency* Aggression is triggered by environmental signals, for example the male stickleback will behave aggressively when it sees anything red (even a Royal Mail van) (Tinbergen, 1951). According to this, humans have a natural 'fighting instinct' which is triggered by environmental signals.
- *An adaptive response* Aggressive behaviour promotes survival and reproductive success because the strongest, most aggressive animal controls food, territory and mating.

- *Not naturally harmful* In non-human animals ritualised forms of aggression evolve to prevent actual harm taking place. For instance, two males will circle each other, make threatening noises and put on displays of strength. Species evolve *evolutionarily stable strategies* to optimise aggression and survival. The classic example is the balance between 'hawks' and 'doves' in any group – a group of all doves is vulnerable to infiltration by one hawk, whereas too many hawks kill each other off. Therefore, in any group, there is an optimum, stable balance between hawks and doves. Both ritual forms of aggression and stable strategies can be seen in sporting teams.

Hydraulic model and catharsis

According to Lorenz's hydraulic model (pictured on the left) aggressive energy builds up until it reaches a certain point and then the individual will act aggressively. However, this stored energy can be released prematurely through physical activity.

EVALUATION

Social learning theory

Individual differences in aggressive behaviour A strength of SLT is that it can explain differences in aggressive and non-aggressive behaviour both between and within individuals. Differences between individuals can be shown in cultural differences. The 'culture of violence' theory (Wolfgang and Ferracuti, 1967), for example, proposes that, in large societies, some subcultures develop norms that sanction violence to a greater degree than does the dominant culture. Some subcultures may emphasise and model non-aggressive behaviour, producing individuals that show low levels of aggression.

Differences within individuals can be related to selective modelling and vicarious reinforcement and **context-dependent learning**. People respond differently in different situations because they have observed that aggression is rewarded in some situations and not others, i.e. they learn behaviours that are appropriate to particular contexts.

Biological contributions One common criticism is the extent to which SLT is a complete explanation of human aggression. Animal studies have shown that animals reared alone, without any opportunity to learn aggression from others, still display aggression. This shows that, in some species at least, aggression does not require social learning. However, Bandura had this covered because he did not deny the importance of biological factors – he claimed that biological factors create the potential for aggression but the actual form of aggression is learned.

Frustration–aggression theory

Research support for the original theory There is some empirical support for the original frustration–aggression hypothesis. For example, Kulik and Brown (1979) arranged for students to telephone strangers (**confederates**) to ask for charity donations. The students were either given high expectations (a high payment for each successful call) or low expectations. The student participants were then frustrated during the calls. Those with higher expectations displayed more verbal aggression towards the confederates. This shows a relationship between level of frustration and level of aggression.

Research support for the reformulation There is a wealth of evidence that shows that frustration doesn't always lead to aggression, supporting Berkowitz's reformulation. For instance, cognitive activity has been shown to eliminate aggression. Burnstein and Worchel (1962) arranged for a confederate to disrupt a group's problem-solving task. If the disruption was blamed on a failing hearing aid, no aggression toward the confederate was observed.

Cognitive factors could increase aggression, for example the presence of aggressive cues in a study by Geen and Berkowitz (1967) led to aggressiveness. They first frustrated their participants and then showed them a film which either had an aggressive or non-aggressive content. Aggression was later assessed through the level of electric shocks the participants administered to a learner. If the participant had watched an aggressive film or there was an aggressive trigger present in the room, such as a gun, the number of shocks given was greater.

Ethological theory

There are several criticisms of this approach. First, it is **determinist** because it suggests that aggression is inevitable unless channelled elsewhere. This may be true of animal behaviour but humans are capable of thinking about what they do and thus can control aggressive impulses.

Second, ethological theory does not account for cultural differences in aggression. Even in non-human animal behaviour social factors have been shown to override biological ones. For example, when an area of the brain (called the **amygdala**) is electrically stimulated in monkeys, docile animals become aggressive, but the monkeys don't behave aggressively in the presence of more dominant monkeys (Aronson, 1999).

More modern ethological theories (**sociobiological** theories) incorporate an element of learning and are not quite so determinist. They do suggest that aggression is an adaptive behaviour but it is only partly controlled by inherited mechanisms.

Catharsis

The physical activity associated with sports may have a beneficial effect – instead of promoting aggression it may reduce its likelihood. According to **catharsis** theory, acting aggressively, or even just viewing aggression in others, is an effective way to purge our own aggressive feelings. This idea, originally attributable to Breuer and Freud (1893), was that expressing anger was much better than bottling it up inside. The principle of catharsis is based on the hydraulic model of aggression (on facing page), whereby frustration leads to anger and aggression, which builds up inside an individual until they are released in some way. Letting out the anger here and there in relatively harmless ways is seen as better than letting it build up to a dangerous 'explosion' of rage.

Almost as soon as researchers started studying this theory, it became clear there was a problem. In a typical experiment, Hornberger (1959) found that participants who had hammered nails after being insulted by a confederate were more aggressive toward the confederate afterwards than participants who had not vented their anger in the same way. In an influential review of catharsis theory, Geen and Quanty (1977) concluded that venting anger does not reduce aggression, but, if anything, it makes people more aggressive afterwards. Geen and Quanty did concede that venting anger can reduce physiological arousal, but only when an individual expresses their anger directly against the person responsible for their frustration (and then only when they believe they will not retaliate). Venting anger against substitute targets, or merely viewing aggressive behaviour in a third party does not, they concluded, reduce aggression. – which clearly has important implications for participating in and watching sports contests.

The main focus of this topic is theories of aggression *in sport* – on this spread we have presented the relevant theories but you must remember to apply these to sport.

CAN YOU...? (No. 11.5)

1... Select **two or more** key points for each of the theories described on this spread.

2... For each key point write about 50 words explaining the point.

3... Identify about **ten** points of evaluation (these can be positive or negative).

4... Elaborate each point (see page 9).

5... Use all of this material to write an answer to the following exam question: *Critically consider theories of aggression in sport*. As good practice you might also write 'building block' essays about the different theories of aggression as applied to sport. Your answers should contain about 300 words of description and 500 words of evaluation.

Don't forget to read the essay-writing guidance on pages 8–9.

IMPROVING MOTIVATION IN SPORT

EXPLANATIONS OF MOTIVATION AND IMPLICATIONS FOR IMPROVING MOTIVATION

Achievement motivation theory
- McClelland *et al.* suggest we are motivated by the drive to succeed and the drive to avoid failure. We will pursue a goal when the motivation to succeed exceeds fear of failure.
- Motivation to succeed comes from intrinsic motives (personal desire) rather than extrinsic ones (e.g. wanting prizes or fame).
- Sports present an approach–avoidance conflict, wanting both to take part (approach) and escape anxiety (avoidance). Individuals with high intrinsic motivation and low anxiety (high approach, low avoidance) succeed at high levels in sport, whereas those low in intrinsic motivation and high in anxiety will find competitive sport difficult (as 'avoidance' exceeds 'approach'). Moderate intrinsic motivation with high anxiety doesn't lead to success at high levels of competition.
- The need to achieve (nAch) can explain individual differences, e.g. high nAch people avoid both high- and low-risk situations.

Self-efficacy
- Bandura suggested that self-efficacy creates motivation. It is cognitive (rather than emotional, so is distinct from self-esteem) and is situation specific.
- Schunk says our beliefs about our sporting ability come from: successful performance (so a good coach raises task difficulty slowly), vicarious experience, verbal persuasion (e.g. praise) and emotional and physiological arousal (e.g. feeling relaxed suggests we can cope with the task).

Goal perspective theory
- Nicholls suggested that people are either task- (mastery) or ego- (competitive) orientated.
- Training environments may be mastery or competitive. Competitive climates punish mistakes and encourage competition. Mastery-oriented climates reward effort and cooperation and raise self-confidence and intrinsic motivation.
- Mastery climate can be achieved through Tasks, Authority, Rewards, Grouping, Evaluation and Timing (TARGET) (Epstein).

EVALUATION

Achievement motivation theory
- The importance of intrinsic motivation is supported by research and the model explains why athletes can respond differently when competing at low and high levels.
- However, the model doesn't predict sporting success so is rarely used. High-achievement motivation (high intrinsic motivation and low anxiety) doesn't always lead to better performance than low-achievement motivation.
- Alternatives include more situation-specific theories (e.g. self-efficacy) or a trait-oriented view (Achievement Motivation Inventory, Schuler and Prochaska).

Self-efficacy
- This doesn't claim to be a complete explanation of sporting motivation but can help in coaching.
- Wells *et al.* found that participants misled into believing they were lifting heavier weights (greater self-efficacy) lifted the most.
- Chalabaev *et al.* found that girls who believed boys were better footballers than girls played worse.

- Myers *et al.* found that high collective efficacy in women's ice hockey teams predicted performance on that day (but not the previous day) suggesting a small effect of performance on collective efficacy but a powerful effect of collective efficacy on performance.

Goal perspective theory
- The matching hypothesis suggests individuals perform best when their goal orientation matches the motivational climate but Newton and Duda found that a mastery climate is best for both task- and ego-oriented individuals.
- Zahariadis and Biddle found that task-oriented young people took part in sport for team spirit and skills (intrinsic rewards) but ego-oriented ones valued extrinsic rewards (e.g. social status).
- The relationship between orientation and performance is complex, e.g. Sarrazin *et al.* found that goal orientation interacted with both self-efficacy and task difficulty to determine effort and performance on a rock-climbing task.

EXTERNAL FACTORS AFFECTING

SOCIAL FACILITATION

- Triplett demonstrated the coaction effect (presence of others enhances sporting performance) using speed of fishing reel winding. Similarly, Zajonc *et al.* found that cockroaches ran a maze faster in pairs.
- An audience effect can be positive (on dominant responses, i.e. well learned, instinctive, simple motor tasks) or negative (on non-dominant responses, i.e. conceptual, novel or complicated tasks) (Zajonc).
- Teams are more likely to win when playing at home than away (home advantage effect, HAE) possibly because a supportive home crowd energises the home team (social facilitation) and inhibits the away team. Being on home territory also raises confidence (Davies and Houston demonstrated with butterflies).
- Wright *et al.* confirmed the home *disadvantage* effect. When teams lack confidence (e.g. under pressure) the home crowd may seem critical, increasing errors.
- Michaels *et al.* found that poor pool players (non-dominant response) played worse with an audience whereas better players improved (dominant response).
- Zajonc *et al.* found that cockroaches performed better with a cockroach audience too, but only on a simple maze (dominant response) not a complex maze (non-dominant response).

EVALUATION

- Audience effect not always observed, e.g. Geisler and Leith studied football penalties.
- In sports the audience may be interacting and therefore audience effect research may not always be relevant, though it can affect research.
- Personality may matter. Grayden and Murphy found that with an audience, extraverts were better than introverts at serving a tennis ball.
- Social facilitation may be explained by drive theory (Zajonc), evaluation apprehension (Cottrell) or distraction–conflict (Sanders).
- Some research has found the effect disappears with a blindfolded audience, supporting evaluation apprehension, but Schmitt *et al.* found the effect did still occur with a blindfolded observer, so the relationship is complex.
- Saunders *et al.* demonstrated distraction–conflict, participants with high distraction (doing same task) performed better on a simple task but worse on a complex one.
- HAE also related to team quality (Bray found high-quality American hockey teams won more home games than low-quality teams) and audience size (Schwartz and Barksy found that HAE increased with home crowd size).

INTERNAL FACTORS AFFECTING SPORTING PERFORMANCE

EFFECTS OF AROUSAL

- 'Arousal' (physical and psychological activation) is related to sympathetic nervous system activity (and adrenaline level).
- The relationship between arousal and performance is an inverted U (Yerkes and Dodson). Performance is best at the optimum arousal level.
- The optimum for complex, fine motor skills is lower than for simple, gross motor skills.

EVALUATION

- Sonstroem and Bernado found basketball players performed worst when arousal was very high or very low, supporting the inverted-U hypothesis.
- Thelwell and Maynard found that county cricketers rated arousal as one of the top four factors affecting batsmen and bowlers.
- Understanding optimum arousal helps in mental preparation for competition. When fine motor skills are needed (e.g. darts) lower arousal is preferable (so alcohol or beta-blocker use is more common) but sports relying on gross motor skills need higher arousal (e.g. 'psyching up' rituals as in rugby).

EFFECTS OF ANXIETY

- Anxiety (negative emotion) consists of cognitive component (state anxiety = worry) and physiological component (somatic anxiety) as an individual difference (how well we cope with anxiety). Trait anxiety refers to an individual difference (how well we cope with anxiety).
- Multidimensional anxiety theory says that somatic anxiety has an inverted-U pattern whereas state anxiety correlates negatively with performance (Martens *et al.*).
- The catastrophe model (Fazey and Hardy) suggests that increases in somatic anxiety lead to the inverted-U pattern but increases in state anxiety lead to a catastrophe.
- Hanin suggested differences in trait anxiety mean each person has an individual zone of optimal functioning (IZOF).

EVALUATION

- Modern sports psychology focuses on state anxiety rather than arousal (somatic anxiety) but the relationship between state anxiety and sporting performance has been found to be weak (meta-analysis by Craft *et al.*).
- Catastrophe model supported by Hardy *et al.*, performance of crown green bowlers fell sharply when cognitive anxiety was high. Many athletes perform best when worried (Jones *et al.*).
- Russell and Cox supported the IZOF by showing that American football and basketball players reporting positive emotions during games (i.e. in their IZOF) played somewhat better than those with negative emotions. However, Randle and Weinburg found no difference for IZOF.

ATTRIBUTION THEORY

- Attribution theory (Heider) says we identify causes of our own and other people's behaviour as internal (dispositional) or external (situational).
- A self-serving bias is when we attribute our success to ability (internal) and failure to task difficulty (external). Without a sense of responsibility for our success/failure we cannot improve, so sporting progress requires attributing failure to our (lack of) effort.
- Weiner suggested self-attribution depends on both the internal/ external attribution and whether this is stable over time and situations. Stability helps to predict future success. However, instability helps us deal with failure as it is seen as temporary.
- Seligman suggested learned helplessness arises in situations where we lack control, so we give up trying.
- People with an internal locus of control have greater potential for change than 'externals' so respond better to coaching/learn from their failures.

EVALUATION

- Gill studied self-serving bias in female basketball players. As predicted, the players attributed their successes to their own team but their failures to the other team. However, when asked to make attributions about their own performance they attributed failure to themselves and success to the team, contrary to the self-serving bias.
- Novice golfers who made unstable attributions (e.g. attributed failure to luck) persisted longer (Foll *et al.*), but stable attributions are better in successful situations.
- Orbach *et al.* used attribution training with novice tennis players. False feedback led to internal attributions for success and later to improved self-esteem and performance.

SPORTING PERFORMANCE

TEAM MEMBERSHIP

- A team may underperform if exceptionally talented individuals members are poorly integrated.
- Holt and Sparkes found four factors enhancing group cohesion in university football teams: clear roles, willingness to make personal sacrifices, good communication and shared goals.
- Coaching that uses a negative style (e.g. ridicule) reduces cohesiveness but team-building exercises increase it (Turman).
- Team underperformance can arise from social loafing (team members work less as group size increases), demonstrated by Ringlemann with tug-of-war teams and Latané et al. with the loudness of shouting. Karau and Williams confirmed this effect with different kinds of task and participant groups.

EVALUATION

- Gould et al. found a positive correlation between group cohesion in US Olympic teams and their performance.
- Gieve et al. investigated whether poor cohesiveness caused poor performance or vice versa. In basketball teams cohesiveness didn't affect performance but good performance improved cohesiveness. However, Slater and Sewell found an effect in both directions in university hockey teams.
- Social loafing isn't inevitable – it doesn't occur if the task is important.
- Swain et al. found individual differences in social loafing in adolescent boys. Many sprinted more slowly in a team than individually (Ringlemann effect) but 'task-oriented' boys ran no more slowly in teams.

EFFECTS ON MENTAL HEALTH

- Babyak et al. showed that adults with clinical depression improved after either exercise or antidepressants but the exercise group were less likely to relapse. Nicoloff and Schwenk found fewer depressive symptoms after childbirth for women in an exercise plus therapy group than therapy alone.
- In a meta-analysis, Herring et al. found that in people with various medical conditions, regular exercise reduced anxiety by up to 20%.
- Brown found that exercise reduced illness in stressed students.
- Exercise makes you feel competent so raises confidence and esteem. Physically active people have higher self-esteem (Frost and McKelvie).
- Exercise improves blood flow to the brain so aids cognitive functioning (important in older people with poorer circulation). Molley et al. found logical memory in older adults improved after one exercise session and Labounty found STM improved in students after 15 minutes of walking.

EFFECTS ON PHYSICAL HEALTH

- Exercise combats obesity through weight loss and fitness, lowering risk in many diseases. Morris et al. found that bus conductors had fewer cardiovascular problems than drivers; perhaps because they are more active (or less stressed).
- Lack of exercise rated as fourth highest risk factor in heart disease (American Heart Association).
- In people with Type 2 diabetes exercise helps control blood sugar level, reducing cardiovascular problems. Lee et al. found that an exercise programme for obese boys improved insulin sensitivity.
- Shapiro et al. found that marathon runners slept longer after a race; however Horne and Minard found that exhausting tasks made participants fall asleep faster but not sleep for longer. Similarly, King et al. found insomniacs fell asleep more readily and slept better after exercising.
- Many problems with ageing may result from lack of exercise, e.g. Smith and Dade found bone mass increased in older women taking exercise.

EVALUATION

Confounding variables
- Variation in the vigour, duration or frequency of exercise may affect the benefits, explaining variation in research findings.
- Long exercise programmes are better than short ones for depression (Craft and Landers) and are more likely to produce cardiovascular benefits (North et al.). Moderate exercise (e.g. brisk walking) may be sufficient (Tully et al.) or vigorous exercise may be necessary (Chomistek and Rimm).
- There are individual differences in exercise patterns. Well-educated people are more likely to exercise (Disman et al.) as are reserved, serious, intelligent, imaginative, forthright and self-sufficient people (Hartung and Farge), so benefits may arise from these differences, not exercise (unless participants are randomly assigned to control or exercise groups).

Potential harm
- Exercise also has risks for physical health, e.g. immune system suppression following heavy exercise (Nieman).
- There are also risks, e.g. becoming addicted to exercise (can happen in anorexia and bulimia nervosa).

Psychological explanations for the benefits
- The cognitive–behavioural hypothesis suggests exercise encourages positive thoughts and feelings, e.g. raises self-efficacy (Bandura).

- The social interaction hypothesis suggests exercise leads to contact with others and social support is good for health, but North et al. found greater reductions in depression when people were exercising at home alone.
- The distraction hypothesis suggests exercise distracts us from worrying. Bahrke and Morgan found that meditation was as effective as exercise in reducing anxiety, so perhaps the mental state during exercise is beneficial.

Physiological explanations for the benefits
- The physiological changes associated with exercise and fitness include: more efficient metabolism (protein production, energy use), improved supply of oxygen, enhanced growth hormone production (stamina and strength), increased brain cell growth, increased neurotransmitter production (e.g. serotonin and dopamine, enhancing mood), more endorphins (elevating mood – although Kraemer et al. found a negative relationship between endorphin levels and mood), reduced sympathetic arousal (lowering stress), immune system protection (e.g. Fleshner found exercising rats deal better with infection).

THEORIES OF AGGRESSION IN SPORT

SOCIAL LEARNING THEORY (SLT)

- Sports people may learn aggressive behaviour from models they admire through social learning, e.g. Bandura et al. showed how children imitate aggressive models.
- Imitation depends on observation vicarious reinforcement (Bandura and Walters) and direct reinforcement.

EVALUATION

- SLT can explain differences between individuals, e.g. the 'culture of violence' theory (Wolfgang and Ferracuti) proposes that subcultures may develop norms sanctioning violence, or may develop norms for less aggressive behaviour.
- SLT can explain differences within individuals, e.g. context-dependent responses.
- SLT may be an incomplete explanation of aggression (animals reared alone still display aggression) but Bandura said that biological factors create the potential for aggression; it is the form of aggression that is learned.

FRUSTRATION–AGGRESSION THEORY

- Frustration, e.g. from lack of success, creates aggression (Dollard et al.). We strive to achieve an aim and arousal is raised if external, social factors block it, leading to frustration and aggression.
- The cognitive–neoassociation model (Berkowitz) says that frustration leads indirectly to aggression via negative feelings (e.g. anger or anxiety). As these can be controlled, e.g. by how you perceive the situation, frustration doesn't automatically lead to aggression.

EVALUATION

- Kulik and Brown found that participants frustrated on a phone call task were more verbally aggressive if they had high expectations, showing that frustration of an aim is related to aggression.
- Many studies show frustration doesn't always lead to aggression, e.g. when cognitions intervened; failing hearing aid didn't lead to aggressive response (Burnstein and Worchel).
- Cognitive factors can also increase aggression, e.g. following frustration, the presence of aggressive cues (like guns in the room or aggressive films) led to greater aggressiveness (Geen and Berkowitz).

ETHOLOGICAL THEORY

- Aggression is governed by natural selection (Lorenz). It is innate and triggered by environmental signals; adaptive (promotes survival and reproduction) and not naturally harmful (ritualised aggression and stable strategies).
- Lorenz's hydraulic model says aggressive energy builds up to a certain point then the individual will act aggressively, but this energy can be diverted through physical activity (catharsis).

EVALUATION

- This approach is determinist (aggression is inevitable unless channelled elsewhere) which may apply to animals but humans can control aggressive urges.
- Ethological theory cannot account for cultural differences; even in animals social factors override biological ones. When the amygdala of a monkey is stimulated it becomes aggressive – unless a more dominant monkey is present (Aronson).
- Sociobiological theories are less determinist, suggesting that whilst aggression is adaptive it is only partly controlled by innate mechanisms.
- Evidence for catharsis is lacking. Hornberger found that participants who hammered nails (catharsis) after being insulted were more aggressive toward the confederate. A meta-analysis by Geen and Quanty found that venting anger generally increases aggression although it reduces physiological arousal if it is expressed directly to the person responsible (and if they won't retaliate).

Question 11 **Describe and evaluate theories of aggression in sport.** *[25]*

Student answer

Paragraph 1 ▶ There are lots of theories that can be used with aggression in sport.

Paragraph 2 ▶ A lot of aggression in sport is meant because e.g. you want to get the ball off the opposition but sometimes you get excited or upset because of fouls and lose your temper.

Paragraph 3 ▶ Firstly there are instinct theories that use animal behaviour. One example is Lorenz who thinks that aggression is normal in humans as we are an ape, and chimpanzees are aggressive like us, although gorillas aren't. Others like to think it is because people are a territorial animal, and all animals defend territory. This is just like in football and rugby and boxing, but if it was just human nature then we'd fight on after the match and that doesn't happen, except in ice hockey perhaps. Most people know it's a game and can have a good laugh and make friends which means this explanation isn't correct. Lorenz used evidence from sticklebacks which are fishes and not even apes so it's not all that relevant. Anyway, people who believe that it's biological think that girls are less aggressive than boys, but this isn't true, if you watch girls playing football or rugby it's just as aggressive.

Paragraph 4 ▶ Then the next theory is aggression/frustration, which was invented by Dollard. Aggression happens when you are stopped from getting what you want, a goal. Then you become aggressive because you get frustrated. This can't be an explanation of everything because you can be aggressive, like in rugby, before anybody frustrates you. It might explain why some people start fouling when they're being beaten. Some people are mardy anyway and are like that all the time. Also it depends on the culture you're in because when I played rugby against a Welsh team it was OK to do some things that you'd get penalised for at home.

Paragraph 5 ▶ Freudians think that we have a sudden burn-up of anger and letting it out is better for us — this is discharging it, and is also an explanation by Lorenz. The evidence isn't too good on this though, all the evidence says we are more aggressive after a blow-up.

Paragraph 6 ▶ Also it might be sex, this is called catharsis when you burn off the energy. There are a lot of people who think you don't have sex before a game because it takes your energy away, but there no evidence for it.

Paragraph 7 ▶ Bandura with his Bobo doll test showed that kids can learn to be aggressive. It's done by imitating people, so you might learn off the TV like shirt-pulling and diving. You then get rewarded with a penalty so you do it all the time. This is positive reinforcement of imitation and there is lots of evidence from Bandura's studies that this happens all the time. Bandura did think that we have a biological aggression, but you socially learn how to express it. You can't really prove there is biological aggression though, but you can show that people learn it like Bandura did, so proper science should go for the proof. There is lots of proof that giving shocks when we've watched a violent film makes us more aggressive and give more shocks.

Paragraph 8 ▶ In rugby and boxing the thing is about aggression anyway, so you learn it at school. You get lots of rewards for being very aggressive, but sometimes you can lose it and then everyone blames you for giving away a free kick. So you learn to be only a bit aggressive instead. This is not like being hostile where you lose your temper. This means that all the theories except learning aren't correct in sport and also that society is more important than animal urges.

[614 words]

Examiner comments

This essay is full of potentially appropriate material, but it is often not well expressed and lacking in the all-important detail and elaboration. This student has covered a good range of theories but the amount of detail provided is basic. The sections that offer evaluation (shaded in grey) are particularly poor. In both the description and evaluation it is clear that the student has some understanding but has failed to grasp the more 'technical' aspects of theory and evaluation – a sports jock version!

Paragraphs 1 and 2 provide some introductory remarks but gain no credit because there is no substance.

Paragraph 3 introduces instinct theory but really tells us very little about the theory, suggesting the student hasn't understood it any more than it relates to animal behaviour. The second half of the paragraph is evaluation which is largely anecdotal – though there is some reference to Lorenz's research.

Paragraph 4 is similar – a very basic explanation of the theory followed by some anecdotal evaluation. It is good to use real-life sporting examples but only when you are illustrating a point (which is sometimes the case). There are some good points made about personality and culture, but these lack clarity.

Paragraphs 5 and 6 relate to ethological/ Freudian explanations. The description is not clear – reading what the student has written probably makes little sense, which illustrates how basic it is. Anything you write should inform the reader otherwise it is basic.

Paragraph 7 is an accurate but weak and non-technical explanation of social learning theory, but it is well set in sports (as required in the question). The evaluation is slightly better than elsewhere, but a precise reference to the research is missing.

Paragraph 8 contains some repetition of previous material, but a conclusion has been drawn.

Overall the essay is basic with little technical detail. The description (**AO1**) is basic in terms of detail but the breadth lifts it to the next band (4–5 marks), **4 out of 10 marks**. The evaluation (**AO2**) does refer to psychological concepts and therefore again is better than basic, lying in the 4–7 mark band but nearer the bottom, so **5 out of 15 marks**.

Total 9/25 marks for an E grade.

Improvement?

To improve the **AO1** mark, the theories would need to be presented in greater detail so that someone with no knowledge of the theory could understand the key points.

To improve the **AO2** mark, comments should be elaborated and supported by identifiable evidence ('technical detail'). For example:

'There is a wealth of evidence that shows that frustration doesn't always lead to aggression. For instance, cognitive activity has been shown to eliminate aggression. Burnstein and Worchel (1962) arranged for a confederate to disrupt a group's problem solving task. If the disruption was blamed on a failing hearing aid, no aggression towards the confederate was observed.

The expression generally needs to be improved. Many sentences are simply not clear and need expansion to be creditworthy, for example the sentence 'It might explain why people start fouling when they're being beaten'.

Chapter 12

Abnormal psychology

Chapter contents

218 Introduction to the study of abnormal psychology

220 Issues of bias in diagnosis

222 Aetiologies of schizophrenia

224 Treatments for schizophrenia

226 Aetiologies of depression

228 Treatments for depression

End-of-chapter review

230 Chapter summary

232 Exam question with student answer

Specification breakdown	
Issues of bias in diagnostic systems (e.g. culture and gender).	Diagnosing psychological disorders is a difficult process, as demonstrated by Rosenhan's classic study which formed part of your AS course. He showed that psychiatric diagnosis was unreliable because it relies unduly on the context in which patients are seen. Psychiatric diagnoses may also be unreliable because of culture or gender biases, i.e. the tendency to treat certain cultures or genders differently. This section looks at such biases.
Aetiologies of schizophrenia, including physiological and psychological explanations.	The term 'aetiology' means studying the causes of a disease. You are required to study both physiological and psychological aetiologies (explanations) of schizophrenia – two physiological and two psychological explanations will be sufficient if you know them in enough depth.
	SPECIAL WARNING – students often confuse the words 'physiological' and 'psychological', which may have disastrous consequences in an exam. For example, if you are asked to write an essay on 'physiological aetiologies of schizophrenia' you may write about psychological aetiologies by mistake. In an exam this would score a zero mark – so be VERY careful.
Two treatments for schizophrenia (e.g. chemotherapy, behavioural therapies, cognitive therapies, humanistic therapies).	You are only required to study TWO treatments for schizophrenia. The options provided in the specification are only examples, so you are free to answer exam questions using any two treatments. These may be physiological methods, psychological methods or both. In this chapter we have selected treatments that will be familiar to you from your AS studies.
Aetiologies of unipolar depression, including physiological and psychological explanations.	The term 'unipolar' is used to distinguish depression from bipolar disorder. Unipolar disorder is only depression, whereas bipolar disorder includes phases of mania as well as depression. 'Unipolar depression' is also referred to as major depressive disorder (MDD). In this chapter we will use the term 'depression' to refer to unipolar depression.
	In this section you will learn about the explanations (aetiologies) of depression, in other words, learn about why people suffer from depression. Is it due to physiological factors or psychological ones, or both?
Two treatments for unipolar depression (e.g. behavioural therapies, cognitive therapies, humanistic therapies).	In this section you again only need to study TWO treatments for the exam. You may find it helpful to be able to compare and contrast the treatments you have chosen to gain a deeper understanding of each treatment.

UNDERSTANDING MENTAL ILLNESS

Approximately one in three people suffer from mental illness during the course of their lifetime, so at some time you will undoubtedly have direct experience of mental illness – either affecting someone close to you or yourself. Such direct experiences are likely to help you to understand the true nature of mental disorders, however there are other ways to experience mental illness, such as through its portrayal in films – there are a number of websites that list films about different kinds of mental illness (try Wikipedia 'films featuring mental illness').

Schizophrenia in the movies

The film *A Beautiful Mind* describes the mathematical genius of John Nash (played by Russell Crowe). As a student at Princeton University he formulated a revised version of game theory and began his descent into schizophrenia, experiencing delusions about being approached by a shadowy government agent to assist with code breaking, and had hallucinations of a non-existent room-mate. Eventually he lost his job and received various treatments for his illness, including insulin shock therapy. He made a partial recovery and his colleagues at Princeton allowed him to use their facilities for the rest of his life. He was awarded the Nobel Prize in 1994 for his earlier work.

Depression in the movies

Sylvia Plath was an American poet and writer, born in 1932. She came to Britain to study at Cambridge University where she met Ted Hughes, later to become UK poet laureate. The film *Sylvia* tells the story of their life together and Plath's episodes of depression and eventual suicide in 1963. She had previously tried to commit suicide and was treated with **electroconvulsive therapy (ECT)**. Her experiences with depression are documented in the semi-autobiographical book *The Bell Jar* and in many of her poems.

Experiencing emotional mental disorder

Another means of gaining insight into mental illness is through chat rooms, where sufferers share their feelings, experiences and ordeals. For example,

I think I'm hearing voices, but I'm not sure, because its my own voice, but I don't feel like its my thoughts, and I keep urging myself to do things that aren't normal like punch and smash things. I also keep getting episodes of hyperactivity, but then the slightest thing will bring me crashing back down, for example earlier I was bouncing off the walls cleaning and making dinner.

www.mentalhealthforum.net/forum

I have found an antidepressant that works for me – Zispin – and have been in regular counselling. Initially I felt so alone and desperate, sometimes wishing I was dead. My husband and I nearly split because of the pressure my depression has caused. I had to give up my job, which was in a call centre, but have just been offered another part-time job working away from the public. Seeking help is the best thing I have ever done, I have learnt so much about myself in the last three months. It is so hard to see any sign of hope when you feel so low but there is light at the end of the tunnel, I can see that now.

www.belljar.co.uk

Should the mentally ill be held responsible for murder?

Larry Robison was born into a middle-class family in 1957. He was a good student but his parents began to notice unusual behaviors when he entered his teens. They sought medical advice but it was not until he was 21 that he was diagnosed with **paranoid schizophrenia**. His parents could not afford to pay for treatment and hospitals would not hold him because he was not violent. He also was not given medication to control his hallucinations and paranoia.

One night in 1982 Larry murdered five people. In prison he was offered no psychiatric help and was executed 16 years later. While on trial, Larry's family discovered that there was a family history of mental illness, including his uncle, brother and grandfather who were all diagnosed and hospitalised with paranoid schizophrenia. Larry's story does not mean that all schizophrenia is inherited nor that all people with schizophrenia have the potential to be murderers, but in his case it is possible that he did inherit the disorder and that his mental illness contributed to his murderous rampage. Should he have been held responsible for his crimes? There was considerable protest about his execution, even from some relatives of the murdered individuals. Should the mentally ill be held responsible for any crimes they commit? How should society deal with such potentially 'dangerous' individuals?

STARTER ACTIVITIES

What is abnormality?

You might put together some photographs of people and TV characters that you are familiar with and consider in what way the individuals are normal or abnormal.

Who is more abnormal?

Can you work out a method of establishing who is more abnormal?

Explaining abnormality

In your AS course you studied four different approaches in psychology – the biological, behaviourist, psychodynamic and cognitive approaches. Use your knowledge of these approaches to suggest explanations for mental disorder.

In order to do this you need to have a clear understanding of different mental illnesses. The two disorders you will study are schizophrenia and depression. These are formally described below, but the films and websites discussed on the facing page will help increase your understanding of these and other disorders.

> **> WWW**
>
> For more accounts of mental disorders, see Ruby's room on the BBC, interviews with people suffering from different mental disorders.
> **www.bbc.co.uk/headroom/rubys**

Depression

Depression is a *mood disorder*. Mood disorders affect a person's emotional state and include **unipolar disorder** (also called **major depressive disorder**) and **bipolar disorder**. Depression and mania are the key emotions in mood disorders. Depression is a low emotional state characterised by significant levels of sadness, lack of energy and self-worth, and feelings of guilt. Mania is a state of euphoria or frenzied activity in which people may have an exaggerated belief that the world is theirs for the taking (Comer, 2003). Most people with a mood disorder suffer only from depression (therefore *uni*polar disorder), whereas others experience states of mania that alternate with their depression (hence *bi*polar disorder). Depression ranks first among the top ten causes of worldwide disability.

Diagnostic criteria The formal diagnosis of depression requires the presence of five of the following symptoms: sad mood, loss of interest in usual activities, difficulties sleeping (insomnia or hypersomnia), becoming lethargic or becoming more agitated than usual, poor appetite and weight loss or increased appetite and weight gain, loss of energy and sense of fatigue, negative self-concept, feelings of worthlessness and guilt, difficulty concentrating, and recurrent thoughts of death or suicide.

The symptoms must cause clinically significant distress or impairment in general functioning, and cannot be better explained by bereavement. For a diagnosis of depression to be given, these symptoms should be present all or most of the time, and should persist for longer than two weeks.

Schizophrenia

There are many misconceptions about this disorder. Schizophrenia is *neither* 'split personality' *nor* 'multiple personality'. People with schizophrenia are not perpetually incoherent nor do they constantly display **psychosis** (i.e. loss of contact with reality). Schizophrenia is characterised by a profound disruption of cognition and emotion, which affects a person's language, thought, perception, affect, and even sense of self.

Positive and negative symptoms The symptoms of schizophrenia are typically divided into positive and negative symptoms.

Positive symptoms are those that appear to reflect an excess or distortion of normal functions. These include delusions (bizarre beliefs that seem real), experiences of control (the person may believe they are under the control of an alien force that has invaded their mind and/or body), hallucinations (bizarre, unreal perceptions of the environment, such as hearing voices, seeing lights or feeling bugs crawling on the skin) and disordered thinking (e.g. believing that thoughts have been inserted or withdrawn from the mind).

Negative symptoms are those that appear to reflect a diminution or loss of normal function, which often persist during periods of low (or absent) positive symptoms. This includes affective flattening (a reduction in the range and intensity of emotional expression), alogia (poverty of speech) and avolition (the reduction of, or inability to initiate and persist in, goal-directed behaviour; it is often mistaken for apparent disinterest).

ISSUES OF BIAS IN DIAGNOSIS

CULTURE BIAS

NOMOTHETIC

In your AS psychology course you studied a variety of the therapies that are used to treat mental disorders, for example **psychosurgery** and **chemotherapy**. The decision to use a particular treatment is usually linked to a diagnosis of a particular mental disorder. In the same way that your doctor might diagnose a particular physical illness and then decide on a suitable course of treatment, a psychiatrist diagnoses a mental disorder and advises on a suitable treatment. This diagnosis is related to a **classification system** – a system that groups symptoms together as named syndromes, such as measles or **schizophrenia**. There are classification symptoms for both physical and mental disorders. A doctor or psychiatrist identifies the symptoms displayed by a patient and then uses these to decide what illness the patient is suffering from.

The process of diagnosis is by no means perfect. There are important issues such as **reliability** and **validity** which were vividly illustrated in one of your AS core studies – Rosenhan's (1973) study 'On being sane in insane places'. Further issues include **culture** and **gender biases** in diagnosis.

A '**bias**' is a tendency to focus on certain aspects of experience rather than on others.

The terms 'culture bias' and 'gender bias' refer to the tendency to treat people differently according to their culture or gender respectively. It tends to be the belief that one culture or gender is inferior to another. These biases are discussed on pages 74–77.

▲ *Research has found that black Afro-Caribbean immigrants in the UK are up to seven times more likely to be diagnosed as schizophrenic than white people. Research has also found that women are more likely than men to be diagnosed with depression and specific phobias. Such variations may be due to bias or to genuine differences.*

Culture bias in the diagnosis of depression

Some cultural groups believe that depression is a social problem rather than a mental disorder. Karasz (2005) illustrated this in a study with two diverse cultural groups in New York – South Asian immigrants and European Americans. Participants were asked to read a vignette describing depressive symptoms. The former group identified the 'problem' in largely social and moral terms, with suggestions for treatment emphasising self-management and referral to non-professional help. The latter (European American) group emphasised biological explanations for the symptoms, including 'hormonal imbalance' and 'neurological problems'.

BIAS IN DIAGNOSIS

Cultural bias in diagnosis

Classification systems Inevitably, these are based on **cultural** assumptions about what counts as normal or abnormal behaviour. For example, in the West it is regarded as abnormal to think you are hearing voices. This is not true for all cultural or **subcultural** groups; some religious groups may even regard it as desirable to hear voices. One of the key methods of defining mental illness is in terms of social **norms** (such as hearing voices or feelings of worthlessness) which inevitably means that Western classification systems are culturally biased. This means that members of other cultural groups may be identified as ill when they exhibit behaviours or describe feelings that are considered normal within their own culture.

Psychological tests Part of the diagnostic process often involves the use of personality or intelligence tests. Such tests have been devised by Western psychologists based on Western ideas about personality and intelligence, and these tests are standardised on Western populations. All of this means that non-Western individuals are likely to be assessed less accurately on such tests.

Research evidence Certain cultural and subcultural groups are treated differently. For example, Cochrane and Sashidharan (1995) found that black Afro-Caribbean immigrants in the UK are up to seven times more likely to be diagnosed with **schizophrenia** than white people. Blake (1973) had also found that when **clinicians** were given a case study, they were more likely to diagnose schizophrenia if the individual was described as Afro-American.

In terms of subcultural bias, Johnstone (1989) found that lower-class patients were more likely to spend longer in hospital, be prescribed physical rather than psychological treatments, and have a poorer prognosis.

Gender bias in diagnosis

Classification systems The practice of psychiatry has, until recently, been male dominated, which means that male behaviours are the standard by which all behaviours are measured. The result is that 'normal' female behaviours are often seen as signs of illness. For example, the clinical characteristics for **anorexia nervosa** include amenorrhea (cessation of the menstrual cycle). This assumes that all sufferers are female.

Rates of diagnosis There are significant differences in the rates of diagnosis for men and women for certain disorders, for example, women are more likely to be diagnosed with **depression** and **specific phobias**, whereas men are more likely to be diagnosed with alcohol abuse or anti-social conduct (Robins *et al.*, 1984). There are no significant differences with disorders such as schizophrenia and **bipolar disorder**.

Why do differences exist with some disorders and not others? One possibility is bias based on gender stereotypes. Ford and Widiger (1989) gave psychiatrists written case studies. **Histrionic personality disorder** was correctly diagnosed 80% of the time when the patient was said to be female, and 30% of the time when male. Worrell and Remer (1992) suggested that bias may be due to traditional sex stereotypes which mean, for instance, that clinicians are more likely to interpret women's behaviours as hysterical or submissive.

Research participation Leo and Cartagena (1999) point out that studies of mental disorder have typically relied on male samples because female behaviour is thought to fluctuate along with monthly hormonal changes. The results of such studies may influence classification systems and be inappropriately applied to women. This furthermore means that clinical vignettes in psychiatric textbooks under-represent women and may lead clinicians to be less able to deal with female patients.

Classification systems

Clinicians make diagnoses using a classification system that lists every recognised psychiatric disorder and the associated symptoms. The clinician notes the symptoms displayed by a patient and decides which disorder is present.

There are a number of such classification systems. The two dominant ones in the West, both representing the medical/biological approach to abnormality, are the *Diagnostic and Statistical Manual of Mental Disorders* (*DSM*), developed in America, and the *International Classification of Diseases* (*ICD*), developed in Europe. Both manuals are constantly revised and updated. The

DIAGNOSTIC AND STATISTICAL MANUAL OF MENTAL DISORDERS
FOURTH EDITION
TEXT REVISION
DSM-IV-TR®
AMERICAN PSYCHIATRIC ASSOCIATION

current versions are referred to as *DSM-IV-TR* (a 5th edition is due out in 2013) and *ICD-10*. In the UK diagnosis is largely carried out using *DSM*.

There are other classification systems, such as those used in non-Western cultures (e.g. the *Chinese Classification of Mental Disorders*) or those used by other theoretical orientations (e.g. the *Psychodynamic Diagnostic Manual*).

At the beginning of the twentieth century there were only twelve recognised mental disorders; the first edition of *DSM* in 1952 listed about 100 disorders and the current *DSM* lists 372.

EVALUATION

Cultural bias in diagnosis

Explaining over-diagnosis It is possible that the over-diagnosis of mental disorders in certain cultural groups is due to **genetic** differences rather than culture bias in diagnosis. For example, it might be that black Afro-Carribbeans have a greater genetic vulnerability for schizophrenia. However, rates of diagnosis for Afro-Caribbeans are not as high elsewhere in the world as they are in the UK.

Another alternative explanation for the high diagnosis rates in the UK may be that members of minority ethnic groups in Britain have more stressful lives and this makes them more likely to develop schizophrenia. Therefore, the difference would be due to social/environmental factors rather than biased diagnosis.

Type 1 and Type 2 errors Malgady (1996) considered the consequences of over- or under-diagnosis in terms of **Type 1** and **Type 2 errors** (discussed on page 32). He argued that if clinicians believe there is no culture bias in diagnosis and this is a mistaken belief then they are doing a disservice to their minority clients by failing to recognise or treat their problem. This is a Type 2 error – they are mistakenly accepting a false **null hypothesis**. If they try to avoid a Type 2 error the result may be that Type 1 errors are committed – they mistakenly reject the null hypothesis (believe there is culture bias when in fact there isn't). The result would be a misdirection of healthy individuals to the mental health service system. Malgady believes that the Type 2 error is more serious and therefore it is desirable to accept that there is culture bias.

Gender bias in diagnosis

Bias or difference? It is possible that at least some cases of differential diagnosis are due to real differences rather than bias. For example, gender differences in social roles and in life experiences (e.g. pregnancy and child rearing) may explain why women are more likely to experience depression than men. Nolen-Hoeksema (1987) suggests that men and women even respond differently to depression; women focus on the negative emotions associated with depression, and are more likely to seek professional help, while men use distractions (e.g. alcohol) to cope with their mood state.

The 'difference' explanation is supported by the fact that, although rates of depression are twice as high in women as men, they are similar for **bipolar disorder**. If there was a systematic gender bias in diagnosis, one would expect it to be reflected in bipolar disorder as well because it relies on some of the same symptoms.

The desirability of diagnostic systems

The fact that diagnoses can be unreliable and inaccurate (invalid) suggests they should not be used. However, the same is at least partly true of medical diagnosis generally, yet we wouldn't suggest abandoning that. Both *ICD* and *DSM* are continually updated, so **reliability** and **validity** are always improving.

A major issue with psychiatric diagnoses is that they result in **labelling**. For example, a person becomes a 'schizophrenic' rather than a person with schizophrenia, a label that tends to stick even when the disorder has disappeared. An invalid psychiatric diagnosis has serious and lifelong implications. For this reason, many critics prefer to avoid the use of such labels. An alternative is to use a more **idiographic approach** that doesn't require classification (which is **nomothetic**) but emphasises analysing each patient's problems individually.

Age bias and treatment

Benek-Higgins *et al.* (2008) claim that depression in elderly individuals is often misdiagnosed because its symptoms are masked by natural changes in elderly individuals and their lifestyles. As a result, antidepressant medication is less likely to be prescribed even when needed. There is the additional problem that elderly people are less likely to seek help for depressive symptoms because they fear the stigma attached to mental illness or that they will lose their independence. Electroconvulsive therapy (ECT) is also effective and well tolerated in the elderly. A meta-analysis found a significant improvement in 83% of cases where ECT was used with elderly patients (Mulsant *et al.*, 1991).

Publication bias

Turner *et al.* (2008) claim that there is evidence of a publication bias towards studies that show a positive outcome of antidepressant treatment, thus exaggerating the benefits of such drugs. The authors found that, not only were positive results more likely to be published, but studies that were not positive were often published in a way that conveyed a positive outcome. The authors consider that such selective publication can lead doctors to make inappropriate treatment decisions that may not be in the best interest of their patients.

CAN YOU...? (No. 12.1)

1... Select **six** key topics related to bias in diagnosis.

2... For each key concept write **three or four** sentences explaining the topic.

3... Identify about **ten** points of evaluation (these can be positive or negative).

4... Elaborate each point (see page 9).

5... Use all of this material to write an answer to the following exam question: *Critically consider issues of bias in diagnosis.* Your answer should contain about 300 words of description and 500 words of evaluation.

Remember that, when writing an essay, you can include material from other spreads – but only if it is made specifically relevant to the essay. For example, in an essay on issues of bias in diagnosis you might include material discussed on culture and gender bias in general (see pages 74–77).

AETIOLOGIES OF SCHIZOPHRENIA

NATURE AND NURTURE

DETERMINISM

GENETIC FACTORS

ENVIRONMENTAL FACTORS

There are many different explanations for the disorder that we call **schizophrenia**, but it is the biological (physiological) explanations that have received the most research support to date (Comer, 2003). The importance of physiological explanations of schizophrenia does not, however, deny the role that psychological factors play in the onset of this disorder. Current thinking is that a '**diathesis–stress**' relationship may be at work, with a *physiological* predisposition (the diathesis) for schizophrenia only developing into the disorder if other significant *psychological* stressors are present in the person's life (Gottesman and Reilly, 2003).

What is a concordance rate? In a sample of, for example, 100 twin pairs, one twin of each pair has schizophrenia. The number of times the other twin also shows the illness determines the concordance rate, so if 40 have schizophrenia, then the concordance rate is 40% (or 0.40).

Brain ventricles

Brain ventricles are the cavities in the brain that contain nutrients. On average, the ventricles of a person with schizophrenia are about 15% bigger than normal (Torrey, 2002). It may be that the enlarged ventricles are the result of poor brain development or tissue damage.

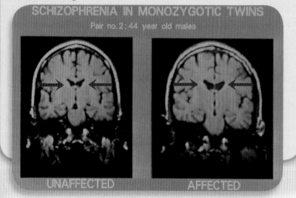

SCHIZOPHRENIA IN MONOZYGOTIC TWINS
Pair no. 2 : 44 year old males

UNAFFECTED   AFFECTED

PHYSIOLOGICAL EXPLANATIONS

Genetic factors

Family studies have established that schizophrenia is more common among genetic relatives of a person with schizophrenia, and that the closer the degree of genetic relatedness, the greater the risk. For example, Varma *et al.* (1997) looked at the first-degree relatives (FDRs) of about 1,000 schizophrenics and 1,000 controls. Psychiatric illness was found in 16% of the FDRs of schizophrenics compared with 7% of the controls.

Twin studies If monozygotic (MZ) twins (who share 100% of their genes) are more concordant (similar) than are **dizygotic (DZ) twins** (who on average share only 50% of their genes), then this suggests that the greater similarity is due to genetic factors. Joseph (2004) calculated that the pooled data for all schizophrenia twin studies carried out prior to 2001 shows a **concordance rate** for MZ twins of 40.4% and 7.4% for DZ twins.

Adoption studies Studies of genetic relatives fail to disentangle the effects of shared genes and shared environment since relatives (e.g. siblings) live together. One alternative is to compare adopted children with and without biological parents diagnosed with schizophenia. For example, Tienari *et al.* (2000) studied 164 adoptees whose biological mothers had been diagnosed with schizophrenia, and found that 11 (6.7%) also received a diagnosis of schizophrenia, compared with just 4 (2%) of the 197 **control** adoptees (born to non-schizophrenic mothers).

The dopamine hypothesis

The dopamine hypothesis states that messages from **neurons** that transmit **dopamine** fire too easily or too often, leading to the characteristic symptoms of schizophrenia. Schizophrenics are thought to have abnormally high numbers of D_2 **receptors** on receiving neurons, resulting in more dopamine binding and therefore more neurons firing. Dopamine neurons play a key role in guiding attention, so disturbances in this process may well lead to the problems of attention, perception and thought found in people with schizophrenia (Comer, 2003).

PSYCHOLOGICAL EXPLANATIONS

Psychodynamic approach

Freud (1924) believed that schizophrenia was the result of two processes, (1) **regression** to a pre-**ego** stage; and (2) attempts to re-establish ego control. Harsh experiences, such as having uncaring parents, leads to regression as an **ego defence**. Schizophrenia was thus seen by Freud as an infantile state, with some symptoms (e.g. delusions of grandeur) reflecting this primitive condition and other symptoms (e.g. auditory hallucinations) reflecting the person's attempts to re-establish ego control.

Cognitive approach

Biological factors cause the initial sensory experiences of schizophrenia, but further features of the disorder appear as individuals attempt to understand those experiences. When schizophrenics first experience voices and other worrying sensory experiences, they turn to others to confirm the validity of what they are experiencing. Other people fail to confirm the reality of these experiences, so the schizophrenic comes to believe that the others must be hiding the truth. They develop delusional beliefs that they are being manipulated and persecuted by others.

Life events

A major factor that has been associated with a higher risk of schizophrenic episodes is the occurrence of stressful **life events**. These are specific stresses, such as the death of a close relative or the break-up of a relationship. For example, a study by Brown and Birley (1968) studied people who had experienced schizophrenia. If they had a subsequent attack it was found that they reported twice as many stressful life events compared with a healthy control group.

Double bind theory

Bateson *et al.* (1956) suggest that children who frequently receive contradictory messages from their parents are more likely to develop schizophrenia. For example, if a mother tells her son that she loves him, yet at the same time turns her head away in disgust, the child receives two conflicting messages about their relationship. The child's ability to respond to the mother is incapacitated by such contradictions. These interactions prevent the development of an internally coherent construction of reality, and in the long run, this manifests itself as schizophrenic symptoms (e.g. flattened affect and withdrawal). These ideas were echoed in the work of psychiatrist R.D. Laing, who argued that what we call schizophrenia is actually a reasonable response to an insane world.

EVALUATION OF PHYSIOLOGICAL EXPLANATIONS

Genetic factors

Family studies Many researchers now accept that family concordance for schizophrenia may be more to do with common rearing patterns or other factors rather than **heredity**.

Twin studies More recent, methodologically sound studies (e.g. those using 'blind' diagnoses where researchers do not know whether the twin they are assessing is MZ or DZ) have tended to report a lower concordance rate for monozygotic twins. However, MZ concordance rates are still many times higher than DZ rates.

There is an alternative explanation for the higher MZ rates. Joseph (2004) points out that MZ twins are treated more similarly, encounter more similar environments (i.e. are more likely to do things together) and experience more 'identity confusion' (i.e. frequently being treated as 'the twins' rather than as two distinct individuals) than DZ twins. As a result, argues Joseph, there is reason to believe that the differences in concordance rates between MZ and DZ twins reflect nothing more than the environmental differences that distinguish the two types of twin.

The dopamine hypothesis

Drug effects Drugs that are known to increase levels of dopamine have also been found to create the characteristic hallucinations and delusions of a schizophrenic episode. This includes the recreational drug *amphetamine* and the drug *L-dopa* used for people with Parkinson's disease, who typically have low levels of dopamine.

Post-mortem studies A major problem for the dopamine hypothesis is the fact that drugs used to treat schizophrenia by blocking dopamine activity can actually increase it as neurons struggle to compensate for the sudden deficiency. Haracz (1982) conducted a review of post-mortem studies of schizophrenics. Most of the patients who showed elevated dopamine levels also had received **antipsychotic** drugs shortly before death, which suggests that the drugs had increased the dopamine levels.

Brain ventricles

Research evidence to support the role of enlarged ventricles is far from consistent. A **meta-analysis** of over 90 brain scan studies revealed a substantial overlap between the schizophrenic and control populations in terms of ventricle size (Copolov and Crook, 2000). A possible explanation for why some schizophrenics have enlarged ventricles may be due to the use of antipsychotic medication. A study by Lyon *et al.* (1981) found that as the dose of medication increased, the density of brain tissue decreased, leading to enlarged ventricles.

▲ **Misleading media**
Schizophrenia is often misrepresented in the media. The voice-over in the 1970s film Schizo erroneously refers to it as 'a mental disorder, sometimes known as multiple or split-personality, characterised by loss of touch with the environment and alternation between violent and contrasting behaviour patterns'.

EVALUATION OF PSYCHOLOGICAL EXPLANATIONS

Psychodynamic approach

There is no research evidence to support Freud's specific ideas concerning schizophrenia, except insofar as subsequent **psychoanalysts** have claimed, like Freud, that disordered family patterns are the cause of this disorder. For example, Fromm-Reichmann (1948) described 'schizophrenogenic' mothers or families who are rejecting, overprotective and dominant, and act as important contributory influences in the development of schizophrenia.

Cognitive approach

There is evidence of a physical basis for the cognitive deficits associated with schizophrenia, for example, research by Meyer-Lindenberg *et al.* (2002) found a link between excess dopamine in the **prefrontal cortex** and **working memory**.

Life events

Not all evidence supports the role of life events. For example, van Os *et al.* (1994) reported no link between life events and the onset of schizophrenia. Patients were equally likely to have had a major life event or not in the three months prior to the onset of their illness (when assessed retrospectively). In fact, in a **prospective** part of the study, those patients who had experienced a major life event went on to have a lower likelihood of relapse.

In any case, evidence that does suggest a link between life events and the onset of schizophrenia is only **correlational**. It could be that the beginnings of the disorder (e.g. erratic behaviour) were the cause of the major life events. Furthermore, life events after the onset of the disorder (e.g. losing one's job, divorce) may be a consequence rather than a cause of mental illness.

Double bind theory

There is some evidence to support this particular account of how family relationships may lead to schizophrenia. Berger (1965) found that schizophrenics reported a higher recall of double bind statements by their mothers than non-schizophrenics. However, this evidence may not be reliable because patients' recall may be affected by their schizophrenia.

CAN YOU...?   No. 12.2

1... Select **four** key concepts from the physiological explanations and **four** key concepts from the psychological explanations.

2... For each key concept write **three or four** sentences explaining the concept.

3... Identify about **ten** points of evaluation (these can be positive or negative).

4... Elaborate each point (see page 9).

5... Use all of this material to write an answer to the following exam question: *Discuss aetiologies of schizophrenia including physiological and psychological explanations.* (Note that this means you must include at least one of each). As good practice you could write two 'building block' essays, one on physiological explanations and one on psychological explanations. Each answer should contain about 300 words of description and 500 words of evaluation.

Don't forget to read the essay-writing guidance on pages 8–9.

TREATMENTS FOR SCHIZOPHRENIA

DETERMINISM AND
EXTERNAL INFLUENCES

NATURE AND NURTURE

ETHICAL ISSUES

If the causes of **schizophrenia** are physiological then it follows that treatments should be physiological. However, as we have seen, the evidence implicates both physiological and psychological factors so it makes sense to consider both forms of treatment. In any case, physiological treatments appear to fail not just because they are ineffective but because, for example, patients often dislike the side effects of drugs and therefore don't take them. As a result, psychological treatments (psychotherapies) are frequently used as an alternative to physiological treatments, or in addition to them.

At AS level you will have studied cognitive–behavioural therapy, psychoanalysis and chemotherapy or psychosurgery. We included ECT because it is much more likely to be used than either psychoanalysis or psychosurgery. However you may prefer to include psychoanalysis or psychosurgery in any essay you write. If you do, it is crucial that you make the treatment relevant to the treatment of schizophrenia rather than just giving a general description of the treatment.

EXAM TIP

Note that the A2 specification requires that you only study any **two** treatments for schizophrenia; they may both be physiological or psychological.

PHYSIOLOGICAL TREATMENTS

Chemotherapy – antipsychotic drugs

Drugs that are effective in treating the most disturbing forms of **psychotic** illness, such as schizophrenia, are called **antipsychotics**.

Conventional antipsychotic drugs (such as chlorpromazine) are used primarily to combat the **positive symptoms** (see page 229) of schizophrenia – such as hallucinations and thought disturbances. The positive symptoms are thought to be products of an overactive **dopamine** system. Conventional antipsychotics reduce dopamine levels. They are dopamine **antagonists** in that they bind to, but do not stimulate dopamine receptors (particularly the D_2 receptors), thus blocking their action (see diagram on right).

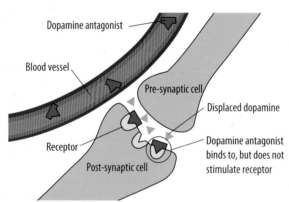

Dopamine antagonist

Blood vessel

Pre-synaptic cell

Displaced dopamine

Receptor

Dopamine antagonist binds to, but does not stimulate receptor

Post-synaptic cell

Atypical antipsychotic drugs (such as *clozapine*) also combat the positive symptoms, but may have some beneficial effects on **negative symptoms** as well. They are thought to act on both dopamine and **serotonin** levels, though there isn't universal agreement on this. Kapur and Remington (2001) suggest that they act on D_2 receptors alone and only occupy the receptors temporarily and then rapidly dissociate to allow normal dopamine transmission. It is this characteristic of atypical antipsychotics that is thought to be responsible for the lower levels of side effects found with these drugs compared with conventional antipsychotics.

Electroconvulsive therapy

Historical origins Electroconvulsive therapy (ECT), developed from the idea that schizophrenia could somehow be cured by inducing **seizures**, following reports that *dementia praecox* (an early name for what we now know as schizophrenia) was rare in patients with severe epilepsy. This led to the belief that seizures in patients with dementia praecox somehow reduced the symptoms of the disorder.

What happens in ECT? An electric current is passed between two scalp electrodes to create a seizure. An electrode is placed above the temple of the non-dominant side of the brain, and a second in the middle of the forehead (unilateral ECT). The patient is first injected with a short-acting **barbiturate**, so they are unconscious before the electric shock is administered, and given a nerve-blocking agent, paralysing the muscles of the body to prevent them contracting during the treatment which might cause fractures. A small amount of electric current (approximately 0.6 amps), lasting about half a second, is passed through the brain. This produces a seizure lasting up to one minute, which affects the entire brain. A patient usually requires between three and 15 treatments. The use of ECT as a treatment for schizophrenia is described in the box at the top of the facing page.

PSYCHOLOGICAL TREATMENT

Cognitive–behavioural therapy

Cognitive–behavioural therapy (CBT) is now the most commonly used form of psychological therapy. The basic assumption of CBT is that people often have distorted beliefs that influence their behaviour in maladaptive ways. For example, someone with schizophrenia may believe that their behaviour is being controlled by someone or something else. CBT is used to help the patient to identify and correct these faulty interpretations.

The learning of maladaptive responses to life's problems is often the result of distorted thinking by the schizophrenic, or mistakes in assessing cause and effect (for example, assuming that something terrible has happened because they wished it). During CBT, the therapist lets the patient develop their own alternatives to these previous maladaptive beliefs, ideally by looking for alternative explanations and coping strategies that are already present in the patient's mind.

CBT techniques CBT usually takes place weekly or fortnightly for between five and 20 sessions. Patients are encouraged to trace back the origins of their symptoms in order to get a better idea of how they might have developed. Understanding where symptoms originate can be crucial for some patients. If, for example, a patient hears voices and believes they are demons, they will naturally be very afraid. Offering a range of psychological explanations for the existence of hallucinations and delusions can help reduce this anxiety.

Patients are also encouraged to evaluate the content of their delusions or of any voices, and to consider ways in which they might test the validity of their faulty beliefs. Patients might also be set behavioural assignments which can enable them to improve their general level of functioning. A therapist may draw diagrams for patients to show them the links between their thinking, behaviour and emotions.

CBT cannot completely eliminate the symptoms of schizophrenia but it can make patients better able to cope with their maladaptive behaviours.

ECT and schizophrenia

Tharyan and Adams (2005) carried out a review of 26 studies to assess whether ECT resulted in any meaningful benefit for schizophrenic patients (e.g. in terms of hospitalisation, change in mental state and behaviour).

They found that when ECT was compared with placebo (i.e. it was simulated) ECT, more people improved in the real ECT condition. However, there was no indication that this advantage was maintained over the medium or long term. When ECT was compared with antipsychotic medication treatment, results favoured the medication groups. There was some limited evidence to suggest that when ECT was combined with antipsychotic medication, this resulted in a greater improvement in mental state. The authors concluded that a combination of ECT and medication may be appropriate when rapid reduction of symptoms is required, or when patients show limited response to medication alone.

Ethical issues

Research on therapies for schizophrenia must be carried out in such a way that does not place vulnerable individuals at unreasonable risk. The *British Psychological Society* (BPS) advise that when participants take part in a psychological investigation they should not be increasing the probability that they would come to any form of harm. The possibility for harm is heightened when dealing with vulnerable groups such as patients with schizophrenia. The potential for harm in outcome studies of schizophrenia include those associated with medication discontinuation, the use of placebo conditions and capacity for informed consent.

EVALUATION OF PHYSIOLOGICAL TREATMENTS

Chemotherapy

Effectiveness There is research support for antipsychotic mediation. For example, Davis *et al.* (1980) analysed the results of 29 studies (3519 people). They found that relapse occurred in 55% of the patients whose drugs were replaced by a **placebo**, but was significantly less (19%) in those who remained on the drug. However, Ross and Read (2004) point out that these figures are misleading, because they also show that 45% of those given a placebo had no relapse, i.e. a significant number did just as well with placebo therapy.

Blocks search for psychological solutions Ross and Read (2004) argue that being prescribed medication reinforces the view that there is 'something wrong with you'. This prevents the individual from looking for, and dealing with, possible stressors (such as life history or current circumstances) that might be responsible for their condition.

Atypical versus conventional antipsychotics Although the introduction of the new 'atypical' antipsychotics raised expectations for the outcomes possible with medication, a **meta-analysis** of studies revealed that the superiority of these drugs compared with conventional antipsychotics was only moderate (Leucht *et al.*, 1999). This analysis found that two of the new drugs tested were only 'slightly' more effective than conventional antipsychotics, while the other two were no more effective.

Side effects Conventional antipsychotics have many worrying side effects, including **tardive dyskinesia** (uncontrollable movements of the lips, tongue, face, hands and feet). About 30% of people taking antipsychotic medication develop tardive dyskinesia, and it is irreversible in 75% of cases (Hill, 1986).

These side effects are lower for atypical antipsychotics. For example, Jeste *et al.* (1999) found tardive dyskinesia rates after nine months of treatment of 30% for conventional antipsychotics but just 5% for atypical antipsychotics. This means that atypical antipsychotics may ultimately be more appropriate because they have fewer side effects, which in turn means that patients are more likely to continue their medications and therefore see more benefits.

Electroconvulsive therapy

Effectiveness An *American Psychiatric Association* (APA) review in 2001 listed 19 studies that had compared ECT with 'simulated ECT' (patients are given general anaesthesia but no ECT – a form of placebo). The review concluded that ECT produced results that were no different from or worse than antipsychotic medication. However, an Indian study (Sarita *et al.*, 1998) found no difference in symptom reduction between 36 schizophrenia patients given either ECT or simulated ECT.

There is some evidence that ECT combined with antipsychotic medication may be more effective than either alone (see study by Tharyan and Adams above).

Appropriateness There are **ethical issues** to consider, most importantly that of side effects. The major side effect is memory loss. This is usually temporary and a single treatment of ECT does not result in serious memory impairment. However, memory problems are cumulative – that is, they get worse over a course of treatment. The *National Institute for Clinical Excellence* (NICE) (2003) has concluded that there is insufficient evidence to recommend ECT as an appropriate treatment for schizophrenia. In the UK, the decline between 1979 and 1999 was 59% (Read, 2004).

EVALUATION OF PSYCHOLOGICAL TREATMENT

Cognitive–behavioural therapy

Effectiveness Outcome studies measure how well a patient does after a particular treatment, compared with the accepted form of treatment for that condition. Outcome studies of CBT suggest that patients who receive such treatment experience fewer hallucinations and delusions and recover their functioning to a greater extent than those who receive antipsychotic medication alone. Drury *et al.* (1996) found benefits in terms of a reduction of positive symptoms and a 25–50% reduction in recovery time with patients given a combination of antipsychotic medication and CBT. This may be because medication allows access to the benefits of CBT.

How much is due to the effects of CBT alone?
A study by Kulpers *et al.* (1997) confirmed the effectiveness of CBT but also noted that there were lower patient drop-out rates and greater patient satisfaction when CBT was used in addition to antipsychotic treatment. In fact, most studies of the effectiveness of CBT have been conducted with patients treated at the same time with antipsychotic medication. It is difficult, therefore, to assess the effectiveness of CBT independent of antipsychotic medication.

Appropriateness of CBT It is commonly believed within psychiatry that not everyone with schizophrenia may benefit from CBT. In a study of 142 schizophrenic patients, Kingdon and Kirschen (2006) found that many patients were not deemed suitable for CBT because **psychiatrists** believed they would not fully engage with the therapy. In particular they found that older patients were deemed less suitable than younger patients (see 'Age bias and treatment' on page 23).

CAN YOU...? No. 12.3

1... There are **three** methods of treatment described on this spread; you should select **two** of them. For each method selected identify **six** key points.

2... Write about 40 words describing each of these key points (you may need to draw on your AS work).

3... Identify about **ten** points of evaluation (these can be positive or negative).

4... Elaborate each point (see page 9).

5... Use all of this material to write an answer to the following exam question: *Describe and evaluate two treatments for schizophrenia.* As good practice you could write two 'building blocks' essays, one on each of your treatments. Your answer should contain about 300 words of description and 500 words of evaluation.

Don't forget to read the essay-writing guidance on pages 8–9.

AETIOLOGIES OF DEPRESSION

Depressive disorders are the most common of the mental disorders, with about one person in six having a diagnosable depressive condition at some time in their lives. Historically, **depression** has been something of a battlefield between those who see it as a biological (physiological) condition and those who see it as psychological. In fact, there is strong evidence for the role of both physiological and psychological factors in depression. It is possible that these explanations fit together, for example, that some factors *cause* the development of depression in the first place, whereas others maintain it.

PHYSIOLOGICAL EXPLANATIONS

Genetic factors

Twin studies Research using twins indicates a **genetic** basis for depression. The basis of twin studies is that identical (or **monozygotic, MZ**) **twins** are naturally occurring clones of each other, having all of their genes in common. On the other hand, non-identical (or **dizygotic, DZ**) **twins** share on average half of their genes. If we assume that the environment shared by twins is roughly the same for both types of twin, then any greater similarities in MZ than DZ pairs shows the action of genes. McGuffin *et al.* (1996) studied 177 **probands** with depression and their same-sex co-twins. The **concordance rate** was 46% for MZ twins and 20% for DZ twins, suggesting that depression has a substantial heritable component.

Genes as diatheses Genetic factors are thought to act as diatheses in a **diathesis–stress** relationship. Such a view would see a genetic predisposition for depression interacting with environmental stressors to produce a depressive reaction. We might expect, therefore, such environmental stressors to affect those with the genetic predisposition differently from those without it. Kendler *et al.* (1995) found that women who were the co-twin of a depressed sibling were more likely to have become depressed than those without this presumed genetic vulnerability. Most significantly, the highest levels of depression were found in the group that was exposed to significant negative **life events** and was most genetically at risk for depression.

Which genes? If depression has a genetic basis then researchers should be able to locate the genes responsible. One candidate is the **serotonin** transporter gene, which is responsible for producing serotonin in the brain. This gene comes in three forms (**alleles**), varying in the length of its two strands: long–long, long–short and short–short. It is believed that the short–short form leads to inefficient serotonin production.

Neurotransmitter dysfunction

It is widely believed that a group of **neurotransmitters** called **monoamines**, which include **noradrenaline** and serotonin, exist in lower levels in the brains of depressed individuals.

Noradrenaline In the 1960s, it was proposed that depression stems from a deficiency of the neurotransmitter noradrenaline in certain brain circuits. Among the findings linking low levels of noradenaline to depression was the discovery that indirect markers of noradrenaline levels (e.g. by-products found in urine) were often low in depressed individuals (Bunney and Davis 1965).

Serotonin Among the findings supporting a link between low **synaptic** serotonin levels and depression is that **cerebrospinal fluid** in depressed, and especially in suicidal, patients contains reduced amounts of a major serotonin by-product, signifying reduced levels of serotonin in the brain itself (McNeal and Cimbolic, 1986). The introduction of *Prozac* and other **antidepressant** drugs that selectively block serotonin reuptake confirmed the association between serotonin and depression (this is discussed on the next spread). Furthermore, Delgado *et al.* (1990) gave depressed patients who were receiving antidepressant medication a special diet that lowered their levels of one of the precursors of serotonin – **tryptophan**. The majority of patients experienced a return of their depressive symptoms, which disappeared again when their diet was returned to normal.

PSYCHOLOGICAL EXPLANATIONS

Psychodynamic approach

Freud (1917) believed that some cases of depression could be explained by 'constitutional' (i.e. genetic) factors, but many cases were linked to childhood experiences of loss or rejection in the family which are **repressed**. Such individuals unconsciously harbour some negative feelings towards those that they love. Later in life, when a loved one is lost or the person experiences other forms of loss (e.g. loss of a job), these repressed feelings resurface but are turned inwards. Freud emphasised the role of anger in both adult mourning and depression. Mourning is the 'normal' response to loss but in some people this extends to permanent melancholia (Freud's term for what we now call depression). Depression, according to this view, is 'anger turned against oneself'.

Cognitive approach

Beck's theory of depression Beck (1967) believed that depressed individuals feel as they do because their thinking is biased towards negative interpretations of the world. Depressed people have acquired a negative **schema** – a tendency to adopt a negative view of the world – during childhood. This may be caused by a variety of factors, including parental and/or peer rejection, criticisms by teachers, or depressive attitudes of parents. These negative schema (e.g. expecting to fail) are activated whenever the individual encounters a new situation (e.g. an examination) that resembles the original conditions (e.g. parental ridicule) in which these schema were learned. Negative schema maintain what Beck calls the negative triad, a pessimistic view of the self, the world (not being able to cope with the demands of the environment) and the future.

Learned helplessness Seligman (1975) proposed that depression may be learned when a person tries but fails to control unpleasant experiences. As a result they acquire a sense of being unable to exercise control over their life, and so become depressed. This '**learned helplessness**' then impairs their performance in situations that can be controlled. This is a characteristic of many depressives who fail to initiate coping strategies in the face of stress. The '*reformulated helplessness theory*' (Abramson *et al.*, 1978) suggests that the depressed person thinks the cause of such events is internal ('It's my fault, I'm stupid'), stable ('People will never want to be my friend'), and global ('Everything I do goes wrong'). A person prone to depression is thus thought to show a depressive **attributional style**.

EVALUATION OF PHYSIOLOGICAL EXPLANATIONS

Genetic factors

Comorbidity In fact, the concordance rates for depression are relatively low when compared with other disorders. This may be explained in terms of **comorbidity**, when two or more mental illnesses occur together and perhaps have some common cause. It is possible that people inherit a vulnerability for a wider range of disorders than depression alone. If this were the case we would expect to see higher concordance when looking at a range of disorders in related individuals. There is some research support for this. For example, Kendler *et al.* (1992) found a higher incidence of mental disorders in twins when looking at depression and generalised anxiety disorder rather than depression alone.

Diathesis–stress model is supported by the research by Kendler *et al.* (above) and further by an Australian study (see right) which provide a link between genetic predispositions (diatheses) and negative life events (stressors).

Neurotransmitter dysfunction

Noradrenaline The role of noradrenaline in depression is supported by the fact that drugs which cause noradrenaline depletion induce depressive states, while those that increase noradrenaline levels show antidepressant effects (Leonard, 2000). Kraft *et al.* (2005) studied 96 patients with depression who were treated for six weeks with a *dual serotonin–noradrenaline reuptake inhibitor* (SNRI). The patients showed a significantly more positive response than those treated with a **placebo**.

Serotonin Some studies have used patients whose depression is currently in remission. The patients are given a tryptophan-deficient amino acid mixture to eat that temporarily decreases serotonin levels in the brain. These patients tend to experience a brief relapse of symptoms during tryptophan depletion, suggesting that a lowering of serotonin levels results in depression (Ruhe *et al.*, 2007).

However, individuals without a personal or family history of depression tend not to show any mood changes following tryptophan depletion, despite the fact that tryptophan depletion alters the activity of the same mood-regulating regions of the brain, such as the **amygdala**, in these individuals as it does in patients with depression. Thus, lowering serotonin levels does not induce depression in all people. One suggestion by aan het Rot *et al.* (2009 – yes that is spelled correctly) is that it is possible that a depressive episode alters the serotonin system such that a person becomes more vulnerable to the effects of future changes in serotonin levels.

EVALUATION OF PSYCHOLOGICAL EXPLANATIONS

Psychodynamic approach

There is some research support for the role of early loss in later depression. For example, studies have found that many people who have suffered depression describe their parents as 'affectionless' (Shah and Waller, 2000), supporting Freud's concept of 'loss' through withdrawal of affection. Barnes and Prosen (1985) found that men who had lost their fathers during childhood scored higher on a depression scale than those whose fathers had not died. Bifulco *et al.* (1992) found evidence that children whose mothers died in childhood were more likely to experience depression later in life. However, they also found that the association could be explained by the lack of care from parents and parent substitutes following the loss, rather than the loss itself.

In any case, loss probably only explains a relatively small percentage of cases of depression. It is estimated that only 10% of those who experience early loss later become depressed (Paykel and Cooper, 1992).

Cognitive approach

Beck's theory of depression is supported by research that bears out many of Beck's predictions. For example, Hammen and Krantz (1976) found that depressed women made more errors in logic when asked to interpret written material than non-depressed participants. Bates *et al.* (1999) found that depressed participants who were given negative automatic-thought-like statements became more and more depressed. However, as with so many explanations, the fact that there is a link between negative thoughts and depression does not mean that the former caused the latter.

Learned helplessness Although Seligman's initial research was based on the study of animals, learned helplessness has subsequently been demonstrated in many human studies. For example, Hiroto and Seligman (1975) showed that college students who were exposed to uncontrollable aversive events were more likely to fail on subsequent cognitive tasks. Another study by Miller and Seligman (1974) found that depressed students performed worst of all on a similar task. These findings suggest that having some degree of control is likely to improve performance, especially for those who are depressed.

Vulnerability factors in depression

Wilhelm *et al.* (2006) conducted a study where 150 Australian teachers were interviewed every five years over a period of 25 years. At each interview they were asked about positive and negative life events (such as bereavement, unemployment and marital break-up) and assessed for **clinical depression** using several standard interviews. The researchers found that negative **life events** were linked to depression but, most importantly, those individuals who had the short–short form of the serotonin transporter gene (see facing page) were particularly vulnerable to depression. Variations in the serotonin transporter gene alone were not associated with depression, but the vulnerability the gene created only became apparent when an individual also experienced negative life events.

CAN YOU...? No. 12.4

1... Select **four** key concepts from the physiological explanations and **four** key concepts from the psychological explanations.

2... For each key concept write **three or four** sentences explaining the concept.

3... Identify about **ten** points of evaluation (these can be positive or negative).

4... Elaborate each point (see page 9).

5... Use all of this material to write an answer to the following question: *Discuss aetiologies of unipolar depression including physiological and psychological explanations.* (Note that this means you must include at least one of each.) As good practice you could write two 'building block' essays, one on physiological explanations and one on psychological explanations. Each answer should contain about 300 words of description and 500 words of evaluation.

Don't forget to read the essay-writing guidance on pages 8–9.

The frequency with which depression occurs, the suffering that it causes, together with the increasing evidence for the physiological *causes* of this disorder has led to pressure to the development of effective forms of treatment that are likewise physiological in nature. However, as for treatments of schizophrenia, psychological forms of treatment for depression offer significant benefit, especially when combined with physiological methods.

Remember that the specification only requires you to study two treatments for depression; however we have covered three to give you some choice. If you studied psychosurgery or psychoanalysis at AS level you may prefer to use one of these. If you do, it is crucial that you make the treatment relevant to the treatment of depression rather than just giving a general description of the treatment.

Note that we have used the term 'depression' instead of the 'proper' term 'unipolar depression' – used to distinguish it from 'bipolar depression' (see discussion on page 229).

PHYSIOLOGICAL TREATMENTS

Chemotherapy – antidepressant drugs

Antidepressants are drugs that relieve the symptoms of depression. There are several different types, although we will only focus on the older 'tricyclic' antidepressants and the newer 'SSRIs' (**selective serotonin reuptake inhibitors**) here. These drugs are used to treat moderate to severe depressive illnesses. Antidepressants are typically taken for at least four to six months, although in some cases they are needed for a longer time.

How do they work? Depression is thought to be due to insufficient amounts of **neurotransmitters** such as **noradrenaline** and **serotonin** being produced in the **neuron** endings to activate their neighbouring cells. In normal brains neurotransmitters are constantly being released at **synapses**, stimulating the neighbouring cells. To terminate their action, neurotransmitters are re-absorbed into the nerve endings or are broken down by an enzyme. Antidepressants work either by reducing the rate of re-absorption or by blocking the enzyme which breaks down the neurotransmitters. Both of these methods increase the amount of neurotransmitter available to excite neighbouring neurons.

Tricyclics block the transporter mechanism that re-absorbs both serotonin and noradrenaline into the presynaptic cell after it has fired. As a result, more of these neurotransmitters are left in the synapse, prolonging their activity, and making transmission of the next impulse easier.

Selective serotonin re-uptake inhibitors (SSRIs) work in much the same way as the tricyclics but, instead of blocking the re-uptake of different neurotransmitters, they block mainly serotonin and so increase the quantity available to excite neighbouring brain cells, thus reducing the symptoms of depression. The best known of these drugs is *Prozac* (*fluoxetine*).

Phases of treatment The treatment of depression has three distinct phases. The treatment of current symptoms takes place during the acute phase of treatment. Once symptoms have diminished, treatment enters the continuation phase for approximately four to six months, after which medication is gradually withdrawn in order to prevent relapse. A third phase, maintenance, is recommended for individuals who have a history of recurrent depressive episodes.

Electroconvulsive therapy

Electroconvulsive therapy (ECT) is generally used in severely depressed patients for whom psychotherapy and medication have proved ineffective. It is used when there is a risk of suicide because ECT often has much quicker results than antidepressant drugs. NICE (2003) suggests that ECT should only be used in cases where all other treatments have failed or when the condition is considered to be potentially life-threatening.

What happens in ECT? The procedural details of ECT are described on page 234. Exactly how or why ECT works is not completely understood, but what is clear is that it is the seizure rather than the electrical stimulus that generates improvement in depressive symptoms. The seizure appears to restore the brain's ability to regulate mood. It may do this by enhancing the transmission of neurotransmitters or by improving blood flow in the brain.

▲ *SSRIs block the reuptake of serotonin at the presynaptic membrane, increasing its concentration at receptor sites on the postsynaptic membrane.*

PSYCHOLOGICAL TREATMENT

Cognitive–behavioural therapy

Cognitive–behavioural therapy (CBT) emphasises the role of maladaptive thoughts and beliefs in the origins and maintenance of depression. When people think negatively about themselves and their life, they become depressed (see previous spread). The aim of CBT is to identify and alter these maladaptive cognitions (the **cognitive** part of therapy) as well as any dysfunctional behaviours that might be contributing to depression (the **behavioural** part). CBT for depression is intended to be relatively brief (usually between 16 and 20 sessions) and is focused on current problems and current dysfunctional thinking. Although there are many ingredients involved in CBT (including 'homework'), two of the main ones are 'thought catching' and 'behavioural activation' (Hammen, 1997).

Thought catching Individuals are taught how to see the link between their thoughts and the way they feel. They might, as part of their 'homework', be asked to record any emotion-arousing events, the automatic 'negative' thoughts associated with these events, and then their 'realistic' thoughts that might challenge these negative thoughts. For example, they may feel distressed about something they overhear, automatically assuming that the person was talking about them. During CBT they are taught to challenge this association, such as asking themselves 'Where's the evidence that they were talking about me? Might they have been talking about someone else? What is the worst that can happen if they were?' By challenging these dysfunctional thoughts, and replacing them with more constructive ones, clients are encouraged to try out new ways of thinking and, ultimately, behaving.

Behavioural activation This is based on the commonsense idea that being active leads to rewards that act as an antidote to depression. A characteristic of many depressed people is that they no longer participate in activities that they previously enjoyed. In CBT, therapist and client identify potentially pleasurable activities and anticipate and deal with any cognitive obstacles (e.g. 'I won't be able to achieve that').

EVALUATION OF PHYSIOLOGICAL TREATMENTS

Chemotherapy

Effectiveness Kirsch *et al.* (2008) reviewed clinical trials of SSRI antidepressants and concluded that only in cases of the most severe depression was there any significant advantage to using SSRIs. Moderately depressed individuals showed the same improvement when given either the drug treatment or a **placebo**. In other words, even the placebo appeared to benefit moderately depressed individuals possibly because it 'offered them hope', which contributed to a lessening of their symptoms. For the most severely depressed group, the expectation of anything working was lessened, thus diminishing any 'placebo effect' and increasing the apparent difference between treatment and **control** conditions.

Children and adolescents Despite their role in the treatment of adults, antidepressants appear less useful when given to children and adolescents (Hammen, 1997). **Double blind** studies (e.g. Geller *et al.*, 1992) have consistently failed to demonstrate the superiority of antidepressant medications over placebo conditions. Ryan (1992) suggests that this may well have something to do with developmental differences in brain **neurochemistry**.

Risk of suicide There has been concern about the safety of SSRIs, particularly the possibility that their use may increase suicidal thoughts in vulnerable people. A review of studies comparing SSRIs with other treatments or with a placebo condition (Ferguson *et al.*, 2005) found that those treated with SSRIs were twice as likely to attempt suicide. A later review of studies (Barbui *et al.*, 2008) found that although the use of SSRIs increased the risk of suicide among adolescents, this risk was decreased among adults. Among adults aged 65 or older, exposure to SSRIs appeared to have a protective effect against suicide attempts.

Electroconvulsive therapy

ECT versus 'simulated' ECT There is a substantial body of evidence to support the effectiveness of ECT, especially in cases of treatment-resistant depression (Folkerts *et al.*, 1997), although there are also studies that have shown no difference in response to ECT in treatment-resistant depression (Hussain, 2002).

ECT versus antidepressants A review of 18 studies with 1,144 patients comparing ECT with drug therapy showed that ECT is more effective than drug therapy in the short-term treatment of depression (Scott, 2004). However, none of these trials compared ECT with newer antidepressant medications such as the SSRIs.

Side effects Possible physical side effects include impaired memory, cardiovascular changes and headaches. In a review of research Rose *et al.* (2003) concluded that at least one-third of patients complained of persistent memory loss after ECT.

Unilateral versus bilateral ECT One way of minimising the cognitive problems associated with ECT is to use unilateral ECT (where electrodes are placed on one side of the skull) rather than bilateral ECT (where electrodes are placed on each side). Studies (e.g. Sackeim *et al.*, 2000) have found that unilateral ECT is less likely to cause cognitive problems than bilateral ECT, yet may be just as effective.

EVALUATION OF PSYCHOLOGICAL TREATMENT

Cognitive–behavioural therapy

Effectiveness There is an impressive body of research supporting the effectiveness of CBT in the treatment of depression. Butler *et al.* (2006) reviewed studies of CBT and found 16 published **meta-analyses**. Based on this very large body of evidence they concluded that CBT was highly effective for treating depression. However, Holmes (2002) claims that the single largest study into effective treatments for depression (carried out by the *National Institute for Mental Health*) showed that CBT was less effective than antidepressant drugs and other psychological therapies. In addition, Holmes argues that the evidence for the effectiveness of CBT comes mainly from trials of highly selected patients with only depression and no additional symptoms. There is far less evidence of effectiveness in more representative patient populations where the majority have complex problems.

Nevertheless, NICE recommends CBT as the most effective psychological treatment for moderate and severe depression.

Therapist competence appears to explain a significant amount of the variation in CBT outcomes. Kuyken and Tsivrikos (2009) lend support to this claim, concluding that as much as 15% of the variance in outcome may be attributable to how effectively therapists conduct treatment.

Research suggests that clients' engagement with 'homework' predicts their outcomes and that therapists who are able to improve clients' engagement with homework have associated benefits in terms of outcomes (Bryant *et al.*, 1999).

Who isn't it suitable for? CBT appears to be less suitable for people who have high levels of dysfunctional beliefs that are both rigid and resistant to change (Elkin *et al.* 1985). CBT also appears to be less suitable in situations where high levels of stress in the individual reflect realistic stressors in the person's life that therapy cannot resolve (Simons *et al.*, 1995).

CAN YOU...?   No. 12.5

1... There are **three** methods of treatment described on this spread, you should select **two** of them. For each method selected identify **six** key points.

2... Write about 40 words describing each of these key points (you may need to draw on your AS work).

3... Identify about **ten** points of evaluation (these can be positive or negative).

4... Elaborate each point (see page 9).

5... Use all of this material to write an answer to the following exam question: *Describe and evaluate two treatments for unipolar depression.* As good practice you could write two 'building block' essays, one on each of your treatments. Your answers should contain about 300 words of description and 500 words of evaluation.

Don't forget to read the essay-writing guidance on pages 8–9.

ISSUES OF BIAS IN DIAGNOSIS
BIAS IN DIAGNOSIS

Cultural bias in diagnosis
- This leads to biased beliefs about mental illness. Karasz gave different cultural groups in New York a description of depression. The South Asian immigrants offered social or moral explanations, whereas European Americans gave biological ones.
- Classification systems are based on cultural assumptions about normality, e.g. in the West hearing hallucinating voices is deemed abnormal but in some other cultures it is not.
- Using a system designed by one culture to diagnose members of another cultural group can result in classifying a person as mentally ill when their behaviours or feelings are normal for their own culture.
- Personality or IQ devised by Western psychologists are likely to be less accurate when used on non-Western individuals.
- Black Afro-Caribbean immigrants in the UK are more likely to be diagnosed with schizophrenia than white people (Cochrane and Sashidharan).
- Lower social class patients are hospitalised for longer, given physical rather than psychological treatments and have a poorer prognosis (Johnstone).

Gender bias in diagnosis
- Classification systems (until recently) were standardised against male behaviours so normal female behaviours could be interpreted as signs of mental illness. A diagnostic criterion for anorexia is the cessation of menstruation, which assumes all sufferers are female.
- Gender bias leads to differences in diagnosis. Women are more likely to be diagnosed with depression or specific phobias and men with alcohol abuse or anti-social conduct (Robins et al.). This discrepancy may result from gender stereotypes.
- There is no difference for some disorders (e.g. schizophrenia or bipolar disorder), presumably because these disorders do not arouse gender stereotypes.
- Ford and Widiger gave psychiatrists written case studies and found that the psychiatrists diagnosed histrionic personality disorder more accurately if they were told the patient was female.
- Studies of mental disorders tended to use male samples in the belief that female behaviour fluctuates with hormonal changes. The findings of such research may influence classification systems which therefore would be inappropriate for women (Leo and Cartagena).
- Psychiatrists may be less well prepared for dealing with female patients as female cases are under-represented in their textbooks.

EVALUATION

Cultural bias
- Over-diagnosis in some cultural groups may be due to genetic differences in vulnerability rather than bias.
- Social factors may affect the risk of mental illness. In Britain, ethnic minorities have more stressful lives making them vulnerable to schizophrenia.
- It is safer to assume there *is* a culture bias and make Type 1 errors (mistakenly diagnose and treat well people) than to assume there is no culture bias and risk Type 2 errors (failing to treat mentally ill patients from cultural minorities) (Malgady).

Gender bias
- Some apparent gender bias in diagnosis may be due to real social role and life experience differences (e.g. pregnancy and childcare).
- Depressed women focus on negative emotions and are more likely to seek professional help. Depressed men use distractions, e.g. alcohol.

- If gender differences were only caused by bias the pattern should be similar for both unipolar and bipolar disorder as they share symptoms; however, they are not.
- *DSM* and *ICD* may be unreliable and invalid like medical diagnoses, but are still useful.
- Classification (a nomothetic approach) leads to the negative consequence of labelling. An idiographic approach avoids labels by focusing on patients as individuals.

Age bias
- Benek-Higgins et al. suggest depression in older adults is often left untreated as other age-related changes mask the symptoms and because older people fear the stigma and consequences (e.g. loss of independence) of diagnosis.

AETIOLOGIES OF SCHIZOPHRENIA
PHYSIOLOGICAL EXPLANATIONS

Genetic factors
- Family studies show that for biological relatives of schizophrenics, closer genetic relatedness is linked to higher risk of also having schizophrenia (e.g. Varma et al.).
- Joseph found concordance rates of 40.4% for MZs but only 7.4% for DZs, suggesting that schizophrenia is partly genetic.
- Adoption studies can separate the effects of genes and the environment. Tienari et al. found that for adults who had been adopted as children, more whose mothers were schizophrenic also had schizophrenia themselves, compared with those with non-schizophrenic mothers.
- The diathesis–stress model suggests that genes only predispose individuals to schizophrenia and that the disorder develops in high-risk individuals who experience stressors (Gottesman and Reilly).

The dopamine hypothesis
- In schizophrenia, neurons using the neurotransmitter dopamine fire too easily or too often. An excess of D_2 receptors means dopamine can bind easily and cause firing.
- Dopamine neurons control attention so could lead to problems in attention, perception and thinking, such as are seen in schizophrenia.

Enlarged ventricles
- The brain ventricles in people with schizophrenia are about 15% bigger than normal (Torrey), which could explain some cognitive problems.

EVALUATION

Genetic factors
- Family patterns of schizophrenia may be due to common parenting behaviour or other environmental factors rather than genes.
- When MZ twins are assessed by researchers 'blind' to whether they are MZs or DZs, concordance rates are lower (although still much higher than for DZs).
- The experiences of MZs may be more alike than those of DZs so the higher concordance for MZs more environmental than genetic.

The dopamine hypothesis
- Drugs that increase dopamine levels (e.g. amphetamine) create hallucinations and delusions similar to schizophrenia.
- However, drugs used to treat schizophrenia (which reduce dopamine action) can cause an *increase* in dopamine levels as neurons compensate for the effect of the antipsychotic drug.
- Haracz (1982) found high levels of dopamine in post-mortem studies of schizophrenics who had been taking antipsychotics.

Brain ventricles
- Copolov and Crook found an overlap in ventricle size of schizophrenic and control groups, suggesting enlarged ventricles are not the cause of schizophrenia. Instead it may be caused by medication.
- Lyon et al. found that with higher doses of antipsychotics, brain tissue density fell, so the ventricles enlarged.

TREATMENTS FOR SCHIZOPHRENIA
PHYSIOLOGICAL TREATMENTS

Chemotherapy – antipsychotic drugs
- Conventional antipsychotics (e.g. *chlorpromazine*) combat positive symptoms, e.g. hallucinations, by reducing the action of dopamine.
- They are dopamine antagonists – block the action of dopamine receptors (especially D_2).
- Atypical antipsychotics (e.g. *clozapine*) combat positive and negative symptoms, possibly by acting on both dopamine and serotonin levels.
- Kapur and Remington suggest atypical antipsychotics bind to receptors only temporarily, then allow normal dopamine transmission. This could explain why they have fewer side effects.

Electroconvulsive therapy (ECT)
- ECT developed to treat schizophrenia.
- ECT induces seizures by passing a small, brief electric current through the brain (usually unilaterally) while the patient is unconscious and paralysed (to avoid fractures).

PSYCHOLOGICAL TREATMENTS

Cognitive–behavioural therapy (CBT)
- CBT is the most common psychological therapy. It aims to identify and correct distorted beliefs.
- During 5–20 weekly or fortnightly sessions, patients identify the origins of their symptoms and consider explanations for the existence of symptoms (e.g. hallucinations or delusions) to reduce anxiety.
- Testing faulty beliefs through behavioural assignments helps to reduce symptoms and enable patients to cope.

EVALUATION

Chemotherapy
- Davis et al. found a 55% relapse rate for patients receiving a placebo compared with 19% taking antipsychotics. Of course, 45% of the placebo group didn't relapse, so that is quite effective too.
- Prescribing medication implies the problem lies within the patient, preventing them from identifying and removing stressors contributing to their condition (Ross and Read).
- Atypical antipsychotics are better than conventional drugs, but only marginally (Leucht et al.).
- Conventional antipsychotics have major and sometimes irreversible side effects (e.g. tardive dyskinesia).
- Atypical antipsychotics have fewer side effects, e.g. tardive dyskinesia rates of 30% for conventional but just 5% for atypical antipsychotics (Jeste et al.).
- Fewer side effects means that patients are more likely to take the drugs and so benefit from them.

Electroconvulsive therapy (ECT)
- A 2001 review by the APA found simulated ECT to be no better or worse than antipsychotic medication.
- Sarita et al. found no difference in effect between real and simulated ECT.
- ECT plus antipsychotics is more effective than either alone (Tharyan and Adams).
- ECT produces memory loss which worsens during treatment. This, and its low effectiveness, means NICE does not recommend ECT as a treatment for schizophrenia and its use in the UK has declined (Read).

EVALUATION

Cognitive–behavioural therapy
- Drury et al. found that after CBT patients have fewer hallucinations and delusions and function better than those on antipsychotics alone.
- CBT has lower drop-out rates and greater patient satisfaction when used in addition to antipsychotics (Kuipers et al.).
- As most studies test CBT in combination with antipsychotics it is hard to judge its effectiveness independently.
- CBT needs the patient to engage to work. Kingdon and Kirschen found many were unsuitable for this reason, especially older ones.

AETIOLOGIES OF DEPRESSION

PSYCHOLOGICAL EXPLANATIONS

Psychodynamic approach
- Freud suggested that schizophrenia resulted from experiences such as harsh parenting. This caused regression to a pre-ego state (producing infantile symptoms, e.g. delusions of grandeur) and attempts to regain ego control (e.g. producing hallucinations).

Cognitive approach
- Biological factors cause the sensory disturbances of schizophrenia but further features result from attempts to understand these effects.
- Schizophrenics try to check the reality of their sensory experiences. As other people cannot confirm them, this leads to the schizophrenic developing delusions about manipulation and persecution.

Life events and schizophrenia
- Brown and Birley found that people with schizophrenia often had major stressful life events prior to a schizophrenic episode.

Double bind theory
- Children who receive conflicting messages from a parent are more likely to develop schizophrenia (Bateson et al.). These contradictions make it hard to build a coherent view of reality so flattened affect and social withdrawal result.

EVALUATION

Psychodynamic approach
- Fromm-Reichmann described schizophrenogenic mothers (who are rejecting, overprotective and moralistic).

Cognitive approach
- Meyer-Lindenberg et al. found that excess dopamine was linked to poor working memory.

Life events and schizophrenia
- Some evidence contradicts the role of life events, e.g. van Os et al. found no link to the onset of schizophrenia. Indeed, their prospective results showed that patients experiencing major life events had a *lower* risk of relapse.
- The evidence is correlational so it could be that disordered behaviour after diagnosis causes the major life events.

Double bind theory
- Berger found that schizophrenics recall more double bind statements by their mothers than non-schizophrenics, but the disorder may make patients' recall unreliable.

PHYSIOLOGICAL EXPLANATIONS

Genetic factors
- McGuffin et al. found a concordance rate of 46% for MZs but only 20% for DZs.
- The diatheses–stress model suggests that genetic factors predispose individuals to respond to environmental stressors with depression.
- Co-twins with a depressed sibling are more likely also to have depression than those without the genetic vulnerability, especially if they have negative life events as well (Kendler et al.).
- The serotonin transporter gene has three forms. The 'short–short' form leads to low serotonin production so may be linked to genetic vulnerability in depression.

Neurotransmitter dysfunction
- Depressed individuals have low monoamine neurotransmitter levels (e.g. noradrenaline and serotonin) in their brains.
- Bunney et al. found low levels of noradrenaline by-products in urine from depressed individuals.
- McNeal and Cimbolic found low levels of serotonin by-products in the cerebrospinal fluid of depressed patients.
- The effectiveness of antidepressants that selectively block serotonin re-uptake confirms the link between serotonin and depression.
- When depressed patients on antidepressants eat too little tryptophan (needed to make serotonin) depressive symptoms tend to return but disappear again with a normal diet (Delgado et al.).

EVALUATION

Genetic factors
- Concordance for depression is low compared with other disorders, perhaps because of comorbidity (when mental illnesses occur together), suggesting that what is inherited is a vulnerability to a range of disorders.
- Kendler et al. found higher rates of depression and anxiety together than depression alone.
- Wilhelm et al. found negative life events were linked to depression, especially in individuals with the short–short form of the serotonin transporter gene, supporting the diatheses–stress model. Variations in the gene alone were not linked to depression, suggesting it creates a vulnerability to respond to stress with depression.

Neurotransmitter dysfunction
- Drugs that deplete noradrenaline induce depression and those that increase noradrenaline levels have antidepressant effects (Leonard).
- Kraft et al. found that a serotonin–noradrenaline reuptake inhibitor had more effect on patients with depression than a placebo.
- Ruhe et al. found that patients in remission from depression relapsed when fed a tryptophan-deficient diet. In non-depressed patients this affected the amygdala without affecting mood.
- A depressive episode may make the individual vulnerable to future changes in serotonin levels (aan het Rot et al.).

PSYCHOLOGICAL EXPLANATIONS

Psychodynamic approach
- Freud suggested some cases of depression were linked to repressed childhood experiences of loss of or rejection by a loved one, e.g. parent. The resulting unconscious negative feelings (e.g. anger) are turned inward and cause depression.

Cognitive approach
- Beck suggested that depression is caused by negative schema (dysfunctional thinking) acquired in childhood, e.g. through rejection, criticism or having depressed parents.
- Negative schema are activated in new situations and maintain the negative triad, giving the depressive a pessimistic view of themselves, their ability to cope and their future.
- According to Seligman, learned helplessness can account for depression if a person tries but fails to control unpleasant experiences that *could* be controlled.
- Abramson et al. suggested the reformulated helplessness theory – helplessness causes a depressive attributional style, so the person thinks the cause of any stressful event is internal, stable and global.

EVALUATION

Psychodynamic approach
- Depressed people often describe their parents as 'affectionless' (Shah and Waller), supporting the link between early rejection and later depression.
- Barnes and Prosen found that boys whose fathers had died were more likely to become depressed as adults than those who had not experienced such a loss. Bifulco et al. found the same pattern for children and death of the mother, though this could be due to poor emotional care after the loss.
- Loss only explains some cases as only about 10% of those experiencing early loss become depressed (Paykel and Cooper).

Cognitive explanations
- Hammen and Krantz found that depressed women made more errors in logic than non-depressed ones, and Bates et al. found that depressed participants given negative statements became more depressed, supporting Beck's ideas.
- However, the link between negative thoughts and depression is not necessarily causal.
- Learned helplessness was initially demonstrated with animals, but Hiroto and Seligman found that students exposed to uncontrollable aversive events were poorer at cognitive tasks and depressed students performed worst of all (Miller and Seligman), supporting the idea that the feeling of being in control improves performance, especially in depression.

TREATMENTS FOR DEPRESSION

PHYSIOLOGICAL TREATMENT

Chemotherapy – antidepressant drugs
- Tricyclics block re-absorption of serotonin and noradrenaline.
- SSRIs (e.g. Prozac) selectively block the re-uptake of serotonin.
- In the acute phase of drug treatment current symptoms are reduced. In the continuation phase (four to six months), gradual withdrawal of the drug prevents relapse. A third (maintenance) phase is used for individuals with recurrent depression.

Electroconvulsive therapy (ECT)
- NICE only recommends ECT where all other treatments have failed or when the condition is potentially life-threatening (suicide).
- How and why ECT works are not fully understood, but it is the seizure (not the electrical stimulus) that reduces symptoms, possibly by restoring the brain's ability to regulate mood by enhancing neural transmission or improving blood flow.

EVALUATION

Chemotherapy
- A review by Kirsch et al. found SSRIs only helped more than a placebo in severe depression. The placebo helped in moderate depression by offering hope. In severe depression, this hope is less likely.
- Antidepressants are less useful for depressed children and adolescents, e.g. Geller et al. found antidepressants were no better than a placebo, perhaps because brain neurochemistry is different in adults (Ryan).
- The safety of SSRIs has been questioned as they may increase suicidal thoughts in vulnerable people. Ferguson et al. found suicide attempts were twice as likely with SSRIs compared with other treatments or a placebo.
- Barbui et al. found that SSRIs increased the risk of suicide in adolescents but *decreased* it in adults over 65.

Electroconvulsive therapy
- Folkerts et al. found considerable evidence to support the use of ECT especially in treatment-resistant cases but some studies have shown no benefit from ECT in treatment-resistant depression (Hussain).
- In a review, Scott found ECT was more effective than drug therapy in the short-term treatment of depression, but this study only considered older drugs (not SSRIs).
- Side effects include impaired memory and headaches. At least one-third of patients have persistent memory loss after ECT (Rose et al.).
- Unilateral ECT causes fewer cognitive problems but is as effective (Sackeim et al.).

PSYCHOLOGICAL TREATMENT

Cognitive–behavioural therapy (CBT)
- CBT aims to identify the dysfunctional thinking and behaviour that contributes to depression.
- During 16–20 sessions, dysfunctional thinking is tackled using different techniques and 'homework'.
- Cognitive element may involve thought catching which shows the individual how their thoughts and feelings are linked. 'Homework' can include recording emotion-arousing events and related automatic 'negative' thoughts, challenging these with 'realistic' thoughts. This enables more positive behaviours.
- The behavioural element involves changing behaviour. Behavioural activation is based on the idea that being active counteracts depression.

EVALUATION

Cognitive–behavioural therapy
- In a review, Butler et al. concluded that CBT was very effective for treating depression, but Holmes claimed that the largest study shows CBT is less effective than antidepressants and other psychological therapies.
- Evidence for CBT is based mainly on patients with no other symptoms, which is unrealistic as many have complex problems (Holmes).
- Nevertheless NICE recommends CBT as the most effective psychological treatment for moderate and severe depression.
- The variation in CBT outcomes may be explained by therapist competence (Kuyken and Tsivrikos), clients' engagement with 'homework' (Bryant et al.) and the selective loss of patients for whom the therapy is not working (Hunt and Andrews).
- CBT is not effective for all depressed patients, e.g. if they have many and rigid dysfunctional beliefs (Elkin et al.) or high stress levels (Simons et al.).
- March et al. (2007) found that combining antidepressants and CBT reduced the risk of suicide in depressed adolescents.

Question 12 Discuss issues of bias in diagnostic systems. *[25]*

Student answer

Paragraph 1 The diagnostic systems developed in Western psychological medicine are the DSM in the USA and ICD in Europe. Both have been modified over time, but there is one very clear bias — cultural. This was demonstrated when the DSM was changed in the 1980s to remove homosexuality as a mental disorder. This was due to cultural change and social pressure from the gay rights movement in the USA.

Paragraph 2 There are other cultural biases too. One of the most investigated is between the dominant white Western cultures and other non-Western or native non-white ones. In the West it is thought strange for people to hear voices, except in a religious context — which shows this is to do with social norms, not medical problems. Supporting evidence from the UK shows that Caribbean immigrants are seven times more likely to be diagnosed with schizophrenia than white natives, and in the USA doctors are more likely to offer schizophrenia as a diagnosis if they know the patient is African American. Even psychological testing is biased as most are rooted in Western culture and are normalised on white native samples.

Paragraph 3 This is not necessarily racist! Firstly there may be real genetic differences, but that is unlikely, as the same pattern of over-diagnosis isn't reflected elsewhere in the world. Secondly, it may reflect the fact that Western society is deeply divided by social class as much as ethnicity and as the Afro-Caribbeans are often in the lower social classes they suffer multiple discriminations causing huge amounts of stress, making them far more vulnerable to disorders. Support for this comes from Johnstone (1989) who found that lower-class white patients spent longer in hospital, were more likely to be given physical treatments and had poorer outcomes than middle-class patients. So it may be social class that is as important as ethnicity. There is even evidence that subcultures in the same country have different interpretations. Karasz (2005) found that Asian immigrants in New York saw depressive symptoms as a social problem but European immigrants saw it as a biological and medical problem.

Paragraph 4 There are other biases, the biggest being gender bias. Stereotypes seem to form the basis of diagnosis, and psychiatry has until recently been male-dominated. Some conditions seem set up to be 'female', such as anorexia, where lack of menstrual periods is a symptom of the disorder — yet men suffer anorexia too!

Paragraph 5 Support for the idea of gender bias comes from Ford (1989) who showed that hysterical personality disorders are more likely to be correctly diagnosed when the symptoms are said to be from a female in a case study rather than a male. Women are more likely to be diagnosed as having depression while men as having anti-social conduct.

Paragraph 6 But is this a reflection of reality? Women may react differently to depression, and look for professional help, while men become alcoholics. Certainly there appear to be no gender differences in diagnosis of bipolar disorder or schizophrenia. This suggests that the alleged gender bias may be partly based on reality and not entirely a bias.

Paragraph 7 An explanation may be that research often uses male subjects. In support of this idea Leo and Cartagena (1999) argue that women are thought to have less stable behaviour due to hormonal changes and used less in research. Results are male-biased and also doctors are less trained to deal with women.

Paragraph 8 There are even age biases as elderly patients are less likely to be given antidepressant medicine due to depressive symptoms being seen as age-related changes (Benek-Higgins et al. 2008) and less likely to have ECT even though it is very successful with 83% of elderly patients.

Paragraph 9 Rosenhan's famous study suggested that medical staff over-diagnose mental disorder. In the first part of the study normal behaviour was seen as ill. In the second part real patients were possibly turned away. These are examples of Type 1 and Type 2 behaviour (over- and under-diagnosis). This was presented as bad, but it is really safer for doctors to show over-diagnosis as then they will help those who need helping rather than rejecting them. It is also important for doctors to assume culture bias exists and work round this.

Paragraph 10 There obviously are biases in diagnostic systems, and these reflect the patriarchal class-dominated societies the doctors operate in. In Western society we would expect to find discrimination against women, the elderly, ethnic minorities and the lower classes in lots of areas of society (like access to jobs, income, housing, etc.) and we find it reflected in diagnosis. But it is important to realise there are real differences and problems as well.

[760 words]

Examiner comments

This is an excellent essay and is clearly well constructed and well written, although there is more on culture bias than on other forms of bias. The essay has breadth and considerable depth related to culture bias.

Paragraph 1 sets out an immediate example of clear culture bias. It is far better to have a firm opening paragraph than a paraphrase of the title (see 8–9 about writing good essays). Paragraph 2 gives basic information on culture bias with good evaluation indicated by phrases like 'supporting evidence'. This evidence could be **AO1** material if it were merely described, but here it has been introduced as **AO2** evaluation. The **AO2** content is highlighted in grey.

Paragraph 3 is a massive evaluative paragraph with accurate and well-structured use of material. The quality and breadth of evaluation here raises the essay into the higher mark bands. PY4 is synoptic, which means using the whole breadth of information available, even if that comes (appropriately) from sociology, politics, art or general studies, as well as other areas of psychology.

Paragraph 4 introduces gender bias, and paragraphs 5, 6 and 7 give excellent and broad evaluation. Paragraph 8 introduces another type of bias and then paragraph 9 deals with Type 1/2 bias using the findings of Rosenhan's study.

Paragraph 10 draws a general conclusion about bias.

The essay is not particularly long but contains a good balance of **AO1** and **AO2**. The **AO1** displays both depth and breadth, though the material on gender bias is briefer, therefore **9 out of 10 marks for AO1**. The **AO2** shows sustained evaluation of the evidence and is both balanced and reasoned but again this applies to the first half of the essay more than the second half so **15 out of 16 marks for AO2**.

23/25 makes this a clear Grade A essay.

Improvement? There is not a lot of room for improvement except to add a little more detail in the second half of the essay to boost the **AO1 + AO2** mark.

REFERENCES

aan het Rot, M., Mathew, S.J. and Charney, D.S. (2009). Neurobiological mechanisms in major depressive disorder. *Canapagedian Medical Association Journal, 180,* 305–313. ▶ **page 237**

Abernethy, E.M. (1940). The effect of changed environmental conditions upon the results of college examinations. *Journal of Psychology, 10,* 293–301. ▶ **page 92**

Abraham, S.C.S., Sheeran, P., Spears, R. and Abrams, D. (1992) Health beliefs and the promotion of HIV-preventative infections among teenagers: a Scottish perspective. *Health Psychology, 11,* 363–370. ▶ **page 173**

Abramson, L.Y., Seligman, M.E.P. and Teasdale, J. (1978). Learned helplessness in humans: critique and reformulation. *Journal of Abnormal Psychology, 87,* 49–74. ▶ **page 236**

Abwender, D.A. and Hough, K. (2001). Interactive effects of characteristics of defendant and mock juror on U.S. participants' judgement and sentencing recommendations. *Journal of Social Psychology, 141,* 603–615. ▶ **page 201**

Akert (1998). *Terminating romantic relationships: The role of personal responsibility and gender.* Unpublished manuscript, Wellesley College. ▶ **page 105**

Adams, G.R., Shea, J.A. and Fitch, S.A. (1979). Toward the development of an objective assessment of ego-identity status. *Journal of Adolescence, 8,* 223–237. ▶ **page 133**

Aggleton, J.O. and Waskett, L. (1999). The ability of odours to serve as state-dependent cues for real-world memories: can Viking smells aid the recall of Viking experiences? *British Journal of Psychology, 90*(1), 1–7. ▶ **page 93**

Agrawal, A., Neale, M.C., Prescott, C.A. and Kendler, K.S. (2004). A twin study of early cannabis use and subsequent use and abuse/dependence of other illicit drugs. *Psychological Medicine, 34*(7), 1227–1237. ▶ **page 166**

Ainsworth, M.D.S., Blehar, M.C., Waters, E. and Wall, S. (1978). *Patterns of Attachment: A Psychological Study of the Strange Situation.* Hillsdale, NJ: Lawrence Erlbaum. ▶ **page 137**

Ajzen, I. (1985). From intentions to actions: a theory of planned behavior. In J. Kuhl and J. Beckman (eds) *Action-control: From Cognition to Behavior.* Heidelberg: Springer. ▶ **page 173**

Ajzen, I. and Fishbein, M. (1980). *Understanding attitudes and predicting social behavior.* Englewood Cliffs, NJ: Prentice-Hall. ▶ **page 172**

Albus, H., Vansteensel, M.J., Michel, S., Block, G.D. and Meijer, J.H. (2005). A GABAergic mechanism Is necessary for coupling dissociable ventral and dorsal regional oscillators within the circadian clock. *Current Biology, 15,* 886–893. ▶ **page 156**

Allen, J.P. and Land, D. (1999). Attachment in adolescence. In J. Cassidy and P.R. Shaver (eds) *Handbook of Attachment Theory and Research,* New York: Guilford. ▶ **page 139**

Allison, T. and Cicchetti, D. (1976). Sleep in mammals: ecological and constitutional correlates. *Science, 194,* 732–734. ▶ **page 161**

Allport, G.W. and Postman, L.J. (1947). *The Psychology of Rumor.* New York: Holt. ▶ **page 209**

American Heart Association (1999). *2000 Heart and Stroke Statistical Update.* Dallas, TX: American Heart Association. ▶ **page 226**

American Psychiatric Association (1953). *Ethics Code.* Washington, DC: American Psychological Association. ▶ **page 235**

American Psychiatric Association (2001). *The Practice of Electroconvulsive Therapy: Recommendations for Treatment, Training and Privileging,* 2nd edn. Washington, DC: American Psychiatric Association. ▶ **page 235**

Amsterdam, B. (1972). Mirror image reactions before age two. *Developmental Psychobiology, 5,* 297–305. ▶ **page 149**

Anderson, S., Avery, D., DiPietro, E., Edwards, G. and Christian, W. (1987). Intensive home-based early intervention with autistic children. *Educational Treatment of Children, 10,* 352–366. ▶ **page 191**

Animals (Scientific Procedures) Act (1986). *Halsbury's Statutes,* 4th edn. *Current Statutes Service, Issue 9,* vol. 2. London: Butterworth. ▶ **page 52**

Antikainen, R., Hanninen, T., Honkalampi, K., Hintikka, J., Koivumaa-Honkanen, H., Tanskanen, A. and Viinamaki, H. (2001). Mood improvement reduces memory complaints in depressed patients. *European Archives of Psychiatry and Clinical Neuroscience, 251*(1), 6–11. ▶ **page 91**

Anton, S.J., Colwell, C.S., Harmar, A.J., Waschek, J.A. and Herzog, E. (2005). Vasoactive intestinal polypeptide mediates circadian rhythmicity and synchrony in distinct subsets of mammalian clock neurons. *Nature Neuroscience, 8,* 476–483. ▶ **page 157**

Antrobus, J., Kondo, T. and Reinsel, R. (1995). Dreaming in the late morning: summation of REM and diurnal cortical activation. *Consciousness and Cognition, 4,* 275–299. ▶ **page 153**

Archer, S. (1982). The lower age boundaries of identity development. *Child Development, 53,* 1551–1556. ▶ **page 137**

Ardila, A. (1995). Directions of research in cross-cultural neuropsychology. *Journal of Clinical and Experimental Neuropsychology, 17,* 143–150. ▶ **page 75**

Argyle, M., Henderson, M., Bond, M., Iizuka, Y. and Contarello, A. (1986). Cross-cultural variations in relationship rules. *International Journal of Psychology, 21,* 287–315. ▶ **pages 110, 111**

Armitage, C.J. and Conner, M. (1998). Efficacy of the theory of planned behaviour: a meta-analytic review. Unpublished manuscript, University of Leeds. ▶ **page 178**

Aronson, E. (1999). *The Social Animal,* 8th edn. New York: Worth Publishers. ▶ **pages 71, 122**

Aronson, J., Lustina, M., Good, C., Keough, K., Steele, C. and Brown, J. (1999). When white men can't do math: necessary and sufficient factors in stereotype threat. *Journal of Experimental Social Psychology, 35,* 29–46. ▶ **page 223**

Asch, S.E. (1955). Opinions and social pressure. *Scientific American, 193,* 31–35. ▶ **pages 197, 200**

Aschoff, J. and Wever, R. (1976). Human circadian rhythms: a multioscillatory system. *Fed Proceedings, 35,* 2326–2332. ▶ **page 157**

Ashton, H. (1997). Benzodiazepine dependency. In A. Baum, S. Newman, J. Weinman, R. West and C. McManus (eds) *Cambridge Handbook of Psychology, Health and Medicine.* Cambridge: Cambridge University Press. ▶ **page 171**

Atchley, R.C. (1977). *The Social Forces in Later Life,* 2nd edn. Belmont, CA: Wadsworth. ▶ **page 143**

Atchley, R.C. (1982). Retirement as a social institution. *Annual Review of Sociology, 8,* 263–287. ▶ **page 142**

Atkinson, R.C. and Shiffrin, R.M. (1968). Human memory: a proposed system and its control processes. In K.W. Spence and J.T. Spence (eds) *The Psychology of Learning and Motivation,* vol. 2. London: Academic Press. ▶ **page 86**

Atkinson, R.C. and Shiffrin, R.M. (1971). The control of short-term memory. *Scientific American,* August, 82–90. ▶ **page 86**

Babyak, M.A., Blumenthal, J.A., Herman, S., Khatri, P., Doraiswamy, P.M., Moore, K.A., Craighead, W.E., Baldewicz, T.T. and Krishnan, K.R. (2000). Exercise treatment for major depression: maintenance of therapeutic benefit at 10 months. *Psychosomatic Medicine, 62,* 633–638. ▶ **page 220**

Bachman, J.G., Freedman-Doan, P., O'Malley, P.M., Johnston, L.D. and Segal, D.R. (1999). Changing patterns of drug use among US military recruits before and after enlistment. *American Journal of Public Health, 89*(5), 672–677. ▶ **page 207**

Bachman, J.G., Johnson, L.D., O'Malley, P.M. and Humphreys, H. (1988). Explaining the recent decline in marijuana use: differentiating the effects of perceived risk, disapproval and general life-style factors. *Journal of Health and Social Behaviour*, *29*, 92–112. ▶ **page 173**

Baddeley, A.D. (1966a). The influence of acoustic and semantic similarity on long term memory for word sequences. *Quarterly Journal of Experimental Psychology*, *18*, 302–309. ▶ **page 87**

Baddeley, A.D. (1966b). Short-term memory for word sequences as a function of acoustic, semantic and formal similarity. *Quarterly Journal of Experimental Psychology*, *18*, 362–365. ▶ **page 87**

Baddeley, A.D. (2000) The episodic buffer: A new component of working memory? *Trends in Cognitive Sciences, 4*(11), 417–23. ▶ **page 88**

Baddeley, A.D. and Hitch, G.J. (1974). Working memory. In G.H. Bower (ed.) *The Psychology of Learning and Motivation,* vol. 8. London: Academic Press. ▶ **page 88**

Baddeley, A.D. and Hitch, G.J. (1977). Recency re-examined. In S. Dornic (ed.) *Attention and Performance*. New Jersey: Erlbaum. ▶ **page 93**

Baddeley, A.D., Grant, S., Wright, E. and Thomson, N. (1975). Imagery and visual working memory. In P.M.A. Rabbitt and S. Dornic (eds) *Attention and Performance,* vol. v. London: Academic Press. ▶ **page 89**

Bahrick, H.P., Bahrick, P.O. and Wittinger, R.P. (1975). Fifty years of memory for names and faces: a cross-sectional approach. *Journal of Experimental Psychology: General*, *104*, 54–75. ▶ **page 87**

Bahrke, M. S. and Morgan, W.P. (1978). Anxiety reduction following exercise and meditation. *Cognitive Therapy and Research*, *2*(4), 323–333. ▶ **page 221**

Baldwin, J. and McConville, M. (1979). *Jury Trials*. London: Oxford University Press. ▶ **page 200**

Bandura, A. (1977). *Social Learning Theory*. Englewood Cliffs, NJ: Prentice-Hall. ▶ **pages 202, 221**

Bandura, A. (1982). Self-efficacy mechanisms in human agency. *American Psychologist*, *37*, 122–147. ▶ **page 214**

Bandura, A. (1997). *Self-efficacy: the exercise of control*. San Francisco, CA: Freeman. ▶ **page 221**

Bandura, A. and Walters, R.H. (1963). *Social Learning and Personality Development*. New York: Holt, Rinehart and Winston. ▶ **pages 182, 222**

Bandura, A., Ross, D. and Ross, S.A. (1961). Transmission of aggression through imitation of aggressive models. *Journal of Abnormal and Social Psychology*, *63*, 575–582. ▶ **pages 73, 202, 203, 222**

Banks, M.S., Aslin, R.N. and Letson, R.D. (1975). Sensitive period for the development of human binocular vision. *Science, 190*, 675–677. ▶ **page 70**

Barbui, C., Furukawa, T.A. and Cipriani A. (2008). Effectiveness of paroxetine in the treatment of acute major depression in adults: a systematic re-examination of published and unpublished data from randomised trials. *Canadian Medical Association Journal*, *178*, 296–305. ▶ **page 239**

Barjonet, P.E. (1980). L'influence sociale et des representations des causes de l'accident de la route. *La Travail Human, 20*, 1–14. ▶ **page 205**

Barnes, G. and Prosen, H. (1985). Parent death and depression. *Journal of Abnormal Psychology*, *94*, 64–69. ▶ **page 237**

Barrett, C.J. (1978). Effectiveness of widows' groups in facilitating change. *Journal of Consulting and Clinical Psychology*, *46*, 20–31. ▶ **page 143**

Bartels, A. and Zeki, S. (2000). The neural basis of romantic love. *NeuroReport*, *11*, 3829–3834. ▶ **page 111**

Bartlett, F.C. (1932). *Remembering*. Cambridge: Cambridge University Press. ▶ **page 204**

Bassett, J.E. and Blanchard, E.B. (1977). The effect of the absence of close supervision on the use of response cost in a prison token economy. *Journal of Applied Behavior Analysis*, *101*(3), 375–379. ▶ **page 207**

Basso, M.R., Carona, F.D., Lowery, N. and Axelrod, B.N. (2002). Practice effects on the WAIS-III across 3- and 6-month intervals. *The Clinical Neuropsychologist*, *16*(1), 57–63. ▶ **page 122**

Bates, G.W., Thompson, J.C. and Flanagan, C. (1999). The effectiveness of individual versus group induction of depressed mood. *Journal of Psychology*, *133*(3), 245–252. ▶ **page 237**

Bateson, G., Jackson, D.D., Haley, J. and Weakland, J.H. (1956). Towards a theory of schizophrenia. *Behavioural Science*, *1*(4), 251–264. ▶ **page 232**

Baumeister, R.F. and Steinhilber, A. (1984). Paradoxical effects of supportive audiences on performance under pressure: the home field disadvantage in sports championships. *Journal of Personality and Social Psychology*, *47*, 85–93. ▶ **page 218**

Baumrind, D. (1975). Metaethical and normative considerations governing the treatment of human subjects in the behavioural sciences. In E.C. Kennedy (ed.) *Human Rights and Psychological Research: A Debate on Psychology and Ethics*. New York: Thomas E. Crowell. ▶ **page 71**

Baxter, L.A. (1994). A dialogic approach to relationship maintenance. In D.J. Canary and L. Stafford (eds) *Communication and Relational Maintenance*. New York: Academic Press. ▶ **page 104**

Beardsley, T. (1997). The machinery of thought. *Scientific American*, August, 58–63. ▶ **page 87**

Beauvoir, S., de (1949). *The Second Sex*. Translated and edited by H.M. Parshley. New York: Knopf. ▶ **page 76**

Beck, A.T. (1967). *Depression: Causes and Treatment*. Philadelphia: University of Pennsylvania Press. ▶ **page 236**

Becker, G.S. and Murphy, K.M. (1988). A theory of rational addiction. *Journal of Political Economy*, 96, 675–700. ▶ **page 166**

Becker, M.H. and Maiman, L.A. (1975). Sociobehavioural determinants of compliance with health and medical care recommendations. *Medical Care*, *13*, 10–24. ▶ **page 172**

Bell, R.A., LeRoy, J.B. and Stephenson, J.J. (1982). Evaluating the mediating effects of social supports upon life events and depressive symptoms. *Journal of Community Psychology*, *10*, 325–340. ▶ **page 107**

Belloc, N.B. (1973). Relationship of health practices and mortality. *Preventative Medicine, 2*, 67–81. ▶ **page 174**

Belmont, L. and Marolla, F.A. (1973). Birth order, family size and intelligence. *Science, 182*, 1096–1101. ▶ **page 126**

Benek-Higgins, M.B., McReynolds, C.J., Hogan, E. and Savickas, S. (2008). Depression and the elder person: the enigma of misconceptions, stigma and treatment. *Journal of Mental Health Counseling, 30*(4), 283–296. ▶ **page 231**

Benham, G., Bowers, S., Nash, M. and Muenchen, R. (1998). Self-fulfilling prophecy and hypnotic response are not the same thing. *Journal of Personality and Social Psychology*, *75*(6), 1604–1613. ▶ **page 151**

Bennett, N. (1976). *Teacher Styles and Pupil Progress*. London: Open Books. ▶ **page 185**

Bennett-Levy, J. and Marteau, T. (1984). Fear of animals: what is prepared? *British Journal of Psychology*, *75*, 37–42. ▶ **page 13**

Bennion, L.D. and Adams, G.R. (1986). A revision of the extended version of the objective measure of ego identity status: an identity instrument for use with late adolescents. *Journal of Adolescent Research*, *1*, 183–198. ▶ **page 133**

Berger, A. (1965). A test of the double-bind hypothesis of schizophrenia. *Family Process, 4*, 198–205. ▶ **page 233**

Berkowitz, L. (1978). Whatever happened to the frustration aggression hypothesis? *American Behavioral Scientist, 21*(5), 691–708. ▶ **page 222**

Berntson, G.G., Shafi, R. and Sarter, M. (2002). Specific contributions of the basal forebrain corticopetal cholinergic system to encephalographic activity and sleep/waking behaviour. *European Journal of Neuroscience, 16*, 2453–2461. ▶ **page 94**

Bifulco, A., Harris, T. and Brown, G.W. (1992). Mourning or early inadequate care? Reexamining the relationship of maternal loss in childhood with adult depression and anxiety. *Development and Psychopathology, 4*, 433–449. ▶ **page 237**

Binet, A. (1905). New methods for the diagnosis of the intellectual level of subnormals. First published in. *L'Année Psychologique*, 12, 191–244. Available at http://psychclassics.asu.edu/Binet/binet1.htm (last accessed May 2010). ▶ **page 116**

Bjerkedal, T., Kristensen P., Skjeret G. and Brevik, J. (2007). Birth order and intelligence. *Intelligence, 35*(5), 503–514. ▶ **page 126**

Blake, W. (1973). The influence of race of diagnosis. *Smith College Studies in Social Work, 43*(3), 184–192. ▶ **page 230**

Blakemore, C. and Cooper, G.F. (1970). Development of the brain depends on the visual environment. *Nature, 228*, 477–478. ▶ **page 70**

Blair, A. (1993). Social class and the contextualization of illness experience. In A. Radley (Ed.) *Worlds of Illness: Biographical and Cultural Perspectives on Health and Disease.* London: Routledge. ▶ **page 175**

Blake, J. (1989). *Family size and achievement*. Berkeley, CA: University of California Press. ▶ **page 127**

Blanco, C., Petkova, E., Ibanez, A. and Saiz-Ruiz, J. (2002). A pilot placebo-controlled study of fluvoxamine for pathological gambling. *Annals of Clinical Psychiatry, 14*, 9–15. ▶ **page 169**

Blau, Z.S. (1973). *Old Age in a Changing Society*. New York: New Viewpoints. ▶ **page 143**

Bleach, K. and Smith, J. (1998). Switching off and dropping out? *Topic, 20*, 1–5. ▶ **page 189**

Blos, P. (1967). The second individuation process of adolescence. *Psychoanalytic Study of the Child*, 22, 162–186. ▶ **pages 136, 138**

Blum, K., Noble, E.P., Sheridan, P.J., Finley, O., Montgomery, A., Ritchie, T., Ozkaragoz, T., Fitch, R.J., Sadlack, F., Sheffiled, D., Dahlmann, T., Halbardier, S. and Nagomi, H. (1991). Association of the A_1 allele of the D_2 dopamine receptor gene with severe alcoholism. *Alcohol, 8*, 409–425. ▶ **page 166**

Blumstein, P. and Schwartz, P. (1983). *American Couples*. New York: William Morrow. ▶ **page 108**

Boekhout, B. Hendrick, S. and Hendrick, C. (1999). Relationship infidelity: a loss perspective. *Journal of Personal and Interpersonal Loss, 4*, 97–123. ▶ **page 105**

Bohman, M. (1996). Predisposition to criminality, Swedish adoption studies in retrospect. *Ciba Foundation Symposium, 194*, 99–109. ▶ **page 203**

Boivin, D.B., Duffy, J.F., Kronauer, R.E. and Czeisler, C.A. (1996). Dose-response relationships for resetting of human circadian clock by light. *Nature, 379*(6565), 540–542. ▶ **page 157**

Bonnet, M.H. and Arand, D.L. (1995). 24 hour metabolic rate in insomniacs and matched normal sleepers. *Sleep, 18*, 581–588. ▶ **page 159**

Bouchard, T.J. Jr. and McGue, M. (1981). Familial studies of intelligence: a review. *Science, 212*, 1055–1059. ▶ **page 124**

Bouhoutsos, J.C., Goodchilds, J.D. and Huddy, L. (1986). Media psychology: an empirical study of radio call-in psychology programs. *Professional Psychology: Research and Practice, 17*(5), 408–414. ▶ **page 60**

Bower, T.G.R. (1981). Cognitive development. In M. Roberts and J. Tamburrini (eds) *Child Development 0–5.* Edinburgh: Holmes McDougall. ▶ **page 91**

Bowlby, J. (1969). *Attachment and Love:* vol. 1: *Attachment.* London: Hogarth. ▶ **page 100**

BPS (2009). Code of ethics and conduct. See www.bps.org.uk/document-download-area/document-download$.cfm?file_uuid=E6917759-9799-434A-F313-9C35698E1864&ext=pdf (accessed May 2010). ▶ **pages 57, 60**

Bradburn, N. (1969). *The Structure of Psychological Well-being.* Chicago, IL: Aldine. ▶ **pages 107, 140**

Braun, A. (1999). The new neuropsychology of sleep: implications for psychoanalysis: commentary. *Neuro-psychoanalysis, 1*(2), 196–201. ▶ **page 153**

Braun, A., Balkin, T., Wesensten, N., Carson, R., Varga, M., Baldwin, P., Selbie, S., Belenky, G. and Herscowitch, P. (1997). Regional cerebral blood flow throughout the sleep-wake cycle: an (H_2O).-O-15 PET study. *Brain, 120*, 1173–1197. ▶ **page 153**

Bray, S.R. (1999). The home advantage from an individual team perspective. *Journal of Applied Sport Psychology, 11*, 116–125. ▶ **page 219**

Brehm, S.S. and Kassin, S.M. (1996). *Social Psychology* 3rd edn. Boston: Houghton Mifflin. ▶ **page 105**

Breuer, J. and Freud, S. (1893). *Studies on Hysteria*, Standard Edition 2. London: Hogarth Press. ▶ **page 223**

Britton, P. (1992). Home Office/ACPO Review of offender profiling, unpublished. Reported in Copson, G. (1996). At last some facts about offender profiling in Britain. *Forensic Update, 46*, 4–10. ▶ **page 199**

Brodbar-Nemzer, J.Y. (1986). Divorce and group commitment: The case of the Jews. *Journal of Marriage and Family, 48*, 329–340. ▶ **page 141**

Brooks-King, M. and Hurrell, H.G. (1958). Intelligence tests with tits. *British Birds, 51*, 514–524. ▶ **page 116**

Brosnan, M. (2008). Digit ratio as an indicator of numeracy relative to literacy in 7-year-old British school children. *British Journal of Psychology, 99*, 75–85. ▶ **page 34**

Broughton, R.J. (1968) Sleep disorders: disorders of arousal? Enuresis, sonambulism, and nightmares occur in confusional states of arousal, not in "dreaming sleep". *Science, 159*, 1070–1078. ▶ **page 159**

Brown, E.L., Deffenbacher, K.A. and Sturgill, W. (1977). Memory for faces and the circumstances of encounter. *Journal of Applied Psychology, 62*, 311–318. ▶ **pages 205, 222**

Brown, G.W. and Birley, J.L.T. (1968). Crises and life: changes and the onset of schizophrenia. *Journal of Health and Social Behaviour, 9*, 203–214. ▶ **page 232**

Brown, G.W. and Harris, T. (1982). Fall-off in the reporting of life events. *Social Psychiatry, 17*, 23–28. ▶ **page 107**

Brown, J.D. (1991). Staying fit and staying well: physical fitness as a moderator of life stress. *Journal of Personality and Social Psychology, 60*(4), 555–561. ▶ **page 220**

Brown, R. and Kulik, J. (1977). Flashbulb memories. *Cognition, 5*, 73–99. ▶ **page 91**

Bruner, J. (1960). *The Process of Education.* Cambridge, MA: Harvard University Press. ▶ **page 184**

Brunner, H.G., Nelen, M., Breakfield, X.O., Ropers, H.H. and van Oost, B.A. (1993). Abnormal behaviour associated with a point mutation in the structural gene for monoamine oxidase A. *Science, 262*, 578–580. ▶ **page 203**

Bryant, M.J., Simons, A.D. and Thase, M.E. (1999). Therapist skill and patient variables in homework compliance: controlling an uncontrolled variable in cognitive therapy outcome research. *Cognitive Therapy and Reearch*, 23(4), 381–399. ▶ **page 239**

Bryant, P. (1995). Jean Piaget. In R. Fuller (ed.) *Seven Pioneers of Psychology*. London: Routledge. ▶ **page 119**

Bryant, P.E. and Trabasso, T. (1971). Transitive inferences and memory in young children. *Nature*, 232, 456–458. ▶ **page 185**

Buchanan, T.W. and Lovallo, W.R. (2001). Enhanced memory for emotional material following stress-level cortisol treatment in humans. *Psychoneuroendocrinology*, 26, 307–317. ▶ **page 91**

Buckhout, R. and Regan, S. (1988). Explorations in research on the other-race effect in face recognition. In M.M. Gruneberg, P.E. Morris and R.N. Sykes (eds) *Practical Aspects of Memory*. Chichester: Wiley. ▶ **page 204**

Buckhout, R. (1974). Eyewitness testimony. *Scientific American*, 231(6), 23–31. ▶ **pages 204, 205**

Bull, R. and McAlpine, S. (1998). Facial appearance and criminality. In A. Memon, A. Vrij and R. Bull (eds) *Psychology and Law, Truthfulness, Accuracy and Credibility*. New York: McGraw-Hill. ▶ **page 201**

Bunney, W.E. and Davis, J.M. (1965). Norepinephrine in depressive reactions: a review. *Archives of General Psychiatry*, 13, 483–494. ▶ **page 236**

Bunting, B.P. and Mooney, E. (2001). The effects of practice and coaching on test results for educational selection at eleven years of age. *Educational Psychology*, 21(3), 243–253. ▶ **pages 37, 123**

Burgoine, E. (1988). A cross-cultural comparison of bereavement among widows in New Providence, Bahamas and London, England. Paper read at International Conference on Grief and Bereavement in Contemporary Society, London, July 12–15. ▶ **page 143**

Buri, J.R. (1991). Parental authority questionnaire. *Journal of Personality Assessment*, 57(1), 110–119. ▶ **page 37**

Burnstein, E. and Worchel, P. (1962). Arbitrariness of frustration and its consequences for aggression in a social situation. *Journal of Personality*, 30, 528–540. ▶ **page 223**

Buss, D.M. (1989). Sex differences in human mate preferences: evolutionary hypotheses tested in 37 cultures. *Behavioral and Brain Sciences*, 12, 1–49. ▶ **pages 72, 103, 141**

Butcher, L.M., Davis, O.S.P, Craig, I.W. and Plomin, R. (2008). Genome-wide quantitative trait locus association scan of general cognitive ability using pooled DNA and 500K single nucleotide polymorphism microarrays. *Genes, Brain and Behaviour*, 7(4), 435–446. ▶ **page 124**

Butler, A.C., Chapman, J.E., Forman, E.M. and Beck, A.T. (2006). The empirical status of cognitive-behavioral therapy: a review of meta-analyses. *Clinical Psychology Review*, 26(1), 17–31. ▶ **pages 22, 239**

Button, T.M., Rhee, S.H., Hewitt, J.K., Young, S.E., Corley, R.P. and Stallings, M.C. (2007). The role of conduct disorder in explaining the comorbidity between alcohol and illicit drug dependence in adolescence. *Drug and Alcohol Dependence*, 87(1), 46–53. ▶ **page 167**

Buunk, B.P. (1996). Affiliation, attraction and close relationships. In M. Hewstone, W. Stroebe and G. Stephenson (eds.) *Introduction to Social Psychology: A European Perspective*. Oxford: Blackwell. Ð page 107

Cahill, L. and McGaugh, J. L. (1995). A novel demonstration of enhanced memory associated with emotional arousal. *Consciousness and Cognition*, 4, 410–421. ▶ **page 91**

Calnan M. (1989). Control over health and patterns of health-related behaviour. *Social Science and Medicine*, 29, 131–136. ▶ **page 175**

Campbell, S.S. and Murphy, P.J. (1998). Extraocular circadian phototransduction in humans. *Science*, 279, 396–399. ▶ **page 156**

Cann, J. (2006). Cognitive skills programmes, impact on reducing reconviction among a sample of female prisoners. *Research Findings 276*. London, Home Office. ▶ **page 207**

Cann, J., Falshaw, L., Nugent, F. and Friendship, C. (2003). Understanding what works, accredited cognitive skills programmes for adult men and young offenders. *Research Findings 226*. London: Home Office. ▶ **page 207**

Canter, D.V. (1994). *Criminal Shadows: Inside the Mind of the Serial Killer*. London: HarperCollins. ▶ **page 199**

Canter, D.V. and Larkin, P. (1993). The environmental range of serial rapists. *Journal of Environmental Psychology*, 13, 63–69. ▶ **page 199**

Canter, D.V., Alison, L.J., Alison E. and Wentink N. (2004). The organised/disorganised typology of serial murder: Myth or model? *Psychology, Public Policy and Law*, 10(3), 293–320. ▶ **page 199**

Canter, D.V. (2004). An empirical test of Holmes and Holmes serial murder typology. *Criminal Justice and Behavior*, 31(4), 489–515. ▶ **page 199**

Capallini, I., Barton, R.A., McNamara, P. and Preston, B.T. (2008). Phylogenetic analysis of the ecology and evolution of mammalian sleep. *Evolution*, 62–67, 1764–1776. ▶ **page 155**

Cappuccio, F.P., D'Elia, L., Strazzullo, P. and Miller, M.A. (2010). Sleep duration and all-cause mortality: a systematic review and meta-analysis of prospective studies. *Sleep*, 33(5), 585–592. ▶ **page 220**

Carmichael, L., Hogan, P. and Walter, A. (1932). An experimental study of the effect of language on the reproduction of visually perceived forms. *Journal of Experimental Psychology*, 15, 73–86. ▶ **page 204**

Carstensen, L.L., Isaacowitz, D.M. and Charles, S.T. (1999). Taking time seriously: a theory of socioemotional selectivity. *American Psychologist*, 54, 165–181. ▶ **page 143**

Carter, H. and Glick, P. (1970), *Marriage and Divorce: A Social and Economic Study*. Cambridge, MA: Harvard University Press. ▶ **page 140**

Caspi, A., Williams, B., Kim-Cohen, J., Craig, I.W., Milne, B.J., Poulton, R., Schalkwyk, L.C., Taylor, A., Werts H. and Moffitt, T.E. (2007). Moderation of breastfeeding effects on the IQ by genetic variation in fatty acid metabolism. *Proceedings of the National Academy of Sciences of the United States of America*, 104, 18860–18865. ▶ **page 125**

Ceci, S. (1991). How much does schooling influence general intelligence and its cognitive components? A reassessment of the evidence. *Developmental Psychology*, 27, 703–722. ▶ **page 126**

Chalabaev, A., Major, B., Cury, F. and Sarrazin, P. (2009). Physiological markers of challenge and threat mediate the effects of performance-based goals on performance. *Journal of Experimental Social Psychology*, 45, 991–994. ▶ **page 215**

Chan, D.W. (2004). Multiple Intelligences of Chinese gifted students in Hong Kong: perspectives from students, parents, teachers, and peers. *Roeper Review*, 27(1), 18–25. ▶ **page 120**

Charlton, T., Panting, C., Davie, R., Coles, D. and Whitmarsh, L. (2000). Children's playground behaviour across five years of broadcast television: a naturalistic study in a remote community. *Emotional and Behavioural Difficulties*, 54, 4–12. ▶ **page 203**

Chase, W.G. and Simon, H.A. (1973). The mind's eye in chess. In W.G. Chase (ed.) *Visual Information Processing*. New York: Academic Press. ▶ **page 185**

Chen, L.Y., Rex, C.S., Sanaiha, Y., Lynch, G. and Gall, C.M. (2010). Learning induces neurotrophin signaling at hippocampal synapses. *Proceedings of the National Academy of Science USA*, 107(15), 7030–7035. ▶ **page 143**

Chicurel, M. (2001). Mutant gene speeds up the human clock. *Science*, *291*(5502), 226–227. ▶ **page 157**

Chomistek, A.K. and Rimm, E.B. (2010). Physical activity and incident cardiovascular disease: investigation of the effect of high amounts of vigorous-intensity activity. *EPI/NPAM* 2010; March 3, 2010. San Francisco, CA. Abstract 2. ▶ **page 221**

Chorney, M.J., Chorney, K., Seese, N., Owen, M.J., Daniels, J., McGuffin, P., Thompson, L.A., Detterman, D.K., Benbow, C., Lubinski, D. and Eley, T. (1998). A quantitative trait locus associated with cognitive ability in children. *Psychological Science*, *9*, 159–166. ▶ **pages 72, 124**

Christianson, S.A. and Hubinette, B. (1993). Hands up! A study of witnesses' emotional reactions and memories associated with bank robberies. *Applied Cognitive Psychology*, *7*, 365–379. ▶ **page 205**

Cina, A., Bodenmann, G. and Blattner, D. (2003). The effects of the CCET in enhancing parenting skills. Paper presented at the 2nd Family Congress, Munich, Germany. ▶ **page 105**

Cleary, J.P., Walsh, D.M., Hofmeister, J.J., Shankar, G.M., Kuskowski, M.A., Selkoe, D.J. and Ashe, K.H. (2005). Natural oligomers of the amyloid-β protein specifically disrupt cognitive function. *Nature Neuroscience*, *8*, 79–84. ▶ **page 95**

Cloward, R.D. (1967). Studies in tutoring. *Journal of Experimental Education*, *36*(1), 14–25. ▶ **page 185**

Clulow, C.F. (1990). Divorce as bereavement: Similarities and differences. *Family and Conciliation Courts Review*, *28*, 19–22. ▶ **page 140**

Coccaro, E.F., Bergman, C.S., Kavoussi, R.J. and Seroczynski, A.D. (1997). Heritability of aggression and irritability: a twin study of the Buss-Durkee Aggression Scales in adult male subjects. *Biological Psychiatry*, *41*, 273–284. ▶ **page 73**

Cochrane, R. (1988). Marriage, separation and divorce. In S. Fisher and J. Reason (eds) *Handbook of Life Stress, Cognition and Health*. New York: John Wiley and Sons. ▶ **pages 140, 141**

Cochrane, R. and Sashidharan, S.P. (1995). *Mental Health and Ethnic Minorities: A Review of the Literature and Implications for Services*. Birmingham University and Northern Birmingham Mental Trust, February. ▶ **page 230**

Coffield, F., Moseley, D., Hall, E. and Ecclestone, K. (2004). *Should we be Using Learning Styles? What Research has to Say to Practice.* London: Learning and Skills Research Centre. ▶ **page 187**

Cohen, P.A., Kulik, J.A. and Kulik, C.L.C. (1982). Educational outcomes of tutoring: a meta-analysis of findings. *American Educational Research Journal*, *19*, 237–248. ▶ **page 185**

Cohen, S. and Lichtenstein, E. (1990). Perceived stress, quitting smoking and smoking relapse. *Health Psychology*, *9*(4), 466–478. ▶ **page 166**

Coleman, J.C. (1961). *The Adolescent Society: The Social Life of the Teenager and its Impact on Education*. Glencoe, IL: The Free Press. ▶ **page 189**

Coleman, J.C. (1974). *Relationships in Adolescence*. London: Routledge and Kegan Paul. ▶ **page 138**

Coleman, J.C. (1980). *The Nature of Adolescence.* London: Methuen. ▶ **page 138**

Coleman, J.C. (1990) *Teenagers and Divorce*. Brighton: Trust for the Study of Adolescence. ▶ **page 138**

Coleman, J.C. and Hendry, L. (1990). *The Nature of Adolescence*. London: Routledge. ▶ **page 138**

Comer, R. (2003). *Abnormal Psychology*, 5th edn. New York: Worth Publishers. ▶ **pages 219, 232**

Comings, D.E., Ferry, L., Bradshaw-Robinson, S., Burchette, R., Chiu, C. and Muchleman, D. (1996). The dopamine D_2 receptor (DRD_2) gene: a genetic risk factor in smoking. *Pharmacogenetics*, *6*(1), 73–79. ▶ **page 167**

Conway, M.A., Anderson, S.J., Larsen, S.F., Donnelly, C.M., McDaniel, M.A., McClelland, A.G.R., Rawles, R.E. and Logie, R.H. (1994). The formation of flashbulb memories. *Memory and Cognition*, *22*, 326–343. ▶ **page 91**

Coolican, H. (1996). *Introduction to Research Methods and Statistics in Psychology*. London: Hodder & Stoughton. ▶ **page 36**

Cooper, M.L., Shaver, P.R. and Collins, N.L. (1998). Attachment styles, emotion regulation, and adjustment in adolescence. *Journal of Personality and Social Psychology*, *74*(5), 1380–1397. ▶ **page 137**

Copolov, D. and Crook, J. (2000). Biological markers and schizophrenia. *Australian and New Zealand of Psychiatry*, *34*, S108–S112. ▶ **page 233**

Copson, G. (1995). Coals to Newcastle? Part 1, a study of offender profiling. Police Research Group, *Special Interest series, 7*. London: Home Office Police Department. ▶ **page 199**

Cottrell, N.B. (1972). Social Facilitation. In C.G. McClintock (ed.) *Experimental Social Psychology.* New York: Holt, Reinehart and Winston. ▶ **page 219**

Cottrell, N.B., Wack, D.L., Sekerak, G.J. and Rittle, R.H. (1968). Social facilitation of dominant responses by the presence of an audience and the mere presence of others. *Journal of Personality and Social Psychology*, *9*, 245–250. ▶ **page 219**

Cowan, N. (2001). The magical number 4 in short-term memory: a reconsideration of mental storage capacity. *Behavioral and Brain Sciences*, *24*(1), 87–114. ▶ **page 87**

Cox, R.H. (2007). *Sport Psychology: Concepts and Applications*, 6th edn. New York: McGraw-Hill. ▶ **page 215**

Craft, L.L. and Landers, D.M. (1998). The effect of exercise on clinical depression and depression resulting from mental illness: a meta-analysis. *Journal of Sport and Exercise Psychology*, *20*, 339–357. ▶ **page 221**

Craft, L.L., Maygar, T.M., Becker, B.J. and Feltz, D.L. (2003). The relationship between the competitive state anxiety inventory-2 and sports performance: A meta-analysis. *Journal of Sports and Exercise Psychology, 25*, 44–65. ▶ **page 217**

Craik, F.I.M. (1973). A 'levels of analysis' view of memory. In P. Pliner, L. Krames and T.M. Alloway (eds) *Communication and Affect: Language and Thought*. London: Academic Press. ▶ **page 88**

Craik, F.I.M. and Lockhart, R.S. (1972). Levels of processing: a framework for memory research. *Journal of Verbal Learning and Verbal Behavior*, *11*, 671–684. ▶ **page 88**

Craik, F.I.M. and Tulving, E. (1975). Depth of processing and the retention of words in episodic memory. *Journal of Experimental Psychology*, *104*, 268–294. ▶ **page 89**

Critchely, M. (1970). *The Dyslexic Child*. Springfield, IL: Thomas. ▶ **page 190**

Crits-Christoph, P., Gibbons, M.B., Barber, J.P., Gallop, R., Beck, A.T. and Mercer, D. (2003). Mediators of outcome of psychosocial treatments for cocaine dependence. *Journal of Consulting and Clinical Psychology*, *71*, 918–25. ▶ **page 169**

Crossley, R. and Remington-Gurley, J. (1992). Getting the words out: facilitated communication training. *Topics in Language Disorders*, *12*, 29–45. ▶ **page 191**

Culnan, M.J. and Markus, M.L. (1987). In F.M. Jablin (ed.) *Handbook of Organizational Communication*. Newbury Park, CA: Sage. ▶ **page 108**

Cumming, E. and Henry, W.E. (1961). *Growing Old*. New York: Basic Books. ▶ **page 142**

Cummings, B.J., Head, E., Afagh, A.J., Milgram, N.W. and Cotman, C.W. (1996a). Beta-amyloid accumulation correlates with cognitive dysfunction in the aged canine. *Neurobiology of Learning and Memory*, *66*, 11–23. ▶ **page 95**

Cummings, B.J., Satou, T., Head, E., Milgram, N.W., Cole, G.M., Savage, M.J., Podlisny, M.B., Selkoe, D.J., Siman, R.,

Greenberg, B.D. and Cotman, C.W. (1996b). Diffuse plaques contain C-terminal A beta 42 and not A beta 40: evidence from dogs and cats. *Neurobiology of Aging, 17,* 653–659. ▶ **page 95**

Cunningham, C.l., Dickinson, S.D., Grahme, N.J., Okorn, D.M. and McMullin, C.S. (1999). Genetic differences in cocaine-induced place preference in mice depends on trail duration. *Psychopharmacology, 146*(1), 73–80. ▶ **page 166**

Curry, L. (1983). Individualised CME: the potential and the problems. *The Royal College of Physicians and Surgeons of Canada Annuals, 16*(6), 521–526. ▶ **page 186**

Curry, L. (1987). *Integrating Concepts of Cognitive or Learning Style: A Review of Attention to Psychometric Standards.* Ottawa: Curry, Adams and Associates. ▶ **page 187**

Dabbs, J.M. Jr and Hargrove, M.F. (1997). Age, testosterone and behavior among female prison inmates. *Psychosomatic Medicine, 59*(5), 477–480. ▶ **page 202**

Dabbs, J.M. Jr, Carr, T.S., Frady, R.L. and Riad, J.K. (1995). Testosterone, crime and misbehaviour among 692 male prison inmates. *Personality and Individual Differences, 18,* 627–633. ▶ **page 202**

Daily Mail (2009). Forget the seals, meet the Navy sea lions: animals clear mines and even detain terrorist divers. See www.dailymail.co.uk/news/worldnews/article-1230814/Forget-Seals-meet-Navy-Sea-Lions-Animals-clear-mines-fight-terrorists.html (accessed June 2010). ▶ **page 61**

Danner, F.W. and Day, M.C. (1977). Eliciting formal operations. *Child Development, 48,* 1600–1606. ▶ **page 185**

Darlington, T.K., Wager-Smith, K., Ceriani, M.F., Staknis, D., Gekakis, N., Steeves, T.D.L., Weitz, C.J., Takahashi, J.S. and Kay S.A. (1998). Closing the circadian loop: CLOCK-induced transcription of its own inhibitors per and tim. *Science, 280*(5369), 1599–1603. ▶ **page 156**

Dave, D., Rashad, I. and Spasojevic, J. (2006). The effects of retirement on physical and mental health outcomes. NBER Working Paper no. 12123. ▶ **page 142**

Davidson, A.J. (2006). Search for the feeding-entrainable circadian oscillator: a complex proposition. *American Journal of Physiology. Regulatory, Integrative and Comparative Physiology, 290*(6), 1524–1526. ▶ **page 156**

Davies, A., Wittebrod, K. and Jackson, J.L. (1997). Predicting the antecedents of a stranger rapist from his offence behaviour. *Science and Justice, 37,* 161–170. ▶ **page 198**

Davies, N.B. and Houston, A.I. (1984). Territory economics. In J.R. Krebs and N.B. Davies (eds) *Behavioural Ecology.* Oxford: Blackwell Scientific Publications. ▶ **page 218**

Davies, P.G., Spencer, S.J. Quinn, D.M. and Gerhardstein, R. (2002). Consuming images: how television commercials that elicit stereotype threat can restrain women academically and professionally. *Personality and Social Psychology Bulletin, 28,* 1615–1628. ▶ **page 122**

Davis, J.M., Schaffer, C.B., Killian, G.A., Kinnard, C. and Chan, C. (1980). Important issues in the drug treatment of schizophrenia. *Schizophrenia Bulletin, 6,* 70–87. ▶ **page 235**

DeCoursey, P.J., Walker, J.K. and Smith, S.A. (2000). A circadian pacemaker in free-living chipmunks: essential for survival? *Journal of Comparative Physiology, 186,* 169–180. ▶ **page 157**

Deffenbacher, K.A., Bornstein, B.H., Penrod, S.D. and McGorty, E.K. (2004). A meta-analytic review of the effects of high stress on eyewitness memory. *Law and Human Behaviour, 28,* 687–706. ▶ **page 205**

Delgado, P.L., Charney, D.S., Price, L.H., Aghajanian, G.K., Landis, H. and Heninger, G.R. (1990). Serotonin function and the mechanism of antidepressant action. Reversal of antidepressant-induced remission by rapid depletion of plasma tryptophan. *Archives of General Psychiatry, 47,* 411–418. ▶ **page 236**

DeLongis, A., Folkman, S. and Lazarus, R.S. (1988). The impact of daily stresses on health and mood: Psychological and social resources as mediators. *Journal of Personality and Social Psychology, 54,* 486–495. ▶ **page 107**

Dennett, D.C. (2003). *Freedom Evolves.* New York: Penguin. ▶ **pages 78, 79, 148**

Dermer, M. and Thiel, D.L. (1975). When beauty may fail. *Journal of Personality and Social Psychology, 31,* 1168–1176. ▶ **page 103**

DeSantis, A. and Kayson, W. (1997). Defendants' characteristics of attractiveness, race and sex on sentencing decisions. *Psychological Reports, 81*(2), 679–683. ▶ **page 200**

D'Esposito, M. (2007). From cognitive to neural models of working memory. *Philosophical Transactions of the Royal Society of London B, 362*(1481), 761–772. ▶ **page 89**

DeVries, R. (1969). Constancy of generic identity in the years three to six. *Monographs of the Society for Child Development, 34* (Serial No. 127). ▶ **page 117**

Dishman, R.K., Sallis, J.F. and Orenstein, D.R. (1985). The determinants of physical activity and exercise. *Public Health Report, 100*(2), 158–171. ▶ **page 221**

Dixon, J.A., Mahoney, B. and Cocks, R. (2002). Accents of guilt? Effects of regional accent, race and crime type on attributions of guilt. *Journal of Language and Social Psychology, 21*(2), 162–168. ▶ **page 200**

Dolcos, F., Miller, B., Kragel, P., Jha, A. and McCarthy, G. (2007). Regional brain differences in the effect of distraction during the delay interval of a working memory task. *Brain Research, 1152,* 171–181. ▶ **page 89**

Dollard, J.R., Doob, L.W., Miller, N.E., Mowrer, O.H. and Sears, R.R. (1939). *Frustration and Aggression.* New Haven, CN: Yale University Press. ▶ **page 222**

Douglas, J.E. (1981). Evaluation of the (FBI) psychological profiling programme, unpublished. Reported in Copson, G. (1996). At last some facts about offender profiling in Britain. *Forensic Update, 46,* 4–10. ▶ **page 199**

Downs, A.C. and Lyons, P.M. (1991). Natural observations of the links between attractiveness and initial legal judgements. *Personality and Social Psychology Bulletin, 17,* 541–547. ▶ **page 200**

Driskell, J.E. and Olmstead, B. (1989). Psychology and the military. *American Psychologist, 44*(1), 43–54. ▶ **page 61**

Druckman, D. and Bjork, R.A. (eds) (1994). *Learning, Remembering, Believing: Enhancing Human Performance.* Washington, DC: National Academy Press. ▶ **page 151**

Druley, J.A. and Townsend, A.L. (1998). Self-esteem as a mediator between spousal support and depressive symptoms: a comparison of healthy individuals and individuals coping with arthritis. *Health Psychology, 17,* 255–261. ▶ **page 106**

Drury, V., Birchwood, M., Cochrane, R. and MacMillan, F. (1996). Cognitive therapy and recovery from acute psychosis: a controlled trial. *British Journal of Psychiatry, 169,* 593–601. ▶ **page 235**

Dubrovsky, V.J., Kiesler, S.B. and Sethna, B.N. (1991). The equalization phenomenon: Status effects in computer-mediated and face-to-face decision-making groups. *Human-Computer Interaction, 6,* 119–146. ▶ **page 109**

Duck, S.W. (1991). *Friends for Life.* Hemel Hempstead: Harvester Wheatsheaf. ▶ **page 104**

Duck, S.W. (2007). *Human Relationships,* 4th edn. London: Sage. ▶ **page 104**

Duck, S.W. and Sants, H. (1983). On the origins of the specious: Are personal relationships really interpersonal states? *Journal of Social and Clinical Psychology, 1,* 27–41. ▶ **page 103**

Dunayer, J. (2002). Animal equality. See www.upc-online.org/thinking/animal_equality.html (accessed May 2010). ▶ **page 59**

Duncan, B.L. (1976). Differential social perception and attribution of intergroup violence: testing the lower limits of stereotyping of Blacks. *Journal of Personality and Social Psychology*, *34*(4), 590–598. ▶ **page 200**

Duncan, J., Seitz, R.J., Kolodny, J., Bor, D., Herzog, H., Ahmed, A., Newell, F.N. and Emslie, H. (2000). A neural basis for general intelligence. *Science*, *289*(5478), 457–460. ▶ **page 121**

Dutton, D.G. and Aron, A.P. (1974). Some evidence for heightened sexual attraction under conditions of high anxiety. *Journal of Personality and Social Psychology*, *30*, 510–517. ▶ **page 42**

Dweck, C. (2007). *Mindset: The New Psychology of Success*. London: Random House. ▶ **page 213**

Dweck, C.S. (1975). The role of expectations and attributions in the alleviation of learned helplessness. *Journal of Personality and Social Psychology*, *31*, 674–685. ▶ **pages 183, 189**

Eagly, A.H. (1978). Sex differences in influenceability. *Psychological Bulletin*, *85*, 86–116. ▶ **page 77**

Eagly, A.H. and Carli, L. (1981). Sex of researchers and sex-typed communications as determinants of sex differences in influenceability: a meta-analysis of social influence studies. *Psychological Bulletin*, *90*, 1–20. ▶ **page 37**

Eagly, A.H. and Johnson, B.T. (1990). Gender and leadership style: a meta-analysis. *Psychological Bulletin*, *108*, 233–256. ▶ **page 77**

Ebbinghaus, H. (1885). *Memory*. New York: Teacher's College Press. ▶ **page 182**

Eberly, M.B. and Montemayor, R. (1999). Adolescent affection and helpfulness towards parents: a 2-year follow up. *Journal of Early Adolescence*, *19*, 226–248. ▶ **page 139**

Eccles, J.S., Midgley, C., Wigfield, A. and Buchanan, C.M. (1993). Development during adolescence: the impact of stage-environment fit on young adolescents' experiences in schools and in families. *American Psychologist*, *48*, 90–101. ▶ **page 139**

Ecker, C., Rocha-Rego, V., Johnston, P., Mourao-Miranda, J., Marquand, A., Daly, E.M., Brammer, M.J., Murphy, C. and Murphy, D.G. (2010). Investigating the predictive value of whole-brain structural MR scans in autism: a pattern classification approach. *Neuroimage*, *49*(1), 44–56. ▶ **page 190**

Edwards, J.A. and Cline, H.T. (1999). Light-induced calcium influx into retinal axons is regulated by presynaptic nicotinic acetylcholine receptor activity in vivo. *Journal of Neurophysiology*, *81*(2), 895–907. ▶ **page 73**

Egner, T., Jamieson, G. and Gruzelier, J.H. (2005). Hypnosis decouples cognitive control from conflict monitoring processes of the frontal lobe. *Neuroimage*, *27*, 969–978. ▶ **page 151**

Eich, E., Macaulay, D. and Ryan, L. (1994). Mood dependent memory for events of the personal past. *Journal of Experimental Psychology. General*, *123*, 201–215. ▶ **page 90**

Eiser, C. (1997). Children's perceptions of illness and death. In A. Baum, S. Newman, J. Weinmann, R. West and C. McManus (eds) *Cambridge Handbook of Psychology, Health and Medicine*. Cambridge: Cambridge University Press. ▶ **page 175**

Ekerdt, D.J., Bosse, R. and Levkoff, S. (1985). An empirical test for phases of retirement: findings from the Normative Aging Study. *Journal of Gerontology*, *40*(1), 95–101. ▶ **page 143**

Elkin, I., Parloff, M.B., Hadley, S.W. and Autry, J.H. (1985). NIMH treatment of depression collaborative research program: background and research plan. *Archives of General Psychiatry*, *42*, 305–16. ▶ **page 239**

Elliott, J. (2005). The dyslexia debate continues – response. *The Psychologist*, *18*(12), 728. ▶ **page 191**

Ellis, H., Shepherd, J. and Davies, G. (1979). Identification of familiar and unfamiliar faces from internal and external features: some implications for theories of face recognition. *Perception*, *8*, 431–439. ▶ **page 204**

Ellis, H.D., Shepherd, J.W. and Davies, G.M. (1975). An investigation of the use of the photofit technique for recalling faces. *British Journal of Psychology*, *66*, 29–37. ▶ **page 205**

Empson, J. (2002). *Sleep and Dreaming*, 3rd edn. London: Palgrave. ▶ **page 155**

Engler, B. (1999). *Personality Theories: An /Introduction*. Boston: Houghton Mifflin. ▶ **page 189**

Epstein, J. (1989). Family structures and student motivation: a developmental perspective. In C. Ames and R. Ames (eds) *Research on Motivation in Education*, vol. 3. *Goals and Cognitions*. New York: Academic Press. ▶ **page 214**

Epstein, R. (2002). Editor as guinea pig. *Psychology Today*, June 2. ▶ **page 111**

Erikson, E.H. (1963). *Childhood and Society*, New York: Norton. ▶ **pages 132, 136, 138, 143**

Erikson, E.H. (1968). *Identity: Youth and Crisis*. London: Faber. ▶ **pages 110, 137**

Eron, L.D. and Huesmann, L.R. (1986). The role of television in the development of antisocial and prosocial behavior. In D. Olweus, J. Block and M. Radke-Yarrom (eds) *Development of Antisocial and Prosocial Behaviour, Theories and Issues*. New York, Academic Press. ▶ **page 203**

Eron, L.D., Huesmann, L.R., Leftowitz, M.M. and Walder, L.O. (1972). Does television violence cause aggression? *American Psychologist 27*, 253–263. ▶ **page 203**

Ertekin-Taner, N., Graff-Radford, N., Younkin, L.H., Eckman, C., Baker, M., Adamson, J. and Ronald, J. (2000). Linkage in plasma AD42 to a quantitative locus on chromosome 10 in late-onset Alzheimer's disease pedigrees. *Science*, *290*, 2303–2304. ▶ **page 94**

Eslinger, P.J. and Damasio, A.R. (1985). Severe disturbance of higher cognition after bilateral frontal lobe ablations: patient EVR. *Neurology*, *35*, 1731–1741. ▶ **page 89**

EU Treaty of Lisbon (2009). The Lisbon Treaty and the European Constitution: a side-by-side comparison. See www.openeurope.org.uk/research/comparative.pdf (accessed May 2010). ▶ **page 58**

Evans, F.J. and Orne, M.T. (1971). The disappearing hypnotist: the use of simulating subjects to evaluate how subjects perceive experimental procedures. *International Journal of Clinical and Experimental Hypnosis*, *19*, 277–296. ▶ **page 150**

Eysenck, H.J. and Eysenck, S.B.G. (1977). Block and psychoticism. *Journal of Abnormal Psychology*, *86*, 651–652. ▶ **page 197**

Eysenck, M.W. (1998). *Psychology: An Integrated Approach*. Harlow: Longman. ▶ **page 93**

Eysenck, S.B.G., Eysenck, H.J. and Barrett, P. (1985). A revised version of the psychoticism scale. *Personality and Individual Differences*, *6*, 21–29. ▶ **page 197**

Farrell, M.P. and Rosenberg, S.D. (1981). *Men at Midlife*. Boston, MA: Auburn House. ▶ **page 135**

Fazey, J.A. and Hardy, L. (1988). *The Inverted-U Hypotheses: A Catastrophe for Sport Psychology*. British Association of Sport Sciences Monograph No. 1 National Coaching Foundation, Leeds. ▶ **page 216**

Feingold, A. (1992). Gender differences in mate selection differences: a test of the parental investment model. *Psychological Bulletin*, *112*, 125–139. ▶ **page 102**

Ferguson, S., Cisneros, F., Gough, B., Hanig, J. and Berry, K. (2005). Chronic oral treatment with 13-cis-retinoic acid (isotretinoin) or all-trans-retinoic acid does not alter depression-like behaviors in rats. *Toxicological Sciences*, *87*, 451–459. ▶ **page 239**

Ferrara, M., De Gennaro, L. and Bertini, M., (1999). Selective slow-wave sleep (SWS), deprivation and SWS rebound: do we need a fixed SWS amount per night? *Sleep Research Online*, *2*(1), 15–19. ▶ **page 155**

Fiatarone, M.A., O'Neill, E.F., Doyle, R.N., Clements, K.M., Solares, G.R., Nelson, M.E., Roberts, S.B., Kehayias, J.J., Lipsitz, L.A. and Evans, W.J. (1994). Exercise training and nutritional supplementation for physical frailty in very elderly people. *New England Journal of Medicine, 330,* 1769–1775. ▶ **page 176**

Fleshner, M. (2000). Exercise and neuroendocrine regulation of antibody production: protective effect of physical activity on stress-induced suppression of the specific antibody response. *International Journal of Sports Medicine, 21,* S14–S19. ▶ **page 221**

Flynn, J.R. (1987). Massive IQ gains in 14 nations: What IQ tests really measure. *Psychological Bulletin, 101,* 171–191. ▶ **page 72**

Folkard, S. (1996). Bags of time to play. *Daily Express.* 28 September. ▶ **page 157**

Folkerts, H.W., Michael, N., Tolle, R., Schonauer, K., Mucke, S. and Schulze-Monking, H. (1997). Electroconvulsive therapy *v.* paroxetine in treatment-resistant depression: a randomized study. *Acta Psychiatrica Scandinavica, 96,* 334–342. ▶ **page 239**

Ford, M.R. and Widiger, T.A. (1989). Sex bias in the diagnosis of histrionic and antisocial personality disorders. *Journal of Consulting and Clinical Psychology, 57,* 301–305. ▶ **page 230**

Fossey, D. (1983). *Gorillas in the Mist.* Orlando, FL: Houghton Mifflin Company. ▶ **page 58**

Foulkes, D. (1997). Misrepresentation of sleep-laboratory dream research with children. *Perceptual and Motor Skills, 83*(1), 205–206. ▶ **page 153**

Fowler, T., Shelton, K., Lifford, K., Rice, F., McBride, A., Nikolov, I., Neale, M.C., Harold, G., Thapar, A. and van den Bree, M.B.M. (2007). Genetic and environmental influences on the relationship between peer alcohol use and own alcohol use in adolescents. *Addiction, 102*(6), 894–903. ▶ **page 167**

Freud, S. (1900). *The Interpretation of Dreams,* translated by J. Crick. London: Oxford University Press. ▶ **page 152**

Freud, S. (1917). Introductory lectures on psychoanalysis. In J. Strachey (ed.) (1961). *The Standard Edition of the Complete Psychological Work of Sigmund Freud,* vol. 16. New York: Norton. ▶ **pages 54, 236**

Freud, S. (1924). The loss of reality in neurosis and psychosis. In *Sigmund Freud's Collected Papers* (vol. 2, 272–282). London: Hogarth Press. ▶ **page 232**

Freud, S. (1925). Some psychical consequences of the anatomical distinction between the sexes. In J. Strachey (ed.) (1961). *The Standard Edition of the Complete Psychological Works of Sigmund Freud,* vol. 19. London: The Hogarth Press. ▶ **page 76**

Frey, C.U. and Rothlisberger, C. (1996). Social support in healthy adolescents. *Journal of Youth and Adolescence, 25*(1), 17–31. ▶ **page 139**

Friendship, C., Blud. L., Erikson, M. and Travers, R. (2002). An evaluation of cognitive behavioural treatment for prisoners. *Research Findings No. 161.* London: Home Office. ▶ **page 207**

Fromm-Reichmann, F. (1948). Notes on the development of schizophrenia by psychoanalystic psychotherapy. *Psychiatry, 11,* 263–273. ▶ **page 233**

Frost, J. and McKelvie, S.J. (2005). The relationship of self-esteem and body satisfaction to exercise activity for male and female elementary school students, high school students and university students, *Athletic Insight, 7*(4). See www.athleticinsight.com/vol.7Iss4/Selfesteem.htm (accessed December, 2005). ▶ **page 220**

Funk, J.L. (1986). Gender differences in the moral reasoning of conventional and postconventional adults. Unpublished doctoral dissertation, University of Texas. ▶ **page 76**

Gabrieli, J.D.E. (1998). Cognitive neuroscience of human memory. *Annual Review of Psychology, 49,* 87–115. ▶ **page 95**

Gallup, G.G., Jr. (1970). Chimpanzees: self-recognition. *Science, 167,* 86–87. ▶ **page 149**

Gardener, B., Davies, A., McAteer, J. and Michie, S. (2010). Beliefs underlying UK parents' views towards MMR promotion interventions: a qualitative study. *Psychology, Health and Medicine, 15*(2), 220–230. ▶ **page 172**

Gardner, B.T. and Gardner, R.A. (1969). Teaching sign language to a chimpanzee. *Science, 165,* 664–672. ▶ **page 13**

Gardner, H. (1983). *Frames of Mind: The Theory of Multiple Intelligences.* New York: Basic Books. ▶ **pages 19, 120**

Gardner, H. (1999). *Intelligence Reframed: Multiple Intelligences for the 21st Century.* New York: Basic Books. ▶ **pages 21, 119**

Garner, D.M., Garfinkel, P.E., Schwartz, D. and Thompson, M. (1980). Cultural expectations of thinness in women. *Psychological Reports, 47,* 483–491. ▶ **page 21**

Garrido, V. and Morales, L.A. (2007). Serious (violent and chronic) juvenile offenders, a systematic review of treatment effectiveness in secure corrections. In *The Campbell Collaboration Reviews of Intervention and Policy Evaluations (C2-RIPE),* July 2007. Philadelphia, PA: Campbell Collaboration. ▶ **page 207**

Geen, R.G. and Berkowitz, L. (1967). Some conditions facilitating the occurrence of aggression after the observation of violence. *Journal of Personality, 35,* 666–676. ▶ **page 223**

Geen, R.G. and Quanty, M.B. (1977). The catharsis of aggression: an evaluation of a hypothesis. In L. Berkowitz (ed.) *Advances in Experimental Social Psychology, 10,* 1–37. New York: Academic Press. ▶ **page 223**

Geisler, G.W.W. and Leith, L.M. (1997). The effects of self esteem, self efficacy and audience presence on soccer penalty shot performance. *Journal of Sport Behavior, 20,* 322–337. ▶ **pages 213, 219**

Gelkopf, M., Levitt, S. and Bleich, A. (2002). An integration of three approaches to addiction and methodone maintenance treatment: the self-medication hypothesis, the disease model and social criticism. *Israel Journal of Psychiatry and Related Sciences, 39*(2), 140–151. ▶ **page 166**

Geller, B., Cooper, T.B., Graham, D.L., Fetner, H.H., Marsteller, F.A. and Wells, J.M. (1992). Pharmacokinetically designed double-blind placebo-controlled study of nortriptyline in 6–12 year olds with major depressive disorder. *Journal of the American Academy of Child and Adolescent Psychiatry, 31,* 34–44. ▶ **page 239**

Gelpin, E., Bonne, O., Peri, T., Brandes, D. and Shalev, A.Y. (1996). Treatment of recent trauma survivors with benzodiazepines: a prospective study. *Journal of Clinical Psychiatry, 57*(9), 390–394. ▶ **page 171**

George, S. and Murali, V. (2005). Pathological gambling: an overview of assessment and treatment. *Advances in Psychiatric Treatment, 11,* 450–456. ▶ **page 168**

Gibson, E.J. and Walk, R.D. (1960). The 'visual cliff'. *Scientific American, 202*(4), 64–71. ▶ **page 13**

Gill, D.L. (1980). Success-failure attributions in competitive groups: an exception to egocentrism. *Journal of Sport Psychology, 2,* 106–114. ▶ **page 217**

Gilligan, C. (1982). *In a Different Voice: Psychological Theory and Women's Development.* Cambridge, MA: Harvard University Press. ▶ **pages 76, 135**

Gilligan, C. and Attanucci, J. (1988). Two moral orientations: gender differences and similarities. *Merrill-Palmer Quarterly, 34,* 223–237. ▶ **page 76**

Glassman, N. (1999). All things being equal: the two roads of Piaget and Vygotsky. In P. Lloyd and C. Fernyhough (eds) *Lev Vygotsky: Critical assessments: Vygotsky's Theory,* vol. i. New York: Routledge. ▶ **page 119**

Glenn, N.D. and McLanahan, S. (1982). Children and marital happiness: a further specification of the relationship. *Journal of Marriage and the Family, 44,* 63–72. ▶ **page 141**

Glick, J. (1975). Cognitive development in a cross-cultural perspective. In E.G. Horowitz (ed.) *Review of Child Development Research*, vol 4. Chicago: University of Chicago Press. ▶ **page 123**

Gokhale, A.A. (1995). Collaborative learning enhances critical thinking. *Journal of Technology Education, 7*(1), 22–30. ▶ **page 185**

Goldacre, B. (2009). *Bad Science*. London: Harper Perennial. ▶ **page 16**

Good, T.L. and Brophy, J.E. (1991). *Looking in Classrooms*. New York: Harper and Row. ▶ **page 189**

Goodwill, A.M. and Alison, L.J. (2006). The development of a filter model for prioritizing suspects in burglary offences. *Psychology, Crime and Law*, August 2006, *12*(4), 395–416. ▶ **page 199**

Goodwin, D.W., Powell, B., Bremer, D., Hoine, H. and Stern, J. (1969). Alcohol and recall: state-dependent effects in man. *Science, 163,* 1358. ▶ **page 92**

Gordon R.A., Bindrim, T.A., McNicholas, M.L. and Walden, T.L. (1988). Black innocence and the White jury. *Michigan Law Review, 83,* 1611–708. ▶ **page 201**

Gottdiener, W.H., Murawski, P. and Kucharski, L.T. (2008). Using the delay discounting task to test for failures in ego control in substance abusers: a meta-analysis. *Psychoanalytic Psychology, 25,* 533–549. ▶ **page 167**

Gottesman, I.I. and Reilly, J.L. (2003). Strengthening the evidence for genetic factors in schizophrenia (without abetting genetic discrimination). In M.F. Lenzenweger and J.M. Hooley (eds) *Principles of Experimental psychopathology*. Washington, DC: American Psychological Association. ▶ **page 232**

Gottfredson, L. (2003). Dissecting practical intelligence theory: its claims and its evidence. *Intelligence, 31,* 343–397. ▶ **page 121**

Gottman, J.M., Levenson, R.W., Gro, J., Frederickson, B.L., McCoy, K., Rosenthal, L., Ruef, A. and Yoshimoto, D. (2003). Correlates of gay and lesbian couples' relationship satisfaction and relationship dissolution. *Journal of Homosexuality, 45*(1), 23–43. ▶ **pages 108, 109**

Gould, D., Russell, M., Damarjian, N. and Lauer, L. (1999). A survey of mental skills training knowledge, opinions and practices of junior tennis coaches. *Journal of Applied Sport Psychology, 11,* 28–50. ▶ **page 219**

Gould, R.L. (1980). Transformation tasks in adulthood. In *The Course of Life,* vol. 3, *Adulthood and Aging Processes*. Bethesda, MD: National Institute of Mental Health. ▶ **page 134**

Gould, S.J. (1981). *The Mismeasure of Man*. New York: Norton. ▶ **page 123**

Grant, K.A., Shively, C.A., Nader, M.A., Ehrenkaufer, R.L., Line, S.W., Morton, T.E., Gage, H.D. and Mach, R.H. (1998). Effects of social status on striatal dopamine D_2 receptor binding characteristics in cynomolgus monkeys assessed with positron emission tomography. *Synapse, 29*(1), 80–83. ▶ **page 167**

Grasha, A.F. (1996). *Teaching with Style*. Pittsburgh, PA: Alliance Publishers. ▶ **page 186**

Gray, J.A. (1991). On the morality of speciesism. *The Psychologist, 14,* 196–198. ▶ **page 58**

Graydon, J. and Murphy, T. (1995). The effect of personality on social facilitation whilst performing a sports related task. *Personality and Individual Differences, 19*(2), 265–267. ▶ **page 219**

Gredler, M. (1992). *Learning and Instruction Theory into Practice*. New York: Macmillan Publishing Company. ▶ **page 119**

Greendale, G.A., Barrett-Connor, E., Edelstein, S., Ingles, S. and Halle, R. (1995). Lifetime leisure exercise and osteoporosis: the Racho Bernardo Study. *American Journal of Epidemiology, 141,* 951–959. ▶ **page 174**

Greenfield, P.M. (1997). You can't take it with you: why ability assessments don't cross cultures. In R. Sternberg (ed.) *American Psychologist – special issue on intelligence through the lifespan*, 1115–1124. ▶ **page 127**

Greenfield, S. (2007). Style without substance. *Times Educational Supplement Magazine*, 27 July. ▶ **page 187**

Grieve, F.G., Whelan, J.P. and Meyers, A.W. (2000). An experimental examination of the cohesion-performance relationship in an interactive team sport. *Journal of Applied Sport Psychology, 12,* 219–235. ▶ **page 219**

Grigorenko, E.L., Geissler, P. W., Prince, R., Okatcha, F., Nokes, C., Kenny, D.A., Bundy, D.A. and Sternberg, R.J. (2001). The organization of Luo conceptions of intelligence: a study of implicit theories in a Kenyan village. *International Journal of Behavioral Development, 25*(4), 367–378. ▶ **page 122**

Gründl, M. (2007). Beautycheck – causes and consequences of human facial attractiveness. See www.uni-regensburg.de/ Fakultaeten/phil_Fak_II/Psychologie/Psy_II/ beautycheck/ english/index.htm. ▶ **page 101**

Gupta, S. (1991). Effects of time of day and personality on intelligence test scores. *Personality and Individual Differences, 12*(11), 1227–1231. ▶ **page 42**

Gyarmathy, V.A. and Latkin, C.A. (2008). Individual and social factors associated with participation in treatment programs for drug users. *Substance Misuse, 43*(12–13), 1865–1881. ▶ **page 169**

Hammen, C. (1997). *Depression*. Hove: Psychology Press. ▶ **pages 238, 239**

Hammen, C.L. and Krantz, S. (1976). Effect of success and failure in depressive cognitions. *Journal of Abnormal Psychology, 85,* 577–586. ▶ **page 237**

Hanin, Y.L. (1986). State-trait anxiety research on sports in the USSR. In C.D. Spielberger and R. Diaz-Guerrero (eds) *Cross-cultural anxiety,* vol. 3. New York: Hemisphere. ▶ **page 216**

Hansen, J., Winzeler, S. and Topolinski, S, (2010). When the death makes you smoke: a terror management perspective on the effectiveness of cigarette on-pack warnings. *Journal of Experimental Social Psychology, 46*(1), 226–228. ▶ **page 172**

Haracz, J.L. (1982). The dopamine hypothesis: an overview of studies with schizophrenic patients. *Schizophrenia Bulletin, 8*(3), 438–469. ▶ **page 233**

Harden, R.M. and Stamper, N. (1999). What is a spiral curriculum? *Medical Teacher, 21,* 141–143. ▶ **page 185**

Hardy, L., Parfitt, G. and Pates, J. (1994). Performance catastrophes in sport: a test of the hysteresis hypothesis. *Journal of Sports Sciences, 12,* 327–334. ▶ **page 217**

Hare-Mustin, R.T. and Marecek, J. (1988). The meaning of difference: gender theory, post-modernism and psychology. *American Psychologist, 43,* 455–464. ▶ **page 74**

Harkness, S. and Super, C. (1992). Parental ethnotheories in action. In I.E. Sigel (ed.) *Parental Belief Systems: The Psychological Consequences for Children*. Hillsdale, NJ: Erlbaum. ▶ **page 122**

Harlow, H.F. (1959). Love in infant monkeys. *Scientific American, 200*(6), 68–74. ▶ **page 58**

Harris, J.R. (1995). Where is the child's environment? A group socialization theory of development. *Psychological Review, 102,* 458–489. ▶ **page 126**

Hartel, D.M. and Schoenbaum, E.E. (1998). Methadone treatment protects against HIV infection: two decades of experience in the Bronx, New York City. *Public Health Reports, 113* (supplement 1), 107–115. ▶ **page 169**

Hartung, G.H. and Farge, E.J. (1977). Personality and physiological traits in middle-aged runners and joggers. *Journal of Gerontology, 32,* 541–548. ▶ **page 221**

Hastie, R., Penrod, S.D. and Pennington, N. (1983). *Inside the Jury*. Cambridge, MA: Harvard University Press. ▶ **page 200**

Hatfield, E. and Walster, G.W. (1981). *A New Look at Love*. Reading, MA: Addison-Wesley. ▶ **page 42**

Havighurst, R.J. (1961). Successful aging. *The Gerontologist, 1*(1), 8–13. ▶ **page 142**

Havighurst, R.J., Neugarten, B.L. and Tobin, S.S. (1968). Disengagement and patterns of aging. In B.L. Neugarten (ed.) *Middle Age and Aging*, Chicago: University of Chicago Press. ▶ **page 143**

Hazan, C. and Shaver, P. (1987). Conceptualising romantic love as an attachment process. *Journal of Personality and Social Psychology, 52*, 511–524. ▶ **page 100**

Heather, N. (1976). *Radical Perspectives in Psychology*. London: Methuen. ▶ **page 78**

Hebb, D.O., Heron, W. and Bexton, W.H. (1952). The effect of isolation upon attitude, motivation and thought. Defence Research Board, Canada, Fourth Symposium, Military Medicine 1, in cooperation with McGill University, Ottawa, Canada. ▶ **page 61**

Heider, F. (1958). *The Psychology of Interpersonal Relations*. New York: Wiley. ▶ **page 216**

Heisenberg, W. (1927). Uber den anschlauchichen Inhalt der quantentheoretischen Kinetik und Mechanik. *Zeitschrift für Physik, 43*, 172–198. ▶ **pages 55, 69**

Hendrie, H.C. (2001). Exploration of environmental and genetic risk factors for Alzheimer's disease: the value of cross-cultural studies. *Current Directions of Psychological Science, 10*, 98–101. ▶ **page 95**

Herring, M.P., O'Connor, P.J. and Dishman, R.K. (2010). The effect of exercise training on anxiety symptoms among patients: a systematic review. *Archives of Internal Medicine, 170*(4), 321–331. ▶ **page 220**

Herrnstein, R.J. and Murray, C. (1994). *The Bell Curve: Intelligence and Class Structure in American Life*. New York: Free Press. ▶ **pages 123, 127**

Hickmon, M. (2008). Paddling vs. ACT scores and civil immunity legislation. See www.stophitting.com/index.php?page=paddlingvsact (accessed August 2010). ▶ **page 183**

Hildalgo, R.B., Barnett, S.D. and Davidson, J.R. (2001). Social anxiety disorder in review: two decades of progress. *International Journal of Neuropsychopharmacology, 4*, 279–298. ▶ **page 171**

Hilgard, E.R. (1965). *Hypnotic Susceptibility*. New York: Harcourt, Brace, Jovanovich. ▶ **page 151**

Hilgard, E.R. (1977). *Divided Consciousness: Multiple Controls in Human Thought and Action*. New York: Wiley-Interscience. ▶ **pages 150, 151**

Hill, D. (1986). Tardive dyskinesia: a worldwide epidemic of irreversible brain damage. In N. Eisenberg and D. Glasgow (eds) *Current Issues in Clinical Psychology*. Aldershot: Gower. ▶ **page 235**

Hinsz, V.B. and Davis, J.H. (1984). Persuasive argument theory, group polarization and choice shifts. *Personality and Social Psychology Bulletin, 10*, 260–268. ▶ **page 201**

Hinton, J. (1967). *Dying*. Baltimore: Penguin. ▶ **page 142**

Hiroto, D.S. and Seligman, M.E.P. (1975). Generality of learned helplessness in man. *Journal of Personality and Social Psychology, 31*, 311–327. ▶ **page 237**

Hitch, G. and Baddeley, A.D. (1976). Verbal reasoning and working memory. *Quarterly Journal of Experimental Psychology, 28*, 603–621. ▶ **page 88**

Ho, D.Y.F. (1986). Chinese patterns of socialisation: a critical review. In M. Bond (ed.), *The Psychology of the Chinese People*. Hong Kong: Oxford University Press, 1–37. ▶ **page 110**

Hobbs, T.R. and Holt, M.M. (1976). The effects of token reinforcement on the behavior of delinquents in cottage settings. *Journal of Applied Behavior Analysis, 9*(2), 189–198. ▶ **page 207**

Hobson, J.A. (1988). *The Dreaming Brain*. New York: Basic Books. ▶ **page 152**

Hobson, J.A. (1994). *Dreaming as Delirium: How the Brain Goes Out of its Mind*. Boston: Little, Brown Book Group. ▶ **page 152**

Hobson, J.A. (2000). The ghost of Sigmund Freud haunts Mark Solms's dream theory. *Behavioral and Brain Sciences, 23*, 951–952. ▶ **page 153**

Hobson, J.A. and McCarley, R.W. (1977). The brain as a dream state generator: an activation-synthesis hypothesis of the dream process. *American Journal of Psychiatry, 134*, 1335–1348. ▶ **page 152**

Hochbaum, G.M. (1958). *Public Participation in Medical Screening Programmes: A Sociopsychological Study* (Public Health Service Publication 572). US government Washington, DC: Printing Office. ▶ **page 172**

Hock, C., Konietzko, U., Streffer, J.R., Tracy, J., Signorell, A., Müller-Tillmanns, B., Lemke, U., Henke, K., Moritz, E., Garcia, E., Wollmer, M.A., Umbricht, D., de Quervain, D.J., Hofmann, M., Maddalena, A., Papassotiropoulos, A., Nitsch, R.M. (2003). Antibodies against β-amyloid slow cognitive decline in Alzheimer's disease. *Neuron, 38*(4), 547–554. ▶ **page 95**

Hogg, M.A. and Vaughan, G.M. (2008). *Social Psychology*, 5th edn. Harlow: Pearson. ▶ **page 111**

Hollander, E., Buchalter, A.J. and de Caria, C.M. (2000). Pathological gambling. *The Psychiatric Clinics of North America, 23*(3), 629–642. ▶ **page 168**

Hollin, C.R., Palmer, E.J., McGuire, J., Hounsome, J.C., Hatcher, R.M., Bilby, C.A. and Clark, C. (2004). *Pathfinder Programmes in The Probation Service: A Retrospective Analysis*. London: RDS Home Office Online Report 66/04. ▶ **page 207**

Holmes, J. (2002). All you need is cognitive therapy? *British Medical Journal, 342*, 288–294. ▶ **page 239**

Holmes, R.M. and Holmes, S.T. (1998). *Serial Murder*, 2nd edn. Thousand Oaks, CA: Sage. ▶ **page 199**

Holmes, T.H. and Rahe, R.H. (1967 The social readjustment rating scale *Journal of Psychosomatic Research, 11*, 213–618. ▶ **page 140**

Holt, N.L. and Sparkes, A.C. (2001). An ethnographic study of cohesiveness in a college soccer team over a season. *Sport Psychologist, 15*(3), 237–259. ▶ **page 218**

Holt, P.A. and Stone, G.L. (1988). Needs, coping strategies and coping outcomes associated with long-distance relationships. *Journal of College Student Development, 29*, 136–141. ▶ **page 105**

Home Office (2000). *Guidance on the Operation of the Animals (Scientific Procedures) Act 1986*. London: The Stationery Office. ▶ **page 59**

Honda, Y., Asake, A., Tanaka, Y. and Juji, T. (1983). Discrimination of narcolepsy by using genetic markers and HLA. *Sleep Research, 1*(2), 254. ▶ **page 158**

Hopfield, J.J., Feinstein, D.I. and Palmer, R.G. (1983). 'Unlearning' has a stabilising effect in collective memories. *Nature, 304*, 158–159. ▶ **page 153**

Horn, J.M., Loehlin, J.C. and Willerman, L. (1979). Intellectual resemblance among adoptive and biological relatives: the Texas Adoption Project. *Behaviour Genetics, 9*, 177–207. ▶ **page 124**

Hornberger, R.H. (1959). The differential reduction of aggressive responses as a function of interpolated activities. *American Psychologist, 14*, 354. ▶ **page 223**

Horne, J. (1988). *Why we Sleep? The Functions of Sleep in Humans and Other Mammals*. Oxford: Oxford University Press. ▶ **page 155**

Horne, J.A. and Minard, A. (1985). Sleep and sleepiness following a behaviourally 'active' day. *Ergonomics, 28,* 567–575. ▶ **page 220**

Horner, B.R. and Scheibe, K.E. (1997). Prevalence and implications of attention deficit hyperactivity disorder among adolescents in treatment for substance abuse. *Journal of the American Academy of Child and Adolescent Psychiatry, 36,* 30–36. ▶ **pages 141, 166**

Horwitz, A.V. and White, H.R. (1998). The relationship of cohabitation and mental health: a study of a young adult cohort. *Journal of Marriage and the Family, 60,* 505–514. ▶ **page 141**

House, J.C. (1997). Towards a practical application of offender profiling: the RNC's criminal suspect prioritization system. In J.L. Jackson and D.A. Bekerian (eds) *Offender Profiling: Theory, Research and Practice*. Chichester: Wiley. ▶ **page 199**

Howlin, P. (1997). *Autism: Preparing for Adulthood*. London: Routledge. ▶ **page 191**

Hsu, F.L.K. (1983). *Americans and Chinese: Two Ways of Life*. New York: Abelard Schuman ▶ **page 110**

Hubel, D.H. and Wiesel, T.N. (1970). The period of susceptibility to the physiological effects of unilateral eye closure in kittens. *Journal of Physiology, 206,* 419–436. ▶ **page 70**

Hublin, C., Kaprio, J., Partinen, M., Heikkila, K. and Koskenvuo, M. (1997). Prevalence and genetics of sleepwalking: a population-based twin study. *Neurology, 48,* 177–178. ▶ **page 158**

Hughes, M. (1975). *Egocentrism in Preschool Children*. Unpublished PhD thesis, University of Edinburgh. ▶ **page 119**

Hultsch, D.F. and Deutsch, F. (1981). *Adult Development and Aging*. New York: McGraw-Hill. ▶ **page 140**

Humphreys, L. (1970). *The Tearoom Trade*. Chicago: Aldine. ▶ **page 170**

Hunsberger, B. and Cavanagh, B. (1988). Physical attractiveness and children's expectations of potential teachers. *Psychology in the Schools, 25*(1), 70–74. ▶ **page 103**

Hunt, C. and Andrews, G. (2007). Drop-out rate as a performance indicator in psychotherapy. *Acta Psychiatrica Scandinavica, 85*(4), 275–278. ▶ **page 239**

Huss, E.T. and Kayson, W.A. (1985). Effects of age and sex on speed of finding embedded figures. *Perceptual and Motor Skills, 61,* 591–594. ▶ **page 186**

Hussain, S.S. (2002). *Electroconvulsive Therapy in Depressive Illness that has not Responded to Drug Treatment*. MPhil thesis, University of Edinburgh. ▶ **page 239**

Ingham, J. (1989). An experimental investigation of the relationships among learning style perceptual preference, instructional strategies, training achievement and attitudes of corporate employees. Doctoral dissertation, St. John's University. ▶ **page 187**

Inhelder, B., Sinclair, H. and Bovet, M. (1974). *Learning and the Development of Cognition*. London: Routledge. ▶ **page 119**

Issac, C.L. and Mayes, A.R. (1999). Rate of forgetting in amnesia: II. Recall and recognition of word lists at different levels of organisation. *Journal of Experimental Psychology: Learning, Memory and Cognition, 25,* 963–977. ▶ **page 94**

Jacobs, J. (1887). Experiments in prehension. *Mind, 12,* 75–79. ▶ **page 87**

Jacobs, M.K., Christensen, A., Snibbe, J.R., Dolezal-Wood, S., Huber, A. and Polterok, A. (2001). A comparison of computer-based versus traditional individual psychotherapy. *Professional Psychology: Research and Practice, 32*(1), 92–96. ▶ **page 135**

Jahoda, G. (1954). A note on Ashanti names and their relationship to personality. *British Journal of Psychology, 45,* 192–195. ▶ **page 203**

James, W. (1890). *Principles of Psychology*. New York: Holt. ▶ **page 78**

Jankowiak, W. and Fischer, E. (1992). Romantic love: a cross-cultural perspective. *Ethnology, 31*(2), 149–155. ▶ **page 111**

Janssen, M., de Wit, J., Hospers, H.J. and Griesven, F. (2001). Educational status and young Dutch gay men's beliefs about using condoms. *AIDS Care, 13*(1), 41–56. ▶ **page 174**

Jarvis, M. (2005). *The Psychology of Effective Learning and Teaching*. Cheltenham: Nelson Thornes. ▶ **page 187**

Jarvis, M. (2006). *Sport Psychology: A Student's Handbook*. London: Routledge. ▶ **page 212**

Jenkins, W.O., Witherspoon, A.D., DeVine, M.D., deValera, E.K., Muller, J.B., Barton, M.C. and McKee, J.M. (1974). *Post-prison Analysis of Criminal Behaviour and Longitudinal Follow-up Evaluation of Institutional Treatment*. Springfield, VA: National Technical Information Service. ▶ **page 207**

Jenness, A. (1932). The role of discussion in changing opinion regarding a matter of fact. *Journal of Abnormal and Social Psychology, 27,* 279–296. ▶ **page 197**

Jeste, D., Lacro, J.P., Nguygen, H.A., Petersen, M.E., Rockwell, E. and Sewell, D.D. (1999). Lower incidence of tardive dyskinesia with risperidone compared with haloperidol in older patients. *Journal of the American Geriatric Society, 47,* 716–719. ▶ **page 235**

Johnson, C. and Scott, B. (1978). Eyewitness testimony and suspect identification as a function of arousal, sex of witness, and scheduling of interrogation. Paper presented at the meeting of the American Psychological Association, Washington, DC. ▶ **page 205**

Johnson, J.D., Simmons, C.H., Jordan, A., MacLean, L., Taddei, J., Thomas, D., Dovidio, J.F. and Reed, W. (2002). Rodney King and O.J. Simpson revisited, the impact of race and defendant empathy induction on judicial decisions. *Journal of Applied Social Psychology, 32*(6), 1208–1223. ▶ **page 201**

Johnson, N., Backlund, E., Sorlie, P. and Loveless, C. (2000). Marital status and mortality: the national longitudinal mortality study. *Annals of Epidemiology, 10,* 224–238. ▶ **pages 107, 140**

Johnson, W. and Bouchard, T.J. Jr. (2005). The structure of human intelligence: it is verbal, perceptual and image rotation (VPR), not fluid and crystallised. *Intelligence, 33,* 393–416. ▶ **page 121**

Johnstone, L. (1989). *Users and Abusers of Psychiatry: A Critical Look at Traditional Psychiatric Practice*. London: Routledge. ▶ **page 230**

Jones, G. (1991). Recent developments and current issues in competitive state anxiety research. *Psychologist, 4,* 152–155. ▶ **page 216**

Jones, G., Swain, A. and Hardy, L. (1993). Intensity and direction dimensions of competitive state anxiety and its relationship to performance. *Journal of Sport Sciences, 11,* 525–532. ▶ **page 217**

Jordan, R. (1985). Signing and autistic children. *Communication, 19,* 9–12. ▶ **page 191**

Jordan, R.H. and Burghardt, G.M. (1986). Employing an ethogram to detect reactivity of black bears (*Ursus americanus*) to the presence of humans. *Ethology, 73*(2), 89–115. ▶ **page 26**

Joseph, J. (2004). Schizophrenia and heredity: why the emperor has no genes. In J. Read, L. Mosher and R. Bentall (eds) *Models of Madness: Psychological, Social and Biological Approaches to Schizophrenia*. Andover: Taylor and Francis. ▶ **pages 72 232, 233**

Josselson, R. (1988). *Finding Herself: Pathways to Identity Development in Women*. New York: Jossey Bass. ▶ **page 76**

Joyce, C.R.B. and Hudson, L. (1968). Student style and teaching styles: an experimental study. *British Journal of Medical Education, 2,* 28–32. ▶ **page 187**

Julien, R.M. (2001). *A Primer of Drug Action*. New York: Worth Publishers. ▶ **page 166**

Kahn, R.J., McNair, D.M., Lipman, R.S., Covi, L., Rickels, K., Downing, R., Fisher, S. and Frankenthaler, L.M. (1986). Imipramine and chlordiazepoxide in depressive and anxiety disorders. II: Efficacy in anxious outpatients, *Archives of General Psychiatry, 43,* 79–85. ▶ **page 171**

Kahn, R.L. and Antonucci T.C. (1980). Convoys over the life course: attachments, roles and social support. In P.B. Baltes and O.G. Brim, Jr (eds) *Life-span Development and Behaviour*, vol. 3. New York: Academic Press. ▶ **page 142**

Kahn, S., Zimmerman, G., Csikszentmihaly, M. and Getzels, J.W. (1985). Relations between identity in young adulthood and intimacy at midlife. *Journal of Personality and Social Psychology*, 49, 1316–1322. ▶ **page 137**

Kahneman, D. and Tversky, A. (1973). On the psychology of prediction. *Psychological Review*, 80, 237–251. ▶ **page 175**

Kalb, C. (2008). Plight of the teenage insomniac. *Newsweek*, 151(14), 10. ▶ **page 159**

Kalmijn, M. and Monden, C. (2006). Are the negative effects of divorce on well-being dependent on marital quality? *Journal of Marriage and Family*, 68(5), 1197–1213. ▶ **page 140**

Kamin, L.J. and Goldberger, A.S. (2002). Twin studies in behavioral research: a skeptical view. *Theoretical Population Biology, 61*, 83–95. ▶ **page 125**

Kapur, S. and Remington, G. (2001). Dopamine D_2 receptors and their role in atypical antipsychotic action: still necessary and may even be sufficient. *Biological Psychiatry*, 50, 873–883. ▶ **page 234**

Karasz, A. (2005). Cultural differences in conceptual models of depression. *Social Science and Medicine, 60*, 1625–1635. ▶ **page 220**

Karau, S.J. and Williams, K.D. (1993). Social loafing: a meta-analytic review and theoretical integration. *Journal of Personality and Social Psychology.* 65, 681–706. ▶ **page 218**

Karon, B.P. and Widener, A.J. (1997). Repressed memories and World War II: lest we forget! *Professional Psychology: Research and Practice*, 28(4), 338–340. ▶ **page 91**

Kelling, G.L. and Wilson, J.Q. (1982). Broken windows, the police and neighborhood safety. *Atlantic Magazine*, March 1982. ▶ **page 206**

Kendler, K.S., Kessler, R.C., Walters, E.E., MacLean, C., Neale, M.C., Heath, A.C. and Eaves, L.J. (1995). Stressful life events, genetic liability and onset of an episode of major depression in women. *American Journal of Psychiatry*, 152, 833–842. ▶ **page 236**

Kendler, K.S., Neale, M.C., Kessler, R.C., Heath, A.C. and Eaves, L.J. (1992). Major depression and generalised anxiety disorder. Same genes, (partly) different environments? *Archives of General Psychiatry*, 49, 716–722. ▶ **page 237**

Kerr, N.L., MacCoun, R.J., Hansen, C.H. and Hymes, J.A. (1987). Gaining and losing social support, momentum in decision making groups. *Journal of Experimental Social Psychology, 23*, 119–145. ▶ **page 201**

Kessler, R.C., Hwang, I., Labrie, R., Petukhova, M., Sampson, N.A., Winters, K.C. and Shaffer, H.J. (2008). DSM-IV pathological gambling in the National Comorbidity Survey Replication. *Psychological Medicine*, 38(9), 1351–1360. ▶ **page 167**

Kiecolt-Glaser, J.K., Garner, W., Speicher, C.E., Penn, G.M., Holliday, J. and Glaser, R. (1984). Psychosocial modifiers of immunocompetence in medical students. *Psychosomatic Medicine*, 46, 7–14. ▶ **page 21**

Kiecolt-Glaser, J.K. and Glaser, R. (1986). Psychological influences on immunity. *Psychosomatics*, 27, 621–624. ▶ **pages 107, 140**

Kiesler, S. and Sproull, L. (1992). Group decision making and communication technology. *Organizational Behavior and Human Decision Processes, 52*(1), 92–123. ▶ **page 109**

Kihlstrom, J.F., Evans, F.J., Orne, M.T. and Orne, E.C. (1980). Attempting to breach post-hypnotic amnesia. *Journal of Abnormal Psychology*, 89, 603–667. ▶ **page 151**

Kilkenny, C., Parsons, N., Kadyszewski, E., Festing, F.W., Cuthill, I.C., Fry, D., Hutton, J. and Altman, D.G. (2009). Survey of the quality of experimental design, statistical analysis and reporting of research using animals. *PLoS ONE, 4*(11). See www.plosone. org/article/info:doi/10.1371/journal.pone.0007824 (accessed October 2010). ▶ **page 59**

Kim, S.W. and Grant, J.E. (2001). An open naltrexone treatment study in pathological gambling disorder. *International Clinical Psychopharmacology*, 16(5), 285–289. ▶ **page 169**

King, A.C., Pruitt, L.A., Woo, S., Castro, C.M., Ahn, D.K., Vitello, M.V., Woodward, S.H. and Bilwise, D.L. (2008). Effects of moderate-intensity exercise on polysomnographic and subjective sleep quality in older adults with mild to moderate sleep complaints. *Journal of Gerontology Series A: Biological Sciences and Medican Science*, 63(9), 997–1004. ▶ **page 220**

Kingdon, D.G. and Kirschen, H. (2006). Who does not get cognitive behavioural therapy for schizophrenia when therapy is readily available? *Psychiatric Services*, 57, 1792–1994. ▶ **page 235**

Kinsey, A.C., Pomeroy, W.B. and Martin, C.E. (1948). *Sexual Behaviour in the Human Male*. Philadelphia, PA: W.B. Saunders Co. ▶ **page 70**

Kirsch, I., Deacon, B.J., Huedo-Medina, T.B., Scoboria, A., Moore, T.J. and Johnson, B.T. (2008). Initial severity and antidepressant benefits: a meta-analysis of data submitted to the food and drug administration, *PLoS Medicine*, 5(2), e45 EP. ▶ **page 239**

Kitayama, S. and Markus, H.R. (1992). Construal of self as cultured frame: implications for internationising psychology. Paper presented at the Symposium in Internationalisation and Higher Education, Ann Arbor, MI. ▶ **page 189**

Klein, G., Juni, A., Waxman, A.R., Arout, C.A., Inturrisi, C.E. and Kest, B. (2008). A survey of acute and chronic heroin dependence in ten inbred mouse strains: evidence of genetic correlation with morphine dependence. *Pharmacology, Biochemistry and Behavior*, 90(3): 447–452. ▶ **page 166**

Klesges, R.C., Shelton, M.L. and Klesges, L.M. (1993). Effects of television on metabolic rate: potential implications for childhood obesity. *Pediatrics*, 91, 281–286. ▶ **page 175**

Klinowska, M. (1994). Brains, behaviour and intelligence in cetaceans (whales, dolphins and porpoises). In *11 Essays on Whales and Man*, 2nd edn. See www.highnorth.no/library/myths/br-be-an.htm (accessed May 2010). ▶ **page 155**

Kohlberg, L. (1969). Stage and sequence: the cognitive-developmental approach to socialisation. In D.A. Goslin (ed.) *Handbook of Socialisation Theory and Practice*. Skokie, IL: Rand McNally. ▶ **page 76**

Kollins, S.H., Newland, M.C. and Critchfield, T.S. (1997). Human sensitivity to reinforcement in operant choice: how much do consequences matter? *Psychonomic Bulletin and Review*, 4, 208–220. Erratum: *Psychonomic Bulletin and Review*, 4, 431. ▶ **page 182**

Kosslyn, S.M., Thompson, W.L., Costantini-Ferrando, M.F., Alpert, N.M. and Spiegel, D. (2000). Hypnotic visual illusion alters color processing in the brain. *American Journal of Psychiatry*, 157, 1279–1284. ▶ **page 150**

Kraemer, R.R., Dzewaltowski, D.A., Blair, M.S., Rinehardt, K.F. and Castracane, V.D. (1990). Mood alteration with treadmill running and its relationship to eta-endorphin, corticotropin and growth hormone. *Journal of Sports Medicine and Physical Fitness, 30*, 241–246. ▶ **page 221**

Kraft, J., Slager, S., McGrath, P. and Hamilton, S. (2005). Sequence analysis of the serotonin transporter and associations with antidepressant response. *Biological Psychiatry*, 58(5), 374–371. ▶ **page 237**

Krause, N. (1987). Life stress, social support and self-esteem in an elderly population. *Psychology and Aging*, 2(4), 349–356. ▶ **page 106**

Kroger, J. (1996). *Identity in Adolescence: The balance between self and other*, 2nd edn. London: Routlledge. ▶ **page 137**

Krueger, J.M., Walter, J. and Levin, C. (1985). Factor S and related somnogens: an immune theory for slow-wave sleep. In D. McGinty, R. Drucker-Colín, A. Morrison and L. Parmeggiani (eds) *Brain Mechanisms of Sleep*. New York: Raven Press. ▶ **page 154**

Kübler-Ross, E. (1969). *On Death and Dying*. London: Tavistock/Routledge. ▶ **page 142**

Kuhn, T.S. (1962). *The Structure of Scientific Revolutions*. Chicago: University of Chicago Press. ▶ **page 69**

Kulik, J.A. and Brown, R. (1979). Frustration, attribution of blame and aggression. *Journal of Experimental Social Psychology, 15*, 183–194. ▶ **page 223**

Kulpers, E., Garety, P., Fowler, D., Dunn, G., Bebbington, P., Freeman, D. and Hadley, C. (1997). London–East Anglia randomized controlled trial of cognitive behavioural therapy for psychosis. I: Effects of the treatment phase. *British Journal of Psychiatry, 17*, 319–327. ▶ **page 235**

Kurdek, L.A. (2003). Differences between gay and lesbian cohabiting couples. *Journal of Social and Personal relationships, 20*(4): 411–436. ▶ **pages 108, 109**

Kurdek, L.A. and Schmitt, J.P. (1987). Partner homogamy in married, heterosexual and cohabiting, gay and lesbian couples. *Journal of Sex Research, 23*, 212–232. ▶ **pages 108, 109**

Kuyken, W. and Tsivrikos, D. (2009). Therapist competence, co-morbidity and cognitive-behavioral therapy for depression. *Psychotherapy and Psychosomatics, 78*, 42–48. ▶ **page 239**

Labounty, L. (2007). Effects of exercise on short-term memory. St. Joseph: Missouri Western State University. See http://clearinghouse.missouriwestern.edu/manuscripts/854. Asp. (accessed 26 February 2008). ▶ **page 220**

Ladouceur, R., Sylvain, C., Boutin, C., Lachance, S., Doucet, C. and Leblond, J. (2001). Cognitive treatment of pathological gambling. *Journal of Mental and Nervous Disorders, 189*, 766–773. ▶ **page 169**

Laing, R.D. (1965). *The Divided Self*. Harmondsworth, Middlesex: Penguin. ▶ **pages 55, 69**

Laird, J.D. (1974). Self-attribution of emotion: the effects of facial expression on the quality of emotional experience. *Journal of Personality and Social Psychology, 29*, 475–486. ▶ **page 40**

Lajunen, T. and Rasanen, M. (2004). Can social psychological models be used to promote bicycle helmet use among teenagers? A comparison of the Health Belief Model, Theory of Planned Behavior and the Locus of Control. *Journal of Safety Research, 35*(1), 115–123. ▶ **page 164**

Landy, D. and Sigall, H. (1974). Beauty is talent: task evaluation as a function of the performer's physical attractiveness. *Journal of Personality and Social Psychology, 29*, 299–304. ▶ **page 103**

Langer, E.J. and Rodin, J. (1976). The effects of choice and enhanced personal responsibility for the aged: a field experiment in an institutional setting. *Journal of Personality and Social Psychology, 34*, 191–198. ▶ **pages 142, 174, 188**

Langlois, J.H. and Roggmann, L.A. (1990). Attractive faces are only average. *Psychological Science, 1*, 115–121. ▶ **page 101**

Larson, R. and Verma, S. (1999). How children and adolescents spend time across the world: work, play and developmental opportunities *Psychological Bulletin, 125*, 701–736. ▶ **page 139**

Larson, R., Richards, M., Moneta, G., Holmbeck, G. and Duckett, E. (1996). Changes in adolescents' daily interactions with their families from ages 10 to 18: disengagement and transformation. *Developmental Psychology, 32*, 744–754. ▶ **page 139**

Lashley, K. (1931). Mass action in cerebral function. *Science, 73*, 245–254. ▶ **page 92**

Latané, B., Williams, K. and Harkins, S. (1979). Many hands make light work: the causes and consequences of social loafing. *Journal of Personality and Social Psychology, 37*, 822–832. ▶ **page 218**

Lawrence, D. (1971). The effects of counselling on retarded readers. *Educational Research, 13*, 119–124. ▶ **page 191**

Le Foll, D., Rascle, O. and Higgins, N.C. (2006). Persistence in a putting task during perceived failure: influence of state-attributions and attributional style. *Applied Psychology: An International Review, 55*, 586–605. ▶ **page 217**

Lea, M. and Spears, R. (1995). Love at first byte? Building personal relationships over computer networks. In J.T. Wood and S. Duck (eds) *Understudied Relationships: Off the Beaten Track*. Newbury Park, CA: Sage. ▶ **page 109**

Lecendreux, M., Bassetti, C., Dauvilliers, Y., Mayer, G., Neidhart, E. and Tafti, M. (2003). HLA and genetic susceptibility to sleepwalking. *Molecular Psychiatry, 8*, 114–117. ▶ **page 159**

Lee, L. (1984). Sequences in separation: a framework for investigating endings of the personal (romantic) relationship. *Journal of Social and Personal Relationships, 1*, 49–74. ▶ **page 104**

Lee, S., Kim, Y., Guerra, N., Prince, A., Bacha, F. and Arslanian, S. (2010). Effects of exercise without calorie restriction on total and abdominal fat and in vivo insulin sensitivity in obese boys: a randomised controlled trial. Paper presented at American Diabetes Society Conference, 70th Scientific Sessions, Orlando, Florida. ▶ **page 220**

LeFrançois, G.R. (2000). *Psychology for Teaching*, 10th edn. Belmont, CA: Wadsworth. ▶ **page 183**

Leo, R.J. and Cartagena, M.T. (1999). Gender bias in psychiatric textbooks. *Academic Psychiatry, 23*(2), 71–76. ▶ **page 230**

Leonard, B.E. (2000). Evidence for a biochemical lesion in depression. *Journal of Clinical Psychiatry, 61*(Suppl. 6), 12–17. ▶ **page 237**

Lepper, M.R., Greene, D. and Nisbett, R.E. (1973). Undermining children's intrinsic interest with extrinsic reward: a test of the overjustification hypothesis. *Journal of Personality and Social Psychology, 28*, 129–137. ▶ **page 183**

Leucht, S., Pitschel-Walz, G., Abraham D. and Kissling, W. (1999). Efficacy and extrapyramidal side-effects. *Schizophrenia Research, 35*(1), 51–68. ▶ **page 235**

LeVay, S. (1991). A difference in hypothalamic structure between heterosexual and homosexual men. *Science, 254*, 1034–107. ▶ **page 100**

Levinson, D.J. with Levinson, J.D. (1996). *Seasons of a Woman's Life*. New York: Knopf. ▶ **page 134**

Levy-Lahad, E., Wijsman, E.M., Nemens, E., Anderson, L., Goddard, K.A.B., Weber, J.L., Bird, T.D. and Schellenberg, G.D. (1995). A familial Alzheimer's disease locus on chromosome 1. *Science, 269*, 970–973. ▶ **page 94**

Libet, B., Gleason, C.A., Wright, E.W. and Pearl, D.K. (1983). Time of conscious intention to act in relation to onset of cerebral activity (readiness-potential). The unconscious initiation of a freely voluntary act. *Brain, 106*, 623–642. ▶ **page 79**

Lillard, L.A. and Waite, L.J. (1995). Till death do us part: marital disruption and mortality. *American Journal of Sociology, 100*, 1131–1156. ▶ **page 141**

Lin, L., Faraco, J., Li, R., Kadotani, H., Rogers, W., Lin, X., Qiu, X., de Jong, P., Nishino, S. and Mignot, E. (1999). The sleep disorder canine narcolepsy is caused by a mutation in the *hypocretin* (orexin) receptor 2 gene. *Cell, 98*(3), 365–376. ▶ **page 158**

Lin, N., Simeone, R.S., Ensel, W.M. and Kuo, W. (1979). Social support, stressful life events and illness: a model and an empirical test. *Journal of Health and Social Behaviour, 20*, 108–119. ▶ **page 107**

Lindemann, E. (1944). Symptomatology and management of acute grief. *American Journal of Psychiatry, 101*, 141–148. ▶ **page 142**

Ling, R. (2001). Adolescent girls and young adult men: two sub-cultures of the mobile telephone. Telenor Research and Development. Telenor R&D Report R 34/2001. ▶ **page 109**

Littlewood, J. (1992). *Aspects of Grief: Bereavement in Adult Life*. London: Routledge. ▶ **page 142**

Liu, D., Wellman, H.M., Tardif, T. and Sabbagh, M.A. (2004). Development of Chinese and North American children's theory of mind. Paper presented at the 28th International Congress. ▶ **page 75**

Lockhart, R.S. and Craik, F.I.M. (1990). Levels of processing: A retrospective commentary on a framework for memory research. *Canadian Journal of Psychology, 44*, 87–112. ▶ **page 89**

Loehlin, J.C., J.M. Horn and L. Willerman (1989). Modeling IQ change: evidence from the Texas Adoption Project. *Child Development, 60*, 993–1004. ▶ **page 124**

Loftus, E.F. and Palmer, J.C. (1974). Reconstruction of automobile destruction: an example of the interaction between language and memory. *Journal of Verbal Learning and Verbal Behavior, 13*, 585–589. ▶ **pages 38, 204, 205**

Loftus, E.F., Loftus, G.R. and Messo, J. (1987). Some facts about 'weapon focus'. *Law and Human Behaviour, 11*(1), 55–62. ▶ **page 204**

Loftus, E.F. and Pickrell, J.E. (1995). The formation of false memories. *Psychiatric Annals, 25*, 720–725. ▶ **page 91**

Logie, R.H. (1995). *Visuo-spatial Working Memory*. Hove: Lawrence Erlbaum Associates, Ltd. ▶ **page 88**

Logie, R.H. (1999). State of the art: working memory. *The Psychologist, 12*, 174–178. ▶ **page 87**

Lombroso, C. (1876) *L'Uomo Delinquente*. Milan: Hoepli. ▶ **page 196**

Lopata, H.Z. (1979). *Women as Widows: Support Systems*. New York: Elsevier. ▶ **page 143**

López-Olmeda, J.F., Madrid, J.A. and Sanchez-Vazquez, F.J. (2006). Light and temperature as zeitgebers of zebrafish (*Danio rerio*): circadian activity rhythms. *Chronobiology International, 23*(3), 537–550. ▶ **page 156**

Lorenz, K.Z. (1966). *On Aggression*. New York: Harcourt, Brace and World. ▶ **page 222**

Lott, I.T. (1982). Down's syndrome, aging and Alzheimer's disease: a clinical review. *Annals of the New York Academy of Sciences, 396*, 15–27. ▶ **page 94**

Lovaas, O.I. (1987). Behavioural treatment and abnormal education and educational functioning in young autistic children. *Journal of Consulting and Clinical Psychology, 55*, 3–9. ▶ **page 190**

Lundrigan, S. and Canter, D. (2001). Spatial patterns of serial murder: an analysis of disposal site location choice. *Behavioural Sciences and the Law, 19*, 595–610. ▶ **page 199**

Lyketsos, C. (2001). Cited in D. Pendick *Depression and Memory*, www.memorylossonline.com/summer2001/depression.html (accessed April 2010). ▶ **page 90**

Lynch, J.J. (1977). *The Broken Heart: The Medical Consequences of loneliness*. New York: Basic Books. ▶ **pages 107, 140**

Lyon, K., Wilson, J., Golden, C.J., Graber, B., Coffman, J.A. and Bloch, S. (1981). Effects of long-term neuroleptic use on brain density. *Psychiatric Research, 5,* 33–37. ▶ **page 233**

Lyons, M.J., True, W.R., Eisen, S.A., Goldberg, J., Meyer, J.M., Faraone, S.V., Eaves, L.J. and Tsuang, M.T. (1995). Differential heritability of adult and juvenile antisocial traits. *Archives of General Psychiatry, 52*, 906–915. ▶ **page 203**

Maccoby, E.E. and Jacklin, C.N. (1974). *The psychology of sex differences.* Stanford, CA: Stanford University Press. ▶ **page 77**

Madon, S., Guyll, M., Spoth, R.L., Cross, S.E. and Hilbert, S.J. (2003). The self-fulfilling influence of mother expectations on children's underage drinking. *Journal of Personality and Social Psychology, 84*, 1188–1205. ▶ **page 203**

Maguire, E.A., Gadian, D.G., Johnsrude, I.S., Good, C.D., Ashburner, J. Frackowiak, R.S. and Frith, C.D. (2000). Navigation-related structural change in the hippocampi of taxi drivers. *Proceedings of the National Academy of Science, 97*(8), 4398–4403. ▶ **page 73**

Malgady, R.G. (1996). The question of cultural bias in assessment and diagnosis of ethnic minority clients: let's reject the null hypothesis. *Professional Psychology: Research and Practice, 27*(1), 73–77. ▶ **page 231**

Malouff, J.M., Rooke, S.E. and Schutte, N.S. (2008). The heritability of human behavior: results of aggregating meta-analyses. *Current Psychology, 27*(3), 153–161. ▶ **page 124**

Maltby, J., Day, E. and Macaskill, A. (2007). *Personality, Individual Differences and Intelligence*. Harlow: Pearson. ▶ **page 126**

Mandel, D.R. (1998). The obedience alibi: Milgram's account of the Holocaust reconsidered. *Analyse and Kritik: Zeitschrift für Sozialwissenschaften, 20*, 74–94. ▶ **page 55**

Mandler, G. (1967). Organisation and memory. In K.W. Spence and J.T. Spence (eds) *The Psychology of Learning and Motivation: Advances in Research and Theory*, vol. 1. London: Academic Press. ▶ **page 89**

March, J.S., Silva, S., Petrycki, S., Curry, J., Wells, K., Fairbank, J., Burns, B., Domino, M., McNulty, S., Vitiello, B. and Severe, J. (2007). The treatment for adolescents with depression study: long-term effectiveness and safety outcomes. *Archives of General Psychiatry, 64*(10), 1132–1143. ▶ **page 239**

Marcia, J. (1966). Development and validation of ego identity status. *Journal of Personality and Social Psychology, 3*, 551–558. ▶ **page 138**

Marcia, J. (1976). Identity six years after: a follow-up study. *Journal of Youth and Adolescence, 5*, 145–160. ▶ **page 137**

Marelich, W.D. Lundquist, J. Painter, K. and Mechanic, M.B. (2008). Sexual deception as a social-exchange process: development of a behaviour-based sexual deception scale. *Journal of Sex Research, 45*(1), 27–35. ▶ **page 103**

Marshall, S.P. (1990). What students learn and remember from word instruction. Paper presented at the Annual Meeting of the American Educational Research Association, Boston. ▶ **page 189**

Martens, R., Burton, D., Vealey, R.S., Bump, L.A. and Smith, D. (1990). Development and validation of the Competitive State Anxiety Inventory-2. In R. Martens, R.S. Vealey and D. Burton (eds) *Competitive Anxiety in Sport* (pp. 117–190). Champaign, IL: Human Kinetics. ▶ **page 216**

Maslow, A. (1954). *Motivation and Personality.* New York: Harper and Row. ▶ **page 188**

Mason, K.L. (2008). Cyberbullying: a preliminary assessment for school personnel. *Psychology in the Schools, 45*(4), 323–348. ▶ **pages 108, 109**

Matthews, S.C., Camacho, A., Mills, P.J. and Dimsdale, J.E. (2003). The Internet for medical information about cancer: help or hindrance? *Psychosomatics: Journal of Consultation Liaison Psychiatry, 44*(2), 100–103. ▶ **page 173**

Mayo Health (2001). Everyone Active: Exercise for Healthy Aging. www.mayohealth.org. ▶ **page 175**

Mazzella, R. and Feingold, A. (1994). The effects of physical attractiveness, race, socioeconomic status and gender of defendants and victims on judgments of mock jurors: a meta-analysis. *Journal of Applied Social Psychology, 24*, 1315–1344. ▶ **page 201**

McClelland, D.C. (1961). *The Achieving Society*. Princeton, NJ: Van Nostrand. ▶ **page 214**

McClelland, D.C., Atkinson, J.W., Clark, R.A. and Lowell, E.L. (1953). *The Achievement Motive*. New York: Appleton-Century-Crofts. ▶ **page 214**

McCoy, A.W. (2007). Science in Dachau's shadow: Hebb, Beecher and the development of CIA psychological torture and modern medical ethics. *Journal of the History of the Behavioral Sciences* (Wiley Interscience), *43*(4), 401–417. ▶ **page 61**

McGarrigle, J. and Donaldson, M. (1974). Conservation accidents. *Cognition*, *3*, 341–350. ▶ **page 117**

McGue, M. (1999). The behavioural genetics of alcoholism. *Current Directions in Psychological Science 8*, 109–115. ▶ **page 166**

McGuffin, P., Katz, R., Rutherford, J. and Watkins, S.A. (1996). Hospital based twin register of the heritability of DSM-IV unipolar depression. *Archives of General Psychiatry*, *53*, 129–136. ▶ **page 236**

McGuire, D.K., Levine, B.D., Williamson, J.W., Snell, P.G., Blomqvist, C.G., Saltin, B. and Mitchell, J.H. (2001). A 30-year follow-up of the Dallas bed rest and training study. *Circulation*, *104*, 1350. ▶ **page 220**

McKelvie, S.J. and Coley, J. (1993). Effects of crime seriousness and offender facial attractiveness on recommended treatment. *Social Behaviour and Personality*, *21*, 265–277. ▶ **page 200**

McLarnon, L.D. and Kaloupek, G.D. (1988). Psychological investigations of genital herpes recurrence: prospective assessment and cognitive-behavioral intervention for a chronic physical disorder. *Health Psychology*, *7*, 231–249. ▶ **page 175**

McLaughlan, A. (1986). The effects of two forms of decision reappraisal on the perception of pertinent arguments. *British Journal of Social Psychology*, *25*, 129–138. ▶ **page 201**

McNaughton, S. and Leyland, J. (1990). Maternal regulation of children's problem-solving behaviour and its impact on children's performance. *Child Development*, *61*, 113–126. ▶ **page 119**

McNeal, E.T. and Cimbolic, P. (1986). Antidepressants and biochemical theories of depression. *Psychological Bulletin*, *99*, 361–374. ▶ **page 236**

Meddis, R. (1975). On the function of sleep. *Animal Behaviour*, *23*, 676–691. ▶ **page 154**

Mednick, S.A., Gabrielli, W.F. Jr and Hutching, S.B. (1987). Genetic factors in the etiology of criminal behavior. In S.A. Mednick, T.E. Moffitt and S.A. Stack (eds) *The Causes of Crime: New Biological Approaches*. Cambridge: Cambridge University Press. ▶ **page 202**

Meichenbaum, D. (1977). *Cognitive-Behaviour Modification: An Integrative Approach*. New York: Plenum Press ▶ **page 170**

Meichenbaum, D. (1985). *Stress Inoculation Training.* New York: Pergamon. ▶ **page 170**

Meilman, P.W. (1979). Cross-sectional age changes in ego identity status during adolescence. *Developmental Psychology*, *15*, 230–231. ▶ **page 137**

Merrick, S. (1992). Multiple intelligences or multilevel intelligence. *Psychological Inquiry*, *3*(4), 365–384. ▶ **page 121**

Meyer-Lindenberg, A., Miletich, R.W., Kohn, P., Esposito, G., Carson, R.E., Quarantelli, M., Weinberger, D.R. and Berman, K.F. (2002). Prefrontal cortex dysfunction predicts exaggerated striatal dopamine uptake in schizophrenia. *Nature Neuroscience 5*, 1809–1817. ▶ **page 233**

Michaels, J.W., Blommel, J.M., Brocato, R.M., Linkous, R.A. and Rowe, J.S. (1982). Social facilitation and inhibition in a natural setting. *Replications in Social Psychology*, *2*, 21–24. ▶ **page 213**

Michels, I.I., Stöver, H. and Gerlach, R. (2007). Substitution treatment for opioid addicts in Germany. *Harm Reduction Journal*, *4*, 5. ▶ **page 169**

Michie, S., Marteau, T.M. and Kidd, J. (1992). Predicting antenatal class attendance: attitudes of self and others. *Psychology and Health*, 7, 225–234. ▶ **page 173**

Mignot, E. (1998). Genetic and familial aspects of narcolepsy. *Neurology, 50*(Suppl, 1), S16–S22. ▶ **page 159**

Mignot, E. (2001). A hundred years of research. See http://med.stanford.edu/school/Psychiatry/narcolepsy/narcolepsyhistory.html (accessed August 2008). Originally published in 2001, *Archives Italiennes de Biologie*, *139*(3), 207–220. ▶ **page 159**

Mignot, E., Hayduk, R., Grumet, F.C., Black, J. and Guilleminault, C. (1997). HLA DQB10602 is associated with cataplexy in 509 narcoleptic patients. *Sleep*, *20*(11), 1012–1020. ▶ **page 159**

Miles, C. and Hardman, E. (1998). State-dependent memory produced by aerobic exercise. *Ergonomics*, *41*(1), 20–28. ▶ **page 92**

Milgram, S. (1963). Behavioural study of obedience. *Journal of Abnormal and Social Psychology*, *67*, 371–378. ▶ **pages 13, 16, 22, 54, 56, 57**

Milgram, S. (1974). *Obedience to Authority: An Experimental View*. New York: Harper and Row. ▶ **pages 22, 71**

Miller, G.A. (1956). The magic number seven, plus or minus two: some limits on our capacity for processing information. *Psychological Review*, *63*, 81–93. ▶ **page 87**

Miller, J. (ed.) (1983). *States of Mind*. London: British Broadcasting Corporation. ▶ **page 68**

Miller, L. (1994). www.radix.net/~reimann/enet/VC94/Msg/msg34.html (accessed March 2003). ▶ **page 119**

Miller, W. and Seligman, M.E.P. (1974). Depression and learned helplessness in man. *Journal of Abnormal Psychology*, *84*, 228–238. ▶ **page 237**

Milner, B. (1962). Les troubles de la mémoire accompagnant des lésions hippocampiques bilaterales. In P. Passouant (ed.) *Physiologie de l'hippocampe*. Paris: Centre de Recherches Scientifiques. ▶ **page 95**

Mita, T.H., Dermer, M. and Knight, J. (1977). Reversed facial images and the mere-exposure hypothesis. *Journal of Personality and Social Psychology*, *35*, 597–601. ▶ **page 40**

Modgil, S., Modgil, M. and Brown, G. (1983). *Jean Piaget: An Interdisciplinary Critique*. London: Routledge. ▶ **page 185**

Moeller, F.G., Dougherty, D.M., Swann, A.C., Collins, D., Davis, C.M. and Cherek, D.R. (1996). Tryptophan depletion and aggressive responding in healthy males. *Psychopharmacology*, *126*, 97–103. ▶ **page 203**

Moghaddam, F.M., Tayler, D.M. and Wright, S.C. (1993). *Social Psychology in a Cross-cultural Perspective*. New York: W.H. Freeman and Company. ▶ **page 110**

Mokros, A. and Alison L.J. (2002). Is offender profiling possible? Testing the predicted homology of crime scene actions and background characteristics in a sample of rapists. *Legal and Criminological Psychology*, *7*(1), 25–43. ▶ **page 199**

Molloy, D.W., Beerschoten, D.A, Borrie, M.J., Crilly, R.G. and Cape, R.D.T. (1988). Acute effects of exercise on neuropsychological function in elderly subjects. *Journal of the American Geriatrics Society*, *36*, 29–33. ▶ **page 220**

Montemayor, R. (1982). The relationship between parent-adolescent conflict and the amount of time adolescents spend alone and with parents and peers. *Child Development*, *53*, 1512–1519. ▶ **page 139**

Moore, S.M. and Leung, C. (2001). Romantic beliefs, styles and relationships among young people from Chinese, Southern European and Anglo-Australian backgrounds. *Asian Journal of Social Psychology*, *4*, 53–68. ▶ **page 110**

Mor, V., McHorney, C. and Sherwood, S. (1986). Secondary morbidity among the recently bereaved. *American Journal of Psychiatry*, *143*, 158–163. ▶ **page 142**

Morgan, E. (1995). Measuring time with a biological clock. *Biological Sciences Review*, *7*, 2–5. ▶ **page 157**

Morgan, H. (1996). An analysis of Gardner's theory of multiple intelligence. *Roeper Review*, *18*, 263–270. ▶ **page 121**

Morris, C.D., Bransford, J.D. and Franks, J.J. (1977). Levels of processing versus transfer appropriate processing. *Journal of Verbal Learning and Verbal Behavior, 16*, 519–533. ▶ **page 89**

Morris, J.N., Heady, J.A., Raffle, P.A.B., Roberts, C.G. and Parks, J.W. (1953). Coronary heart-disease and physical activity of work. *Lancet, 2,* 1053–1057. ▶ **page 220**

Morris, P.E., Gruneberg, M.M., Sykes, R.N. and Merrick, A. (1981). Football knowledge and the acquisition of new results. *British Journal of Psychology, 72,* 479–483. ▶ **page 86**

Moscovici, S., Lage, S. and Naffrechoux, M. (1969). Influence of a consistent minority on the responses of a majority in a color perception task. *Sociometry, 32,* 365–380. ▶ **page 200**

Mulsant, B.H., Rosen, J., Thornton, J.E. and Zubenko, G.S. (1991). A prospective naturalistic study of electroconvulsive therapy in late-life depression. *Journal of Geriatric Psychiatry and Neurology, 4,* 3–13. ▶ **page 231**

Murphy, M.P. and LeVine, H. (2010). Alzheimer's disease and the β-amyloid peptide. *Journal of Alzheimers Disease, 19*(1), 311–323 (accessed February 2010). ▶ **page 95**

Murray, M. and McMillan, C. (1993). Health beliefs, locus of control, emotional control and women's cancer screening behaviour. *British Journal of Clinical Psychology, 32,* 87–100. ▶ **page 173**

Murstein, B.I. (1972). Physical attractiveness and marital choice. *Journal of Personality and Social Psychology, 22,* 8–12.
▶ **page 38**

Myers, D.G. and Kaplan, M.F. (1976). Group-induced polarization in simulated juries. *Personality and Social Psychology Bulletin, 2*(1), 63–66. ▶ **page 201**

Myers, J.E., Madathil, J. and Tingle, L.R. (2005). Marriage satisfaction and wellness in India and the United States: a preliminary comparison of arranged marriages and marriages of choice. *Journal of Counselling and Development, 83,* 183–190. ▶ **page 111**

Myers, N.D., Payment, C.A. and Feltz, D.L. (2004). Reciprocal relationships between collective efficacy and team performance in women's ice hockey. *Group Dynamics: Theory, Research and Practice, 8,* 182–195. ▶ **page 215**

Nairne, J.S., Whiteman, H.L. and Kelley, M.R. (1999). Short-term forgetting of order under conditions of reduced interference. *Quarterly Journal of Experimental Psychology, 52A,* 241–251. ▶ **page 87**

Naish, P. (2006). Detecting hypnotically altered states of consciousness. *Contemporary Hypnosis, 22*(1), 24–30. ▶ **page 151**

Nemeth, C. (1977). Interactions between jurors as a function of majority vs. unanimity decision rules. *Journal of Applied Social Psychology, 7,* 38–56. ▶ **page 200**

Nemeth, G.J. and Brilmayer, A.G. (1987). Negotiation versus influence. *European Journal of Social Psychology, 17,* 45–56. ▶ **page 201**

Nestler, S. and Egloff, B. (2010). When scary messages backfire: influence of dispositional cognitive avoidance on the effectiveness of threat communications. *Journal of Research in Personality, 44*(1), 137–141. ▶ **page 173**

Newton, M. and Duda, J.L. (1999). The interaction of motivational climate, dispositional goal orientations and perceived ability in predicting indices of motivation. *International Journal of Sport Psychology, 30,* 63–82. ▶ **page 215**

NICE (National Institute for Clinical Excellence) (2003). *Electroconvulsive Therapy (ECT): Guidance, Technology Appraisal 59*. London: National Institute for Clinical Excellence. ▶ **page 235**

NICHD Early Child Care Research Network (2003). Social functioning in first grade: associations with earlier home and child care predictors and with current classroom experiences. *Child Development, 74,* 1639–1663. ▶ **page 21**

Nicholls, J.G. (1984). Conceptions of ability and achievement motivation. In R.E. Ames and C. Ames (eds) *Research on Motivation in Education: Student Motivation*, vol. 1. New York: Academic Press. ▶ **page 214**

Nicoloff, G. and Schwenk, T.S. (1995). Using exercise to ward off depression. *The Physician and Sports Medicine, 23*(9), 44–58. ▶ **page 220**

Nieman, D.C. (2000). Is infection risk linked to exercise workload. *Medicine and Science in Sports and Exercise, 32,* S406–411. ▶ **page 221**

Nishino, S., Ripley, B., Overeem, S., Lammers, G.L. and Mignot, E. (2000) Hypocretin (orexin) transmission in human narcolepsy. *The Lancet, 355,* 39–40. ▶ **page 159**

Noble, E.P. (2000). Addiction and its reward process through polymorphisms of the D2 dopamine receptor gene: a review. *European Psychiatry, 15*(2): 79–89. ▶ **page 167**

Noble, E.P., Blum, K., Ritchie, T., Montgomery, A. and Sheridan, P.J. (1991). Allelic association of the D₂ dopamine receptor gene with receptor-binding characteristics in alcoholism. *Archives of General Psychiatry, 48,* 648–654. ▶ **page 166**

Nolen-Hoeksema, S. (1987). Sex differences in unipolar depression: evidence and theory. *Psychological Bulletin, 101,* 259–282. ▶ **page 231**

North, T.C., McCullagh, P. and Tran, Z.V. (1990). Effect of exercise on depression. *Exercise and Sport Science Reviews, 18,* 379–415. ▶ **page 221**

Nuremberg Code (1947). In A. Mitscherlich and F. Mielke (1949). *Doctors of Infamy: The Story of the Nazi Medical Crimes* (pp. xxiii–xxv). New York: Schuman. ▶ **page 56**

O'Brien, S. and Lee, L. (1990). Effects of videotape intervention on Pap smear knowledge, attitudes and behavior. Special Issue: Behavioural research in cancer, *Behaviour Changes, 7,* 143–150. ▶ **page 173**

Oakley, D. (1999). Hypnosis and consciousness: a structural model. *Contemporary Hypnosis, 16,* 215–223. ▶ **page 150**

Ohayon, M.M. and Roth, T. (2003). Place of chronic insomnia in the course of depressive and anxiety disorders. *Journal of Psychiatric Research, 37*(1), 9–15. ▶ **page 159**

Oliviero, A. (2008). cited in article: Why do some people sleepwalk? *Scientific American,* January. See see www.sciam.com/article.cfm?id=why-do-some-people-sleepwalk, accessed October 2010. ▶ **page 158**

Oliviero, A., Della Marca, G., Tonali, P.A., Pilato, F., Saturno, E., Dileone, M., Rubino, M. and Di Lazzaro, V. (2007). Functional involvement of cerebral cortex in adult sleepwalking. *Journal of Neurology, 254*(7), 1066–1072. ▶ **page 158**

Olmstead, T.A. and Petry, N.M. (2009). The cost-effectiveness of prize-based and voucher-based contingency management in a population of cocaine- or opioid-dependent outpatients. *Drug and Alcohol Dependence, 1, 102*(1–3), 108–115. ▶ **page 169**

Olmstead, T.A., Sindelar, J.L. and Petry, N.M. (2007). Cost-effectiveness of prize-based incentives for stimulant abusers in outpatient psychosocial treatment programs. *Drug and Alcohol Dependence, 87*(2–3), 175–182. ▶ **page 169**

Onika, D., Burton, K.S. and Reese-Durham, N. (2008). The effects of the multiple intelligence teaching strategy on the academic achievement of eighth grade math students. See www.thefreelibrary.com/The+effects+of+the+multiple+intelligence+teaching+strategy+on+the.-a0181365766 (accessed April 2010). ▶ **page 121**

Orbach, I., Singer, R.N. and Price, S. (1999). An attribution training program and achievement in sport. *The Sport Psychologist, 13*(1), 69–82. ▶ **page 217**

Orne, M.T. (1970). Hypnosis, motivation and the ecological validity of the psychological experiment. In W.J. Arnold and M.M. Page (eds) *Nebraska Symposium on Motivation*, vol. 18. Lincoln, University of Nebraska Press. ▶ **page 151**

Orne, M.T., Seenan, P.W. and Evans, F.J. (1968). Occurrence of post-hypnotic behaviour outside the experimental setting. *Journal of Personality and Social Psychology*, 9, 189–196. ▶ **page 150**

Orth, U., Trzesniewski, K.H. and Robins, R.W. (2010). Self-esteem development from young adulthood to old age: a cohort-sequential longitudinal study. *Journal of Personality and Social Psychology*, 98(4), 645–658. ▶ **page 142**

Osborn, S.G. and West, D.J. (1979). Conviction records of fathers and sons compared. *British Journal of Criminology*, 19, 120–133. ▶ **page 202**

Oswald, I. (1980). Sleep as a restorative process: human clues. *Progress in Brain Research, 53*, 279–288. ▶ **page 154**

Paffenbarger, R.S. (1994). 40 years of progress: physical activity, health and fitness. *Medicine and Science in Sports and Exercise, 4*, 93–109. ▶ **page 220**

Pagel, M.D., Erdly, W.W. and Becker, J. (1987). Social networks: we get by with (and in spite of) a little help from our friends. *Journal of Personality and Social Psychology*, 53, 793–804. ▶ **page 107**

Palmer, E.J., McGuire, J., Hatcher, R.M., Hounsome, J.C., Bilby, C.A. and Hollin, C.R. (2008). The importance of appropriate allocation to offending behaviour programmes. *International Journal of Offender Therapy and Comparative Criminology*, 55(2), 206–211. ▶ **page 207**

Palmer, E.J., McGuire, J., Hounsome, J.C., Hatcher, R.M., Bilby, C.A. and Hollin, C.R. (2007). Offending behaviour programmes in the community: the effects on reconviction of three programmes with adult male offenders. *Legal and Criminological Psychology*, 12, 251–264. ▶ **page 207**

Palmere, M., Benton, S.L., Glover, J.A. and Ronning, R. (1983). Elaboration and recall of main ideas in prose. *Journal of Educational Psychology*, 75, 898–907. ▶ **page 89**

Park, S., Püschel, J., Sauter, B., Rentsch, M. and Hell, D. (1999). Spatial working memory deficits and clinical symptoms in schizophrenia: a 4-month follow-up study. *Biological Psychiatry*, 46(3), 392–400. ▶ **page 88**

Parkes, C.M. (1987). *Bereavement: Studies of Grief in Adult Life*, 2nd edn. Madison: International Universities Press. ▶ **page 142**

Parkes, K.R. (1984). Locus of control, cognitive appraisal and coping in stressful episodes. *Journal of Personality and Social Psychology*, 46, 655–668. ▶ **page 175**

Parrott, A.C. (1998). Nesbitt's paradox resolved? Stress and arousal modulation during cigarette smoking. *Addiction*, 93(1), 27–39 ▶ **page 166**

Pascual-Leone, A., Nguyet, D., Cohen, L.G., Brasil-Neto, J.P., Cammarota, A. and Hallett, M. (1995). Modulation of muscle responses evoked by transcranial magnetic stimulation during the acquisition of new fine motor skills. *Journal of Neurophysiology*, 74(3), 1037–1045. ▶ **page 73**

Pashler, H., McDaniel, M., Rohrer, D. and Bjork, R. (2009). Learning styles: Concepts and evidence. *Psychological Science in the Public Interest*, 9, 105–119. ▶ **page 187**

Patel, N. (2007). The BPS should do more. British Science Association. See www.britishscienceassociation.org/web/news/reportsandpublications/magazine/magazinearchive/SPAArchive/SPAMarch07/_PatelMarch07.htm (accessed May 2010). ▶ **page 61**

Pavlov, I.P. (1902). *The Work of the Digestive Glands*. London: Charles Griffin. ▶ **page 68**

Paykel, E.S. and Cooper, Z. (1992). Life events and social stress. In E.S. Paykel (ed.) *Handbook of Affective Disorders*. Guilford Press: London Read. ▶ **page 237**

Pearlin, L.I., Menaghan, E.G., Lieberman, M.A. and Mullan, J.T. (1981). The stress process. *Journal of Health and Social Behavior*, 22, 337–356. ▶ **page 107**

Peterson, L.R. and Peterson, M.J. (1959). Short-term retention of individual verbal items. *Journal of Experimental Psychology*, 58, 193–198. ▶ **page 87**

Petrides, K.V., Chamorro-Premuzic, T., Frederickson, N. and Furnham, A. (2005). Explaining individual differences in scholastic behaviour and achievement. *British Journal of Educational Psychology*, 75, 239–25. ▶ **page 122**

Pfeifer, J.E. and Ogloff, J.R. (1991). Ambiguity and guilt determinations: a modern racism perspective. *Journal of Applied Social Psychology*, 21, 1713–1725. ▶ **page 200**

Piaget, J. (1954). *The Construction of Reality in the Child*. New York: Basic Books. ▶ **page 118**

Piaget, J. (1970). Piaget's theory. In P.H. Mussen (ed.) *Carmichael's Manual of Child psychology*, vol. 1. New York: Wiley. ▶ **page 185**

Piccione, C., Hilgard, E.R. and Zimbardo, P.G. (1989). On the degree of stability of measured hypnotizability over a 25-year period. *Journal of Personality and Social Psychology*, 56(2), 289–295. ▶ **page 151**

Pinker, S. (2002). *The Blank State: The Modern Denial of Human Nature*. New York: The Penguin Group. ▶ **page 127**

Pinker, S. (2003). *The Blank Slate*. London: Penguin. ▶ **page 73**

Pinker, S. (2008a). Crazy love. *Time, 28 January*. ▶ **page 111**

Pinker, S. (2008b). The fear of determinism. In J. Baer, J.C. Kaufman and R. Baumeister (eds) *Are We Free? Psychology and Free Will*. New York: Oxford University Press. ▶ **pages 79, 148**

Plomin, R., DeFries J.C. and Loehlin, J.C. (1977). Genotype–environment interaction and correlation in the analysis of human behavior. *Psychological Bulletin*, 84(2), 309–322. ▶ **pages 73, 141**

Pollard, C. (1998). Zero Tolerance, short-term fix, long-term liability? In N. Dennis (ed.) *Zero Tolerance, Policing a Free Society*. IES Health and Welfare Unit, Lancing: Hartington Fine Arts Ltd. ▶ **page 207**

Popper, K. (1935). *Logik der Forschung*. Vienna: Julius Springer Verlag. Translation (1959) *The Logic of Scientific Discovery*. London: Hutchinson. ▶ **page 69**

Povey, R., Conner, M., Sparks, P., James, R. and Shepherd, R. (2000). Application of the theory of planned behaviour to two dietary behaviours: role of perceived control and efficacy. *British Journal of Health Psychology*, 5, 121–139. ▶ **page 173**

Quigley, B.M., Johnson, A.B. and Byrne, D. (1995). Mock jury sentencing decisions, a meta-analysis of the attractiveness–leniency effect. Paper presented at the meeting of the American Psychological Society. New York. ▶ **page 200**

Rahe, R.H., Mahan, J. and Arthur, R. (1970). Prediction of near-future health-change from subjects' preceding life changes. *Journal of Psychosomatic Research*, 14, 401–406. ▶ **page 140**

Rainville, P., Duncan, G.H., Price, D.D., Carter, B. and Bushnell, M.C. (1997). Pain affect encoded in human anterior cingulated but not somatosensory cortex. *Science*, 277, 968–971. ▶ **page 151**

Ramirez, C. and Avila, A.G. (2002). Influence of teachers' causal attributions on students' academic achievements. *Psicotherma*, 14, 444–449. ▶ **page 189**

Randle, S. and Weinberg, R. (1997). Multidimensional anxiety and performance: an exploratory examination of the Zone of Optimal Functioning hypothesis. *The Sport Psychologist*, 11, 160–174. ▶ **page 217**

Rawson, R.A., Huber, A., McCann, M., Shoptaw, S., Farabee, D., Reiber, C. and Ling, W. (2002). A comparison of contingency management and cognitive-behavioral approaches during methadone maintenance treatment for cocaine dependence. *Archives of General Psychiatry*, 59(9), 817–824. ▶ **page 169**

Read, J. (2004). Electroconvulsive therapy. In J. Read, L.R. Mosher and R.P. Bentall. *Models of Madness*. London: Routledge. ▶ **page 235**

Reed, J.M. and Squire, L.R. (1998). Retrograde amnesia for facts and events: findings from four new cases. *Journal of Neuroscience, 18*, 3943–3954. ▶ **page 95**

Regan, T. (1984). *The Case for Animal Rights*. New York: Routledge. ▶ **page 58**

Reicher, S. and Haslam, S.A. (2006) Rethinking the psychology of tyranny: the BBC prison study. *British Journal of Social Psychology, 45*, 1–40. ▶ **page 70**

Reif, A., Jacob, C.P., Rujescu, D., Herterich, S., Lang, S., Gutknecht, L., Baehne, C.G., Strobel, A., Freitag, C.M., Giegling, I., Romanos, M., Hartmann, A., Rösler, M., Renner, T.J., Fallgatter, A.J., Retz, W., Ehlis, A.C. and Lesch, K.P. (2009). Influence of functional variant of neuronal nitric oxide synthase on impulsive behaviors in humans. *Archives of General Psychiatry, 66*(1), 41–50. ▶ **page 202**

Reitman, J.S. (1974). Without surreptitious rehearsal, information in short-term memory decays. *Journal of Verbal Learning and Verbal Behaviour, 13*, 365–377. ▶ **page 93**

Reitzes, D.C. and Mutran, E.J. (2004). The transition to retirement: stages and factors that influence retirement adjustment. *International Journal of Aging and Human Development, 59*(1), 63–84. ▶ **page 142**

Remondes, M. and Schman, E.M. (2004). Role for a cortical input to hippocampal area CA1 in the consolidation of a long-term memory. *Nature, 431*, 699–703. ▶ **page 95**

Retz, W., Retz-Junginger, P., Supprian, T., Thome, J. and Rösler, M. (2004). Association of serotonin transporter promoter gene polymorphism with violence, relation with personality disorders, impulsivity and childhood ADHD psychopathology. *Behavioral Sciences and the Law, 22*(3), 415–425. ▶ **page 202**

Revenson, T.A., Schaiaffino, K.M., Majerovitz, S.D. and Gibofsky, A. (1991). Social support as a double-edged sword: The relation of positive and problematic support to depression among rheumatoid arthritis patients. *Social Science and Medicine, 33*, 807–813. ▶ **page 107**

Richardson, V. and Kilty, K.M. (1991). Adjustment to retirement: continuity vs. discontinuity. *International Journal of Aging and Human Development, 33*, 151–169. ▶ **page 143**

Riding, R. and Grimley, M. (2002). Cognitive style, gender and learning from multi-media materials in 11 year old children. *British Journal of Educational Technology, 30*(1), 43–56. ▶ **page 186**

Ridley, M. (2003). *Nature via Nurture*. London: Fourth Estate. ▶ **page 79**

Riechmann, S.W. and Grasha, A.F. (1974). A rational approach to developing and assessing the construct validity of a student learning style scales instrument. *The Journal of Psychology, 87*, 213–223. ▶ **page 187**

Rimer, B.K., Trock, B., Lermon, C. and King, E. (1991). Why do some women get regular mammograms? *American Journal of Preventative Medicine, 7*, 69–74. ▶ **page 173**

Ringelmann, M. (1913). Recherches sur les moteurs animés: travail de l'homme [Research on animate sources of power: the work of man]. *Annales de l'Institut National Agronomique*, 2nd series, vol. 12, 1–40. ▶ **page 212**

Roberts, A.D. and Bruce, V. (1988). Feature salience in judgements of sex and familiarity of faces. *Perception, 17*, 475–481. ▶ **page 204**

Roberts, P. and Newton, P.M. (1987). Levinsonian studies of women's adult development. *Psychology and Aging, 2*, 154–163. ▶ **page 135**

Roberts, R.E., Roberts, C.R. and Duong, H.T. (2008). Chronic insomnia and its negative consequences for health and functioning of adolescents: a 12-month prospective study. *Journal of Adolescent Health, 42*, 294–302. ▶ **page 159**

Robins, L.N., Helzer, J.E., Weissman, M.M., Orvaschel, H., Gruenberg, E., Burke, J.K. and Regier, D.A. (1984). Lifetime prevalence of specific psychiatric disorders in three cities. *Archives of General Psychiatry, 41*, 949–958. ▶ **page 230**

Rogers, C.R. (1959). A theory of therapy, personality, and interpersonal relationships as developed in the client-centred framework. In S. Koch (ed.) *Psychology: A Study of a Science*. New York: McGraw-Hill. ▶ **page 220**

Rogers, R.L., Meyers, J.S. and Mortel, K.F. (1990). After reaching retirement age physical activity sustains cerebral perfusion and cognition. *Journal American Geriatric Society, 38*, 123–128. ▶ **page 220**

Rohlfing, M. E. (1995). Doesn't anybody stay in one place anymore? An exploration of the understudied phenomenon of long-distance relationships. In J.T. Wood and S.W. Duck (eds) *Understudied Relationships: Off the Beaten Track*. Thousand Oaks, CA: Sage, 173–196. ▶ **page 105**

Rollie, S.S. and Duck, S.W. (2006). Stage theories of marital breakdown. In J.H. Harvey and M.A. Fine (eds) *Handbook of Divorce and Dissolution of Romantic Relationships*. Mahwah, NJ: Lawrence Erlbaum Associates, 176–193. ▶ **page 104**

Rose, D., Fleischmann, P., Wykes, T., Leese, M. and Bindman, J. (2003). Patients' perspectives on electroconvulsive therapy: systematic review. *British Medical Journal, 326*, 1363–1365. ▶ **page 239**

Rosenhan, D.L. (1973.) On being sane in insane places. *Science, 179*, 250–258. ▶ **page 22**

Ross, C.A. and Read, J. (2004). Antipsychotic medication: myths and facts. In J. Read, L.R. Mosher and R.B. Bentall (eds) *Models of Madness*. London: Routledge. ▶ **page 235**

Ross, G.J., Pate, R.R., Casperson, C.J., Domberg, C.L. and Svilar, M. (1987). Home and community in children's exercise habits. *Journal of Physical Education, Recreation, and Dance, 58*, 85–92. ▶ **page 174**

Rotter, J. (1966). Generalized expectancies for internal versus external control of reinforcement, *Psychological Monographs, 80*(1), Whole No. 609. ▶ **page 165**

Rubin, Z. (1973). *Liking and Loving: An Invitation to Social Psychology*. New York: Holt, Rinehart and Winston. ▶ **page 142**

Ruhe, H.G., Mason, N.S. and Schene, A.H. (2007). Mood is indirectly related to serotonin, norepinephrine and dopamine levels in humans: a meta-analysis of monoamine depletion studies. *Molecular Psychiatry, 12*, 331–359. ▶ **page 237**

Rusbult, C.E. and Martz, J.M. (1995). Remaining in an abusive relationship: an investment model analysis of nonvoluntary commitment. *Personality and Social Psychology Bulletin, 21*, 558–571. ▶ **page 103**

Russell, C.S. (1974). Transition to parenthood: Problems and gratifications. *Journal of Marriage and the Family, 36*, 294–302. ▶ **page 141**

Russell, J. and Jarvis, M. (2003). *Angles on Applied Psychology*. Cheltenham: Nelson Thornes. ▶ **page 215**

Russell, W.D. and Cox, R.H. (2000). A laboratory investigation of positive and negative affect within individual zones of optimal functioning theory. *Journal of Sport Behaviour, 23*, 164–180. ▶ **page 217**

Russell, W.M.S. and Birch, R. (1959). *The Principles of Humane Experimental Technique*. Methuen, London. ▶ **page 59**

Rutter, M., Graham, P., Chadwick, D.F.D. and Yule, W. (1976). Adolescent turmoil: fact or fiction. *Journal of Child Psychology and Psychiatry, 17*, 35–56. ▶ **page 139**

Ryan, J.D., Althoff, R.R., Whitlow, S. and Cohen, N.J. (2000). Amnesia is a deficit in relational memory. *Psychological Science, 11*, 454–461. ▶ **page 95**

Ryan, J.J., Glass, L.A. and Bartels, J.M. (2009). Internal consistency reliability of the WISC-IV among primary school students. *Psychological Reports*, 104(3), 874–878. ▶ **page 123**

Ryan, N.D. (1992). The pharmacologic treatment of child and adolescent depression. *Psychiatric Clinics of North America*, 15, 29–40. ▶ **page 239**

Ryan, R.M. and Lynch, J.H. (1989). Emotional autonomy versus detachment: revisiting the vicissitudes of adolescence and young adulthood. *Child Development*, 60, 34–64. ▶ **page 139**

Sackeim, H.A., Prudic, J. and Devanand, D.P., Nobler, M.S., Lisanby, S.H., Peyser, S., Fitzsimons, L., Moody, B.J. and Clark, J. (2000). A prospective, randomised, double blind comparison of bilateral and right unilateral electroconvulsive therapy at different stimulus intensities. *Archives of General Psychiatry*, 57(5), 425–434. ▶ **page 239**

Sadler-Smith, E. and Tsang, F. (1998). A comparative study of approaches to studying in Hong Kong and the United Kingdom. *British Journal of Educational Psychology*, 67, 81–93. ▶ **page 186**

Saladin, M., Saper, Z. and Breen, L. (1988). Perceived attractiveness and attributions of criminality: what is beautiful is not criminal. *Canadian Journal of Criminology*, 30, 251–259. ▶ **page 200**

Samuel, J. and Bryant, P. (1984). Asking only one question in the conservation experiment. *Journal of Child Psychology and Psychiatry*, 25(2), 315–318. ▶ **page 117**

Sanders, G.S. (1981). Driven by distraction: an integrative review of social facilitation theory and research. *Journal of Experimental Social Psychology*, 17, 227–251. ▶ **page 219**

Sanders, G.S., Baron, R.S. and Moore, D.L. (1978). Distraction and social comparison as mediators of social facilitation effects. *Journal of Experimental Social Psychology*, 14, 291–303. ▶ **page 219**

Sanjuan, P.M., Langenbucher, J. and Labouvie, E. (2009). The role of sexual assault and sexual dysfunction in alcohol/other drug use disorders. *Alcoholism Treatment Quarterly* 27(2), 150–163. ▶ **page 167**

Santtila, P., Häkkänen, H., Alison, L. and Whyte, C. (2003). Juvenile firesetters, crime scene actions and offender characteristics. *Legal and Criminological Psychology*, 8(1), 1–20. ▶ **page 199**

Sarita, E.P., Janakiramaiah, N. and Gangadhar, B.N. (1998). Efficacy of combined ECT after two weeks of neuroleptics in schizophrenia: a double-blind controlled study. *National Institute of Mental Health and Neurosciences Journal*, 16, 243–251. ▶ **page 235**

Sarrazin, P., Roberts, G., Cury, F., Biddle, S. and Famose, J. (2002). Exerted effort and performance in climbing among boys: the influence of achievement goals, perceived ability and task difficulty. *Research Quarterly for Exercise and Sport, 73*, 425–436. ▶ **page 215**

Sassin, J.F., Parker, D.C., Mace, J.W., Gotlin, R.W., Johnson, L.C. and Rossman, L.G. (1969). Human growth hormone release: relation to slow-wave sleep and sleep-waking cycles. *Science*, 165(3892), 513–515. ▶ **page 154**

Savin, H.B. (1973). Professors and psychological researchers: Conflicting values in conflicting roles. *Cognition, 2*, 147–149. ▶ **page 71**

Scammacca, N., Roberts, G., Vaughn. S., Edmonds, M., Wexler, J., Reutebuch, C.K. and Torgesen, J.K. (2007). *Interventions for Adolescent Struggling Readers: A Meta-analysis with Implications for Practice*. Portsmouth, NH: RMC Research Corporation, Center on Instruction. ▶ **page 191**

Scarr, S. and McCartney, K. (1983). How people make their own environments: a theory of genotype-environment effects. *Child Development, 54*, 424–435. ▶ **page 73**

Schacter, D.L. (1987). Implicit memory: history and current status. *Journal of Experimental Psychology: Learning, Memory and Cognition, 13*, 501–518. ▶ **page 94**

Schacter, D.L., Church, B.A. and Bolton, E. (1995). Implicit memory in amnesic patients: impairment of voice-specific priming. *Psychological Science, 6*, 20–25. ▶ **page 95**

Schellenberg, G., Turcotte, M. and Ram, B. (2005). What makes retirement enjoyable? Canadian Social Trends. See www.statcan.gc.ca/pub/11-008-x/2005002/article/8453-eng.pdf (accessed July 2010). ▶ **page 142**

Schellenberg, G.D., Bird, T.D., Wijsman, E.M., Orr, H.T., Anderson, L., Nemens, E., White, J.A., Bonnycastle, L., Weber, J.L. and Alonso, M.E. (1992). Genetic linkage evidence for a familial Alzheimer's disease locus on chromosome 14. *Science, 258*, 668–671. ▶ **page 94**

Schmitt, B., Gilovich, T.K., Goore, N. and Joseph, L. (1986). Mere presence and social facilitation: one more time. *Journal of Experimental Social Psychology, 22*, 242–248. ▶ **pages 213, 218, 219**

Schuler, H. and Prochaska, M. (2000). Entwicklung und Konstrukt-validierung eines berufsbezogenen Leistungsmotivationstest. *Diagnostica, 46*(82), 61–72. ▶ **page 215**

Schunk, D.H. (1991). Self-efficacy and academic motivation. *Educational Psychologist, 26*, 207–232. ▶ **page 214**

Schwartz, B. and Barksy, S.F. (1977). The home advantage. *Social Forces, 55*, 641–661. ▶ **page 219**

Schweinhart, L.J., H.V. Barnes and D.P. Weikart. (1993). Significant benefits: the High/Scope Perry preschool study through age 27. *Monographs of the High/Scope Educational Research Foundation, 10*, Ypsilanti, MI: High/Scope Press. ▶ **page 126**

Scott, A.I.F. (2004). *The ECT Handbook*, 2nd edn. The third report of the Royal College of Psychiatrists' Special Committee on ECT. Royal College of Psychiatrists: London ECT Review Group. ▶ **page 239**

Scoville, W.B. and Milner, B. (1957). Loss of recent memory after bilateral hippocampal lesions. *Journal of Neurology, Neurosurgery and Psychiatry, 20*, 11–21. ▶ **pages 87, 95**

Seeman, M. and Evans, J.W. (1962). Alienation and learning in a hospital setting. *American Sociologial Review, 27*, 772–782. ▶ **page 175**

Seligman, M.E.P. (1975). *Helplessness: On Depression, Development and Death*. San Francisco: W.H. Freeman. ▶ **pages 216, 236**

Seligman, M.E.P. (1995). *The Optimistic Child*. New York: Houghton Mifflin Company. ▶ **page 216**

Selkoe, D.J. (2000). Toward a comprehensive theory for Alzheimer's disease. *Annals of the New York Academy of Sciences, 924*, 17–25. ▶ **page 94**

Selye, H. (1936). A syndrome produced by diverse nocuous agents. *Nature, 138*, 32. ▶ **pages 16, 164**

Severiens, S.E. and ten Dam, G.T.M. (1994). Gender differences in learning styles: a narrative review and quantitative meta-analysis. *Higher Education, 27*, 487–501. ▶ **page 186**

Sewall, T.J. (1986). *The Measurement of Learning Style: A Critique of Four Assessment Tools* (ERIC No. ED267247): University of Wisconsin, Wisconsin Assessment Center, U.S. Educational Research Information Center. ▶ **page 187**

Shaffer, D.R. (1993). *Developmental Psychology: Childhood and Adolescence*, 3rd edn. Pacific Grove, CA: Brooks/Cole. ▶ **page 139**

Shah, R. and Waller, G. (2000). Parental style and vulnerability to depression: the role of core beliefs. *The Journal of Nervous and Mental Disease, 188*, 19–25. ▶ **page 237**

Shallice, T. (1967). Temporal summation and absolute brightness threshold. *British Journal of Mathematical and Statistical Psychology, 20*, 129–162. ▶ **page 93**

Shallice, T. and Warrington, E.K. (1970). Independent functioning of verbal memory stores: a neuropsychological study. *Quarterly Journal of Experimental Psychology, 22*, 261–273. ▶ **page 89**

Shapiro, C.M., Bortz, R., Mitchell, D., Bartel, P. and Jooste, P. (1981). Slow-wave sleep: a recovery period after exercise. *Science*, *214*, 1253–1254. ▶ **pages 155, 220**

Shaver, P.R., Furman, W. and Buhrmester, D. (1985). Transition to college: network changes, social skills and loneliness. In S. Duck and D. Perlman (eds) *Understanding Personal Relationships: An Interdisciplinary Approach*. London: Sage. ▶ **page 104**

Sheehy, R.S. and Horan, J.J. (2004). The effects of stress-innoculation training for first year law students. *International Journal of Stress Management*, 11, 44–55. ▶ **page 171**

Sheingold, K. and Tenney, Y.J. (1982). Memory for a salient childhood event. In U. Neisser (ed.) *Memory Observed*. San Francisco: W.H. Freeman. ▶ **page 90**

Sheldon, W.H. (1942). *The Varieties of Temperament: A Psychology of Constitutional Differences*. New York and London: Harper and Brothers. ▶ **page 196**

Sheline, Y.I., Sanghavi, M., Mintun, M.A. and Gado, M.H. (1999). Depression duration but not age predicts hippocampal volume loss in women with recurrent major depression. *Journal of Neuroscience*, *19*, 5034–5043. ▶ **page 91**

Sherif, M., Harvey, O.J., White, B.J., Hood, W.R. and Sherif, C.W. (1961). *Intergroup Co-operation and Conflict: The Robbers Cave Experiment*. Norman: University of Oklahoma Press. ▶ **page 61**

Shumaker, S.A. and Hill, D.R. (1991). Gender differences in social support and physical health. *Health Psychology*, *10*, 102–111. ▶ **page 141**

Siddique, C. and D'Arcy, C. (1984). Adolescence, stress and psychological well-being. *Journal of Youth and Adolescence*, *13*, 459–474. ▶ **page 139**

Sieber, J.E. and Stanley, B. (1988). Ethical and professional dimensions of socially sensitive research. *American Psychologist*, 43, 49–55. ▶ **pages 56, 127**

Siegel, J.M. (2003). Why we sleep. *Scientific American*, November, 92–97. ▶ **page 154**

Siegel, J.M. and Rogawski, M.A. (1988). A function for REM sleep: regulation of noradrenergic receptor sensitivity. *Brain Research Review*, *13*, 213–33. ▶ **page 154**

Siegel, J.M., Nienhuis, R., Gulyani, S., Ouyang, S., Wu, M.F., Mignot, E., Switzer, R.C., McMurry, G. and Cornford, M. (1999). Neuronal degeneration in canine narcolepsy. *Journal of Neuroscience*, *19*(1), 248–257. ▶ **page 159**

Sigall, H. and Ostrove, N. (1975). Beautiful but dangerous: effects of offender attractiveness and nature of the crime on juridic judgement. *Journal of Personality and Social Psychology, 31*, 410–414. ▶ **pages 103, 201**

Simmons, R. and Blyth, D. (1987). *Moving into Adolescence: The Impact of Pubertal Change and School Context*. New York: Aldine de Gruyter. ▶ **page 139**

Simon, H.A. (1974). How big is a chunk? *Science*, *183*, 482–488. ▶ **page 87**

Simons, A.D., Gordon, J.S., Monroe, S.M., and Thase, M.E. (1995). Toward an integration of psychologic, social, and biologic factors in depression: effects on outcome and course of cognitive therapy. *Journal of Consulting and Clinical Psychology*, *63*, 369–377. ▶ **page 239**

Simpson, J., Collins, W.A., Tran, S. and Haydon, K. (2007). Attachment and the experience and expression of emotion in romantic relationships: a developmental perspective. *Journal of Personality and Social Psychology*, *92*(2), 355–367. ▶ **page 103**

Sindelar, J., Elbel, B. and Petry, N.M. (2007). What do we get for our money? Cost-effectiveness of adding contingency management. *Addiction*, *102*(2), 309–316. ▶ **page 168**

Singer, P. (1975). *Animal Liberation*. New York: Avon. ▶ **page 58**

Slater, M.R. and Sewell, D.F. (1994). An examination of the cohesion-performance relationship in university hockey teams. *Journal of Sports Sciences*, *12*, 423–431. ▶ **page 219**

Slavin, R.E. (1991). *Educational Psychology: Theory into Practice*, 3rd edn. Englewood Cliffs, NJ: Prentice-Hall. ▶ **page 185**

Sloan, F.A. and Wang, Y. (2008). Economic theory and evidence on smoking behavior of adults. *Addiction*, *103*(11), 1777–1785. ▶ **page 167**

Smith, C. and Lloyd, B. (1978). Maternal behaviour and perceived sex of infant: revisited. *Child Development*, *49*, 1263–1265. ▶ **page 21**

Smith, E.R. and Mackie. D.M. (1995). *Social Psychology*. New York: Worth Publishers, Inc. ▶ **page 200**

Smith, K. and Crawford, S. (1986). Suicidal behavior among 'normal' high school students. *Suicide and Life Threatening Behavior*, *16*, 313–325. ▶ **page 139**

Smith, P. and Bond, M.H. (1998). *Social Psychology Across Cultures: Analysis and Perspectives*, 2nd edn. New York: Harvester Wheatsheaf. ▶ **page 74**

Snook, B., Cullen, R.M., Mokros, A. and Harbort, S. (2005). Serial murderers' spatial decisions: factors that influence crime location choice. *Journal of Investigative Psychology and Offender Profiling*, *2*, 147–164. ▶ **page 199**

Snowman, J. and Biehler, R. (2000). *Psychology Applied to Teaching*. Boston: Houghton Mifflin. ▶ **page 188**

Snyder, E.M., Yong, Y., Almeida, C.G., Paul, S., Moran, T., Choi, E.Y., Nairn, A.C., Salter, M.W., Lombroso, P.J., Gouras, G.K. and Greengard, P. (2005). Regulation of NMDA receptor trafficking by amyloid-beta. *Nature Neuroscience*, *8*(8), 1051–1058. ▶ **page 95**

Snyder, F. (1970). The phenomenology of dreaming. In L. Madow and L. Snow (eds) *The Psychodynamic Implications of the Physiological Studies on Dreams*. Springfield, IL: Thomas. ▶ **page 153**

Solms, M. (2000). Dreaming and REM sleep are controlled by different brain mechanisms. *Behavioral and Brain Sciences*, *23*, 843–850. ▶ **page 153**

Sommers, S.R. and Ellsworth, P.C. (2003). How much do we really know about race and juries? A review of social science theory and research. *Chicago–Kent Law Review*, *78*, 997–1031. ▶ **page 201**

Sonstroem, R.J. and Bernardo, P.B. (1982). Intraindividual pregame state anxiety and basketball performance: a re-examination of the inverted-U curve. *Journal of Sport Psychology*, *4*, 235–245. ▶ **page 217**

Soon, C., Brass, M., Heinze, H. and Haynes, J. (2008). Unconscious determinants of free decisions in the human brain. *Nature neuroscience, 11*(5), 543–545. ▶ **page 79**

Spanos, N.P. (1986). Hypnosis and the modification of hypnotic susceptibility: a social psychological perspective. In P. Naish (ed.) *What is Hypnosis?* Philadelphia: Open University Press. ▶ **page 151**

Spanos, N.P., Cobb, P. and Gorassini, D. (1985). Failing to resist hypnotic suggestions: a strategy for self-presenting as deeply hypnotised. *Psychiatry*, *48*, 282–293. ▶ **page 151**

Spearman, C. (1927). *The Abilities of Man: Their Nature and Measurement*. London: Macmillan Publishing. ▶ **page 120**

Spears, R., Lea, M. and Lee, S. (1990). De-individuation and group polarization in computer-mediated communication. *British Journal of Social Psychology*, *29*, 121–134. ▶ **page 109**

Spencer, S.J., Steele, C.M. and Quinn, D.M. (1999). Stereotype threat and women's math performance. *Journal of Experimental Social Psychology*, *35*, 4–28. ▶ **page 122**

Sperling. G. (1960). The information available in brief visual presentations, *Psychological Monographs*, *74*, Whole no. 498, 1–29. ▶ **page 87**

Spielman, A.J. and Glovinsky, P.B. (1991). The varied nature of insomnia. In Hauri, P.J. (ed.) *Case Studies in Insomnia*. New York: Plenum Medical Book Co. ▶ **page 159**

Squire, L.R., Ojemann, J.G., Miezin, F.M., Petersen, S.E., Videen, T.O. and Raichle, M.E. (1992). Activation of the hippocampus in normal humans: a functional anatomical study of memory. *Proceedings of the National Academy of Science USA*, 89, 1837–1841. ▶ **page 87**

St George-Hyslop, P.H. (2000). Genetic factors in the genesis of Alzheimer's disease. *Annals of the New York Academy of Sciences*, 924, 1–7. ▶ **page 95**

Stasser, G. and Stewart, D. (1992). Discovery of hidden profiles by decision-making groups: solving a problem versus making a judgement. *Journal of Personality and Social Psychology*, 63, 426–434. ▶ **page 201**

Sternberg, R.J. (1985). *Beyond IQ: A Triarchic Theory of Human Intelligence*. Cambridge: Cambridge University Press. ▶ **page 120**

Sternberg, R.J., Grigorenko, E.L., Ferrari, M. and Clinkenbeard, P. (1999). The triarchic model applied to gifted identification, instruction, and assessment. In N. Colangelo and S.G. Assouline (eds) *Talent Development III: Proceedings from the 1995 Henry B. and Jocelyn Wallace National Research Symposium on Talent Development*. Scottsdale, AZ: Gifted Psychology Press. ▶ **page 121**

Stevens, R.G. (2006). Artificial lighting in the industrialized world: circadian disruption and breast cancer. *Cancer Causes Control*, 17, 501–507. ▶ **page 157**

Stewart, J.E. III (1980). Defendant's attractiveness as a factor in the outcome of criminal trials: an observational study. *Journal of Applied Social Psychology*, 10, 348–361. ▶ **page 103**

Stickgold, R. (2005). Sleep-dependent memory consolidation. *Nature*, 437, 1272–1278. ▶ **page 154**

Stickgold, R., Malia, A., Maguire, D., Roddenberry, D. and O'Connor, M. (2000). Replaying the game: hypnagogic images in normals and amnesics. *Science*, 290, 350–353. ▶ **page 95**

Stigler, J.W. and Perry, M. (1990). Mathematics learning in Japanese, Chinese and American classrooms. In J.W. Stigler, R.A. Shweder and G. Herdt (eds) *Cultural Psychology: Essays on Comparative Human Development*. New York: Cambridge University Press. ▶ **page 185**

Storms, M.D. and Nisbett, R.E. (1970). Insomnia and the attribution process. *Journal of Personality and Social Psychology*, 16, 319 328. ▶ **page 159**

Strickland, B.R. (1978). Internal-external expectancies and health related-behaviour. *Journal of Consulting and Clinical Psychology*, 46(6): 1192–1211. ▶ **page 174**

Striegel-Moore, R.H., Silberstein, L.R. and Rodin, J. (1986). Toward an understanding of risk factors for bulimia. *American Psychologist*, 41, 246–263. ▶ **page 174**

Swain, A. (1996). Social loafing and identifiability: the mediating role of achievement goal orientation. *Research Quarterly for Exercise and Sport*, 67(3), 337–344. ▶ **page 219**

Sylva, K. (1987). Plowden: history and prospect. *Oxford Review of Education*, 13(1), 3–12. ▶ **page 185**

Sylvain, C., Ladouceur, R. and Boisvert, J.M. (1997). Cognitive and behavioural treatment of pathological gambling: a controlled study. *Journal of Consulting and Clinical Psychology*, 65, 727–732. ▶ **page 167**

Symister, P. and Friend, R. (2003). The influence of social support and problematic support on optimism and depression in chronic illness: a prospective study evaluating self-esteem as a mediator. *Health Psychology*, 22(2), 123–129. ▶ **page 106**

Takano, Y. and Osaka, E. (1999). An unsupported common view: Comparing Japan and the U.S. on individualism/collectivism. *Asian Journal of Social Psychology*, 2(3), 311–341. ▶ **page 74**

Tang, Y.P., Shimizu, E., Dube, G.R., Rampon, C., Kerchner, G.A., Zhuo, M., Liu, G. and Tsien, J.Z. (1999). Genetic enhancement of learning and memory in mice. *Nature*, 401(6748), 25–7. ▶ **page 125**

Tashiro, T. and Frazier, P. (2003). 'I'll never be in a relationship like that again.' Personal growth following romantic relationship breakups. *Personal Relationships*, 10, 113–128. ▶ **page 105**

Taylor, S.E. (1995). *Health Psychology*. London: McGraw-Hill. ▶ **page 172**

Taylor, S.E., Klein, L.C., Lewis, B.P., Grunewald, T.L., Gurung, R.A.R. and Updegraff, J.A. (2000). Biobehavioral responses to stress in females: tend-and-befriend, not fight-or-flight. *Psychological Review*, 107(3), 411–429. ▶ **page 77**

Tharyan, P. and Adams, C.E. (2005). Electroconvulsive therapy for schizophrenia. *The Cochrane Database for Systematic Reviews*, Issue 2. ▶ **page 235**

Thelwell, R.C. and Maynard, I. W. (2000). Professional cricketers' perceptions of the importance of antecedents influencing repeatable good performance. *Perceptual and Motor Skills*, 90, 649–658. ▶ **page 217**

Thibaut, J.W. and Kelley, H.H. (1959). *The Social Psychology of Groups*. New York: John Wiley and Sons. ▶ **page 102**

Thompson, D.M. (1988). Context and false recognition. In G.M. Davies and D.M. Thompson (eds) *Memory in Context: Context in Memory*. New York: Wiley. ▶ **page 205**

Thompson, P. (1980). Margaret Thatcher: a new illusion. *Perception*, 9(4), 483–484. ▶ **page 205**

Thurstone, L.L. (1938). Primary mental abilities. *Psychometric Monographs*, 1. ▶ **page 120**

Tienari, P., Wynne, L.C., Moring, J., Laksy, K., Nieminen, P. and Sorri, A. (1994). Finnish adaptive family study: sample selection and adoptee DSM-III-R diagnoses. *Acta Psychiatrica Scandinavica*, 101, 433–443. ▶ **page 232**

Tinbergen, N. (1951). *The Study of Instinct*. Oxford: Clarendon Press. ▶ **page 222**

Tindale, R.S., Davis, J.H., Volrath, D.A., Nagao, D.H. and Hinsz, V.B. (1990). Asymmetrical social influence in freely interacting groups: a test of three models. *Journal of Personality and Social Psychology*, 58, 438–449. ▶ **page 201**

Ting-Toomey, S. (1986). Conflict communication styles in black and white subjective cultures. *International and Intercultural Communication Annual*, 10, 75–88. ▶ **page 110**

Tonkin, A., Alderson, C. and Roberts, G. (2008). Spiral of learning. *Nursery World*, 108(4119), 26–26. ▶ **page 184**

Torrey, E.F. (2002). Studies of individuals never treated with antipsychotic medications: a review. *Schizophrenia Research*, 58(2–3), 101–115. ▶ **page 232**

Trevana, J. and Miller, J. (2009). Brain preparation before a voluntary action: Evidence against unconscious movement initiation. *Consciousness and Cognition*, 19(1), 447–456. ▶ **page 79**

Triplett, N. (1897). The dynamogenic factors in pacemaking and competition. *American Journal of Psychology*, 9, 507–533. ▶ **page 212**

Tsai, S.P., Wendt, J.K., Donnelly, R.P., de Jong, G. and Ahmed, F.S. (2005). Age at retirement and long-term survival of an industrial population: prospective cohort study. *British Medical Journal*, 21 October 2005, online doi: 10.1136/bmj.38586.448704.E0. ▶ **page 142**

Tuckey, M.R. and Brewer, N. (2003). How schemas affect eyewitness memory over repeated retrieval attempts. *Applied Cognitive Psychology*, 17, 785–800. ▶ **page 205**

Tully, M.A., Cupples, M.E., Hart, N.D., McEneny, J., McGlade, K.J., Chan, W-S. and Young, I.S. (2007). Evidence based public health policy and practice: randomised controlled trial of home-based walking programmes at and below current recommended levels of exercise in sedentary adults. *Epidemiology and Community Health*, *61*, 778–783. ▶ **page 221**

Tulving, E. and Psotka, J. (1971). Retroactive inhibition in free recall: inaccessibility of information available in the memory store. *Journal of Experimental Psychology*, *87*, 1–8. ▶ **page 93**

Turkheimer, E., Haley, A., Waldron, M., Onofrio, B. and Gottesman, I. (2003). Socioeconomic status modifies the heritability of IQ in young children. *Psychological Science*, *14*(6), 624–628. ▶ **page 72**

Turman, P.D. (2003). Coaches and cohesion: the impact of coaching techniques on team cohesion in the small group sport setting. *Journal of Sport Behavior*, *26*, 86–103. ▶ **page 218**

Turner, E.H., Matthews, A.M., Linardatos, E., Tell, R.A. and Rosenthal, R. (2008). Selective publication of antidepressant trials and its influence on apparent efficacy. *New England Journal of Medicine*, *358*(3), 252–260. ▶ **page 221**

Turner, J.C. and Helms, D.B. (1989). *Contemporary Adulthood*, 4th edn. Fort Worth, FL: Holt, Rinehart and Winston. ▶ **page 140**

UK Office of Statistics (2010). See www.statistics.gov.uk/cci/nugget.asp?id=949 (accessed July 2010). ▶ **page 143**

Ulmer, R.G., Preusser, D.F., Williams, A.F., Ferguson, S.A. and Farmer, C.M. (2000). Effect of Florida's graduated licensing program on the crash rate of teenage drivers. *Accident Analysis and Prevention*, *32(4)*, 527–532. ▶ **page 207**

Underwood, J. (1957). Interference and forgetting. *Psychological Review*, *64*, 49–60. ▶ **page 92**

United Nations (2004). Divorces and crude divorce rates by urban/rural residence: 2000–2004. See http://unstats.un.org/unsd/demographic/products/dyb/DYB2004/Table25.pdf (accessed July 2010). ▶ **page 141**

USDHHS (United States Department of Health and Human Services) (1998). *Preliminary Results from the 1997 National Household Survey on Drug Abuse*. DHHS Publication no. SMA 98–3251. Washington, DC: US Government Printing Office. ▶ **page 174**

Valentine, E.R. (1992). *Conceptual issues in Psychology*, 2nd edn. London: Routledge. ▶ **page 78**

Valins, S. (1966). Cognitive effects of false heart-rate feedback. *Journal of Personality and Social Psychology*, *4*(4), 400–408. ▶ **page 150**

Valzelli, L. (1973). The 'isolation syndrome' in mice. *Psychopharmacologia*, 31, 305–320. ▶ **page 202**

Van Cauter, E. and Plat, L. (1996). Physiology of growth hormone secretion during sleep. *Journal of Pediatrics*, *128*(2), S32–S37. ▶ **page 154**

van Den Brink, W. and Haasen, C. (2006). Evidence based treatment for opioid dependence. *Canadian Journal of Psychiatry*, *51*(10), 621–623. ▶ **page 169**

van Os, J., Fahy, T.A., Bebbington, P., Jones, P., Wilkins, S., Sham, P., Russell, A., Gilvarry, K., Lewis, S., Toone, B. and Murray, R. (1994). The influence of life events on the subsequent course of psychotic illness: a prospective follow-up of the Camberwell Collaborative Psychosis Study. *Psychological Medicine*, *24*(2), 503–513. ▶ **page 233**

Varma, S.L., Zain, A.M. and Singh, S. (1997). Psychiatric morbidity in the first degree relatives of schizophrenic patients. *American Journal of Medical Genetics*, *74*(1), 7–11. ▶ **page 232**

Virkkunen, M., Nuutila, A., Goodwin, F.K. and Linnoila, M. (1987). Cerebrospinal fluid monoamine metabolite levels in male arsonists. *Archives of General Psychiatry*, *44*, 241–247. ▶ **page 202**

Virkkunen, M., DeJong, J., Bartko, J., Goodwin, F.K. and Linnoila, M. (1989). Relationship of psychobiological variables to recidivism in violent offenders and impulsive fire setters. *Archives of General Psychiatry*, *46*, 600–603. ▶ **page 202**

Vogel, G. (1960). Studies in psychophysiology of dreams III. The dream of narcolepsy. *Archives of General Psychiatry*, *3*, 421–428. ▶ **page 159**

Volkow, N.D., Wang, G., Fowler, J.S., Logan, J., Gerasimov, M., Maynard, L., Ding, Y., Gatley, S.J., Gifford, A. and Franceschi, D. (2001). Therapeutic doses of oral methylphenidate significantly increase extracellular dopamine in the human brain. *Journal of Neuroscience*, *21*(2), 1–5. ▶ **page 167**

Voracek, M. and Haubner, T. (2008). Twin-singleton differences in intelligence: a meta-analysis. *Psychological Reports*, *102*(3), 951–62. ▶ **page 125**

Vygotsky, L.S. (1962). *Thought and Language*. Cambridge, MA: MIT Press. ▶ **page 118**

Vygotsky, L.S. (1987). The development of scientific concepts in childhood. In R.W. Rieber and A.S. Carton (eds) *The Collected Works of L.S. Vygotsky*, vol. 1. New York: Plenum Press. ▶ **page 185**

Wadeley, A. (2000). Adulthood. In M. Cardwell, L. Clark and C. Meldrum (eds) *Psychology for A2 Level*. London: Collins. ▶ **page 141**

Wagstaff, G.F. (1986). Hypnosis as compliance and belief. In P. Naish (ed.) *What is Hypnosis?* Philadelphia: Open University Press. ▶ **page 150**

Wahlsten, D. (1997). The malleability of intelligence is not constrained by heritability. In B. Devlin, S.E. Fienberg and K. Roeder (eds) *Intelligence, Genes and Success: Scientists Respond to the Bell Curve*. New York: Springer, 71–87. ▶ **page 127**

Wakefield, A.J., Murch, S.H., Anthony, A., Linnell, J., Casson, D.M., Malik, M., Berelowitz, M., Dhillon, A.P., Thomson, M.A., Harvey, P., Valentine, A., Davies, S.E. and Walker-Smith, J.A. (1998). Ileal-lymphoid-nodular hyperplasia, non-specific colitis and pervasive developmental disorder in children. *Lancet*, *351* (9103), 637–641. ▶ **page 16**

Walkerdine, V. (1984). *The Mastery of Reason: Cognitive Development and the Mastery of Reason*. London and New York: Routledge. ▶ **page 185**

Wallston, K.A., Wallston, B.S. and DeVellis, R. (1978). Development of the multidimensional health locus control scales. *Health Education Monographs*, *6*, 161–170. ▶ **page 174**

Walster, E. (1966). The assignment of responsibility for an accident. *Journal of Personality and Social Psychology*, *5*, 508–516. ▶ **page 205**

Walster, E., Aronson, V., Abrahams, D. and Rottman, L. (1966). The importance of physical attractiveness in dating behaviour. *Journal of Personality and Social Psychology*, *4*, 508–516. ▶ **pages 38, 103**

Walther, J.B. (1993). Impression development in computer-mediated interaction. *Western Journal of Communication*, 57, 381–398. ▶ **page 109**

Walther, J.B. and Tidwell, L.C. (1995). Nonverbal cues in computer-mediated communication and the effects of chronemics on relational communication. *Journal of Organizational Computing*, *5*(4), 355–378. ▶ **page 109**

Warrington, E. and Weiskrantz, I. (1968). New methods of testing long-term retention with special reference to amnesic patients. *Nature*, *217*, 972–974. ▶ **page 95**

Waterman, A.S. (1985). Identity in the context of adolescent psychology. *New Directions for Child Development*, *30*, 5–24. ▶ **page 137**

Watkins, D., Reghi, M. and Astilla, E. (1991). The-Asian-learner-as-a-rote-learner stereotype: myth or reality? *Educational Psychology*, *11*(1), 21–34. ▶ **page 186**

Watson, J.B. (1913). Psychology as the behaviourist views it. *Psychological Review*, *20*, 158–177. ▶ **page 68**

Watson, J.B. (1925). *Behaviorism*. New York: People's Institute Publishing Company. ▶ **page 72**

Watson, N.F., Goldberg, J., Arguelles, L. and Buchwald, D. (2006). Genetic and environmental influences on insomnia, daytime sleepiness and obesity in twins. *Sleep, 29*(5), 645–649. ▶ **page 159**

Waugh, N.C. and Norman, D. (1965). Primary memory. *Psychological Review, 72*, 89–104. ▶ **page 93**

Waynforth, D. and Dunbar, R.I.M. (1995). Conditional mate choice strategies in humans: evidence from 'lonely hearts' advertisements. *Behaviour, 132*, 755–779. ▶ **page 103**

Webb, W.B. (1982) Sleep and biological rhythms. In W.B. Webb (ed.), *Biological rhythms, sleep and performance*. Chichester, UK: John Wiley and Sons. ▶ **page 154**

Weiner, B. (1992). *Human Motivation: Metaphors, Theories and Research*. Thousand Oaks, CA: Sage. ▶ **pages 188, 216**

Wells, C.M., Collins, D. and Hale, B.D. (1993). The self efficacy-performance link in maximum strength performance. *Journal of Sports Sciences, 11*, 167–175. ▶ **page 215**

West, R. (2006). *Theory of Addiction*. Oxford: Blackwell. ▶ **pages 166, 167**

Westcott, M.R. (1982). Quantitative and qualitative aspects of experienced freedom. *Journal of Mind and Behavior, 3*, 99–126. ▶ **page 78**

White, C. and Edgar, G. (2010). Inequalities in healthy life expectancy by social class and area type: England, 2001–03. *Health Statistics Quarterly, 45*, 28–56. ▶ **page 174**

White, G.L., Fishbein, S. and Rutstein, J. (1981). Passionate love and the misattribution of arousal. *Journal of Personality and Social Psychology, 41*, 56–62. ▶ **page 42**

Whitty, M. and Gavin, J. (2001). Age/sex/location: uncovering the social cues in the development of online relationships. *Cyberpsychology and Behavior, 4*(5): 623–630. ▶ **page 109**

Whitty, M.T. (2002). Liar, liar! An examination of how open, supportive and honest people are in chat rooms. *Computers in Human Behavior, 18*, 343–352. ▶ **page 109**

Whitty, M.T. (2003). Cyber-flirting: playing at love on the Internet. *Theory and Psychology, 13*(3), 339–357. ▶ **page 109**

Wickless, C. and Kirsch, I. (1989). Effects of verbal and experiential expectancy manipulations on hypnotic susceptibility. *Journal of Personality and Social Psychology, 57*, 762–768. ▶ **page 151**

Wiederhold, B.K. and Wiederhold, M.D. (2008). Virtual reality for posttraumatic stress disorder and stress inoculation training. *Journal of Cybertherapy and Rehabilitation, 1*(1), 23–25. ▶ **page 171**

Wilcox, S. and Storandt, M. (1996). Relations among age, exercise, and psychological variables in a community sample of women. *Health Psychology, 15*, 110–113. ▶ **page 175**

Wilhelm, S., Steketee, G., Reilly-Harrington, N.A., Deckersbach, T., Buhlmann, U. and Baer, L. (2006). Effectiveness of cognitive therapy for obsessive-compulsive disorder: an open trial. *Journal of Cognitive Psychotherapy, 19*, 173–179. ▶ **page 237**

Williams, H.L., Lubin, A. and Goodnow, J.J. (1959). Impaired performance with acute sleep loss. *Psychological Monographs, 73*(14), whole no. 484. ▶ **page 155**

Williams, J.D. and Gruzelier, J.H. (2001). Differentiation of hypnosis and relaxation by analysis of narrow band theta and alpha frequencies. *International Journal of Clinical and Experimental Hypnosis, 49*, 185–206. ▶ **page 151**

Williams, L.M. (1994). Recall of childhood trauma: a prospective study of women's memories of childhood abuse. *Journal of Consulting and Clinical Psychology, 62*, 1167–1176. ▶ **page 91**

Williams, T.M. (1981). How and what do children learn from television? *Human Communication Research, 7*(2),180–192. ▶ **page 203**

Williams, W.M., Blythe, T., White, N., Li, J., Gardner, H. and Sternberg, R.J. (2002). Practical intelligence for school: developing metacognitive sources of achievement in adolescence. *Developmental Review, 22*, 162–210. ▶ **page 121**

Wilson, C.M. and Oswald, A.J. (2005). How does marriage affect physical and psychological health? A survey of the longitudinal evidence. See http://wrap.warwick.ac.uk/1466/1/WRAP_Wilson_twerp728.pdf (accessed July 2010). ▶ **page 140**

Wilson, D. (2005) Big Brother damages our health. *Guardian*, 13 August. See www.guardian.co.uk/media/2005/aug/13/bigbrother.comment (accessed May 2010). ▶ **page 60**

Winkleby, M.A., Robinson, T.N., Sundquist, J. and Kraemer, H.C. (1999). Ethnic variations in cardiovascular disease risk factors among children and young adults: findings from the third National Health and Nutrition Examination Survey, 1988–94. *Journal of the American Medical Association, 281*, 1006–1013. ▶ **page 174**

Wober, M. (1974). Towards an understanding of the Kiganda concept of intelligence. In J.W. Berry and P. Dasen (eds) *Culture and Cognition: Readings in Cross-cultural Psychology*. London: Methuen. ▶ **page 122**

Wolfgang, M.E. and Ferracuti, F. (1967). *The Subculture of Violence: Towards an Integrated Theory in Criminology*. London: Tavistock Publications. ▶ **page 223**

Wood, D.J. and Middleton, D.J. (1975). A study of assisted problem solving. *British Journal of Psychology, 66*, 181–191. ▶ **page 185**

Wood, D.J., Bruner, J.S. and Ross, G. (1976). The role of tutoring in problem-solving. *Journal of Child Psychology and Psychiatry, 17*, 89–100. ▶ **page 184**

Wood, J.T. and Duck, S. (eds) (1995) *Understudied Relationships: Off the Beaten Track*. Thousand Oaks, CA: Sage. ▶ **page 108**

Wood, W., Lundgren, S., Ouellette, J.A., Busceme, S. and Blackstone, T. (1994). Minority influence, a meta-analytic review of social influence processes. *Psychological Bulletin, 115*, 323–345. ▶ **page 201**

Worrell, J. and Remer, P. (1992). *Feminist Perspectives in Therapy: An Empowerment Model for Women*. Chichester: Wiley. ▶ **page 230**

Wright, D.B. (1993). Recall of Hillsborough disaster over time: systematic biases of 'flashbulb' memories. *Applied Cognitive Psychology, 7*, 129–138. ▶ **page 91**

Wright, E.F., Voyer, D, Wright, R.D. and Roney, C. (1995). Supporting audiences and performance under pressure: the home-ice disadvantage in hockey championships. *Journal of Sport Behavior, 18*, 21–28. ▶ **page 218**

Xiaohe, X. and Whyte, M.K. (1990). Love matches and arranged marriages: a Chinese replication. *Journal of Marriage and the Family, 52*(3), 709–722. ▶ **page 111**

Yamagishi, T. (2002). *Big-hearted Japanese: Illusion of Cultural Collectivism*. Tokyo: Nippon Keizai Shinbunsha. ▶ **page 75**

Yelsma, P. and Athappilly, K. (1988). Marital satisfaction and communication practices: comparisons among Indian and American couples. *Journal of Comparative Family Studies, 19*, 37–54. ▶ **page 141**

Yerkes, R.M. and Dodson, J.D. (1908). The relation of strength stimulus to rapidity of habit-formation. *Journal of Comparative Neurological Psychology, 18*, 459–482. ▶ **pages 212, 216**

Young, A.W., Hellawell, D. and Hay, D.C. (1987). Configural information in face perception. *Perception, 16*, 747–759. ▶ **page 205**

Young, E. (2008). Sleep tight. *New Scientist*, 15 March, 30–34. ▶ **page 154**

Zahariadis, P.N. and Biddle S.J.H. (2000). Goal orientations and participation motives in physical education and sport: their relationships in English schoolchildren. *Athletic Insight: The Online Journal of Sport Psychology, 2*(1). See www.

athleticinsight.com/Vol2Iss1/English_Children.htm (accessed October 2010). ▶ **page 215**

Zajonc, R.B. (1965). Social facilitation. Science, *149*, 269–274. ▶ **pages 218, 219**

Zajonc, R.B. (1968). Attitudinal effects of mere exposure. *Journal of Personality and Social Psychology* (Monograph), *9*, 1–29. ▶ **page 40**

Zajonc, R.B., Heingarter, A. and Herman, E.M. (1969). Social enhancement and impairment of performance in the cockroach. *Journal of Personality and Social Psychology*, 13, 83–92. ▶ **page 218**

Zebrowitz, L.A. (1997). *Reading Faces: Window to the Soul?* Boulder, CO: Westview Press. ▶ **page 101**

Zepelin, H. and Rechtschaffen, A. (1974). Mammalian sleep, longevity and energy metabolism. Brain, Behaviour and Evolution, *10*, 425–470. ▶ **page 155**

Zhang, J. (2005). Continual-activation theory of dreaming. *Dynamical Psychology*. See www.goertzel.org/dynapsyc/2005/ZhangDreams.htm (accessed May 2010). ▶ **page 153**

Zhang, L.F. and and Sternberg, R.J. (eds) (2009). *Perspectives on the Nature of Intellectual Styles*. Springer Publishing Company: New York. ▶ **page 187**

Zigler, E. and Butterfield, E.C. (1968). Motivational aspects of change in IQ test performance of culturally deprived nursery school children. *Child Development*, *39*, 1–14. ▶ **page 122**

Zimbardo, P.G., Banks, P.G., Haney, C. and Jaffe, D. (1973). Pirandellian prison: the mind is a formidable jailor. *New York Times Magazine*, 8 April, 38–60. ▶ **page 22**

INDEX AND GLOSSARY

3Rs Stands for replace, reduce and refine as a way to deal with ethical issues raised by the use of non-human animals in research. 59, 63

Abernethy, E.M 92

Abnormal psychology 227–42

Absolutist Morality. The view that some things are simply right or wrong and there is no relative position. For example, murder is wrong regardless of the circumstances. 58, 59

Accommodation In Piaget's theory of cognitive development, the process of adjusting or changing existing schemas because new, conflicting information creates disequilibrium. 118–19, 129

Achievement Motivation Inventory (AMI) 215

Acoustic 87

Activation-synthesis hypothesis 152–3

Activation 152

Active influence 73

Activity theory 142

Actor-observer effect People tend to make situational attributions for their own behaviour but dispositional attributions for the behaviour of others (those who are being observed). 204, 205, 209

Adams, G.R., Shea, J.A. and Fitch, S.A 133

Adaptive Any physical or psychological characteristic that enhances an individual's survival and reproduction, and is thus likely to be naturally selected. 12, 84, 157, 171, 225, 100, 138, 222, 102, 167, 111, 223, 125, 103, 155, 158, 170

Adaptive pressures 102

Adaptive value 111

Addiction A repetitive behaviour that increases the risk of disease and/or associated personal and social problems. Addictive behaviours continue despite moderate use or attempts to abstain. 164, 177, 167, 168–9, 170, 58, 172, 221, 63, 166, 222

Adolescence 131–46

Adoption studies 124, 127

Adrenaline A hormone associated with arousal of the autonomic nervous system, and also a neurotransmitter. 76, 91, 216, 221, 224

Adulthood 140–3

Afrocentrism 75

Ageing 220

Aggression 73, 80, 222

Aims A statement of what the researcher(s) intend to find out in a research study. 22, 24, 47, 164

Alcohol 166

Allele One of two (or more) forms of the DNA sequence in a particular gene. 124, 236

Allport, G. W. and Postman, L. J. 204

Alpha bias A tendency to exaggerate differences between men and women. 74, 76, 77, 81

Alternative hypothesis A testable statement about the relationship between two variables. 30–1, 32–3, 35, 36, 37, 38, 39, 41, 43

Alzheimer's disease/disorder A progressive disease where gradually more and more parts of the brain are damaged, leading to lapses of memory, confusion and other mental problems. 78, 83, 87, 94, 95, 97

Amnesia A profound loss of memory caused by physical damage or psychological trauma. 70, 83, 91, 94, 95, 96–7, 150–1

Amsterdam, B. 149

Amygdala A group of nuclei in the brain forming part of the limbic system and involved in emotional processing and memory. 95, 223, 225, 241

Anal stage In psychoanalytic theory, the second stage of psychosexual development when the organ focus of the id is on the anus.

Analgesia Something that relieves pain. 150

androcentric bias 76

Androcentric Centred or focused on men, often to the neglect or exclusion of women. 76, 81

Animal rights 58

Animal studies 95

Anorexia nervosa (AN) A type of eating disorder in which an individual, despite being seriously underweight, fears that she or he is or might become obese and therefore engages in self-starvation to prevent this happening. 221, 225, 230

Antagonist A drug that binds to a receptor but does not alter the activity of the receptor so reduces the potential for a response in the neuron, as distinct from an agonist. 169, 177, 234, 240

Anterior cingulate cortex A region of the brain involved in various autonomic functions as well as rational cognitive functions, such as reward anticipation, decision making, empathy and emotion. 202

Anterograde amnesia Loss of ability to create new memories after the event that caused the amnesia, as distinct from retrograde amnesia. 94–5, 97

Antidepressants A group of stimulant drugs which increase the production of serotonin and/or noradrenaline, and thus reduce symptoms of depression. 22, 59, 171, 220, 238, 239, 241

Antipsychotic A drug used to reduce psychotic symptoms. 233, 234, 235, 240

Anxiety 27, 90, 124, 134, 136, 138, 166, 170–1, 212–13, 216–17, 220–1, 224

Anxiety disorders A group of mental disorders whose primary symptom is extreme worry – the fear that something unpleasant is about to happen. 22, 124

Appearance–reality distinction What something looks like (its appearance) does not represent how things really are (reality). The ability (or inability) to understand this. 117–18, 129

Applied behaviour analysis The application of the principles of behaviorism to modify behaviour. 183, 190–1, 192–3

Approach-avoidance 214

Arousal 216–17

Articulatory process A component of the phonological loop which acts as an 'inner voice', i.e. words/sounds are verbally repeated. 88, 96

Asch, S.E. 13, 197, 200

Asperger's syndrome An autistic spectrum disorder where individuals are deficient in social skills, but, unlike others on the spectrum, have a normal IQ. Many individuals (although not all) exhibit exceptional skill or talent in a specific area. 190, 193

Assimilation In Piaget's theory of cognitive development, the process of fitting new experiences into existing schemas without making any change to the schema. 118, 128, 198

Association 24

Atchley, R.C. 142

Atkinson, R.C. and Shifrin, R.M. 86

Attachment is an emotional bond between two people. It is a two-way process that endures over time. It leads to certain behaviours such as clinging and proximity-seeking, and serves the function of protecting an infant. 100, 137, 139, 144

Attention deficit hyperactivity disorder (ADHD) A developmental disorder which is characterised by inappropriate inattention, impulsiveness and motor hyperactivity which is inappropriate for a child's age.

Attribution theory An account of how we explain the causes of our own and other people's behaviour to ourselves. 159, 161, 188, 189, 192, 201, 204, 216–17, 224

Attribution training A patient learns to attribute the causes of a target behaviour, such as insomnia, to another source and thus remove the problem. 189, 217

Attributional style An aspect of personality that indicates how people explain to themselves why they experience a particular event. 236

Attrition The loss of participants from a study over time, which is likely to leave a biased sample or a sample that is too small. 23, 46, 109, 239

Audience effects The observation that performance is enhanced if an audience is present. 212, 218

Autism A mental disorder on the autistic spectrum which usually appears in early childhood and typically involves avoidance of social contact, abnormal language and so-called 'stereotypic' or bizarre behaviours. 16, 121, 190, 191, 193

Autistic savants 121

Babyface hypothesis The suggestion that animals have an innate tendency to find infant-like features appealing (e.g. small nose, high forehead, little chin). 101, 103, 112

Baddeley, A.D. 87, 88

Baddeley, A.D. and Hitch, G.J. 88, 93, 96

Baddeley, A.D., Grant, S., Wright, E. and Thomson, N. 89

Bahrick, H.P., Bahrick, P.O. and Wittinger, R.P. 87

Bandura, A. 73, 202, 203, 214, 215, 221, 222

Bandura, A. and Walters, R.H. 222

Bar chart A graph used to represent the frequency of data. The categories on the x-axis have no fixed order and there is no true zero. 44, 47

Barbiturate A class of drugs that depresses the central nervous system. They were popular as an anti-anxiety treatment, but were very addictive and have now largely been replaced by benzodiazepines. 172, 177, 234

Bargaining 102

Bartlett, F.C. 204

Basal forebrain 'Basal' refers to the fact that this region is found in the 'basement' of the brain. The basal forebrain is a group of structures related to the production of acetylcholine which is involved in communication between brain cells. It is important in learning and memory as well as wakefulness and REM sleep. 94

Bateson, G., Jackson, D.D., Haley, J. and Weakland, J.H. 232

Baumrind, D. 71

Beck, A.T. 236

Becker, G.S. and Murphy, K.M. 166

Behaviour checklist A list of the behaviours to be recorded during an observational study. 19, 21, 26, 46–7

Behaviour management/behaviour modification treatment Techniques based on classical and operant conditioning (learning theory) where undesirable behaviours are changed through conditioning. 183

Behavioural categories Divisions of a target behaviour (such as stress or aggression) into subsets that can be measured. This can be done using a behaviour checklist (list of the behaviours to be recorded during an observational study) or a coding system (a systematic method for recording observations in which individual behaviours are given a code for ease of recording). 24, 26, 55, 136

Behavioural therapy Methods of treating psychological disorders through conditioning (classical and operant conditioning). Undesirable behaviours are unlearned. 22, 206–7

Behaviourism/behaviourist/behaviourist approach An approach to explaining behaviour that holds the view that all behaviour can be explained through experience – as a result of classical or operant conditioning (i.e. nurture or environment), referring only to the behaviours themselves rather than any internal mechanisms in order to explain behaviour. 11, 12–13, 68, 69, 182, 189, 212

Bell, R.A., LeRoy, J.B. and Stephenson, J.J. 107

Benek-Higgins, M.B., McReynolds, C.J., Hogan, E. and Savickas, S. 231

Bennett-Levy, J. and Marteau, T. 13

Benzodiazepines (BZs) A class of drug used to treat anxiety. BZs act as an inhibitory transmitter to slow down the activity of the central nervous system. 171, 177

Bereavement 142–3, 145

Berger, A.

Berkowitz, L. 222–3

β-amyloid (β-amyloid protein 42) A small protein produced in the brain, differing in structure from the normal β-amyloid protein 40, which builds up in the gaps between neurons in the brains of people with Alzheimer's disease, causing plaques. 94–5, 97

Beta bias A tendency to minimise differences between men and women. 74, 76–7, 81

Beta-blockers Drugs that decrease anxiety by reducing the activity of adrenaline and noradrenaline which are part of the sympathomedullary response to stress. 217

Bias A systematic distortion. 19, 20, 21, 23, 24, 25, 27, 28, 32, 69, 74–5, 76–7, 81, 90, 109, 137, 138, 143, 146, 174, 204, 205, 230–1, 236, 239, 241

Binet-Simon Scale 116

Biological approach The view that all behaviour can be explained in terms of biological mechanisms, such as hormones, neurotransmiitters, brain activity and inherited influences (via genes). 11, 12, 75–6, 91, 164, 167, 202–3, 231

Biological determinism 78, 81

Biological influences 100

Biological rhythms Cyclical changes in the way bodily systems behave. 148, 157–8, 160

Bipolar disorder A mental illness which includes both manic and depressive episodes. Mania is characterised by an elevated and expansive mood, delusions, overactivity and impulsive behaviour. 227, 229, 230–1, 238, 240

Blos, P. 137, 138

Blos's psychoanalytic theory 136–7, 144

Blumstein, P. and Schwartz, P. 108

Bohman M. 203, 208

Bottom-up Processing which starts from the base elements of the system (the physical stimulus or data itself), as distinct from top-down processing. 198, 208

Bowlby, J. 100

BPS guidelines 59, 60, 62

Bradburn, N. 107

Brain scan A technique used to investigate the functioning of the brain by taking images of the living brain. This makes it possible to match regions of the brain to behaviour by asking participants to engage in particular activities while the scan is done. Brain scans are also used to detect brain abnormalities, such as tumours. Examples are CAT scan, PET scan, MRI scan. 59, 70, 80, 87, 89, 96, 233

Brain ventricles 232, 233

Brain-damaged patients 89

Brainstem The region of the brain connecting the brain to the spinal cord. Controls vital functions such as a heartbeat. 152–3, 159, 161

Bray, S.R. 219

Breast cancer 173

Breastfeeding 125

Briefing Discussion with participants before their active participation in a research study, including information on which to base informed consent. Contrast with 'debriefing'. 28

British Crime Survey (BCS) 196

Brooks-King, M. and Hurrell, H.G. 116

Brosnan, M. 34

Brown, R. and Kulik, J. 91

Bruner, J. 184, 193

Brunner, H.G., Nelen, M., Breakfield, X.O., Ropers, H.H. and van Oost, B.A. 203

Bryant, P 119

Buffering hypothesis 106, 107

Bulimia nervosa (BN) A type of eating disorder in which a person habitually engages in episodes of uncontrollable eating followed by self-induced vomiting or other compensatory behaviours. 221

Bunting, B.P. and Mooney, E. 123

Burnout The feeling of physical exhaustion and loss of motivation resulting from prolonged stress or frustration, usually associated with a stressful job. 189, 192

Buss, D.M. 13

Butler, A.C., Chapman, J.E., Forman, E.M. and Beck, A.T. 22

Cann, J., Falshaw, L., Nugent, F. and Friendship, C. 207

Canter, D.V. 199

Capacity This is a measure of how much can be held in memory. It is measured in terms of bits of information, such as number of digits. STM has a very limited capacity (fewer than seven 'chunks' of information), whereas LTM has potentially unlimited capacity. 86–7, 88, 92, 96–7

Cardiovascular disease Refers to any disorder of the heart (e.g. coronary heart disease, CHD) and circulatory system (e.g. hypertension – high blood pressure). 220

Carmichael, L., Hogan, P. and Walter, A. 204

Case study A research method that involves a detailed study of a single individual, institution or event. Case studies provide a rich record of human experience but are hard to generalise from. 21, 46, 70–1, 80, 89, 91, 96, 153, 230

Cataplexy Sudden and temporary loss of muscle tone. 158–9, 161

Catastrophe model 216–17

Catharsis The process of releasing pent-up psychic energy. 222–3, 225

Causal inference A conclusion drawn about the causes of an event. 188, 192

CBT *See Cognitive–behavioural therapy*

Ceci, S. 126, 127

Central executive A hypothetical construct in working memory that monitors and coordinates all other mental functions in working memory. 88, 89, 96

Central nervous system Comprises the brain and spinal cord. 155, 170

Central Tendency 47

Cerebral cortex The surface layer of the forebrain covering the brain like a tea cosy. 94, 97, 152, 161

Cerebrospinal fluid A clear fluid found in the spinal cord and between the skull and brain. Acts as a cushion for the brain and also has an immunological function. 159, 236, 241

Chance The extent to which something occurs randomly, i.e. in the absence of a discoverable cause. 30, 31, 35, 38, 174

Change blindness People's poor ability to notice large alterations in the visual scene. 16, 28

Chaos theory The understanding that small changes in initial conditions produce large differences in outcomes, meaning that simple determinist predictions are impossible, i.e. the world is more probabilistic ('chaotic') than determinist. 78

Charlton, T., Panting, C., Davie, R., Coles, D. and Whitmarsh, L. 203

Chemotherapy Treating psychological or physical illness using drugs. 230

Chi-squared test 36–7, 44, 47

Chromosome The X-shaped bodies that carry all the genetic information (DNA) for an organism. 21, 94, 124

Chunks/chunking Miller proposed that the capacity of STM can be enhanced by grouping digits or letters into meaningful units or 'chunks'. For example, it is easier to remember 100 1000 10 10000 than 10010001010000. 86–7, 96

Circadian rhythm A pattern of behaviour that occurs or recurs approximately every 24 hours, such as the sleep–wake cycle. 148, 156–7, 158–9, 160

Circular definition 89

Circular reactions A feature of the sensorimotor stage in Piaget's theory, to describe the repetitive actions which enable an infant to learn new schema linking sensory and motor experiences. 118

Classical conditioning Learning that occurs through association. A neutral stimulus is paired with an unconditioned stimulus, resulting in a new stimulus–response (S–R) link. 11, 68, 80, 179, 182–3, 192

Classification system Any system that groups similar things together. In psychopathology mental symptoms are grouped together as syndromes or illnesses, such as phobias or obsessive compulsive disorder, and these syndromes are grouped together into types, such as anxiety disorders. 198, 230–1, 240

Clinical depression A term used when a person has symptoms that fit the clinical characteristics of depression, i.e. their depression is considered to be a mental disorder. 91, 220, 225, 229–30, 237

Clinician A health professional, such as a doctor, psychiatrist, psychologist or nurse who deals with the diagnosis and treatment of mental disorder. 230–1

Closed question Questions with a range of answers from which respondents select one; produces quantitative data. Answers are easier to analyse than those from open questions. 20, 27, 46–7

Coaching A form of social facilitation, when two (or more) people) perform the same activity at the same time, enhancing each other's behaviour. 212, 219

Coaction effects The observation that performance is enhanced when working side by side (but not interacting) with another. 212, 218

Cochrane, R. 107

Code of Ethics and Conduct 28

Coding system A systematic method for recording observations in which individual behaviours are given a code for ease of recording. 19, 26, 46–7

Cognition The process of thought; knowing, perceiving or believing. 115, 119, 229, 238

Cognitive approach An approach to explaining behaviour which suggests that the key influence on behaviour is how an individual thinks about the situation. 11, 13, 78, 86, 164, 170, 184, 189, 232–3, 236–7, 241

Cognitive–behavioural hypothesis 221

Cognitive–behavioural therapy (CBT) An approach to the treatment of mental disorders combining both cognitive and behavioural approaches. 22, 78, 168, 169, 170, 176, 188, 192, 206, 234–5, 238–9

Cognitive development The changes in a person's mental structures, abilities and processes that occur over their lifespan. 13, 117–18, 119, 128, 184–5

Cognitive map An internal spatial representation of an individual's surrounding area. It includes landmarks and routes and enables the individual to find their way. 198, 208

Cognitive-neoassociation model 222

Cognitive style An individual's characteristic way of thinking. 121, 128, 186–7, 206

Cohort effect A group of participants that has unique characteristics because of time-specific experiences during their development, such as growing up during the Second World War. This can affect both cross-sectional studies (because one group is not comparable with another) and longitudinal studies (because the group studied is not typical). 23, 135, 144

Coleman, J.C. 138

Coleman, J.C. and Hendry, L. 138

Coleman's focal theory 138

Collaborative group work/learning Learners work together on the same task simultaneously, challenging each other's ideas and taking joint responsibility for the work. 184–5, 187, 193

Collectivist A culture characterised by the extent to which things are shared. Groups live and work together sharing tasks, belongings and valuing interdependence. Japan and Israel are examples of collectivist societies. 12, 74–5, 79, 81, 110–11, 112–13, 118, 119, 128, 137, 141, 143, 185, 189, 193

Commitment 102

Comorbidity The presence of two or more coexisting unhealthy (morbid) conditions or diseases. 237, 241

Comparison level A term used in social exchange theory to describe the standard against which all our relationships are judged. 102–3, 112

Comparison level for alternatives A term used in social exchange theory to describe the standard generated by other possible relationships. 102–3, 112

Competence 57

Compliance 150

Computer-mediated communication Any communication which takes place through computers. 108, 113

Concrete operational stage A stage in Piaget's theory of cognitive development that occurs between the ages of approximately seven and eleven. Logical thinking (operations) depends on concrete representation. 117–18, 128, 184

Concurrent validity A means of establishing validity by comparing an existing test/questionnaire with the one you are interested in. 19, 46

Condensation In psychoanalysis, an element of dreamwork that enables latent content of a dream to be transformed into manifest content by reducing detailed experiences to the fleeting images of a dream. 152, 154, 161

Conditioned response (CR) In classical conditioning the response elicited by the conditioned stimulus, i.e. a new association, has been learned so that the neutral stimulus (NS) produces the unconditioned response (UCR) which is now called the CR. 182–3

Conditioned stimulus (CS) In classical conditioning, the neutral stimulus (NS) after it has been paired with the unconditioned stimulus. The NS elicits the unconditioned response UCR, now called a conditioned response (CR). 182

Conditioning Learning a new response. 73, 184

Confederate An individual in a study who is not a real participant and has been instructed how to behave by the investigator/experimenter. Can act as the independent variable. 25, 200, 223

Confidentiality A participant's right to have personal information protected. 29, 34, 47, 56, 60, 62, 105

Conflict 138–9

Conformity A form of social influence that results from exposure to the majority position and leads to compliance with that position. It is the tendency for people to adopt the behaviour, attitudes and values of other members of a reference group. 18, 37, 197, 200–201, 208

Confounding variable A variable that is not the intended independent variable but which has an effect on the dependent variable. 18, 20, 24, 46, 174, 221, 225

Connectedness The extent to which a person is emotionally linked to another person. 137, 138–39, 145

Consciousness Being aware. 79, 134–5, 148–62

Conservation The ability to distinguish between reality and appearance, for example to understand that quantity is not changed even when a display is transformed. 117, 119

Consolidation The process by which memories are permanently stored. 94–5, 97, 153–4

Consonant syllables 87

Construct validity A means of assessing the validity or trueness of a psychological test by demonstrating the extent to which performance on the test measures an identified underlying theoretical belief. 19, 46, 122, 129

Content analysis A kind of observational study in which behaviour is observed indirectly in written or verbal material, such as interviews, conversations, books, diaries or TV programmes. 21, 46, 92, 97, 223

Content validity A means of assessing the validity or trueness of a psychological test or measurement. It aims to demonstrate that the content (e.g. questions) of the test/measurement represents the area of interest. 19, 46, 122, 129

Context dependent learning People respond differently in different situations because they have observed that a particular behaviour (such as aggression) is rewarded in some situations and not others. 92, 168, 239

Contextualization 48

Contingency management 169

Continual–activation theory of dreaming 153

Continuity 110–11

Continuity hypothesis 100

Control condition/group The condition (in a repeated measures design) or group (in an independent groups design) that provides a baseline measure of behaviour without the experimental treatment (IV), so that the effect of the experimental treatment can be assessed. 24, 155, 161

Controlled observation A form of investigation in which behaviour is observed but under artificial/fixed/contrived conditions, as opposed to a naturalistic observation. 21–2, 26, 46, 65–82

Conway, M. A., Anderson, S. J., Larsen, S. F., Donnelly, C. M., McDaniel, M. A., McClelland, A.G.R., Rawles, R. E. and Logie, R. H. 91

Core sleep Sleep that is vital to physical and psychological health, as distinct from optional sleep. 155

Correlation coefficient A number between −1 and +1 that tells us how closely the co-variables in a correlational analysis are related. 32, 34, 35

Correlation/correlational analysis Determining the extent of a relationship between two variables; co-variables might not be linked at all (zero correlation), they could both increase together (positive correlation) or as one co-variable increases, the other decreases (negative correlation). Usually a linear correlation is predicted, but the relationship can be curvilinear. 16, 20, 24, 32, 34, 35, 44, 46–7, 106, 108, 120, 124

Cortex *See Cerebral cortex*

Cortisol A hormone produced by the adrenal gland that is associated with stress. 91

Cost-benefit approach 71, 80

Cost–benefit analysis A comparison between the costs of something and the related benefits, in order to decide on a course of action. If the costs are too great or the benefits too small, then no action will be taken. 70, 80, 172, 177

Cottrell, N.B. 219

Counterbalancing An experimental technique used to overcome order effects. Counterbalancing ensures that each condition is tested first or second in equal amounts. 41

Counterconditioning Being taught a new association that is the opposite of the original association, thus removing the original association. 183, 192

Couples Coping Enhancement Training (CCET) 105

Co-variable A variable in a correlation analysis that is believed to vary systematically with another co-variable. 20, 34, 35

Covert observation Observing people without their knowledge, e.g. using one-way mirrors. Knowing that your behaviour is being observed is likely to alter your behaviour. 26, 47, 80

Craik, F.I.M. and Lockhart, R.S. 88, 96

Craik, F.I.M. and Tulving, E. 89

Crime 196, 198, 202–3, 209

Crime scene analysis The process used in US profiling of offenders which takes information from the incident to place it within a 'type' from a pre-existing classification. 198

Criterion validity A means of assessing validity by demonstrating the extent to which people who do well on the test do well on other things that you would expect to be associated with the test. 122, 129

Critical period A limited window in biological development during which certain characteristics develop. 70

Critical value The value that a test statistic (observed value) must reach in order for the null hypothesis to be rejected. 33–4, 35, 36–7, 47

Cross-cultural research/study A kind of natural experiment in which the IV is different cultural practices and the DV is a behaviour such as attachment. 23, 46, 75, 81, 95, 103, 110–11, 112, 186, 189, 193

Cross-race effect The decreased ability to recognise people from a different racial group to one's own. 204

Cross-sectional study One group of participants of a young age is compared with another older group of participants with a view to investigating the effect of age on the behaviour in question. 23, 46

Cue-dependent forgetting Failure to remember as a result of the absence of suitable retrieval cues. People are able to remember more (forget less) if they are given the category names (cues) of words they have to memorise. 92–3, 97

Cued recall A method of testing memory where participants are given material to be learned and then they are given cues (such as category names) to enhance recall when they are tested. This allows a researcher to discover all the words that are available, not just those that are currently accessible. 93, 94, 97

Culnan, M.J. and Markus, M.L. 108

Cultural inflences 118

Cultural neuropsychology The study of how the social environment affects the development and function of the human brain and nervous system. 75

Cultural relativism The view that one cannot judge a behaviour properly unless it is viewed in the context of the social environment in which it originates. 72, 74, 80–1

Culture bias The tendency to judge all people in terms of your own cultural assumptions. This distorts or biases your judgement. 74–5, 81, 120, 122, 127, 129, 135, 143, 144, 185, 189, 193, 230–1, 240

Culture The rules, customs, morals and ways of interacting that bind together members of a society or some other collection of people. 12, 23, 46, 55, 72, 74, 75, 80–1, 100, 103, 110–11

Cumming, E. and Henry, W.E. 142

Curry, L. 186

Curry's onion model 186–7, 192

Cycle safety 164

D$_2$ receptors Part of the dopaminergic system in the brain. This type of receptor is targeted by antipsychotic drugs during the treatment of the positive symptoms of schizophrenia. 234

Davies, P.G., Spencer, S.J. Quinn, D.M. and Gerhardstein, R. Debriefing 28

Davies, N.B. and Houston, A.I. 218

Debriefing A post-research interview or questionnaire designed to inform the participants of the true nature of the study and to restore them to the same state they were in at the start of the study. It can also gain useful feedback about the procedures used in the study. 28, 47, 57, 62, 71

Decay An explanation for forgetting where the memory trace in our brain disintegrates over time and so is lost. 86, 92–3, 97

Decentration The ability to focus on more than one aspect of a problem, overcoming the problem of centration. 118

Deception Not telling a participant the true aims of a study (e.g. what participation will involve) and so they cannot give truly informed consent. 28–9, 47, 56–7, 62, 71, 103

Declarative memory A subdivision of long-term memory concerned with knowledge related to 'knowing that' as distinct from 'knowing how' (procedural memory). 94

Deductive model A form of reasoning from the general to the particular, e.g. developing a 'hypothesis from a theory'. 54

Deep processing 89

Degrees of freedom (*df*) The number of values which are free to vary given that the overall total values are known. 33, 36, 37, 47

Deindividuation A psychological state in which individuals have lowered levels of self-evaluation (e.g. when in a crowd or under the influence of alcohol) and decreased concerns about evaluation by others. 108–9, 113

Delayed sleep phase disorder A disorder where a person's major sleep episode is delayed by two or more hours of the desired bedtime. 157, 158–9, 160

Demand characteristics A cue that makes participants aware of what the researcher expects to find or how participants are expected to behave. Demand characteristics can change the outcome of a study because participants will often change their behaviour to conform to the expectations. This may act as a confounding variable. 18, 20, 46, 5, 62, 69, 117

Dennett, D. 78, 148

Dependent variable (DV) A measurable outcome of the action of the independent variable in an experiment. 18, 20, 22, 23–4, 26, 54, 62, 93

Depression A common mental disorder characterised by feelings of sadness, lack of interest in everyday activities, and a sense of worthlessness. Depression can be triggered by a stressful life event or by biological changes. 8, 22, 68, 78, 90–1, 94, 96, 106–7, 158, 159, 170, 220–1, 225, 228–9, 230–1, 236–7, 238–9, 241

Derived etic approach A technique used to study people in different cultures that acknowledges the bias that is inherent in such studies. A derived etic may, for example, consider how such biases affect the data collected or the theory developed from the data. 75, 81

Descriptive statistics Methods of summarising a data set, such as measures of central tendency and dispersion, and the use of graphs. 32, 44, 47

Determinism/determinist The view that an individual's behaviour is shaped or controlled by internal or external forces rather than an individual's will to do something. 11, 12, 13, 66, 69, 78–9, 80–1, 91, 167

Detoxification 168

Developmental approach 13

Developmental psychology 132

Diabetes 220

Diathesis–stress model The view that individuals inherit a susceptibility (diathesis) for a disorder which develops only if the individual is exposed to certain environmental conditions (stress). 72, 80, 159, 161, 167, 176, 232, 237, 240

Digit span technique A technique to assess the span of immediate (short-term) memory. Participants are given progressively more digits in a list to see how many can be recalled. 87, 96

Directional hypothesis States which of the conditions or groups of participants will be higher scoring, i.e. the nature of the predicted difference between them. 24, 33, 35–6, 41, 43, 47

Discontinuity 110–11

Discovery learning Learning through personal enquiry and constructing your own knowledge, rather than being told the answers to questions and presented with pre-constructed categories. 184–5, 193

Disorders of memory 94–5

Displacement An explanation for forgetting, where existing information is pushed out of memory by new information. 92–3, 97

Dissatisfaction 104

Dissociation occurs when a person's psychological functions lose integration and become separated into isolated units, as in dissociative amnesia and dissociative personality disorder (multiple personality disorder). 150–1, 160

Dissolution of relationships 104–5, 107

Distraction hypothesis 221

Divorce 140–1, 145

Dizygotic (DZ) twins Non-identical twins formed from two fertilised eggs (or zygotes). 72, 124, 130, 203, 232, 236

Dollard, J.R., Doob, L.W., Miller, N.E., Mowrer, O.H. and Sears, R.R. 222

Dopamine A neurotransmitter produced in the brain, involved in sexual desire and the sensation of pleasure. Unusually high levels of dopamine can be associated with schizophrenia. 154, 167–8, 176, 221, 225, 232–3, 234, 240–1

Double blind technique Neither the participant nor the experimenter dealing with the participants is aware of the research aims and other important details, and thus have no expectations. 18, 46, 233, 239

Down's syndrome (or Down syndrome) A mental and physical disorder caused by an innate but not inherited genetic condition (the presence of a third chromosome in pair 21). Individuals with Down's syndrome have distinctive facial features, mental retardation and may have some physical defects such as heart or gastrointestinal problems. 94, 96

DRD_2 gene 166

Dreaming 149, 152–3

Dreamwork In psychoanalysis, the processes that transform the latent content of a dream into manifest content. 152–3, 160

Drug use 58, 166

DSM The Diagnostic and Statistical Manual of Mental Disorders. A classification system of mental disorders published by the American Psychiatric Association. It contains typical symptoms of each disorder and guidelines for clinicians to make a diagnosis. The most recent version is DSM-IV-TR. 169, 231, 240

Dual-task performance An experimental technique where participants are presented with two or more stimuli and asked to attend or respond to all of them. 88

Duck, S.W. 104

Duration A measure of how long a memory lasts before it is no longer available. STM has a very limited duration (a memory in STM doesn't last long) whereas LTM has potentially unlimited duration. A memory in LTM could, theoretically, last for the whole of a person's life. 86–7, 92, 96, 108, 113

Dutton, D.G. and Aron, A.P. 42

Duty of care 60

Dweck 183, 189, 192, 213

Dyslexia A learning disability that affects literacy- and language-related skills; literally means 'difficulty with words'. 190–1, 193

DZ twins See Dizygotic twins

Ebbinghaus, H. 182

Ecker, C., Rocha-Rego, V., Johnston, P., Mourao- Miranda, J., Marquand, A., Daly, E.M., Brammer, M.J., Murphy, C. and Murphy, D.G. 190

Ecological validity A form of external validity concerning the ability to generalise a research effect beyond the particular setting in which it is demonstrated to other settings. Ecological validity is established by representativeness (mundane realism) and generalisability (to other settings). 9, 18–19, 20–1, 46, 54, 93, 201

ECT See Electroconvulsive therapy

Educational psychologist A psychologist trained to tackle the problems experienced by young people in education. This may include learning difficulties as well as social and behavioural problems. 180–94

EEA *See Environment of evolutionary adaptation*

EEG Electroencephalograph. A method of detecting activity in the living brain. Electrodes are attached to a person's scalp to record general levels of electrical activity. 79, 81, 148, 152, 155, 158, 161

Effect size A measure of the strength of the relationship between two variables. 22

Ego control The extent to which the ego can resist the demands of the id. 167, 176, 232, 241

Ego defence Unconscious methods, such as repression and displacement, which help the ego deal with feelings of anxiety and thus 'defend' the ego. 11, 136, 244, 232

Ego The conscious rational part of the personality. It develops by the end of an infant's first year, as a child interacts with the constraints of reality and thus is governed by the reality principle. 11, 90, 96, 136, 144, 153, 160, 167, 214

Ego-oriented People who measure their success in terms of outperforming others. 214–15, 224

Egocentric Seeing things from your own viewpoint and being unaware of other possible viewpoints. 118

Eich, E., Macaulay, D. and Ryan, L. 90

Elaborative rehearsal The deep semantic processing of information to be remembered resulting in the production of durable memories. This is in contrast to maintenance rehearsal, which involves simple rote repetition. 86, 96

Electroconvulsive therapy (ECT) The administration of a controlled electrical current through electrodes placed on the scalp induces a convulsive seizure which can be effective in relieving an episode of major depression. 228, 231, 234–5, 238–9, 240–1

Electroencephalogram *See EEG*

Electromyograph (EMG) A method of detecting the electrical potential generated by muscle cells (e.g. to identify loss of muscle tone in REM sleep). 79, 81

Elementary mental functions In Vygotsky's theory of cognitive development, those mental abilities that are innate, such as attention and perception. 118, 128

Elliott, J. 191

Embedded Figures Test (EFT) 181, 186

Emic approach 75

Emic–etic distinction 75

Empirical Relating to a method of gaining knowledge which relies on direct observation or testing. 54, 62, 136–7, 144, 180, 187, 189, 192, 233

Encoding specificity principle An explanation for enhanced memory recall. Memory is best when there is a large overlap between the information available at the time of retrieval and the information in the memory trace. 93

Encoding The way information is changed so it can be stored in memory. Information enters the brain via the senses (e.g. eyes and ears). It is then stored in various forms, such as visual codes (like a picture), acoustic forms (sounds) or semantic forms (the meaning of the experience). Information in STM is mainly encoded acoustically (i.e. information is represented as sounds), whereas information in LTM tends to be encoded semantically (i.e. information is represented by its meaning). 86–7, 96, 204

Endogenous pacemakers Internal mechanisms that govern internal, biological bodily rhythms. 156–7

Endorphins Neurotransmitters released in response to pain that act as the body's natural painkiller. 221, 225

Energy conservation 154

Engram 92

Enhanced memory 90

Enhanced Thinking Skills (ETS) 206–7

Entrainment The process of bringing bodily rhythms into synchronisation with an external influence. 156

Environment All the factors that can affect development aside from those that are inherited, i.e. nurture rather than nature. 72–3, 80–1, 118, 124, 126–7, 132

Environment of evolutionary adaptation (EEA) The environment to which a species is adapted and the set of selection pressures that operated at this time. For humans, this is thought to be the African savannah approximately two million years ago. 12, 102, 112

Epigenetics The study of heritable changes in gene function that occur without a change in the DNA sequence. 72, 80

Episodic buffer Receives input from many sources, temporarily stores this information, and then integrates it in order to construct a mental episode of what is being experienced right now. 88, 96

Episodic memory Memory for events. 87, 96, 154

Epstein, J. 214

Equilibration A balance between existing schemas and new experiences. 118, 128

Erikson, E.H. 110, 132–8

Erikson's lifespan theory 134–5, 144

Erikson's psychosocial theory 136–7, 144

Eron, L.D., Huesmann, L.R., Leftowitz, M.M. and Walder, L.O. 203

Esteem needs 188

Ethical committee A group of people within a research institution that must approve a study before it begins. 28–9, 47, 57, 62, 71, 80

Ethical costs 71

Ethical guidelines Concrete, quasi-legal documents that help to guide conduct within psychology by establishing principles for standard practice and competence. 56–7, 62–3, 71, 80

Ethical issues These arise in research where there are conflicting sets of values concerning the goals, procedures or outcomes of a research study. 13, 22, 26, 28–9, 46–7, 52, 55, 56–7, 58, 60–1, 62–3, 70–1, 80, 105, 117, 125, 173, 183, 206, 209, 235

Ethnocentricism Believing that one's own ingroup (e.g. religious group, nation, gender) is superior to other cultures. 74, 81, 99

Ethology/ethologists Promote the use of naturalistic observation to study animal behaviour and focus on the importance of innate capacities and the functions of behaviours in making an individual better adapted to its environment. 58, 63, 222–3, 225

Etic approach 75

Eugenics 73, 116

Eurocentrism A special form of ethnocentricism, based on a European perspective. 74

Evaluation apprehension The concern or anxiety felt when being assessed by someone else. 213, 219, 225

Event sampling An observational technique in which a count is kept of the number of times a certain behaviour (event) occurs. 25, 26, 47

Event-specific amnesia 91

Evolution The constant process of change in all species. 84, 90, 100, 109

Evolutionary approach Explaining species' different physical and behavioural characteristics in terms of the principle of natural selection. 12, 69, 80, 103, 138, 154–5, 157

Exogenous zeitgebers Time-givers that are externally caused and entrain biological rhythms. 156–7, 161

Experiment/experimental A research method to investigate causal relationships by observing the effect of an independent variable on the dependent variable. 18–19, 20–1, 24, 26, 38, 46–7, 68

Experimental condition/group The condition (in a repeated measures design) or group (in an independent groups design) containing the independent variable. 24

Experimenter bias The effect that the experimenter's expectations have on the participants and thus on the results of the experiment. 69, 80

Experimenter effect Anything that the experimenter does that has an effect on a participant's performance in a study, other than what was expected. 20, 46, 69

Explicit memory Memory that is based on conscious recollection as distinct from implicit memory which is beyond conscious awareness. 94–5, 97

Exposure effect 40, 104

External attribution A belief that a behaviour has been caused by factors outside personal control (i.e. situational rather than situational attribution). 188, 216

External cues 92

External locus of control (LoC) The belief that one's behaviour and experience are caused by events outside their own control (externals). 174

External reliability A calculation of the extent to which a measure varies from another measure of the same thing over time. This can be assessed using the test–retest method. 19, 46, 122, 129, 130

External validity (EV) The degree to which a research finding can be generalised to, for example, other settings (ecological validity), other groups of people (population validity) and over time (historical validity). 18–19, 20, 24, 46, 55, 62, 122, 129, 173, 177

Extramarital affairs 104

Extraneous variable In an experiment, any variable other than the independent variable that might potentially affect the dependent variable and thereby confound the results. 18, 20, 24, 46, 54, 62, 111, 185, 193

Extrinsic motives Factors arising outside the individual which increase the likelihood of a behaviour being performed. 188, 214, 224

Extrovert An individual who is outgoing and impulsive, and seeks greater excitement and more dangerous pastimes. This is because they have a lower level of cortical arousal and therefore need more stimulation to experience the same sense of excitement as introverts. 119, 197, 219

Eyewitness testimony (EWT) The evidence provided in court by a person who witnessed a crime, with a view to identifying the perpetrator of the crime. The accuracy of eyewitness recall could be affected during initial encoding, subsequent storage and eventual retrieval. 16, 24, 42, 204, 209

Eysenck Personality Questionnaire (EPQR-S) 197

Eysenck, H.J. and Eysenck, S.B.G. 197

Face validity A means of establishing validity by considering the extent to which a test or questionnaire looks as if it is measuring what it intends to measure. 122

Facet theory 198

Facilitated communication 190, 191

Factor analysis A statistical technique used to identify the variables that explain correlations between scores on tests of different abilities. 120, 122

False belief A mistaken opinion resulting from incorrect reasoning. 168, 176, 202

False memories 91

Falsification/falsify The attempt to prove something wrong. 54, 62, 69, 153

Family 100

FBI 198

Feminist psychologists Psychologists who emphasise the importance and value of women, as well as issues related to power imbalance and minority groups. 77, 81

Field dependence A tendency to see the perceptual field as a whole. A field-dependent learner is less analytical, not attentive to detail. 181, 186, 192

Field experiment A controlled experiment conducted outside a laboratory. The IV is still manipulated by the experimenter, and therefore causal relationships can be demonstrated. 18, 20, 46, 205

Fight or flight response A term which literally means an animal is energised either to engage in a retaliatory response or run away, but now means a general state of energised readiness. 76, 77, 81, 216, 221

Flashbulb memory Accurate and long-lasting memories formed at times of intense emotion, such as significant public or personal events. It is a memory of the context rather than the event itself. 90–1, 96

Flynn effect 72

fMRI scans (Functional magnetic resonance imaging) A method used to scan brain activity while a person is performing a task. It enables researchers to detect those regions of the brain that are rich in oxygen and thus are active. 89, 111

Focal theory A framework for considering how adolescents cope with age-related psychosocial transitions by focusing on issues one at a time. 138–9, 145

Foraging requirements 154

Forensic psychology 196–210

Forgetting 92, 97

Formal operational stage/formal operation In Piaget's theory of cognitive development, the fourth and final stage of development where an individual is capable of abstract, systematic and reflective thinking. 118–19

Free recall In a memory study, participants are allowed to recall items in any order they wish. 93, 97

Free will The view that our behaviour is determined by our own will rather than by other forces (the determinist position). 11, 12, 78–9, 81

Freud , S. 90, 91, 236

Freud's psychoanalytic theory of dreaming 152–3, 160

Freudian Anything related to the works of Sigmund Freud, or a follower of Freud's personality theory and therapy. 78–9, 81, 100, 148

Frontal cortex The front region of the cerebral cortex, contains the motor cortex and prefrontal cortex. Involved in fine motor movement and thinking. 150

Frontal lobe A region in each hemisphere of the forebrain. It is located in front of (anterior to) the central sulcus and above the lateral fissure. It contains the prefrontal cortex. 121, 128, 152,

Frustration-aggression theory 222–3, 225

Fundamental attribution error (FAE) The tendency to explain the causes of another person's behaviour in terms of their personality rather than in terms of situational factors. 204–5, 209

GABA (Gamma-amino-butyric acid) A neurotransmitter that regulates excitement in the nervous system, thus acting as a natural form of anxiety reducer. 158, 161, 170, 176

Gabrieli, J.D.E. 95

Gallup, G.G. 149

Gambling 168–9, 176

Gardner, B.T. and Gardner, R.A. 13

Gardner, H. 120–1

Garner, D.M., Garfinkel, P.E., Schwartz, D. and Thompson, M. 1980 21

Geisler, G.W.W. and Leith, L.M. 213

Gelkopf, M., Levitt, S. and Bleich, A. 166

Gender bias The differential treatment or representation of men and women based on stereotypes rather than real differences. 65, 76–7, 81, 122, 129, 135, 137, 144, 201, 207, 230–1, 240

Gender stereotypes 21

Gene mapping Determining the effect of a particular gene on physical or psychological characteristics. 72, 80

General adaptation syndrome (GAS) Selye's GAS model describes how, through physiological changes in the body, an organism copes with stress in an adaptive way. The model is characterised by three progressive stages that are part of this adaptive process: alarm, resistance and exhaustion. 16, 106

General intelligence 120

Generalisability The extent to which research findings can be applied from a particular research study to the population from which the sample was drawn, or to the world in general. 18, 20, 25, 46, 157

Genes/genetic A unit of inheritance which forms part of a chromosome. Genes control the characteristics (traits) that we inherit from parents. 12, 23, 68, 72–3, 79, 80–1, 94–5, 97, 102–3, 116, 124–5, 129, 132, 135, 141, 158–9, 166–7, 196, 202, 208, 231–2, 233, 236–7, 240–1

Genetic determinism 78, 81

Genetic engineering The deliberate manipulation of the genes of an unborn child, with the intent of making them 'better' in some way, e.g. less aggressive. 125, 129

Genetic heritability 124

Genetic influences 80

Genetic markers 124, 125

Genital stage In psychoanalytic theory, the final stage of psychosexual development when the organ focus is on the genitals, as it was in the phallic stage, but this time in relation to the onset of puberty and adult sexual relations. 132, 136

Geographical profiling A technique for predicting likely characteristics of an offender (e.g. where they live or work) using information about the location of crimes. 198–9, 208

Gibson, E.J. and Walk, R.D. 13

Gifted children 191

Gill, D.L. 217

Gilligan, C. 76, 77

Goal perspective theory 214–15, 224

Goldacre, B. 16

Gollin test A psychological test used to assess a person's implicit and explicit memory using a series of previously seen drawings that become progressively more complete and thus more recognisable. 94–5, 97

Gould's consciousness theory 134–5

Gould's evolution of adult consciousness theory 144

Graphs 44, 47

Grasha-Riechmann Student Learning Style Scale 186

Grasha, A.F. 186–7

Grasha's six learning styles 186–7

Gredler, M. 119

Greendale, G.A., Barrett-Connor, E., Edelstein, S., Ingles, S. and Halle, R. 174

Greenfield, P.M. 127

Grieve, F.G., Whelan, J.P. and Meyers, A.W. 219

Group cohesion 218–19

Group drug counseling 169

Group polarisation The tendency for opinions within a group to shift towards a more extreme view than the views held by individual group members. 201, 208

Group socialisation theory 127

Group-based relationships 110–11

Growth hormone (GH) A hormone that stimulates growth and cell reproduction. 148, 154, 161, 221

Halo effect The tendency for the total impression formed about an individual to be unduly influenced by one outstanding trait. 102, 112

Hardy, L., Parfitt, G. and Pates, J. 217

Hare-Mustin, R.T. and Marecek, J. 74

Harlow, H. 58

Hatfield, E. and Walster, G.W. 42

Hazan, C. and Shaver, P. 100

Head shape 196

Health belief model (HBM) Aims to explain and predict health behaviours based on the attitudes and beliefs of individuals. 164, 172–3, 221

Health locus of control (HLC) The degree of control that people believe they possess over their personal health: an external HLC means they feel they have little control. 174

Health psychology 163–78

Heart disease 220

Heisenberg, W. 69

Hemisphere The forebrain is divided into two halves – also called hemispheres. Each half is largely the same, containing the same specialised regions with the exception of those functions that are lateralised, such as language. 40, 156

Heredity The process by which traits are passed from parents to their offspring, usually referring to genetic inheritance. 116, 132, 233

Heritability The ratio between (a) genetic variability of the particular trait, and (b) total variability in the whole population. 124–5, 129, 166

Heroin 168–9, 176

Herrnstein, R.J. and Murray, C. 127

Hibernation theory A variation of the evolutionary theory of sleep which suggests that sleep serves a similar adaptive purpose to hibernation. 154, 160–1

Hidden observer 151

Hierarchy of Needs 188, 193

High Scope/Perry Preschool Project 1226

Higher mental functions Vygotsky distinguished between lower and higher mental functions. The latter are socially acquired, mediated by social meanings, voluntarily controlled and exist as a link in a broad system of functions rather than as an individual unit. 118

Hilgard, E. 150, 151

Hindbrain An area of the brain located toward the rear and lower portion of a person's head, linking the brain with the spinal cord. It contains the cerebellum, pons, and medulla oblongata which co-ordinate motor activity, posture, equilibrium and sleep patterns, and regulate unconscious but essential functions, such as breathing and blood circulation. 152

Hippocampus A structure in the subcortical area of each hemisphere of the forebrain, associated with memory. It is part of the limbic system, therefore involved in motivation, emotion and learning. 73, 87, 91, 94, 95, 96–7

Histrionic personality disorder An enduring pattern of behavior consisting of unstable emotions, attention seeking and inappropriate flirtatiousness. The person's self-esteem is dependent on the approval of others rather than arising from a true feeling of self-worth. The word histrionic means dramatic or theatrical. 230, 240

HLA (Human leukocyte antigen) A group of proteins that are essential elements of the immune system. They differentiate self cells and non-self cells (any cell displaying that person's HLA type belongs to that person and therefore is not an invader). 158–9, 161

HM case study 70, 71, 80, 87, 94, 95

Hobbs, T.R. and Holt, M.M. 207

Hobson, A. & McCarley, R. 152

Hobson, J.A. 152

Holism/holists Perceiving the whole display rather than the individual features and/or the relations between them.

Holmes, T.H. and Rahe, R.H. 140, 142

Home advantage effect The observation that home teams are likely to be more successful than visiting teams. 76–7, 91, 202–3, 218–19, 222

Hormones Chemical substances that circulate in the blood and only affect target organs. They are produced in large quantities but disappear quickly. Their effects are very powerful. 77, 91, 158, 161

Horne, J. 155

Horner, B.R. and Scheibe, K.E. 166

Hsu, F.L.K. 110

Hughes, M. 119

Humanistic approach Emphasises the uniqueness of each individual, their capacity for self-determination (free will) and drive for self-actualisation, and the importance of subjective experience. Humanistic psychology is a relatively recent development in psychology (post 1950). It is derived from the wider principles of humanism. 12, 189

Humphreys, L. 70, 71, 80

Hunt, C. and Andrews, G. 239

Hypnosis 150–1, 160

Hypnosis A wakeful state of focused attention and heightened suggestibility, with diminished peripheral awareness. 150–1, 160

Hypocretin A neurotransmitter that regulates sleep, appetite and energy conservation. 158–9, 162

Hypothalamus A part of the brain that functions to regulate bodily temperature, metabolic processes such as eating, and other autonomic activities including emotional responses. 156, 160

Hypothesis A precise and testable statement about the assumed relationship between variables. 20, 22, 24, 44, 47, 53, 77, 106, 107

Hypothetico-deductive reasoning An approach to problem solving where a person starts with many possible hypotheses and eliminates erroneous ones through testing, thus arriving at the correct solution. 118, 128

Id The irrational, primitive part of personality. It is present at birth, demands immediate satisfaction and is ruled by the pleasure principle, an innate drive to seek immediate satisfaction. 11, 152, 153

Identical twins The same as monozygotic twins, from one egg. 72, 78, 124, 129, 141, 236

Idiographic approach An approach to research that focuses more on the individual case as a means of understanding behaviour rather than formulating general laws of behaviour (the nomothetic approach). 12, 55, 62, 69, 80, 231

IGF2R 125

Immune response/system Produced by a system of cells within the body that is concerned with fighting against intruders such as viruses and bacteria. White blood cells (leucocytes) identify and eliminate foreign bodies (antigens). 21, 95, 154, 158, 161

Implicit memory A memory that is not based on conscious recollection, as distinct from explicit memory. 90, 94–5, 97

Imposed etic A technique or theory developed in one culture and then used to study the behaviour of people in a different culture with different norms, values, experiences, etc. 23, 46, 74–5, 81

Inattentional blindness The failure to notice a fully visible, but unexpected, object because attention was engaged on another task. 16

Independent groups design An experimental design where participants are allocated to two (or more) groups representing different experimental conditions. Participants are usually allocated using random techniques. 23–4, 33, 38, 42, 43, 44, 47

Independent variable (IV) An event that is directly manipulated by an experimenter in order to test its effect on another variable, the dependent variable (DV). 18, 20, 22, 24, 26, 42, 54, 75

Indigenous psychologies 75

Individual relationships 110–11

Individual zone of optimal functioning 216–17

Individualist A culture that values independence rather than reliance on others, in contrast to many non-Western cultures that could be described as collectivist. 74, 79, 103, 110, 119, 135, 137, 141, 144, 189

Individuation The process of becoming an individual, as distinct from others. The integration of separate characteristics into a well-functioning whole. 136, 139

Inductive model A form of reasoning from the particular to the general, e.g. developing a theory on the basis of a series of research studies. 54, 120

Inferential test statistics Procedures for drawing logical conclusions (inferences) about the population from which samples are drawn. 30–1, 32, 44, 45, 47

Informed consent A decision to participate based on comprehensive information given to potential participants in research about the nature and purpose of the research and their role in it. 28–9, 34, 47, 56–7, 60, 62, 80, 117, 235

Infradian rhythm A pattern of behaviour that occurs more often than once a day, such as the cycle of sleep stages that occurs every 90 minutes during sleep. 156

Inhelder, B., Sinclair, H. and Bovet, M. 119

Inherited Passed on usually from a previous generation. In psychology this usually refers to genetic inheritance. 72, 80, 123–4

Innate Behaviours that are a product of genetic factors. These may be apparent at birth or appear later through the process of maturation. 73, 101, 118, 122, 222, 225

Innate schema 118

Inner scribe A component of the visuo-spatial sketchpad of the working memory model, it is an active rehearsal component dealing with spatial and movement information. There also may be some storage component. 88

Insomnia Problems with falling asleep or staying asleep despite the opportunity to do so. 94, 149, 158–9, 161, 229

Institutional review board 29

institutionalisation 102

Integrity 57

Intelligence tests Tests of mental ability based on a theoretical view of what intelligence is. 23, 74, 116, 120, 122–3, 126, 190

Intelligence The ability to acquire information, to think and reason well, and to deal effectively and adaptively with the environment. 18, 72, 74, 80, 116, 120–1, 122, 172, 190, 198

Inter-interviewer reliability The extent to which two interviewers produce the same outcome from an interview. 19, 46

Inter-observer reliability The extent to which there is agreement between two or more observers involved in observations of a behaviour. 19, 46

Interference theory An explanation of forgetting whereby one set of information competes with another, causing it to be 'overwritten' or physically destroyed. There are two kinds of interference: proactive and retroactive. 92, 93

Internal attribution In attribution theory, accounting for an individual's behaviour in terms of their personality or disposition. 189, 192, 209, 216–17, 224

Internal cues 92

Internal Locus of control (LoC) Explaining your own behaviour in terms of personal control rather than external factors such as luck or the influence of others. 174, 188, 213, 216, 224

Internal reliability A measure of the extent to which something is consistent with itself. For a psychological test to have high internal reliability, all test items should be measuring the same thing. 19, 46, 122–3, 129

Internal validity Whether a study has tested what it set out to test; the degree to which the observed effect was due to the experimental manipulation rather than other factors such as extraneous variables. 18–19, 20, 46, 55, 62, 122–3, 129

Interpersonal coherence The assumption that an individual is consistent in their personality and behaviour (so predictions can be made from crime scene evidence about the offender's day-to-day life). 198, 208

Interval data A level of measurement where units of equal intervals are used, such as when counting correct answers or using any 'public' unit of measurement. 31, 40, 44, 47

Intervening variable A variable that comes between two other variables that is used to explain the relationship between those two variables. 20, 46, 143, 145

Interview A research method or technique that involves a face-to-face, 'real-time' interaction with another individual and results in the collection of data. 19, 20, 24, 27, 46, 106, 134, 141, 199

Intrapsychic process 104

Intrinsic motivation Goal-oriented behaviour that comes from inside an individual rather than from any external or outside rewards. 183, 214–15, 224

Introvert An individual who is more inward-focused and thoughtful than an extravert. 119

Inverted U hypothesis 216–17

Investigator effect Anything that the investigator does that has an effect on a participant's performance in a study, other than what was expected. 18, 23, 46, 55

Invincibility fable The tendency of adolescents to believe that they are immune from misfortune. 175, 177

IQ A person's score (their intelligence quotient) used to be calculated by dividing their test score by age. More recent tests use norms to work out a person's IQ based on their score and age. 18, 72, 78, 116, 120, 122, 123, 124, 129

IQ tests *See Intelligence tests*

Issac, C.L. and Mayes, A.R. 94

James, W. 78

Jenness, A. 197

Jeopardy surface A 3D model used in profiling which illustrates the time, distance and movement of an offender between crime scenes which is used to indicate, with differing levels of probability, the location for the individual's home, work place, etc. 198

Jordan, R.H. and Burghardt, G.M. 26

Julien, R.M. 166

Juries 200–1

Kahn, R.J., McNair, D.M., Lipman, R.S., Covi, L., Rickels, K., Downing, R., Fisher, S. and Frankenthaler, L.M. 137

Kamin, L.J. and Goldberger, A.S. 125

Kelling, G.L. and Wilson, J.Q. 206

KF, case study 89

Kiecolt-Glaser, J.K., Garner, W., Speicher, C.E., Penn, G.M., Holliday, J. and Glaser, R. 21

Kirsch, I., Deacon, B.J., Huedo-Medina, T.B., Scoboria, A., Moore, T.J. and Johnson, B.T. 239

Kohlberg, L. 76

Krause, N. 106–7

Kroger, J. 137

Kübler-Ross, E. 142

Kuhn, T. 13

Kurdek, L.A. 109

Kurdek, L.A. and Schmitt, J.P. 108, 109

Lab experiment An experiment carried out in a controlled setting. Lab experiments tend to demonstrate high internal validity and low external validity, but this isn't always true. 18, 20, 46, 54–5, 62, 77, 111, 205, 209

Labelling The effect of attaching a 'label' to a psychological condition; such labels tend to be enduring and self-fulfilling. 231, 240

Lajunen, T. and Rasanen, M. 164

Langer, E.J. and Rodin, J. 13

Lashley, K. 92

Latané, B., Williams, K. and Harkins, S. 218

Latent content According to Freud, the hidden and 'real' meaning of a dream. 152, 160

Leading (misleading) question A question that, either by its form or content, suggests to the witness what answer is desired or leads him/her to the desired answer. 18, 27, 55, 204

Learned helplessness Occurs when an animal finds that its responses are ineffective, and then it learns that there is no point in responding and behaves passively in future. 183, 189, 192, 216, 236–7, 241

Learning strategy The specific technique an individual uses to acquire new information or understanding which changes from one situation to another (i.e. you use a different strategy when dealing with different kinds of task); in contrast, learning style is relatively stable across situations. 187

Learning style The application of a person's cognitive style (their characteristic way of thinking, perceiving, problem solving, etc.) to the learning situation. 180–1, 186–7, 192

Lee, L. 104

Lee's model 104–5, 113

LeFrançois, G.R. 183

Lesioning Severing connections in the brain as a method of investigating cortical functioning. Temporary lesions can be achieved using anaesthetics. 95

Level of measurement The different ways of measuring a psychological ability, emotion, attitude, etc. Each level expresses a different amount of information about the thing we are measuring. 31–2, 44, 47

Level of significance Equivalent to the probability (p) of a result being due to chance. 31–2, 33

Levels of processing (LOP) The view that enduring memories are created through depth of processing; depth is determined in terms of the meaning extracted rather than by repetition. 86, 88–9, 96, 144

Libet, B. 79

Life event Commonplace experiences that involve change from a steady state. 107, 135, 139, 140–1, 142–3, 144–5, 170, 233, 237, 241

Life events approach 143

Life structure 134

Lifespan psychology 132, 134

Limbic system A system of structures lying beneath the cortex (subcortical), including the amygdala, hippocampus and hypothalamus. The region is associated with emotional behaviour. 79

Lin, N., Simeone, R.S., Ensel, W.M. and Kuo, W. 107

Locus of control (LoC) An aspect of our personality; people differ in their beliefs about whether the outcomes of their actions are contingent on what they do (internal control) or on events outside their personal control (external control). 164–5, 174–5, 177, 188, 192, 213, 216

Loftus, E.F. and Pickrell, J.E. 91

Loftus, E.F., and Palmer, J.C. 13, 24, 38, 204, 205

Loftus, E.F., Loftus, G.R. and Messo, J. 204

Long-term memory (LTM) Your memory for events that have happened in the past. This lasts anywhere from two minutes to 100 years. The long-term memory store has potentially unlimited duration and capacity. 86–7, 88–9, 92–3, 94, 96

Long-term potentiation The process of strengthening connections between neurons when they are repeatedly stimulated which enhances synaptic communication and results in a more permanent channel so can represent learning or memory. 94

Longitudinal/longitudinal study Observation of behaviour over a long period of time, possibly looking at the effects of age on a particular behaviour (such as moral development) by repeatedly testing/interviewing a group of participants at regular intervals. 21, 23, 46, 109, 142

Lorenz, K. 222

Lovaas method See Applied behaviour analysis

Lower mental functions Vygotsky distinguished lower and higher mental functions – the former are genetically inherited, by structure they are unmediated, by functioning they are involuntary, and with regard to their relation to other mental functions they are isolated individual mental units. 118, 128

Main effect hypothesis 106, 107

Maintenance rehearsal The process of repeating an item over and over again in order to remember it. 86, 88

Maintenance treatment (addiction) 168

Major depressive disorder (MDD) Also known as 'major depression', 'clinical depression', or 'unipolar disorder', MDD is a condition characterised by a long-lasting depressed mood or marked loss of interest or pleasure in all or nearly all activities. 227, 229

Majority influence See Conformity

Makaton 190, 191

Malouff, J.M., Rooke, S.E. and Schutte, N.S. 124

Maltby, J., Day, E. And Macaskill, A. 126

Mandel, D.R. 70

Mandler, G. 89

Manifest content The content of a dream that is recalled by a dreamer which, according to Freud, disguises the latent content. 152–3, 160

Mann–Whitney U Test 42–3, 44, 47

MAOI Monoamine oxidase inhibitor. Drugs which create higher levels of neurotransmitters of the monamine group such as serotonin, noradrenaline and dopamine. 154, 161

March, J.S., Silva, S., Petrycki, S., Curry, J., Wells, K., Fairbank, J., Burns, B., Domino, M., McNulty, S., Vitiello, B. and Severe, J. 239

Marcia, J. 133, 138

Marcia's theory 136–7, 144

Marelich, W.D. Lundquist, J. Painter, K. and Mechanic, M.B. 103

Marriage 140–1, 145

Maslow, A. 193

Mastery oriented learning 189

Matched pairs An experimental design where participants who are alike in terms of key variables such as age and IQ, are paired. One member of each pair is placed in the experimental group and the other member in the control group. 18, 24, 38, 40, 46–7

Matching hypothesis An explanation for the formation of relationships suggesting that individuals choose a partner who 'matches' them in terms of certain criteria. The term is also used to refer to other forms of matching, for example in sports psychology a match between goal orientation and motivational climate. 38, 112, 215, 224

Maturation The process of ripening. In psychological terms it means a change that is due to innate factors rather than learning. 72, 80, 118, 128

Maynard the cat 117

McClelland, D. 214

McGarrigle, J. and Donaldson, M. 117

McNaughton, S. and Leyland, J. 119

Mean The arithmetic average of a group of scores, taking the values of all the data into account. 44

Measure of central tendency A descriptive statistic that provides information about a 'typical' number for a data set. 44, 47

Measure of dispersion A descriptive statistic that provides information about how spread out a set of scores is. 44, 47

Meddis, R. 154

Media 60, 63

Median The middle value in a set of scores when they are placed in rank order. 44

Mediated communication 109

Mediated relationships 113

Mednick, S.A., Gabrielli, W.F. Jr and Hutching, S.B. 202, 203, 208

Meichenbaum, D. 170

Melatonin A hormone mainly produced in the pineal gland which induces sleep. 156, 157, 160

Memory The encoding, storage and retrieval of experience. 84–98, 154, 174, 204–5, 209

Memory trace The physical record or 'trace' of a memory. 87, 92

Mental health 220, 225

Mental illness 72, 80, 228–31

Meta-analysis The findings from a number of different studies used to reach a general conclusion about a particular hypothesis. 22, 46, 77, 124, 126, 167, 169, 182, 186, 200, 207, 217–18, 233, 235

Metabolic rate The rate at which the body burns up calories as a result of the chemical processes that produce energy. 154–5, 161

Methadone 168–9, 176

Michaels, J.W., Blommel, J.M., Brocato, R.M., Linkous, R.A. and Rowe, J.S. 213

Microenvironment The experiences (environment) particular to one individual. 73, 80

Microsleep Small periods of sleep during the day which possibly enable some physiological recovery to take place. The individual may not be aware they have been asleep. 155, 161

Midlife crisis 135

Milgram, S. 13, 16, 22, 70, 71, 80

Military 61, 63

Minority influence A form of social influence where people reject the established norm of the majority of group members and move to the position of the minority. 200–1, 208

Mirror test An investigative technique used to assess self-awareness by, for example, putting red colour on an individual's nose and showing them their image in a mirror. The individual demonstrates self-awareness if they touch their nose. 149

Miss America 21

MMR vaccine 16

Mode The most frequently occurring score in a data set. 44

Modelling The process of imitating another's behaviour, which involves cognitive representations of the modelled activities as well as abstractions of the underlying rules of the modelled behaviours. 170, 182, 192, 223

Monoamines A group of neurotransmitters that are chemically similar, including serotonin, dopamine and noradrenaline. 236

Monogamous Having only one sexual partner at any one time. 109

Monozygotic (MZ) Identical twins formed from one fertilised egg (or zygote). 72, 124, 129, 203, 232–3, 236

Mood dependent memory (MDM) 90

Moore, S.M. and Leung, C. 110

Moral responsibility 79

More knowledgeable other (MKO) A term used by Vygotsky to refer to 'experts', people who have greater understanding or information who assist the learning process. 184, 193

Moscovici, S., Lage, S. and Naffrechoux, M. 200

Motivation 188–9, 214–15, 224

MRI scan (Magnetic resonance imaging) Produces a three-dimensional image of the static, living brain which is very precise and provides information about the function of different regions. 79, 89, 91, 95, 96, 111, 190, 193

Multi-method approach 22

Multi-sensory teaching 190

Multi-store model (MSM) The conception of memory as consisting of several kinds of store (sensory, short-term and long-term) in which data are passed from one to the other by attention or rehearsal. 87–8, 96

Mundane realism Refers to how well a study mirrors the real word. The experimental environment is realistic to the degree to which experiences encountered in the environment will occur in the real world. 18, 20, 46

Murray, M. and McMillan, C. 173

MZ twins *See Monozygotic twins*

Narcolepsy A disorder in which individuals experience sudden and uncontrollable attacks of sleep lasting seconds or minutes at irregular and unexpected times. 158–9

National Institute of Child Health and Human Development 21

Natural experiment A research method in which the experimenter cannot manipulate the independent variable directly, but where it varies naturally, and the effect on a dependent variable can be observed. 18, 20, 23, 87, 91, 93, 97, 203, 205, 209

Natural selection The process that explains evolution whereby inherited traits that enhance an animal's reproductive success are passed on to the next generation and thus 'selected', whereas animals without such traits are less successful at reproduction and their traits are not selected. 12, 84, 100, 124, 222, 225

Naturalistic observation A research method carried out in a real-life setting, in which the investigator does not interfere in any way, but merely observes the behaviour(s) in question (this is likely to involve the use of structured observations). 12, 19, 21, 26, 46–7, 58, 63

Nature Those aspects of behaviour that are innate and inherited. 'Nature' does not simply refer to abilities present at birth but to any ability determined by genes, including those that appear through maturation. 69, 72–3, 80, 103, 116, 119, 124, 132, 203, 208

Nature versus nurture The discussion about whether behaviour is due to innate or environmental factors. 124

Naughty teddy 117

Negative correlation A correlation where, as one co-variable increases, the other decreases. 20, 34, 44, 46, 200, 208, 212

Negative punishment Decreases the probability that a behaviour will be repeated through the withdrawal of something pleasant. 182, 192

Negative reinforcement Increases the probability that a behaviour will be repeated because it leads to escape from an unpleasant situation. 182–3, 192

Neo-state view 150

Neodissociationist 150–1, 160

Neural networks A system of highly interconnected neurons which means that the whole network behaves in a way that would not be predicted from the behaviour of individual neurons. 154, 160

Neural plasticity 73, 80

Neuroanatomy The study of the structure and function of the nervous system. 100

Neurobiological The biological basis of the nervous system. 152

Neurochemical/neurochemistry Substances that are involved in the activity of the brain and nervous system. 167

Neuron A specialised cell in the nervous system for transmission of information. 92, 94, 97, 143, 159, 164, 170, 182, 232, 238, 240

Neurotransmitter Chemical substance, such as serotonin or dopamine, that plays an important part in the workings of the nervous system by transmitting nerve impulses across a synapse (gap between neurons), causing the adjacent neuron to be excited or inhibited. 78, 81, 94, 97, 100, 154, 158, 161, 164, 170, 202, 236–7, 238, 240–1

Neutral stimulus (NS) In classical conditioning, the stimulus that initially does not produce the target response, i.e. it is neutral. Through association with the unconditioned stimulus (UCS), the NS acquires the properties of the UCS and becomes a conditioned stimulus (CS) producing a conditioned response (CR). 182

Niche picking The selection of particular environments or experiences as a consequence of genetic predispositions. 73, 80, 125, 129

Nicholls, J.G. 214, 215

Nicotine replacement therapy 168

Night terrors A parasomnia related to sleep walking, where nightmares occur during slow-wave sleep. It may not be possible to wake a person suffering from night terrors. 149, 158–9

NMDA 94

Nominal data A level of measurement where data are in separate categories. 31, 36, 39, 40, 44

Nomothetic approach An approach to research that focuses more on general laws of behaviour than on the individual, possibly unique, case (the idiographic approach). 55, 62, 69, 80, 231, 240

Non-directional hypothesis Predicts that there will be a difference between two conditions or two groups of participants, without stating which condition will produce higher scores. 24, 33, 36–7, 39, 47

Non-human animals 58–9, 63, 80

Non-rapid eye movement (NREM) sleep Includes slow wave sleep. 148, 153, 155, 158, 161

Non-state explanations 150–1

Non-voluntary relationships 110–11, 113

Noradrenaline A neurotransmitter found mainly in areas of the brain that are involved in governing autonomic nervous system activity, e.g. blood pressure and heart rate. 152, 161, 236–7, 238, 241

Norms Something that is standard, usual or typical of a group. 22, 74, 102, 108, 110–11, 112–13, 172–3, 174–5, 177, 230

NREM sleep *See Non-rapid eye movement sleep*

Null hypothesis An assumption that there is no relationship (difference or association) in the population from which a sample is taken with respect to the variables being studied. 30–1, 32–3, 35, 36–7, 38–9, 41, 43, 47, 54, 231

Nurture Those aspects of behaviour that are acquired through experience, i.e. learned from interactions with the physical and social environment. 69, 72–3, 80, 103, 116, 119, 124, 132, 180, 203

Oakley, D. 150

Obedience 22, 71, 80

Objective Measure of Ego Identity Status 133

Observational learning Learning by being aware of what someone else does and modelling their behaviour (social learning theory). 182, 222

Observational studies A form of research where data is collected through observation of participants. No independent variable is manipulated but a dependent variable may be measured. 19, 21, 24–5, 26, 55

Observational techniques The application of systematic methods of observation in an observational study, experiment or other study. 18–19, 21, 26, 46

Observed value The value of a test statistic calculated for a particular data set. 32–3, 34–5, 36–7, 39, 41, 43, 47

Observer bias The tendency for observations to be influenced by expectations or prejudices. 19, 21, 23, 46–7

Oedipus conflict Freud's explanation of how a boy resolves his love for his mother and feelings of rivalry towards his father by identifying with his father. Occurs during the phallic stage of psychosexual development. In Greek mythology Oedipus unknowingly killed his father and married his mother. 76

Oestrogen The primary female hormone, though also present in males in small amounts. Regulates the menstrual cycle and female development in puberty. 34

Old age 142–3

One-tailed test Form of statistical test used with a directional hypothesis. 33, 35, 36–7, 39, 41, 43, 47

Open question A question that invites respondents to provide their own answers rather than to select an answer that has been provided. Tends to produce qualitative data. 20, 27, 46–7

Operant conditioning Learning that occurs when we are reinforced for doing something, which increases the probability that the behaviour in question will be repeated in the future. Conversely, if we are punished for behaving in a certain way, there is a decrease in the probability that the behaviour will recur. 174, 177, 182–3, 192, 206, 209

Operationalise Defining variables in a form that can be easily tested. 20, 24, 26, 47, 55, 75, 119, 133, 136

Opportunity sample A group of participants produced by selecting people who are most easily available at the time of the study. 25, 47, 109, 199, 208

Optimum arousal 204, 205

Optional sleep Sleep that is not required for physical and psychological health, as distinct from core sleep. 155, 161

Oral stage In psychoanalytic theory, the first stage (0–18 months) of psychosexual development when the organ focus is on the mouth. 132

Orbach, I., Singer, R.N. and Price, S. 217

Order effect In a repeated measures design, an extraneous variable arising from the order in which conditions are presented, e.g. a practice effect or fatigue effect. 24

Ordinal data A level of measurement where data are ordered in some way. 31, 35, 40, 43, 44, 47

Oscillators In the human body, a group of cells creating a repetitive rhythm to entrain biological rhythms. 156–7, 160

Overt observation An observational technique where observations are 'open', i.e. the participants are aware that they are being observed. 26, 47

Palmere, M., Benton, S.L., Glover, J.A. and Ronning, R. 89

Paradigm A shared set of assumptions about the subject matter of a discipline and the methods appropriate to its study. 13, 69, 80

Paranoid schizophrenia A form of schizophrenia where the individual feels persecuted. 228

Parasomnias Sleep disorders that occur around periods of sleep, such as sleepwalking and night terrors, as distinct from disorders of being able to sleep, such as insomnia. 158

Parental investment (PI) Any investment by a parent in an offspring that increases the chance that the offspring will survive at the expense of that parent's ability to invest in any other offspring (alive or yet to be born). 102, 112, 141, 145

Parenthood 140–1, 145

Park, S., Püschel, J., Sauter, B., Rentsch, M. and Hell, D. 88

Parrott, A.C. 166

Participant variable Characteristics of individual participants (such as age, intelligence, etc.) that might influence the outcome of a study. 18, 23, 24, 42, 46–7

Pashler, H., McDaniel, M., Rohrer, D. and Bjork, R. 181

Passive influence 73

Peer tutoring Being taught by people of a similar age to yourself who may be more expert. 184–5, 193

Penis envy A girl's recognition of not having a penis, and her desire to have one. Leads to a process similar to the resolution of the Oedipus complex. 76

PET scan (Positron emission tomography) A brain scanning method used to study activity in the brain. Radioactive glucose is ingested and can be detected in the active areas of the brain. 121, 128, 151, 153, 160–1

Peterson , L.R. and Peterson, M.J. 87, 92, 93

Phallic stage In psychoanalytic theory, the third stage of psychosexual development when the organ focus is on the genitals. Resolution of this stage results in the development of a superego. 136

Phase model 142

Phenylketonuria 72, 80

Phobia A mental disorder characterised by high levels of anxiety that, when experienced, interfere with normal living. 171, 182–3, 230

Phonemic processing 89

Phonological loop Encodes speech sounds in working memory, typically involving maintenance rehearsal (repeating the words over and over again), which is why this component of working memory is referred to as a 'loop'. 88–9, 96

Phonological store A component of the phonological loop which acts as an 'inner ear', i.e. storing sounds. 88–9, 96

Phylogenetic signal This refers to the behavioural similarities between species that are genetically similar, i.e. close on the phylogenetic or evolutionary scale. 155, 161

Physical attractiveness 102

Physical environment 119

Physiological approach 13

Physiological dependence Decreasing sensitivity to a drug and negative physical symptoms on discontinuation that arise with persistent drug use. 166, 171

Piaget , J. 116, 118, 119, 128, 184–5, 193

Pilot study A small-scale trial of a study run to test any aspects of the design, with a view to making improvements. 25, 27

Pineal gland Small gland in the brain that is stimulated by darkness or by the SCN to release melatonin, inducing sleep. 156–7, 160

Pinker, S. 111, 127, 148

Placebo A drug or other form of treatment that contains no active ingredients or therapeutic procedure. 19, 169, 171, 235, 237, 239, 240–1

Plaques In Alzheimer's disease, deposits of ß amyloid in the grey matter of the brain. 94–5, 97

Plastic interval scale A kind of interval measurement scale, where the intervals between units are numerically equal but they are not, in reality, the same size. 31

Pleasure centre A collection of structures in the brain, such as the nucleus accumbens, that produce a sense of enjoyment when activated. 166, 176

Plomin, R., DeFries J.C. and Loehlin,J.C. 73

Population In psychological research, all the people about whom we wish to make a statement, also called the 'target population'. 24, 30, 32

Positive correlation Refers to when, in a correlation, two co-variables increase together. 20, 34–5, 38, 44, 120, 122, 128, 185, 203, 219, 225

Post-event information In eyewitness testimony, information supplied after the event, such as a leading question. 205, 209

Post-traumatic stress disorder An anxiety disorder where anxiety is caused by the aftermath of a traumatic experience such as disasters, accidents, or military combat. 61, 63, 171, 176

Postsynaptic membrane The covering of the neuron that is receiving the information at the synapse. 238

Pre-operational stage A stage in Piaget's theory of cognitive development where a child (aged between two and seven years) is able to use symbols to represent experience (e.g. language) but lacks the ability to operate on concepts with internally consistent, adult logic. 118

Precipitating factors 104

Predator avoidance 154

Prefrontal cortex Section of the cerebral cortex at the front of the brain associated with working memory and planning. 79, 87, 89, 96, 152, 153, 160–1, 233

Premenstrual syndrome (PMS) A disorder experienced by some women just prior to menstruation, when they experience mood swings and increased aggression. 77, 81

Presumptive consent A method of dealing with lack of informed consent or deception, by asking a group of people who are similar to the participants whether they would agree to take part in a study. If this group of people consents to the procedures in the proposed study, it is presumed that the real participants would agree as well. 28–9, 47, 57, 62

Presynaptic membrane The covering of the neuron that is sending the information at the synapse. 238

Primary insomnia Sleeplessness that cannot be explained by a medical, psychiatric or environmental cause. 158–9, 161

Primary Mental Abilities (PMAs) 120

Primary-process thought In Freudian theory, thinking that is not organised, is concrete and emotion-driven, visual rather than verbal and, above all, irrational. 152

Primates A group of mammals including humans, apes, monkeys and lemurs. 95

Prison study 70, 80

Privacy The zone of inaccessibility of mind or body and the trust that this will not be 'invaded'. A person's right to control a flow of information about themselves. 26, 29, 47, 56, 60, 62–3, 71, 105, 169

Proactive interference (PI) Forgetting due to interference where previous learning interferes with current learning/recall. 92, 97

Probabilistic Relating to or based on probability. 78, 81

Probability (p) A numerical measure of the likelihood or chance that certain events will occur. 30–1, 47, 235

Proband The first person who seeks treatment for a genetic disorder; other relatives are then contacted to see if they also have the disorder in order to investigate genetic factors. 236

Procedural memory A subdivision of long-term memory, 'knowing how' as opposed to 'knowing that' (declarative knowledge). 87, 93–94, 96–7, 154

Profiling 198–9, 208

Programmed instruction 183

Projection In psychoanalytic theory, a form of ego defence whereby one unknowingly displaces one's own unacceptable feelings onto someone else. 11

Propaganda 61

Prospective study A research study where participants of interest are identified (e.g. those with high blood pressure or who were adopted) and then followed over time to assess later behaviours, attitudes or experiences, as distinct from a retrospective study. 174, 233

Protection from harm 29, 56

Pseudoscience A practice or approach that claims to be scientific but does not adhere to the key principles of the scientific process. 53, 68

Psychoanalysis Form of psychotherapy, originally developed by Sigmund Freud, that is intended to help patients become aware of long-repressed feelings and issues by using such techniques as free association. 12, 54, 62, 189, 234, 238

Psychoanalyst A therapist who uses psychoanalysis to treat patients with mental disorders. 132, 135, 233

Psychodynamic approach Literally an approach that explains the dynamics of behaviour – what motivates a person. The approach has become synonymous with Freud's theory of personality. Freud suggested that unconscious forces and early experience are the prime motivators. 12, 73, 78, 91

Psychological dependence The increasing need for a drug because of the feelings of well-being that results from persistent drug use. 166

Psychological harm Steps are taken to ensure that during a research study, participants do not experience negative physical or psychological effects, such as physical injury, lowered self-esteem or embarrassment, as a result of the research. 28–9, 55, 57, 62, 71, 117

Psychological test *See Psychometric*

Psychometric The measurement of any psychological ability, such as personality or intelligence. 116, 120–1, 123, 127, 128–9, 187, 192, 217

Psychosexual stages In psychoanalytic theory, the developmental stages that are related to the id's changing focus on different parts of the body. 11

Psychosurgery Surgery that involves severing fibres or removing brain tissue with the intention of treating disturbed behaviour for which no physical cause can be demonstrated. Modern psychosurgery techniques, such as deep brain stimulation, do not involve permanent damage. 230

Psychotherapy Any psychological form of treatment for a mental disorder, as distinct from physical forms of treatment. 220

Psychotic/psychoticism/psychosis A loss of contact with reality, consistent with serious mental illness, which typically includes delusions, hallucinations and disordered thinking. 155, 196–7, 234

PsyOps 61

Publication bias The tendency for academic journals to publish only positive findings or findings that agree with existing theory. 201, 208, 231

Punishment In operant conditioning, the application of an unpleasant stimulus such that the likelihood of the behaviour that led to it reoccurring is decreased. 57, 62, 81, 180, 182–3, 192

Qualitative data Data that express the 'quality' of things involving descriptions, words, meanings, pictures, texts and so on. Qualitative data cannot be counted or quantified but they can be turned into quantitative data by placing them in categories. 20–1, 27, 46, 69

Quantitative data Data that represent how much or how long, or how many, etc. there are of something, i.e. a behaviour is measured in numbers or quantities. 20, 27, 46

Questionnaire Written questions that are used to collect data. 18–19, 20, 24, 26–7, 46–7, 55, 104, 106, 134–5, 141

Quota sample Groups of participants are selected according to their frequency in the population. Within each group, individuals are selected using opportunity sampling. 25, 47

Rahe, R.H., Mahan, J. and Arthur, R. 13, 16, 34

Railway rapist 199

Random sample A group of participants chosen in such a way that every member of the target population has an equal chance of being selected. 25, 47, 200

Randomly allocated/random allocation Allocating participants to experimental groups or conditions using random techniques. 20, 24, 47, 126, 168

Range The difference between the highest and lowest score in a data set. 44, 47

Rapid eye movement (REM) sleep During this time the body is paralysed except for the eyes. REM sleep is often equated with dreaming, but dreams also occur in NREM sleep. 148, 152

Rating scale A means of assessing attitudes or experience by asking a respondent to rate statements on a scale of 1 to 3 or 1 to 5, etc. Produces ordinal data. 31, 34, 38

Ratio data A measurement where there is a true zero point and equal intervals between units, as in most measures of physical quantities. 31

Rational choice theory 166–7, 176

Raven's Progressive Matrices 123

Reactive influence 73

Reasoning and Rehabilitation (R&R) 206–7

Recidivism Repeating an undesirable behaviour after receiving some form of treatment or punishment. 202, 207, 209

Reconstructive memory The view that recall is not a matter of passively accessing a piece of information and 'reading it' (as suggested buy the multi-store model). Instead memory involves active reconstruction based on expectations and stereotypes (schema). 204–5, 209

Reduced cues theory 108–9

Reductionist An approach which breaks complex phenomena into more simple components, implying that this is desirable because complex phenomena are best understood in terms of a simpler level of explanation. 13, 55, 62, 69, 80, 189

Reformulated theory 222

Regan, T. 58

Regression A form of ego defense where an individual deals with anxiety by returning to an earlier ego state rather than coping with unacceptable impulses in an adult way. 136, 144, 232, 241

Reification 122

Reinforcement If a behaviour results in a pleasant state of affairs, the behaviour is 'stamped in' or reinforced. It then becomes more probable that the behaviour will be repeated in the future. Can be positive or negative reinforcement: both lead to an increased likelihood that the behaviour will be repeated. 168–9, 176, 182, 186, 192, 202, 206

Reinforcement schedules 182

Reinforcers Any consequence that creates reinforcement. 182, 192

Reitman 1974 93

Relational memory building 95

Relationships 99–114

Reliable/reliability A measure of consistency both within a set of scores or items (internal reliability) and also over time so that it is possible to obtain the same results on subsequent occasions when the measure is used (external reliability). 18–19, 46, 122–3, 129, 135, 187, 230–1

Remondes, M. and Schman, E.M. 95

Repeated measures design An experimental design where each participant takes part in every condition under test. 18, 23, 24, 38, 40, 46–7

Replicability/replication Repeating a research study to see if the same findings are produced. This confirms both the reliability and trueness (validity) of the finding. 19, 54, 62

Representative sample 27

Repression/repressed A form of ego defense whereby anxiety-provoking material is kept out of conscious awareness as a means of coping. 54, 62, 90–1, 96, 152, 236

Research design 47

Research issues 51–64

Research methods 15–48

Resolution 104

Respect 57

Responsibility 57

Restoration theory 154–5

Retirement 142–3, 145

Retrieval failure occurs when information received is stored in long-term memory but is difficult or impossible to access. 92

Retroactive interference Forgetting due to interference where current learning interferes with past learning/recall. 92–3, 97

Retrograde amnesia Form of amnesia where someone is unable to recall events that occurred before the development of the amnesia. 94–5, 97

Retrospective study A research study where participants of interest are identified (e.g. those with high blood pressure or who were adopted) and then information is collected about past experiences, as distinct from a prospective study. 174

Retz, W., Retz-Junginger, P., Supprian, T., Thome, J. and Rösler, M. 203

Reverse alphas bias 77

Rhyming recognition test 89

Right to withdraw The right of participants to refuse to continue with participation in a study if they are uncomfortable in any way, and to refuse permission for the researcher to use any data produced before they withdrew. 28, 47, 56, 62, 71, 80, 197

Ringlemann effect See Social loafing

Role play A controlled observation in which participants are asked to imagine how they would behave in certain situations and act out the part. This method has the advantage of permitting the study of certain behaviours that might be unethical to study or difficult to find in the real world. 22, 46

Rollie, S.S. and Duck, S.W. 104–5, 113

Romance 110

Rosenberg Self-Esteem (RSE) scale 106

Rosenhan, D.L. 13, 16, 22

Ross, C.A. and Read, J. 234

Rotter, J. 165

Same-sex relationships 108, 113

Sample/sampling/sampling method The process of taking a group of participants intended to be a representative selection of a target population. 19, 24–5, 27, 32, 46–7, 102, 109, 191

Samuel, J. and Bryant, P. 117

Sanders, G.S., Baron, R.S. and Moore, D.L. 219

Scaffolding An approach to instruction that aims to support a learner only when absolutely necessary, i.e. to provide a support framework (scaffold) to assist the learning process. 184–5, 193

Scarr, S. and McCartney, K. 73

Scattergraph A graphical representation of the relationship (i.e. the correlation) between two sets of scores, each dot representing one pair of data. 44, 47

Schacter, D.L. 94

Schema A cluster of related facts based on previous experiences, and used to generate future expectations. 118, 128, 184, 204–5, 209, 236, 241

Schizophrenia A mental disorder where an individual has lost touch with reality and may experience symptoms such as delusions, hallucinations, grossly disorganised behaviour and flattened emotions. 12, 55, 62, 68–9, 72–3, 78, 228–35, 240–1

Schmitt, B., Gilovich, T.K., Goore, N. and Joseph, L. 213, 219

Schwartz, B. and Barksy, S.F. 219

Scientific determinism 78, 81

Scientific method An objective means of testing hypotheses in order to develop empirically based explanations/theories. 54–5, 62, 68–9, 70, 87

Screening tests 190

Secondary insomnia Sleeplessness that occurs because of a medical, psychiatric or environmental cause. 158–9, 161

Secure attachment This is a strong and contented attachment of an infant to his or her caregiver, which develops as a result of sensitive responding by the caregiver to the infant's needs. Securely attached infants are comfortable with social interaction and intimacy. Secure attachment is related to healthy subsequent cognitive and emotional development. 100, 137, 139, 144

Secure base A sense of emotional safety which is necessary for independent behaviour; in infancy it is provided by a secure attachment. 137, 144

Seizures Characterised by sudden powerful muscular contractions and unconsciousness, induced by sudden, abnormal electrical activity in the brain. 234, 240

Selective pressure In evolutionary theory, demand created by the environment resulting in one set of genes being favoured over another. This is the mechanism of natural selection. 12

Selective serotonin reuptake inhibitors See SSRIs

Self-actualisation A person's motivation to maximise their achievements and fulfil their potential. 12, 188, 193

Self-awareness The state or ability to perceive, feel or to be conscious of your own existence. 58, 75, 149, 150

Self-concept The self as it is currently experienced; all the attitudes we hold about ourselves. 229

Self-efficacy The belief that we can perform competently in a given situation. 173, 177, 182, 214–15, 220, 224

Self-esteem The feelings that a person has about their self-concept. 37, 57, 106–7, 112, 137, 139, 142, 172, 188, 191, 202, 209, 214, 220, 224–5

Self-fulfilling prophecy A prediction made about another comes true simply because of the expectation. Our beliefs generate expectations which affect our own perception and other people's behaviour. 202, 209

Self-medication model 166, 167, 176

Self-report methods Any research method where participants are asked to report their own attitudes, abilities and/or feelings, such as a questionnaire, interview or psychological test. 20

Self-selected sample See Volunteer sample

Self-serving bias A kind of attributional bias. Individuals prefer to make internal (dispositional) attributions about their successes and external (situational) attributions about their failures. 216–17, 224

Seligman, M.E.P. 216

Selye, H. 16, 164

Semantic coding 87

Semantic memory A subdivision of long-term memory that contains organised knowledge about the world and about language, i.e. facts that have meaning. 87, 88, 96, 154

Semiotics The study of cultural sign processes, such as language and mathematical concepts. 118, 128

Sensori-motor The co-ordination of sensory and motor experiences, such as hand–eye coordination. 119, 128

Sensory deprivation A procedure that reduces or removes stimulation from one or more of the senses. 58, 61, 63

Sensory memory (SM) This is the information collected by your eyes, ears, nose, fingers and so on. Information is retained for a very brief period by the sensory registers. We are only able to hold accurate images of sensory information momentarily (less than half a second). The capacity of sensory memory is very large. The method of encoding depends on the sense organ involved, i.e. visual for the eyes, acoustic for the ears. 86–7, 96

Sentient/sentience Having the ability to feel or sense; a form of consciousness where one is aware of one's own being, but consciousness may not be necessary for sentience. 58, 63

Serial killers Murderers who have killed three or more people, spread over a period of at least 30 days. 198

Serial probe technique A Participant listens to a string of digits and at the end one of them is given as the probe. The participant has to remember the digit that came after the probe. 93, 97

Serotonin A neurotransmitter found in the central nervous system and implicated in many different behaviours and physiological processes, including aggression, eating behaviour, sleep and depression. 152, 154, 161, 168, 170, 176, 202–3, 208, 234, 236–7, 238, 240–1

SES *See Socio-economic status*

Shallice, T. 93

Shallice, T. and Warrington, E.K. 89

Shallow processing 89

Shaping A process whereby a desired behaviour is gradually conditioned by reinforcing behaviours that progressively move closer and closer to the behaviour in question. 182–3, 190, 192–3, 206

Sheingold, K. and Tenney, Y.J. 91

Sheldon, W.H. 196

Shift work Work schedule where workers start and finish work at different times through the day and night. 158, 161

Short-term memory (STM) Your memory for immediate events. Short-term memories last for a brief time and disappear unless they are rehearsed. Short-term memory is sometimes referred to as working memory because it is necessary to use that memory to comprehend language, solve problems and so on. 86, 92–3, 96

Siegel, J.M. and Rogawski, M.A. 154

Sign test 38–9, 44, 47

Significance level The level of probability (p) at which it has been agreed to reject the null hypothesis. 31, 32–3

Significant A statistical term indicating that a set of research findings are sufficiently strong for us to accept the research hypothesis under test. 30, 33–4, 47

Singer, P. 58

Situational attributions In attribution theory, accounting for an individual's behaviour in terms of aspects of the environment or external factors, such as another person's behaviour or luck. 201, 204, 208–9

Situational variables Factors in the environment that could affect the DV, such as noise, time of day or the behaviour of an investigator. 18, 46

Skinner, B.F. 61

Slave system 88, 89

Sleep 148–9, 154–5, 220

Sleep deprivation 155

Sleep disorders 158–9

Sleepwalking A parasomnia that occurs during slow-wave sleep and entails a range of activities normally associated with wakefulness (such as eating, getting dressed or walking); the person has no conscious knowledge of what they are doing. 149–50, 158–9

Slow-wave sleep (SWS) Stages 3 and 4 of NREM sleep when brain waves have low frequency and high amplitude. This stage of deep sleep is associated with bodily growth and repair, such as the production of growth hormones. 154

Smallest space analysis A technique for identifying common elements between crimes which helps to find the most useful crime scene evidence by indicating which characteristics rarely occur together; if they do on more than one occasion, this might indicate a single perpetrator. 198, 208

Smith, C. and Lloyd, B. 21

Smith, E.R. and Mackie. D.M. 200

Smith, P. and Bond, M.H. 75

Smoking 166

Snapshot study A research study that takes place over a short priod of time, as opposed to a longitudinal study. 23, 46, 109, 113

Social approach 13

Social constructionist An approach to studying and explaining human behaviour in terms of its social context rather than any objective reality. If behaviour is separated from social context then its true meaning is lost. 77

Social desirability bias A tendency for respondents to answer questions in a way that they think will present them in a better light. 20, 27, 144–5, 149, 169

Social disengagement theory 142, 145

Social environment 119

Social exchange theory 102–3, 112

Social facilitation A form of social influence, where performance is enhanced when working in the presence of other people. 218–19, 224–5

Social identity model of deindividuation effects (SIDE) 108, 109, 113

Social interaction hypothesis 221

Social learning theory (SLT) The basic assumption of this theory is that people learn through observing the behaviour of models, mentally rehearsing the behaviours they display, then later imitating them in similar situations. 73, 80, 100, 174, 182, 202, 209, 222–3

Social loafing The reduction of individual effort when people work in groups as compared with when they work alone. 212, 218–19, 224–5

Social norms Something that is standard, usual or typical of a group of people. 22, 172, 174–5, 177, 206, 230

Social Readjustment Rating Scale (SRRS) 140, 142

Social support 106, 107

Socially sensitive research Any research that might have direct consequences on particular groups on society. 56, 62, 127

Socio-cognitive theory of hypnosis (SCT) 150–1

Socio-economic status (SES) A measure of an individual's or family's social and economic position, based on income, education and occupation. 72, 174

Sociobiology An approach to explaining social behaviour in terms of evolutionary processes. 102–3, 112

Soft determinism The belief that free will and determinism are compatible ideas. 78, 81

Solms, M. 153

Somatic anxiety 216–17

Somatotypes 196

Sommers, S. R. and Ellsworth, P. C. 201

Spearman's correlation test 34–5, 44, 47, 120–1, 128

Special educational needs 190–1

Speciesism The assumption that some individuals are superior based solely on the grounds that they are members of the species *Homo sapiens*. Speciesim is similar to sexism or racism where superiority is defined by sex or race. 58, 63

Specific abilities 120

Specific phobia A phobia of specific activities or objects, such as bathing or spiders. 230, 240

Sperling, G. 87

Spiral curriculum An approach to teaching that suggests learning is more effective if concepts are repeatedly revisited, gradually creating a more sophisticated understanding. 184–5, 193

Split-half method A method of assessing internal reliability by comparing two halves of, for example, a psychological test to see if they produce the same score. 19, 46

Sport psychology 212–26

SRRS (Social Readjustment Rating Scale) Developed by Holmes and Rahe to be able to test the idea that life changes are related to stress-related illnesses such as anxiety and depression. 34, 140, 142

SSRIs (selective serotonin re-uptake inhibitors) Commonly prescribed drugs for treating depression. They work by selectively preventing the re-uptake of serotonin from the synaptic gap, thus leaving more serotonin available at the synapse to excite surrounding neurons. 152, 154, 161, 168, 170, 176, 202–3, 208, 234, 236–7, 238–9, 240–1

Stage theory approach 135, 143

Standard deviation A measure of dispersion that shows the amount of variation in a set of scores. It assesses the spread of data around the mean. 44, 47, 116

Standardised instructions A set of instructions that are the same for all participants to ensure that any differences between participants are not due to different expectations or understanding. 45

Standardised procedures A set of procedures that are the same for all participants in order to be able to repeat a study. This includes standardised instructions. 18, 62

Stanford-Binet Intelligence Scale 116, 122

State anxiety 216–17

State explanations 150–1

State-dependent learning A form of cue-dependent learning (or forgetting) where things are recalled better when you are in the same state you were as when they were initially learned, such as being happy or depressed or drunk. 92, 97

Statistical tests *See Inferential statistics*

Stereotype A social perception of an individual in terms of some readily available feature, such as their group membership or physical attractiveness, rather than their personal attributes. 102, 186, 202, 204–5

Sternberg's triarchic theory of intelligence 120–1, 128

Storm and stress 138, 144

Stratified sample Groups of participants selected according to their frequency in the population. Within each strata individuals are selected using random sampling. 25, 47

Stress inoculation training (SIT) A type of CBT which trains people to cope with anxiety and stressful situations by learning certain skills and thus 'inoculate' (i.e.protect) themselves against the damaging effects of future stressors. 170–1

Stress The subjective experience of a lack of fit between a person and their environment, i.e. where the perceived demands of a situation are greater than a person's perceived ability to cope. 21, 34, 72, 106, 112, 138, 164, 166, 170–1, 176, 220

Structured (systematic) observations An observer uses various 'systems' to organise observations, such as behavioural categories and sampling procedures. 26, 47

Structured interview Any interview in which the questions are decided in advance. 20, 26, 46

Structured language programmes 190

Structured observation 26

Structured questionnaires 20

Sub-scales Psychological tests produce measurements of abilities, attitudes, etc. by providing a score for each individual. This score is expressed on a scale, a system of ordered marks at fixed intervals. Such scales may be subdivided into separate subscales measuring different aspects of the same thing, such as separating an intelligence test score into verbal and nonverbal intelligence. 129

Subcultural A term used to refer to separate groups of people within one culture. Like cultural groups, a subculture is a group who share a distinct set of rules, morals and so on. 125, 230

Subjective experience 79

Subjectivity 109

Suicide 239

Superego develops between the ages of three and six, and embodies our conscience and sense of right and wrong. 76

Suprachiasmatic nucleus (SCN) A tiny cluster of nerve cells in the hypothalamus of each hemisphere that acts as the main endogenous pacemaker. 156, 160

Susceptibility 151

Swain, A. 219

SWS See Slow-wave sleep

Symbolism In psychoanalysis, an element of dreamwork that enables the latent content of a dream to be transformed into manifest content by replacing elements of the dream with symbols. 156, 160

Symister, P. and Friend, R. 106

Sympathetic arousal/sympathetic nervous system The part of the autonomic nervous system that is associated with physiological arousal and 'fight or flight' responses. 42, 216, 224–5

Synapse/synaptic cleft A small gap separating neurons. It consists of the presynaptic membrane (which discharges neurotransmitters), the postsynaptic membrane (containing receptor sites for neurotransmitters) and a synaptic gap between the two. 94, 143, 164, 238

Synopticity 13

Synthesis 152

Systematic desensitisation A form of cognitive–behavioural therapy used to treat phobias and other behaviour problems involving anxiety. A client is gradually exposed to (or imagines) the threatening situation under relaxed conditions until the anxiety reaction is extinguished. 171, 183, 192

Systematic sample A method of obtaining a representative sample by selecting every Nth person. This can be a random sample if the first person is selected using a random method and then every Nth person is selected. 25, 47

Table of critical values A table of data showing the critical values for each inferential test. 33, 34–7, 39, 41, 43

Tangles Damaged brain tissue found in Alzheimer's patients associated with a build-up of tau protein. 94–5, 97

Tardive dyskinesia Dyskinesia refers to involuntary repetitive body movements. Tardive refers to a slow onset. It is a common side effect of antipsychotic drugs. 235, 240

TARGET 214

Target population The group of people that the researcher is interested in. The group of people from whom a sample is drawn. The group of people about whom generalisations can be made. 24–5, 32, 47

Task-oriented individuals are concerned with the mastery of a particular skill and measure success in terms of improvement from one point in time to the next. 214–15, 219, 224–5

Tau protein A protein found in the brain that normally helps to provide the structure of neurons. 94–5

Taylor, S.E., Klein, L.C., Lewis, B.P., Grunewald, T.L., Gurung, R.A.R. and Updegraff, J.A. 77

Teaching 180, 184–5, 189

Team membership 218, 224–5

Tearoom trade study 70, 71, 80

Temporal gradient Describes the fact that older memories are preserved better than more recent remote memories in amnesiacs. 94, 97

Temporal lobe A region in each hemisphere of the forebrain. It is located on the left and right, behind (posterior to) the frontal lobe and below the Sylvian fissure, approximately in line with temples (near the ears). It contains structures associated with memory, such as the hippocampus. 95, 97

Termination 104

Test of association An inferential test that compares two attributes in a sample of data to determine if there is any relationship between them. 38, 44

Test of difference An inferential test that compares two samples of data to determine if they come from the same or different populations. 44

Test statistic The numerical value that is calculated for any inferential test. The 'name' of the observed value. 30, 32–3

Test–retest method/reliabilities A method used to check external reliability. The same test or interview is given to the same participants on two occasions to see if the same results are obtained. 19, 46, 187

Testosterone A hormone produced mainly by the testes in males, but also occurrs in females. It is associated with the development of secondary sexual characteristics in males (e.g. body hair), but has also been implicated in aggression and dominance behaviours. 34, 77, 202, 208

Tests of difference 38–9, 40–1

Thatcher effect An illusion where it is difficult to detect local feature changes when viewing a face upside down. 204, 205

Theory of planned behaviour (TPB) explains how attitudes, norms and beliefs lead to behaviour, and thus can be used to understand how to change behaviour. 164, 173, 177

Theory of reasoned action (TRA) suggests that behaviour is determined by intentions to perform the behavior and that these intentions are, in turn, a function of attitudes toward the behaviour and subjective norms. 172–3, 177

Thibaut, J.W. and Kelley, H.H. 102

Three mountains task 119

Thurstone's multifactor theory 120–1, 128

Time sampling An observational technique in which the observer records behaviours in a given time frame, e.g. noting what a target individual is doing every 30 seconds. 25, 26, 47

Ting-Toomey, S. 110

Token economy A form of behaviour modification, which uses operant conditioning to positively reinforce appropriate behaviours using tokens (secondary reinforcers) that are exchanged for primary reinforcers (food or privileges). 168, 176, 190, 193, 206–7, 209

Tolerance The progressive reduction of the effect of a drug due to its continued use. 168

Top-down Processing that starts from an overview of a system, as opposed to bottom-up processing, such as using previous experience and context to enrich sensory input. 198, 208

Torture 61

Transfer-appropriate processing Memory is strengthened if the way information is initially encoded is the same as how it is later retrieved. 89

Triangulation Comparing three or more views of the same thing to establish validity. 69

Triplett, N. 212, 218

Tryptophan An essential amino acid found in the diet, particularly in milk, cheese, fish, nuts and chocolate. Tryptophan is a precursor of the neurotransmitter serotonin, and melatonin, a hormone related to sleep. 203, 208, 236–7, 241

Tulving, E. and Psotka, J. 93

Turkheimer, E., Haley, A., Waldron, M., Onofrio, B. and Gottesman, I. 125

Turner, E.H., Matthews, A.M., Linardatos, E., Tell, R.A. and Rosenthal, R. 231

Twin studies Research conducted using twins. If nature is a more important influence then we would expect monozygotic (MZ) twins to be more similar than dizygotic (DZ) twins in terms of a target behaviour such as intelligence or personality. Such studies may look at twins reared apart to reduce the confounding variable of shared environment. 72, 124–5, 129, 159, 208, 232–3, 236

Two-tailed test Form of test used with a non-directional hypothesis. 33, 36–7, 39

Type 1 error Rejecting a null hypothesis that is true. This is more likely to happen if the significance level is too high (lenient, e.g. 10%). 15, 30, 32, 47, 231, 240

Type 2 error Accepting a null hypothesis that is in fact not true. This is more likely to happen if the significance level is too low (stringent, e.g. 1%). 15, 30, 32, 47, 231, 240

Ultradian rhythm A pattern of behaviour that occurs less often than once a day, such as the human female menstrual cycle. 148, 156

Uncertainty principle You cannot observe something without changing it. First formulated in the context of quantum mechanics, you cannot determine both the position and velocity of a subatomic particle simultaneously because when you undertake to measure one, you change the other measure. 55, 62, 69, 80

Unconditioned response (UCR) In classical conditioning, the innate reflex response to a stimulus, such as salivating when presented with food. 182–3

Unconditioned stimulus (UCS) In classical conditioning, the stimulus that inevitably produces an innate reflex response, such as food producing a salivation response. 182

Unconscious Lacking consciousness or awareness. In psychoanalytic theory, the unconscious part of your mind contains information that is either very hard or almost impossible to bring into conscious awareness. It holds your repressed thoughts which are too anxiety-provoking to allow into one's conscious. However, such material exerts a powerful influence over behaviour. 148, 152

Understudied relationships 108–11

Unipolar depression Depression (or major depressive disorder) as distinct from bipolar disorder where periods of depression alternate with periods of mania. 22, 229

Unstructured interview An interview that starts out with some general aims and possibly some questions, and lets the interviewee's answers guide subsequent questions. 20, 46

Unstructured observation An observer records all relevant behaviour but has no system. This technique may be chosen because the behaviour to be studied is largely unpredictable. 20, 26, 47

Utilitarian A theoretical framework for morality where decisions about what is right or wrong is based on the principle of what is useful or practical for the majority of people. Established by weighing costs and benefits for individuals and society. 58–9

Valid/validity Refers to the legitimacy of a study, the extent to which the findings can be applied beyond the research setting as a consequence of the study's internal and/or external validity. 18–19, 20, 46, 54, 69, 87, 107, 122–3, 129, 230–1

Valins, S. 150

Variance A measure of dispersion of a set of scores. It is the square of the standard deviation. 72, 129

Vicarious reinforcement Learning not through direct reinforcement of behaviour, but through observing someone else being reinforced for that behaviour. 73, 80, 100, 202, 222–3, 225

Virtual reality 171

Visual cache A component of the visuo-spatial sketchpad of the working memory model, a passive store that holds information about form and colour. 88

Visual cache 88

Visual cortex The part of the cortex that processes visual data, located at the back (posterior part) of the brain. 70

Visuo-spatial sketchpad Encodes visual information in terms of separate objects as well as the arrangement of these objects in one's visual field. 88–9, 96

Voluntary relationships 110–11, 113

Volunteer bias A form of sampling bias caused by the fact that volunteer participants are usually more highly motivated than randomly selected participants. 25, 47

Volunteer sample A sampling technique that relies solely on people who chose to respond to requests from the environment. 25, 47, 109

Voracek, M. and Haubner, T. 125

Vygotsky, L.S. 118, 119, 128, 184–5, 193

Wagstaff, G. 150

Wahlsten, D. 127

Walther, J.B. 109

Walther, J.B. and Tidwell, L.C. 109

Waste of time hypothesis 154

Waugh, N.C. and Norman, D. 93

Weapon effect The consequence of a witness focusing on a frightening aspect of the crime scene (e.g. a weapon) rather than important details such as the perpetrator's face, which reduces the accuracy of their recall. 204–5, 209

Weightlifters 215

Weiner, B. 188, 216

Well-being 106

Wells, C.M., Collins, D. and Hale, B.D. 215

Whitty, M.T. 109

Wilcoxon Matched Pairs Signed Ranks Test 40

Wilcoxon *T* Test 40–1, 44, 47

Williams, L.M. 91

Wiltshire, S. 121

Wish fulfillment 152–3

Working memory An aspect of memory that deals with information that is being worked on, equivalent to short-term memory. It is divided into separate stores representing different modalities. 86, 88–9, 122, 233

Working memory model (WMM) An explanation of short-term memory, called 'working memory'. Based on four components, some with storage capacity. 86, 88–9

Wright, D.B. 91

Wright, E. F., Voyer, D, Wright, R. D. and Roney, C. 218

Yerkes–Dodson law The curvilinear relationship between arousal and performance. People do not perform well when they are very relaxed; they perform best when moderately aroused and performance drops off again at high levels of arousal. 209

Yerkes, R. & Dodson, J. 212

Yerkes, R. 123

Zahariadis, P.N. and Biddle S.J.H. 215

Zajonc, R.B. 40, 218, 219

Zepelin, H. and Rechtschaffen, A. 155

Zero correlation In a correlation co-variables are not be linked at all. 44

Zero-tolerance policy An approach to reducing crime by taking a hard line on minor offences to prevent escalation of the scale and seriousness of criminal behaviour. 206, 209

Zhang, J. 153

Zimbardo, P.G. 22, 70, 71, 80

Zone of proximal development (ZPD) In Vygotsky's theory, the 'region' between a person's current abilities, which they can perform with no assistance, and their potential capabilities, which they can be helped to achieve with the assistance of 'experts'. 118, 128, 184, 193